The Story of the Latter-day Saints

Building the Nauvoo Temple, a 1975 painting by Gary Smith.
(Courtesy the artist)

The Story of the Latter-day Saints

James B. Allen and Glen M. Leonard

Published in Collaboration
with the Historical Department of
The Church of Jesus Christ of
Latter-day Saints

Deseret Book Company
Salt Lake City, Utah
1976

To Our Wives
Renée and Karen

© 1976 by Deseret Book Company
All rights reserved
ISBN 0-87747-594-6
Library of Congress Catalog Card No. 76-20376
Printed in the United States of America

Contents

4

5

List of Maps

FOREWORD

In 1921 Elder Joseph Fielding Smith, apostle and Church Historian, prepared a manual for the Melchizedek Priesthood classes under the title *Essentials in Church History.* This was published in hardback the next year. In the years that followed, this useful distillation of the history of The Church of Jesus Christ of Latter-day Saints was continually expanded and brought up to date, eventually going through twenty-eight editions. The most recent printing was in 1973.

Upon the death of Elder Smith, then president of the Church, in July 1973, officials of the Church and the Deseret Book Company recommended that the Historical Department prepare a history that might serve the same needs that *Essentials in Church History* had provided for so many years. Much new material has been acquired by the Church Archives dealing with the events of Church history, and there has been a need for more attention to important events that have taken place in recent years.

With the approval of the First Presidency, we asked two of our finest historians, James B. Allen and Glen M. Leonard, to undertake the task of preparing this history. Dr. Allen, a native of Logan, Utah, with degrees in history from Utah State University, Brigham Young University, and the University of Southern California, taught Church history in the institutes of religion and at Brigham Young University. He is now assistant Church historian as well as professor of history at BYU. Dr. Leonard is a native of Farmington, Utah, and received degrees in history from the University of Utah. Formerly managing editor of *Utah Historical Quarterly*, he is now senior historical associate in the Historical Department of the Church. Both historians have served proselyting missions for the Church and have been active in their wards and stakes, Dr. Allen having been a bishop and high councilor and Dr. Leonard a seventies quorum president.

Although the authors bear primary responsibility for their interpretation, the work was read by a committee consisting of myself as Church Historian; Dr. Davis Bitton, assistant Church historian; and Dr. Maureen Ursenbach Beecher, editor of the Historical Department. We have found that the authors were conscientious in their efforts to keep abreast of current scholarship and to portray the exciting, often controversial history of the Saints as fairly and dispassionately as possible. At the same time, of course, their interpretation reflects their own orientation as devout believers in the restored gospel of Jesus Christ.

We are grateful for the guidance of Elder Alvin R. Dyer and Elder Joseph Anderson, who served as managing directors of the Historical Department while this book was being prepared. Earl E. Olson, assistant managing director of the department, and Donald T. Schmidt, Church Librarian and Archivist, have given full support. We are particularly pleased that the book appears on the one-hundredth anniversary of the birth of President Joseph Fielding Smith, who for half a century served with distinction as Church Historian.

Leonard J. Arrington
Church Historian

The history of The Church of Jesus Christ of Latter-day Saints has been written many times before, and will be written again as new information becomes available and as succeeding generations ask fresh questions about their past. Our intent in *The Story of the Latter-day Saints* is to offer, principally in narrative form, a compact, introductory overview of Church history that takes advantage of recent scholarship as well as considerable new material available in the Church Archives. We also concentrate more heavily on the events of the past fifty years than do earlier works. Within each chapter we focus on a brief period—varying from three or four to a dozen years—and attempt to explain the events with as much detail, interest, and meaning as possible while keeping in mind the broader trends as well as the limitations imposed by the size of the book.

There are many themes in the history of the Latter-day Saints, but four seem to stand out. While we made no effort to structure the work artificially around those themes, they influenced our interpretation and are significant enough to mention here.

First, we are convinced that the Latter-day Saints were basically a religious people and not, as sometimes has been asserted, motivated largely by personal economic or political considerations. Anyone who reads the first-person accounts of the Saints' religious experiences, many in their own handwriting, must become convinced, as we are, that they genuinely believed in the authenticity of their faith and were deeply concerned with sharing it with their fellowmen. From the time of Joseph Smith's first vision, the Saints bore constant testimony that the Church was divinely inspired, directed by revelation from God. Even though the Saints and their leaders were constantly involved in secular affairs, concern for these things was secondary to a quest for salvation in the restored kingdom of God. Only by understanding this motivation can we perceive what led Latter-day Saints in all periods to sacrifice personal concerns so that the message of the gospel could spread to the people of the world. It was all done in the hope of preparing a righteous people for the millennial reign of Christ.

A second theme is that the Church was always influenced to some degree by the events of the world around it. We think it important to see the institution in the context of its environment, and where appropriate we have tried to demonstrate that relationship. The early persecutions, the economic problems of the Saints, their choice of various places of refuge, and their changing religious and social programs were all related in some way to the broader setting. Understanding that relationship is essential to understanding the Church itself.

Third, we see The Church of Jesus Christ of Latter-day Saints as a religious body that began in America as a tiny organization and expanded in nearly 150 years to claim an international membership. How and why that expansion took place is one of the essential themes of its history. Only in recent times, and only after the end of a policy of gathering to a central place of refuge, has the Church become a genuinely worldwide church, yet the quest for global influence was a continuing theme from the beginning.

Finally, we are impressed with the dynamics of change within the Church. We have tried to suggest how and why new programs were adopted, old policies reevaluated and changed, and new doctrinal information presented to the Saints. We have also tried to suggest some of the things that have remained constant. The Church is based on the principle of continuing revelation, and as new conditions arise, the Saints are continually impressed with the importance of heeding the counsel of the living prophet. This central Mormon teaching helps explain the ready acceptance by most members of new programs and directions. How the Church maintained its constant commitment to certain central religious truths and at the same time remained flexible enough to adapt to the ever-present but always changing challenges of the world is an essential part of its history.

In the preparation of this book we have relied heavily on the impressive body of new scholarship that has appeared in the past twenty years, and for this work we are most grateful. We have been helped by the standard historical works listed in the first section of the bibliography, and owe respect and gratitude to such early scholars as B. H. Roberts, Joseph Fielding Smith, Orson F. Whitney, Hubert Howe Bancroft, and Andrew Jenson. We have had the full cooperation of the personnel of the library and archives of the Historical Department, as well as our colleagues in the history division. We have also benefited greatly from conversations with other fellow historians, especially those who are preparing the forthcoming sixteen-volume sesquicentennial history of the Church. Many have generously provided materials and suggestions.

As a matter of style, we have attempted to avoid an abundance of footnotes. We have been careful, however, to include all basic sources in the bibliographic essay at the end of the book. In general, footnotes have been used only to identify direct quotations that are not otherwise clearly identifiable from the context. Further, we have adopted the policy used by many textbook writers of not providing a footnote if the quotation is very short and used mainly for literary effect.

We acknowledge the valuable help of the following people who, under assignment from the Church Historian, assisted us by providing research material and preliminary drafts in selected areas: Bruce D. Blumell, John F. Yurtinus, Evelyn Wendel, Craig Johnson, Christian Thorup, Edward J. Thompson, John Bluth, Betty Barton, Robert G. Mouritsen, Richard L. Jensen, and Gordon I. Irving. Credit for the basic map work goes to Merrill K. Ridd and Burt Merkley. We are indebted to Sharon Swenson for much editorial help, to Thomas G. Alexander for reading and critiquing the manuscript, and to Valerie Searle for skillfully directing the process of typing and retyping it in its many stages. She was assisted by Debbie Lilenquist, Karen Hulet, and Kathleen Davidson. In the production of the book, Wm. James Mortimer, Eleanor Knowles, and Michael Graves of Deseret Book have given encouragement and technical direction. The handsome design is the work of Bailey-Montague and Associates. Finally, we are deeply grateful for the skill, sensitivity, and sense of responsibility with which Leonard J. Arrington, Davis Bitton, and Maureen Ursenbach Beecher read the manuscript. In each case the suggestions given were invaluable.

James B. Allen
Glen M. Leonard

PART I

Laying the Foundations of Zion, 1820-1839

This portrait of Joseph Smith, probably painted by W. Majors after the death of the Prophet, is based on a daguerreotype made in Nauvoo. It is thought to be the most authentic likeness of Joseph Smith extant. (Published by permission of the Reorganized Church of Jesus Christ of Latter Day Saints)

IN THE MID-1970s more than twenty thousand young men and women of many nationalities were participating in full-time religious missions in more than eighty nations, attempting to acquaint others with the restored gospel of Jesus Christ. The message delivered by those Mormon missionaries was something like this:

"We represent The Church of Jesus Christ of Latter-day Saints. The Lord has sent us to you with this important message. Throughout history, when the Lord has had important truths to communicate to his children, he has revealed them through his prophets. Today we live in a time of trouble and turmoil. Many people are confused, discouraged, and searching for something better. . . . Our message and testimony to you is that God continues to guide his children today through living prophets. We particularly want you to know about a prophet whose name was Joseph Smith. In 1820 Joseph Smith, then still a young man, was living in the state of New York (in the United States). In his own words he gives the following account. . . ."

The missionaries then told the story of Joseph Smith and the rise of the church he was influential in founding. Wherever they were and whether they were Brazilians, Koreans, Danes, or Americans, they carried the same message: Joseph Smith was the instrument in the hands of God for restoring to the earth the ancient church of Jesus Christ, with all the knowledge and authority necessary to bring about the salvation of mankind. Like the tiny stone that the ancient prophet Daniel described as cut out of a mountain without hands, The Church of Jesus Christ of Latter-day Saints began as a small American body that believed its message universal and felt under obligation to carry its gospel to the world.

This unique message was repeated many times a day as the missionaries worked to build the Church in many lands. But despite this worldwide thrust, Latter-day Saints had always taught that the United States was specially prepared for its role in the restoration of the gospel, and that the environment in which Joseph Smith lived was especially well suited to receive that message. The growth of the Church from an obscure religion to one of worldwide magnitude is one of the themes of this volume.

At the time of its origin in 1830 The Church of Jesus Christ of Latter-day Saints was, indeed, characterized by much that was distinctively

American. The special revivalistic fervor of western New York helped prepare Joseph Smith for his earliest spiritual experiences. The necessity of restoring the gospel of primitive Christianity, the nearness of the Millennium, temperance, faith in miracles, and spiritual manifestations were accepted by many seekers of true religion in the 1820s and 1830s and helped prepare prospective converts for the message of Mormonism, as it was soon called. The Book of Mormon proclaimed America to be a land of promise, "choice above all other lands," and the site of a New Jerusalem to be established in preparation for Christ's millennial reign. Within ten years after the Church's organization in 1830, scores of missionaries had covered much of the United States and gathered thousands of converts to Ohio and Missouri. These converts made a valiant effort to establish ideal Christian communities in these two gathering places, but internal problems as well as conflict with non-Mormon neighbors resulted in their expulsion from both states. The Saints, however, never lost faith that one day there would be a return to Missouri, where Zion, the New Jerusalem, would be built upon the American continent.

The American roots of Mormonism in these years is also seen in a revelation that proclaimed the Constitution of the United States divinely inspired. In 1839 about fifteen hundred members lived outside the United States, but the overwhelming majority of Saints were native-born Americans whose habits, values, and hopes were intimately connected with the land of their birth and whose faith in the gospel intensified their expectations of America's destiny.

Since the Latter-day Saints of the 1830s were so intensely American, it may seem strange they were unable to live peacefully with their American neighbors. Religious persecution, however, was not uncommon in that early period. Many Americans feared secretive or close-knit groups, suspecting subversive plots to overthrow their free and pluralistic society. Some even detected foreign influences in religion, particularly Catholicism, and often connected those influences with charges of disloyalty. Others simply ridiculed the revivalists or other groups claiming special spiritual manifestations. In short, America was a fluid, diverse society—some people accepted new ideas, others ignored them, and others became actively involved in opposing new, hard-to-understand movements.

To some of their contemporaries, the clearly American traits of the Mormon people did not overshadow their distinctive solidarity and their unique claim that the Church was established by divine revelation as the only church on the face of the earth that carried the authority of God himself. Only the Roman Catholics and a few small, insignificant sects claimed as much—but Mormonism was not insignificant to neighboring residents of frontier Missouri and western Illinois.

This formative period of Latter-day Saint history was dominated by the powerful figure of Joseph Smith. As a leader he directed both temporal and spiritual activities, and suggested that actually there was little difference between the two. "All things unto me are spiritual," the Lord said to him in a revelation as early as September 1830, "and not at any time have I given unto you a law which is temporal."[1] From the beginning people came to "Brother Joseph" to ask the will of the Lord concerning them. Joseph instructed the Saints in the law of consecration, which they hoped would establish a series of ideal communities and promote temporal and spiritual equality. He led a small army from Ohio to Missouri, hoping to restore his followers to their homes, and he established both a banking enterprise and a temple in Ohio. The schools of Kirtland, the communities in Missouri, the printing houses in Ohio and Missouri, the publication of the Book of Commandments, and the willingness of thousands to uproot their lives and relocate were all results of the conviction that Joseph Smith was a prophet. Young Joseph's vision of the Father and the Son, the appearances of Moroni and other angels, the translation of the Book of Mormon, the more than 120 revelations recorded by Joseph Smith, and countless incidents of healing, speaking in tongues, and other spiritual manifestations—all provided the strength of Mormonism in these early years. For believers, these things were "the substance of things hoped for, the evidence of things not seen"; they were the foundation of their faith.

---

[1] *The Doctrine and Covenants of The Church of Jesus Christ of Latter-day Saints,* 29:34. *Hereinafter cited as D&C.*

CHAPTER 1

The Religious Setting for the Restoration

T his is my Beloved Son. Hear Him!"

That, recorded Joseph Smith, is what he heard in the spring of 1820 as he prayed in a secluded spot in a grove of trees near his home in western New York, and in vision beheld two heavenly Personages. The message he received was that he should join no church but rather wait until the Lord saw fit, through him, to restore the ancient gospel of Jesus Christ.

From this profound experience young Joseph emerged a man of destiny whose story would one day be known worldwide. But in a sense this did not mark the beginning of the history of the Latter-day Saints, for what Joseph Smith did was, in part at least, intimately related to the religious environment of his time. Many people were ready for his message, but how they became so can be fully understood only by examining a long period of religious history that culminated in the great revivals of the early nineteenth century. The Saints believe that in some way the hand of God directed the historical events that prepared America for a restoration of the ancient faith.

The Protestant Reformation

The preparation began as early as the Protestant Reformation in Europe, for religious life in the New World was largely the outgrowth of that important movement. As Protestantism was adapted to the colonial environment, it went through many changes, but by the nineteenth century it contained many ideas that would provide a fertile field for the rise of Mormonism.

Martin Luther is usually credited with precipitating the Reformation, though he was not the first to criticize the powerful Catholic Church. In 1517 he attacked the practice of selling indulgences (partial relief from the temporal penalties of sin) and this, together with other disagreements, eventually led to his trial for heresy. In 1521 he formally broke from Catholicism and, at the urging of certain German rulers, assisted in establishing the Lutheran Church. Luther had no intention of destroying Catholicism; he wanted only to purify it and return it to the ancient tenets of Christianity as he understood them.

In England, one of the least radical Protestant movements began after the Catholic Church failed to sanction a divorce sought by King Henry VIII. Angered, in 1534 the king proclaimed the English church independent of the papacy and established himself as the head of the new Church of England, or Anglican Church. A hundred years later Anglicanism was the established (state-supported) church not only in England but also in many of her American colonies.

Like Luther, most reformers hoped to purify the church by returning to the simple practices and fundamental doctrines of early Christianity. They rejected elaborate priesthood forms and adopted simple patterns of worship. Many taught that salvation was a question of one's individual relationship with God, rather than the result of a series of sacraments that could be administered only by a priest. Others contended that the ordinance of baptism must be performed only for those old enough to believe.

But the man who had the greatest influence on Joseph Smith's New England heritage was the Swiss reformer John Calvin. It was his theology that the Puritans of England promoted in their attempts to purify the Anglican Church; and when they failed in their homeland, they took Calvinism to America.

Religion in Colonial America

From John Calvin, the Puritans of New England inherited at least two distinctive doctrines: belief in man's total depravity and

South Royalton, Vermont, as it appeared in 1912, was representative of New England villages. (George E. Anderson photograph, Church Archives)

the concept of predestination and election. Through the fall of Adam, they taught, man became utterly depraved—incapable of goodness and totally undeserving of anything but damnation. Salvation came only to those whom God, for his own purposes, chose or elected to be saved. Christ's atonement provided the power for this salvation, but it was only for those who had been thus predestined.

An ironic twist in the Calvinist-Puritan doctrine compelled believers to adhere strictly to God's laws, as they interpreted them, and created the moral climate of Joseph Smith's homeland. Through faith and obedience to God's will, his elect could learn of their chosen state. Further, he would bless the elect with success— particularly economic success—which led the Puritan fathers to emphasize thrift, industry, and hard work as characteristics of God's chosen. These virtues became essential elements of the Puritan ethic that typified much of colonial America.

The Puritans saw themselves as a chosen people, commissioned by God to build a New Jerusalem, or a City of Zion, in America—an exemplary community that all could observe and emulate. The church consisted of a number of elected or "regenerated" individuals who voluntarily formed a "covenant community" that agreed to obey the will of God. Children born to church members were said to be born "under the covenant." Pastors and other church officers received their authority only by common consent of the members of each congregation, and this formed the basis for what later became known as Congregationalism.

Puritanism became the established faith in nearly all New England colonies, and initially no other religion was tolerated. After all, the leaders reasoned, if this were the true faith, it would be wrong in the sight of God to allow the existence of any other.

But the Puritan way did not long remain the only way in New England. Roger Williams was a particularly prominent dissenter. He believed Calvinism could be maintained as a vital faith only by voluntary association, not by a state-imposed conformity. The formation of other non-Puritan congregations could not long be forestalled, even in Massachusetts, as population increased and as the younger generation demanded less rigid conformity to tradition.

Outside New England, the Church of England became the established faith in most colonies, although the Quakers, Presbyterians, Baptists, and Lutherans gained sizeable followings. The continuing immigration from Europe introduced a variety of smaller Protestant sects as well as a number of Catholic congregations; and by the time of the American Revolution, a significant religious diversity prevailed in all colonies, even in New England. Few people maintained formal membership in any church—only an average of 8 percent in all the colonies—but religious values maintained a significant influence in colonial society.

At the beginning of the eighteenth century a movement known as the Great Awakening swept America, reaching its peak in the 1730s and early 1740s. Essentially it was a fervent effort to restore righteousness and religious zeal, and in New England Jonathan Edwards attempted to restore the crumbling foundations of early Puritanism. Its most ambitious objectives were not achieved, but the Great Awakening did have certain long-range influences, some of which contributed to the social and intellectual climate conducive to the rise of Mormonism. It kindled a warm glow of religious commitment that had not been felt in America for years, and gave rise to a new evangelistic pattern that resulted in itinerant preachers, especially Baptists, establishing many new churches along the frontier. It also helped promote greater participation by laymen in the affairs of organized religion, a characteristic that would become essential to the church founded by Joseph Smith.

Still, total freedom of religion had not been achieved in America, for established churches existed in nearly every colony. The American Revolution helped create a climate leading to disestablishment, that is, separation of church and state. The Declaration of Independence and the American Constitution were both products of the eighteenth century enlightenment, and both assumed that man was capable of discovering correct political principles for himself and formulating his own political institutions. Implicitly this meant that government should be free to respond to the needs of the people, uninfluenced by the pressures of organized religion. On the other hand, religion should be a matter of personal conscience, and no one should be required, through payment of taxes, to support a religion teaching doctrines that he did not believe.

Before the ink could dry on the Declaration of Independence, agitation for disestablishment began in many colonies. Virginia was one of the first, and in 1785 it adopted a Bill for Establishing Religious Freedom. Its author, Thomas Jefferson, regarded this and the Declaration of Independence his most significant achievements. The move for disestablishment spread throughout the new nation, though it found opposition in many quarters and was not totally achieved until well into the nineteenth century. The separation of church and state eventually became one of the nation's most characteristic political traditions.

Another period of religious fervor, the Second Great Awakening, began in New England in the 1790s and spread throughout the nation. It was characterized by circuit-riding preachers, fiery-tongued evangelists, new grass-roots religious movements, fervent emotionalism, and the manifestation of certain physical excesses that demonstrated to new converts divine acceptance. After the War of 1812, the revival swept the country in periodic waves, reaching a peak between 1825 and 1827.

Western New York was so intensely affected that it was called the Burned-over District. It was populated largely by former New Englanders, including the family of Joseph Smith, whose deep-rooted religious heritage made them especially sensitive to the call for a spiritual reawakening. An impressive series of revival meet-

Typical camp meeting at the time of the Second Great Awakening.
(*Library of Congress*)

ings in the Burned-over District during Joseph Smith's early years gave the future prophet ample opportunity to become familiar with them and to think seriously about his own salvation.

The Christian Primitivists: Precursors of the Restoration

The Great Awakening, the growing religious freedom and pluralism in America, and the Second Great Awakening prepared a fertile field for the spread of religious ideas and a multiplication of sects. One impulse common to many of the new movements was Christian primitivism: the desire to restore the ancient doctrines and practices of the New Testament church. As early as 1639 Roger Williams taught that the primitive church had been destroyed by apostasy and that the authority to perform ordinances had been lost. He thus became a seeker, looking forward to a time when the true church would be restored by special commission. A growing number of seekers followed him, and by Joseph Smith's time the search for the restoration of the ancient church was not uncommon among Protestants both in America and Europe.

To most primitivists the restoration of the ancient gospel was a necessary precursor to the second coming of Christ. Millennialism—the belief that the Savior's second advent was imminent—was commonplace by the early nineteenth century, and many people fervently expected it within their own lifetimes. Millennialism helped spark the revivals of the Second Great Awakening, and restorationist publications such as Alexander Campbell's *Millennial Harbinger* kept the idea constantly before believers.

The long list of primitivists in Joseph Smith's time was impressive, but all such movements were overshadowed by the Campbellites, or Disciples of Christ. One of their early leaders was Sidney Rigdon, who later became second to Joseph Smith in the leadership of the Latter-day Saints.

Thomas Campbell and his son Alexander were initially concerned with reforming the Presbyterian Church, but after Rigdon heard the younger Campbell discuss the "restoration of the ancient order of things," he persuaded him to join a liberal Baptist group. Campbell, in turn, persuaded Rigdon to accept a call to head the First Baptist Church of Pittsburgh in 1822. When Campbell decided to break with the Baptists, Sidney Rigdon's followers became the third group to declare itself a part of Campbell's new movement. Rigdon soon became popular among the Disciples of Christ, largely because of his eloquent preaching and profound biblical scholarship. As a restorationist he taught faith, repentance, and baptism, and promised the Holy Ghost to those who would believe. He was well prepared for the message of the Mormon missionaries when they came to him in 1830.

Many other seekers and restorationists were spiritually prepared for the gospel. After hearing both Sidney Rigdon and Alexander Campbell in 1829, Parley P. Pratt joined the Disciples, recognizing much of the pure gospel he was seeking, though he still wondered about proper authority to administer holy things. Wilford Woodruff early in life asked God in prayer to "restore the ancient Gospel, to restore the ancient gifts, to restore the ancient power,"[1] and he received assurance he would see it happen.

At age fifteen Joel Johnson sat up all night reading the Bible and thrilling with a spiritual confirmation that someday he would possess the ancient gospel. Jesse Crosby at age sixteen wondered which of the churches was right, attended different denominations, and continually sought solitude in the woods to pray for guidance.

---

[1] *Journal of Discourses,* 26 vols. (London: Latter-day Saints' Book Depot, 1854-86), 25:171.

And as young Eliza R. Snow studied the New Testament, she too yearned for the spiritual gifts of which the ancient apostles testified.

John Taylor, a Methodist preacher in Canada, met regularly with a group that concluded that no existing religious sect was the church of Christ, and that all lacked divine authority. They sought a church with the same organization as the original church, including apostles, but disagreed on how to find it. Some felt they should ask God to commission them by revelation with the ancient authority of apostles and prophets, while others wondered if the Lord had not already ordained apostles somewhere in the world. Such incidents happened many times in early nineteenth-century America, and such seekers were soon attracted to the message of the Mormon missionaries.

The Smiths of New England

The family history of Joseph Smith, Jr., the first Latter-day Saint prophet, intimately reflected his historical New England heritage. His ancestors on both sides migrated to Massachusetts in the seventeenth century. His grandparents, Asael and Mary Smith, spent their early married years on the Smith family farm at Topsfield, where in 1772 their three children were baptized in the Congregational Church. Both Asael and Mary "owned the covenant," or made a personal confession of their faith. Asael, however, did not remain an active Congregationalist, for his religious views acquired some of the more liberal overtones of the Age of Enlightenment.

Asael became an enthusiastic supporter of the American Revolution and enlisted in the army. His attitude toward the war was not unlike that of other patriots of his day. He expressed it in a 1799 "address" written to members of his family:

> Bless God that you live in a land of liberty, and bear yourselves dutifully and conscionable toward the authority under which you live. See God's providence in the appointment of the Federal Constitution.[2]

In 1778 Asael moved his family to Derryfield, New Hampshire, where he became prominent in civic affairs. His ill health, however, made it difficult for him to work his farm. Then in 1785

---

[2]As quoted in Richard Lloyd Anderson, *Joseph Smith's New England Heritage* (Salt Lake City: Deseret Book Company, 1971), p. 128.

his father died, and the following year, with their eleven children, the Smiths returned to the family farm at Topsfield. Asael assumed the responsibility of paying the family debts, caring for his aged stepmother, and managing a hundred-acre farm. He began these tasks in the midst of a serious postwar depression. His success is an exemplary story of thrift and industry. After only five years he was able to settle all his father's debts. He later took his family to Tunbridge, Vermont, where he pioneered eighty-five acres of uncleared land, soon purchased more farms, and became a community leader. Sometime between 1810 and 1820 he moved to northern New York state, where he died in 1830, the year his grandson organized a new church.

On his mother's side, Joseph Smith's grandfather was Solomon Mack, son of the Congregational pastor at Lyme, Connecticut. Financial misfortune struck the Mack family when Solomon was only four, and he was apprenticed to a neighborhood farmer. He worked long, hard hours, with no opportunity for either education or religious training, and after he had served his apprenticeship he enlisted to fight in the French and Indian War. Later he followed several professions: merchant, land developer, shipmaster, mill operator, and farmer. He was apparently a model of the Puritan ethic in practice, for he was known for industry, hard work, honesty in business dealings, and generosity almost to a fault.

Although Solomon joined no church until late in life, his wife, Lydia, provided the family with strong religious training, which Solomon deeply appreciated. The daughter of a Congregationalist deacon, Lydia had been a schoolteacher before her marriage. When he was nearly eighty, Solomon seriously turned to religion and, with his wife as his teacher, read the Bible, received some singular spiritual manifestations, and was converted. This seems to have had a miraculous influence on his health, and during the rest of his life he labored to bring others to religion. He even wrote an autobiography designed to persuade others to Christianity.

Lucy Mack, Joseph's mother, was the youngest daughter of Solomon and Lydia Mack; she was born at Gilsum, New Hampshire, in 1775. About twenty years later she met Joseph Smith, son of Asael, while she was visiting her brother at Tunbridge, Vermont. The two were married in 1796 and immediately took up

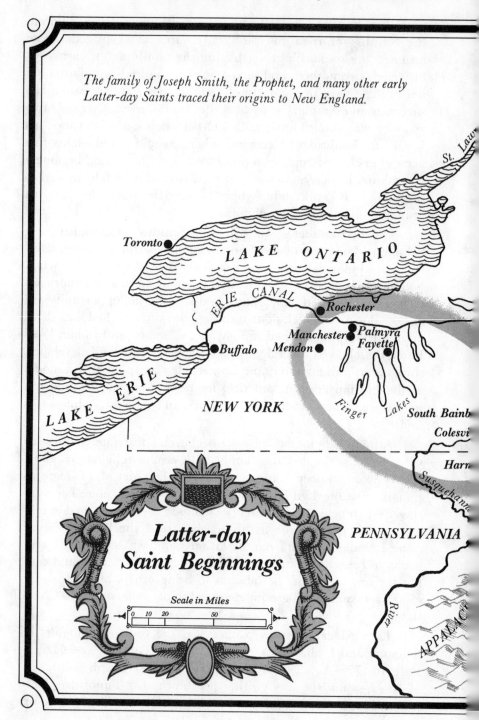

The family of Joseph Smith, the Prophet, and many other early
Latter-day Saints traced their origins to New England.

Toronto

LAKE ONTARIO

St. Law

ERIE CANAL

Rochester

Manchester   Palmyra
Fayette

Buffalo   Mendon

LAKE ERIE

NEW YORK

Finger   Lakes   South Bainb

Colesvi

Harn

Susquehann

*Latter-day
Saint Beginnings*

PENNSYLVANIA

Scale in Miles

0   10   20   50

River

APPALAC

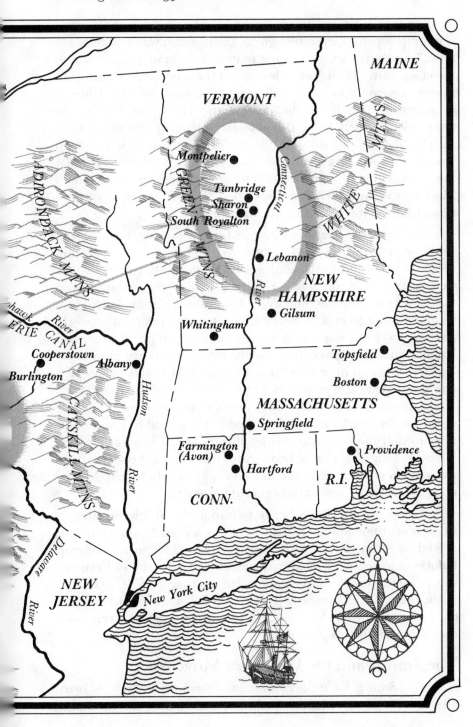

farming in Tunbridge. But farming in the rocky soil of Vermont was not prosperous, even though, as Lucy said, it was a "handsome farm," and after six years they rented their land and went into merchandising. Then Joseph learned of the large profits possible in raising ginseng root and selling it to China, for the Chinese considered this herb a valuable medicine. He invested heavily in the enterprise, only to be disappointed when the son of his shipping partner absconded with the profits. The Smiths were forced to sell their farm and use Lucy's dowry to pay their debts. In 1804 they moved to Sharon, Vermont, where they rented Solomon Mack's farm, and there, on December 23, 1805, the third of their nine children, Joseph Smith, Jr., was born.

In Vermont, Joseph, Sr., worked the farm, and taught school in the winter. In 1811 the family moved to Lebanon, New Hampshire. They looked ahead with great optimism, but in 1813 they were struck by a devastating epidemic of typhus, which killed thousands in Vermont and New Hampshire. All their children contracted the fever and recovered, but young Joseph, two weeks after his recovery, was seized with an infection in his shoulder and left leg. After failing to cure it, the doctors decided to amputate the leg. The boy and his mother refused to consent to this drastic step and persuaded them to try once more to cut out the infected part. Since anesthetics were not yet in use, the doctors tried to tie him down for the operation, but he refused. They tried to give him liquor to dull the pain, but this he also refused. The surgeons then removed a large section of bone. After the successful operation, he was sent to recuperate at the home of his uncle in Salem, Massachusetts, where he gradually regained his health.

The epidemic took a heavy toll upon the Smith fortunes, as sickness continued in the family for nearly a year. Again the family moved, this time to Norwich, Vermont, but three successive crop failures depleted their meager resources. The poor soil of Vermont was discouraging, but when snow fell in June of 1816 and frost killed the replanted crops in July, many Vermont farmers moved on. Emigration from Vermont reached a floodtide that year, and the Smith family was part of it.

The Smiths and the Westward Movement

The Smiths were latecomers to western New York. Shortly after the Revolution, land speculators, anticipating the inevitable settlement west of the Adirondacks, purchased all available state-owned land and then actively promoted the golden opportunities of the West. In western New York, especially, the land was rich, fertile, and easy to cultivate. All a prospective settler needed was enough money for a down payment and enough manpower to clear away the trees.

The emigration to western New York began as early as the 1790s, and by 1800 it had become a mass movement. By 1812, two hundred thousand people lived in the area, over two-thirds of them New Englanders. So great was the migration through the Mohawk Valley, in fact, that many of the more conservative New Englanders became alarmed. Not only did they see the rate of their population growth fall woefully behind that of the rest of the nation, but land values were declining, the social structure was threatened with disruption, and their best and youngest citizens were moving away. Newspaper propaganda bristled with alarming descriptions of danger on the frontier, as every effort was made to persuade the migrants to stay home.

But the warnings were to no avail. Those who left were seeking better economic opportunity, and they were willing to risk the dangers and pay the price in work to find it.

In this atmosphere in the summer of 1816 Joseph Smith, Sr., left his family and headed west in search of new opportunities. Several weeks later he wrote and told them to follow him—not to Ohio, as they had expected, but to the vicinity of Palmyra in western New York. Lucy and her eight children, the youngest only a few months old, packed all they could into a wagon, used the last of their financial resources to pay off their creditors, and sometime during that winter joined Joseph, Sr., in Palmyra.

The township of Palmyra suffered from inflation at the time of their arrival. It had been settled for twenty-five years and boasted a population of nearly three thousand people. Only thirteen miles to the south was Canandaigua, the economic center of the region. Everyone expected the present boom to continue, and immigrants, including the Smiths, paid highly inflated prices for their land. Unfortunately, the boom in the vicinity of Palmyra did not last. Before long many transplanted New Englanders found themselves once again moving west, to Ohio. The Smiths, however, decided to remain.

They rented a small home in Palmyra, and everyone old

enough worked at odd jobs to help secure a livelihood. Joseph, Sr., was a cooper. He set about making the buckets and barrels in demand because of the abundance of maple trees in the area. Wooden containers were needed to store and collect the sap, which was made into sugar and syrup. He also knew enough masonry to case wells, cisterns, and basement walls. One such job came from Martin Harris, a well-to-do farmer, who hired him and his second son, Hyrum, to case a well. Alvin, the oldest son, worked as a carpenter's helper. Lucy, meanwhile, set up a home business of her own. She painted and sold oilcloth table coverings and made and sold such sundries as gingerbread, pies, boiled eggs, and root beer. She did an especially lively business at public celebrations on the Fourth of July and other holidays. Within two years the family had saved enough to make a down payment on a hundred-acre farm in Farmington (later Manchester) township, a few miles south of Palmyra.

The family all continued to work in order to support themselves and pay for their land. During the first year Joseph, Sr., and his sons cleared thirty acres of timber and planted wheat. They also tapped twelve to fifteen hundred maple trees in order to draw the precious sap and make maple sugar. Though some neighbors later described the family as lazy and irresponsible, at least one recalled, "They have all worked for me many a day; they were very good people. Young Joe (as we called him then) has worked for me, and he was a good worker; they all were."[3]

The Smiths soon built a two-room log cabin with two attic bedrooms. Joseph was twelve years old when the family moved in. In mid-1821, needing additional sleeping quarters after their youngest child was born, they added a lean-to. They later began to build a new and larger frame house, which was completed in the late fall of 1825.

Young Joseph's educational opportunities were extremely limited. School terms normally lasted a maximum of three months, and children were taught little more than the basics of reading, writing, and arithmetic. Joseph attended school for only a term or two, but he also studied on his own. His mother noted that "he seemed much less inclined to the perusal of books than any of the rest of our children, but far more given to meditation and deep

---

[3]*Saints' Herald* 28 (1881): 165.

study."[4] He was also inquisitive and interested in contemporary news and issues. He regularly read the *Palmyra Register* and participated in a young people's debating club.

Joseph Smith was a "remarkably quiet, well-disposed child," his mother said. He admired his parents, always expressing great love and loyalty for them, and was apparently an obedient son. Some of his contemporaries remembered him as "good natured, very rarely if ever indulging in any combative spirit toward anyone," as having a "jovial easy, don't care way with him and made him a lot of friends," and as "a real clever jovial boy."[5]

Until about 1820, none of the Smith family joined any religious denomination, though they were staunchly believing Christians. Like many other unchurched Americans, they were seekers and not eager to be too quick to join a particular church. Joseph's father was deeply spiritual, and Lucy later recorded several remarkable dreams and visions he experienced, which seemed to foreshadow the coming restoration of the gospel through their son. Under the tutelage of their father, the family studied the scriptures together and were led by him in family prayer. No pains were spared, the Prophet recalled later, in instructing him in the principles of Christianity.

What is it that shapes a man? From his family, as well as from the religious and social crosscurrents in early America, Joseph Smith received a heritage steeped in the Puritan ethic of thrift and industry, faith in God and a realization of man's dependence upon him, a longing for the establishment of God's ideal community, and belief that America was a land chosen for a divine destiny. By the time he came of age, America was a land of religious freedom, and although new movements were often ridiculed and scoffed at, no legal barriers barred their growth. His religious environment contained seeds of teachings that later became part of Mormon doctrine, but more importantly, it fostered a strong and active faith that one day the ancient order of things would be restored. The immediate vicinity of Joseph Smith's home burned with the

---

[4]Lucy Smith, *Biographical Sketches of Joseph Smith the Prophet and His Progenitors for Many Generations* (Liverpool: Published for Orson Pratt by S. W. Richards, 1853), p. 84.

[5]Pomeroy Tucker, *Origin, Rise and Progress of Mormonism* (New York: D. Appleton & Co., 1867), pp. 16-17; *Saints' Herald* 28 (1881): 167. For an insightful analysis of this general issue, see Richard Lloyd Anderson, "Joseph Smith's New York Reputation Reappraised," *Brigham Young University Studies* 10 (Spring 1970): 283-314.

fervor of the Second Great Awakening, and ministers and laymen commonly debated the question of which church was right.

But such historical forces alone would not produce a prophet. Not until he was determined and ready to open himself to the mind and will of God—to allow divine inspiration to help mold his character and destiny—would he become different from what he was. By 1820 he was ready.

CHAPTER 2

The Restoration Commences, 1820-1831

J oseph Smith could not avoid the spiritual awakenings of the Burned-over District. During a twelve-month period beginning in mid-1819, religious revivals took place in at least ten towns within a twenty-mile radius of his home. In July 1819 the Methodists of the Genesee Conference held their annual meetings in Phelps Village (then called Vienna) about ten miles from the Smith farm. A hundred ministers met to deliberate policy, then began to hold camp meetings throughout the area. During the next year this process sparked a flaming spiritual advance as Methodists, Baptists, and Presbyterians all participated, and their churches showed uncommon membership gains.

In the midst of this religious excitement, the contemplative young Joseph was deeply touched. Later, when he became more mature, he dictated recollections of the memorable events of that year to scribes and confided more intimate details to close friends. On the basis of these accounts from the 1830s, we are able to re-construct his remarkable story.[1]

Joseph Smith's attendance at revivals while in his early teens,

[1]In the following reconstruction, the direct quotations are taken from various accounts. The standard account is found in Joseph Smith, Jr., *History of the Church of Jesus Christ of*

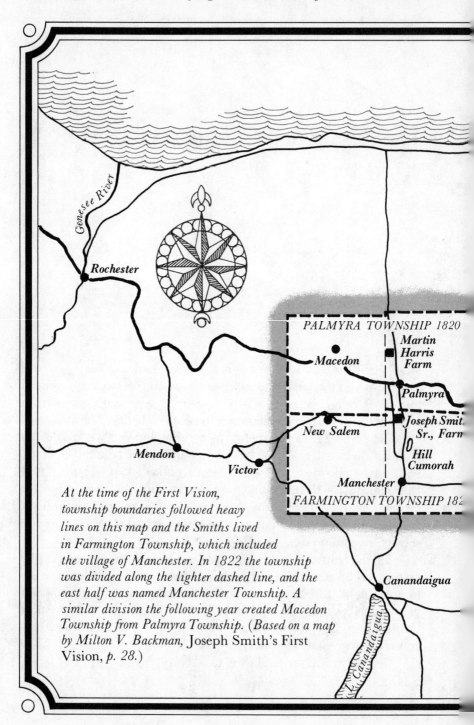

At the time of the First Vision, township boundaries followed heavy lines on this map and the Smiths lived in Farmington Township, which included the village of Manchester. In 1822 the township was divided along the lighter dashed line, and the east half was named Manchester Township. A similar division the following year created Macedon Township from Palmyra Township. (Based on a map by Milton V. Backman, Joseph Smith's First Vision, p. 28.)

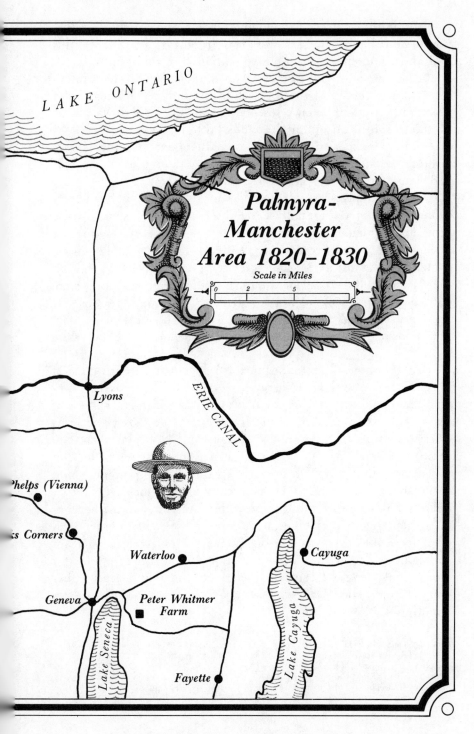

LAKE ONTARIO

Palmyra-
Manchester
Area 1820–1830

Scale in Miles

0   2   5

Lyons

ERIE CANAL

Phelps (Vienna)

Corners

Waterloo

Cayuga

Geneva

Peter Whitmer
Farm

Lake Seneca

Lake Cayuga

Fayette

and his family's concern for religion, made his own quest for salvation urgent. He became seriously concerned for the welfare of his soul and commenced an intensive searching of the scriptures. No doubt he was somewhat torn when his mother, two brothers, and a sister joined the Presbyterians, while his father remained aloof from organized religion. Joseph began to lean toward the Methodists. Still uncommitted to any faith, he longed for the kind of emotional experience he witnessed in others. At one revival meeting, he later told a friend, he intensely desired to get religion and wanted to feel the spirit and shout like the rest.

As the young seeker examined various denominations he became disillusioned, especially as he observed the ministers' intense competition for converts. So contentious was this proselyting, he later wrote, "great confusion and bad feeling ensued—priest contending against priest, and convert against convert; so that all their good feelings one for another, if they ever had any, were entirely lost in a strife of words and a contest about opinions." "I knew not who was right or who was wrong," he recalled in 1835, "but considered it of the first importance to me that I should be right."

At the same time, he began to suspect that perhaps none of the churches were right. Like other seekers, he observed that mankind "had apostatized from the true and living faith and there was no society or denomination that built upon the Gospel of Jesus Christ as recorded in the New Testament." His mind was soon drawn to James 1:5. "If any of you lack wisdom," he read, "let him ask of God, that giveth to all men liberally, and upbraideth not, and it shall be given him." He was ready for that message: "Never did any passage of scripture come with more power to the heart of man than this did at this time to mine. It seemed to enter with great force into every feeling of my heart. I reflected on it again and again, knowing that if any person needed wisdom from God, I did. . . . At length I came to the conclusion that I must either remain in darkness and confusion, or else I must do as James directs, that is, ask of God."

Latter-day Saints, ed. B. H. Roberts, 7 vols., 2nd ed. rev. (Salt Lake City: Deseret Book Co., 1964), 1:2-8. Other accounts are reproduced in Dean C. Jessee, "The Early Accounts of Joseph Smith's First Vision," *Brigham Young University Studies* 9 (Spring 1969): 275-94, and in James B. Allen, "Eight Contemporary Accounts of Joseph Smith's First Vision: What Do We Learn from Them?" *Improvement Era* 73 (April 1970): 4-13. The quotations referring to the visit from Moroni are all taken from the standard account in Joseph Smith's *History of the Church*.

Stained-glass representation of Joseph Smith's first vision, once located in the Adams Ward meetinghouse in Los Angeles, California, was one of many fine artistic representations of this sacred event. (Church Archives)

On a beautiful spring morning in 1820 Joseph went to a familiar spot in the woods near his home. At least three serious concerns were on his mind. Could he find forgiveness of sins and salvation for his soul? Secondly, what about the welfare of mankind? "I felt to mourn for my own sins and for the sins of the world," he said. Finally, he longed to know which, if any, of the churches was right, and which he should join. For the first time in his life, he tried to utter a vocal prayer.

No one knows how long Joseph Smith remained alone in the woods, but before his objective was accomplished he experienced a desperate struggle. As he tried to pray, he said, "immediately I was seized by some power which entirely overcame me, and had such astonishing influence over me as to bind my tongue so that I could not speak." While he attempted to loose his tongue, several strange things happened. Distracting thoughts ran through his mind, threatening to keep him from his goal. At one point, he later recalled, "I heard a noise behind me like someone walking towards me. I strove again to pray, but could not; the noise of walking seemed to draw nearer. I sprang upon my feet and looked around, but saw no person, or thing." Presently "thick darkness" seemed to gather around him, and he felt that he was "doomed to sudden

An excerpt from Joseph Smith's 1832 account of his first vision. This is the earliest known document in which the vision was recorded and the only one in the Prophet's own handwriting. (Church Archives)

destruction" and must abandon himself to the power of "some actual being from the unseen world."

Despite his alarm, he continued to pray inwardly for deliverance. It was then that he saw a pillar of light, which shone "above the brightness of the sun at noon day." It gradually descended until it enveloped him, and immediately he was freed from the invisible opposition. Within the light the astonished young man saw two persons who resembled each other. They seemed to be standing above him in the air, the brightness of their presence defying all description. One of them called him by name, then pointed to the other and said, "This is My Beloved Son. Hear Him!"

As the solemn vision of the Father and the Son continued, Joseph received assurances concerning the religious questions that had perplexed him. "Joseph my son, thy Sins are forgiven thee," he was told. He began to gain a deeper understanding of the universal nature of salvation when the Savior testified in plainness that he had been crucified so that all those who believed in him might have eternal life.

Astounded at what was happening, Joseph nevertheless gained his composure enough to ask which of all the churches he should join. He was informed that all of them taught incorrect doctrines and none were acknowledged by God as his church. He was warned that certain professors of religion were "corrupt; that 'they draw near to me with their lips, but their hearts are far from me; they teach for doctrines the commandments of men: having a form of godliness, but they deny the power thereof.' " A second time he was warned against joining any of the existing churches, but received the firm assurance that "the fulness of the gospel should at some future time be made known" to him. He later confided to friends that he also saw "many angels" in his vision.

As the vision ended, Joseph again became aware of his environment. He found himself lying on his back looking skyward through the trees. Weak at first and unable to rise, he eventually regained enough strength to return home. His mother sensed that something was affecting him, but her first inquiries were met with "Never mind, all is well—I am well enough off." Then he looked at her and said, "I have learned for myself that Presbyterianism is not true."

The heavenly vision had a profound effect upon young

The Sacred Grove, Palmyra, New York. (George E. Anderson photograph, Church Archives)

Joseph. His mind, once agitated by uncertainty, was comforted now, reassured by "a state of calmness and peace indescribable." In addition, he said, "my soul was filled with love, and for many days I could rejoice with great joy and the Lord was with me." In this spirit he began to relate his experience to selected friends and acquaintances, but he "could find none that would believe the heavenly vision." He was particularly disappointed with the reaction of a Methodist minister who had been active in the religious awakening around Palmyra. The preacher treated his story "not only lightly, but with great contempt, saying it was all of the devil, that there were no such things as visions or revelations in these days; that all such things had ceased with the apostles, and that there would never be any more of them."

For a time Joseph Smith attempted to communicate his message to people around him, but to his neighbors it seemed incredible that any fourteen-year-old should make such claims. The criticism became so intense that it seemed as if he were being attacked from every side. It may have been because of this ridicule of his most sacred experience that he finally decided it would be folly, perhaps even sacrilege, to keep on sharing it publicly. Although he continued to tell it privately to a few close associates, it was not until several years after the organization of the Church that he decided to prepare an account of his first vision for publication, and then only to counteract the false and distorted reports that were circulating.

The Visit of Moroni

It would be more than three years before Joseph would experience other spiritual manifestations. In the meantime, despite the profound message of his vision, he was not a teenage religious recluse. Rather, he grew up like other young men in western New York and was probably more fun-loving—even mischievous—than many of his associates. In fact, he confessed later, "I was left to all kinds of temptation; and, mingling with all kinds of society, I frequently fell into many foolish errors, and displayed the weakness of youth, and the foibles of human nature; which, I am sorry to say, led me into divers temptations, offensive in the sight of God." This is not to say that he engaged in any gross misconduct. "I was guilty of levity," he explained, "and sometimes associated with jovial company, etc., not consistent with that character which ought to be maintained by one who was called of God as I had been. But this will not seem very strange to any one who recollects my youth, and is acquainted with my native cheery temperament." Lest anyone expected him to be more than human, never in his life did he claim perfection: rather, he recognized and, when he felt it appropriate, admitted his human failings.

Perhaps it is only by understanding his humanness that the reader of Latter-day Saint history can comprehend what makes a prophet. Though imperfect, Joseph Smith was striving toward perfection. When he made mistakes or sometimes succumbed to temptation, he took seriously the scriptural promise of God's forgiveness if he would overcome his weaknesses through prayer and effort. The Prophet exhibited such boundless faith in Christ's promise that even with, or in spite of, his weaknesses, he could apparently draw closer to the Divine than others and become an instrument in restoring the gospel.

On the night of September 21, 1823, Joseph Smith, now seventeen, retired to one of the sleeping rooms of the old log house. In bed he began to pray earnestly for forgiveness of his sins and follies and for further information on his standing before the Lord. Then, according to his own account, his room was filled with light, and appearing at his bedside, seemingly standing in the air, was a personage dressed in a brilliant white robe. Calling Joseph by name, the visitor announced that he was a messenger from the presence of God and that God had a work for the youth to do. The angel described an ancient record buried on a hillside not far from Joseph's home, a book giving an account of the early inhabitants of the American continent. The messenger, whose name was Moroni, was their last historian. He told Joseph that the book, written on "gold plates," contained the fulness of the gospel as it had been delivered by the resurrected Savior to these ancient people. With the record were "two stones in silver bows" which could be fastened to a breastplate. Called the Urim and Thummim, they were to be used in translating the book. The messenger told Joseph that when he obtained the plates, he should show them to no one. In vision he was shown where the plates were buried, and then the angel left as quickly as he had appeared.

As Joseph lay marveling at this experience, suddenly Moroni visited him again, repeating the same message. The messenger returned a third time, adding the caution that Satan would tempt him to use the plates to acquire wealth. He was admonished that the glory of God must be his only object in this work. Joseph had no sleep that night.

The next morning he went with his father to work in the fields as usual, but was so exhausted that Joseph, Sr., sent him home. Attempting to climb the fence at the edge of the field, the young man fainted. When he awoke he was again confronted by the angel Moroni, who repeated a fourth time the message of the night before and then instructed him to inform his father of the experience. He did so, and his father believed.

Joseph Smith, Sr., advised his son to follow Moroni's instructions, which he did. Proceeding immediately to the hill, he recognized the spot he had seen in vision. He located the plates, along with the breastplate and the Urim and Thummim, in a stone box buried in the hill. When he tried to .take them, Moroni appeared again. He was not yet ready, he was told, and the angel chastized him for allowing thoughts of potential wealth to obsess him while traveling to the hill. Already the young man was thinking contrary to instructions. As if to reiterate the awesomeness of his task, another vision was opened to his mind. In it he first saw the glory of the Lord resting upon him, and then the "Prince of Darkness" surrounded by his "innumerable train of associates." Moroni told the awe-struck young man: "All this is shown, the good and the evil, and holy and impure, the glory of God and the power of darkness, that you may know hereafter the two powers and never be influenced or overcome by that wicked one." Joseph was then told that he must return to that spot every year for four years. There he would meet Moroni. At each meeting, said Joseph, he received "instruction and intelligence . . . respecting what the Lord was going to do, and how and in what manner His kingdom was to be conducted in the last days." Finally, on September 22, 1827, he was entrusted with the plates.

Four Important Years

Joseph Smith's activities between the ages of seventeen and twenty-one, when he took the ancient record from the hill, are vague because of the dearth of authentic contemporary information. Yet this was a critical time in the life of the young prophet, as he developed from a teenage boy attracted to the wealth of the world—even after his remarkable spiritual manifestations—into a young man who had overcome such desires and was entrusted with a sacred record.

His detractors have emphasized every negative scrap of evidence, while others have countered with evidence of his religious nature. From Joseph Smith's own viewpoint, he was not without fault, but was growing in his ability to live as God wished. While en route to Missouri just two years after the Book of Mormon was published, he wrote a tender letter to his wife. Recalling his earlier years, he poured out his soul to Emma:

I have visited a grove which is Just back of the town almost every day where I can be Secluded from the eyes of any mortal and there give vent to all the feeling of my heart in meaditation and prayer. I have Called to mind all the past moments of my life and am left to morn [and] shed tears of sorrow for my folly in Sufering the adversary of my Soul to have so much power over me as he has had in times past. But God is merciful and has forgiven my Sins and I rejoice that he Sendeth forth the Comferter unto as many as believe and humbleth themselves before him.[2]

This heartfelt outpouring, along with other expressions in Joseph's own handwriting from this early period, confirm the genuineness of his religious conviction.

The religious activities of the Smith family initially remained unchanged by his experiences. Joseph, his father, and at least one brother, William, steadfastly refused to join any church. His mother and two brothers, Hyrum and Samuel, continued their membership in the Presbyterian church and evidently attended regularly until about 1828. On March 29, 1830, however, they were suspended for nonattendance, but that was only a week before they were to become members of the restored church, organized on April 6.

In the meantime, the family struggled to get out of debt, pay off the mortgage on their property, and complete their new home. The guiding hand in the building of the new home was the oldest son, Alvin, but on November 19, 1823, he died of what his mother later described as an overdose of calomel to cure the "bilious colic." Almost his last thoughts had to do with the most important things in the Smith family life at the moment: the sacred record and the new home. Not long before his death he said to his brother Hyrum: "I want to say a few things which I wish to have you remember. I have done all I could to make our dear parents comfortable. I want you to go on and finish the house." To Joseph he said, "I want you to . . . do everything that lies in your power to obtain the Record. Be faithful in receiving instruction, and in keeping every commandment that is given you." [3]

In the process of completing the house, the Smiths employed a carpenter by the name of Calvin Stoddard, who apparently took a covetous liking to the commodious home. At the time the Smiths were to make their last payment on the property, they received an extension allowing them to harvest their crops and get their wheat

---

[2]Joseph Smith to Emma Smith, June 6, 1832, as reproduced in *Brigham Young University Studies* 11 (Summer 1971): 519-20.
[3]Lucy Smith, *Biographical Sketches*, p. 88.

Smith family home in Palmyra, New York, completed in the late 1820s, is maintained as a historic memorial by the Church. (Charles B. Hall engraving, Church Archives)

to the mill. When Joseph, Sr., and his son Joseph left town to raise the money, Stoddard and two neighbors used a legal technicality to accuse them of running away to avoid payment. On the basis of this false testimony, the land agent gave Stoddard title to the property for the amount still owing. Friends of the Smiths heard of this deception, and Stoddard was soon forced to sell his title to a Mr. Durfee, the high sheriff of the county. Durfee then rented the home and farm back to the Smiths, but they never gained title to it. A surprising sequel to the story is that Calvin Stoddard fell in love with Joseph's sister, Sophronia, whom he married in 1827.

In the meantime, Joseph, Jr., continued to work with his father as well as hire out to other people. One of the curious sidelines with which he became involved was seeking for buried treasure. A mild craze of this activity excited the farmers of New York in the 1820s, based partly on superstitious reliance on folk magic, partly on belief in legend and folklore of buried Indian treasure and hidden Spanish pirate hoard. Some credence was lent to the rumors when Indian burial mounds, some not far from the Smith home, actually yielded artifacts of stone, copper, and sometimes silver. It was not unusual to find men and boys spending time following tales of buried wealth, and apparently some of the Smith family, including Joseph, became involved for a time. In a way, it might be said that this was part of Joseph's rude awakening to reality. Already he had been chastened for thinking of the gold plates as a source of income, and it is not improbable that the economic privation he knew could lead him to less sacrilegious schemes for acquiring wealth.

In the process, Joseph apparently acquired a reputation for possessing certain psychic powers to locate buried treasure. Neither the original source of such rumors nor whether they had any basis in fact is known, but Josiah Stowel (or Stoal) of Bainbridge, New York, believed them. On that belief, in October 1825 he hired Joseph, along with several other workers, to dig for treasure supposedly buried by the Spanish in an abandoned mine near Bainbridge. For nearly a month they worked without success until Joseph, as he later related the story, finally persuaded Stowel to abandon the enterprise. The incident only served to add to Joseph's reputation as a money-digger, an image that was revived later and enhanced with disparaging overtones.

All this led to young Joseph's first experience with the law. Early in 1826 someone brought charges against him and he was brought to trial in Chenango County, New York. The documents are so few and so contradictory that, although it is certain the trial was held, neither the precise charges nor the outcome of the trial are known. It is clear only that the charges somehow involved mystical money-seeking activities. According to one account, Joseph admitted once doing that kind of thing, but said that he had now given it up and did not solicit such work. Perhaps this was the maturity he needed before he could be entrusted with the sacred records denied him three years earlier.

These years also held other steps forward for Joseph Smith. During the winter that he worked for Josiah Stowel, he went to school. In addition, he became acquainted with persons who became lifelong friends. Mr. Stowel himself testified in favor of Joseph at the 1826 trial and remained a friend and supporter. Across the county line, in Broome County, lived Joseph Knight, a prosperous farmer and miller. Joseph also worked for him at times and became close friends with his son, Joseph Knight, Jr. According to the latter, Joseph told the family about the visits of Moroni and of the sacred record. This association would eventually lead members of the Knight family, at great sacrifice, to follow Joseph from New York to Ohio, Missouri, and Illinois, and later to follow Brigham Young to Utah.

Joseph Smith also found romance that year. While working for Stowel, he boarded with the family of Isaac Hale, a locally famous hunter. There he met and began to court the gracious Emma Hale. Courtship was not easy, for Emma's parents had heard and believed the negative stories about the young prophet, and they refused to give their consent to the marriage. At twenty-two, however, she was of age and could legally marry without their permission. Seeing no other alternative, Joseph and Emma eloped and were married by a justice of the peace on January 18, 1827. Emma's father was later reconciled to Joseph and became a believer.

At length the time came for Joseph to receive the sacred plates from which he would translate the Book of Mormon. Immediately after his marriage he quit working for Josiah Stowel and took his wife to his father's home, where he helped with the farming. On September 20, 1827, Stowel and Joseph Knight, Sr., came to visit with the Smiths. During the early morning hours of Sep-

Portrayal of Joseph Smith returning home with the plates of the Book of Mormon was painted by J. Leo Fairbanks and hangs in the Logan Temple. Much of the doctrine and sacred history of the Church is depicted in such paintings commissioned for display in temples and chapels.
(Internal Communications Department of the Church)

tember 22, Joseph borrowed Mr. Knight's horse and wagon and drove to the Hill Cumorah, where he met Moroni and obtained the ancient plates. At this point he received his final charge and warning. It was, he wrote, "that I should be responsible for them; that if I should let them go carelessly, or through any neglect of mine, I should be cut off; but that if I would use all my endeavors to preserve them until he, the messenger, should call for them, they should be protected."[4] He would soon have cause to remember that warning.

The Sacred Records

Joseph Smith said that the ancient records

were engraven on plates which had the appearance of gold, each plate was six inches wide and eight inches long, and not quite so thick as common tin. They were filled with engravings, in Egyptian characters, and bound together in a volume as the leaves of a book, with three rings running through the whole. The volume was something near six inches in thickness, a part of which was sealed. The characters on the unsealed part were small, and beautifully engraved. The whole book exhibited many marks of antiquity in its construction, and much skill in the art of engraving.[5]

There has been much speculation on how much such a book would weigh, for if it were pure gold, it would be much too heavy for anyone to carry. The implication within the book was that the metal was an alloy, hence Joseph's statement that it had the appearance of gold. It was not an uncommon practice for ancient people to keep records on plates made of various metals.

The most mysterious part of Joseph Smith's story is the use of the two stones called the Urim and Thummim, which were deposited with the plates. All he said about them was that they were "transparent stones set in the rim of a bow fastened to a breastplate." He implied that the "bow" was something like the rims of spectacles, which attached to a metal breastplate so that the person using it could concentrate and retain free use of his hands.

Biblical writers referred to an instrument called the Urim and Thummim, which somewhat resembled that described by Joseph Smith. The precise use of the instrument is not fully clear, but it is interesting that while the Israelites were wandering

---

[4]Joseph Smith, *History of the Church*, 1:18.
[5]Joseph Smith, *History of the Church*, 4:537.

between Egypt and Palestine, the priestly Levites wore as part of their sacred clothing a breastplate, or pouch, into which they were told to place the Urim and Thummim. It was apparently believed that this would somehow assist in divine communications. When Moses consecrated his brother Aaron, he placed a breastplate on him, and in it placed the Urim and Thummim. Aaron apparently used them in his role as a judge.

Joseph Smith left no firsthand description of how he used the Urim and Thummim in the translation process. Various associates have left sometimes contradictory descriptions of the process, but· Joseph Smith himself simply stated, "Through the medium of the Urim and Thummim I translated the record by the gift and power of God."[6] He also reported that he received several early revelations after inquiring of the Lord through the Urim and Thummim.

One key left by Joseph Smith to the method of translation, or revelation, came in April 1829 when Oliver Cowdery expressed a desire to translate. After he was unable to do so, the Lord spoke through Joseph Smith:

> Behold, you have not understood; you have supposed that I would give it unto you, when you took no thought, save it was to ask me.
> But, behold, I say unto you that you must study it out in your mind; then you must ask me if it be right, and if it is right I will cause that your bosom shall burn within you; therefore, you shall feel that it is right.
> But if it be not right you shall have no such feelings, but you shall have a stupor of thought that shall cause you to forget the thing which is wrong; therefore, you cannot write that which is sacred save it be given you from me.[7]

Because of this comment, many Latter-day Saints conclude that the translation process was not one in which words miraculously appeared, or a literal translation was placed in Joseph's mind. Rather, they believe that he was forced to concentrate deeply, attempting to determine the meaning for himself, and once he had the idea correct, he would know by a divine confirmation that he was right. No good translation is ever literal, for words express ideas, and ideas are expressed differently in different languages and by different personalities. The best translations convey the spirit and meaning of the material in the best form of the new

---

[6]Joseph Smith, *History of the Church*, 4:537.
[7]D&C 9:7-9.

language possible. They also always carry the marks of the translator himself, who inevitably uses certain idioms and expressions
characteristic of his training and background. For the faithful
Latter-day Saint, this explains why the English version of the Book
of Mormon carries unmistakable marks of the language of Joseph
Smith's time, and why grammatical problems were not uncommon, especially in the first edition.

Briefly, the Book of Mormon gives an account of three groups
of people who migrated to the American continent in ancient
times. It focuses primarily on the family of Lehi, who left
Jerusalem about 600 B.C. His descendants split into two groups,
called Nephites and Lamanites, and the book traces their constant
conflicts as well as the religion taught by their prophets. It also
tells of the visit by the resurrected Christ to these people, who were
said to be some of the other sheep to which he alluded while teaching his apostles in Palestine. Within two hundred years after this
visit, corruption and conflict again prevailed, and eventually the
Lamanites completely overwhelmed and destroyed the Nephite
people. Mormon was one of their last historians; he collected and
abridged all available records. His son Moroni finished the work
and before his death buried the record in a hill, where it would rest
until it came forth in the last days. Its primary purpose, as stated
in the preface, was not to tell the history of these people, but to be
another witness of the divinity of Christ—"to the convincing of the
Jew and Gentile that Jesus is the Christ, the Eternal God,
manifesting himself unto all nations."

The Latter-day Work Begins

Whatever his neighbors may have thought of the twenty-one-
year-old Joseph Smith, evidence suggests that some of them
believed he actually possessed plates of gold. Within only a few
days after Joseph received the plates, Preserved Harris asked his
brother Martin if he had heard about Joseph Smith having a
"golden bible," and Martin merely shrugged it off with the statement that the money-diggers had unearthed something interesting.
But the next day, in the village of Palmyra, he was again asked the
same question. With such rumors flying quickly in an area already
saturated with stories of buried wealth, it is not surprising that almost immediately various schemes were developed to get the plates
from Joseph Smith. Constantly on his guard, he changed the hid-

ing place several times, on some occasions immediately before the arrival of a mob.

Some of those who hoped to steal the plates sought the help of a local clairvoyant, Sally Chase, who claimed that by peering into her personal peepstone she could tell where "Joe Smith kept his gold bible hid." It is probable that she and her brother Willard were involved in searching and digging for treasure, and because of their disappointment at failing, they joined in the raids. According to Joseph's mother, Willard was "Methodist class-leader" at the same time that he led at least one group in search of the plates.

The Prophet despaired of proceeding with the translation while in such constant danger of losing the plates. He and his believing wife, Emma, therefore decided to move to Harmony, Pennsylvania, to live with her father. But they were without money until Martin Harris unexpectedly gave them fifty dollars to help make the 150-mile move. A prosperous farmer in the area, Harris had been acquainted with the Smiths for some time and had great confidence in Joseph. That he believed the account of the plates would have great consequences in his life in the near future.

In Harmony, Joseph copied some of the characters from the plates and translated them. Martin Harris had previously agreed to take such a transcription to learned people in the East. Accordingly, Harris arrived in Harmony sometime in February 1828, then proceeded to New York City with the transcript in his pocket.

According to Martin Harris's own account, he first called on Dr. Charles Anthon, a professor of classical studies at Columbia College. A prolific scholar, Professor Anthon produced at least one book a year for over thirty years and in his day had a profound influence on the study of the classics in the United States. Harris later visited a certain "Dr. Mitchell," probably Samuel L. Mitchill, M.D., of New York City. Both scholars acknowledged that the transcription seemed correct. The question arises, of course, as to whether either of them was qualified to make such a statement, since the Book of Mormon text was supposedly written in a reformed Egyptian. They may have recognized the characters' resemblance to Egyptian or other ancient languages, but they probably could not verify the translation. Either they were simply pontificating, or Martin Harris read too much into what they did say. In later years Professor Anthon denied having said the translation was correct, although he did acknowledge Martin Harris's visit. According to Harris, when Professor Anthon asked how Joseph Smith got the gold plates and Harris told him about the angel, Anthon disgustedly tore up the paper he had signed verifying the authenticity of the transcript. He told Harris to bring the plates to him to translate, and when told that part of the record was sealed, he replied, "I cannot read a sealed book."

The consequences of this journey for Martin Harris were great. At this time he was a well-respected farmer, trusted by Palmyra residents for his integrity. When he returned from New York City he was so certain of the authenticity of the work Joseph Smith was doing that he subsequently worked full time to help in the translation (despite constant nagging from his unbelieving wife), eventually lost the support of his wife, mortgaged his farm to raise the money to publish the Book of Mormon, and generally subjected himself to public ridicule. But he also became honored in the Church as one of three chosen witnesses of the gold plates.

Martin Harris played another role in the story of the Book of Mormon. After his return from New York City he went to Harmony, Pennsylvania, again to serve as a scribe for Joseph Smith. For two months he wrote as Joseph translated, and by June 14 he had recorded 116 pages of manuscript. Then the influence of Harris's nagging wife threatened the work they had so carefully put together. Mrs. Harris had constantly expressed disgust for what her husband was doing, and would apparently do anything possible to discredit Joseph Smith. In order to give her some evidence that what he was doing was good and right, Harris repeatedly pressured Joseph Smith to allow him to take the manuscript of the translation to show her. Twice the Prophet replied that he had inquired of the Lord and received a negative answer. Finally, Joseph said the Lord had relented, and he loaned the manuscript to Harris on condition that he show it to only five specified individuals. But the harassed disciple did not restrain himself and soon began exhibiting it to almost every visitor. Whether his wife conspired to steal it is not certain, but the manuscript soon disappeared and was never recovered. Harris was crushed—so much so that he was afraid for a time even to return to Harmony. But he was not nearly so discouraged as Joseph Smith.

In the meantime Emma gave birth to a son who soon died, and Emma herself lay close to death for several weeks. This sorrow, together with the prolonged absence of Martin Harris, weighed heavily on Joseph. Finally he traveled to Palmyra, where Martin Harris reluctantly told him what had happened. Shocked, disillusioned, and feeling severely chastened, Joseph returned to Harmony. For a time, he said, he lost not only the power to translate, but also the plates and the Urim and Thummim, both of which were restored to him only after severe soul searching. Once again he was reminded of his weaknesses, and chastened through revelation for being careless with sacred things.

But all was not lost. In a subsequent revelation Joseph was forgiven of his transgressions and told that these events were part of a plan to thwart the designs of those who had stolen the manuscript. The thieves, according to the revelation, were planning to wait for a second translation. Then, if it followed the first translation verbatim, they would change parts of the original in order to prove that Joseph did not have the gift of translation. Joseph, therefore, was not to translate the same records. The Book of Mormon plates, he was told, contained two accounts of the material already translated: one from a secular perspective and a second covering the religious concerns of the Book of Mormon people. Joseph had translated from the secular account; he was now to begin translating the spiritual. Since he would not translate the same material twice, the plans of his enemies would be frustrated. The first fourth of the Book of Mormon is the result of that new beginning.

The work of translation proceeded only intermittently during the fall and winter of 1828-29, with Emma acting as a scribe. In the meantime, a young man named Oliver Cowdery began teaching school in Palmyra and boarded with Joseph's parents. From them he learned of Joseph's work, and after receiving his own witness that it was divine, he insisted on going to Harmony as soon as the school term closed. He arrived on April 5 and two days later began working as Joseph's scribe. It was Oliver Cowdery who recorded the major portion of the Book of Mormon as the Prophet dictated.

These were days of tremendous spiritual growth and satisfaction for Joseph Smith. In the year following the loss of the first manuscript, he received fourteen of his recorded revelations, foreshadowing such important events as the appointment of three witnesses to view the Book of Mormon plates, the organization of the Church, the appointment of Twelve Apostles, and the spread of missionary work. But according to Joseph and Oliver, the most memorable experience came on May 15, 1829, when they came upon a passage dealing with the ordinance of baptism. Immediately the question that had been asked repeatedly by other restorationists came into their minds: Who had the authority to administer the saving ordinance? They retired to the woods to pray about it and were visited by a heavenly messenger who announced that he was John the Baptist, sent to confer upon them the Aaronic Priesthood. Here, according to Latter-day Saint doctrine, was one of the first steps in the restoration of the ancient order of things, for as the heavenly messenger laid his hands upon their heads, he restored to them authority to baptize as well as to administer other ordinances. Since this was the lesser priesthood, it did not carry the power to confer the gift of the Holy Ghost by the laying on of hands, but for Joseph and Oliver it was an essential step. The angel commanded them to baptize each other, which they did in the Susquehannah River; then they ordained each other again to the Aaronic Priesthood. John the Baptist told them that he acted under the direction of Peter, James, and John, the ancient apostles who would later restore to them the higher, or Melchizedek, priesthood, which would give them authority to organize the Church. No date for the apostles' visit has been preserved, but it probably happened during May or June 1829.

The Three Witnesses to the Book of Mormon. (Charles B. Hall engravings, Church Archives)

The importance of Joseph Smith and Oliver Cowdery's proclaiming the visit of John the Baptist and Peter, James, and John cannot be minimized in understanding the rapid rise of Mormonism in the 1830s. In the midst of a period when primitivism and restoration of the ancient gospel were principal religious themes, Joseph and Oliver declared that not only were they going to restore the ancient church, but they had also been given direct, divine authority to do so. Many primitivists had earlier raised the question of authority, and some, like Charles G. Finney, had solved the problem by receiving spiritual manifestations they believed were calls to preach. But few, if any, had proclaimed so forcefully that they had received a personal visitation from one with divine authority who personally bestowed it upon them. For many seekers of the day, the claim of divine authority was a major attraction of Mormonism, and they were prepared both to test a prophet who made that claim and to follow him if they were convinced the claim was true. The quest for authority was especially important to the early success of the Mormon movement.

Completion of the Book of Mormon, 1829-30

During the month of May 1829, Joseph and Oliver remained at Harmony steadily translating and writing. Other believers helped them in the process. Joseph Knight supplied them with provisions, and Isaac Hale protected them from antagonists who threatened violence. Feeling the need for more peaceful surroundings, Joseph asked Oliver to write his friend David Whitmer and ask if they might move to his home in Fayette, New York. Whitmer had received a testimony of the sacred work and soon arrived with a wagon to take them to Fayette, where the translation was completed.

Pressure continued on Joseph Smith to allow others to see the plates, and as the translation drew to a close the record itself declared that when it came to light, certain witnesses would be allowed that privilege. Accordingly, Martin Harris, Oliver Cowdery, and David Whitmer were shown the plates, and later eight other friends and family members were given the same opportunity. Their testimonies, which they never rescinded, are printed with the Book of Mormon.

In the meantime, Joseph secured the copyright on June 11, 1829, and made arrangements for publishing the book. Egbert B.

Grandin, a Palmyra printer, initially refused the job, but was later persuaded by friends that he could accept it as a strictly business matter, with no implication of religious involvement. Martin Harris agreed to pay Grandin $3,000 for the work, and Joseph was able to return to his little farm in Harmony.

Cowdery, Harris, and the Smith family supervised the printing, but the task was beset with unforeseen problems. In September 1829, Abner Cole, using the pseudonym Obediah Dogberry, began a newspaper in Palmyra called the *Reflector*. He printed it on Sunday, using the press of E. B. Grandin. After printing derogatory remarks about the forthcoming "Gold Bible," he announced that he would begin to publish extracts from it in January. Cole had access to the printer's manuscript, and soon a few excerpts did appear. Hyrum Smith and Oliver Cowdery could not persuade him to desist and sent for Joseph. Eventually the matter was submitted to arbitration, and Cole was obliged to stop violating the copyright.

But that was not the end of publication difficulties. A few residents of Palmyra were determined to block the project and persuaded Grandin that he would never be paid if he proceeded with the printing. They threatened to boycott the book, and noted that without local sales the Smiths could hardly raise the money to pay their debt. Grandin stopped, and only after Martin Harris persuaded him that he would, indeed, be paid for his services did the printing of the 5,000 copies resume. On March 26, 1830, a newspaper advertisement announced publication of the Book of Mormon. A year later Martin Harris, true to his word, paid the $3,000, but only after he was forced to sell his farm to raise the money.

Press, owned by E. B. Grandin, on which the first edition of the Book of Mormon was printed. (Church Archives)

The time was now ready for the organization of the Church, an event foreshadowed by the Book of Mormon and by revelation to Joseph Smith. The Prophet and his friends had preached the gospel whenever possible, and on April 6, 1830, at least thirty believers met together in the Whitmer log home in Fayette, New York. Some of them had already been baptized. Six of those present were officially listed as the organizers, and after an opening prayer Joseph asked the congregation if they would accept him and Oliver Cowdery as their teachers. A unanimous vote was recorded, after which he ordained Oliver Cowdery an elder of the Church, and Oliver ordained Joseph.

The name of the new church, as given in an April 6 revelation, was the Church of Jesus Christ, and until 1834 the members called it either that or the Church of Christ. The use of the term "Saints" came gradually, but as early as August 1831 members of the Church were referred to as Saints in a revelation. Very early, however, nonmembers had begun to use the terms "Mormon" or "Mormonite" to designate the followers of Joseph Smith. On May 3, 1834, a conference of the Church in Kirtland, Ohio, accepted a resolution proclaiming that thereafter the Church would be known as The Church of the Latter-day Saints. This was apparently to establish a more distinctive title and to escape the use of the term "Mormonite." Finally, on April 23, 1838, another revelation designated the name as The Church of Jesus Christ of Latter-day Saints. This has been the official title ever since.

Even though the term "Mormon" was used partly in derision in the early days of the Church, it no longer carries that connotation and members are no longer offended by it. They prefer, however, to use the official name of the Church whenever possible, and to be called Saints, or Latter-day Saints. In modern history all three terms are used interchangeably.

The Work Begins to Spread

The next few months were busy, crucial months for Joseph and the infant church. Ironically the Latter-day Saints had now rejected the evangelism and revivalism of the Burned-over District. Revival leaders had preached the importance of being converted and coming to Christ, and although they contended bitterly for members, ultimately the specific church one joined was to them of little consequence. The Mormons, on the other hand, taught that salvation could come only through the Church of Jesus Christ. They suggested that the Millennium was close at hand, and that all who remained a part of spiritual Babylon, that is, even church-going New Yorkers, would suffer if they were not a part of the restored kingdom. "But those who harden their hearts in unbelief, and reject it," one of the revelations received by the Prophet said, "it shall turn to their own condemnation."[8] This attitude led to ridicule, bitterness, and even violence against the Saints. Twice during the summer of 1830 Joseph Smith was arrested and tried on charges of disorderly conduct. Numerous witnesses testified, but nothing substantial could be proven, and in both cases the Prophet was acquitted. Only by moving could the Saints temporarily avoid such conflict. In the meantime, persecution served only to further unify the believers.

Between April 1830 and January 1831 several important developments helped determine the progress of the Church of Jesus Christ. Small pockets of followers lived in various towns in western New York. One group was in Colesville, where the Knight family provided a nucleus and where in April Newel Knight received the first miraculous healing performed through Joseph Smith. In June the first conference of the Church was held there with thirty members and several prospective converts. Joseph Smith expressed his ecstasy during these early months in the following words:

> To find ourselves engaged in the very same order of things as observed by the holy Apostles of old; to realize the importance and solemnity of such proceedings; and to witness and feel with our own natural senses, the like glorious manifestations of the powers of the Priesthood, the gifts and blessings of the Holy Ghost, and the goodness and condescension of a merciful God unto such as obey the everlasting Gospel of our Lord Jesus Christ, combined to create within us sensations of rapturous gratitude, and inspire us with fresh zeal and energy in the cause of truth.[9]

Even though the followers of Joseph Smith rejected Protestant evangelism, they soon developed an unequaled missionary system of their own. Every convert considered himself a missionary and was fired with a zeal to tell friends and neighbors. "Therefore, if ye have desires to serve God ye are called to the work," Joseph

---

[8]D&C 20:15.
[9]Joseph Smith, *History of the Church*, 1:85-86.

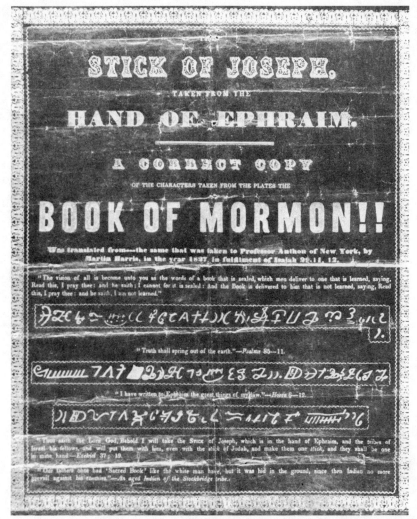

Broadside used in the early days of the Church to publicize the Book of Mormon reproduces the characters Joseph Smith copied from the plates. The broadside was printed in gold letters on black paper. (Church Archives)

had said by revelation in 1829. "For behold the field is white already to harvest; and lo, he that thrusteth in his sickle with his might, the same layeth up in store that he perisheth not, but bringeth salvation to his soul."[10] Within two months a formal

---

[10]D&C 4:3-4.

missionary system was inaugurated. Samuel Smith, brother of the Prophet, was called as the first missionary. He came home saddened by his lack of immediate success, but he had left copies of the Book of Mormon wherever possible. One of them eventually found its way into the hands of several people who subsequently joined the Church, including a carpenter named Brigham Young. In northern New York, Joseph Smith's father and his brother Don Carlos described the restoration to their family, and most of the Prophet's uncles and aunts, as well as his grandfather, Asael, accepted and believed.

During these months the Church also laid the foundation for various publications. Emma Smith was told by revelation to compile a hymnbook. Joseph Smith and John Whitmer began copying and arranging for publication of Joseph's revelations. In December he received a series of revelations known as the Writings of Moses. As a result of this, he began a revision of the King James Bible, attempting to make it conform more closely with his enlightened understanding of the gospel truth.

Even in this early stage, misunderstanding and disagreement arose within the Church, and in the summer of 1830 Joseph had his first frustrating experience attempting to keep harmony among the faithful. The result strengthened his position as prophet and undisputed leader. Oliver Cowdery challenged the wording of a revelation and in a letter from Fayette commanded Joseph to erase it. The Prophet traveled to Fayette and found not only Cowdery but the entire Whitmer family rejecting his phrasing. With "labor and perseverance," he reports that he was able to persuade them that his wording harmonized with the scriptures, and thus he strengthened his own position as the only one authorized to receive divine revelations for the Church as a whole. Later a young convert named Hiram Page claimed to receive revelations for the Church through the use of a so-called seer stone, and some Church members, including Oliver Cowdery and some of the Whitmers, believed him. Another revelation quickly set the matter to rest. Directed to Oliver Cowdery, it read, in part:

Verily, verily, I say unto thee, no one shall be appointed to receive commandments and revelations in this church excepting my servant Joseph Smith, Jun. . . .

And if thou art led at any time by the Comforter to speak or teach, or at all times by the way of commandment unto the church, thou mayest do it.

But thou shalt not write by way of commandment, but by wisdom;

And thou shalt not command him who is at thy head, and at the head of the church.[11]

From the beginning it was clear that only one individual could receive revelation for the entire church, but even such clarity did not keep the problem from recurring.

Seekers Find Salvation

For Joseph Smith, these things were the beginning of the restoration of the ancient order of things. A revelation had proclaimed that it was "the beginning of the rising up and the coming forth of my church out of the wilderness—clear as the moon, and fair as the sun, and terrible as an army with banners."[12] The soldiers of the restored Christian army were to put on the whole armor of God, that they might be able to "withstand the evil day, having done all." No revelation could more effectively fire the zeal of any true believer than the one which urged all to

Stand, therefore, having your loins girt about with truth, having on the breastplate of righteousness, and your feet shod with the preparation of the gospel of peace, which I have sent mine angels to commit unto you;

Taking the shield of faith wherewith ye shall be able to quench all the fiery darts of the wicked;

And take the helmet of salvation, and the sword of my Spirit, which I will pour out upon you, and my word which I reveal unto you, and be agreed as touching all things whatsoever ye ask of me, and be faithful until I come, and ye shall be caught up, that where I am ye shall be also. Amen.[13]

And so the little army marched forth, small in number but, like Daniel of old, high in expectation.

Whom could they persuade to join their ranks? Other New Englanders with a Puritan background might find a familiar note in such sentiments as "ye are called to bring to pass the gathering of mine elect; for mine elect hear my voice and harden not their hearts."[14] Or perhaps the Mormon message would appeal to the Universalist, who insisted upon a rational faith, rejected the pessimistic doctrines of limited atonement and eternal damnation, and

[11]D&C 28:2, 4-6.
[12]D&C 5:14.
[13]D&C 27:15-18.
[14]D&C 29:7.

believed that man was largely responsible for working out his own salvation. How much more reasonable to him would be the revelation which explained that there was no such thing as endless punishment, for the term "endless punishment" merely meant God's punishment, since Endless was his name.[15] Or perhaps it would appeal to the seeker who rejected all churches or went from church to church seeking a restoration of the ancient gospel.

At age eighteen Parley Parker Pratt had joined the Baptists, despite the feeling that he had not found the church of Christ. Four years later he heard the preaching of Sidney Rigdon and was impressed that here was the ancient gospel. Rigdon and the Campbellites preached the gospel as Pratt thought it should be— except for the question of authority to administer the sacred ordinances. But he joined the movement anyway. In 1830, at age twenty-three, he was prompted to forsake his little frontier home in Ohio and travel east to preach as the Spirit directed. Not far from Newark, New York, he came upon the Book of Mormon, read it, and was so overwhelmed that he interrupted his mission to go to Palmyra seeking Joseph Smith. The Prophet was in Pennsylvania, but Pratt sat up all night conversing with Hyrum Smith. Soon he became convinced that Mormonism was what he had been looking for—the ancient gospel restored, complete with proper authority. He interrupted his mission again to return to Palmyra where, about September 1, he was baptized by Oliver Cowdery. The next day he was ordained an elder of the Church and soon continued on his mission, a new and zealous recruit in the tiny Mormon band. Parley Pratt's younger brother Orson had been told by his father to use caution in accepting any denomination, and had refused to unite with any. When his brother brought news of the restoration of the ancient church, Orson also joined.

Newel Knight, a youthful friend of Joseph Smith, was early convinced that there had been an apostasy and that a restoration of the ancient gospel was needed. When he heard of Mormonism, he accepted it gladly. Joseph Knight, his father, had refused to join any religious sect, but accepted the doctrines of the Universalists. He too believed Joseph Smith and joined the Church. Such men were typical of the Mormon converts while the Church was yet in New York.

---

[15]D&C 19:7-12.

Looking Westward

The same revelation that reminded Oliver Cowdery of his position in relationship to Joseph Smith called him on a mission to the Indians. About the middle of October he set out in the company of Peter Whitmer, Jr., Parley P. Pratt, and Ziba Peterson. Together they headed for the far western borders of the United States and the Indian territory that lay beyond.

Those who believed the Book of Mormon had a special interest in the American Indians. The record declared that one day its message would be taken to that people, and Oliver Cowdery and others had been anxious to know when. To them, this 1830 mission was the fulfillment of that dream. On the western borders of Missouri were several eastern tribes recently forced to move from their native lands.

As white Americans pushed westward, it was at the expense of Indian tribes unable to halt the onrush of settlement. Many federal officials felt that the only solution was to persuade Indians to move west beyond the ninety-fifth meridian, where the government would help them begin anew and guarantee them a new home in the "permanent Indian frontier." At that time it was an area no white man wanted. After forcefully persuading the Indians already there to move further out on the Great Plains, the government offered various inducements to persuade the tribes east of the Mississippi to move. From Ohio went the Shawnee, who settled on a twenty-five-mile-wide reservation south of the Kansas River. They were soon joined in 1829 by the Delaware, their former neighbors in Ohio, who accepted land immediately to the north. The Delaware were hardly settled in their new surroundings when the first Mormon missionaries to the Indians appeared among them.

This mission had another meaning for the Church. A venture to the cutting edge of the frontier, it was a first official look westward, foreshadowing future dramatic activities. When Oliver Cowdery was instructed to pursue this mission, he was promised that a site would soon be chosen for the city of Zion. The exact location was not specified, but he was told, "it shall be on the borders by the Lamanites." Few places fulfilled this prediction as well as Missouri, the westernmost state in the United States whose farthest border was the Indian frontier. Not only was the Church beginning to look westward, but one reason for the eventual move had also been foreshadowed: the building of Zion, the New Jerusalem, somewhere in western Missouri.

The four eager missionaries left New York in the middle of October. For Parley P. Pratt, this was a fitting climax to the journey he had begun only two months earlier when he left northeastern Ohio to preach in New York. Now, as a Mormon elder, he called upon his friend and former pastor Sidney Rigdon, leader of a congregation in Mentor, Ohio. When the missionaries presented Rigdon with a copy of the Book of Mormon, he was skeptical, but he promised to read it and find out for himself. He gave them permission to use his chapel, and Oliver Cowdery and Parley P. Pratt presented their message to his congregation. Impressed, this minister, who had long taught the idea of the restoration of the ancient gospel, told his congregation neither to accept nor reject without careful investigation. In about two weeks Rigdon announced his readiness for baptism. The authenticity of the Book of Mormon, he declared, had been revealed to him. Rigdon's congregation followed him into Mormonism. In the meantime, the missionaries preached throughout the vicinity, and converts, many of them former Campbellites, began to flock in. Suddenly Ohio's Western Reserve became a more fruitful field than the Burned-over District in New York. Before the missionaries left, approximately 130 converts had been baptized. When Joseph Smith heard the good news, he sent John Whitmer to preside in Ohio, and by the summer of 1831 about a thousand had joined the new church. As a result of the Ohio preaching, a powerful preacher was brought into the leadership of the Church, and the Church itself soon headed westward.

Parley Pratt could not have approached Sidney Rigdon at a better time. For months Rigdon had been at odds with Alexander Campbell over one aspect of the restoration of the ancient order of things. Rigdon saw in the New Testament that the early Christians shared all things in common, and he wanted to establish a religious community to exhibit this brotherly love. Campbell objected. He did not share Rigdon's interpretation of the New Testament and believed such an economic experiment would lead to confusion when practiced by large numbers, especially if some merely wanted to avoid earning their own living. This created a bitter break between the two, and Rigdon immediately led all the people he could out of Campbell's movement. Some of his followers actually set up a common-stock community that sought complete economic equality. When the Mormon missionaries came to Rigdon, he was struggling with the dilemma of whether his congregation should remain independent or join another group. The answer for him was Mormonism.

Rigdon, however, would not be satisfied until he met the Prophet, and in December he and a young hatter named Edward Partridge traveled together to New York. Partridge had not joined the Church, and his main purpose was to learn for himself about the character of Joseph Smith. The two stopped at the Smith home in Manchester, and when the family was not there, they began to ask neighbors about their character. They were told it was unimpeachable except in the subject of religion. They then proceeded to Waterloo, New York, where they met Joseph himself. After staying with the Smith family for a time, Partridge became convinced and was baptized by the Prophet. Joseph described him as "a pattern of piety, and one of the Lord's great men"[16]—in less than a year he would become the first bishop in the Church.

Joseph Smith must have been as immediately impressed by Sidney Rigdon as most were who heard him preach. Immediately the two were drawn together. Rigdon's years as an associate of Alexander Campbell had well prepared him to teach the doctrines of his new faith and to stand next to the Prophet in expounding them. A revelation through Joseph Smith soon recognized this: "Behold, verily, verily, I say unto my servant Sidney, I have looked upon thee and thy works. I have heard thy prayers, and prepared thee for a greater work." He was sent forth like John the Baptist, he was told, to prepare the way for the Lord, assuring him that much that he had been teaching was correct. Only one thing was lacking. "Thou didst baptize by water unto repentance, but they received not the Holy Ghost," but now through him they would also receive the Holy Ghost by the laying on of hands, "even as the apostles of old." Through Joseph, according to the revelation, the fulness of the gospel had been sent forth, "and in weakness have I blessed him." Rigdon now was to strengthen Joseph. He was to "watch over him that his faith fail not," to write for him as he received revelation of ancient scripture, and to "preach my gospel and call on the holy prophets to prove his words, as they shall be

---

[16]Joseph Smith, *History of the Church*, 1:28.

given him."[17] Rigdon's years of preaching and his knowledge of the scriptures would now be marshaled to discover texts to prove the truth of Mormon teachings. Three years later he was designated a spokesman for Joseph Smith, and in December 1830 he began helping in Joseph's revision of the Bible.

The time was ripe for a move. The Church was gaining members slowly in New York, but grew by leaps and bounds in Ohio. Persecution plagued the Prophet in New York, and perhaps he could find relief and refuge in Ohio. Undoubtedly Sidney Rigdon helped persuade him that Ohio held great promise. The first revelation to come to Rigdon had said, "And now I say unto you, tarry with him, and he shall journey with you." Not long afterward, the two were told in another revelation that they should stop translating and go to Ohio, and the whole church in New York was told, "It is expedient in me that they should assemble together at the Ohio."[18]

By the end of the month Joseph and Emma Smith had left New York, accompanied by Sidney Rigdon and Edward Partridge, and early in February they arrived in Kirtland. There the Smiths were welcomed into the home of Newel K. Whitney, a merchant and former Campbellite who followed Sidney Rigdon into the new faith. Some New Yorkers were uncertain about the move, but during the rest of the winter they nevertheless prepared to participate in this first migration of the Mormons. In the spring several groups assembled and traveled from Colesville, Fayette, and Palmyra to the Erie Canal, where they took a canal boat to Buffalo. From there they went by steamer along Lake Erie to Fairport, Ohio, and from there a short distance overland to Kirtland.

Even though Ohio was, in one sense, a new beginning, it was in New York that the foundations were laid and the direction set for the growth of Latter-day Saint doctrine. The restoration was by no means complete, for the body of doctrine continued to develop as new circumstances prepared the Saints for new instructions. Never, in fact, was it anticipated that church doctrine would be static, and even today the Saints believe that God "will yet reveal many great and important things pertaining to the Kingdom of God." But the New York period established essential directions.

---

[17]D&C 35:3-6, 17, 19, 23.
[18]D&C 37:3; see also 38:32.

These early Saints believed that Jesus Christ had established his church in its purity in New Testament times, but that an apostasy had taken place over the centuries that demanded divine restoration of the ancient gospel. They believed that the modern church of Jesus Christ should have the same authority as the ancient church, and that this priesthood authority had been restored by the ancient apostles and prophets themselves. They looked forward to establishing the hierarchy of the ancient church, headed by twelve apostles. Although the early organization in New York was very simple, with Joseph Smith and Oliver Cowdery simply called first and second elders, they were also designated as apostles, and it was believed twelve apostles would soon be appointed. The duties of various priesthood officers were outlined, and it was obvious from the beginning that this was a lay priesthood. Joseph Smith was clearly in charge as the accepted prophet, seer, and revelator for the Church, and the doctrine of continued revelation was well established.

Along with the Bible, the Saints accepted the divinity of the Book of Mormon, and any doctrines it proclaimed were therefore part of Mormonism. These included the principles of faith, repentance, baptism by immersion for those who have reached the age of understanding, the laying on of hands for the gift of the Holy Ghost, miracles, spiritual gifts, and the sacrament of the Lord's supper in remembrance of his atonement. The Book of Mormon also taught the fall of man but rejected the Calvinist doctrine of his total depravity. It testified of the reality of Christ's atonement and emphasized that man attained salvation by a combination of faith, good works, and the grace of Jesus Christ. It proclaimed man's free agency and the universality of the gospel. Also fundamental in the Book of Mormon was the doctrine of millennialism: that Christ would return and reign for a thousand years in peace. Mormons expected this to happen soon and believed their mission was to prepare for his coming. They were his Saints, and they believed they must establish the Kingdom before he came. These principles provided the foundation for more elaborate doctrines that would be proclaimed as the Church grew numerically, as its members were prepared to receive new ideas and challenges, and as Joseph Smith matured in his role as prophet.

CHAPTER 3

Unfolding Latter-day Zion, 1831-1836

On a summer day early in August 1831, a small group of Latter-day Saints recently transplanted from Colesville, New York, by way of northern Ohio assembled at an isolated spot twelve miles west of Independence, Jackson County, Missouri, to participate in a symbolic act of new beginnings. Twelve men representing the tribes of Israel solemnly placed the first log for a house, signifying the laying of the foundation of Zion. Assisting them was Joseph Smith, who had journeyed to the westernmost state of Jacksonian America to examine the spot revelation identified as the Center Place. In this area the Prophet envisioned a great city around a complex of sacred temples. It was a New Jerusalem—a city of refuge, a gathering place where the latter-day kingdom could be established in anticipation of the millennial reign of Jesus Christ.

A Place of Refuge

The gathering was a dominant concept of the early restored church. The righteous from all nations, searched out by proselyting elders, were to congregate in a place of refuge. This location would guarantee protection against wars, plagues, and other

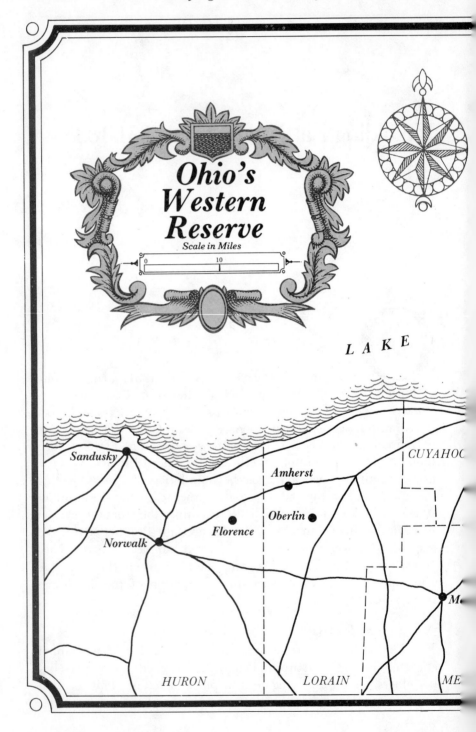

Ohio's
Western
Reserve

Scale in Miles

0   10

LAKE

Sandusky

Amherst

Oberlin

Florence

Norwalk

CUYAHO

M

HURON   LORAIN   ME

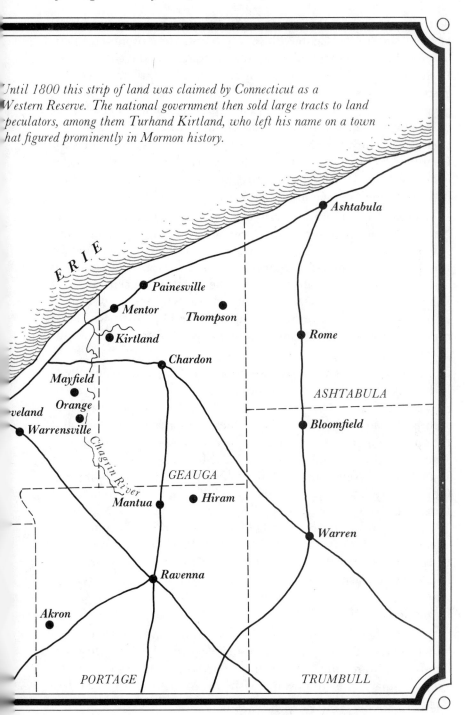

Until 1800 this strip of land was claimed by Connecticut as a Western Reserve. The national government then sold large tracts to land speculators, among them Turhand Kirtland, who left his name on a town that figured prominently in Mormon history.

ERIE

Ashtabula

Painesville

Mentor

Thompson

Rome

Kirtland

Chardon

Mayfield

ASHTABULA

Orange

Bloomfield

veland

Warrensville

Chagrin River

GEAUGA

Mantua

Hiram

Warren

Ravenna

Akron

PORTAGE

TRUMBULL

destructive forces of the last days. As if to underscore the necessity of migrating to the Center Place, the Saints were promised safety only in the holy city of Zion—a place of peace and righteousness. If the Indians beyond the boundaries of Missouri accepted the gospel, these sons of Lehi would also help build the New Jerusalem promised in the Book of Mormon. But the completion of such plans always depends on men and circumstances, and in this case stresses developed that determined that at this time Jackson County, Missouri, was only a brief wintering place on the trail of Mormon history. After three short years the Saints would unwillingly abandon their Zion.

From the beginning, Church leaders knew that the proposed gathering place required support. So, while an advance contingent struggled to lay the groundwork for a millennial city on the frontier, other Latter-day Saints remained in scattered branches eastward along the route to Zion. The greatest concentration of Saints centered in northern Ohio, where Kirtland and nearby Hiram became nerve centers of the growing church. It was here, rather than at Jackson County, that Joseph Smith created a temporary headquarters.

The area designated by revelation as an assembly place "for a little season" lay along the northern edge of the Allegheny Plateau in northern Ohio. The New York Saints found hundreds of members ready to welcome them when they arrived in Ohio, and the law of consecration (which will be discussed in detail later) was soon to be introduced among them. Members of the Colesville Branch from New York followed Newel Knight to Thompson, Ohio, where they squatted on land offered to the Church by Leman Copley's consecration. Frederick G. Williams and Isaac Morley of Kirtland and Philo Dibble, who lived near Mentor, also opened their farmland to the new arrivals. Bishop Edward Partridge and his assistants apportioned the consecrated lands to arriving Saints according to need, and additional property was purchased with funds obtained when the New York Saints liquidated private holdings.

In September, Joseph and Emma Smith and the twins they had recently adopted took up residence with the John Johnson family of Hiram, thirty miles from Kirtland. First, however, the Prophet made an important visit to Missouri. With Sidney Rigdon, Martin Harris, Edward Partridge, William W. Phelps,

Joseph Coe, and A. Sidney Gilbert, he set out in mid-June to discover a settlement site and dedicate the land of Zion. Also heading west about this time were twenty-two elders assigned by the Kirtland conference of June 3-6 to travel in pairs, preaching along different routes toward Missouri. In addition, the entire Colesville Branch abandoned its site at Thompson, Ohio, after Leman Copley reneged on his agreement to share his property. This congregation had been instructed in March to begin saving funds to purchase an inheritance in Zion; now they went to claim it. Arriving in Jackson County during the week of July 16, 1831, they settled in the Kaw Township, later part of Kansas City.

The arriving disciples discovered a remote frontier, largely undeveloped but not without promise. Their immediate task was to establish a claim to the area "appointed and consecrated for the gathering of the saints. . . , the land of promise, and the place for the city of Zion."[1] Following the log-laying ceremony at Kaw township, Sidney Rigdon dedicated the land as a permanent inheritance for the Saints. On the following day, August 3, at a spot one-half mile west of Independence, the Prophet set a cornerstone for a new temple. Joseph Smith had issued instructions for establishing the law of consecration for the government of the Zion society. A revelation appointed Edward Partridge as bishop, Sidney Gilbert as land agent and merchant, William W. Phelps as printer, and Oliver Cowdery (who, unlike the others, returned to Ohio) as editor. After the Prophet and his companions returned to Kirtland, those left behind adjusted to frontier life. They harvested wild hay for livestock, sowed a little grain, and prepared land for cultivation.

A letter from William W. Phelps in July spoke glowingly of the sage-grass prairie and thickly timbered plain. So that the church at large might know of Zion's potential, Sidney Rigdon prepared a similar description, boasting of mild climate, fertile soil, and natural resources. He acknowledged the disadvantages that might be expected on a frontier—lack of industry, education, and the refinements of society—but both he and Phelps were impressed with "the rolling prairies . . . decorated with a growth of flowers so gorgeous and grand as to exceed description."[2]

The optimism nurtured by this virgin land and enthusiasm

---

[1]D&C 57:1-2.
[2]Joseph Smith, *History of the Church*, 1:197. For reproductions of both letters, see Richard

for Zion was soon tempered by the realities of pioneering. Within a year, after a poor harvest and other problems, the Church newspaper in Zion was cautioning:

> Although Zion, according to the prophets, is to become like Eden or the garden of the Lord, yet at present it is as it were but a wilderness and desert, and the disadvantages of settling in a new country, you know, are many and great. Therefore, prudence would dictate at present the churches abroad, come not up to Zion, until preparations can be made for them.[3]

The Mormon population in Missouri thus remained intentionally small. By November 1832, the *Evening and the Morning Star* counted 830 gathered Saints preparing the land for additional immigrants. Meanwhile, those remaining in Ohio postponed their departure and concentrated on developing a secondary gathering place in a less remote region, closer to the field of potential converts and to the resources of the developed East. Thus two centers of Mormonism slowly gained strength—Zion, designated as the center place, though briefly left to its own resources, and Kirtland, a stake to Zion, a temporary headquarters where the Lord instructed the Saints to "retain a strong hold . . . for the space of five years."[4]

A People of God and Their Quest for Community

The Latter-day Saints were committed to becoming true disciples of Christ, and in a yearning for Christian unity, they congregated in their designated places of refuge. Here they would find relief from concerns of Babylon and begin to erect the Kingdom of God on earth. That community would be built upon a search for spiritual gifts, the claim to new revelation and scripture, and active missionary zeal.

To most restorationists a sign of the true faith was the outpouring of spiritual gifts. It became the task of Joseph Smith to temper the religious enthusiasm of some converts and channel it in more acceptable directions. In the Kirtland area some young former Shakers persisted in certain "spiritual operations" that even

---

Lloyd Anderson, "Jackson County in Early Mormon Descriptions," *Missouri Historical Review* 65 (April 1971): 274-76, 285-87.
[3]*Evening and the Morning Star* 1 (July 1832).
[4]D&C 64:21.

Emma Hale Smith,   *Sidney Rigdon,*   *Edward Partridge,*
wife of the   *designated by revelation as*   *first bishop*
Prophet Joseph.   *"spokesman" to the Prophet.*   *of the Church.*
(Church Archives)   *(Church Archives)*   *(Church Archives)*

most Shakers had abandoned, including rolling and turning exercises, facial grimaces, and mock warfare. John Whitmer reported:

> Some had visions and could not tell what they saw. Some would fancy to themselves that they had the sword of Laban, and would wield it as expert as a light dragoon; some would act like an Indian in the act of scalping; some would slide or scoot on the floor with the rapidity of a serpent, which they termed sailing in the boat to the Lamanites, preaching the gospel. And many other vain and foolish maneuvers that are unseemly and unprofitable to mention.[5]

These manifestations, even when adapted to Mormon forms and terminology, were not considered acceptable spiritual experiences, and Joseph Smith denounced them. He had already defined the true and profitable gifts of the spirit: wisdom, knowledge, healing, miracles, prophecy, discerning of spirits, and the gift of tongues. Church members and leaders exercised these gifts, but Joseph Smith warned against seeking after signs. The legitimate gifts, he said, would follow after believers. Believing Mormons did witness the miraculous healing of Mrs. Luke S. Johnson's paralyzed arm, see evil spirits cast out during a June 1831 conference in Kirtland, and report a miraculous parting of the ice at Buffalo harbor for the departure of the Colesville Saints.

Among the most distinctive characteristics of Mormonism

---

[5]John Whitmer, "The Book of John Whitmer, Kept by Commandment," *Journal of History* (Lamoni, Iowa) 1 (January 1908): 55.

was its claim to revelation. Unlike many advocates of the primitive gospel movement, the Saints did not believe the Bible was an infallible, final religious authority. They agreed with the Campbellites that the King James Bible required correction, but also claimed new revelation to restore lost truths. A challenge to orthodoxy, this view of modern revelation, visions, and prophetic utterances provided ammunition for critics of the new religion.

Nevertheless, Joseph Smith found it necessary to again define limits to revelation and establish his preeminent role as prophet, seer, and revelator. In Ohio, for example, a Mrs. Hubble sanctimoniously claimed new revelations as a prophetess, and a servant on Isaac Morley's farm likewise asserted the right to direct the Saints. Against such interlopers the Prophet declared by revelation, as he had done before, that the Lord had appointed only one person to receive revelations and commandments for the entire church.

Through the Prophet modern revelation brought direction for the Saints in their personal lives, instructions on church procedures, and doctrinal expositions. In the 1830s the Prophet also expanded doctrinal understanding through restoration of lost scriptures. The Book of Mormon spoke of other scripture hidden from the world, and Mormons were interested when newspapers reported the discovery of several supposedly lost books of the Bible. Millennial sects were particularly interested in the books of Jasher and Enoch, which contained apocalyptic and communitarian messages. A *Book of Enoch* had been published in English in 1821, but in June and December of 1830 Joseph Smith gave to the Church his own restorations of the Prophecy of Enoch and the Visions and Writings of Moses. The following spring he formally began revising the Old and New Testaments, a project that continued for more than two years. As the Prophet neared the completion of his inspired revision, he cautioned the Saints against accepting the so-called lost books and specifically labeled the Apocrypha a mixture of truth and falsehood.

Except for selected segments, the Prophet's work on the Bible was not published in his lifetime. Nevertheless, the three-year project was a valuable learning experience. Intensive study of the Bible raised questions whose answers were later included in the Doctrine and Covenants and other doctrinal expositions. Among the new insights was the vision of the degrees of glory, the separateness of the Father and the Son as members of the Godhead, and

man's place in the universe as an uncreated, preexistent child of
God. The Prophet also recorded important instructions on priesthood and prophecies of the second coming of Christ.

Another byproduct of the Bible revision and the general
interest in antiquities was the Prophet's intensified interest in Hebrew and other ancient languages. This, along with his reputation
as a translator of golden plates and restorer of ancient writings,
quite naturally led to purchase of certain Egyptian mummies and
scrolls in 1835. Joseph Smith identified the scrolls as a record of
Abraham in Egypt, and spent several weeks attempting to
translate them. He apparently progressed as far as the second
chapter of the record later known as the Book of Abraham, but did
not return to the task until 1842. It was first published that same
year, and ultimately appeared in the Pearl of Great Price.

*A damaged section of the Egyptian papyri that provided the basis for the
Book of Abraham. (Church Archives)*

The exact relationship between the ancient scrolls and the printed text of the Book of Abraham has been a matter of controversy. The scrolls themselves were lost after Joseph's death, but in 1967 papyrus fragments were discovered in a New York museum and presented to the Church. Although translations by both LDS and other scholars made it clear that they were not part of the Abraham text, Church scholars were quick to observe that they had only eleven fragments. They suggested that the scrolls themselves may simply have been the catalyst that turned Joseph's mind back to ancient Egypt and opened it to revelation on the experiences of Abraham. The published Book of Abraham contains important ideas about man and the universe, but Joseph may have received these ideas the same way he did those of the inspired translation of the Bible. In that instance, acting without original documents, the Prophet's only claim was that by divine inspiration he was able to replace incorrect with correct ideas and restore the original biblical meaning. He studied Hebrew and Egyptian but never claimed fluency in ancient languages. Even the Book of Mormon was translated by the gift and power of God rather than through any prior knowledge of ancient language. When applied by Mormons to Joseph Smith, the term "translator" thus has a special meaning.

From the first the Saints eagerly sought copies of the Prophet's translations and revelations. Recognizing this, as early as 1830 he began arranging the revelations in chronological order and making editorial corrections to prepare them for publication. In November 1831 six new revelations were incorporated, including a preface and an appendix to the proposed book. But the compilation was not unchallenged. William E. M'Lellin, an experienced teacher, was critical of the lack of erudition in the language of the commandments. The Prophet invited him to equal them, and the humbled teacher could not. In contrast, most of the elders at a special conference that October testified of the divine origin of the revelatory writings and offered their witness in a brief preface to the book.

Oliver Cowdery and John Whitmer personally carried the collection to Independence, Missouri, for printing, and during Joseph Smith's next visit these two and W. W. Phelps were authorized to proceed with publication. This they did, but when about two-thirds of the revelations had been set in type and sheets run off, a mob destroyed the press and scattered the printed forms. This interruption delayed publication another two years, though local members retrieved the printed sheets and bound a few copies of the incomplete volume, the Book of Commandments for the Government of the Church of Christ, which later became collectors' items.

When finally published in the fall of 1835, the Doctrine and Covenants of The Church of Jesus Christ of Latter-day Saints had been enlarged, corrected, and rearranged by the First Presidency. Also included in the volume were several doctrinal essays, "Lectures on Faith," which were not revelations but had been used as lessons in a School of the Elders the previous winter. The whole publication, giving the Saints easy access to the Prophet's revelations, set forth the regulations or covenants of church membership and clarified doctrinal matters.

The Prophet had elaborated on many central concepts in the five years since the establishment of the Church. But revelation, Mormons believe, usually comes in response to present needs and specific problems, and much of Joseph Smith's new revelation reflected the contemporary search for a harmonious world view that would reconcile otherworldliness and materialism. He thus provided answers to questions that also prompted other religious leaders and philosophers to suggest new world views. One of these was Thomas Dick, whose *Philosophy of a Future State* (appearing in a second edition in 1830) projected an eternally progressive afterlife. Though no direct evidence exists that Dick's study was discussed among the Saints before 1836, the views of this Christian materialist have striking parallels with the Prophet's revelations of the early 1830s on the degrees of glory and the eternal nature of the elements.

Another concept probably first revealed during the Prophet's Old Testament study in 1831 was recorded in 1843 as a revelation on the new and everlasting covenant of marriage. During the early 1830s rumors of clandestine polygamy spread among both the Saints and their detractors. Official pronouncements denied its existence, since at that time the Prophet did not intend to make the principle a matter of church doctrine. Some members, told by the Prophet that a new marriage system eventually would be introduced, assumed the prerogative of practicing it without authorization. These aberrations led to some apostasy during the mid-1830s. The brief statement on marriage appended to the 1835 Doctrine and Covenants gave a direct answer to charges of immorality and polygamy among the Saints; it correctly asserted that the law of the Church at that time affirmed only the monogamous marriage relationship.

Whatever their validity, these rumors about unorthodox sexual practices damaged the Church's public image. Those speaking and writing against Mormonism—including ministers, editors, disaffected Mormons, businessmen, and local government officials—sometimes included charges of polygamy in their scoffing diatribes. They also challenged the Prophet's revelations.

Eber D. Howe was among the earliest newsmen in Ohio to revive the controversies the Saints hoped they had left behind in New York. In his Painesville *Telegraph,* Howe reprinted the earlier Dogberry articles and added his own ridicule. Others joined the chorus. The *Millennial Harbinger,* issued as the voice of Alexander Campbell's religious movement, denounced the Prophet as an imposter. And well it might, for so many Campbellites were being converted to Mormonism that it threatened the Campbellite stronghold in Ohio. Campbell's sixteen-page *Delusions . . .* directly challenged the Book of Mormon and was the first of a steady stream of books and pamphlets from the Campbellite press. No other group matched the Campbellites' attacks on Mormonism.

The literary harassment reached its zenith in 1834 with the publication of *Mormonism Unvailed* [sic], an anthology that was the genesis of many later anti-Mormon works. A citizens committee sponsored this spurious collection, turning first to Doctor Philastus Hurlbut (Doctor was his given name), an ambitious convert and missionary to Pennsylvania who had been excommunicated for immorality and then turned to lecturing against the Church. Hurlbut's usefulness to the publications committee was weakened when a court in Chardon convicted him of threatening the Prophet's life, so the book was issued under Eber D. Howe's name. It contained a mixture of old and new charges against Joseph Smith's credibility and attempted to weaken the believability of the Book of Mormon by asserting a link with Solomon Spaulding's fanciful novel *Manuscript Found,* which told of Romans shipwrecked among the Indians in America. Joseph Smith, the theory suggested, was too unlearned to write the Book of Mormon himself, and so Sidney Rigdon wrote it for him by adding religious material to Spaulding's narrative novel. This theory was discredited early, even by anti-Mormon writers.

Despite its claim to inside information, *Mormonism Unvailed* disappointed its sponsors. Few Mormons left the Church because of it, and anticipated sales to nonmembers were sluggish. Joseph Smith's response was equally restrained to this and other forms of literary harassment. It was physical abuse that troubled the Prophet most. Here and there hecklers punctuated threats of beatings or tar and feathers by throwing eggs, inkstands, or books at preaching elders. Occasionally Latter-day Saint preachers created resentment themselves with unrestrained enthusiasm or dogmatic insistence on the superiority of their religion. "For these things," the Prophet wrote, "we are heartily sorry."[6]

Certain residents of Hiram, Ohio, vented their personal feelings with mob action directed against the Prophet and Sidney Rigdon. Stimulated by whiskey and hidden behind blackened faces, a gang of more than two dozen men dragged Joseph from his bed during the night of March 24, 1832. Choking him into submission, they stripped him naked, scratched his skin with their fingernails, tore his hair, then smeared his body with tar and feathers. A vial of nitric acid forced against his teeth splashed on his face; a front tooth was broken. Meanwhile other members of the mob dragged Rigdon by the heels from his home, bumping his head on the frozen ground, which left him delirious for days. The Prophet's friends spent the night removing the tar to help him keep a Sunday morning appointment. He addressed a congregation that included Simonds Ryder, organizer of the mob.

Newspaper reports of the mob action in Hiram strongly denounced it, but the Prophet's antagonists did not relent. When he left a week later on his second visit to Missouri, they pursued him three hundred miles to Cincinnati before he sought the protection of a steamer captain and safely completed the trip. After his return to Kirtland, he was almost continuously accompanied by a guard. Likewise, Sidney Rigdon sought protection, moving first to Kirtland, then Chardon; and the Saints took precautions and accelerated the manufacture of guns for defense. Joseph instructed his wife to take refuge in Kirtland while he was away. Emma did so, still sorrowing over the death of Joseph Murdock,

---

[6]*Latter-day Saints' Messenger and Advocate* 1 (September 1835).

one of their adopted twins. The child, already weakened from a case of measles, died from complications of a cold probably contracted through exposure on the night of the Hiram mobbing.

Spreading the Gospel Message

Such troubles did not halt the Saints' efforts to publicize their message. In Missouri, the Church printing house commenced publishing the scriptures, hymns, and a newspaper. The first number of the *Evening and the Morning Star* appeared in September 1832, and the publication continued until the ransacking of its office less than two years later. The *Latter Day Saints' Messenger and Advocate* was then published at Kirtland until 1837. Church agents also issued two secular newspapers during this period, the *Upper Missouri Advertiser,* at Independence, and the *Northern Times,* published in 1835 at Kirtland. Although short-lived, these various papers provided a much needed voice in the clarification of doctrine and Latter-day Saint views on matters of current interest.

Dispersal of the restoration message was not left to the printed media alone, for the disciples of Mormonism in the early 1830s exhibited a spontaneous missionary zeal. New members were fired with a desire to share the good news, to speak with a "warning voice, every man to his neighbor." Soon after the Church established itself in Ohio, the Prophet organized the work. At the conferences at Kirtland in June 1831 and at Amherst in January 1832, elders who had volunteered for service were assigned companions and in some instances directed to specific areas and routes

Masthead of first issue of the first Mormon newspaper. The revelation is now published as section 20 of the Doctrine and Covenants. (Church Archives)

of travel. Beginning in 1834 the missionaries were issued preaching licenses as authorized Church representatives.

During the early 1830s missionaries heavily canvassed the communities close to their homes. Short-term missionary excursions were common as elders traveled to nearby towns during slack seasons on the farm. Ohio was crisscrossed many times in this fashion, and every departing set of elders was expected to preach along the way.

If Ohio was saturated with missionaries, other parts of the continent were not forgotten. By the end of the Kirtland period people in every organized state in the Union, much of Upper Canada, the Fox Islands off the coast of Maine, and Great Britain were contacted. Wherever the missionaries went, they organized branches, and between 1831 and 1837 an estimated twenty thousand persons were baptized. Conversions were slowest in the southern states, where missionaries found difficulty penetrating the well-established traditions and dealing with the complications of slavery and rigid class structure. The work spread most rapidly along the corridor from New York and Pennsylvania through Ohio to the outpost in Missouri.

Wherever they were called to labor, these early Mormon missionaries preferred contacts in public meetings—in courthouses, schools, churches, barns, homes, or on street corners. But they also went from door to door with Book of Mormon in hand. They found their strongest opposition among the clergy. Though encountering much difficulty and opposition from ministers, indifferent frontiersmen, and jeering, mud-throwing pranksters and skeptics, the missionaries nevertheless displayed an overpowering optimism in a field ready for the harvest. Convinced they were engaged in the Lord's errand of gathering the righteous out of Babylon, they found satisfaction in helping to establish Zion.

The Latter-day Kingdom: Economic Affairs

Many of the revelations and preaching of the 1830s referred to the kingdom that gathered Israel would establish in preparation for the second advent of Christ and the Millennium. Along with a site for this premillennial community, Zion's people required a righteous law and an ecclesiastical government.

A revelation delivered to the final conference at Fayette, New York, in January 1831 gave the Saints a comforting promise:

Wherefore, hear my voice and follow me, and you shall be a free people, and ye shall have no laws but my laws when I come, for I am your lawgiver, and what can stay my hand? . . .

And let every man esteem his brother as himself, and practice virtue and holiness before me. . . .

And that ye might escape the power of the enemy, and be gathered unto me a righteous people, without spot and blameless—

Wherefore, for this cause I gave unto you the commandment that ye should go to the Ohio; and there I will give unto you my law; and there you shall be endowed with power from on high.[7]

The promised law was not long in coming. Soon after Joseph Smith's arrival in Kirtland he declared the "Law of the Church" in the presence of twelve elders. This revelation of February 9, 1831, introduced an important new economic order among the Saints, the law of consecration and stewardship. A people of Zion who were of one heart and one mind and dwelt in righteousness with no poor among them had been described in the Prophecy of Enoch revealed to the Prophet in June 1830. Similar societies with all things held in common were the ideal Christian communities described in the Book of Mormon and the New Testament; this new order was an important step in the restoration of the ancient order of things.

The law of consecration and stewardship met practical as well as spiritual needs. Among the Ohio Saints were converts from the communitarian orders of the Shakers and members of Isaac Morley's "Family," a system of common property among the followers of Sidney Rigdon. Joseph Smith disapproved of plans under which everyone simply put their possessions together in a strictly communal system and all had access to everything. For converts reluctant to abandon the practice, "the more perfect law of the Lord" was an acceptable alternative. In addition, the new law would provide land in Ohio for transplanted New York Saints to farm and supply surplus funds to support the poor and finance Church publications, and would provide a living for full-time officers, such as the bishop.

Under the new system, each individual was counted equal, and all who entered the order were expected to consecrate their property and personal possessions to the Church "with a covenant and a deed which can not be broken." This was the ultimate eco-

---

[7]D&C 38:22, 24, 31-32.

nomic sacrifice. Every member of the order was entitled to receive an inheritance, or stewardship, "sufficient for himself and family." Any excess would be distributed to those without enough for their needs or used for other general improvements. Each year the faithful stewards were to give their surpluses to the bishop's storehouse. Stewards were admonished to avoid debt, dress plainly in homespun, and avoid the Shaker practice of helping themselves to personal belongings of fellow members of the order.

Economically, the law of consecration and stewardship was designed to accomplish four related objectives. First, it would eliminate poverty and create an economic equality tempered by individual needs, circumstances, and capacities. Second, through the continuing consecration of excess production into the storehouse, there would be a sharing of surplus, creating capital for business expansion and for church programs. Third, the system relied heavily on individual initiative. Each steward operated under a system of free enterprise in the management of property. He was subject to profits and losses, the laws of supply and demand, and the price system. But despite this involvement in the capitalistic system, the stewards were part of a united community working toward a fourth objective, group economic self-sufficiency.

In practice the imperfections of the Saints made it impossible to live in unity under the "law for the government of the church." The order inaugurated by the Colesville Branch at Thompson, Ohio, ended in confusion and lawsuits before it had scarcely begun in the spring of 1831. It dissolved when Leman Copley withdrew his offer of land for the common pool. The Colesville Saints then moved to Missouri, where other members were gathering for a second attempt to live the law.

Some important changes were made at this time in the way the order functioned. The difficulties over land titles at Thompson suggested the need for legally binding, written documents to transfer property. In Jackson County Bishop Edward Partridge prepared a deed of consecration listing as a perpetual conveyance all items transferred to the order. On another document he listed the items returned to the donor as a stewardship and spelled out the restrictions on this inheritance. Transmitted for life on condition of good behavior, the stewardship could be forfeited through transgression. In this case the steward would lose the real estate leased from the bishop but could retrieve his loaned personal property if he paid for it. The agreement included an insurance provision that bound the bishop to care for the steward's family in case of infirmity, old age, or widowhood.

More adjustments soon became necessary. Those not fully converted to the system interpreted their lease or stewardship as a legal title, irrevocable even if they apostatized. In May 1833 a Missouri court ruled in favor of a member who sued for the return of a fifty-dollar donation. After this Bishop Partridge abandoned his attempt to establish a perpetual deed of consecration.

These adjustments in the law of consecration were incorporated into the revelations published in the 1835 edition of the Doctrine and Covenants. Under the modified plan, the donor retained personal ownership and stewardship of income-producing property and personal effects. Each year he was to decide for himself how much was surplus and consecrate it to the bishop, in an annual voluntary irretrievable offering. Any inheritance given the poor was conveyed under similar, irretrievable contract. All these changes were consistent with what church leaders learned through experience, and with a revelation of August 1831 that commanded members to subject themselves to the law of the land. Contemporary legal opinion tended to disapprove of churches holding property in trust, and the law of consecration was now harmonized with that view. But for faithful Saints who wanted to live it, real sacrifice and brotherhood were still required.

The eagerness of some Saints to gather to Zion and enjoy the benefits of the law of consecration created other problems. Too many wanted to gather before the order could accommodate them. To restrain the poor from coming too quickly and to ensure an orderly migration, Joseph Smith issued regulations in 1831 and 1832 keyed to the ability of the Missouri bishop to provide for new arrivals. Before leaving Ohio, each candidate was required to obtain a certificate from three elders or the bishop, and only with this certificate would he receive a share of the common wealth in Zion.

By early 1832 the administration of the new economic order was becoming complicated and, like its legal aspects, required changes. The basic institution was the bishop's storehouse. But there was also a Mercantile Establishment (stores in both Ohio and Missouri), a Printing Establishment (the press in Missouri), and a Literary Establishment (a committee of six men in Ohio appointed "stewards over the revelations and commandments" who were responsible for all literary activities of the Church). In addition, Newel K. Whitney was ordained a bishop in Ohio with authority to collect consecrations but not dispense inheritances. That duty remained with the bishop in Zion.

To simplify this, the Prophet and others went west in April 1832 and created a new administrative agency known as the United Firm. At first the United Firm consisted of five members: Bishop Whitney, Joseph Smith, and Sidney Rigdon, all of Ohio; and Oliver Cowdery and Martin Harris, residents of Zion. The new agency received authority to manage everything concerning the bishopric, both in Zion and in Kirtland, centralizing the administration of the United Order in Kirtland, where Bishop Whitney lived. This naturally disturbed some Church leaders in Missouri, for it seemed to weaken Zion's role in favor of the supposedly subordinate stake in Ohio. They criticized Joseph Smith for failure to move Church headquarters to Missouri; a revelation responded that this would come only in the Lord's due time. Clearly there were advantages to the new system, for it consolidated Church financial concerns and gave the Prophet and his Kirtland associates more authority in business affairs. Kirtland emerged as the financial capital of the Church, just as it already claimed precedence as the spiritual center.

The Government of the Kingdom Grows

When the Church left New York, its ecclesiastical organization consisted of elders, priests, teachers, and deacons, led by its first and second elders, Joseph Smith and Oliver Cowdery. For over two years the general government of the Church consisted simply of conferences of elders that convened every three months. As the Church grew, so did its organization. The office of high priest, not originally identified in the revelation of church government, was soon added, and a clearer distinction was made between the two main branches of the priesthood: the Aaronic, or lesser, priesthood, and the Melchizedek, or higher, priesthood. By 1835 other important changes had been made that would characterize the permanent ecclesiastical structure of The Church of Jesus Christ of Latter-day Saints.

Originally the bishopric was the chief ecclesiastical office in Missouri, and whenever conferences of elders met to conduct church business, Bishop Partridge was usually named moderator of

Engraving showing the Kirtland Temple and nearby buildings. (From the Illustrated American, *December 27, 1890, Church Archives)*

the session. Sometime in the fall of 1832 the elders' role was assumed by a council of high priests, but the bishop continued to be recognized as the head of the Church in Zion and to preside at high priests council meetings. This continued until the expulsion from Jackson County, after which the council of high priests was replaced by a newly formed high council at Far West, and the bishop's primacy as presiding high priest ended.

Bishop Partridge's primary responsibility in Jackson County was administration of the Church's economic law. In September 1831 Newel K. Whitney became his agent in Ohio, and three months later Whitney was ordained a bishop. The bishops only handled questions of consecrations and inheritances, leaving the high priests to regulate spiritual matters.

Church officials referred to the Prophet in Ohio matters not provided for in already revealed guidelines. Joseph Smith, meantime, became part of a new presiding quorum. On January 25, 1832, he was sustained at a conference at Amherst, Ohio, as president of the high priesthood, and he was so ordained by Sidney Rigdon. The First Presidency was soon organized, and a revelation dated March 8 recognized Sidney Rigdon and Jesse Gause as counselors to Joseph Smith. Gause, however, became disaffected and Frederick G. Williams filled the vacancy. The Prophet and his counselors held the keys of the kingdom and presided over the entire church.

As the gathering of the Saints continued, church government continued to expand. Kirtland was designated as a stake, a term that suggested major activity, but until 1834 its affairs were handled by a council of high priests under the direction of the bishop. On February 17, 1834, the Kirtland high council was organized. Acting under the direction of a presidency, this council consisted of twelve high priests and was to be the official judicial body for the stake. The First Presidency at first functioned also as the presidency of the Kirtland Stake, but after Kirtland was abandoned, these functions were separated. In July 1834 a stake was also organized in Clay County, Missouri, with a presidency and a high council. Thus the stake became one of the basic administrative units of the Church.

At the same time, Joseph Smith recognized the need for more help in the First Presidency. On December 5, 1834, Oliver Cowdery was named assistant president, and the following day Joseph Smith, Sr., and Hyrum Smith received the same calling. Although officially the First Presidency was a quorum of three, this action established the precedent for later leaders to call needed special assistants.

Another new office announced was that of patriarch. On December 18, 1833, Joseph Smith and his two counselors ordained Joseph Smith, Sr., as the first patriarch in the Church, responsible for giving individual patriarchal blessings to the members. Subsequently other patriarchs were called to serve in various stakes and missions, and the elder Smith served as patriarch to the whole church. According to a revelation of March 28, 1835, this position was to be given only to his direct descendants.

In 1835, the basic hierarchy of the Church was completed with the organization of the Council of the Twelve Apostles and the First Council of the Seventy. On March 28, at a special meeting of the Twelve, the Prophet dictated a special revelation that clarified the duties of many church officers and distinguished more clearly between the two priesthoods. Now section 107 of the Doctrine and Covenants, it is one of the basic references on the operation of church government.

As early as 1829 the three witnesses to the Book of Mormon

had been instructed to seek out twelve apostles, but only at the urging of Joseph Smith did they finally accomplish this important task. After receiving proper authority from the First Presidency, Oliver Cowdery, David Whitmer, and Martin Harris ordained nine of the twelve on February 14 and 15, 1835, and the other three were ordained later. The primary function of the Twelve was to be special witnesses of Christ, although they also served as a traveling high council, authorized to set in order Church affairs anywhere in the world outside the stakes of Zion. In 1841 their authority was expanded to include conduct of affairs within the stakes.

The original Council of the Twelve was a dedicated body of young men. The president of the group was the eldest—Thomas B. Marsh, thirty-five. The youngest four were all twenty-four. All twelve had served in Zion's Camp (discussed below) and, like the seventies who would soon be chosen, were told that this march had been a trial of their faith, a test that now qualified them for their new responsibilities.

The office of seventy was introduced into the Church by Joseph Smith about two weeks after the organization of the Twelve. Unlike other priesthood groups, this body was given seven presidents to preside over each quorum, and a First Council of seven presidents was to lead all the seventies. The seventies were to be missionaries; and the First Council of the Seventy, and eventually the First Quorum, were to become General Authorities of the Church. The revelation that delineated their duties indicated they were to form a quorum equal in authority to that of the Twelve Apostles, but it also said that they were to act under the direction of the Twelve in preaching and administering the gospel. The phrase "equal in authority" has been interpreted to apply only if something should happen to the entire First Presidency and the Twelve: the First Council of the Seventy was next in line to assume leadership.

By early 1835, nearly all the basic ecclesiastical units had been organized. The principal administrative responsibility was given to the First Presidency, consisting of a president and two counselors. The twelve apostles were traveling ministers, special witnesses of Christ authorized to set in order church business anywhere outside the stakes. The Seventy were to assist the apostles in this task, and sometimes were even called the seventy apostles. The Patriarch had the special calling of giving blessings. These officers, along with the Presiding Bishopric and whatever assistants have been called, have since then constituted the General Authorities of the Church.

In addition, the organization of 1835 included two stakes of Zion, each presided over by a stake presidency assisted by a high council of twelve high priests. The high council was then basically a judicial body, although it later assumed greater advisory and administrative functions under the direction of the stake president. There were also bishops in each stake presiding over the Aaronic, or lesser, priesthood, whose basic responsibility was economic. The responsibilities of various priesthood positions would be augmented in years to come, but these offices remained basic to the Church's ecclesiastical administration.

The City of Zion and Disruptions in the Gathering

On June 25, 1833, the Prophet sent a plan for the city of Zion and its temple to his brethren in Zion. This ideal city was to be one

Temple lot, Independence, Missouri, in 1907. (George E. Anderson photograph, Church Archives)

mile square, with ten-acre blocks, divided into one-half-acre lots, one house to the lot; a complex of temples was located on two city blocks. The ideal, according to Joseph Smith, was to fill this city, then another one next to it, and so on as needed to "fill up the world in these last days." Independence, Missouri, would be the Center Place.

But the Saints would have to postpone the building of Zion, for even as they eagerly anticipated it, conflict and persecution planted seeds for their forceful removal from Jackson County. Lack of adequate, unbiased sources makes the reasons for this conflict difficult to assess, but several differences between the Mormons and the old settlers of the area may be identified.

To the original settlers, one cause of conflict may have been economic. The communalism of the Latter-day Saints required substantial land holdings to accommodate the anticipated gathering, and the Saints were rapidly buying property in Jackson County. At the same time Mormon merchants and tradesmen established stores and shops that competed with those of the old settlers and grasped a portion of the lucrative Santa Fe trade previously dominated by Missourians. Impressed by the Mormon image of group solidarity, some old settlers expressed fears that as a group the Mormons were determined to take over all their lands and business.

They also viewed the body of Saints as a political threat. Members in Jackson County did not form a separate political faction or party and held no public office during their short stay, yet leaders in county government feared Mormon domination by sheer numbers. By July 1833 the population included about twelve hundred Latter-day Saints, nearly one-third the total population, and the Church was growing rapidly. Local citizens were suspicious of a religious zeal that predicted the imminent establishment of a millennial kingdom in which Latter-day Saints, under the King of kings, would rule the world from their Missouri capital. The Saints seemed to be religious aliens threatening political domination.

The gathering Saints also collided with their neighbors in matters of religion. Protestant ministers, challenged everywhere by the proliferation of new sects, resented the intrusion of a people they quickly tagged as fanatics. The religious views of the Saints on the gathering of Zion, consecration, millennial politics, and new revelation set them apart even from their Christian neighbors, who quickly agreed with the Mormons themselves that they were a "peculiar people."

Cutting across economic, political, and religious lines were two other issues important to the Missouri frontiersmen: Mormon attitudes toward the Indians and toward slavery. The first Saints in Missouri had come to convert the Indians just beyond the western borders. Though they failed, the local citizens did not forget this strange interest in uniting two cultures in a religious venture of city building.

Similarly, Missouri farmers suspected Mormon subterfuge among their slaves. Residents of the state shared a long-standing hostility toward free Negroes, for they seemed to threaten the institution of slavery. When Missouri was admitted to the Union under the famous Compromise of 1820, restrictions were placed upon further entry of free blacks into the state. In 1830 fewer than six hundred lived in Missouri, and none in Jackson County. Rumors early in 1832 accused the Saints of attempting to persuade slaves to disobey their masters, rebel, or run away. The issue of free blacks soon triggered a confrontation that had been brewing for months in an atmosphere of religious intolerance.

The Saints themselves may not have been totally without blame in the matter. The feelings of the Missourians, even though misplaced, were undoubtedly intensified by the rhetoric of the gathering itself. They were quick to listen to the boasting of a few overzealous Saints who too-loudly declared a divine right to the land. As enthusiastic millennialists, they proclaimed that the time of the gentiles was short, and they were perhaps too quick to quote the revelation that said that "the Lord willeth that the disciples and the children of men should open their hearts, even to purchase this whole region of country, as soon as time will permit."[8] Even though the Saints were specifically and repeatedly commanded to be peaceful and never to shed blood, some seemed to unwisely threaten warfare if they could not fulfill the commandment peacefully. In July 1833 Church leaders reemphasized the importance of legally purchasing land, but by then a combination of factors was leading to confrontation.

Whatever some unwise and imperfect Saints may have done,

---

[8]D&C 58:52.

a revelation after their expulsion placed at least partial blame on them. "I, the Lord, have suffered the affliction to come upon them," rang the words that came through Joseph Smith, "in consequence of their transgressions. . . . Behold, I say unto you, there were jarrings, and contentions, and envyings, and strifes, and lustful and covetous desires among them; therefore by these things they polluted their inheritances. They were slow to hearken unto the voice of the Lord their God: therefore, the Lord their God is slow to hearken unto their prayers, to answer them in the day of trouble."[9] The redemption of Zion must be postponed until Zion's people had become more perfect, but the same revelation promised that "Zion shall not be moved out of her place," and that one day her redemption would surely come.

Confrontation and Expulsion

Most of the Saints struggled to apply the principles of restored Christianity and live peacefully with their neighbors. But charges against them mounted, and the truth of the matter became unimportant: certain influential Missouri settlers simply did not want the Saints to live among them, and the indictments they spread were readily believed.

In April 1833 about three hundred leading citizens met in Independence to plan the removal or destruction of their unwanted neighbors. Nothing concrete was accomplished, but feelings on both sides were soon intensified. The Reverend Benton Pixley, a long-time missionary to the Indians, wrote anti-Mormon articles and made house-to-house visits denouncing the Saints. In July William W. Phelps, editor of the *Evening and the Morning Star,* answered Pixley's charges with an article entitled "Beware of False Prophets."

The same issue of the Church newspaper carried a notice, entitled "Free People of Color," designed to warn free blacks who were members of the Church of the Missouri law that forbade them to enter the state unless they carried a certificate of citizenship from another state. The notice touched a nerve among the Missourians, who interpreted it as encouragement of immigration and therefore a threat to the slave system. In response, eighty prominent citizens signed a manifesto. Known as the "secret

---

[9]D&C 101: 2-7.

constitution," it denounced the Mormons and called for a meeting on July 20. The manifesto claimed that Mormons were tampering with slaves, encouraging sedition, and inviting free Negroes and mulattoes to join the Church and immigrate to Missouri. It openly declared the intent of the signers to remove the Mormons "peaceably if we can, forcibly if we must."[10]

When William W. Phelps heard of the secret constitution, he issued an "Extra" in an attempt to clarify the controversial notice. It was actually intended, he said, to halt the immigration of free blacks, and even to "prevent them from being admitted as members of the church." But the clarification failed. The "Extra" was ignored.

The meeting on Saturday, July 20, attracted four or five hundred citizens opposed to the Latter-day Saints. They released a public document repeating the assertions of the secret constitution and pronouncing a bitter ultimatum. Mormon immigration and settlement must halt, and the Saints must sell their land and businesses and leave the country within a reasonable time. All this must be accomplished under a pledge which, if broken, would justify the proponents in consulting again on further steps. Though the Saints were astounded, this unbelievable mob proposal was soon presented to six Church leaders. Denied time to consider it, they rejected the plan. The impatient assembly, after waiting two hours for an answer, voted to take immediate action. About a hundred men proceeded to the Church printing office, kicked in the door, and evicted Mrs. Phelps and her children. They tossed the press from a second-story window, pulled off the roof, and tore down the walls of the building. Damages were estimated at about $5,000, and the attack halted the printing of the Book of Commandments and the two newspapers. The mob next attacked the store, the blacksmith shop, and two men, Edward Partridge and Charles Allen. They were hauled to the public square, partially stripped of their clothing, and, after failing to admit guilt or promising to leave, were covered with tar and feathers. Violence had erupted and would not cease until the Saints were gone.

The mob appeared again on July 23, carrying rifles, pistols, clubs, and whips, and compelled Mormon leaders to assemble in the public square. They were forced to sign a written agreement to

---

[10]Joseph Smith, *History of the Church*, 1:374.

leave the county, one group before January 1 and another before April, although John Corrill and Sidney Gilbert would be allowed to remain as agents in selling the property of the Saints.

This agreement allowed the Saints a little time to seek advice from Joseph Smith and consult with state officials. Oliver Cowdery was immediately dispatched to Kirtland, where a council met and sent a message to the Saints in Zion to seek redress under the law. A letter from Frederick G. Williams in October recommended that only those who actually signed the pledge should leave, and that no one should sell his inheritance in Zion. The Saints could hardly consider the agreement legally binding, for it was signed under mob duress.

The leaders in Zion, meanwhile, petitioned Missouri Governor Daniel Dunklin for help and protection. The state attorney general considered the request, criticized the citizens for lawlessness, and urged the Saints to seek both redress and protection under the laws by petitioning the circuit judge and justices of the peace. To pursue their case in the courts, the Church retained the legal firm of Doniphan, Atchison, Rees, and Wood in late October. In addition, Church leaders ended their policy of passive resistance and counseled the Saints to arm themselves for the defense of their families and homes. A delegation to Clay County purchased powder and lead, and Church officials announced on October 20 their intent to defend themselves against any physical attack.

The Missourians quickly interpreted this as a violation of the Mormon promise to evacuate. They spread the word through the county, and on Thursday, October 31, the citizens took their first concerted action. That night forty or fifty men attacked the Whitmer settlement just over the Big Blue River, eight miles west of Independence, unroofed and demolished ten houses, and whipped several men as the Mormons fled. Church leaders sought a peace warrant against the captains of the raiding party, but after a justice of the peace refused it, the elders decided to post guards. Each branch was instructed to organize its own defense and be prepared to march at a moment's notice.

Violence continued throughout the county, and judges repeatedly refused to issue warrants against the mobsters. Early in November the Saints in Independence were forced to leave their homes and camp together on the temple lot under the protection of two or three dozen men. In another raid on a settlement on the Big Blue a Missourian was wounded, prompting his cohorts to organize for battle and the Saints, in turn, to congregate in even larger bodies for protection. On November 4 several Missourians captured a Mormon ferry on the Big Blue, and soon thirty or forty angry men from each side confronted each other in the fields. Shots were fired and the Missourians departed, with the Mormons in hot pursuit. Two Missourians were killed; on the Mormon side, Philo Dibble's injury crippled him for life, and Andrew Barber died of his wounds the following day.

Meanwhile, a few Mormon leaders were jailed in Independence, and rumors that the Mormons were planning to bring Indians against the town began to spread. More citizens rallied, but eventually the leaders either escaped or were freed from jail. By then, they had informed the sheriff of their intention to evacuate the county.

Lilburn W. Boggs, then lieutenant governor of the state, acted as intermediary between the two opposing groups and persuaded the Saints to surrender their arms and leave within ten days in order to avoid more bloodshed. The Saints understood that Boggs would also collect the arms of their enemies and that all would be returned to their rightful owners after they had evacuated. In this they were sadly misled.

The prisoners were released in a cornfield near Independence, and immediately they began planning for the exodus from Jackson County. But as if to reinforce their determination to rid themselves of their neighbors, the Missourians continued harassing Mormon settlements. Mounted bands threatened the Saints with physical violence, searched their homes for weapons, whipped some, and chased others from their property. One group of about 130 women and children, left alone while the men hunted wagons, were harassed by over one hundred armed men. When ordered out within two hours, they loaded supplies into four available wagons and moved across the river into Clay County.

A few of the Saints found refuge in Ray, Lafayette, and Van Buren counties, but the largest congregation assembled in Clay County, to open another chapter in the history of the Church in Missouri. The citizens of Liberty, the principal town of Clay County, offered work, shelter, and provisions. The refugees moved into abandoned slave cabins, built crude huts, and pitched tents.

When spring arrived they rented land and found work splitting rails, grubbing brush, or as day laborers. Women served as domestics and teachers. Because of their friendliness toward the beleaguered Saints, the helpful citizens of Clay and other counties were criticized by hostile elements in Jackson County and dubbed "Jack Mormons," a term applied widely in the nineteenth century to friendly non-Mormons.

The removal from Jackson County deeply concerned the Prophet. Not only had it brought suffering to the Saints, but it had also interrupted a principal dream of the restoration. By revelation in October the Saints were assured, "Zion shall be redeemed, although she is chastened for a little season." Until that could be accomplished, the Prophet encouraged the eastern branches to continue gathering funds for land purchases in Jackson County and told the Missouri faithful to retain title to their lands and seek redress through constitutional means. These important instructions set the tone for Latter-day Saint policy toward Jackson County in following years, and the concept of redeeming Zion became a permanent part of Mormon millennial expectations.

Following the instructions of the Prophet, the exiled Missouri Saints made further attempts to recover their property and damages through the courts. They asked the governor to provide a military escort as they reoccupied their homes, and guards for witnesses who would testify in the Jackson County court. Governor Dunklin agreed to furnish arms if the Saints would organize themselves into a local militia, but, he explained to the dismay of the Saints, he would have to work through proper channels, meaning the Jackson Guard.

When the court of inquiry was finally held, the governor did authorize the Clay County militia, the Liberty Blues, to guard the witnesses. A circuit court hearing was held in late February, and a cadre of fifty Blues accompanied the Mormon witnesses across the river into Jackson County. It soon became evident that the excitement of the Jackson County citizens made criminal prosecution impossible, so Church leaders decided to abandon the effort.

The Church next petitioned the president of the United States, Andrew Jackson, for a federal guarantee of protection once the lost property was regained. For the first time the Church encountered national politics and discovered that no matter how just their cause, other considerations made it impossible for the federal

The Saints begin to leave Jackson County. This painting is one of a series begun by C. C. A. Christensen in 1869 to illustrate his lectures on Church history. The paintings were sewed together on a long wooden pole and unrolled as the artist talked. (From the Permanent Collection of Brigham Young University)

government to act. One of the great national debates of the day concerned the sovereign rights of states and the degree to which the federal government could intervene in a state's internal affairs. Just a year earlier the United States had come close to civil war when South Carolina had claimed the right to nullify an act of Congress within its borders. President Jackson went so far as to assemble troops, declare South Carolina in rebellion, and threaten to march on the state if it did not conform to the federal law. South Carolina backed down, but only with a strong proclamation that it was sovereign and had a right to do what it had done. Joseph Smith was so concerned by the issue that he had it recorded in his history of the Church, calling South Carolina's action a rebellion. Then, on Christmas Day in 1832, he received one of his best-known revelations, which predicted that "beginning at the rebellion of South Carolina," civil war would surely come to the United States.

When the Mormons presented their grievances to the United States, it was in an atmosphere charged with tension over the states' rights issue, and the general feeling was that the federal government had no authority to intervene in such matters. The Mormon question was referred to Secretary of War Lewis Cass, who replied on May 2, 1834, that the offenses listed as religious persecution appeared to be violations of state, not federal, law. According to the Constitution, the president could not call out the militia unless the governor declared a state of insurrection. Having just survived the nullification controversy, the Jackson administration was not prepared to intervene in another states' rights question.

Governor Dunklin continued efforts to help the Mormons, but the tense situation prevented effective action, through either the courts or the legislature. By 1834 he was complaining in despair to the legislature that "under our present laws, conviction for any violence committed upon a Mormon, cannot be had in Jackson County."[11] Mormon appeals continued until well after the final expulsion from the state in 1838, but under the circumstances a fair court decision seemed impossible.

Zion's Camp

The Ohio Saints, in the meantime, were preparing to make a bold and dramatic effort to rescue their beleaguered comrades: the march of Zion's Camp. Joseph Smith's revelations of December 16, 1833, and February 24, 1834, suggested direct action, though veiled in well-worded parable and hyperbole. A parable of a nobleman and his vineyard was given "that you may know my will concerning the redemption of Zion."[12] The Lord of the vineyard instructed his servant (i.e., Joseph Smith) to gather the young and middle-aged "warriors" and redeem the land that had been captured by an intruding enemy. By February, when the Prophet announced the intention to go to Missouri, he had enlisted more than thirty volunteers. The high council sent eight enlistment officers to the eastern congregations to seek out additional volunteers and contributions. It was not intended that this would be merely an invading army. The plan envisioned a return of the Saints to their homes in Jackson County in cooperation with state authorities and under state protection.

On the first day of May the advance guard of Kirtland

---

[11] As quoted in Warren A. Jennings, "Zion Is Fled: The Expulsion of the Mormons from Jackson County, Missouri" (Ph.D. diss., University of Florida, 1962), p. 238.
[12] D&C 101:43-62; 103:15-22.

volunteers began its thousand-mile trek. Additional units followed, and on May 6 the Prophet organized his 150 men into companies of twelve. Buying supplies as it traveled, the camp marched across Ohio, Indiana, and Illinois, adding volunteers from other branches until it grew to an estimated 205 members, including ten women (wives of recruits) who went along as cooks and washerwomen.

While the little Mormon army moved westward, the Clay County Saints proceeded to rearm themselves. On June 5 they informed Governor Dunklin that they were ready for a state escort for their return. But Jackson County citizens were also preparing by securing pledges from surrounding counties for support to resist reestablishment of the Saints in Jackson County. Rumors of imminent Mormon invasions across the Missouri during the last week of April brought a hasty mustering of the Jackson Guard, but when no invasion materialized, the Missourians vented their tension by burning the remaining Mormon houses. Then they slipped across the river in small groups to harass the settlers near the river.

Zion's Camp left its Salt River encampment June 12, having asked the Missouri governor for a military escort. Governor Dunklin, fearing that any attempts to cooperate with the Mormons would spark a civil war, withdrew his earlier offer to escort the refugees back to their homes and advised the Saints to sell contested lands and move elsewhere. Zion's Camp received word of the refusal with dismay, but the governor had already launched a compromise. Acting through Colonel John Thornton, a wealthy landowner in Clay County, the governor acknowledged the Mormons' right to live in Missouri, but concluded that their religious eccentricity made isolation advisable. Jackson County officials agreed to negotiate a peaceful solution, and the governor outlined the alternatives for the Latter-day Saints: sell out and leave the county, persuade the Missourians they should rescind their illegal resolves and abide by the law, or occupy separate territories and isolate themselves from their antagonists.

The two sides met at Liberty on June 16 in a crowded meeting at the courthouse. Judge John F. Ryland presided. After a tirade of inflammatory speeches by local citizens, a committee of ten proposed to buy out the Mormons if they agreed never to return. Prices would be established by disinterested arbitrators. Alternatively, the old residents said they would sell on the same terms if the Mormons wanted to purchase their holdings. Both offers were impractical, since neither side was actually inclined to sell to the other.

The meeting adjourned to allow the attending elders to seek the consensus of the Church. In the meantime, they promised to keep Zion's Camp outside Jackson County. The camp moved to a site between two branches of Fishing River, just east of the Clay County line. There they were warned that about three hundred armed mobocrats from several nearby communities were planning an attack. A fierce squall, however, prevented a clash, and the following day the Mormon army moved to a Mormon farm five miles away.

Church leaders soon rejected the Jackson County offer and proposed their alternative. They suggested that a committee of twelve, six from each side, be appointed to determine the value of the property of the citizens wishing to leave and the cost of damages. The Saints would use the credits for damages to buy out the old citizens and pay any differences within a year. The plan was rejected, however, and the stalemate continued.

The citizens of Jackson County, meanwhile, were still disturbed by the presence of the Kirtland militia on their borders. On June 22 the sheriff of Clay County visited the camp to secure a statement of intent, as requested by Judge Ryland. "It is our intention," camp officials declared, "to go back upon our lands in Jackson county, by order of the Executive of the State if possible."[13] But the Saints lacked the necessary military support from the governor, although negotiations were in progress, and Joseph Smith soon recognized the impossibility of reoccupation without that support.

On June 22 the Prophet received a revelation at Fishing River declaring that Zion would not be redeemed at that time. The reason given was the failure of the Church as a whole to observe the law of consecration and to support Zion's Camp financially. The Saints were learning the difficult lesson that the Lord does not always fight their battles for them, and that political and physical realities often require that fulfillment of his commandments be delayed. Those who had met a trial of faith by responding to the call were promised a special endowment, and the Saints were urged to continue their efforts to obtain legal

---

[13]*Evening and the Morning Star* 2 (July 1834): 176.

redress and to purchase Jackson County land. Zion would still, one day, be redeemed.

On June 30 the Prophet announced that the members of Zion's Camp were discharged. Several had died of cholera; many drifted back to Kirtland in small parties, while others remained in Missouri. On July 7 the Prophet attended a conference which drafted an "Appeal to the American People," explaining the Latter-day Saints' refusal to accept the Missouri offer to buy them out and declaring, "To sell our land would amount to a denial of our faith."[14]

Kirtland: Way Station for a Season

Even while the Saints in Zion were suffering displacement, important developments occurred in Ohio. Particularly significant were Latter-day Saint involvements in the economic and political life of Geauga County, the establishment of an educational program, a reorganization of the United Firm, and completion and dedication of the Kirtland Temple.

Kirtland had been designated as a way station for five years, and many members willingly accepted the challenge to help retain a strong hold there. Latter-day Saints crowded into Kirtland, overflowed all available houses, and then sought out abandoned shops, simple huts, barns, or wagon boxes for temporary living quarters.

In Ohio, as in Missouri, older settlers reacted negatively to the prospect of large numbers of Mormons living together in one place. Established communities were fully willing to allow the Saints to participate in their own religious practices and to share in the economic and political life of the community as long as they remained a scattered, integrated minority. But the policy of gathering—of congregating in self-contained, exclusive sub-communities—seemed to challenge the original citizens' traditions.

Many of the Saints were destitute of worldly possessions, but those with resources contributed generously toward land purchases, home building, and construction of the temple. The Saints had their own dry goods stores, inn, sawmills, gristmill, and fulling mill, plus various craftsmen. In this way, they contributed to the development of the community. Because of the general

---

[14]*Evening and the Morning Star* 2 (August 1834): 183-84.

poverty of the Saints, however, older citizens feared the burden of charity might be shifted to the town. Their fears were compounded by the worsening economic conditions of 1835. Some non-Mormons wanted to force the Saints out of the Kirtland area, and two leading businessmen refused to employ the newcomers in their factory and sawmill. When grain became scarce that summer, merchants expanded their boycott by refusing to sell to the Latter-day Saints, hoping to starve them out. But there were Mormon mills outside Kirtland, and other supplies were available fifty miles from the community.

The Saints in Ohio participated more broadly in public affairs than those in Jackson County, and Joseph Smith, who lived in Kirtland, took great interest in both local and national politics. The Mormons in general supported the national administration and gave allegiance to Andrew Jackson's Democratic party. But Ohio's Western Reserve was mixed politically, and the Whigs in Geauga County were suspicious of the potential political threat presented by a bloc of Mormon votes. Several Latter-day Saints in Kirtland, including Oliver Cowdery, Sidney Rigdon, and Frederick G. Williams, held elective offices, and the Whigs saw this as a possible first step toward Mormon control of local government. The unity of the Mormons thus created the potential for jealousies, even though the Prophet made no attempt to urge political conformity.

Already rumors spread that because of their exclusiveness Mormons were anti-American and part of a secret, autocratic society. To quash such tales, Frederick G. Williams founded the *Northern Times* in 1834. Another effort to quiet false political assertions was the statement on government, adopted in 1835 and printed in the first edition of the Doctrine and Covenants. This statement, probably written by Oliver Cowdery, emphasized freedom of religion, freedom of opinion, and the need for government free from the influence of any particular religion.

Contemporary Church leaders were not hesitant to speak out on many issues of both local and national concern. Through the *Northern Times* and other publications they denounced abolitionism, supported Andrew Jackson in his campaign against the United States Bank, and became involved in the question of changing the Geauga County Seat. Despite their religious exclusiveness, it was important to them that they be recognized as part of the larger body politic in America and as loyal citizens.

Intemperance was an important social issue in Ohio and many other places in Jacksonian America, and the Mormon solution eventually played an important role in setting the Latter-day Saints apart as a distinctive people. By 1833, the year the Word of Wisdom was given, the temperance movement in America had five thousand local societies claiming over a million members. Temperance articles were regular fare in the public press. Diet, too, was receiving considerable attention, with stress on fruits, vegetables, and moderation in meat.

In Kirtland, local politicians watched for the Latter-day Saint reaction. The Owenites (a communitarian group) and the Campbellites had endorsed the temperance movement, and the Kirtland Temperance Society had been organized since October 1830. The society closed the local distillery, first by refusing to sell it grain and then, when the distillers imported grain, by pooling resources to purchase the business. A distillery at Mentor closed at the same time. Even though some Saints belonged to the society, critics complained of lack of Mormon support, and the society folded in October 1835.

During the height of the movement to close the Geauga County distilleries, the Prophet gave the Saints their own guidelines on temperance. The Word of Wisdom denounced the drinking of wine, strong drink, and hot drinks. It outlined the proper medicinal uses of tobacco, advised the moderate use of meat, and encouraged the use of grain and fresh fruits with thanksgiving. The "hot drinks" prohibited were later interpreted to mean specifically tea and coffee. At first written "not by commandment or constraint, but by revelation and the word of wisdom," this revelation eventually became a standard of health as well as a symbol of obedience among the Latter-day Saints.

In addition to such political and social concerns, the Church led Kirtland in education. One of the First Presidency's duties was to develop a training school for church officers—the School of the Prophets. According to the "Olive Leaf" revelation, recorded December 27, 1832, it was to be a temple school, conducted in the House of the Lord. One important task of the school was to train prospective missionaries, but the Prophet also recognized the need for knowledge of temporal as well as spiritual matters. He had been urged by revelation to "study and learn, and become acquainted with all good books, and with languages, tongues, and people."[15] With this philosophy, the School of the Prophets established a division for secular education as well as theology classes, and participants discussed current issues and signs of the times along with the doctrines of the Kingdom.

The School of the Prophets opened in January of 1833 but was disrupted in April. When it reopened in the fall of 1834 it had been divided into the Elder's School for theological training and the Kirtland School for temporal education. "Lectures on Faith," a series of lessons subsequently published with the Doctrine and Covenants between 1835 and 1921, was a basic test for missionaries. Burdick's *Arithmetic,* Kirkham's *Grammar,* and Olney's *Geography* guided nearly one hundred students in the secular division, where they were also tutored in the rudiments of penmanship by William E. M'Lellin. Both schools met during the winter of 1835-36 with increased enrollment and with new evening grammar classes. Beginning in late November the school sponsored a seven-week Hebrew class taught by Joshua Seixas of Hudson, Ohio. The classwork for both schools moved into the temple in January 1835 and a second term of Hebrew commenced. In November 1837 the Kirtland High School assumed the general education curriculum pioneered by the Kirtland School.

Except for the mob violence against Joseph Smith and Sidney Rigdon in March 1832, anti-Mormon activities in Ohio in the early 1830s remained at a relatively low pitch. But the Prophet found it necessary to employ guards, and the Saints were constantly harassed by threats and lawsuits. Joseph Smith spent thousands of dollars defending himself against various charges, many of which proved to be simply the venting of personal animosity.

At least some of the Prophet's troubles stemmed from internal problems. Sylvester Smith, for example, accused him of lying and of using insulting and abusive language during the march of Zion's Camp. In a trial held in August 1834, however, the accuser admitted that he had misrepresented the facts, and he later made a voluntary public statement in the *Messenger and Advocate* clearing the Prophet. Such cases pitting one member against another often brought unwelcome publicity and were used by the Church's

---

[15]D&C 90:15.

enemies to build a negative public image of Mormonism.

After the tragic expulsion of the Saints from Jackson County, it again became necessary to adjust the administration of the Church's economic affairs. Because of persecution, the law of consecration had become virtually nonexistent in Missouri, and most of the Saints now provided for themselves. In April 1834 the Prophet reorganized the United Firm and separated it into two distinct divisions: Ohio and Missouri. The property of the Ohio United Firm was then divided among the seven officers as their stewardships and personal responsibility. The printing agency was transferred to Kirtland, where publication of the church newspaper resumed. Two treasuries were created under the Ohio United Firm, one for collecting money from book sales and the other for collecting income produced by management of church property.

In the long run, the Saints were simply unable to live a law of perfect economic equality. "For if ye are not equal in earthly things ye cannot be equal in obtaining heavenly things,"[16] they had been told, but as long as imperfections existed they could not attain that ideal. Even when all they had to do was donate their annual surplus to the bishop's storehouse, it was difficult to recognize their "surplus." By 1839 any effort to live the law of perfect economic equality was abandoned, though it remained the ideal. In the meantime, full participation in an economic system based on the profit motive and private ownership was the only workable substitute. The scriptural law of tithing replaced the law of consecration as a means of providing funds for church expenses.

The Promised Endowment

Their admitted imperfections did not prevent the Saints from enjoying the outpouring of spiritual blessings, and they were still anxiously engaged in building the Kingdom. Missionary work grew, the Prophet received revelations for spiritual guidance, and the Saints proceeded toward the fulfillment of a major goal, a temple in Kirtland.

When the Saints outgrew the log meetinghouse in Kirtland, a conference of Church leaders met to plan a replacement. Most assumed they would build another simple log or frame structure,

---

[16]D&C 78:6.

but the Prophet had a grander plan in mind. In December the important "Olive Leaf" revelation not only spelled out significant doctrine, but also commanded the elders to establish a house, "even a house of prayer, a house of fasting, a house of faith, a house of learning, a house of glory, a house of order, a house of God."[17] This would be the first Latter-day Saint temple. A later revelation specified that the lower floor would be a meetinghouse and the upper level a school. The building committee, composed of Hyrum Smith, Reynolds Cahoon, and Jared Carter, issued a circular distributed to all branches requesting money for the new project. Funds began to arrive from everywhere—even the beleaguered Zion in Missouri.

According to a revelation, the plans for this temple-school were to be "after the manner which I shall show unto three of you, whom ye shall appoint and ordain unto this power."[18] Members of the First Presidency, with Frederick G. Williams as draftsman, were the three, and they created a plan resembling a modified New England meetinghouse. It was a striking building that utilized traditional motifs arranged in an unorthodox pattern, with two main doors instead of three, a vertically unaligned center window used to light both floors, and a second story replacing the more typical gallery. Inside, two sets of pulpits gave the assembly room an unusual double front. Four tiers of lavishly carved pulpits for the Melchizedek Priesthood were placed on the west (where other denominations placed a single pulpit), and pulpits for the Aaronic Priesthood were placed on the east. Veils or curtains lowered by hidden ropes and pulleys divided the room into quarters and covered the pulpits when the presiding officers wished privacy.

The temple was built of sandstone covered with plaster. The cornerstone was laid on July 23, 1833, and the project had an immediate impact on the Church and the community. It spurred a lagging economy and employed those unable to find work elsewhere, including refugees from troubled Missouri. When fundraising fell short, Joseph Smith borrowed money to meet the estimated $60,000 cost. The project rallied members to a cause that demanded sacrifice and financial commitment and helped resolve

---

[17]D&C 88:119.
[18]D&C 95:14.

some of the discord that had followed Zion's Camp. Despite the Saints' difficulties in keeping the law of consecration, they demonstrated exemplary cooperation. Typical of the enthusiasm the Saints felt for building the temple was the experience of Vilate Kimball. She spent the summer spinning wool to provide clothes for those working on the project and was supposed to receive half the wool as pay. She kept nothing but gave all to those working on the temple. Many women participated in similar generous ways, and when the exterior coating was being applied to the sandstone walls, the women donated glassware to be crushed and worked into the plaster to give a gleaming appearance to the sacred building. To the Latter-day Saints the temple was more than a meetinghouse or a school. It was the visible symbol of the Kingdom of God.

But the Saints had something else to anticipate once the building was complete. Even before they left New York they had been promised that they would be "endowed with power from on high,"[19] and by mid-1833 this special blessing was specifically promised as a function of the Lord's house. This was not the endowment later performed in the Nauvoo and other temples, but it was a special outpouring of spiritual manifestations resembling those of Pentecost.

Events surrounding the dedication of the temple in March 1836 were a spiritual highpoint in the history of the Church in Kirtland. Two months before the dedication ceremonies the Prophet introduced among the leaders an ordinance of washing and anointing with oil, which symbolized the spirituality and cleanliness they desired. At an impressive meeting in the attic rooms of the temple, the Prophet and others reported visions of the celestial kingdom, and the Prophet saw his deceased brother Alvin in that kingdom. Marveling at how this could happen, since Alvin had died before the restoration of the gospel, the Prophet received a revelation concerning the salvation of those who die without hearing the gospel, and this eventually led to the Latter-day Saint practice of baptism of the dead.

On the day of the dedication, March 27, nearly half the crowd had to be turned away, but the ceremonies were later repeated for them. Morning and afternoon meetings were held, the

---

[19]D&C 38:32.

Appearance of the Savior in the Kirtland Temple, as depicted in a 1975 painting by Utah artist Gary Smith. (Reproduced courtesy the artist)

sacrament of the Lord's supper was served, a new hymn was sung, several testimonies were heard, and the event concluded with the whole congregation shouting together three times: "Hosanna, Hosanna, Hosanna to God and the Lamb, Amen, Amen, Amen."

But the day was not complete. That night members of the priesthood met in the temple to be instructed in the ordinances of washing of feet and anointing with oil. Suddenly, they reported, they heard the room filled with sounds of wind. People outside the temple heard the sound and said they saw a shaft of light on the temple steeple, and inside the priesthood members spoke in tongues. In an atmosphere like the day of Pentecost, the Prophet admonished the Twelve to carry the gospel to the nations. Two days later priesthood members spent an all-night session receiving washings and anointings, and on March 30 another day of Pentecost was recorded. Several testified to visions of the Savior and of angels. A final outpouring of such experience came on April 3 following two meetings attended by a thousand Saints. Joseph Smith and Oliver Cowdery dropped the curtains that surrounded the west pulpits and, after solemn prayer, received visions of the Savior and the ancient prophets Moses, Elias, and Elijah, each of whom restored certain keys pertaining to the last days.

After these climactic events the temple was put to thorough use. This included regular Sunday meetings at 10 A.M. and 4 P.M., fast meetings on the first Thursday of each month with Patriarch Joseph Smith, Sr., presiding, school classes during the week, and separate meetings for the Melchizedek Priesthood quorums on weekday evenings. Soon a new corps of missionaries left, having received the "endowment from on high" promised when the Saints left their New York homelands to gather in Ohio. Within three years, the same Saints would once again be uprooted from their homes, joining their Missouri brethren in a new attempt at community building in the westernmost corner of Illinois.

CHAPTER 4

The Saints Move On, 1836-1839

On three successive nights in November 1833, the banks of the Missouri River north of Independence were covered with terrified, homeless refugees. Over twelve hundred Latter-day Saints were being driven from what they believed would be their place of refuge. Jamming the riverbank at Wayne Landing, they waited to board a ferry to cross into Clay County. Many distraught families had been separated, and even as they sought each other, their tormentors hunted them down, fired on them, and whipped them.

Among the harried group were the twenty-six-year-old apostle Parley P. Pratt and his wife, Thankful. About midnight on November 5 the two escaped their home on horseback. The next morning they crossed the river and camped with the growing number of Saints huddled among the cottonwood trees in the river bottoms of Clay County. Elder Pratt pathetically reported:

Hundreds of people were seen in every direction, some in tents and some in the open air around their fires, while the rain descended in torrents. Husbands were inquiring for their wives, wives for their husbands; parents for children, and children for parents. Some had the good fortune to escape with their families, household goods, and some provisions, while others knew not the fate of their friends, and had lost all their goods. The scene was indescribable.[1]

The Latter-day Saints in Missouri were again seeking a place of refuge. They found it, temporarily, in Clay County, but within thirty months they would be on their way to another county; and finally, in another three years, they would find themselves completely driven from the state.

In Kirtland, meanwhile, the Prophet himself would find little peace, and in 1838 he would join his exiled followers in northern Missouri, only to be imprisoned within the year and left behind as the Saints sought new refuge in Illinois. His distress would come not only from bitter anti-Mormons, but from those within who would lose confidence in him, attempt to replace him, and fight against all that he was trying to accomplish. By the end of the decade two of the three witnesses to the Book of Mormon, the president of the Council of the Twelve, and several other friends and close associates would turn against him. The last years of the 1830s produced both one of the most pathetic scenes in the history of the Church and a surprising note of faith and optimism. This perseverance suggests a good deal about Mormonism, just as the reasons for their difficulties tell much about the society of western America in the 1830s.

Clay County Rejects the Saints

As mentioned earlier, the Saints received a kindly reception from the citizens of Clay County. For more than two years the Saints lived and worked there, hoping for the day when Zion would be restored. During this time many Saints became landowners in the new location, and members from other parts of the country swelled their numbers. The citizens of Clay County had welcomed the Mormon refugees in a humanitarian gesture. But they considered it a temporary arrangement, and the same concerns that had disturbed their neighbors in Jackson County soon began to stir them. Even though the Saints were peaceful in their conduct, the people of Clay County were anxious to see them leave. They did not want the Mormons among them permanently, but it looked as if the Latter-day Saints were planning to stay.

---

[1]Parley Parker Pratt, *Autobiography of Parley Parker Pratt*, ed. Parley P. Pratt, 3rd ed. (Salt Lake City: Deseret Book Co., 1938), p. 102.

On June 29, 1836, a mass meeting of Clay County settlers was held in the Liberty courthouse. The accusations leveled at the Saints in Jackson County were reiterated in four basic objections: their religious differences were exciting prejudice, they were easterners whose customs and even dialect were essentially different from those of the Missourians, they were non-slave holders opposed to slavery, and they were constantly communicating with the Indians whom they proclaimed were God's chosen people who would inherit with them the land of Missouri. "We do not vouch for the correctness of these statements," said the report of the committee, "but whether they are true or false, their effect has been the same in exciting our community."[2] The committee believed that the very existence of such charges aroused hostility. To avoid bloodshed, the Saints were asked to leave the county. The report made no direct threat of hostility, but committee members said the invitation to move would spare the county a civil war.

The accusations of Clay County spokesmen and the reply of the Saints reflect the stresses of frontier society, as well as the process by which tragic misunderstandings often occur. In Missouri, slavery was vigorously defended. Not that slavery was essential to the state's economy—it was only marginal—but many Missourians had migrated from the South during the struggle for statehood to ensure Missouri's slave-holding status. Deeply held sympathies for slavery had become part of their social structure. As abolitionists in the North and East gained momentum and sometimes reached extremes, Missourians looked with trepidation at anything that seemed to threaten the system. The Saints had unequivocally declared that they had no intention of interfering with slavery, and that they believed any interference would be both unlawful and unjust. But the fact remained that most Mormons were from the East, where abolitionism was strongest, and none of them were known to have held slaves. Despite Mormon denials, some Missourians seemed incapable of believing what seemed inconsistent.

It was understandable, too, that the Missourians were wary of Indian uprisings. The tribes along their western borders had recently been transplanted there against the Indians' will, and the

---

[2] Joseph Smith, *History of the Church*, 2:450.

Missouri settlers knew all too well the smoldering resentment many native Americans must have felt. The Indians probably posed no actual threat, but the settlers could never know for sure. The Mormons denied any communications with the Indians and announced their readiness to assist in defense against any threatened Indian attack. To encourage the Indians in an uprising would be sedition and rebellion, they said.

The Saints were sincerely attempting to be good citizens, but to the Missourians, circumstantial evidence to the contrary seemed strong enough to cause worry. The first Mormons to enter Missouri had come as missionaries to the Indians, and although they made no converts, it was as a result of this mission that Missouri was designated as the gathering place for the Saints. Besides, the Book of Mormon declared that the Indians were a choice people, and actually promised that one day these descendants of the Book of Mormon people would assist in building the New Jerusalem. The Latter-day Saints had no thought of promoting violence or Indian rebellion, but anyone in Missouri who had another interpretation had some basis on which to build. The totally different religious outlook of the Missouri Protestants combined with the small element of truth in the generally false rumors about the Mormons to create misunderstandings and potential violence. Even if both sides had only the best intentions, the situation was explosive and reflected the kind of misunderstanding that is a tragic but persistent part of human history.

The Saints, recognizing the accuracy of Clay County citizens' assessment of the situation's explosiveness, sadly but graciously acceded. They agreed to discourage further Mormon immigration and to accept the offer from the committee to assist them in selecting and moving to a new location.

The area selected was in the region of Shoal Creek, north and east of Clay County, and there the Saints began another gathering place. They petitioned the state legislature for organization of a new county, and suddenly it seemed that a possible solution had been found. That area was sparsely settled, and to the politicians it seemed appropriate for an exclusively Mormon county. Two new counties were quickly formed, Caldwell and Daviess counties, and there was a general understanding that Caldwell would be primarily for the Saints. This was simply a gentlemen's agreement, with no legal force, but the Saints happily agreed. Everyone already living in the new county who could be induced to sell to the Mormons did so, and the Saints agreed they would settle in other counties only with the consent of settlers already there. Soon Mormon settlements dotted both Caldwell and Daviess counties, but the major immigration was into Caldwell.

The most important settlement was at Far West, in Caldwell County. The site was chosen in the summer of 1836 by John Whitmer and W. W. Phelps, who purchased it with money collected among Saints in Kentucky and Tennessee. Unfortunately a misunderstanding arose when these men acted independently of the high council in laying out the town and assigning to themselves the profits from the sale of lands, but after a hearing before the high council, the matter was settled. The profits from land sales on the townsite as well as other land titles were turned over to Bishop Partridge for the benefit of the Church.

The Saints poured in and within two years more than 4,900 of them lived in the county, along with a hundred non-Mormons. At Far West there were 150 homes, four dry goods stores, three family grocery stores, several blacksmith shops, two hotels, a print-ing shop, and a large schoolhouse that doubled as a church and courthouse. In the hard-drinking atmosphere of western Missouri, Far West was unique. The Mormons attempted to live temperate lives and in October 1837 voted not to support any shops selling spiritous liquors, tea, coffee, or tobacco.

In Daviess County, meanwhile, another important settlement was located on the Grand River. This was Adam-ondi-Ahman, usually abbreviated "Di-Ahman." By May 1838 a number of Saints were there when Joseph Smith officially designated it as a spot for settlement. It came to hold a special place in the hearts of the Latter-day Saints, for he told them that here Adam called his posterity together shortly before his death, and here he would return. A stake was soon organized, many residences and a store erected, and a site dedicated for a temple block. In 1838 there were approximately fifteen hundred settlers.

In addition to the religious symbolism of its location, Adam-ondi-Ahman was also strategically situated on the banks of the Grand River, which emptied into the Missouri fifty miles down-stream. This provided the Saints with an important shipping route for agricultural products, as well as for immigration and other travel. Water transportation was necessary for a viable economy, as

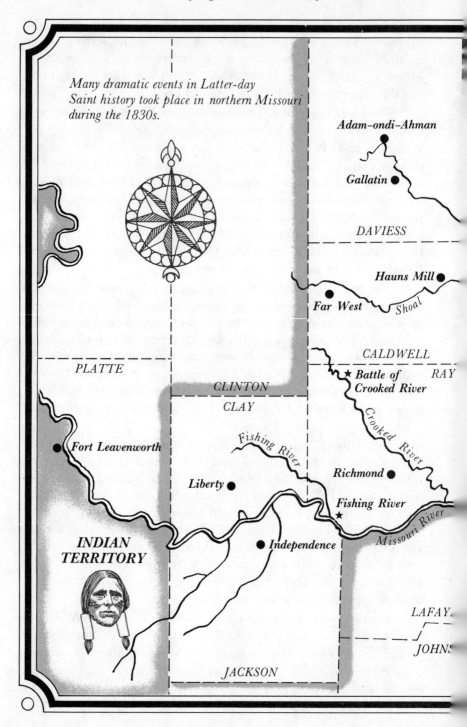

Many dramatic events in Latter-day
Saint history took place in northern Missouri
during the 1830s.

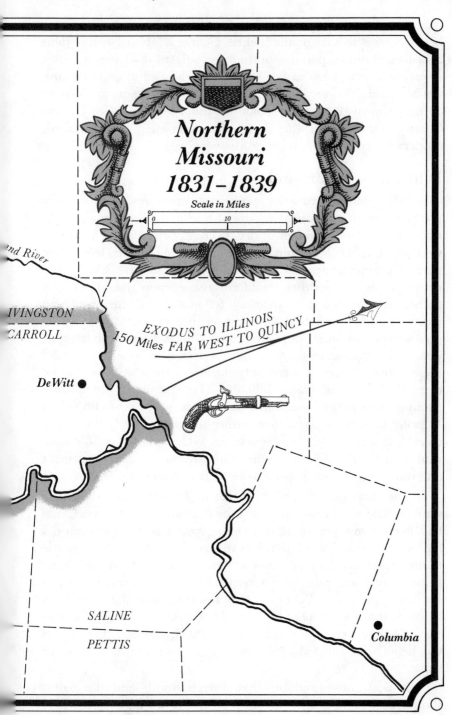

Northern
Missouri
1831–1839

Scale in Miles

0   10

Grand River

LIVINGSTON
CARROLL

EXODUS TO ILLINOIS
150 Miles FAR WEST TO QUINCY

DeWitt ●

SALINE

PETTIS

Columbia ●

roads were few and poor in that frontier wilderness. In order to better control this economic lifeline, George M. Hinckle and John Murdock obtained permission from the citizens of Daviess County to create a settlement at the spot where the Grand emptied into the Missouri. This settlement, named DeWitt, became a Mormon outpost amidst the gentile or non-Mormon settlements of Daviess County. Once again the Saints were building a permanent, cooperative economy in western Missouri.

Difficulties at Kirtland

In Kirtland, meanwhile, problems were developing. By 1836 the Saints were in political control of Kirtland township and were numerically strong enough to decide county elections. The Whigs were irked at the Mormons' apparent favoring of the Democratic party. Continued rumors that the Mormons were practicing plural marriage created another smoldering issue, even though Church authorities threatened to withdraw fellowship from anyone found guilty of such a practice. In addition, the intensity of Mormon preaching occasionally antagonized the Ohio settlers, who felt they were being condemned by certain over-zealous missionaries. All these things, however, were only minor irritants and would not cause the Saints any major difficulty. The Mormons were not proclaiming that Ohio was Zion, and there was no likelihood of Missouri-style antagonism over either slavery or the Indians. The chief difficulty in Ohio was economic, as the almost boundless optimism of the Prophet and some of his associates led to investment and indebtedness that proved to be their undoing in that state.

The economy of northern Ohio in 1836 and 1837 was in a state of flux, with high optimism for the future. The Ohio Canal had been completed in 1834, opening new trading opportunities for Ohio farmers. Population was still growing, especially with the immigration of Mormons to the vicinity of Kirtland, and land prices were rising rapidly. To most settlers, paying inflated prices seemed appropriate. Buyers were optimistic about the future and believed that the value of land would continue to rise. Credit was easy. Businessmen were willing to lend money because they shared the belief that the land they mortgaged could only increase in value.

It was understandable that Joseph Smith and the Saints should be caught up in the spirit of the times and incur heavy debts in efforts to build personal as well as community economic strength. In the 1830s, building lots in Kirtland jumped from $50 an acre to $2,000, and outside of town land prices rose from $10 an acre to $150. The Church undertook such projects as a steam saw-mill, a tannery, and a print shop; and the building of the Kirtland Temple provided employment and some commercial activity. But the Saints, like other western settlers, had little liquid capital, and their business enterprises were begun only on credit. Joseph Smith himself went into debt to purchase land, anticipating an increase in value with the continuing boom. He also purchased mer-chandise on credit for his Kirtland store, and when he began the Kirtland bank, he borrowed money from other banks to help finance it. To some it may appear that he was borrowing too heavily, but the bankers, merchants, and land jobbers of the day would hardly have extended him such credit if they had not believed he had the potential to repay.

By late 1836 it was clear that something more was needed. The Prophet knew that he and the others could not borrow forever, and that somehow their assets needed to become more liquid. The answer seemed to be a bank that could print and circu-late notes. If the notes were accepted at face value, a circulating medium would be created, debts paid, and the economy stimu-lated. On November 2, 1836, Church leaders organized the Kirt-land Safety Society Bank. Orson Hyde was sent to Columbus, Ohio, to obtain a state charter, and Oliver Cowdery went to Penn-sylvania to secure plates and printed bank notes.

Unfortunately for Joseph Smith's plans, Orson Hyde re-turned without the charter. Even though the Prophet considered this as evidence of prejudice against his people, there was another reason the charter was not granted. In the latest election the anti-banking wing of the Democratic party had won control of the new legislature, which refused to issue any new bank charters. The Saints were victims of a temporary political reverse, for their request came at a time when all such requests were being rejected. Thus thwarted, Church leaders turned instead to a joint stock company that, while not officially a bank, could issue notes and take in money. The legality of such an enterprise was questionable, but it seemed the only solution to the money problem. The com-pany was reorganized as the Kirtland Safety Society Anti-Banking Company, the printed notes had the new name over-printed, and on January 6, 1837, the new bank notes began circulating. About $20,000 had been acquired for purchase of stock, though it is not certain how much of this was in gold coin and how much merely some form of paper security.

Almost immediately, it seemed, Kirtland's economic life was beginning to pick up as local citizens were able to turn their assets into cash. Townspeople began to borrow from the bank, often using land as their collateral, and they received the Kirtland bank notes. These notes circulated at face value in Kirtland and some surrounding communities, and as long as people had confidence in this paper money, they used it to purchase goods and to pay old debts.

Such banking practices, it should be remembered, were common, especially in western America where the need for credit was urgent. Joseph Smith was doing nothing unusual: between 1829 and 1837 the number of banks in America jumped from 329 to 788, and bank loans increased from under $200 million to over $500 million.

But the Kirtland boom ended almost before it began. Within three weeks the bank announced that it must stop redeeming its notes in specie (that is, gold coin). This signaled to those holding the notes that the company was in trouble. Reasons for these difficulties are hard to determine, but a few things are apparent. It is doubtful that the bank, as with other banks of the time, had enough gold coin in its vault to meet any sustained demand. In ad-

Kirtland Safety Society bank note, signed by Joseph Smith. The word "Bank" was changed to "Anti-Banking Co." when officials were unable to obtain a state charter. (Church Archives)

dition, there had been public criticism of the bank by non-Mormon editors cynical of its possibilities for success. Perhaps more important was the lack of a state charter. State law prescribed a heavy fine for anyone involved in banking without a charter or in passing the notes of such a bank. Kirtland bank officers doubted the constitutionality of such law and so argued in court tests, but they lost their case. In the meantime, major state banks refused to accept the Kirtland notes, probably because the bank had no charter. When this happened, the notes came pouring back into Kirtland. As the notes were presented to the bank for redemption in increasing numbers, Joseph Smith and other officers were forced to suspend specie payment. The notes were redeemable only in land.

For all practical purposes the Kirtland bank had failed even before the famous panic of 1837. In May other economic forces combined to create the crisis that closed hundreds of banks throughout the United States. One factor was Andrew Jackson's Specie Circular of mid-1836, which declared that henceforth the federal government would sell public land only for specie. Suddenly both hard money and bank notes assumed new meaning, and when runs on the banks began in 1837, specie payments in the entire country ended, and the less solvent banks began to fail.

The Kirtland bank struggled on through the spring and summer, with its notes circulating at greatly discounted values. Some members accepted them for goods and services in the belief that one day they would again be worth their face value. Joseph Smith did everything he could to build confidence and make the institution work, but early in the summer he recognized the inevitability of failure, and he resigned his position as cashier. By the end of the summer the bank was forced to close its doors permanently. Warren Parrish, who succeeded the Prophet as cashier, was accused of absconding with a large amount of money, though the charge was never proved. The whole venture left the Saints shocked and bewildered, as many had lost both money and property.

Perhaps the greatest impact was on Joseph Smith and a few of the leaders. The Prophet was in debt for about $100,000, and when the bank failed, his creditors clamored for their money, threatening lawsuits if necessary. The Prophet controlled substantial assets or he could not have obtained the credit initially, but these holdings—particularly his store and land—could not be turned into ready cash. Besides, many of his notes had been co-signed by other men, complicating attempts to meet the demands of the creditors.

Some of Joseph Smith's closest associates failed to separate his roles as prophet and religious leader from his activities in the temporal world. In part, this reflected his own view. He looked at all he did as part of the effort to build the Kingdom, and realized that the spiritual kingdom must have a strong economic base. He struggled like every other man to earn a living. In addition, as a committed leader he was striving to build a viable economy for the Saints in Kirtland. His failure in business had nothing to do with the integrity of his religious experiences. Other honest men failed too, and so did much of the economy of western America in 1837.

Throughout the summer the spirit of apostasy fomented within the Church, with economics as a central issue. On September 27 Joseph Smith and Sidney Rigdon left for a trip to Missouri, and in their absence the internal strife became so serious that the Church in Kirtland seemed threatened with dissolution. Even the temple became the scene of violent arguments as factions and bitterness grew. An attempt was made to replace the Prophet as head of the Church, and even some of the leaders began to turn against him as a fallen prophet. A number, however, remained firm in their convictions, and Brigham Young, especially, proclaimed loudly and publicly that Joseph was still the prophet and true leader of the Church. So forceful was Elder Young in his denunciation of those who were attempting to replace the Prophet that they turned their fury on him. On December 22, convinced that his life was in danger, he left his wife and children behind and fled on horseback toward Missouri.

Joseph Smith and Sidney Rigdon, meanwhile, had returned to Kirtland and were dismayed to find the Church in disarray. Unable to reason with those who were now his enemies, Joseph had a hard decision to make. Threats were being made against his life, and he had reason to believe they would be carried out; creditors were pressing him from every side, and the most recent lawsuit seriously threatened imprisonment. Should he leave Kirtland, apparently running out on this debts, or should he stay and face prison and possible assassination? On the night of January 12, 1838, he and the ailing Sidney Rigdon finally decided that they must leave Kirtland to escape mob action, and they fled on horseback; their families would join them later in Missouri. Thus, Kirtland's brief period as the administrative center of the Church ended. Later the Prophet made a list of all his Ohio debts and employed an agent to help settle with his creditors. Though he made every effort, he was never able to fully meet these obligations.

Joseph Smith's trip to Missouri was both pathetic and dramatic. Heading west, the two leaders stopped about sixty miles from Kirtland and waited three days for their families to join them. While tarrying, the Prophet began looking for work cutting and sawing wood, but was unable to earn enough to meet his needs. At Dublin, Ohio, a member sold his farm and gave three hundred dollars to the Prophet to help him on his way. Not everyone had lost faith in him. The weather was cold that January, and the travelers were still pursued by their enemies. Elder Rigdon was ill and remained briefly in Illinois, but the Prophet and his family continued. In March they were in Missouri, and as they neared Far West they saw members of the Church coming to assist them with teams and money. On March 14 they entered Far West with their escort, and the Saints greeted them with open arms. It was a welcome sight after the disappointment and tragedy of Kirtland.

With the Prophet now living in Missouri, many of the faithful who remained in Kirtland wanted to follow him. On March 6, 1838, the seventies met in the temple to plan the migration. They extended the privilege of joining the exodus to all members of the Church. The result was the pioneer party known as Kirtland Camp, which left the city on July 6 with 515 people, 27 tents, 59 wagons, 97 horses, 22 oxen, 69 cows, and 1 bull. Foreshadowing the later migration from Illinois, the party was divided into companies of tens, with a captain over each. As they traveled westward, the Saints were frequently hampered by muddy roads and by the need to work at odd jobs along the way in order to earn enough money to continue. Discouragement was great, and before reaching Springfield, Illinois, the group had been reduced to about 260 persons. On October 2, after traveling 866 miles, the remaining Saints were met by Joseph Smith, Sidney Rigdon, and others and happily escorted into Far West. Two days later they began to settle at Adam-ondi-Ahman.

Kirtland, meanwhile, did not immediately lose all its Saints. As late as 1841 there were still about five hundred there, but in

October of that year Hyrum Smith wrote to the faithful in Kirtland to inform them that they were commanded to leave the town.
It took a number of years, but eventually most of the former Kirtland Saints either migrated or joined schismatic groups.

Brighter Prospects

The troubles in Missouri and Ohio did not prevent the
Church from growing elsewhere. Missionary work continued to be
successful in various parts of the United States, and in 1836 and
1837 two especially significant missions by members of the Council
of the Twelve Apostles remarkably demonstrated that prospects for
growth had never been brighter.

In April 1836 Parley P. Pratt was sent to Canada, where he
preached in and around Toronto. There he met John Taylor, a
Methodist preacher who had become a restorationist and was looking for the establishment of the ancient church of Christ. At first
John Taylor received Elder Pratt coolly, but he decided to investigate. To his friends Taylor said:

> Mr. Pratt has come to us under circumstances that are peculiar; and
> there is one thing that commends him to our consideration; he has come
> amongst us without purse or scrip, as the ancient apostles traveled; and
> none of us are able to refute his doctrine by scripture or logic. I desire to
> investigate his doctrines and claims to authority, and shall be very glad if
> some of my friends will unite with me in this investigation. But if no one

John Taylor,
Methodist preacher who became
an apostle and LDS Church
President. (Church Archives)

Parley P. Pratt,
a preacher of the Disciples of Christ
who became an LDS
apostle. (Church Archives)

will unite with me, be assured I shall make the investigation alone. If I find his religion true, I shall accept it, no matter what the consequences may be; and if false, then I shall expose it.[3]

After three weeks of investigation John Taylor and his wife were baptized, and within less than two years the former Methodist preacher had·himself become one of the Twelve.

Elder Pratt converted others besides John Taylor, and many new converts had friends and relatives in England to whom they wrote letters about the restoration of the gospel and their conversion. Soon Joseph Fielding, Isaac Russell, John Goodson, and John Snyder became anxious to proclaim the gospel in England, and thus prepared for the opening of missionary work across the Atlantic.

In Kirtland, Joseph Smith was concerned with much more than the financial problems of the Church. In the midst of his troubles of May and June 1837, when it seemed as if the Church was passing through its severest crisis yet, Joseph Smith declared, "God revealed to me that something new must be done for the salvation of His Church."[4] That "something new" was expansion of the Church to England, the first mission outside the United States and Canada.

Already the groundwork had been laid for this mission. For years Joseph Smith had anticipated the spread of the gospel in foreign lands, and both Heber C. Kimball and Orson Hyde had displayed interest in such a prospect. In February and March Elder Kimball became especially concerned with the need to go to a foreign land. In the spring Elder Pratt returned to Canada to discuss prospects for a mission to England with new converts there, and he found favorable response. By the time the Prophet received his revelation, enthusiasm was high for an overseas mission, and if this course would help save the Church, he would have no difficulty in finding men to go. Early in June he called Heber C. Kimball, Orson Hyde, and Willard Richards, along with the four Canadian converts, to open a mission in England, and by the middle of the month they were on their way.

The missionaries left their homes almost destitute, arrived in their fields of labor penniless, and yet made friends and attained a

---

[3]B. H. Roberts, *The Life of John Taylor* (1892; reprint ed., Salt Lake City: Bookcraft, 1963), pp. 37-38.
[4]Joseph Smith, *History of the Church*, 2:489.

success many would have thought impossible. When they left in June friends and relatives gave them small amounts of money, which, together with sixty dollars in Kirtland Safety Society notes that John Goodson was able to exchange with a New York broker, provided money to purchase passage on the ship *Garrick*. The fare was eighteen dollars apiece, and they had to supply their own provisions. They arrived at the port of Liverpool on July 20, 1837.

In England, as in America, conditions were right for the missionaries, though opposition was also present. Joseph Fielding's brother, the Reverend James Fielding of Preston, at first opened his chapel to them, but when they acquired converts he accused them of "sheep stealing" and turned against them. After this the missionaries secured a meeting place known as the "Cockpit" in Preston, where they could preach more freely. They also spread the work to Bedford and other communities in the northwestern part of England.

The elders' methods were simple, plain, and sincere. They emphasized the impending end of the world and the Millennium, the restoration of the ancient church through Joseph Smith, and the importance of repentance and baptism for the remission of sins. They utilized friends and relatives as much as possible, preached in established churches when they could, and went door to door only as a last resort. They were careful to give prospective converts only those points of doctrine for which they seemed ready, rarely mentioning the gathering to the new world, the law of consecration, or Joseph Smith's vision of the three degrees of glory. Elder Goodson actually slowed the work in Bedford when he violated Heber C. Kimball's instructions and publicly read the vision from the Doctrine and Covenants. Such unfamiliar doctrine before the people were ready to hear it "turned the current of feeling generally, and nearly closed the door in all that region."[5]

Most converts were from the impoverished industrial classes. Orson Hyde wrote to his wife:

Those who have been baptized, are mostly manufacturers and some other mechanics. They know how to do but little else than spin and weave cotton and make cambrick, mull and lace, and what they would do in Kirtland or the city "Far West," I cannot say. They are extremely poor, most of them not have a change of clothes decent to be babtized in, but they

---

[5] Joseph Smith, *History of the Church*, 2:505.

A TIMELY WARNING

TO THE PEOPLE OF ENGLAND,

Of every Sect and Denomination, and to every Individual into whose hands it may fall.

BY AN ELDER OF THE CHURCH OF LATTER DAY SAINTS, LATE FROM AMERICA.

PRESTON, 19th August, 1837.

First published in Toronto for distribution in eastern Canada and the United States, Orson Hyde's essay was published widely in England as a missionary tract of the restoration. (Church Archives)

have open hearts and strong faith. We have taught them nothing about the gathering for they have no means to bring them to America, let along procuring them a place to live after they get there.[6]

The elders met little violent opposition, although many preachers spoke against the restored gospel, and in one instance Catholics threatened to stone one of Elder Kimball's converts. A few potential converts refused baptism, fearing that when the elders returned to the United States they would be left alone to face persecution. By April 1838 the missionaries had gained over four hundred members in Preston and more than fifteen hundred scattered throughout the western part of England. Heber C. Kimball alone was credited with more than a thousand converts. Elders Goodson and Snyder had returned to America earlier, and on April 20, 1838, the two apostles and Elder Russell also sailed for home. Joseph Fielding was left in charge of the mission, with Willard Richards as first counselor and William Clayton, a convert from the industrial town of Penwortham, as second counselor. Two years later nearly the full Council of the Twelve would return to build on this foundation and launch the massive immigration program that would be the main source of the Church's growth in Nauvoo and the West. The mission to England was not the salvation of the Church in Kirtland, but it provided the basis for unprecedented future growth.

---

[6]*Elders' Journal of the Church of Jesus Christ of Latter-day Saints* 1 (November 1837): 20-21.

Missouri Difficulties

Even as the missionaries in England enjoyed success and as Saints in America continued to flock to Missouri, 1838 and 1839 brought another period of ordeal for the Church and its leaders in Missouri. Not even the leaders themselves were immune from disagreement and misunderstanding, and in February 1838 the presidency of the Church in Missouri—David Whitmer, W. W. Phelps, and John Whitmer—were tried by a general Church council and released. A major charge was that they had sold their land in Jackson County. To some members, this constituted a denial of the faith. David Whitmer was also charged with violating the Word of Wisdom, and the others with claiming money that belonged to the Church. This action was controversial, for it was not clear what body had proper authority to judge a stake presidency, but on April 6 Thomas B. Marsh was made stake president with Brigham Young and David W. Patten as counselors.

On April 7 Oliver Cowdery was charged with a series of transgressions. He wrote a letter in reply but refused to appear before the high council, and he was subsequently excommunicated. Elder Cowdery, too, had sold his interests in Jackson County, and this was one of the original charges against him. It was dropped after he insisted in his letter that the Church could not dictate to him in such affairs. But his general disagreement with the Church's administrative procedures in Missouri, as well as his own request to withdraw from a society that claimed that degree of temporal authority, led to his excommunication. The same high council soon dropped from membership David Whitmer and Lyman E. Johnson, a member of the Twelve.

All three of these men had shown sympathy for the dissenters at Kirtland and were publicly finding fault with Joseph Smith to the extent of justifying lawsuits against him. Their excommunication was, in effect, a purging from the leadership of those who could not work harmoniously. The action took two of the three witnesses to the Book of Mormon as well as an apostle. Within a year three more apostles would be excommunicated, and others would find their standing in the Church seriously jeopardized.

By the summer of 1838 conditions had reached an impasse within the Church. There were so many dissenters in Missouri that some who remained loyal felt threatened. Sidney Rigdon undoubtedly remembered the brutal beating he had received from apostates in 1832, and other Saints feared the dissenters would join with other enemies to intensify their Missouri troubles. It was a time of tension and pressure from within and without.

On June 19 Sidney Rigdon's feelings welled up and burst forth in a heated oration sometimes called the "salt sermon." He drew from the scriptural text, "Ye are the salt of the earth: but if the salt have lost his savour, wherewith shall it be salted? it is thenceforth good for nothing, but to be cast out, and to be trodden under foot of men."[7] In his direct and powerful way President Rigdon applied the test to the dissenters, and the implication was obvious. They must either leave or face the consequences.

Not long afterward a document appeared addressed to Oliver Cowdery, David and John Whitmer, W. W. Phelps, and Lyman E. Johnson, the leading dissenters. Signed by eighty-four members, it pointedly ordered them to leave the county or face "a more fatal calamity." Undoubtedly some dissenters were an embarrassment to the Church, for they had been accused of theft, counterfeiting, and tampering with the mails, but such a document proved equally embarrassing. It now appeared that the Mormons were taking the law into their own hands, though the document was apparently signed spontaneously without the formal sanction of Church leaders, except possibly Sidney Rigdon. Whatever its purpose, it quickly prompted the dissenters to leave. Such action by Church members was unfortunate, because their assumption of such power provided evidence against them that fed the anti-Mormon hostility again growing among their neighbors.

The situation did not end here, however. Another more tragic event made the Saints look even worse. About the time of Sidney Rigdon's "salt sermon" a secret society called the Danites was formed by Sampson Avard, who was the first signer of the document threatening the dissenters. Initially the society was formed against the dissenters, but after they left, it continued operating. The old settlers of Missouri were renewing their threats, and the Danites were told by Avard that now their duty was to defend the Church against mobs. Eventually they went beyond the bounds of legality or propriety and began retaliation against those who had committed crimes against the Saints. Avard was very skillful at persuading his followers and the Church's enemies not only that he

---

[7]Matthew 5:13.

had the backing of the leaders of the Church, but also that the Danites were authorized to rob, plunder, lie, and even kill to avenge themselves. The Danites were bound together by oaths of secrecy and had secret signs for identification and warning. Avard was ruthless as well as hotheaded, and when he and others were finally arrested and brought to court after five months of terrorizing the territory, he accused Joseph Smith and Sidney Rigdon of being directly behind all that his misguided band had done.

The degree of actual involvement of Church leaders in the plans of the Danites remains unclear, particularly that of Sidney Rigdon. Joseph Smith was unaware of the extent of Avard's perfidy until the matter came to light in the courts. Avard was an impressive man who probably told President Smith only enough of his plans to make them appear consistent with the Prophet's own concerns. While in jail sometime later, the Prophet wrote:

> We have learned . . . since we have been prisoners, that many false and pernicious things, which were calculated to lead the Saints far astray and to do great injury, have been taught by Dr. Avard as coming from the Presidency, and we have reason to fear that many other designing and corrupt characters like himself, having been teaching many things which the Presidency never knew were being taught in the Church by anybody until after they were made prisoners. Had they known of such things they would have spurned them and their authors as they would the gates of hell. Thus we find that there have been frauds and secret abominations and evil works of darkness going on, leading the minds of the weak and unwary into confusion and distraction, and all the time palming it off upon the Presidency, while the Presidency were ignorant as well as innocent of those things.[8]

The summer of 1838 was tense, and Joseph Smith was forced to make some difficult and harsh decisions. He hated violence, but once again the old Missouri charges were being repeated, violence was threatened, and the Saints had only begun their new communities in northern Missouri. After many had been driven from New York, Ohio, Jackson County, and Clay County within an eight-year period, it seemed unthinkable that another relocation should be forced upon them. It was a wonder that some Saints restrained themselves as long as they did, and it was very human and understandable that the Prophet apparently decided that this time, at least, they must stand and fight. This was no invitation to mob ac-

---

[8] Joseph Smith, *History of the Church*, 3:231.

tion on the part of the Saints or to excesses like those of the Danites, but in the hot summer of 1838 it could well be construed by the wily Avard as support for his own objectives. It could also be distorted by the enemies of Joseph Smith.

Independence Day, July 4, 1838, was crucial. At Far West the Saints celebrated the national holiday and laid the cornerstones of a temple. Orator for the day was Sidney Rigdon, who, despite recent illness, maintained the ability to whip feelings into high emotion. His speech, approved by Joseph Smith and other Church leaders, was a declaration of independence for the Saints from any further mob violence or illegal activity. He concluded his long and stinging oration with words that must have sunk deep into the heart of every listener:

> We take God and all the holy angels to witness this day, that we warn all men in the name of Jesus Christ, to come on us no more forever, for from this hour, we will bear it no more, our rights shall no more be trampled on with impunity. The man or the set of men, who attempts it, does it at the expense of their lives. And that mob that comes on us to disturb us; it shall be between us and them a war of extermination; for we will follow them, till the last drop of their blood is spilled, or else they will have to exterminate us: for we will carry the seat of war to their own houses, and their own families, and one party or the other shall be utterly destroyed.—Remember it then all MEN.
>
> We will never be the agressors, we will infringe on the rights of no people; but shall stand for our own until death. We claim our own rights, and are willing that all others shall enjoy theirs.
>
> No man shall be at liberty to come into our streets, to threaten us with mobs, for if he does, he shall atone for it before he leaves the place, neither shall he be at liberty, to villify and slander any of us, for suffer it we will not in this place.
>
> We therefore, take all men to record this day, that we proclaim our liberty this day, as did our fathers. And we pledge this day to one another, our fortunes, our lives, and our sacred honors, to be delivered from the persecutions which we have had to endure, for the last nine years, or nearly that. Neither will we indulge any man, or set of men, in instituting vexatious law suits against us, to cheat us out of our just rights, if they attempt it we say wo unto them.
>
> We this day then proclaim ourselves free, with a purpose and a determination, that never can be broken, "no never! *no never!!* NO NEVER"!!![9]

The jubilant audience responded: "Hosannah, hosannah, hosan-

---

[9]The entire oration is reproduced in *Brigham Young University Studies* 14 (Summer 1974): 517-27.

nah! Amen. Amen. Amen!" and repeated it three times. Much of the oration was obviously heated rhetoric, but it represented the determination of the Saints to fight back. When distorted reports reached the mobs and other Missouri citizens, the speech provided a basis for charges of treason and violence against the Saints that were fostered by those who wanted to drive them from the state.

The rest of the long hot summer of 1838 was almost predictable. The first blows of the so-called Mormon War were struck at Gallatin, in Daviess County. August 6 was election day, and William Peniston, a candidate for the state legislature and an old enemy of the Mormons, was determined to keep them from voting. Election days in the West were rarely orderly anyway, and when Peniston began to harangue the voters, many of whom were filled with whiskey, a fight was inevitable. It broke out when a drunken citizen picked a fight with one of the Saints, and as others ran to assist him, the fracas became general. Sticks, stones, clubs, and whips—anything available was used by both sides, and although the Mormons claimed the victory, men were beaten and bloodied in both camps.

Reports, probably exaggerated, soon reached Far West, and immediately Joseph Smith and others armed themselves and formed bands to ride to Daviess County. They met at the home of Lyman Wight in Adam-ondi-Ahman with several who had been in the battle, and there they learned with relief that no one had been killed. Tempers were high, but the Prophet and his companions did what they could to promote peace. They visited several old settlers in the vicinity, including Adam Black, the newly elected judge for Daviess County. Perhaps the fact that they were armed intimidated the judge, or perhaps he simply wanted to get rid of them; whatever the reason, he signed an affidavit certifying that he would not associate himself with any mob against the Mormons. By the end of August, however, he swore an affidavit against the Mormons alleging he had been threatened with death if he did not sign the document. Peniston, in the meantime, also brought charges against the Saints, and on these and other affidavits, warrants were issued for the arrest of Joseph Smith and Lyman Wight, charging them with insurrection.

Joseph Smith was willing to submit to arrest, but when the sheriff came, the Prophet requested that the trial take place in his own county, for he feared a trial at Gallatin would be a pretext for lynching. A hearing was finally held before Judge King in Daviess County, and to the surprise of the Saints he ordered the Prophet and Lyman Wight to stand trial before the circuit court. They were released on $500 bond while awaiting the proceedings.

Rumors and exaggerated stories now circulated on both sides, and false reports of Mormon uprising reached the desk of Governor Lilburn W. Boggs. Indisposed to help the Mormons (he had been an enemy earlier in Jackson County), Boggs chose to believe the worst and did little to quell the threats against the Saints. He did, however, order General David R. Atchison, of the state militia, and other generals to raise a force of mounted, armed men to stand ready to quell civil disturbances in Caldwell, Daviess, and Carroll counties. The Saints, meantime, enlisted in the militia of Caldwell County and began to act in self-defense. One group even intercepted and confiscated a shipment of arms intended for a mob in Daviess County.

The mob threatened to attack Adam-ondi-Ahman, where Lyman Wight and a contingent of Mormon militia prepared to defend themselves. Only the actions of Generals Alexander Doniphan and David R. Atchison prevented violence. At the same time, a committee of "old citizens" in Daviess County agreed either to buy all the property of the Saints there or to sell theirs to the Saints. Joseph Smith was informed, and he immediately sent messengers to Church branches in the East and South to try to raise the necessary money, but the continuing conflict made this tentative agreement impossible to fulfill.

In Carroll County, mob forces next besieged DeWitt. When Joseph Smith heard of it he rode for DeWitt, which he had to enter secretly. He found the Saints in great distress, without food, and the mob growing daily. When it became apparent that even the militia supposed to protect them would probably side with the mob, there was nothing to do but capitulate and leave the county.

Encouraged by what they heard from DeWitt, the Daviess County mobs threatened the Saints at Adam-ondi-Ahman more seriously. Near Millport, a short distance from "Di-Ahman," several Mormon homes and haystacks were burned. General H. G. Parks instructed Lyman Wight, a colonel in the state militia, to put down mobs wherever he found them, and Wight immediately organized the Mormons into two companies of militia. Generals Parks, Atchison, and Doniphan knew that the Mormons

Haun's Mill Massacre of October 1838 as depicted by C. C. A. Christensen. (From the Permanent Collection of Brigham Young University)

only acted defensively against mobs, and they did all they could to persuade the governor that an action against the Saints would be unjustified. But Boggs remained unconvinced, as his later actions indicated.

In the midst of this external turmoil, another shock from inside the Church awaited Joseph Smith. On October 24, Thomas B. Marsh, president of the Council of the Twelve, and Orson Hyde, a member of the Twelve, signed affidavits in Richmond that seemed to support the most damaging reports of Danite activities accusing the Prophet of promoting the violence. The tenseness of the summer and the confusing rapidity of incriminations had affected even the most prominent Church leaders. Thomas Marsh was excommunicated and Orson Hyde was dropped from the Council. The latter was restored the following June, after a long, sad repentance and confession of his error. Marsh was rebaptized in 1857 and died in Utah a member of the Church, though never again a member of the Twelve. But for the time being, the fact that two more apostles had turned against the Prophet only added fuel to the fire already raging against the Saints.

Captain Samuel Bogart was a Methodist minister in charge of a company of Caldwell County militia. On October 24 Bogart's men accosted at least two Mormon settlers in their homes, ordering them to leave the state, and took three Mormons prisoner. When word reached Far West, Captain David W. Patten, a member of the Twelve, took a small detachment of militia and marched on Bogart's camp at Crooked River to rescue the prisoners. It was ironic for two different companies of the same state militia to face each other, but it was typical of the civil war developing in northern Missouri. A hand-to-hand battle ensued in which Patten and Gideon Carter were killed, as well as one member of Bogart's group.

Highly exaggerated reports of these activities soon reached Governor Boggs, and it appeared to him that the Mormons were burning towns, driving old settlers from their homes, and generally undermining civil authority. The known proclivities of the Danites for vengeance did not help the Mormon cause. Finally, on October 27, 1838, heedless of any information he may have had about the Mormon viewpoint, Boggs issued his infamous "Order of Extermination." "The Mormons," he wrote to General John B. Clark of the state militia, "must be treated as enemies and *must be exterminated* or driven from the state, if necessary for the public good. Their outrages are beyond all description."[10] Clark was ordered to immediately carry out his instructions.

Events soon followed a predictable course. On October 30 more than two hundred men of the state militia were involved in the most brutal massacre of the conflict, part of an apparent effort to literally carry out the governor's extermination order. Mormon Jacob Haun owned a small mill on Shoal Creek and had been joined there by about thirty families. They had made a peace treaty with militia leaders on October 28, but the militia, under the command of Colonel Thomas Jennings, attacked the tiny settlement. The Saints cried for peace but no respite was granted. Though men and women fled to a blacksmith shop or into the woods, the mob fired mercilessly. In all, seventeen Mormons were killed, including one elderly man who was hacked to death. Ten-year-old Sardius Smith was found trembling with fear in the blacksmith shop and summarily shot to death. His murderer

---

[10]Joseph Smith, *History of the Church*, 3:175.

bragged afterward, "Nits will make lice, and if he had lived he would have become a Mormon."[11]

The next day the state militia was at Far West, and General Samuel Lucas made four demands of the Saints: their leaders were to surrender for trial and punishment, Mormon property was to be confiscated to pay for damages, the balance of the Saints were to leave the state under the protection of the militia, and they were to yield their arms. Colonel George M. Hinckle, a Mormon militia officer, simply told Joseph Smith, Sidney Rigdon, Lyman Wight, Parley P. Pratt, and George W. Robinson that the militia officers wanted to talk to them. They consented but were shocked and surprised when Hinckle turned them over to General Lucas as prisoners. Perhaps Hinckle thought this was the only way to end the violence, but Church leaders considered it treachery. Hyrum Smith and Amasa Lyman were taken prisoner the next day. The Saints were defenseless as the unruly militia entered Far West, plundered the town, and brutally ravished some of the women. It was a very uneasy peace that rested on Caldwell County.

When the Prophet and the others were arrested, a court-martial by the state militia was quickly held. The prisoners were not present, but the decision of the court was that they should be shot the following morning at eight o'clock. General Lucas ordered General Doniphan to carry out the order, but Doniphan, indignant at the brutality and injustice of the affair, replied to his superior with the following memo:

> It is cold-blooded murder. I will not obey your order. My brigade shall march for Liberty tomorrow morning, at 8 o'clock; and if you execute these men, I will hold you responsible before an earthly tribunal, so help me God.
>
> A. Doniphan
> Brigadier-General[12]

Doniphan's response prevented the execution.

November and December 1838 were months of relative calm, though the Saints knew that eventually they would have to leave the state. With Joseph Smith and his counselors in prison, responsibility to begin the preparations for the exodus fell to Brigham Young as senior member of the Council of the Twelve.

---

[11]As quoted in B. H. Roberts, *A Comprehensive History of the Church of Jesus Christ of Latter-day Saints*, 6 vols. (Salt Lake City: Deseret News Press, 1930), 1:482.
[12]Joseph Smith, *History of the Church*, 3:190-91 note.

*Alexander Doniphan statue, Richmond, Missouri. Doniphan has become a
legendary hero to the Saints for his fearlessness in refusing an order to execute
the Prophet. (Church Archives)*

By January a committee to superintend the exodus had been appointed, and before the winter ended the threat of further mob
activity finally forced the Saints to begin their wearisome march.
In February Brigham Young was forced to flee from Far West for
his life, and by April 20 nearly all the Saints in Missouri had
crossed the Mississippi River and found refuge near Quincy,
Illinois.

In the meantime, the Saints again sought relief from the
Missouri legislature. Their grievances were clearly defined and
much sympathy was shown by many members of the legislature. A
bill was introduced that would have initiated an investigation of
the affair, but it was never acted upon. Instead, the legislature appropriated $2,000 for the relief of the citizens of Caldwell County,

an act that actually provided little help. Later the lawmakers furnished the militia about $200,000 for the expenses of the conflict. The "Mormon War" in Missouri was officially at an end.

Five Months in Prison

Joseph Smith and those arrested with him on October 31 were taken to Independence for four days, then transferred to Richmond, Missouri, to await trial. They were charged with treason. At Richmond there was discussion about whether they should be tried by a military court-martial or by civil authorities, but it was finally decided that a civil trial was appropriate. It began on November 13, with Judge Austin A. King presiding. The evidence seems to have been stacked against the Prophet. Sampson Avard, the first witness, accused the Prophet of responsibility for the wrongs of the Danites. Other witnesses were equally bitter, but when the prisoners tried to get their own witnesses in court, the individuals named were simply arrested and jailed by their old enemy Captain Bogart, and they were not allowed to appear. Those few who did appear in behalf of the prisoners were abused and threatened so that they were unable to tell all they wanted. Finally the judge bound the prisoners over for further trial and ordered them placed in prison in Clay County. At the end of November Joseph and Hyrum Smith, Sidney Rigdon, Lyman Wight, Alexander McRae, and Caleb Baldwin were imprisoned in a town ironically named Liberty, a spot where they would remain for four and a half months. At the same time Parley P. Pratt and several others were confined in Richmond.

Liberty Jail was a small, twenty-two-foot-square building. Its heavy stone walls were timbered inside with logs. The interior was divided into an upper and lower room, or dungeon, very dimly lighted by two small windows in the upper room. The prison fare was described as "so filthy we could not eat it until we were driven to it by hunger," and the general treatment given the prisoners was unfair. They were sometimes allowed visitors, however, and maintained contact with the outside world through letters. Twice they tried to escape from jail, but both times their efforts failed.

Yet the months in Liberty Jail were of special significance to Joseph Smith and to the Church. They demonstrated the abilities of such men as Brigham Young, John Taylor, and Heber C. Kimball, who organized the exodus from Missouri and resettlement in

Illinois. More importantly, the Prophet had time to pray and meditate about the Church and its meaning, time to formulate new ideas and put them into writing. Some of his most profound revelations and writings came from Liberty Jail. Surprisingly, his letters exuded optimism, though they also pointed to the weaknesses of the Saints and called for overcoming them. The Prophet displayed love and compassion along with sharpness.

On December 18 he wrote to Church members briefly reviewing their problems, condemning the actions of their enemies, and denying the charges levied against them. His letter also contained these words of counsel:

> Brethren, from henceforth, let truth and righteousness prevail and abound in you; and in all things be temperate; abstain from drunkenness, and from swearing, and from all profane language, and from everything which is unrighteous or unholy; also from enmity, and hatred, and covetousness, and from every unholy desire. Be honest one with another, for it seems that some have come short of these things, and some have been uncharitable, and have manifested greediness because of their debts towards those who have been persecuted and dragged about with chains without cause, and imprisoned. Such characters God hates—and they shall have their turn of sorrow in the rolling of the great wheel, for it rolleth and none can hinder. Zion shall yet live, though she seem to be dead.[13]

To his wife Emma the Prophet wrote on April 4:

It is I believe now about five months and six days since I have been under the grimace of a guard night and day, and within the walls, grates, and screaking iron doors of a lonesome, dark, dirty prison. . . .

I think of you and the children continually. . . . I want you should not let those little fellows forget me. Tell them Father loves them with a perfect love and he is doing all he can to get away from the mob to come to them. Do teach them all you can, that they may have good minds. Be tender and kind to them. Don't be fractious to them, but listen to their wants. Tell them Father says they must be good children and mind their mother. My dear Emma there is great responsibility resting upon you in preserving yourself in honor and sobriety before them and teaching them right things to form their young and tender minds, that they begin in right paths and not get contaminated when young by seeing ungodly examples.[14]

---

[13]Joseph Smith, *History of the Church*, 3:233.
[14]Joseph Smith to Emma Smith, April 4, 1839, as quoted in Leonard J. Arrington, "Church Leaders in Liberty Jail," *Brigham Young University Studies* 13 (Autumn 1972): 22. Original at Yale University.

Toward the end of March he wrote a long letter to the Church, parts of which now appear as sections 121, 122, and 123 of the Doctrine and Covenants. These statements enjoin upon the writer, and all who read them, patience and long-suffering, the assurance of continuing revelation, a reminder that the powers of the priesthood should be exercised in righteousness, hope for the future, and the need to keep a record of all that transpired.

During all this, Joseph Smith still retained the uncanny ability to attract and impress people—even his avowed enemies. One of the most interesting descriptions of the Prophet in Missouri was later recorded by Peter H. Burnett, a non-Mormon attorney who helped defend him in the trial in Daviess County in early April:

> Joseph Smith, Jr., was at least six feet high, well-formed, and weighed about one hundred and eighty pounds. His appearance was not prepossessing, and his conversational powers were but ordinary. You could see at a glance that his education was very limited. He was an awkward but vehement speaker. In conversation he was slow, and used too many words to express his ideas, and would not generally go directly to a point. But, with all these drawbacks he was much more than an or-

Jail at Liberty, Missouri. (C. C. A. Christensen painting, from the Permanent Collection of Brigham Young University)

dinary man. He possessed the most indomitable perseverance, was a good judge of men, and deemed himself born to command, and he did command. His views were so strange and striking, and his manner was so earnest, and apparently so candid, that you could not but be interested. There was a kind, familiar look about him, that pleased you. He was very courteous in discussion, readily admitting what he did not intend to controvert, and would not oppose you abruptly, but had due deference to your feelings. He had the capacity for discussing a subject in different aspects, and for proposing many original views, even on ordinary matters. His illustrations were his own. He had great influence over others. As evidence of this I will state that on Thursday, just before I left to return to Liberty, I saw him out among the crowd, conversing freely with every one, and seeming to be perfectly at ease. In the short space of five days he had managed so to mollify his enemies that he could go unprotected among them without the slightest danger. Among the Mormons he had much greater influence than Sidney Rigdon. The latter was a man of superior education, an eloquent speaker, of fine appearance and dignified manners; but he did not possess the native intellect of Smith, and lacked his determined will.[15]

In February Sidney Rigdon was released on bail. He hurried to Illinois, where he began making plans for an appeal to Washington and, rather unrealistically, to "impeach" the state of Missouri. In April the remaining prisoners were ordered to Daviess County for trial. On the ninth a grand jury brought in a bill against them for "murder, treason, burglary, arson, larceny, theft, and stealing." The accused were unable to obtain a change of venue for trial on these charges, but as they were being taken to another county, it became clear that the judge, the sheriff, and the guards had connived to allow their escape. A guard even helped them saddle their horses. With the sheriff and other guards filled with whiskey and asleep, Joseph and Hyrum rode the two horses while the others walked, and they escaped to Illinois. On April 22 Joseph arrived at Quincy to once again enjoy the embraces of his family and friends. Later Parley P. Pratt also escaped from prison, and before the year ended all the Missouri prisoners had left that state.

The exodus from Missouri marked the end of an important period in the history of the Church. The years in Ohio and Missouri were marked by the building of a magnificent temple, new revelations of doctrine, the expansion of the work overseas,

[15]Peter H. Burnett, *Recollections and Opinions of an Old Pioneer* (New York: D. Appleton & Co., 1880), pp. 66-67.

and the designation of a land of Zion. They were also marred by financial tragedy, bitter persecution, apostasy, and the expulsion of the Saints from Zion. But something miraculous was happening. In the midst of all this trouble the Church was still growing, and even while the Prophet was in jail some twelve to fifteen thousand people followed him, figuratively speaking, across the frozen fields of Missouri to Illinois. For the fourth time in less than a decade they sought and began to build a place of refuge. A letter from Liberty Jail had struck the note of optimism:

. . . and if thou shouldst be cast into the pit, or into the hands of murderers, and the sentence of death passed upon thee; if thou be cast into the deep; if the billowing surge conspire against thee; if fierce winds become thine enemy; if the heavens gather blackness, and all the elements combine to hedge up the way; and above all, if the very jaws of hell shall gape open the mouth wide after thee, know thou, my son, that all these things shall give thee experience, and shall be for thy good. The Son of Man hath descended below them all; art thou greater than he?

Therefore, hold on thy way, the Priesthood shall remain with thee, for their bounds are set, they cannot pass. Thy days are known, and thy years shall not be numbered less; therefore, fear not what man can do, for God shall be with you forever and ever.[16]

---

[16] Joseph Smith, *History of the Church*, 3:300-1; D&C 122:7-9.

PART *II*

New Directions, 1839-1856

*These views represent two new beginnings in this period of Mormon history.
The engraving of a peaceful Nauvoo about 1844 is by Herrmann J. Meyer,
and the engraving of Great Salt Lake City in 1853 is by Frederick Piercy.
The major building on the left of Salt Lake's Main Street is the Deseret
Store and Tithing Office. (Church Archives)*

*THE EXODUS FROM MISSOURI was a sorrowful time for the
Saints, but it opened an era of renewed vitality in the Church and
provided a catalyst for the reorientation of Latter-day Saint economic,
political, and religious life. At Nauvoo and again later at Salt Lake
City the Saints built impressive cities—this time accepting an economic
system more closely resembling free enterprise than the
communitarianism tried unsuccessfully in Ohio and Missouri. For the
first time they negotiated with the federal government, although they
received little cooperation until the Mexican War of 1846. In religious
life, the Saints received many new insights concerning man's eternal
destiny, expanded their organization, and adopted important new
practices. Thus, in ways besides geographical displacement, the exodus
of 1839 and the one that followed seven years later set the Church
moving in new directions.*

*At Nauvoo Joseph Smith reached the zenith of both his temporal and
spiritual influence. As a secular leader he became mayor of one of the
two largest cities in Illinois, editor of its newspaper, a leading
entrepreneur, and a candidate for the presidency of the United States.
As a spiritual leader he announced important new doctrinal ideas,
began the erection of a magnificent temple, introduced a sacred temple
ceremony that helped increase brotherhood and spirituality among the
Saints, and laid the foundation for expanding the Kingdom worldwide.
His tragic martyrdom in 1844 became a rallying point for a greater
spiritual unity among the Saints and strengthened the Kingdom instead
of destroying it as his antagonists had hoped.*

*The following years found the Saints inclined westward, where the
Church under the firm hand of Brigham Young once again established a
distinctive society, but outside the realms of American civilization in the
somewhat foreboding Great Basin. The Saints were willing to help
wrest that area from Mexico for the United States, and there they
entrenched themselves with a determination never again to be driven
from their homes.*

*In this new gathering place the Church faced its first direct conflict
with federal officials, a challenge opening a political struggle that
lasted until the end of the century. This friction was caused in part by
two distinctive practices: plural marriage and the widely misunderstood*

*participation of Church leaders in Utah's civil and business affairs.
The foundations for these involvements had been laid in Nauvoo but they
did not receive national attention until the 1850s.*

*The course of Church history in this period fit naturally into the
cultural tempo of the times. For instance, in England, as in America,
many humble Christians were searching for a restoration of the ancient
order of things. In this religious climate missionaries reaped hundreds of
converts for the expanding church. In fleeing to the Great Basin, too, the
Saints were part of a larger thrust. The westward movement in
America was a dominant theme throughout the nineteenth century. It
began with steady settlement of the area from the Appalachians to the
Mississippi; then in the 1840s pioneers began a series of jumps to
widely separated places, skipping completely the Great Plains, which
later became America's breadbasket. By the time the Latter-day Saints
joined this movement in 1846-47, American settlers had established
outposts in Oregon and in the Mexican province of Upper California.
Other settlers were moving rapidly into Texas, which had just been
taken into the Union. In the Great Basin the Latter-day Saints found
themselves at a crossroads for other westering Americans and
established an outpost that they envisioned as a self-sufficient place of
religious refuge from the troubled world.*

CHAPTER 5

Building the City Beautiful, 1839-1842

The expulsion of the Latter-day Saints from northern Missouri reopened the question of a single gathering place. Previously, Mormon communities established as enclaves within existing societies had resulted in conflict and expulsion. Some members thought these experiences proved that the policy of gathering should be abandoned. Joseph Smith retained the plan for a gathered community of the faithful, however, and over a seven-year period the Latter-day Saints built an impressive city, one of the largest in Illinois at the time. These same years saw both church doctrine and administration mature significantly.

A New Community for the Saints

As the Saints scattered from Missouri during the winter of 1838-39, they moved eastward, uncertain of their final destinations. Most headed for the Mississippi River ferry at Quincy, Illinois, where they found temporary quarters just out of reach of their antagonists. Throughout the winter, companies of wagons, two-wheeled carts, and families on foot trekked the 150 miles to the Missouri border. Other families made the journey on river boats from Richmond. Levi Hancock's outcast family built a

*Exodus of the Saints from Missouri, as depicted by C. C. A. Christensen.
(From the Permanent Collection of Brigham Young University)*

horse-drawn cart, filled it with corn, and set out from Far West
through snow deep enough to half bury the young Mosiah. They
carried few clothes or blankets and no household goods—Mosiah
traveled barefoot. Eating roasted corn, elm bark, and herbs, and
sleeping in the open, the family made its way to the river and
crossed it early one January morning before the ice broke.

General supervision of the migration was handled by a seven-
member relocation committee appointed in January with William
Huntington as chairman. Its most urgent task was helping remove
the poor. In response to a committee plea, at least four hundred
Missouri Saints willingly committed their property to help the
more destitute members. Headquartered at Far West, the committee directed the migration until mid-April, when mob pressure
forced them to leave with the dispersing Saints.

The refugees received additional aid from non-Mormon
citizens in Quincy. The town's Democratic Association quickly organized a sympathetic reception committee, which sponsored humanitarian relief measures, such as helping provide food, housing,
and temporary employment. To emphasize their compassion, the
Quincy citizens met on February 27 and adopted resolutions
officially and bluntly denouncing the Missouri mobs and govern-

ment officials. Soon Illinois Governor Thomas Carlin and others were encouraging the Saints to locate in the Prairie State, while across the river Iowa Territorial Governor Robert Lucas extended a similar invitation.

It was not a foregone conclusion that the Saints should continue to congregate in special gathering places. When a conference of elders debated the question in February, Bishop Edward Partridge and Far West's President William Marks argued that the Missouri persecutions left no choice but to scatter "to different parts." Initially their view prevailed, but when Brigham Young arrived in Quincy he proposed settlement by immigrant companies or branches as a better plan. Soon afterward Joseph Smith wrote a letter from Liberty Jail that promoted the spirit of gathering and suggested that the Saints "fall into the places and refuge of safety that God shall open unto them, between Kirtland and Far West . . . in the most safe and quiet places they can find."[1] Late in April Joseph Smith presided at a conference in Quincy that affirmed the policy suggested by Brigham Young; the conference appointed the Prophet, Bishop Vinson Knight, and Alanson Ripley to select a relocation site.

In most respects the situation in Illinois and eastern Iowa favored the Latter-day Saints. In Illinois the government was underfinanced and the general economy still suffered from the panic of 1837. During the preceding decade tens of thousands of new residents had poured into the upper Mississippi River valley, spurring the sale of land, which was widely available though often at inflated prices. New citizens, including the Mormons, were welcomed in the hope they would stimulate the economy. Office seekers considered them politically important as voters.

The selection of gathering sites in Hancock County, Illinois, and Lee County, Iowa, followed careful exploration and a thorough investigation of available land. One tract of 20,000 acres was offered at two dollars an acre on a twenty-year contract by land agent Isaac Galland, a resident of Commerce, Illinois. Galland's offer appealed to Joseph Smith, who wrote from Liberty Jail in late March encouraging both parties to close the deal. No action was taken until the Prophet arrived in Illinois; then he and other priesthood officers inspected lands in the Commerce area

---

[1]Joseph Smith, *History of the Church*, 3:301.

and Iowa's "Half Breed Tract." Beginning on April 30 with the purchase of a 123-acre farm from Hugh White and 47 acres near Commerce from Isaac Galland, Church leaders secured thousands of acres on liberal terms in the two counties fronting the Mississippi. A general conference May 4-6 sanctioned these purchases. On May 10 Joseph Smith moved with his family to a two-room log cabin, known later as the "Homestead," on the White farm about one mile south of Commerce.

Other purchases around Commerce included the 400-acre Horace Hotchkiss tract and Galland's 15,000-acre tract surrounding the Nashville townsite in Lee County, Iowa. Mormon land agents also bought the Montrose, Iowa, settlement where Fort Des Moines army barracks provided much-needed temporary housing for several families. In Illinois alone, Latter-day Saints settled at least nineteen different townsites.

Commerce was soon being promoted as the central gathering place. By summer it was unofficially renamed Nauvoo, a word that the Prophet said was derived from the Hebrew and suggested a beautiful place of rest. The following spring federal officials renamed the Commerce post office Nauvoo, and in December state legislators granted the city a charter. Nauvoo became the new headquarters of the Church, and gathering to that new place of

Joseph Smith, Jr., purchased this log home in Nauvoo and built the one-story addition. His son Joseph III added the frame portion and named the residence "The Homestead." (Church Archives)

refuge was soon vigorously encouraged among the Saints.

It was not easy for the Saints to build a new gathering place along the Mississippi. The area was swampy and unhealthy, and malaria was endemic in the region. As soon as the Saints began to settle, an epidemic struck. "It was a very sickly time," said Wilford Woodruff. "Joseph had given up his home in Commerce to the sick, and had a tent pitched in his dooryard and was living in that himself."[2] The Prophet called upon the power of God and, according to Woodruff, went among the sick on both sides of the river. Many miraculous healings were reported, but the following summer the epidemic increased and many died. It reached calamitous proportions in 1841, when so many died that it was necessary for Sidney Rigdon to preach a "general funeral sermon."

An Appeal to Washington

As Church leaders attempted to resolve the issues that had forced them from Far West, the Missouri legislature rejected their petitions for investigation. Their next appeal was to the United States government. It was the Prophet himself and Judge Elias Higbee who made the trip to the nation's capital.

By this time Joseph Smith had learned some valuable lessons in political astuteness. A few Mormons placed the blame for the Missouri persecutions on political parties, and in letters to the *Quincy Whig*, Lyman Wight had even extended the blame to the national Democratic party. On May 17 the First Presidency issued an immediate disclaimer. Clearly, it would be unwise to make redress a political issue, especially when the last hope for assistance lay with a Democratic administration in Washington.

In a political sense, the Latter-day Saint prophet's personal mission to Washington was significant. He revered the United States Constitution and while in Liberty Jail had written his disciples that it "is a glorious standard; it is founded in the wisdom of God. . . . It is like a great tree under whose branches men from every clime can be shielded from the burning rays of the sun."[3] He felt that the constitutional guarantees protecting freedom of religion, the right to petition the government for redress of grievances, and the right to property meant that, if necessary, the federal

---

[2]Matthias Cowley, *Wilford Woodruff* (Salt Lake City: Deseret News, 1909), p. 104.
[3]Joseph Smith, *History of the Church*, 3:304.

government could intervene within a state to protect a distressed people. His major goal was to win federal intervention in Missouri. His failure in this mission demonstrated how widely constitutional interpretations varied in that day. It so affected his own views that four years later he uttered his only recorded criticism of the Constitution:

I am the greatest advocate of the Constitution of the United States there is on the earth. . . . The only fault I find with the Constitution is, it is not broad enough to cover the whole ground.

Although it provides that all men shall enjoy religious freedom, yet it does not provide the manner by which that freedom can be preserved, nor for the punishment of Government officers who refuse to protect the people in their religious rights, or punish those mobs, states, or communities who interfere with the rights of the people on account of their religion. Its sentiments are good, but it provides no means of enforcing them.[4]

Joseph Smith and Elias Higbee arrived in Washington, D.C., on November 28, 1839, and the next day obtained an interview with President Martin Van Buren. They received little encouragement from him, but contacted various senators and representatives. The Illinois delegation treated them especially well, and Illinois Senator Richard E. Young promised to introduce their petition to Congress. Early in February they had another interview with Van Buren, who, according to the Prophet's report, listened reluctantly to their message and simply replied: "Gentlemen, your cause is just, but I can do nothing for you. . . . If I take up for you I shall lose the vote of Missouri."

Joseph Smith continued his quest and obtained interviews with other important political figures, including Senator John C. Calhoun of South Carolina, the leading advocate of states' rights. These interviews clearly reflected the national debate over the Constitution and states' rights that would culminate two decades later in civil war. The essential issue was sovereignty of the states, and the prevailing opinion, especially among southern politicians, was that questions like those raised by the Latter-day Saints were clearly state concerns. The Constitution provided no authority for national intervention. Joseph Smith's more liberal views resulted from the tragic experiences in Missouri but were expressed twenty years too soon. Only after the Civil War were guarantees of federal

[4]Joseph Smith, *History of the Church*, 6:56-57.

intervention more specifically written into the Constitution in the Fourteenth Amendment. For the time being the Mormon question was only one part of the constitutional debate that was already dividing the nation.

Disappointed, Joseph Smith returned to Nauvoo and joined the growing protest against the President. Van Buren was being blamed by his political enemies for the economic crisis of the late 1830s. To this criticism the Prophet added Van Buren's rejection of the Mormon plea. "May he never be elected again to any office of trust or power, by which he may abuse the innocent and let the guilty go free,"[5] Joseph Smith proclaimed. Not surprisingly, in that fall's national election the Mormons voted for the successful Whig candidate for president, William Henry Harrison. In their oppressed condition it was impossible for the exiled Saints to separate political from religious considerations.

Elias Higbee, meanwhile, remained in Washington for a time to see the Mormon petition through the Senate Judiciary Committee. But the unanimous committee report echoed feelings expressed earlier by Van Buren, Calhoun, and other political leaders. The appropriate places to seek relief, according to the report, were in the courts of Missouri or in the United States courts having jurisdiction within that state. The Saints were disappointed, for they had already tried unsuccessfully to plead their case in the Missouri courts.

A general conference of the Church in April could do little more than adopt a resolution complaining that the committee report was both unconstitutional and subversive of freedom. The final appeal, the Saints acknowledged, must be to "the Court of Heaven." Frustrated by the unsatisfactory answers on this constitutional issue, Joseph Smith soon rejected the national leaders of both political parties, and in the next presidential election he declared himself a candidate for the U.S. presidency.

The Gathering from Europe

The spring of 1840 marked the beginning of a new kind of Latter-day Saint migration with important consequences. On the sixth of June, forty English Saints boarded the *Britannia* at Liverpool and sailed for New York. This first group of Mormon emi-

---

[5] Joseph Smith, *History of the Church*, 4:89.

grants from Europe was led by Elder John Moon. Five months later, in a letter from Nauvoo to family members in England, Moon favorably described the economic conditions in his new location, expressed gratitude for spiritual blessings, and listed "two important things in the gathering." First, the Lord had prepared the well-planned city as a "hiding place from the tempest" of the last days. "Another reason for gathering the people of God is . . . that they may build a sanctuary to the name of the Most High."[6] These reasons prompted 4,733 British Mormons to sail to America before the end of the Nauvoo period, and boosted the population of Nauvoo by nearly one-third.

This great movement of new members from Britain resulted primarily from a special mission of the Council of the Twelve Apostles, whose members had been called by revelation in July 1838 "to go over the great waters" to preach the gospel. Apostates warned that this particular revelation would never be fulfilled in detail, for it specified a date (April 26, 1839) and a place (the temple site at Far West) for the departure of the Twelve. With the Saints so recently driven from the state, this seemed impossible. Nevertheless, before dawn on the appointed day Brigham Young, Heber C. Kimball, Orson Pratt, John E. Page, John Taylor, Wilford Woodruff, and George A. Smith assembled as commanded and with eighteen other members held brief religious services. The apostles then quickly left for Nauvoo, where they spent the summer helping settle their families.

They were soon joined by Parley P. Pratt, who had escaped from jail in Columbia, Missouri, and by mid-September all who had accepted the call were on their way. Some were seriously ill, all left their families destitute, and all traveled without purse or scrip. Willard Richards, already in England, was added to the council in April 1840, making a total of eight apostles in the British Isles.

The first in England were Elders John Taylor and Wilford Woodruff, accompanied by Theodore Turley. They docked in Liverpool on January 11, 1840, and immediately went to work in that vicinity and southward. Here Wilford Woodruff began the work that made him one of the most productive missionaries in the Church's history. He preached first in the Staffordshire Potteries,

[6]*Millennial Star* 1 (February 1841): 253.

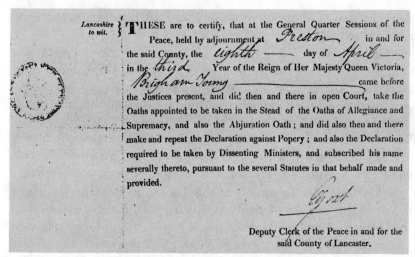

Lancashire to wit. THESE are to certify, that at the General Quarter Sessions of the Peace, held by adjournment at *Preston* in and for the said County, the *eighth* day of *April* in the *third* Year of the Reign of Her Majesty Queen Victoria, *Brigham Young* came before the Justices present, and did then and there in open Court, take the Oaths appointed to be taken in the Stead of the Oaths of Allegiance and Supremacy, and also the Abjuration Oath; and did also then and there make and repeat the Declaration against Popery; and also the Declaration required to be taken by Dissenting Ministers, and subscribed his name severally thereto, pursuant to the several Statutes in that behalf made and provided.

Deputy Clerk of the Peace in and for the said County of Lancaster.

Brigham Young's license to preach in England, issued at Preston in 1840. (Reproduced from S. Dilworth Young, Here Is Brigham . . . , *p. 255)*

working from the homes of members among their friends.

One member with whom Elder Woodruff worked closely was William Benbow. He preached in the Benbow home and spent several nights there, and undoubtedly William told the apostle about his brother John, a prosperous farmer in Herefordshire who sought a church that taught the ancient gospel. John had joined a sect known as the United Brethren. In early March Elder Woodruff noted in his diary that "the Lord warned me to go to the South." Immediately he and his host journeyed to Herefordshire. Within two days after their arrival, John Benbow, his wife, and four friends were baptized, the first of a dramatic harvest. In the Benbow home and some United Brethren chapels, Elder Woodruff preached the gospel to hundreds of willing listeners. The converted United Brethren soon formed the nucleus for many Latter-day Saint branches. For example, Thomas Kington, superintendent of the local United Brethren organization, was baptized on March 21, ordained an elder the next day, and within three months presided over the Gadfield Elm Conference. When Elder Woodruff left Herefordshire to meet the other apostles early in April, he counted 158 converts, including 48 preachers, a former Anglican clerk, a constable sent to stop his preaching, and several wealthy farmers. Nearly 200 others awaited baptism. Before he finished his mission he had baptized more than 600 persons in a pool at the

Benbow farm, and a total of more than 1,800 converts in southern England.

While other missionaries had less dramatic success than Wilford Woodruff, their progress was nevertheless steady and satisfying. After the second group of apostles arrived, the Twelve and their co-workers preached in many cities of England, Scotland, Ireland, and the Isle of Man. In January 1840, about 1500 Saints lived in Great Britain, but when the apostles left fifteen months later, there were 5,814 members—and another 800 had emigrated to America. The mission had indeed been prosperous.

The remarkable success of the Twelve in England no doubt reflected the impact of their convincing testimonies, devotion to the work, and powerful preaching. They also found a people well prepared to receive the gospel. Their greatest success was among the working classes, who were distressed by troublesome economic conditions, high food prices, and general urban poverty and unrest. To many of these people the Mormon testimony that the Millennium was about to be inaugurated was more appealing than either the socialist utopias preached by certain reformers or the continuing poverty which, it seemed, was all their country had to offer. The doctrine of the gathering also appealed to many. Thousands of British citizens had already fled the country in search of better economic opportunity, and in America the Mormon converts could find such opportunity as well as a chance to help establish the Kingdom of God on earth. In addition, there was a religious movement in England, as in America, that emphasized the need for the restoration of the primitive gospel; and when the Mormon elders appeared among people of this persuasion, conversion was often not long in coming.

Materials produced in an extensive publishing program established by the Twelve were essential to the missionary work in Great Britain. Under Brigham Young's direction, the apostles printed 5,000 copies of the Book of Mormon and 3,000 copies of a hymnal in 1841. Under the editorship of Parley P. Pratt they inaugurated a monthly periodical, *The Latter-day Saints' Millennial Star*, which served the British Saints for 130 years. Another important publication was Orson Pratt's missionary tract, *Remarkable Visions and the Late Discovery of Ancient American Records*, which included the first printed account of Joseph Smith's first vision.

Perhaps the most significant activity of the apostles in England was preaching the gathering and organizing emigration. Originally they gave only reluctant approval to emigration, but within three months they promoted it more actively. They soon established an orderly system, which required each emigrant to obtain a recommend from a local leader. As an expression of concern for the poor, the Twelve insisted that the more wealthy be denied recommends unless they assisted the needy. By the turn of the century the massive migration begun in 1840 had transferred to America more than fifty-one thousand European Saints, including an estimated thirty-eight thousand from England.

Nothing illustrates the spirit of the gathering better than the migration of William Clayton with two hundred Saints in 1840. His eleven-week journey from Liverpool to New York included cold weather, storms, poor conditions aboard ship, and even a fire at sea. He traveled up the Hudson River, through the Erie Canal, through Lakes Erie, Michigan, and Superior to Chicago, overland across Illinois, then down the Rock River into the Mississippi, and finally to Nauvoo. The day he stepped ashore in the still rustic community of the Saints, he wrote in his diary, "We were pleased to find ourselves once more at home and felt to praise God for his goodness." Clayton had never seen the swampy peninsula on the Mississippi, but home was where the Saints were.

In April 1841 the Council of the Twelve left England, though Parley P. Pratt remained for another eighteen months with his family to supervise Church affairs. Amos Fielding was appointed supervisor of the trans-Atlantic migration, and the Twelve encouraged the Saints to travel in companies that could charter boats and purchase provisions wholesale. They were told to travel to Nauvoo via New Orleans instead of New York, for that was the less expensive route.

For the English Saints who arrived in the undeveloped countryside of Illinois, conversion changed their lives spiritually and brought them new and unexpected economic and political problems. Since homesteading on the frontier was often beset with hard work, deprivation, and illness, not to mention the unbrotherly behavior of some Mormons, the immigrants were bound to be disappointed if their expectations were too high.

William Clayton, for example, followed the advice of Hyrum Smith and took his family across the Mississippi into Iowa Territory to begin a new career as a farmer. There, in the cold month of

January 1841, the former English bookkeeper found shelter in a rented house that had such poor ventilation that the family had to cook outdoors. He was disappointed to find that the Saints in Iowa held no regular religious services, and was discouraged even more when a fellow member presented a conflicting claim to his land and tried to drive him off. He had been induced to invest in a steamboat, but that venture failed. After frequent spells of illness and the destruction of his corn crop by cattle, he finally moved back across the river to Nauvoo. Some lesser men lost the faith.

The First Presidency anticipated such problems when they warned in a proclamation in January 1841:

> We would wish the Saints to understand that, when they come here, they must not expect perfection, or that all will be harmony, peace, and love; if they indulge these ideas, they will undoubtedly be deceived, for here there are persons, not only from different states, but from different nations, who, although they feel a great attachment to the cause of truth, have their prejudices of education, and, consequently, it requires some time before these things can be overcome. Again, there are many that creep in unawares, and endeavor to sow discord, strife, and animosity in our midst, and by so doing, bring evil upon the Saints. These things we have to bear with, and these things will prevail either to a greater or less extent until "the floor be thoroughly purged," and "the chaff be burnt up." Therefore, let those who come up to this place be determined to keep the commandments of God, and not be discouraged by those things we have enumerated, and then they will be prospered—the intelligence of heaven will be communicated to them, and they will, eventually, see eye to eye, and rejoice in the full fruition of that glory which is reserved for the righteous.[7]

Although expansion of missionary work during the Nauvoo period centered in Great Britain, proselyting continued in southeastern Canada and the United States. Additional missionaries carried the message of Mormonism to Australia, India, Jamaica, South America, and Germany. The work in these new areas was limited and resulted in only scattered conversions. One of the most publicized special missions was Orson Hyde's call at the April 1840 conference to dedicate Palestine for the gathering of the Jews. His commission to visit the Jews took him to New York, London, Amsterdam, and then to Jerusalem, where on Sunday morning, October 24, 1841, with pen and paper in hand, he

---

[7]Joseph Smith, *History of the Church*, 4:272-73.

offered a prayer of dedication. He invoked a tempering of the sterile land and prayed for a gathering of the Jews, the rebuilding of Jerusalem, the creation of a Jewish state, and the rearing of a temple. As a symbol of these goals, Elder Hyde erected a pile of stones on the Mount of Olives and another atop Mount Moriah. Like other missionaries of the 1840s, he was responding to the call of the Church and doing his part to further God's designs for the latter days.

The Government of Nauvoo

The new gathering place encompassed several settlements in Hancock County and neighboring regions in Illinois and Iowa. Nauvoo, however, was the center place, and soon gained political and economic influence in western Illinois.

By September 1840 serious discussions on the form of government had begun. The arrival of John C. Bennett, quartermaster general of Illinois, precipitated positive action. Bennett offered his political support to the Saints and soon accepted baptism. In October Bennett, Joseph Smith, and Robert S. Thompson were appointed to draft a bill incorporating the town. Bennett carried the proposal to the Illinois legislature, where both political parties cooperated in supporting it.

The Nauvoo charter became law December 16, 1840. The sixth city charter granted in Illinois, it was similar to the others. Church leaders considered it a "very broad and liberal" document, one designed to their advantage. Nauvoo's legislative and executive powers resided in the mayor, four aldermen, and nine councilors. The mayor and aldermen also served as judges of the municipal court, a change in the pattern of other chartered cities, so that five men controlled the legislative, executive, and judicial branches of government.

The first municipal elections, on February 1, 1841, made Bennett the mayor. Several Church leaders, including Joseph Smith, Sidney Rigdon, and Hyrum Smith, were elected as aldermen and councilors, ensuring that local civil government would be friendly to the Church. While participation of Latter-day Saints in government was perfectly normal, the interlocking of church and state occasioned some criticism from neighbors who saw it as a violation of the American principle of separation of church and state.

The Nauvoo city council faced problems common to all

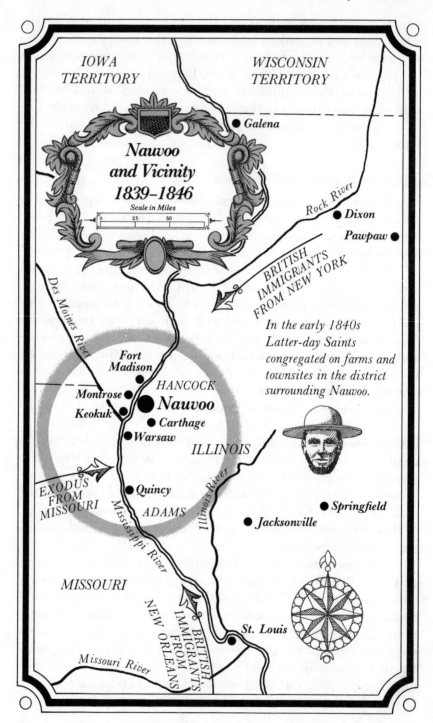

IOWA TERRITORY

WISCONSIN TERRITORY

● Galena

Nauvoo and Vicinity 1839–1846

Scale in Miles
0   25   50

Rock River

● Dixon

Pawpaw ●

Des Moines River

BRITISH IMMIGRANTS FROM NEW YORK

In the early 1840s Latter-day Saints congregated on farms and townsites in the district surrounding Nauvoo.

Fort Madison
●
HANCOCK

Montrose ●
Keokuk ●
Nauvoo

● Carthage

● Warsaw

ILLINOIS

Illinois River

EXODUS FROM MISSOURI

● Quincy

Mississippi River

ADAMS

● Springfield

● Jacksonville

MISSOURI

BRITISH IMMIGRANTS FROM NEW ORLEANS

St. Louis ●

Missouri River

towns and met them traditionally by appointing special officers and enacting laws. Two of the first laws passed guaranteed the right of peaceful assembly and freedom of conscience to all religions. A forty-member police force under Cáptain Hosea Stout enforced laws against the robbers, counterfeiters, horse thieves, confidence men, and renegades who were attracted to all Mississippi River towns. To help unemployed immigrants, the city sponsored a public works program to build stores, hotels, homes, and eventually the temple. It also planned to rid Nauvoo of the mosquito infestation by draining swamps in the lowlands and on the Mississippi River islands.

One important act of the city council was the creation on February 3, 1841, of the Nauvoo Legion. Most local militias in the state were organized at the county level, but the Nauvoo Legion was a city militia directly controlled by the mayor. Enlistment was open to all Hancock County citizens between the ages of fourteen and forty-five. The legion enjoyed broad and unusual legislative power, for unlike other armies in the state, its court-martial could enact its own regulations. Although a branch of the state militia and subject to the governor's call, the Mormon militia's internal government was independent of state interference. As the legion's top officer, Joseph Smith held the unusual rank of lieutenant general. With the exception of George Washington, no other military officer outside Nauvoo held a rank that high until 1847. After Illinois officials approved Joseph Smith's election, he discovered that only a court-martial of his equals could remove him, thus assuring him lifelong tenure.

Major General John C. Bennett handled routine administrative affairs of the legion. The two cohorts, or brigades, could accommodate more than five thousand men, but the legion probably enlisted no more than three thousand members at its peak.

The Saints viewed the Nauvoo Legion as both a means of self-protection and a sign of their patriotism. "It will enable us," the First Presidency proclaimed, "to show our attachment to the state and nation, as a people, whenever the public service requires our aid."[8] But the showy trappings and bold talk of some Mormons created apprehension among non-Mormon neighbors. Comments about the legion's activities became a standard part of anti-

---

[8]Joseph Smith, *History of the Church*, 4:269.

Mormon rhetoric as opponents of the Saints condemned weapons stockpiling, criticized the militia as an undemocratic concentration of military power, and accused the Prophet of becoming a "second Mahomet" who sought religious conquest by the sword.

Economics of the Kingdom

Although the Saints in Nauvoo were engaged in a cooperative enterprise to build the Kingdom of God on earth, their economy was based primarily on private initiative, the profit motive, and free enterprise. In that respect it was different from the earlier law of consecration and the United Firms. In March 1839 Joseph Smith had written from Liberty Jail:

> And again, we further suggest for the consideration of the Council, that there be no organization of large bodies upon common stock principles, in property, or of large companies of firms, until the Lord shall signify it in a proper manner, as it opens such a dreadful field for the avaricious, the indolent, and the corrupt hearted to prey upon the innocent and virtuous, and honest.
>
> We have reason to believe that many things were introduced among the Saints before God had signified the times; and notwithstanding the principles and plans may have been good, yet aspiring men, or in other words, men who had not the substance of godliness about them, perhaps undertook to handle edged tools. Children, you know, are fond of tools, while they are not yet able to use them.[9]

Clearly this was not a rejection of the principle of consecration, but recognition that it may have been applied too soon. In its place, members were instructed to contribute one-tenth of all their possessions at first, then one-tenth of their annual increase. Those without means were expected to labor one day in ten for the Church, and much of this tithing labor helped complete the temple.

Nauvoo's economy centered around the exchange of property, typical of the barter economy of the western United States. Its residents also looked forward to the possibility of commercial development. Primarily a religious, residential, and agricultural center, Nauvoo developed little major manufacturing or transportation. Land and buildings were its chief economic assets.

Because Joseph Smith had signed on behalf of the Church in its massive land purchases, in October 1839 the Nauvoo high

---

[9]Joseph Smith, *History of the Church*, 3:301.

council appointed him church treasurer with responsibilities for property transactions. A conference fifteen months later elected him trustee-in-trust in conformity with the business transactions regulating most religious corporations. Consequently, during his first two years in Nauvoo he was directly involved in church land business, and evidently earned a living from it. Church officials urged all immigrants to purchase lots and farms through Church agents. Land could also be obtained through private investors, including Hyrum Smith, Brigham Young, Ethan Kimball, and Daniel H. Wells.

Of greatest concern in the Nauvoo land business were the problems associated with land values and property titles. Speculation had inflated land prices, and in Nauvoo itself property values varied greatly. Special consideration was often given to the poor, who received land at little or no cost. Some refugees traded titles to abandoned Missouri land for lots in Nauvoo, and the Church used these Missouri titles as part payment on notes falling due to Galland, Hotchkiss, and others. In 1841 the Church began transferring deeds in Kirtland and other eastern Mormon properties that the Saints were urged to trade for Nauvoo property. For convenience in recording land transactions usually handled at the county seat in Carthage, Nauvoo created its own registry of deeds in the spring of 1842 and named Joseph Smith chief registrar.

The settlers established farms, homes, and businesses. Major farming was relegated to land outside the city, but garden plots flourished inside city limits. Lots in Nauvoo included flower and vegetable gardens, orchards, fences, and outbuildings—summer kitchens, smokehouses, privies, barns, and stables. Construction quickly became Nauvoo's principal industry and employed hundreds of craftsmen. Early residents lived in temporary housing and then built log and block cabins. After several years, more impressive brick and frame homes in the New England tradition appeared.

Many small shops and factories in Nauvoo's pre-industrial economy directly served the building boom. Local businesses in the burgeoning city included sawmills, several brickyards, a lime kiln, a tool factory, a carpenter's and joiner's shop, and cabinetmakers. Nauvoo craftsmen produced matches, leather goods, rope and cord, gloves, bonnets, pottery, jewelry, and watches. Advertisements in local newspapers also identified a brewery, gristmills, a cast-iron foundry, a comb manufactory, a spinning wheel maker, a printing office and book bindery, a bakery and confectionery, and several tailors, weavers, cobblers, cordwainers, and wagoners.

Major industry, however, did not develop in Nauvoo. English emigrants seemed particularly interested in establishing corn mills, weaving enterprises, textile mills, potteries, and carriage manufactories, but such dreams did not materialize. "The difficulty is that men are not employed at what they ought to be," said John Taylor in a *Nauvoo Neighbor* editorial in May 1843. "Men that have been accustomed to manufacturing cotton goods are making ditches on the prairie," he lamented, "woolen manufacturers are carrying the hod, and working at day labor . . . and potters have been metamorphosed into builders and wood choppers."

To provide the lumber required to build a city from the swamplands, the Church sent Bishop George Miller and a team of lumbermen to Wisconsin in 1842. The original intent was to provide materials for the temple and Nauvoo House, but large quantities were diverted for houses, barns, and other buildings.

The river offered opportunities for passenger transportation, and ferrying became a reliable business. In 1840, under a franchise granted to the First Presidency by the high council, Joseph Smith arranged to purchase a steamboat, the *Nauvoo*. Two years later Dan Jones and Levi Moffatt built the *Maid of Iowa* to transport converts from New Orleans. The Prophet obtained half interest in the *Maid* in 1843 and exclusive ferry rights between Nauvoo and Montrose, Iowa.

Considering contemporary economic conditions, the Saints at Nauvoo accomplished an amazing feat. The United States was in a depression during the late 1830s and early 1840s, and public and private credit was strained. In Illinois, the state was deeply in debt, two large banks failed, and the general economy hovered near collapse. In this setting, visitors to Nauvoo were amazed at the apparent economic vitality, a reflection of local construction and the influx of immigrants.

Despite the general appearance of prosperity in Nauvoo, the First Presidency carried heavy debts, including several thousand dollars in obligations from the years at Kirtland. Certain eastern creditors pressed for payment, but the October 1841 general conference instructed the trustee-in-trust to withhold payment.

*Joseph Smith's store, Nauvoo, Illinois. The upper floor served as a
President's office and meeting hall, and the Relief Society was organized here
in 1842. (Church Archives)*

The conference resolved "not to appropriate Church property to
liquidate old claims that may be brought forward from Kirtland
and Missouri."[10] Six months later the Twelve encouraged general
debt forgiveness within the Church and suggested that members
voluntarily cancel debts to eliminate internal discord and animosity in preparation for temple blessings. Both actions eased the
burden of indebtedness.

In a further effort to relieve the pressure of financial obligations, many Latter-day Saints tried another approach. A national
Bankruptcy Act, effective February 1, 1842, allowed individuals to
legally petition for relief. In April, Joseph Smith and several other
leading Latter-day Saints engaged lawyers and filed bankruptcies
under the untried law, hoping to eliminate debts and losses
suffered in the removal from Missouri. The courts did not accept
Joseph Smith's appeal, however, and his debts were ultimately left
for settlement by his estate after his death.

---

[10] Joseph Smith, *History of the Church*, 4:427.

Education and Society among the Saints

Besides authorizing municipal government and a militia, the Nauvoo charter allowed establishment of the University of the City of Nauvoo and delegated the city council to select a twenty-three-man board of regents. In practice the council and school shared common leadership. Founded February 3, 1841, the university was governed by a chancellor, Mayor John C. Bennett, and a board of regents that included all city councilmen. The council soon gave regents responsibility for all public education in the city, from the common school on up. Education in Nauvoo was thus a closely controlled arm of municipal government. The First Presidency projected an educational system devoted to "knowledge and learning, in the arts, sciences, and learned professions," and hoped to make the university "one of the great lights to the world" for the diffusion of "that kind of knowledge which will be of practicable utility, and for the public good, and also for private and individual happiness."[11]

Plans for a separate university campus were never realized. Classes convened in homes, public buildings, the Masonic Hall, and the temple. The university offered secondary level classes in the sciences, philosophy, literature, history, music, and the languages. Orson Pratt taught mathematics and related subjects, Orson Spencer specialized in foreign languages, and Sidney Rigdon was appointed to teach religion.

At the common school level, classes functioned in all municipal wards, with three wardens or trustees supervising the work. At least eighty different men and women served as teachers in the city schools, utilizing standard contemporary texts selected from a list approved by the regents.

Besides the enlightenment available through public schools, Nauvoo citizens enjoyed private lectures, debates, and social activities. Visiting dramatic companies and lecturers attracted audiences after Nauvoo became an established city. A circus visited in 1843, and phrenologists several times stopped to prepare head charts. Excursion boats regularly brought visitors to the river docks. These things, however, were only occasional parts of Nauvoo's social life. Local initiative created most leisure activities,

----

[11] Joseph Smith, *History of the Church*, 4:269.

and except for such voluntary organizations as the debate and literary clubs, the choir, and the bands, most fraternizing was carried out by families, at home or between households.

Entertainments for larger groups were held in the Concert Hall, north of the temple, or in the Masonic Hall. The Mansion House, an official residence built for the Church president in 1843, rapidly became a social center. Self-improvement was fostered by the Nauvoo Lyceum, organized in 1842 to conduct weekly debates on current issues, and by the Nauvoo Library and Literary Institute, founded two years later to encourage the reading of good books. University music professor Gustavus Hills helped create the Teacher's Lyceum of Music in December 1841 to foster improvements. The church choir offered occasional concerts, as did two brass bands, one led by William Pitt. The bands played for private parties, where dancing became a religiously acceptable practice among the Latter-day Saints. Useful pastimes included corn husking and rag and quilting bees. Young men enjoyed swimming and exploring small islands in the river. Horsemanship and sports, including running, jumping, wrestling, and weight throwing, filled rare idle afternoons. For the Nauvoo resident seeking diversion from the routine of daily life, a great variety of homemade recreation was available.

Another important voluntary activity opened with installation of a lodge of York Rite Freemasons in Nauvoo. Organized in December 1841, it filled an immediate fraternal need for Freemason members of the Church. Hyrum Smith and Heber C. Kimball, for example, dated their affiliation with the Masons from the 1820s, and Newel K. Whitney, Lucius N. Scovil, George Miller, and many others had been Freemasons before settling at Nauvoo. But William W. Phelps and Ebenezer Robinson joined others who opposed the movement. John C. Bennett had been expelled from Ohio lodges but endorsed the solicitations in the early summer of 1841, which finally brought a dispensation for a Nauvoo lodge in mid-October.

The Nauvoo lodge grew rapidly. Within five months, the Mormons had more members than all other Illinois lodges combined. Latter-day Saints also organized the Rising Sun Lodge at Montrose, Iowa, in August 1842. The Mormon lodges began building a Masonic temple that year. About the same time, the Grand Lodge of Illinois launched an investigation of "irregularities" in Nauvoo. A major concern was the rapid advancement of applicants, particularly Joseph Smith and Sidney Rigdon, who moved immediately to the highest degree of Freemasonry within a day of the lodge's formal installation, March 15, 1842. Fearful that Mormon members would soon control the fraternity in Illinois, a non-Mormon lodge at nearby Quincy petitioned state officers for an inquiry. The Nauvoo Lodge was temporarily suspended until October 1844, when recognition was formally withdrawn. In the meantime, two additional lodges—the Helm and Nye—had been created at Nauvoo. Ultimately most adult males in Nauvoo affiliated with one of the lodges, and despite the suspension, Freemasons in the city completed their Masonic temple and dedicated it on April 5, 1844. Until this time lodge meetings had convened in the upper room of Joseph Smith's store, then at the City Hotel, and later in George Miller's home. Now their own three-story building became a busy community center for social and cultural gatherings, city council meetings, schools, and surplus grain storage.

On March 4, 1842, during the same month that prominent men in the community were initiated into Freemasonry, several women met to organize their own society. Sarah M. Kimball and other women had expressed a desire to provide shirts for workmen on the temple. Those sharing this benevolent concern drafted a plan of government for their sewing group. When consulted, Joseph Smith offered to assist in forming an organization, not after worldly constitutional patterns, but "after the pattern of the priesthood." Under his direction, the Female Relief Society of Nauvoo was organized on March 17, with Emma Smith as its founding president. The Prophet counseled the women to "provoke the brethren to good works in looking to the wants of the poor, searching after objects of charity, and in administering to their wants—[and] to assist, by correcting the morals and strengthening the virtues of the community."[12]

The Relief Society was immediately popular. Under Emma Smith's direction meetings were conducted in each of the city's four ecclesiastical wards. Membership by September 1842 was 1,142, and enrollment increased by another 200 during the next

---

[12]"Nauvoo Relief Society Minutes, March 17, 1842-March 16, 1844," March 19, 1842, Ms., Church Archives, Historical Department of The Church of Jesus Christ of Latter-day Saints, Salt Lake City.

eighteen months. The last meetings of the Nauvoo Relief Society were held in March 1844. The organization was later revived in the Salt Lake Valley.

The Prophet's desire to have the Saints cooperate with impoverished members was also evident in remarks to an informal meeting of young people. At Heber C. Kimball's invitation, capacity gatherings of young men and women began to meet in homes or private halls in January 1843 to hear practical advice on the wise use of their time. The majority of the evening lectures, usually delivered by Elder Kimball, advised against excessive parties, dances, and entertainments. He contended that a young person would be better balanced with some nights devoted to scripture study, and the young people agreed.

When Joseph Smith addressed the informal Young People's Meeting, he encouraged them to organize not for self-improvement but for service to the poor. He particularly referred to an ailing English immigrant who had collected materials for a home but was too lame to build it himself. The Prophet challenged the young men to help the worthy convert. No report is available of the outcome of this project, but the youth did organize the Young Gentlemen and Ladies Relief Society of Nauvoo. This voluntary organization's focus, like the women's Relief Society, was charitable benevolence.

The Church: Expanding Settlement and Administration

Following the disruptive removal from northern Missouri, formal church programs were gradually reinstituted and then enhanced to meet the needs of an expanding membership. The general conference of October 1839 appointed a stake presidency and high council for Nauvoo and a similar organization for the Saints in Lee County, Iowa, later known as Zarahemla Stake. A bishop served Lee County as a stake officer, continuing an earlier pattern. But in Nauvoo the conference appointed three bishops for the city and gave them geographical jurisdictions: the upper, middle, and lower wards. This introduced the bishop's ward as a geographical subdivision of the Church. Not yet a fully developed administrative unit, the ward was simply a convenient division for administering financial and welfare concerns. In many American cities the term "ward" had been used to designate political precincts, and the first Latter-day Saint ecclesiastical wards were apparently created with this precedent in mind.

In the meantime, Latter-day Saint settlements were expanding. Church leaders initially encouraged gathering to central locations at Nauvoo and Montrose, where the Prophet had purchased land for resale to members. Other farm sites south of Nauvoo toward Quincy, in Adams County, and at locations surrounding Hancock and Adams counties soon attracted small congregations. In April 1840 Joseph Smith officially approved retention of these peripheral settlements, an action that brought several requests for stake organizations from the satellite communities. In July the Nauvoo high council approved a request to organize the Ramus Stake at the Crooked Creek settlement, twenty-two miles southeast of Nauvoo. The October conference reestablished a stake at Kirtland, Ohio, and began procedures that soon resulted in eight more stakes in Illinois, five of them in Adams County.

At the same time, certain adverse conditions in the Nauvoo-Montrose area made it less attractive to many Saints. Nauvoo citizens had suffered greatly from malarial fever during the summers of 1839 and 1840, discouraging immigration and inducing some new residents to leave. Land speculators and squatters in Lee County, Iowa, were challenging Mormon title to lands purchased from Dr. Galland. In addition, stake leaders disturbed some members with a debt repudiation policy in December 1839 and an attempt to instigate an unapproved system of consecration soon afterward. At Kirtland, stake president Almon Babbitt began encouraging European immigrants headed for Nauvoo to stop and help rebuild that partially abandoned Mormon community.

All this caused Church leaders to reconsider the policy of expanding settlements. During the early months of 1841 Joseph Smith decisively reestablished the importance of gathering to the twin settlements in Lee and Hancock counties. In January a proclamation from the First Presidency designated Nauvoo as the official site for a general gathering. It spoke glowingly of Mormon accomplishments there, the friendly reception among Illinoisans, and the expectations of improved health conditions. In revelations later that month and in March, the Saints were commanded to build a temple in Nauvoo and to raise cities in Iowa.

The small Mormon farming towns in Adams County, Illinois, were accepted as natural satellites of an expanding Zion for a time, because they were near Nauvoo. In contrast, Kirtland seemed to be rapidly mounting a schismatic challenge to Nauvoo's primacy. Gradually President Babbitt lost favor with other leaders of the Church as he continued to ignore their counsel on gathering. In May 1841 in the *Times and Seasons* the Prophet announced a First Presidency decision to discontinue all stakes except those authorized for Hancock County (Nauvoo, Warren, and Ramus) and Lee County (Zarahemla and Nashville). This action came within a month after stakes had been organized in Philadelphia and New York City. It meant the end of a centrifugal movement, the official disorganization of the troublesome Ohio Stake, and discontinuance of eight stakes in Illinois. Babbitt was disfellowshipped in October for continuing to encourage European Saints to stop at Kirtland, which had been designated as a gathering place only for Saints in the eastern states.

At the beginning of 1841 Nauvoo held about three thousand inhabitants and was by far the Church's largest stake. The renewed effort to focus the gathering there rapidly increased its population, and the organization of Nauvoo into ten urban and three country wards in August 1842 was an indication of its growth. Contributing further to Nauvoo's ecclesiastical ascendancy was the discontinuance of stakes at Ramus and Zarahemla in December 1841 and January 1842, though these areas were still approved for settlement. At the same time, in reconsidering the Kirtland question, the First Presidency authorized the reinstituted Almon W. Babbitt to proceed with caution. "Do what you can in righteousness to build up Kirtland," the instruction read, "but do not suffer yourselves to harbor the idea that Kirtland will rise on the ruins of Nauvoo."[13] The threatened dissolution of Nauvoo had been averted.

To guide Nauvoo's development, the Prophet called on the experienced Council of the Twelve and, in the process, significantly expanded the council's ecclesiastical authority. For nearly two years, until the municipal government became effective, the Nauvoo high council had managed city affairs. In addition, this and other high councils were authorized to handle all affairs within their own stakes, and at first not even the Twelve could intervene in their decisions. At a special conference on

---

[13]Joseph Smith, *History of the Church,* 4:476.

August 16, 1841, however, the Prophet announced it was time for
the Twelve, who had so ably proved themselves in their European
missions, to remain at home where they could support their
families, relieve the First Presidency of some financial duties, and
attend to the needs of immigrants. They would also continue to
direct missionary work, but "the time had come," said the
Prophet, "when the Twelve should be called upon to stand in their
place next to the First Presidency."[14] Originally a "travelling high
council," the apostles, under the direction of the First Presidency,
were now given responsibility for the business of the Church within
the stakes. The relationship between the stakes and the council was
now changed, and the Twelve became general Church authorities
in the stakes as well as in the missions.

In their expanded role, the Twelve encouraged new arrivals
to locate at Nauvoo and invited the Kirtland Saints to sign over
their holdings to the Church in exchange for Nauvoo property. For
British immigrants, the Twelve promoted a new and short-lived
settlement at Warren, near Warsaw. Other converts were directed
to Morley's Settlement, sometimes known as Yelrom. By the end of
1841 seven of the Twelve were serving as Nauvoo city councilmen;
three others were elected later. The apostles became close advisers
of the prophet-mayor and effective administrators of both church
and civic programs. As active assistants to the First Presidency,
they took a direct hand in the ecclesiastical decision-making
process, issued missionary calls, and began assigning fields of labor,
a task previously handled by other quorums. This close direction of
affairs prepared Brigham Young and his associates to exercise the
leadership of the Church after the death of Joseph and Hyrum
Smith.

The Twelve also took a direct hand in the Church's publications program. Don Carlos Smith had established the *Times and
Seasons* in November 1839 as a private business venture in
partnership with Ebenezer Robinson. After Smith's death in 1841,
Robinson inaugurated policies that the Twelve disliked. Robinson
finally agreed to sell the paper to the Twelve if they would also
buy his job printing business. On February 15, 1842, Joseph
Smith's name appeared as editor and publisher of the *Times and
Seasons.* John Taylor served as chief editorial assistant and after

---

[14]Joseph Smith, *History of the Church,* 4:403.

November as editor. Wilford Woodruff supervised the printing office and, in addition to publishing the newspaper, issued an edition of the Book of Mormon, three printings of the Doctrine and Covenants, a second edition of the hymnbook, and several private books and pamphlets.

One of the most important items published in Church periodicals was the Prophet's own history of the restoration. For years Joseph had been dictating his history to scribes and had directed the gathering of relevant documents by his associates. Various efforts had been made to prepare the history for publication, but in 1838 the Prophet began the final effort. Under his direction scribes and other committee members compiled the documents and wrote the history. By the time of his martyrdom in 1844 it was complete only through 1838; but the records were carefully packed before the exodus to the Great Basin, and the history was finally completed in 1856. Before the Prophet died, early portions of the manuscript were printed in the *Times and Seasons* and the *Millennial Star*. Eventually the completed work was published in six volumes as the *History of the Church of Jesus Christ of Latter-day Saints: Period I: History of Joseph Smith, the Prophet, by Himself.*

New Revelations and the Refinement of Church Doctrine

Much of Nauvoo's religious life centered around its Sunday meetings. There were no regular meetinghouses or chapels, and most preaching services were outdoor, city-wide affairs. Such large meetings had become regular by 1840, and they continued until the fall of 1845, when the temple was sufficiently completed that temporary seating could be provided indoors. Though small gatherings were held in homes, every Sunday at 10:00 A.M. the Saints in Nauvoo, across the river in Iowa, and in other nearby settlements knew that, weather permitting, an outdoor preaching meeting would convene. Joseph Smith was often the principal speaker.

As he preached to the Saints month after month, the Prophet explained the scriptures and introduced many important religious doctrines. In Nauvoo the teachings of the Latter-day Saints assumed the distinctive qualities that set them apart more clearly than before from other religions.

The Prophet still faced the necessity of explaining Mormon

beliefs to the world in a way that those unfamiliar with Mormonism could understand. The famous Wentworth letter was a case in point. In the spring of 1842 John Wentworth, a Chicago editor, requested a short history of the Church. The Prophet complied and included several short statements of Latter-day Saint beliefs. These statements were later extracted from the Wentworth letter and became known as the Articles of Faith. Intended for non-Mormons, these articles were never meant to be a complete summary of the gospel, for they included none of the more advanced doctrines first presented to the Church in Nauvoo, nor did they contain such obvious practices as prayer or the sacrament of the Lord's Supper. The Articles of Faith were simply a summary of the Latter-day Saint position on some contemporary religious issues, and in that sense they became an important message to the religious world. Trinitarianism, the fall of man, predestination, election, Christian baptism, the restoration of the ancient church, spiritual gifts, millennialism, and other doctrines—all of which were frequently debated in nineteenth-century America—were approached in the Articles of Faith.

For the Saints, however, the Prophet opened new vistas. Things hidden from ancient times, he said, must now be taught as part of the restoration. He told the Saints they were living in the final dispensation of the gospel, in which all past knowledge and authority would be gathered together through the power of the priesthood. This idea was first suggested as early as 1836, when Moses, Elias, and Elijah appeared in vision to Joseph Smith and Oliver Cowdery in the Kirtland Temple and committed to them the keys of their own dispensations. On October 5, 1840, the Prophet expounded this doctrine more fully, marking the beginning of his efforts to open the minds of the Saints to some of the long-hidden mysteries of the gospel. A year later he told a general conference that "the dispensation of the fulness of times will bring to light the things that have been revealed in all former dispensations; also other things that have not been before revealed." As if to emphasize how revolutionary these new doctrines were, Brigham Young told the elders at the same conference that they must teach abroad "the first principles of the Gospel, leaving the mysteries of the kingdom to be taught among the Saints."[15]

---

[15]Joseph Smith, *History of the Church,* 4:426.

Even for the Saints, some of the newly revealed doctrines were difficult to accept. Only five months before his death the Prophet preached a Sunday sermon to several thousand people in Nauvoo on salvation for the dead, but concluded with a discouraged recognition of how hard it was to accept such things. As recorded by Wilford Woodruff, the Prophet said:

But there has been a great difficulty in getting anything into the heads of this generation. It has been like splitting hemlock knots with a corn-dodger for a wedge, and a pumpkin for a beetle. Even the Saints are slow to understand.

I have tried for a number of years to get the minds of the Saints prepared to receive the things of God; but we frequently see some of them, after suffering all they have for the work of God, will fly to pieces like glass as soon as anything comes that is contrary to their traditions; they cannot stand the fire at all. How many will be able to abide a celestial law, and go through and receive their exaltation, I am unable to say, as many are called, but few are chosen.[16]

The doctrines of the nature of the Godhead, the eternal nature of man, and the relationship between God and man are fundamental to Latter-day Saint theology, yet these doctrines were not fully revealed until the 1840s. The "Lectures on Faith," published in 1835, had defined the Godhead as consisting of two persons, the Father and the Son, and the Holy Ghost as the combined mind of the Father and the Son. At a conference in Ramus, Illinois, in April 1842, Joseph Smith corrected this concept and declared:

The Father has a body of flesh and bones as tangible as man's; the Son also; but the Holy Ghost has not a body of flesh and bones, but is a personage of Spirit. Were it not so, the Holy Ghost could not dwell in us.[17]

As early as 1833 Joseph Smith had taught by revelation that man was eternal and had existed from the beginning with God, but only in Nauvoo did he provide further insight into man's pre-earth existence. In pre-earth life, he taught, God had created the spirits of men—man literally became his offspring. One purpose of mortal life was to provide each spirit with a physical body and a testing ground. It was at this point that Mormon doctrine departed significantly from some current, well-established religious

[16]Joseph Smith, *History of the Church*, 6:184-85.
[17]D&C 130:22.

tenets of the day. Presbyterians, Congregationalists, Baptists, and the reformed churches were still influenced by the Calvinist doctrine that man was helpless to determine his own salvation—he was predestined to be either saved or damned, according to God's will. In addition, they believed man was fallen and thus totally evil in the sight of God. Joseph Smith taught that man, far from being an enemy or mere tool of God, was actually a god in embryo. The Father had achieved godhood only by going through the same experiences man is now enduring. Having successfully met all tests, he progressed in knowledge and power to become God. In turn, he instructed his spirit children in the plan of salvation before they came to earth and promised them that if they lived faithfully in their mortal life, one day they, too, might become gods. This was the doctrine of eternal progression, which became another hallmark of the restored gospel.

Especially important to Joseph Smith was the doctrine of free agency. Even in his pre-earth life, man had the choice of accepting or rejecting the gospel plan, and in this life he still has that free choice. Such teachings totally rejected the doctrines of predestination and man's depravity. This view enobled man and promised him a potential almost unthought-of elsewhere. It added new meaning to Christ's atonement, for the Saints were taught that the plan of redemption had been presented to them in pre-earth life.

Essential to all this was the teaching that certain principles must be accepted and certain ordinances performed by the power of the priesthood before man could attain exaltation, and only in the restored church was that priesthood found. What, then, would happen to those who died without a knowledge of the restored gospel? This question led to another hallmark of the Latter-day Saint faith: the doctrine of salvation for the dead. Joseph Smith first publicly discussed baptism for the dead in a funeral sermon in August 1840. The following month the Church began baptisms for the dead in the Mississippi River. Living proxies stood for dead ancestors in the belief that their loved ones would hear the gospel in the spirit world. Acceptance of the message in the spirit world would validate this earthly proxy ordinance. In January 1841 the Prophet announced by revelation that baptism for the dead was a temple ordinance. Even though the temple was far from completion, a temporary, oval baptismal font was hewn from pine and placed on the backs of twelve wooden oxen. It was dedicated in

November 1841, and no more baptisms for the dead were performed in the river.

Many of the new doctrines taught in Nauvoo, including baptism for the dead, were directly related to temple ordinances. Back in Kirtland it had been clear that temples were to be a channel through which the Saints could receive great spiritual blessings. Now, in Nauvoo, a temple was to be built that would play an expanded role in the religious life of devout Church members. On January 19, 1841, the Saints were commanded by revelation to build a temple to perform baptisms and other ordinances for both the living and the dead; and if they failed, they were cautioned, "ye shall be rejected as a church, with your dead." Great blessings were promised if they completed it.

The temple was built at great sacrifice. Financial problems and the persecutions of 1843 and 1844 continually interfered with its construction. In fact, only after most Mormons were on their way west in 1846 was the temple completed and dedicated. Portions were dedicated earlier, however, and the important priesthood ordinances were performed.

One important temple ordinance was the endowment ceremony, in which special washings and anointings, symbolic signs, instructions, and sacred covenants gave the Saints new insight into their relationship with God, their eternal destinies, and their earthly responsibilities. Like the Masonic rituals, many parts of the endowment can be seen in ancient religious ceremonies. The meaning attached to them, however, made them distinctly a part of Latter-day Saint faith, and the Prophet taught that this ceremony was one more step in the restoration of ancient truths.

So strongly did Joseph Smith feel about instituting the endowment that in May 1842 he selected a small group of members and introduced it to them on the second floor of his brick store in Nauvoo. Other small groups received the endowment ceremony under his direction prior to his death in 1844.

By November 1845 the upper floor of the temple was nearing completion, and the Saints were anticipating this new spiritual experience with great enthusiasm. Church leaders and their wives provided drapes for the windows and canvas to divide the main hall into four rooms, borrowed carpets for the floor, and decorated the walls with borrowed paintings and mirrors. The Saints had been raising potted plants and shrubs in their homes during the winter, and these were taken to the temple, the House of the Lord, to create a setting of beauty and peace for the presentation of the temple ceremony. Beginning December 11, 1845, the endowment ceremony was performed regularly for eager groups of Saints, and as soon as enough were familiar with it to help administer it to others, sessions were held around the clock. The endowment ceremony in behalf of the dead was postponed until temples could be built in the Great Basin, but about five thousand members received their own promised endowments in Nauvoo.

Perhaps the most controversial doctrines taught at Nauvoo were those relating to sealing and plural marriage. According to the important revelation first committed to writing on July 12, 1843, no covenant or vow made between people on this earth is of force after death unless sealed by priesthood authority. This includes the marriage covenant. If marriage is performed or sealed by that authority, the marriage partners are promised that if they do not violate their sacred obligations, their marriage covenant will "be of full force when they are out of the world." This is the "new and everlasting covenant." In Nauvoo many husbands and wives were sealed by the power of the priesthood in the temple. Since the doctrine also provided that sealings could be performed in behalf of the dead, many whose spouses had passed on were sealed to them by proxy. For the most part, however, sealings for the dead had to wait until the move west.

The same revelation that clarified the sealing power also explained the doctrine of plural marriage. Under priesthood authority, it declared, ancient prophets had been given more than one wife, and if the Lord for any reason should command it again, the practice was right and valid when entered into under the direction of the priesthood. To Joseph Smith, this far-reaching doctrine was only one of several necessary parts of the restoration of the ancient order of things in the dispensation of the fulness of times.

Because of the controversial nature of this doctrine, the Prophet initially taught it to only a few of his closest associates. Historical evidence suggests that he understood the principle as early as 1831 and may have begun taking plural wives as early as 1835. Officially, however, the practice began in 1841 when Louisa Beaman was sealed to the Prophet by Joseph Bates Noble. Then, after the Twelve returned from England, Joseph took them and other close associates aside individually and taught them the doctrine. All had difficulty accepting it, some more than others. Because of Orson Pratt's forceful rejection, he and his wife were excommunicated. Later, however, when converted to the doctrine, they were rebaptized, and in 1843 Elder Pratt was restored to the Council of the Twelve. Nine years later he delivered the first public address on the subject, and he wrote most of the early Church literature explaining plural marriage.

Though several prominent men were sealed to additional wives, the practice remained confidential. Nevertheless, the widening circle of persons taken into the Prophet's confidence and the increasing number participating in the practice led to rumors and speculations. Apostates, especially, grasped distorted word-of-mouth reports in 1842 and 1843 and twisted them into sensational exposés and charges of adultery, attempting to discredit the Church. It is not clear whether Joseph Smith lived as husband with any of his plural wives or whether they were only sealed to him as he attempted to introduce the principle. In any case, he rightly denied the charges of adultery, for according to the revelation plural marriages were morally acceptable under the new and everlasting covenant of the priesthood. He could also deny that the Church was teaching plural marriage, for members generally were not aware of it, and certainly it was yet neither a command nor an official doctrine. It became official only when openly preached after 1852 and when the revelation was published.

All this was only part of the rich development of doctrine that characterized the Nauvoo period. Little wonder the Saints congregated by the thousands to hear the Prophet each week, anticipating new and exciting things. Such doctrines as the plurality of gods and man's potential for becoming like God excited the imagination and added meaning to life. Joseph Smith taught that spirit was not immaterial, but refined matter, and he explained that the creation of the earth could be understood as an organizing of already-existing matter rather than a creation from nothing. He expounded on the second coming of Christ, the resurrection, God's reckoning of time, the nature of angels, life in other worlds, and the nature of paradise and spirit prison.

The Nauvoo years, then, were of pivotal historical importance to the growth, organization, and doctrines of The Church of Jesus Christ of Latter-day Saints. A new gathering place was designated and a beautiful, influential city built. Responsibilities of priesthood leaders were expanded and clarified, and the Council of the Twelve gained its full authority in Church affairs. An expanded missionary program brought in new converts more rapidly than ever before, revitalized the Church in England, and laid the foundation for a vast emigration program. In addition, Joseph Smith expounded upon Church doctrines until the Saints' understanding of the gospel plan of salvation was greatly expanded. These doctrines laid the foundation for the advanced religious outlook of the Latter-day Saints and accounted for such modern hallmarks as the temple endowment, marriage for eternity, salvation for the dead, genealogical research, understanding of the Godhead, and the doctrines of pre-earth life and eternal progression. While the 1840s moved the Church forward in new directions, however, conflict and apostasy were leading to new tragedies.

CHAPTER 6

Difficult Days: Nauvoo, 1842-1845

T he accomplishments that brought political influence and relative economic strength to Nauvoo during the early 1840s carried with them the possibilities of both peace and conflict. By 1842 Nauvoo so dominated Hancock County and surrounding areas that older residents feared its population was becoming a political threat. It was true that during the final two years of Joseph Smith's life politics became crucial and he and his close advisers became more politically active. In 1842 he accepted the Nauvoo mayorship. Two years later he became a candidate for national office. Other Latter-day Saints sought and won elective office in Nauvoo, Hancock County, and Illinois. The survival of the Church in Illinois seemed dependent upon its political strength, as the highly politicized climate of the mid-1840s revealed stresses within and jealousies without. But in mid-1844 a stunned membership suddenly found itself without its prophet-leader and facing complicated new challenges, including questions of leadership and threats of another exile. Politically the years between 1842 and 1845 were indeed difficult ones for Nauvoo.

Political Events, 1842-1844

The difficulties between the Latter-day Saints and their

neighbors around Nauvoo grew from the volatile politics of frontier Illinois. Party politics in the state were in the formative stage, and feelings were easily inflamed. In 1838, just before the Saints arrived in Commerce, progressive Democrats had elected Thomas Carlin governor and had won control of state government. The Whigs, a minority party statewide, had drawn substantial support from a region north and west of Springfield, including Hancock County. Local politicians were understandably concerned about the political attitudes of the growing Mormon community at Nauvoo, for it could have a pivotal influence on the fortunes of either party.

Until Joseph Smith's visit with Martin Van Buren in 1839, the Saints generally favored the Jacksonian Democratic party. This quickly changed. Even though the Prophet remained officially neutral in the election of 1840, he was known to favor Whig presidential candidate William Henry Harrison and the Saints probably cast an anti-Van Buren vote. In county balloting, the Mormon vote was divided, thus helping maintain a two-to-one edge for the Whigs, whose traditional concern for property rights elicited an appreciative response from the Missouri exiles. The unified votes in 1841 helped to elect a Whig congressman, but political allegiances remained fluid.

Not long after the 1840 election, political feelings in Hancock County began polarizing around religious issues, and the Saints found themselves deeply involved in state and local politics. Without this involvement, Nauvoo's existence as a political entity and a place of refuge seemed threatened. A small but vocal group of non-Mormons, alarmed at the concentration of political power at Nauvoo, formed an anti-Mormon party. Thomas Sharp's *Warsaw Signal* vocalized the resentment. In some county contests the new anti-Mormon alignment succeeded at the polls in August 1841.

Meanwhile, the Whigs lost ground with the Saints because of their opposition to granting the franchise to non-naturalized residents, including the growing British immigrant population at Nauvoo. Concern over this issue led some Whig newspapers to become openly anti-Mormon. Then the Democrats, with Mormon support, won control of the state legislature. After legalizing the vote for resident male aliens, the Democratic-controlled legislature reorganized the state supreme court. Governor Carlin was enabled to appoint five friendly justices willing to overturn Whig victories in the circuit courts.

Both parties had supported the Nauvoo charter, but the Democrats most actively capitalized on this support to gain the Mormon vote. In addition, Stephen A. Douglas furthered his political aims by patronage. A former secretary of state and an aspiring congressman, Douglas was a state supreme court justice in 1841. Through his influence, Nauvoo Mayor John C. Bennett was named master in chancery for Hancock County. Douglas also listened favorably when Joseph Smith brought some Missouri writs before him for a hearing. By 1842, therefore, Mormon leanings seemed Democratic, for in that party the Saints seemed to be finding their most effective friends. When the Democrats nominated as their candidate for governor Adam Snyder, who had befriended the Mormons in the state legislature, Joseph Smith immediately endorsed him. Attempting to reconcile such endorsement with continuing claims that the Church was nonpartisan, he wrote in the *Times and Seasons:* "In the next canvass, we shall be influenced by no party consideration . . . ; so the partizans in this county, who expect to divide the friends of humanity and equal rights will find themselves mistaken—we care not a fig for Whig or Democrat; they are both alike to us, but we shall go for our friends, our tried friends, and the cause of human liberty, which is the cause of God."[1]

Predictably, the *Quincy Whig,* the *Sangamo Journal* at Springfield, and other Whig papers denounced the Saints. To them, the Mormons were not ignoring party labels but were in collusion with the Democrats. Former governor Joseph Duncan, the Whig candidate for governor, campaigned on an anti-Mormon platform, pledging, if elected, to repeal the Nauvoo charter and drive the Saints from the state. The Saints were equally open in their criticism of Duncan. Joseph Smith indulged in a little political ridicule in July when he named his new horse "Joe Duncan." The Whig papers also eagerly published the shabby exposé written by John C. Bennett, recently disaffected from the Church. Charges of moral depravity and political conspiracy were hurled at the Mormons.

In May, when the Democratic candidate suddenly died, the

---

[1] Joseph Smith, *History of the Church,* 4:480.

Governor Thomas Ford of Illinois. (Courtesy Illinois State Historical Library)

party faced a difficult choice. With the anti-Mormon campaign gaining ground, anyone known as a friend of the Mormons would be a political liability. The Democrats made a shrewd choice—Illinois Supreme Court Justice Thomas Ford, who had not taken a public position on the Mormon issue. He could assure hesitant Democrats that he had never favored the Mormons, while in Nauvoo Douglas could assure the Mormons that the cause of liberty was safe in Democratic hands. Even though Ford actually supported repeal of the Nauvoo charter, the tactic worked. Ford won the election handily and the Saints' support helped him carry Hancock County.

Although the alignment of Mormon votes with friendly

Democrats was not significant statewide, it had powerful emotional impact in Hancock County, where the anti-Mormon party was revived in September 1842. At issue in the fall election of 1842 was the candidacy of Apostle William Smith, the Prophet's brother, who ran on the Democratic ticket for the state House of Representatives. Some legislators were advocating repeal of the charters of all six chartered cities in Illinois, including Nauvoo, and William Smith hoped to join those in the state assembly opposed to the movement. His opponent was Thomas C. Sharp, editor and publisher of the *Warsaw Signal.* To answer Sharp's anti-Mormon comments, William Smith founded his own weekly paper, the *Wasp.* Unlike the *Times and Seasons,* the *Wasp* was exclusively secular. It carried advertising and general news and also engaged in a lively editorial battle. With the Mormon vote behind him, the apostle easily won the election.

Sharp's defeat only strengthened his antagonism. The hostile editor broadened his attack against Mormonism and began criticizing Latter-day Saints over a ten-county area. Realizing that no enemy of the Mormons could win office while the Saints voted as a bloc, Sharp revived the cry for extermination or expulsion.

The Prophet, uncomfortable with his brother's partisan editorializing, persuaded William Smith to resign as *Wasp* editor in April 1843. John Taylor succeeded as editor, enlarged the newspaper, and renamed it the *Nauvoo Neighbor.* The new name was intended to reflect a nominally nonpartisan editorial stance.

When the question of charter repeal was debated in the assembly in December 1842, William Smith cooperated with representatives of other threatened cities. He found the majority of Democrats supporting the Nauvoo charter, the Whigs evenly divided, and some from both parties seeking to replace the franchise with one less powerful. No conclusive action resulted, but the question would appear again.

Other stresses surfaced in the Church's political struggles in Illinois, some of them extending back to 1840. Reapportionment of legislative districts following publication of the 1840 census increased Latter-day Saint influence. The new boundary cut along the Hancock-Adams county line, placing substantial Mormon populations in both sections and making the Mormon vote important in both counties.

Actually, the Democrats were not always reliable in their support of the Mormons. Governor Carlin's Democratic administration rejected its first opportunity to assist the Saints when armed Missourians kidnapped four Mormons in Hancock County in July 1840. The small mob forced Alanson Brown, Benjamin Boyce, Noah Rogers, and James Allred across the river and detained them for several days. Rogers and Boyce were stripped and severely beaten and Brown was strangled to unconsciousness with a rope. Petitions to the Illinois governor for help went unheeded.

Two months later, when Missouri officers sought to extradite Joseph Smith and five others as fugitives from justice, Governor Carlin approved. The sheriff serving the papers failed to locate the wanted men, so the matter rested until the following summer. On June 4, 1841, Joseph Smith had what seemed to be a friendly interview with the governor. Immediately afterward, however, Carlin sent Adams County Sheriff Thomas King, accompanied by a Missouri officer, to arrest the Prophet. Judge Stephen A. Douglas heard the case in Monmouth the following week and ruled that the writ had become ineffective when the Hancock County sheriff returned it to the governor after failing to serve it the previous year. This favorable opinion reinforced the nonpartisan attitudes of Mormon officials. They had seen a lack of sympathy for their cause from the Democratic governor's office, yet friendliness from Democrat Stephen A. Douglas. The individual, not the party, earned their support.

In July 1842 former Missouri governor Lilburn W. Boggs appeared before a justice of the peace in Independence to charge Orrin Porter Rockwell, one of Joseph Smith's bodyguards, with attempted murder. Under an assumed name, Rockwell had been living in Independence with his in-laws while his wife awaited the birth of a child. On the rainy evening of May 6, an unknown assailant fired a pistol loaded with buckshot through the window of Boggs's home, severely injuring him. Shortly thereafter a bedraggled Rockwell arrived in Nauvoo. Rumors placed responsibility for the crime on the Mormons. The *Quincy Whig* reported that Joseph Smith had prophesied a year earlier that Boggs would meet a violent death. The Prophet quickly denied responsibility for the crime, but John C. Bennett urged Boggs to file a complaint. On August 8, on a warrant issued by Governor Carlin in response to a requisition from Governor Thomas Reynolds of Missouri, Joseph Smith was arrested as an accessory before the fact.

The extradition request contended erroneously that Joseph Smith had fled from Missouri following the shooting. Because the Prophet could readily establish his whereabouts in Illinois on the day of the shooting, he and Rockwell sought writs of habeas corpus through the Nauvoo municipal court. When Adams County officers challenged the court's jurisdiction, the city council enacted an ordinance broadening the court's powers. The arresting officers returned to Quincy disgruntled. Because the council's action was legally suspect, the Prophet secured a release from the master in chancery to be certain proper legal action had been taken. Then the two accused men went into hiding, the Prophet in the Nauvoo area, Rockwell in Pennsylvania and New Jersey.

John C. Bennett, influential associate of Joseph Smith, who later wrote much inflammatory literature against the Church. (From his book, The History of the Saints)

It was during these uncertain months of 1842 that the Prophet apparently first looked seriously toward the Rocky Mountains as a place of refuge. A few could go at first, perhaps fifty pioneers, followed by others who would establish a stake, perhaps in Oregon. Increased immigration would eventually make the Saints a powerful people, united with the Indians of the Rocky Mountain West. But these vague ideas were shelved for a year while extensive legal efforts cleared the way for the Prophet's acquittal in the Boggs case.

Letters from Emma Smith, the Female Relief Society, and prominent Nauvoo citizens failed to persuade Governor Carlin of the impropriety of the extradition order. He offered a reward for the fugitives' arrest. To counter the tide of hostile public opinion, a special conference on August 29 prepared documents answering assertions being circulated by John C. Bennett and others. A volunteer force of 380 elders was appointed to carry them to public officials and Church members in various states. Meantime, a legal opinion from Justin Butterfield, the United States district attorney in Chicago, urged the Prophet to seek dismissal of the charges from the governor or state supreme court. In December 1842, the court advised newly elected Governor Thomas Ford that the writ was illegal. Upon Ford's recommendation, and with Butterfield as his defense attorney, Joseph Smith went before Federal District Judge Nathan Pope, who discharged him on grounds that the requisition and warrant of the two state governors went beyond the statements in Boggs's original affidavit and therefore lacked foundation.

A third attempt by Missouri officials to return Joseph Smith to Independence for trial occurred during the congressional campaign of 1843. In this instance John C. Bennett instigated the action in a grand jury hearing in Daviess County, Missouri. The hearing revived the old charge of treason and followed the usual legal channels of a requisition from Governor Reynolds and a warrant for extradition from Governor Ford. The Prophet and his family were visiting with Emma's sister near Dixon, Lee County, Illinois, when the warrant servers took him into custody. The prisoner was carried to Dixon, where he obtained counsel. At the same time, Stephen Markham, who had been sent from Nauvoo with William Clayton to warn of the arresting officers' approach, filed warrants against the two lawmen involved, Sheriff Joseph H. Reynolds of Jackson County, Missouri, and Constable Harmon T.

Wilson of Hancock County, charging them with threatening Joseph's life and with false imprisonment. In this almost comic-opera situation all three indicted men sought hearings and headed toward Stephen A. Douglas's court in Quincy. Joseph, meantime, convinced his friends that the Nauvoo court had the power to try his case. Ushered into town by the mounted posse that had been sent to rescue him and by cheering citizens, this unusual party stopped in the Mormon city on June 30. Sheriff Reynolds refused to acknowledge the city court's jurisdiction or to present his writ for examination, but the court promptly released the Prophet on a writ of habeas corpus.

Disturbed by this development, the arresting officers proceeded quickly to Carthage and attempted to rouse public indignation. The sheriff sent a petition to the governor calling for a posse to retake the Prophet, but Ford honored the Nauvoo municipal court's decision. Certain Hancock County citizens, meanwhile, protested the legal maneuvering in Nauvoo. Reacting precipitously, the city council made it illegal to arrest Joseph Smith on Missouri grievances and required the mayor's approval of all outside warrants. Both measures strained the city charter and weakened Latter-day Saint arguments in the courts.

One of the attorneys who defended the Prophet against this third extradition attempt was Cyrus Walker, a Whig candidate for Congress in 1843, who agreed to provide legal assistance in return for the Prophet's vote in the upcoming election. This pledge placed President Smith in an awkward position when it appeared that opposing candidate Joseph P. Hoge, a Democrat, would better represent Mormon interests. In January 1843 Governor Ford had advised the Prophet to avoid "all political electioneerings." The Church leader replied that he had not created the political unity of his people by his own initiative, but that the Mormons had been united by persecution. In the congressional campaign, he let it be known that he would vote for Walker, but that his brother, Hyrum Smith, felt differently. In this way the Prophet kept his promise to cast his personal vote for the Whig candidate, while Hyrum Smith and John Taylor's *Nauvoo Neighbor* advised the Saints to vote for Hoge. Both congressional candidates, uncertain of Mormon leanings, spent four days campaigning in Nauvoo. The Mormon vote decided the election in Hoge's favor.

Understandably, the Whigs viewed the 1843 voting as a

Hyrum Smith, Church Patriarch and brother to the Prophet. Oil painting attributed to S. Maudsley. (Church Curator)

misuse of corporate political power. Even Democrats, who benefited from Mormon votes, joined the chorus of anti-Mormon feeling, for they saw that the power which worked for them might also work against them. Joseph Smith's attempt to keep the Church aloof from partisanship had been unsuccessful. Recognizing his own great political influence, he decided that he must use it wisely, though attempting to separate politics from religious doctrine. In February 1843 he told a group of workers on the Nauvoo Temple:

It is our duty to concentrate all our influence to make popular that which is sound and good, and unpopular that which is unsound. 'Tis right, politically, for a man who has influence to use it, as well as for a man who has no influence to use his. From henceforth I will maintain all the influence I can get. In relation to politics, I will speak as a man; but in relation to religion I will speak in authority.[2]

To many Saints, he also spoke with convincing authority in politics. To the non-Mormon citizens of Adams and Hancock Counties his authority had created an unwanted political voting bloc. The resulting fear and hatred would soon prove fatal to the Mormon community on the Mississippi.

Quest for Political Refuge

The ultimate aim of all Joseph Smith's political and legal activities was protection of himself and of the Kingdom. In this search for refuge he considered many options, including a politically independent Mormon enclave. If working within the system would not prevent conflict, perhaps peace could be found in Mormon political independence. One manifestation of this was territorial; the Saints considered removing themselves from involvement in gentile political society and forming an independent government. Another option was the formation of a new national political party.

During the troubles of 1843 the city council considered creating an essentially independent city-state within Illinois. Recognizing the impossibility of achieving such a goal through state and local politicians, a committee was appointed to petition the U.S. Congress. The lawmakers would be asked to establish Nauvoo as a federal district, with rights similar to those of territories. The new enclave would be regulated under the existing municipal charter and the Nauvoo Legion would be recognized as a federal army. This would provide a barrier of legal protection against non-Mormon intruders and a protective force to discourage mob invasions from Missouri. The city named Orson Hyde its delegate to Washington. Before his departure, however, other developments changed the nature of his mission.

In January 1843 Joseph Smith proposed an expansion of missionary work that would increase the gathering "by thousands

---

[2]Joseph Smith, *History of the Church*, 5:286.

and tens of thousands." Immigration of such vast numbers would require new stakes and new settlements, and the Prophet elaborated an enlarged vision of the Kingdom of God. As early as 1839 Henry Clay had recommended a Mormon state in Oregon Country, an area then held jointly by the United States and Great Britain. That same fall the *Quincy Whig* and James Arlington Bennett, a New York friend of the Church, independently recommended creation of a self-governing Mormon empire in the Northwest. Other Americans, imbued with the spirit of Manifest Destiny, also looked west to California, Oregon, and Texas; and Mormon leaders exhibited an increasing interest in identifying possible sites beyond the Mississippi for an expanding Mormon community.

The first direct exploration of routes west came in July and August 1843, when a small party under Jonathan Dunham examined lands in the western part of Iowa Territory. The following February Joseph Smith instructed the Twelve to prepare another group of volunteers to examine sites in California, which in that day extended eastward to the Rockies. Early in March 1844 Lyman Wight and George Miller presented an immediate colonizing plan. Their small company in the Black River valley pineries of Wisconsin had produced sufficient lumber to complete the temple and Nauvoo House. Government agents were moving Indians onto the land, and these Indians had expressed an interest in joining the Mormon settlers for an expedition to the warmer climate of the Texas tablelands. The leaders of the Wisconsin Branch, therefore, proposed a Texas gathering place that would be an Indian mission and a colony for converted southern slaveholders. The latter would preserve southern culture and allow southern Mormons to make a unique contribution to the Kingdom.

In response to the Wight-Miller proposal, Joseph Smith convened a special council on March 11, 1844, and charged it to study the plan. This council, called a "municipal department of the Kingdom," was known as the General Council, or the Council of Fifty. It was a secular committee designed to relieve the First Presidency and the Twelve of temporal responsibilities, though many Church leaders actually belonged. A few non-Mormons were also part of the group. In addition to considering the immediate proposal, the council drafted petitions to Congress seeking Mormons' civil rights and considered ways to "secure a resting place in the mountains, or some uninhabited region, where we can enjoy the liberty of conscience guaranteed to us by the Constitution."[3]

On the Texas question, the General Council designated Lucien Woodworth as its agent to make arrangements for an independent Mormon state in southwestern Texas. He left for Austin in mid-March and six weeks later reported progress toward a partial treaty permitting settlement. Contemplating the establishment of western cities as satellites to the Nauvoo headquarters, the General Council drafted a memorial to Congress asking permission to raise 100,000 volunteers as an army of settlers to protect those moving into uninhabited regions. The plan was presented as an economy measure to the government: the army would secure Texas for the Union and protect Oregon country against foreign intervention. It was this position that Orson Hyde finally carried to Washington, along with an alternative should Congress reject it.

By late April it was apparent to Elder Hyde that the Mormon plan was politically unacceptable. A better alternative, he told the General Council, would be to establish a base in Texas and then expand into California. In Congress, as expected, the Oregon proposal was rejected without a formal hearing. Stephen A. Douglas, meantime, provided the Latter-day Saint delegate with a map and description of Oregon and California. This description, the published report of John C. Frémont's recent explorations, was carefully studied by the Twelve two years later in planning the move west.

While Orson Hyde was discussing the Mormon dream of empire building with friendly congressmen, a general conference in April heard Joseph Smith proclaim a new doctrine that fit well with the Church's expanding political vision:

You know there has been great discussion in relation to Zion—where it is, and where the gathering of the dispensation is, and which I am now going to tell you. The prophets have spoken and written upon it; but I will make a proclamation that will cover a broader ground. *The whole of America is Zion itself from north to south.*[4]

In the same conference both Brigham Young and Hyrum Smith emphasized this enlarged concept of Zion. After they received

---

[3]Joseph Smith, *History of the Church,* 6:261.
[4]Joseph Smith, *History of the Church,* 6:318-19.

their temple endowments, the elders were to renew their missionary efforts, and the gathering was to take place all over both North and South America. Brigham Young called the plan "a perfect knockdown to the devil's kingdom," for the Church was to be built up in many places. Hopefully it would have enough political influence to create a more righteous nation.

These ideas may have been related to the Prophet's growing concept of his own role in government, for three months earlier he had declared his candidacy for the presidency of the United States. At the April conference Brigham Young said: "It is now time to have a President of the United States. Elders will be sent to preach the Gospel and electioneer. The government belongs to God." Hyrum Smith remarked: "Don't fear man or devil; electioneer with all people, male and female, and exhort them to do the thing that is right. We want a President of the U.S., not a party President, but a President of the whole people. . . . Lift up your voices like thunder: there is power and influence enough among us to put in a President."[5]

The decision to conduct a national political campaign was one aspect of the Prophet's search for ways to ensure the Saints' civil rights. Governor Ford had decided he could extend no executive protection without causing a local civil war, the national government had refused to involve itself, and Mormon political unity had alienated both political parties. In this setting the Prophet and his associates launched a full-scale effort to implement their ideal political concepts.

Implicit in the millennial concept of history held by most Latter-day Saints was the idea that the governments of men would ultimately fail, to be replaced by the just rule of the King of kings. Latter-day Saints during the 1830s and early 1840s often spoke of the establishment of this political kingdom. Sometimes they failed to distinguish between this anticipated government, which would rule people of all beliefs, and the existing priesthood, which would continue to regulate only the affairs of the Saints. Daniel's vision of a kingdom rolling forth to fill the earth was usually applied in a spiritual sense, but in the early 1840s it was increasingly given political interpretation. At least as early as 1842 those closest to Joseph Smith anticipated the establishment of a political entity

---

[5] Joseph Smith, *History of the Church*, 6:322-24.

outside the regular organization of the Church, although dominated by priesthood leaders. Known as the Kingdom of God, it
would prepare politically for the coming of the Savior and the
Millennium. The governing body was the Council of Fifty.
Though critics of the Church misinterpreted the actions of the
council, its main concern was to influence the establishment of
righteous government that would protect the rights of all, including the Saints, and prepare for the Millennium. The year 1844
seemed the right time to make the first great effort.

On October 1, 1843, the *Times and Seasons* printed an editorial
asking, "Who Shall Be Our Next President?" and concluding that
it must be a man willing to support the rights of the Saints. To ascertain the attitudes of five leading potential candidates on this
question, Joseph Smith sent letters to John C. Calhoun, Henry
Clay, Lewis Cass, Richard M. Johnson, and Martin Van Buren.
The letter spoke of mistreatment of the Latter-day Saints, "who
now constitute a numerous class in the school politic of this vast republic," and of their unsuccessful efforts to gain redress. It then
pointedly asked, " *'What will be your rule of action relative to us as a
people,'* should fortune favor your ascension to the chief
magistracy?" Only Clay and Calhoun replied. Clay refused to
make any commitment, while Calhoun echoed the arguments
heard from Washington in 1839—that such affairs were state matters over which the federal government had no jurisdiction. Both
prompted irate replies from Joseph Smith, who again emphasized
his more liberal views of the federal government's powers. "Who
shall be our next President?" echoed the *Nauvoo Neighbor* in its February 7, 1844, issue. The answer could only be: *"General Joseph
Smith."*

Already, on January 29, the Twelve had decided to press for
Joseph Smith's candidacy. On that date Joseph began working
with William W. Phelps on a statement of his own "Views of the
Powers and Policy of the Government of the United States." Soon
available in pamphlet form, the Prophet's platform did not mention religion but focused on current political concerns and incorporated planks adapted from the leading political parties. He advocated presidential intervention when states refused to suppress
mobs interfering with individual human rights. Further, he advocated the abolition of slavery before 1850 under state initiative,
but went beyond the abolitionist Liberty Party plank by suggest-

ing federal compensation to slave owners. His economic policy followed Henry Clay's "American System." He endorsed a judicious tariff whose revenues might foster economic expansion, and a federally owned national bank. Bank profits, he said, would pay government expenses, and he hoped to reduce taxes by encouraging economy in government and drastically trimming the size of Congress. The Prophet's foreign affairs plank called for annexation of Texas, Oregon, and any liberty-loving people. As a social reformer, he advocated prison reforms, proposed making civil felonies punishable by labor on highways or public works projects, and suggested imprisoning only those convicted of capital crimes. Even these men would be encouraged to reform themselves in penitentiaries that would become "seminaries of learning." Overall, the Prophet's "Views on . . . Government" leaned heavily toward the conservative economic views of leading Whigs, but included broad interpretation of federal responsibilities in civil affairs conditioned by his past experiences and the important abolitionist and expansionist planks of the Liberty and Democratic parties. It was, in essence, an attempt to formulate a "union" program.

The platform was essentially a secular document. Joseph Smith offered himself as a candidate on his personal merits as an involved citizen and not as a religious leader with peculiar insights into national policy. The direction of his campaign fell to his secular advisory body, the General Council. Even so, the distinction between the political and ecclesiastical kingdoms blurred. The Prophet accepted the nomination on the condition that the machinery of church government would work for his election. At the April conference, speakers endorsed and the congregation unanimously affirmed Joseph Smith's candidacy. More than three hundred people volunteered to preach the restored gospel and campaign for him across the nation. The Council of the Twelve appointed elders to supervise these political missionaries in each state and set dates for a series of thirty-seven state and regional conferences. Sidney Rigdon, first counselor in the First Presidency, was named vice-presidential candidate. The National Reform party confirmed the nomination of its candidates in a state convention at Nauvoo May 17 and scheduled a national meeting for Baltimore, Maryland, in mid-July. The Council of Fifty adjourned on April 25 to join the campaigning. These political missions took the majority of Mormon leaders away from Nauvoo during the spring and early summer of 1844.

In their own view the elders of Israel went forth to win converts to the idea that the nation's strength lay in unity. Reacting against fierce partisanship, they supported a candidate who sought peace and justice. Joseph Smith envisioned an American government led by righteous men and ultimately a political kingdom under the Man of Righteousness himself. Perhaps it was politically impractical, and the candidate may have realized the unlikelihood of his actual election. But given the controversies that alienated him from all other parties, he felt that it was a necessary campaign.

The Martyrdom

The search for political and religious refuge ended abruptly for Joseph Smith in June 1844. While his supporters campaigned on a platform designed to unite factions under an inspired government ruled by good men, a disgruntled cabal plotted dissension at home. Mormon apostates, influential men once close advisers to the Prophet, were setting in motion events that would lead to his murder.

The rumors that fed the fears of non-Mormons in Hancock County burgeoned after several key Latter-day Saints became disaffected and joined the opposition. The most prominent defector was John C. Bennett, whose much-publicized departure from Nauvoo in May 1842 created a sensation in both camps. The break had come gradually. Not long after Bennett's arrival in Nauvoo in September 1840, an old acquaintance wrote to Joseph Smith that the supposed bachelor had a wife and family in Ohio from whom he was estranged because of adulterous activities there. Affiliation with the Church in Nauvoo apparently did not reform him, for Bennett seduced a young woman there through a misapplication of the doctrine of plural marriage. Church leaders privately confronted Bennett with his past in mid-1841, and the following spring began publicly refuting the argument he was using to cover his amours. At a parade ground maneuver of the Nauvoo Legion on May 7, 1842, Joseph learned that Bennett had planned to assassinate him. Bodyguards foiled the plot, and ten days later Bennett resigned as mayor of Nauvoo. During the following month he and others confessed licentious conduct and pleaded for mercy.

Expelled from the Church, he shortly left Nauvoo.

Immediately Bennett began publicizing his rift in area newspapers, accusing Mormon leaders of threatening his life, swindling local residents, immorality, and plotting the conquest of several midwestern states. His serialized exposé in the *Sangamo Journal* during the summmer of 1842 was collected and published a few months later as *The History of the Saints; or, an Exposé of Joe Smith and the Mormons.* To counteract these scandalous accounts, Church leaders published an extensive review of the entire affair and sent special missionaries into neighboring settlements.

Bennett's distorted exposures caused some Saints to waver and a few to leave the Church. In April 1844 several of those who disagreed with the Prophet over the plurality of wives and other new doctrines withdrew and organized a reform church based on teachings as they had stood in 1838. The dissenters included William Law of the First Presidency, his brother Wilson Law, Austin Cowles of the Nauvoo high council, James Blakeslee, Charles G. Foster, Francis M. Higbee, and businessmen Robert D. Foster, Chauncey Higbee, and Charles Ivins. The grievances of these men and about two hundred others who joined with them extended beyond polygamy. Joining the seceders, for example, were the land agents who had been chastized for selling lots in upper Nauvoo in competition with the more expensive church-owned lots on the flat. Other leading participants claimed they had been unjustly excommunicated. Denouncing Joseph Smith as a fallen prophet, a political demagogue, an immoral scoundrel, and a financial schemer, these men publicized their charges in a newspaper inaugurated June 7, 1844, as the *Nauvoo Expositor.*

Reaction came quickly from those attacked in the paper. The city council met in long sessions on Saturday, June 8, and again the following Monday. The councilmen suspended one of their own number, non-Mormon Sylvestor Emmons, who was editor of the *Expositor,* and discussed the identity of the publishers and the intent of the newspaper. After analyzing legal precedents and municipal codes, the council decided the paper was a public nuisance that had slandered individuals in the city. Public indignation threatened mob action against the paper, they reasoned, and if the council failed to respond, the libelous newspaper would arouse anti-Mormon mobs. Early Monday evening the council acted under the nuisance ordinance. The mayor, Joseph Smith, then

Well-known Charles B. Hall engraving of the Carthage Jail. (Church Archives)

ordered the city marshal to destroy the press, scatter the type, and burn available papers. Within hours the order had been executed. The publishers, ostensibly fearing for their personal safety, fled to Carthage, where they obtained an arrest warrant against the Nauvoo city council on a charge of riot.

The council had acted legally in its right to abate a nuisance, though contemporary legal opinion allowed only the destruction of published issues of an offending paper, not destruction of the printing press itself. The city fathers had not violated the constitutional guarantees of freedom of the press, though they had probably erred in violating property rights. Witnesses affirmed that even this intrusion had been orderly, and, contrary to the publishers' claims, there had been no riot. Joseph Smith was released on June 13 following a habeas corpus hearing before the municipal court of Nauvoo. On the following day, as judge of the same court, he dismissed the other defendants.

Authorized only to hold a preliminary hearing, the Nauvoo court had exceeded its authority in deciding a riot case with finality. A few days later, to quiet public indignation and at the suggestion of the state circuit judge, Joseph Smith and fifteen others named in the complaint repeated the process of examination before Justice Daniel H. Wells. Again they were discharged, but again the inquiring judge was only a justice of the peace without authority to acquit. A few of the defendants later submitted to a trial before a circuit court jury and were legally acquitted. This release came too late to calm the storm that eventually claimed two lives at Carthage.

The brashness and swiftness of the city council's retaliatory action against the *Expositor* and the easy release from trial of those responsible gave those plotting against the Prophet's life ammunition for their scheme. Anti-Mormon newspapers called for the Saints' extermination. At Warsaw and Carthage, citizens' committees sustained this feeling with formal resolutions. In response, Joseph Smith mobilized his guards and the Nauvoo Legion, and on June 18 he placed the city under martial law. At the same time he furnished detailed information on the matter to Governor Ford and requested a thorough investigation. The citizens of Hancock County, meantime, importuned the governor to mobilize the state militia to ensure justice for the Nauvoo offenders.

So intense was the excitement on both sides that the chief executive published an open letter urging calmness, then personally traveled to Carthage to neutralize a situation that threatened civil war. At the county seat he found a large citizens' posse being formed. Ford obtained a pledge of strict legality and nonviolence toward the defendants. At the governor's request, Joseph Smith ordered the Nauvoo Legion to surrender its state arms to equalize forces and as a demonstration of good faith.

Governor Ford believed that the only way to settle the *Expositor* charges would be a trial at Carthage, the county seat. Therefore, on June 25, after negotiations over the legal procedures to be followed and after receiving a guarantee of protection from Ford, the fifteen men named in the riot charge voluntarily presented themselves to officials at the county seat. A justice of the peace reviewed the case and freed the defendants on bonds pending a trial at the October term of the circuit court. The Nauvoo party retired to the Hamilton House, a nearby hotel, but later that evening Joseph and Hyrum were jailed under an improperly issued writ granted by Robert F. Smith, a justice of the peace and captain of the Carthage Greys. The writ was issued in response to a warrant charging the Smiths with treason for declaring martial law. It was enforced without a hearing.

John Taylor, Willard Richards, Dan Jones, Stephen

Markham, and John S. Fullmer accompanied Joseph and Hyrum to jail. When Jones, Markham, and Fullmer left on errands, they were refused reentrance. On June 26, Governor Ford visited the jail. In the discussion that followed, Joseph Smith defended his mobilization of the legion as a precautionary measure. He explained that he had had no intention of invading non-Mormon regions as his accusers claimed. He also satisfied the governor concerning the city council's action and offered to pay for the property damaged if that would appease those plotting for his destruction.

A week before leaving Nauvoo, Joseph had climbed atop the framing of an unfinished building to address the Nauvoo Legion. In his last public statement to an assemblage at Church headquarters, he noted that the *Warsaw Signal* had called for his death and for the expulsion of the Saints. With sword drawn, the Mormon leader had secured the militia's solemn pledge to fight with him, to the death if necessary, in defense of their rights. During the following week, when faced with arrest, and amid open threats against his life, the Prophet's first reaction had been to flee. On June 23 he crossed the Mississippi, intending to seek refuge in the safety of the Rocky Mountains, hoping that this would protect his life and save the Church further harassment. Some of his friends, however, believed mobs would drive the Saints from their homes despite the Prophet's departure. Pleas from them and from Emma urged him to submit to the law, which he did. Uncertain that justice would be fairly administered in the hands of his enemies, he expressed hints of his fears to those on the road with him to Carthage. One of them remembered his words: "I am going like a lamb to the slaughter, but I am calm as a summer's morning. I have a conscience void of offense toward God and toward all men. If they take my life I shall die an innocent man. . . . "[6]

Now the death of Joseph Smith appeared certain. After his interview with the imprisoned prophet, Governor Ford disbanded the state militia at Carthage, except for two companies of the anti-Mormon Carthage Greys assigned to guard the jail. He took a third company with him to Nauvoo. Although warned of a plot to kill the Prophet, he resisted the rumor and left for the city of the Saints on the morning of June 27, ignoring his promise to allow the prisoners to accompany him. Ford found Nauvoo alert but quiet.

---

[6]Joseph Smith, *History of the Church,* 6:555.

"Last Public Address of Lieut. General Joseph Smith," an 1887 painting by Utah artist John Hafen. The painting is an idealization of the Nauvoo period and incorporates a number of historical inaccuracies, such as the Nauvoo Legion in full uniform and a tower that was not erected on the temple until after Joseph's death. (Church Archives)

At Carthage, meanwhile, a body of men from the disbanded Warsaw regiment daubed their faces with mud and gunpowder, rushed the jail, and quickly overpowered the cooperative guards, who had agreed in advance to load their guns without balls. The assailants rushed upstairs to the jailer's sleeping room where the four Latter-day Saint leaders waited. John Taylor and Willard

Richards were armed with stout canes; the Prophet carried a six-barrel revolver and his brother a single-shot pistol.

Suddenly, shots from the narrow hallway punctured the thin bedroom door. One ball struck Hyrum Smith in the face; another from outside hit him in the back. He fell, mortally wounded. Opening the door partway, Joseph Smith shot into the hallway; three of the six barrels misfired. Two additional balls through the doorway punctured the dying Hyrum's chest and leg. Then, with bayonets and muskets threatening through the doorway, John Taylor moved toward an outside window. A ball from the doorway struck his leg; another, from outside, smashed into the watch in his vest pocket, knocking him to the floor. Elder Taylor was hit next in the wrist, then the knee. He rolled under a bed in the far corner, where he was hit a fifth time with a ball that tore away the flesh of his hip. Leaving Willard Richards alone behind the door, Joseph Smith tried the same escape. Two balls hit him from the open door, another from outside the window. Mortally wounded, he plunged through the window, exclaiming in a last plea for help, "Oh Lord, my God. . . ."

Immediately the attackers inside the jail rushed outside to assure themselves that the object of their attack was dead. Elder Richards and the wounded Elder Taylor remained in the inner prison cell. Part of the mob reentered the jail but finding only Hyrum at first glance, they left amid cries from outside that a posse of Mormons was coming. Though the rumor was untrue, the mobbers fled.

Of the four Latter-day Saints at Carthage Jail, only Willard Richards remained uninjured. Samuel Smith, who happened on the scene soon after the murders, helped Elder Richards arrange for removal of the bodies to the Hamilton House, where John Taylor was also carried. Elder Richards participated in the coroner's inquiry before Justice of the Peace Robert F. Smith, and wrote a quick note informing the Church at Nauvoo: "Joseph and Hyrum are dead."

A cannon's booming notified conspirators waiting in Warsaw and across the river in Missouri that the deed was accomplished. At about the same time, Governor Ford was addressing the Saints in Nauvoo. Cutting short his stay in the city, he was on the road toward Carthage when two messengers hurrying to Nauvoo informed him of the murders. Fearing retaliation from the Nauvoo

Legion, Ford urged the citizens of Carthage to evacuate and ordered county records moved to Quincy for safety. Uncertain of further action by anti-Mormons, he also wrote a message to the citizens of Nauvoo urging them to prepare to defend themselves. Just before midnight he consulted with Willard Richards, who sent another message to Nauvoo urging the Saints to remain calm, stay in the city, and take precautions against a mob attack. Neither side, however, was disposed to be the aggressor, and the alarm soon quieted as the implications of the murders settled on those concerned. A melancholy calm pervaded Nauvoo.

On June 28 the bodies of Mormonism's two leading figures were transported by wagon to the city. A solemn crowd waited in the streets and along the road toward Carthage. The bodies lay in state the following day at the Mansion House while thousands filed silently past the coffins and William W. Phelps preached a funeral sermon in the grove. The next event displayed the tension of the times. Just before the scheduled burial on the temple block, the simple coffins were removed from their pine burial vaults. The vaults, weighted with sandbags, were interred before a sorrowing congregation. The coffins containing the bodies were destined for a secret midnight burial in the basement of the unfinished Nauvoo House to keep them from mutilation by the mob. A few months later Emma had the bodies secretly transferred to a spot behind the Homestead. Here they remained, in an unmarked grave, until 1928, when the two martyrs were reburied beside the grave of Emma Smith at Nauvoo.

Reactions of the Illinois press to the assassinations were mixed. Thomas C. Sharp of the *Warsaw Signal* applauded the deaths and reiterated his call for the Saints' removal. Many other local editors reacted with disbelief, astonishment, and disgust. Newspapers elsewhere in the United States generally echoed this denunciation. In their view the mob had violated the canons of justice by interfering with the due process of law in a cowardly act of cold-blooded murder.

Lists of persons believed implicated in Joseph Smith's murder were compiled by Sheriff J. B. Backenstos and Willard Richards. By late October indictments had been issued for eight men. Three of them left town, and a two-week trial the following May acquitted the remaining defendants. In June 1845 a jury gave a similar verdict to those accused of Hyrum Smith's murder. Contradictory evidence and the reluctance of guards to testify were key factors in the juries' decisions. Counsel for the accused argued that the murders had been a consensus of public opinion and thus no individual could be held responsible for what the populace decreed was legal. In essence, the murders had been justified by recourse to lynch law. Joseph Smith's opponents had turned vigilante, but in doing so they had misused even that extralegal means of popular justice.

At the death of the Prophet Joseph Smith, a universal sadness spread among the Saints, for he was revered as a man who had talked with God and who had guided the Church by revelation. His cheerful temperament combined with his profound ability to impress and inspire left a deep and permanent impact on the lives of those who knew him best. All this was accompanied by the creation of an impressive body of literature designed to perpetuate his memory and give recognition to his role as the Prophet of the Restoration. It was most profoundly expressed in an important essay, now part of the Doctrine and Covenants, which declared that "Joseph Smith, the Prophet and Seer of the Lord, has done more, save Jesus only, for the salvation of men in this world, than any other man that ever lived in it."[7] It was also expressed in such hymns as "Oh Give Me Back My Prophet Dear," and "The Seer, Joseph, the Seer," by John Taylor, as well as "Praise to the Man Who Communed with Jehovah," by W. W. Phelps. Other hymns, such as "Oh, How Lovely Was the Morning" by George Manwaring and "I Saw a Mighty Angel Fly" by George Careless, found a permanent place among the Saints and helped keep alive in their consciousness Joseph's role in the restoration. Typical of the deep feelings of those who knew him best was a poem by Eliza R. Snow on "The Assassination of Generals Joseph and Hyrum Smith," part of which reads:

> For never, since the Son of God was slain
> Has blood so noble flow'd from human vein.

The Interlude: Energizing the Prophet's Program

The private war of Mormonism's chief opponents quieted briefly after the martyrdom. For Nauvoo there was an interlude of

---

[7]D&C 135:3.

peace and an opportunity for renewed growth. The immediate question facing the Saints was one of leadership. The Prophet's role had been partly charismatic. Could his associates in the presiding councils fill the void? To whom did the leadership rightfully belong? To some Mormon-haters, Joseph Smith's death meant the end of Mormonism. To the Saints, life necessarily went on much as usual. With a commitment beyond the loyalty they felt to one man, they looked to the existing organization, expecting it to build upon the foundation Joseph had laid in his mission of restoration.

The question of leadership was complicated, partly because it had never been faced before, and amid the many problems of the Church, it had not been thoroughly discussed. William Law of the First Presidency had been excommunicated in April 1844 and his position as second counselor not filled. The Prophet had intended to replace Sidney Rigdon with Amasa Lyman, but the nomination was never made because Rigdon's impassioned pleadings at the October 1843 general conference induced the congregation to retain him as first counselor, contrary to the Prophet's wishes. Even so, the unstable Rigdon's participation in church affairs had been minimal during the Nauvoo years, and at his own request he had been appointed to a local presidency in Pittsburgh.

President Rigdon was much less well known by the general membership in Nauvoo than were the active members of the Twelve. At the time of the martyrdom, however, all the apostles except John Taylor and Willard Richards were away on campaigning and preaching missions. When word of the murders reached them about mid-July, all except John E. Page and William Smith recognized the responsibility they must bear in continuing the Prophet's work, and they headed for Nauvoo. Brigham Young remembered his reaction to the news:

> The first thing which I thought of was, whether Joseph had taken the keys of the kingdom with him from the earth; brother Orson Pratt sat on my left; we were both leaning back on our chairs. Bringing my hand down on my knee, I said the keys of the kingdom are right here with the Church.[8]

On July 18 Brigham Young, Wilford Woodruff, Orson Hyde,

---

[8]Eldon J. Watson, ed., *Manuscript History of Brigham Young, 1801-1844* (Salt Lake City: Eldon J. Watson, 1960), p. 171.

Heber C. Kimball, and Orson Pratt held a tearful reunion in Boston. Then they issued an epistle instructing all quorum presidents and authorities away from Nauvoo to gather there immediately.

Joseph Smith had ordained his brother Hyrum both patriarch and assistant president. The latter calling could have given Hyrum a claim to the presidency had he lived, and the precedent of this ordination encouraged Sidney Rigdon to advance his own claim as the sole remaining member of the presiding quorum of three presidents. Arriving in Nauvoo on Saturday, August 3, the ambitious Rigdon spurned an invitation to meet with the available apostles. He presented himself instead at the regular Sunday morning service in the grove. There he announced a vision outlining the need for a guardian to "build the church up to Joseph," and suggested that the ancient prophets had foreseen that Rigdon himself should step forth as "guardian" (meaning president and trustee). Rigdon asked stake president William Marks to call a special conference for Tuesday, August 6, to confirm selection of a new leader, but Marks called it for August 8. This providential delay allowed Brigham Young and three of his traveling companions to be present for the deliberations, joining the five members of the Twelve already in the city.

On the morning of the seventh, though weary from their long journey, the Twelve immediately began to fill the leadership gap. They called in the high council and high priests at the Seventies' Hall to hear President Rigdon's proposal. "Joseph sustains the same relationship to this church as he has always done," Rigdon said. "No man can be the successor of Joseph. . . . The martyred Prophet is still the head of this church. . . . I have been consecrated a spokesman to Joseph, and I was commanded to speak for him. The church is not disorganized though our head is gone." The senior apostle, Brigham Young, replied:

> I do not care who leads the church, even though it were Ann Lee; but one thing I must know, and that is what God says about it. I have the keys and the means of obtaining the mind of God on the subject. . . .
>
> Joseph conferred upon our heads all the keys and powers belonging to the Apostleship which he himself held before he was taken away, and no man or set of men can get between Joseph and the Twelve in this world or in the world to come.
>
> How often has Joseph said to the Twelve, "I have laid the founda-

tion and you must build thereon, for upon your shoulders the kingdom rests."[9]

Rigdon believed that a counselor to Joseph Smith was in direct line of succession. To Brigham Young, the counselor stood *beside* the President, not between him and the Twelve.

Despite their differences, the spokesmen for these two claims to leadership agreed that the priesthood of the Church should be assembled to rule on the matter. President Young suggested a solemn assembly for the following Tuesday, but as the call had already gone out for a meeting the next day, he attended. The gathering was larger than usual for outdoor meetings in Nauvoo, and the Saints strained to hear what was being said over the noises of the wind and the crowd. Speaking from a wagon box, President Rigdon rehearsed his claim for an hour and a half during the morning meeting. In the afternoon President Young discussed the nature of church government, the claim of the Twelve to the keys of the priesthood, and the authority of that quorum to ordain a new president if and when one would be chosen. "We have a head," he explained, "and that head is the Apostleship, the spirit and power of Joseph, and we can now begin to see the necessity of that Apostleship."[10] Following remarks by three other speakers, the congregation lifted its hands to sustain the Twelve as recognized leaders—specifically, to act in the office of the First Presidency. This sustaining action was repeated dozens of times as local conferences convened in quarterly sessions throughout the Church. To the satisfaction of most members the problem of leadership was resolved, though conflicting claims would later be advanced by others.

In other business, the Nauvoo conference voted to continue contributions for the temple, agreed to allow the Twelve to delegate management of church finances to bishops, and admonished the Twelve to select a new Church Patriarch. The membership also sustained President Rigdon in full fellowship. Several weeks later, however, the disappointed counselor asserted claims to an authority superior to that of the Twelve, and on September 8 he was excommunicated. He returned to Pittsburgh and the following spring organized a "Church of Christ" with apostles, prophets,

---

[9]Joseph Smith, *History of the Church*, 7:229-30.
[10]Joseph Smith, *History of the Church*, 7:235.

priests, and "kings," which attracted a few who opposed the Twelve or who had rejected the teaching on plural marriage.

For many who remained with the body of the Church in Nauvoo, Brigham Young's calling as President of the Twelve and the First Presidency had been sanctioned by a divine witness. Some of the Saints in the congregation on August 8 had heard their new leader's voice as if it were the voice of Joseph Smith. "If I had not seen him with my own eyes, there is no one that could have convinced me that it was not Joseph Smith," Wilford Woodruff declared later in recalling the event.[11] The mantle of the Prophet had fallen upon a man who would direct the affairs of the Latter-day Saints for more than three decades. He began that task immediately.

The policies that Brigham Young and the Twelve endorsed in accepting the responsibility of the Kingdom were those previously outlined by Joseph Smith. They put the missionary work in order, studied Joseph Smith's plan for an expansion of gathering places, and vigorously pushed industrial development and construction in Nauvoo, especially the erection of the temple. At the October conference the new leaders were formally sustained. Brigham Young's firm-handed approach and administrative skills were clearly evident in frequent councils with the apostles, the Council of Fifty, the city council, church trustees, and temple committees. Epistles over his signature on behalf of the Twelve instructed the Church frequently on matters of temporal and spiritual urgency.

These months were a time for setting the affairs of the Church in order. The Twelve found a place for Amasa M. Lyman among their number, and in May 1845 ordained William Smith to his inherited position as Church Patriarch. Wilford Woodruff was sent to preside in England, with jurisdiction over all of Europe. Supervision of affairs in North America was given to a committee of three who would become the First Presidency three years later: Brigham Young, Heber C. Kimball, and Willard Richards. Before year's end, Parley P. Pratt was called to New York as president, publisher, and immigration agent in the eastern states and provinces. To handle the managerial and clerical functions of the Church, the Twelve appointed senior bishops Newel K. Whitney and George Miller to the office of trustee, which Joseph Smith had

---

[11]*Deseret Semi-weekly News*, March 15, 1892.

Seventies Hall, Nauvoo, Illinois, rebuilt in early 1970s by Nauvoo Restoration, Incorporated. (Nauvoo Restoration, Inc.)

held, freeing Brigham Young from details of financial affairs; Willard Richards continued as historian and recorder.

The administrative committee for the American continent, recognizing that administration of the hundreds of scattered branches needed to be tightened, decided to organize them after the pattern established by the Twelve in England and Scotland. The plan was to appoint a high priest over each congressional district in the United States and a bishop in each larger branch. Presiding elders in the branches would be accountable to the district president at quarterly conferences. At the October 1844 general conference eighty-five names were presented as district presidents. Each president was instructed to move permanently to his assigned location and raise up a stake. Reuben McBride, for example, was assigned to Kirtland, Ohio, and George P. Dykes was established on a one-hundred-acre townsite named Norway, among the Norwegian Saints he had helped convert in LaSalle County, Illinois. Unfortunately, this ambitious design, a fulfillment of Joseph Smith's pronouncement that all of America was Zion, was curtailed by the evacuation of 1846.

At Nauvoo, the local priesthood received encouragement for greater activity. President Young urged the Aaronic Priesthood to visit regularly the homes of the Saints, and the deacons to fulfill their responsibility in assisting the bishops in their care for the poor. Within the Melchizedek Priesthood, the number of seventies multiplied rapidly. The sixty-three members of the first quorum became presidents over nine new quorums, and additional quorums were created under the supervision of the first seven presidents. By January 1846 at least thirty quorums were functioning—holding quorum meetings, participating in missionary work, and assisting in local assignments. In addition, the Seventies Hall was pushed to completion. To increase use of this two-story brick meetinghouse, George A. Smith of the Twelve urged the quorums to organize a preparatory school for missionaries.

The Twelve also gave attention to Joseph Smith's plans for western colonizing missions beyond United States boundaries, but they were simultaneously confronted with troublesome schisms and unauthorized western plans. Joseph Smith had authorized Elder Lyman Wight and Bishop George Miller to establish a stake in Texas. Initially, the Twelve endorsed the still unrealized proposal, but when its sponsors' solicitations aroused talk of a general exodus, Church leaders reconsidered. By late August Elder Wight was being counseled to limit his company to those with him at the pineries and to go north instead of south. He rejected this last advice and took the Wisconsin Saints on a long trek beyond the Red River, where he moved from place to place in successive settlement attempts. In April 1845 the Council of Fifty invited the Texas Saints back to Nauvoo, but Elder Wight, whom William W. Phelps had dubbed the "Wild Ram of the Mountains" because of his independent spirit, persisted in his separatist course. Refusal to cooperate with his colleagues led to his disfellowshipment in 1848.

Another man who led an expedition against the will of the Twelve was James Emmett, a member of the Oregon-California exploring party organized by the Prophet in February 1844. Without the sanction of the Twelve, Emmett left Nauvoo for the West about September with one hundred persons. He placed them under covenant to hold all property in common and to stand together in their venture. The Twelve on at least two occasions sent emissaries to consult with the migrating party, which Brigham Young's manuscript history labeled as excessively fanatic. Though Emmett confessed his error and sought forgiveness in the fall of 1845, he continued to disregard counsel, moved across Iowa into Sioux country, and finally was reprimanded by disfellowshipment two years later. Unlike Wight, Emmett was headed geographically in the right direction. His journey toward the setting sun was simply ahead of its time.

Church leaders characterized those leading groups away from the City of Joseph as opponents of the Prophet's revealed program of building a city and a temple. If fear of hostile action or expectations of a better life elsewhere influenced too many members to scatter, the Twelve reasoned, the dispersion would endanger the incomplete projects at the central gathering place. It was important to build up branches in the East, but it was wrong to leave Nauvoo for premature settlements in the West.

The energetic direction of the Twelve launched Nauvoo into its most visible prosperity. Though foodstuffs remained scarce at times and industry failed to materialize, the city of log and frame residences acquired an impressive new look. Construction once again dominated economic life. Numerous new frame and brick homes were erected. Brigham Young added two wings on his house for an office and for his growing family late in 1844; Heber C. Kimball and Willard Richards built their two-story brick houses the following year; John D. Lee completed his residence; and the authorities began a home for Lucy Mack Smith, widowed since the death of Joseph Smith, Sr., in 1840.

Public construction projects complemented the residential building boom. Besides the Seventies' Hall, a Concert Hall was completed. The Twelve also attempted to implement the Prophet's plan for a large hotel facing Main Street and the river, known as the Nauvoo House. In late 1845, brickwork commenced atop the stone foundations, only to be abandoned the following spring with part of the first-story walls erect. Another business enterprise left incomplete was the Mississippi River stone dike intended as a ship lock and waterhead for shops and machinery.

Both before and after the martyrdom, Nauvoo's most important building project was the Latter-day Saint temple, and the Twelve gave it priority over all other physical programs. Completion of the temple became a rallying point for those who retained

Charles B. Hall engraving of Brigham Young home at Nauvoo. (*Church Archives*)

their allegiance to the apostolic leadership. Brigham Young and the Twelve met frequently with temple committeemen Reynolds Cahoon and Alpheus Cutler and architect William Weeks. Relief Society sisters recommitted themselves to contribute a penny a week per member for glass and nails. Limestone blocks for the second story were laid by the fall of 1844, and the first of the large sunstones was raised into place. By late spring of the following year the trumpet stones and capstones had been positioned. The placing of the capstones was celebrated on May 24 with an appropriate ceremony accompanied by shouts of "Hosanna!" Workers next assembled the roof, finished the interior, removed the temporary baptismal font, and started carving a stone basin and oxen. Formal dedication was planned for April 1846.

While this work proceeded, the peaceable détente in Hancock County fell apart. Stresses that had led to the death of Joseph and Hyrum Smith reappeared, eventually leading to the abandonment of Nauvoo. Latter-day Saint officials publicly spoke as if the Nauvoo settlement would be permanent, but at the same time they quietly laid plans for evacuation. They hoped to buy time to complete the monument to Joseph before surrendering it.

In August 1844, as an election neared, Brigham Young informed the Saints he intended to avoid politics. Individual members, too, should remain aloof from the electioneering, he advised, although in this they had their agency. No national presidential candidate received Church endorsement. Locally, two of the three county commissioners elected in Hancock County were Latter-day Saints. Church members now controlled county government in cooperation with the sympathetic Sheriff Jacob B. Backenstos. The county also elected Mormon Representative Almon W. Babbitt to speak for it in the state assembly.

At Springfield Babbitt faced revival of an effort to repeal the Nauvoo charter. Less radical elements hoped merely to amend it, to remove the power of the municipal court and clip the Legion's independent strength, but highly vocal opponents of Nauvoo's political strength advocated total repeal. When the issue came to a vote, the Democratically controlled legislature announced nearly two-to-one for repeal. The final tally on January 24, 1845, left Nauvoo without government.

The repeal of chartered government concerned the Saints most in matters of police protection and the courts. These arms of government, along with the Nauvoo Legion, had been effective in affording a defense against harassment. Recognizing an urgent need for continued defensive preparedness, Nauvoo militia officers initially decided to reorganize as an extralegal citizens' army, or "new police." During an organizational meeting in March, however, they evolved an unusual alternative. They gave their protective force quasi-legal standing by organizing it under the structure of the priesthood. Thereafter, a countywide militia or police force composed of "quorums" of twelve men acting as "deacons" under the supervision of "bishops" patrolled the streets day and night and served as bodyguards for General Authorities. Brigham Young called this new interim government "The City of Joseph," a name approved at a special April conference.

In the meantime the Twelve asked Governor Ford about reorganizing the city under existing state legislation for towns. Ford was encouraging, and on April 16, 1845, citizens incorporated a one-mile-square section of the city, the maximum size allowed under the law, as a new town called Nauvoo. This government provided for justices of the peace, a council of five trustees, and other officers. The old police who had served faithfully under the charter were appointed en masse to serve the new town under their captain, Hosea Stout. Besides these regular officers, Nauvoo was watched by a "whistling and whittling brigade" of young men and boys armed with knives and sticks. Like a swarm of flies, they followed unwanted visitors as an unspeaking annoyance until the irritated persons left town. The brigade was a further protection for beleaguered Church leaders.

The disincorporated Nauvoo Legion, reorganized as the New Police, or Deacons, continued as an extralegal emergency force (under the priesthood) after the incorporation of the town of Nauvoo. Charles C. Rich had succeeded John C. Bennett as major general of the Nauvoo Legion, and Brigham Young had become lieutenant general. New titles were necessary when the municipal army became a priesthood-sponsored militia. Thus, in a letter in September 1845, President Young addressed Rich as "President of all the Organized Quorums of the Church of Jesus Christ of Latter-day Saints in Hancock County." Elder Rich was told to hold the quorums in readiness to act in response to threats against Morley's Settlement. This was consistent with Governor Ford's advice in April when he urged the Saints to prepare for self-defense.

Public cries against the Saints quieted after the martyrdom, but during the summer of 1845 antagonistic local newspapers again raised their voices. Thomas C. Sharp's *Warsaw Signal* revived its opposition to Mormon officeholders, reopening the debate over Mormon political activity and providing a smokescreen for a barrage of vandalism on Mormon property. Anti-Mormons and cooperating apostates hoped to drive the Saints from scattered settlements into Nauvoo and ultimately to force the entire religious community from Illinois.

Even before this direct harassment commenced, Church leaders reactivated plans for removing the entire membership beyond the borders of the United States. At a New Year's Day party in 1845 attended by several of the Twelve and their wives, and later the following week, the "Great Western Measure" was discussed. During consultations in February and early March, the Council of Fifty instructed Lewis Dana to lead a party of six or eight men to search for a settlement site. Dana, an Oneida Indian convert, had been recently installed as a member of the council. The party's departure in April was recorded in the official annals as "a mission to the Lamanites." Little is known of its efforts, except that the men were back in Nauvoo by summer's end.

The Latter-day Saint resettlement committees considered all three great western territories as potential sites: Texas, then an independent nation; Upper California, an ill-defined and loosely governed Mexican province; and Oregon, the entire American Northwest, jointly claimed by the United States and England. In early 1845 the Mormon leaders were privately favoring a central location somewhere in the middle Rockies or along the eastern rim of the Great Basin. At the same time they also asked non-Mormon friends and government officials for advice. Contacts in Illinois suggested asking Congress for a land grant for exclusive Mormon use. Governor Ford, who had known for nearly a year of Joseph Smith's colonizing plans, quietly proposed an independent Mormon government in California. He warned, however, that the federal government would feel obligated to oppose any such invasion of foreign soil if notified in advance. In March and April a Church committee invited President James K. Polk and governors of states outside Illinois and Missouri to propose solutions to the Mormon problem. The committee itself projected three alternatives: (1) the existing state or federal governments should provide

Charles B. Hall engraving of Heber C. Kimball home, Nauvoo, Illinois. (*Church Archives*)

an asylum free from persecution for the Saints; (2) they should support the Mormon attempt to seek redress for losses; or (3) the Church would find it necessary to withdraw from American society and settle in a remote region. The very few chief executives who responded favored this last alternative.

Private talk of abandoning Nauvoo did not interrupt public activities to strengthen the city during 1845. Industrial development received special attention from the Council of Fifty during these last months in Nauvoo. With encouragement from John Taylor, a meeting of local trade committees urged the development of manufacturing, home industry, and youth enterprises such as the weaving of straw hats and willow baskets. In January 1845 Elder Taylor helped organize the Mercantile and Mechanical Association. The following month Nauvoo's Agriculture and Manufacturing Society began work on the long-envisioned Mississippi River dam.

Despite these activities and Church officials' quiet plans for the evacuation of the city, all surplus energies were directed toward completion of the temple. The edifice that the Saints had been commanded of God to build must be finished so that worthy members could participate in the sacred endowment ceremony before the exodus. Early in 1845 an appeal went out to scattered members for volunteers to work during the summer. Special missionaries visited the branches to collect tithing, and John M. Bernhisel was appointed traveling bishop. In May the capstone was laid, and the finishing touches were added to the attic story during late November. On December 10 the full ordinance of endowment was administered for the first time in a Latter-day Saint temple. This work continued steadily, with sessions for small companies of twelve continuing into the night and on Saturdays until by February 7 more than 5,600 ordinances had been administered to tithe-paying members. During that last month of feverish activity officials performed numerous sealings, including new plural marriages.

Mormon leaders apparently did not reveal plans for the exodus until forced to do so in mid-September 1845 by the actions of their enemies. Public announcement of removal surprised many Saints, and some small factions within the Church openly opposed abandonment of the nearly completed temple and the physically expanding city. At the October general conference, held in the temple, officials assured the anxious Saints that the removal was a well-planned transplanting necessary to give the Church needed room for growth. The conference was largely devoted to assuring an orderly and unified departure, for the events of the previous few weeks had made it clear that Nauvoo would indeed be abandoned.

For three weeks before the conference, two emigration companies of one hundred families each had been in the process of formation. The first company included the apostles. Twenty-three other companies would now be created in a pyramidal organization resembling an army, with captains over tens, fifties, and hundreds. The assembly heard the Prophet's widowed mother, Lucy Mack Smith, declare her intention of joining in the orderly migration if her surviving children accompanied the Saints. In other action, the congregation appointed committees in each settlement to dispose of property and voted to discontinue Church newspapers. In a revival of the spirit of consecration that had aided removal of the poor from Missouri, the conference affirmed its intent to transport the entire membership to a new gathering place in the West. Latter-day Saints unable to attend the meetings were informed of plans by an epistle from the Twelve. They were advised to travel to Nauvoo for their endowments in the temple after its completion, projected for April.

Though Church authorities continually cautioned against haste, a spirit of anxiety pervaded Nauvoo. For more than a year, anti-Mormon forces had sporadically harassed the Saints. A rumored marauding, called a wolf hunt, against outlying settlements in September 1844 was thwarted when Governor Ford ordered the state militia to intervene. The mobsters then tried legal harassments. They swore out arrest warrants against settlers at Yelrom (Morley's Settlement), threatened Sheriff Backenstos with expulsion for his friendliness toward the Mormons, interfered with witnesses in the trials of the murderers of Joseph and Hyrum, and sought to incarcerate Brigham Young and several others on charges of treason.

In September 1845 the anti-Mormons under Colonel Levi Williams began burning Mormon homes, first at Morley's in southwestern Hancock County, then in other settlements. One after another, unprotected families were forced from their log farm homes to watch the vigilantes set the torch. In all, more than two hundred homes and farm buildings, plus many mills and grain stacks, were destroyed. The friendly Sheriff Jacob B. Backenstos vainly attempted to preserve order. He drove off the initial incendiaries with a posse of Mormon legionnaires; then, after occupying Carthage with his militia, he dispatched a number of scouting parties to protect frightened farmers against further raids. But the lives of Backenstos and other county officers who refused to sanction lawlessness were threatened. Confronted by several mobsters on the plains between Warsaw and Carthage, the sheriff fled toward Nauvoo, overtaking three Mormons, whom he immediately deputized. One of the pursuing horsemen raised his gun, and deputy Porter Rockwell fired. Frank A. Worrell, who had supervised the guard at the Carthage Jail on the day of the martyrdom, was mortally wounded. Rockwell and the sheriff were later indicted for murder, but acquitted on grounds of self-defense. Nevertheless, the act intensified hostile feelings in the county. Accordingly, Governor Ford sent General John J. Hardin with four hundred militia to supersede the sheriff. The state army was to act as an independent police force during the uncertain period of civil unrest. Hardin ended the Mormon posse's occupation of Carthage and halted plundering on both sides. As a mediator between the contending parties, he tried to please both sides and stall open confrontation until the Mormons could be evacuated.

Brigham Young's reaction to the home burnings was pacifistic. He ordered a total evacuation of all Latter-day Saints from rural areas and urged members to sell their property if possible, but cautioned against retaliation. In the move to Nauvoo he prohibited defensive measures. This policy, he hoped, would demonstrate to the many uninvolved citizens that the Mormons were not the aggressors. The governor's on-the-spot advisory committees included General Hardin, Mayor W. B. Warren, Attorney General J. A. McDougal, and Judge Stephen A. Douglas. This group concluded that despite the mob's flagrant denial of property rights, nothing could be done to protect the Saints. The only solution was removal.

A group of Quincy citizens, at a meeting on September 22, issued a formal request to that effect. Two days later Church spokesmen replied, "We desire peace above all other earthly blessings."[12] The Saints revealed that they had already taken steps to

---

[12]Brigham Young, "Manuscript History," September 25, 1845, Church Archives.

evacuate between five and six thousand people in the spring, with thousands more to follow when ready. The Church committee asked for help in selling or renting Mormon property in order to procure supplies necessary for the migration. Both sides agreed to end legal prosecution and to promote an end to mobocracy. Representatives from the nine surrounding counties met at Carthage October 1 and adopted similar resolutions. Citizens in Lee County, Iowa, meantime, echoed the call for removal. Neither of the Illinois citizens groups would promise to buy the vacated Mormon property, however, and the Carthage convention threatened to use force if necessary to assure a total evacuation.

Preparations for the exodus kept the artisans of Nauvoo employed throughout the fall and early winter. Each organized emigrant company established its own wagon shop by converting available shops or other buildings. Craftsmen in related fields joined the urgent task of wagon building. By Thanksgiving a published report identified 1,508 wagons ready to leave and another 1,892 under construction.

On August 23, 1845, the Council of the Twelve approved a pioneer expedition of 3,000 men to leave for the Great Salt Lake Valley in the spring. Later, the Council of Fifty, which was responsible for planning the expedition, resolved to send a smaller advance company of 1,000 men. These pioneers, traveling without their families, were to scout appropriate routes, locate sites, and plant crops.

Beginning with the October conference, public discussion of a precise relocation site seemed to center on Vancouver Island. Since the Great Salt Lake Valley was located in Mexican territory, it was recognized that the federal government would oppose any plan to locate there; that would violate Mexican sovereignty and might cause an international incident. Talk of Vancouver may have been a ploy to divert potential critics from a knowledge of the intended place of refuge west of the Rockies, but at least the island was under consideration as a place for a gathering of British Mormons. Late in 1845 Brigham Young asked the United States government for help in transporting the Saints into Oregon Territory. He proposed a contract to build blockhouses to help protect other pioneers or to carry the mail, but as before, the request for help fell on deaf ears.

Late in December 1845 several of the Twelve commenced

One of the rare photographs of the completed Nauvoo temple. (Church Archives)

reading John C. Frémont's report of explorations in California and Oregon and Lansford Hasting's *Emigrant Guide to Oregon and California,* published earlier that year. Brigham Young carefully examined Frémont's map of the unsettled regions west of the Rocky Mountains, and three other maps hung from the walls of the temple. Officials were also familiar with the expeditions of Charles Wilkes and B. L. E. Bonneville. A Nauvoo high council circular in January, announcing the expected departure of the advance company in early March, said that the "resting place" would be sought "in some good valley in the neighborhood of the Rocky Mountains."[13] Those planning that expedition had narrowed the site to a few unclaimed valleys along the western slopes of the Wasatch Mountains.

In New York, meantime, Samuel Brannan was advertising for passengers for a five-month sea voyage to San Francisco Bay. He had been encouraged by Brigham Young in September to gather eastern Saints for the trip. The Nauvoo congregation had planned its overland trek for late spring, when water and livestock feed

---

[13] *Times and Seasons,* January 15, 1846.

would be available on the plains, but mob pressures in Hancock County prompted an early departure. So it was a coincidence that the eastern and Nauvoo Saints departed at the same time: as the ship *Brooklyn* sailed from New York harbor on February 4, the first contingent of Nauvoo refugees ferried across the cold Mississippi toward the rolling plains of Iowa. The Twelve had declared in their September epistle that the exodus West "forms a new epoch, not only in the history of the church, but of this nation. . . . Wake up, wake up, dear brethren, we exhort you, from the Mississippi to the Atlantic, and from Canada to Florida, to the present glorious emergency in which the God of heaven has placed you to prove your faith."[14] Beginning a new chapter in Mormon history, the exiles were heading west, as one pioneer put it, "to find a suitable place for a City of Refuge."[15]

---

[14]Joseph Smith, *History of the Church*, 7:478-80.
[15]Alfred Cordon, "Journal," October 6, 1845, Ms. in Church Archives.

CHAPTER 7

Exodus to a New Zion, 1846-1850

From the eastern United States and Canada, from the American South, from Great Britain, and from scattered branches along the Mormon trail through upstate New York and northern Ohio came Latter-day Saints responding to the appeal of the Council of the Twelve for united action. They packed their trunks, sold their homes and farms, and loaded their wagons to join the trek to a new gathering place. For some this was the fourth move in less than sixteen years. But Parley P. Pratt was optimistic: "The people must enlarge in numbers and extend their borders," he told the general conference of October 1845; "they cannot always live in one city, nor in one county. . . . The Lord designs to lead us to a wider field of action." He compared the exodus to transplanting fruit trees from a small nursery to a field where they would have room to grow. "It is so with us," he said. "We want a country where we have room to expand."[1] That country was the unsettled American West, in a remote corner of Mexico's province of Upper California, near the eastern edge of the Great Basin.

The Mormon westward migration has been recognized as a

---

[1] Joseph Smith, *History of the Church*, 7:463-64.

Trek
Across Iowa
1846
Scale in Miles
0   10   20   50

UNORGANIZED AREA

Potawatomi
Reservation
1833–46

Winter Quarters •

Miller's
Hollow

UNORGANIZED

TERRITORY

Camp of Israel Trail

Mt. P

Missouri River

County organized 1848

MISSOURI

Mormon route westward from Nauvoo crossed the largely unsettled tablelands of Iowa, shown here with county boundaries established by the time of statehood in December 1846.

UNORGANIZED TERRITORY

WISCONSIN TERRITORY

Mississippi River

Counties authorized anuary 1846

Moines

Iowa City

Counties Created 1838-46

Des Moines River

ILLINOIS

Alternate Trail

rden Grove

Burlington

●Chariton River Camp

Sugar Creek Camp● **●Nauvoo**

Keokuk●

major triumph in the settlement of the West. In the process, an entire religious society transplanted itself to a new place of refuge and spent a generation defending its institutions. While some of the scattered Saints who stayed behind attempted to restore a pre-Nauvoo variety of Mormonism, the larger congregation in the Great Basin labored to create a new religious society patterned after the one they had known in their abandoned Zion.

The Mormons on the Move

The evacuation of the Saints from western Illinois was originally scheduled for sometime in April 1846. By then grass would be available on the plains to sustain livestock, and streams would be free from ice. During the winter the citizens of Nauvoo negotiated to sell their homes, shops, and farms and were busy stocking foodstuffs, building wagons, buying teams, and organizing emigrant companies. Suddenly, however, two new threats prompted an early and hasty exit.

An indictment issued by the U.S. District Court in Springfield against Brigham Young and eight other apostles was the first. They were accused of instigating and harboring a Nauvoo counterfeiting operation actually conducted by transient river traffickers. Government officials attempted to serve the warrants but failed when William Miller offered himself as a decoy to prevent President Young's arrest. Dressed in a cloak and wearing Brigham Young's cap, Miller left the temple, where the apostles were gathered, and stepped into the president's carriage. The waiting marshals arrested Miller and transported him the eighteen miles to Carthage before discovering the ploy. A second threat was contained in warnings reported by Governor Ford and confirmed in a letter from Sam Brannan. According to these unfounded reports, federal troops from St. Louis were planning to interfere with the orderly removal planned for spring.

Rather than risk such interference, the Twelve, the Church trustees, and others decided on February 2 to depart immediately. At least two thousand emigrants were prepared to go with them and thousands more could be ready within weeks. The first group, Church authorities and their families, crossed the Mississippi on February 4, utilizing skiffs and flatboats. In succeeding days, under the supervision of Nauvoo police, the evacuation rapidly gained momentum, and on February 24 the river froze, expediting the

Saints' exodus. Within weeks several hundred exiles were assembled in temporary camps in Iowa. Late in February Brigham Young joined his emigrating company at Sugar Creek, nine miles into Iowa.

Joseph Young, senior president of the First Council of the Seventy, was left to preside over the dwindling Mormon population at Nauvoo. His principal tasks were to hasten organizing for removal and to complete the temple for final dedication. During the late winter months blacksmiths, carpenters, and cabinetmakers accelerated the forging of wheel rims and fashioning of wagon boxes, hubs, and spokes. The Saints were also trying to sell their property, and before final evacuation they succeeded in disposing of eighty to ninety percent of their holdings.

The Saints were determined that nothing would hinder them in their religious obligation of completing and dedicating the sacred temple, even though they might never use it again. As artisans added finishing touches to the first floor of the building, Joseph Young conducted daily prayer meetings with small, selected groups. By April the temple was ready for dedication and simultaneous abandonment. No buyer had been found, nor anyone even interested in leasing under agreeable terms. On the last day of the month, in a secret session directed by Elders Wilford Woodruff and Orson Hyde, Joseph Young delivered the building over to the Lord. On the following day 300 people assembled for a brief public dedication. By this time at least 5,615 Saints had received endowments, but for those not so blessed Brigham Young had promised other temples in the West.

Nearly twelve thousand Saints had crossed the river by mid-May, and more than six hundred remained in Illinois. Some were detained by illness or poverty and a few sympathized with the seceders, but to some anti-Mormons it appeared that total evacuation might not be accomplished. This precipitated a final confrontation. Guerrilla warfare was revived against isolated settlers. Then, in June, the mobbers gathered four hundred volunteers, marched to Nauvoo, and demanded surrender. The remaining Nauvoo residents quickly united under former Nauvoo Legion officers and prevented an invasion, but the attacks against farmers in outlying areas continued. In late August Governor Ford responded to a Mormon petition for protection by dispatching an officer with ten men to organize a volunteer militia at Nauvoo.

With both sides in readiness, the stage was set for battle.

In September the Carthage guerrillas under Thomas S. Brockman mustered about eight hundred men to enforce their ultimatum. Adequately armed, and with six cannons, they positioned themselves on the outskirts of Nauvoo and repeated the demand for all Mormons and Mormon sympathizers to leave. Inside the city about three hundred residents organized under Major Benjamin Clifford and Nauvoo Legion officers. For cannon they had five makeshift artillery pieces built from sawed-off steamboat shafts. The defenders positioned themselves behind barricades less than a mile from their challengers.

For two days the opposing forces exchanged gunfire in minor skirmishes, and on the third day, September 12, the invaders attacked in force. Flanking the defenders on the south, they headed for the city while the Mormons and their friends retreated to new positions behind stout blockades. Captain William Anderson, his fifteen-year-old son, August, and David Norris were killed when their "Spartan Band" attempted to cut off the attackers; several in the invading force also died.

Death, wounds, and the realization that further bloodshed was in the offing finally prompted both sides to seek a truce. A committee from Quincy mediated terms, and the holdouts in Nauvoo surrendered their arms and the city itself. In return, they were promised safety while crossing the river and allowed to designate a committee of five to remain long enough to sell their property. Those able to do so left immediately. Others were subjected to more plundering, harassment, and forcible expulsion in direct violation of the agreements.

Approximately 640 destitute Latter-day Saints were forced to cross the river in September. They crowded into makeshift tents on the river bottoms, where many contracted chills and fever in the cold September rains. Word of the condition of the "poor camp" reached the Twelve, and a relief company was sent with provisions, tents, and wagons. On October 9, still practically destitute, the "poor camp" organized for the journey west. On that day flocks of quail, exhausted from a long flight, settled for forty miles along the bottom lands. The hungry Saints easily and gratefully caught them with their hands. Food had been provided when it was badly needed.

The Camp of Israel

Those who had departed earlier moved westward across Iowa. Despite extensive advance preparation, many had neglected to accumulate the suggested year's supply of food required for extended survival on the Iowa prairies. To supply themselves, some families drifted to St. Louis, which became an important outfitting depot. At numerous locations in Missouri and nearby states the Saints chopped wood, split rails, built fences, and performed other labor in exchange for needed supplies. Supervisors of the emigrant companies purchased additional provisions, and families with adequate stocks shared their goods. Gradually even those who started out amply provisioned were left with inadequate supplies.

On March 27, 1846, Brigham Young formed three new companies of one hundred families each among the Saints who had been separated from their intended companies and were gathered on the Chariton River. The military-style organization he established was not uncommon in westward travel and soon became the pattern for Mormon exiles. About fifty families comprised the basic unit of travel. Each fifty, sometimes subdivided into groups of ten, was led by a captain who supervised the march, maintained discipline, and oversaw the work of commissarians, guards, herdsmen, and other officers.

The homeless Saints dubbed themselves, symbolically, the Camp of Israel, and Brigham Young was their Moses. He originally planned that the three companies organized at the Chariton River would forge ahead to the Great Basin in 1846 and plant crops there. Muddy soil, a shortage of supplies, and cold weather plagued the camp for six weeks, though after mid-April the journey became easier.

It was under these conditions that William Clayton composed new words to a traditional English tune, "All Is Well." When the Saints left Nauvoo, he was assigned to act as scribe for Brigham Young, but he became discouraged when he could find little time or money to provide wagons and provisions for his family. In addition, one of his wives, the lovely but frail, teenaged Diantha, had been left behind in Nauvoo, for she was about to have a baby. Concern for her health weighed heavily on his mind. It had been a rainy, cool, and unhappy week for him when he received word on April 15 that Diantha had had her child and that both were well.

His mood changed, and that evening he even held a long-distance christening party for his new son. A musician and poet at heart, he poured out his soul to the tune of a hymn that he had sung all his life. "Come, come, ye Saints," he wrote, "no toil nor labor fear,"

> But with joy wend your way.
> Though hard to you this journey may appear,
> Grace shall be as your day.
> 'Tis better far for us to strive
> Our useless cares from us to drive;
> Do this, and joy your hearts will swell—
> All is well! all is well!

As the Camp of Israel proceeded west, the leaders searched out unclaimed land and appointed agents to establish farms. Two principal encampments were located. At Garden Grove, about 145 miles west of Nauvoo, 715 acres were enclosed for grain and other crops, and an orderly village was laid out. Twenty-seven miles further on, William Huntington supervised a larger operation of several thousand acres. When surveying the area from a rocky knoll, Parley P. Pratt was reminded of the hill from which Moses

A Mormon encampment on Mosquito Creek, about three miles east of Council Bluffs, Iowa. The original painting was by frontier artist George Simons, who once had a studio in Council Bluffs. The painting probably depicted a pioneer group of the 1850s. (Joslyn Art Museum, Omaha, Nebraska)

first viewed the Promised Land, and thus named it Mt. Pisgah.

The principal task of path-finding was delegated to Stephen Markham, who, with an advance party of a hundred men, scouted roads and campsites and built rough bridges when necessary. Following his trail, Brigham Young and Heber C. Kimball reached the Missouri River in mid-June, with other travelers close behind. They established temporary headquarters on the lands of the Pottawattomie Indians, and soon an estimated five hundred wagons had assembled along Mosquito Creek. Willard Richards' tent served as a post office for letters going east and as a meeting place for Church leaders.

The Twelve and the General Council still anticipated that as many as four hundred men would be able to cross the mountains and plant fall wheat in the Great Basin that year. They sought information on routes west, supplies, Indian rights, and other information from the Indian agents and fur traders who knew the area. Their immediate concern, however, was getting the emigrants across the Missouri River, and they finally decided to build a ferryboat. They quickly mobilized the camp for this urgent task. As one crew hauled timber to the Pottawattomie sawmill ten miles away and returned with cut-to-order planks, another fashioned timber for framing. Along both sides of the river workmen prepared boat landings and cut dugways down the gullies and through the jagged bluffs to aid the wagon crossing. On the afternoon of June 29 four Nauvoo Legion cannons were floated across on the new Mormon ferry, and the work of ferrying emigrant wagons commenced immediately.

The Mormon Battalion

Even as the river crossing began, word arrived that Captain James Allen was en route from Mt. Pisgah seeking volunteers for military service. He was representing Colonel Stephen W. Kearny of the U.S. Army of the West, soon to be engaged in the war that Congress had declared a month earlier against Mexico.

In 1845 the United States had annexed Texas, but in the process had wounded the pride of Mexico, which still claimed much of Texas territory. War broke out after a skirmish between Mexican and United States troops in the disputed territory. The conflict was popular with American expansionists, for it meant the possibility of new territory for the United States. At the request of

President James K. Polk, Congress authorized the enlistment of fifty thousand men to augment regular military forces. Within two years the Mexican provinces of Upper California and New Mexico would be added to the American Union. Upper California included the Great Basin, the destination of the Saints.

Captain Allen had gone first to Mt. Pisgah, where he presented his request for Mormon volunteers to Wilford Woodruff and the local high council. They studied his "Circular to the Mormons," but were suspicious of government intentions and unwilling to commit the Church to such an undertaking. They sent him to Brigham Young at the Mosquito Creek campground. Hosea Stout's reaction to Captain Allen's request for volunteers was typical of the feelings of many at Mt. Pisgah. The Saints were indignant, he said, and looked on it as another plot against them. If they did not comply, they could be denounced as enemies of the country, and if they did comply, the army would "then have 500 of our men in their power to be destroyed as they had done our leaders at Carthage. I confess that my feelings was uncommonly wrought up against them."[2] Though such feelings were understandable after so many previous rebuffs, the Saints had a false impression. They were unaware of efforts in Washington in their behalf.

To the surprise of many Latter-day Saints, Brigham Young immediately reacted in favor of the requisition. In a public meeting called to explain the government action, he supported the call as "the first offer we have ever had from the government to benefit us."[3] The men would serve one year and proceed at government expense first to Santa Fe and then to California. After discharge they would retain their arms and supplies. Meantime, the soldiers' pay would help transport their families west. Here was evidence, said President Young, that the government intended not to hinder but to help the Saints reach Upper California. In addition, the Mormons would be able to demonstrate their loyalty. Though President Young did not mention it, it was also a significant symbol for the Saints to help win for the United States the territory they were about to colonize.

---

[2]Juanita Brooks, ed., *On the Mormon Frontier; The Diary of Hosea Stout,* 2 vols. (Salt Lake City: University of Utah Press, 1964), 1:172.
[3]Young, "Manuscript History," July 1, 1846.

If further assurance was needed of the sincerity of the government motives, it came with Jesse C. Little, who met Brigham Young and Heber C. Kimball on their way to recruit soldiers at Mt. Pisgah on July 6, and Colonel Thomas L. Kane, who arrived at Council Bluffs from Fort Leavenworth five days later. Both men had been directly involved in the negotiations in Washington, D.C., which led to the call of the Mormon Battalion.

Elder Little, who was the presiding Church officer in the East and official Church agent in Washington, had met Colonel Kane in Philadelphia in May while seeking means to transport the eastern Saints to Upper California by ship. Kane, a young adventurer who became an articulate, if self-appointed, guardian for the interests of the Saints, suggested the political tactic that Elder Little later used to persuade President Polk to aid the Mormons.

Armed with letters of introduction from Kane and others, Elder Little sought an audience with Polk. He had been told by Brigham Young to seek government contracts to build blockhouses and forts along the Oregon Trail. Failing that, he was authorized to embrace any offer that would aid the emigration. His first hope was for a shipping contract that would provide money as well as inexpensive transportation. His request was timely, for the government needed to send supplies around Cape Horn for its forces in California. Former Postmaster General Amos Kendall told Elder Little that he would urge the cabinet to authorize one thousand Mormons to travel by sea and another thousand overland to California.

When five days passed without a response, Elder Little addressed a personal letter to Polk. He threatened, as Kane had suggested, that lack of federal aid to help the Mormons migrate "under the outstretched wings of the American Eagle" might "compel us to be foreigners." This was indeed a clever ploy, for the Mormons had no intention of becoming disloyal. Yet the government had heard rumors of British interest in the Pacific Coast. An independent Mormon state that might gain the support of England was not an impossibility, and this would certainly complicate American interests in the West. Polk decided, however, to give the shipping contract to others, and he opted against marching a thousand armed Latter-day Saints into California. If they arrived before Kearny's forces, he reasoned, the Missourians in the Army of the West would be distraught, for he knew well the antagonism

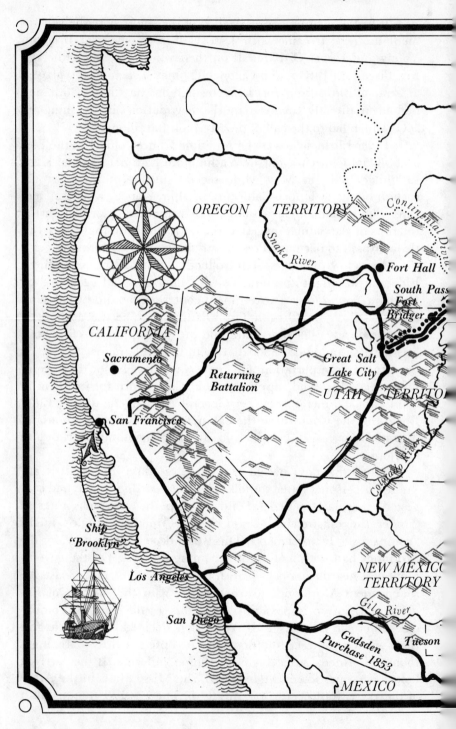

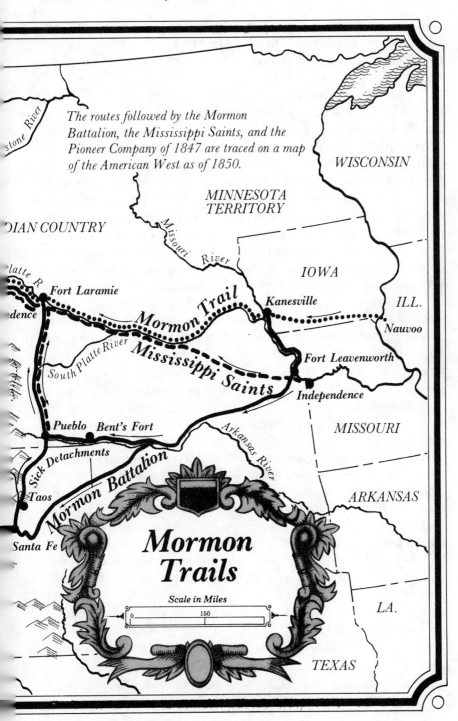

The routes followed by the Mormon
Battalion, the Mississippi Saints, and the
Pioneer Company of 1847 are traced on a map
of the American West as of 1850.

WISCONSIN

MINNESOTA
TERRITORY

DIAN COUNTRY

IOWA

ILL.

Fort Laramie

Kanesville

Mormon Trail

Nauvoo

dence

South Platte River

Mississippi Saints

Fort Leavenworth

Independence

Pueblo   Bent's Fort

MISSOURI

Arkansas River

Sick Detachments

Mormon Battalion

ARKANSAS

Taos

Santa Fe

Mormon
Trails

Scale in Miles

0   150

L.A.

TEXAS

between the Mormons and the Missourians. Besides, he did not need additional soldiers. The existing Army of the West, supplemented by a thousand Missouri volunteers, could secure New Mexico and, if the season was not too late, still enter California.

As an alternative, Polk asked Little in an interview on June 5 if the Mormons would offer five hundred volunteers to enlist *after* the Mormon exiles reached California. This, the president confided in his diary, was a move to placate the Mormons and retain their loyalty. Kane's strategy was working. Little pressed for an immediate enlistment, but the request was turned down. Two days earlier orders had been sent to Kearny authorizing the Mormon enlistment, but in vague terms. Even though President Polk apparently intended the enlistment to take place in California, Kearny interpreted his instructions differently, and on June 19 he ordered the enlistment to take place immediately. Thus the way was paved for an important episode in Mormon history.

The provisioned conveyance west of five hundred men under salary from the government was the kind of financial aid Brigham Young had been seeking. He led the enlistment drive himself and promised that if they were faithful, the Mormon soldiers would not be required to fight. He also arranged for part of each volunteer's pay and his $42 clothing allowance to be returned to his family.

The group that left Council Bluffs on July 20 included 541 soldiers and nearly a hundred other Latter-day Saints, including wives and children of some of the officers and twenty Battalion wives who served as laundresses. The Battalion consisted of five companies under Captain Allen, who was promoted to lieutenant colonel when he assumed command. Church leaders were allowed to choose the other officers. The Battalion was given a gala farewell on June 15. Later the officers met privately with six of the Twelve, who admonished them "to be as fathers to the privates, to remember their prayers, to see that the name of the Deity was revered, and that virtue and cleanliness were strictly observed." According to Sergeant William Hyde, "They also instructed us to treat all men with kindness . . . and never take life when it could be avoided."[4]

The new soldiers marched to Fort Leavenworth, where they

---

[4]Daniel Tyler, *A Concise History of the Mormon Battalion in the Mexican War, 1846-1847* (1881; reprint ed., Chicago: Rio Grande Press, 1964), pp. 128-29.

were outfitted with muskets and supplies. Colonel Allen was suddenly taken ill and remained behind when the Battalion left the fort on August 12, and on August 23 he died. Allen was well liked by the Mormons, and his death caused great sorrow, which turned to bitter disappointment when Lieutenant Andrew Jackson Smith was named his successor. The Mormon soldiers disliked Smith, and seeds of tension were sown.

Lieutenant Smith pushed ahead more rapidly than the men thought proper. In addition, he imposed upon them his own military doctor, George B. Sanderson of Missouri. Sanderson clearly disliked the Mormons, and the feeling was quickly reciprocated. Evidence suggests that many of his treatments were less than adequate, and the Mormons accused him of not caring whether they lived or died. Another element of tension crept in when Lieutenant Smith delegated Captain Nelson Higgins and ten men to convey most of the soldiers' families up the Arkansas River to Pueblo, Colorado, for the winter. The decision proved to be wise, since many of the women and children were clearly unprepared for the arduous journey ahead. Later, at Santa Fe, a second sick detachment and all but five of the remaining women were sent under the direction of Captain James Brown to join the earlier group at Pueblo.

At Santa Fe the remaining members of the Battalion were placed under the command of Lieutenant Colonel Philip St. George Cooke, whose leadership the men learned to appreciate and respect. Cooke had orders to blaze a wagon trail from Santa Fe to California. The best available maps were of little use, but the company had the services of knowledgeable guides. Veering south, the Mormon soldiers at times followed Spanish or Mexican trails but generally cut new roads. This late-summer march also took its toll in sickness, and on November 10 a third detachment of worn and weakened men turned back. Lieutenant William W. Willis led them to Pueblo, Colorado, where the Mormon colony grew to about 150 men and their families.

About 350 officers and men remained, and on reduced rations they continued southward. For a month they struggled across the sandy valley of the lower Rio Grande, then, on November 21, turned toward Tucson. On the way they had an exciting encounter with a herd of wild cattle. Sixty of the beasts were killed by gunfire when the Battalion was attacked by enraged bulls. This "battle of

The Mormon Battalion's only military action—a fight with wild bulls—is portrayed here by C.B. Hancock. (Church Archives)

the bulls" turned out to be the only battle fought in the entire expedition.

Beyond Tucson the Battalion soon rejoined Kearny's route along the Gila River. Guides arrived on December 23 to lead them beyond the Colorado River. The route lay across a trackless desert, where water was obtained only by digging deep wells. Beyond the desert they conveyed wagons through the narrow mountain passes of the coastal range with ropes and pulleys. On January 29, 1847, they reached Mission San Diego at the end of their 2,030-mile march and reported to General Kearny at the nearby seaport settlement.

California had already surrendered, and the Mormon Battalion was not required to do battle. The men filled out the remainder of their enlistment as occupation troops, serving garrison duty in San Diego, San Louis Rey, and Los Angeles. On July 16 they were discharged, though eighty-one reenlisted for an additional six months. The others headed for the Great Salt Lake Valley. Some of these men spent the winter at Sutter's Fort, where employment was available, and thus several Mormons were at New Helvetia in January 1848 for the famous discovery that began the California gold rush. The following summer they abandoned their opportunity to get rich quick and joined their families and friends in the new gathering place of the Saints.

The Mississippi Saints

The sick detachments of the Mormon Battalion went to Pueblo, Colorado, specifically to join a company of Saints from Mississippi who were also on their way to the Rocky Mountains. This small group of emigrants came from Monroe County, where a group of perhaps 150 Church members was located. One of their number, John Brown, had moved his family to Nauvoo, and in January 1846, Brigham Young appointed him to carry a message back to Mississippi that the main body of the Saints would leave Nauvoo in the spring and intended to settle somewhere in the Great Basin, possibly the Bear River Valley. Eager to gather with the Saints, a small company of forty-three under the leadership of William Crosby left Mississippi on April 8, and by May 26 they had traveled 640 miles to Independence, Missouri. There they were joined by fourteen other persons and turned their wagons west.

On July 6 the migrating southern Saints reached Chimney Rock in Wyoming, about eight hundred miles from Independence. There they met some trappers returning from California, who informed them that there were no Mormons ahead of them. They were unaware that Brigham Young had decided to establish winter quarters in Nebraska. They soon decided to take up the offer of John Renshaw, a French trapper, who invited them to spend the winter near the trading post at Pueblo. They reached Pueblo on August 7 and soon learned where Brigham Young was spending the winter. They selected a site to build their own community, erected a row of simple cottonwood log dwellings, and planted crops: turnips, pumpkins, beans, and melons.

The three detachments from the Mormon Battalion arrived at Pueblo in November and December. Together with the Mississippi Saints, they constituted a community of about 275 Mormons camped more than a thousand miles further west than the main body of the Saints. They erected another row of eighteen cabins and completed a meetinghouse at the head of Main Street.

Life in the temporary little Mormon village was typical of life on the frontier. The Saints subsisted in part by trading as well as

hunting venison in the forest. They were generally well supplied
with goods obtained from Bent's Fort, and some were able to use
their skills, such as blacksmithing, to obtain some income. The
Mormon Battalion members kept up regular military drills, and
the Saints enjoyed frequent dances in the meetinghouse, which
also doubled as a schoolhouse and community jail. Seven women
gave birth to babies during the winter, and Indian wives of the
mountain men assisted in caring for their families. Nine deaths
were also recorded during the winter, as well as one marriage. As
spring approached, an advance party left to meet the main pioneer
company at Fort Laramie. The remainder arrived in Salt Lake
Valley a few days after Brigham Young's vanguard company.

Winter Quarters, 1846-47

While the Mormon Battalion was being organized in 1846,
plans for the remaining exiles were in constant flux. The Battalion
claimed many of the best teamsters and left large herds of cattle
without manpower to manage them. For a time Brigham Young
still hoped that a vanguard company could enter the Great Basin
in 1846, but the needs of the stranded camps on the Missouri soon
took precedence. The journey to the new promised land would
have to wait another year.

In the meantime, Church officials secured permission from
the Pottawatomie Indians to winter on their lands in western Iowa.
Several companies of Saints had already crossed the Missouri
River, however, in anticipation of continuing farther west. There
on the lands of the Omaha Indians they found equally desirable
rangeland for their horses, mules, sheep, and an estimated thirty
thousand head of cattle. In order to remain on friendly terms with
the Indians, Church members helped them in various ways, including the occasional donation of a beef.

The temporary Mormon encampments on the west side of the
river soon became the largest. By the end of September a town of
820 lots had been surveyed, and Winter Quarters came into being.
Before Christmas 700 log homes, roofed over with clapboards or
with willows and dirt, were occupied by about 3,500 people. Other
dwellings, including a few dugouts, were added before spring. The
exiles on the Iowa side spread out their winter camps in all directions. Around one site, renamed Kanesville in 1848, grew the
modern Council Bluffs. The winter of 1846-47, then, saw thou-

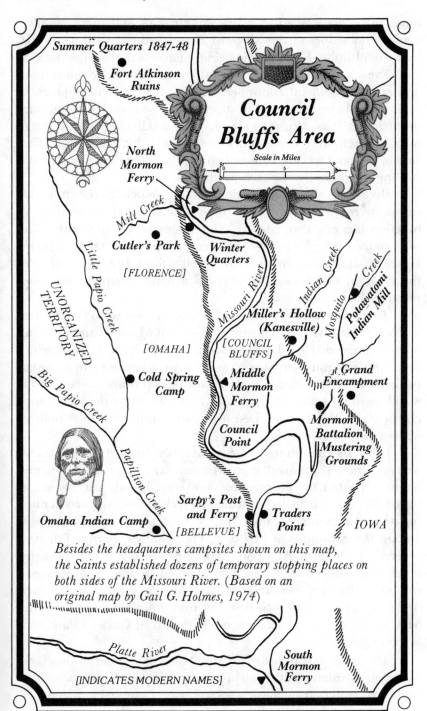

Summer Quarters 1847-48

Fort Atkinson Ruins

Council Bluffs Area

Scale in Miles

0   5

North Mormon Ferry

Mill Creek

Cutler's Park

[FLORENCE]

Winter Quarters

Indian Creek

Mosquito Creek

Potawatomi Indian Mill

Little Papio Creek

UNORGANIZED TERRITORY

Missouri River

Miller's Hollow (Kanesville)

[COUNCIL BLUFFS]

[OMAHA]

Cold Spring Camp

Middle Mormon Ferry

Grand Encampment

Big Papio Creek

Council Point

Mormon Battalion Mustering Grounds

Papillion Creek

Sarpy's Post and Ferry

[BELLEVUE]

Traders Point

IOWA

Omaha Indian Camp

Besides the headquarters campsites shown on this map, the Saints established dozens of temporary stopping places on both sides of the Missouri River. (Based on an original map by Gail G. Holmes, 1974)

Platte River

South Mormon Ferry

[INDICATES MODERN NAMES]

sands of Saints located in a few large camps and many smaller ones on both sides of the Missouri River, and eastward along the trail from Illinois. For the time being, Zion was in the wilderness.

Even in these temporary locations the need for organization and civil government continued. At the principal encampments, high councils were created to superintend both ecclesiastical and municipal affairs. Winter Quarters was subdivided into thirteen wards, which were expanded to twenty-two by early 1847. The care of the poor was apportioned out, with two or three families accepting responsibility for each needy one.

Because of their dual functions, high councils in the emigrant camps were called municipal high councils and authorized to function like city councils. At Winter Quarters, for example, the high council levied a three-fourths percent property tax to support Hosea Stout's transplanted Nauvoo police force. It also encouraged the creation of schools and oversaw general discipline in camp through the town marshal.

To enhance their economic well-being, the wintering Saints actively traded with settlements in northern Missouri and in Iowa, offering unneeded goods or available cash for hogs, grain, vegetables, and emigrant supplies. Young men otherwise unemployed turned local resources into willow baskets, half-bushel measures, or washboards for trade. Under a franchise granted by the high council, Brigham Young organized a private company, which built a water-powered gristmill.

Diets in the camps were necessarily limited. One much-needed product obtained from Missouri was potatoes, but many Saints subsisted on little more than corn bread, salt bacon, a little milk, and a little fresh meat. The lack of fresh vegetables during the first summer caused many to contract scurvy, known among the Mormons as blackleg. The potatoes, horseradish discovered at old Fort Atkinson, and cold weather finally brought relief, but not before disease had claimed its toll. The numbers who died of scurvy, consumption, and chills and fever during that first summer were not recorded, but from mid-September 1846 to May 1848 these ailments caused 359 deaths at Cutler's Park and Winter Quarters.

To some, the industry of the Mormon farmers raised the question of intent. Although announced as temporary way stations, the migrant wintering places were acquiring a look of permanence. Anyone inquiring about plans for removal, however, was quickly assured that an advance company would leave in the spring and that complete evacuation would follow as fast as possible in the next year or two. In the meantime, these villages would provide important rest and supply stations for those who followed the early companies on their way west.

Church leaders and the Council of Fifty turned again to plans for the westering venture as soon as they could. Corresponding frequently with the trustees remaining in Nauvoo, they endeavored to secure badly needed funds through sale of the temple and remaining property, but without success. In the fall of 1846 a visit from Father Jean DeSmet, returning from five years among the Indians of Oregon Country, allowed camp leaders to gather firsthand information about the Rocky Mountains. DeSmet had traversed the Great Salt Lake Basin on his outward journey in 1841. The General Council considered the possibility of sending three hundred men to open farms at the headwaters of the Yellowstone, but discussion of a resting place still centered, as it had done for several years, on the valley of the Great Salt Lake and on nearby Bear River Valley.

On January 14, 1847, Brigham Young set forth "the word and will of the Lord" concerning the pattern of migration "to the place where the Lord shall locate a stake of Zion." Accepted by assembled priesthood quorums as a revelation to the Church, this document became a constitution governing the westward trek from Winter Quarters, reaffirmed the organizational scheme of emigrant companies already tested in the march across Iowa, and urged proper preparation. It reminded the Saints of their responsibility to care for the poor, widows, orphans, and Battalion families; advised the continuation of way stations; and required a covenant of obedience to principles of honesty, cooperation, diligence, and moderation. Comparing the migrating band to ancient Israel, the revelation recommended trust in God and promised divine protection:

If thou art merry, praise the Lord with singing, with music, with dancing, and with a prayer of praise and thanksgiving.

If thou art sorrowful, call on the Lord thy God with supplication, that your souls may be joyful.

Fear not thine enemies, for they are in mine hands and I will do my pleasure with them.

My people must be tried in all things, that they may be prepared to receive the glory that I have for them, even the glory of Zion; and he that will not bear chastisement is not worthy of my kingdom.[5]

A few emigrants declared themselves unwilling to undergo further refining in the wilderness. They returned to civilized comforts or remained in Iowa and disappeared into American society. Those who retained their commitment to a gathered Israel prepared to follow the vanguard, which recommenced its westward trek in April. They would make history.

Sea-going Mormons: The First to Reach the West

The Camp of Israel, the Mormon Battalion, and the southern Saints were not the only Mormons headed west in 1846. On February 4, the same day the first group from Nauvoo crossed the icy Mississippi, a company of Saints numbering 70 men, 68 women, and 100 children sailed out of New York harbor aboard the ship *Brooklyn.* Recruited by Samuel Brannan, they were headed for California with the expectation that they would help choose and establish the final destination for the thousands of Latter-day Saints who would cross the Great Plains.

Elder Orson Pratt of the Council of the Twelve was presiding over the Church in the eastern states when word arrived late in 1845 of the decision to hasten the departure from Nauvoo. Immediately he issued a dramatic call for the Saints in that area to join the exodus. Angered at the treatment the Church was receiving, he perhaps overstated the case when he declared: "We do not want one saint to be left in the United States" after the following spring. "Let every branch," he wrote, "in the East, West, North and South, be determined to flee out of Babylon, either by land or by sea."[6] Elder Samuel Brannan, publisher of the *Prophet,* the Church paper in New York, was appointed to charter a ship and direct a company that would go by sea as soon as possible.

By the end of December Brannan had chartered the ship and begun to recruit passengers, offering the full voyage for $75 per adult, including provisions, and half price for children. The company consisted of farmers and mechanics from the area, and they

---

[5]D&C 136:28-31.
[6]*Times and Seasons,* December 1, 1845.

took with them all tools necessary for building a new society in the West, including the press on which the *Prophet* had been printed and a large quantity of schoolbooks.

The voyage of the *Brooklyn* was pleasant but eventful. It rounded Cape Horn; touched at Juan Fernandez, legendary as the Robinson Crusoe island; spent ten days in the Hawaiian islands; then arrived at Yerba Buena (San Francisco Bay) on July 29, 1846. On the way two severe storms were encountered, one in each ocean. Ten passengers died—nine were buried at sea and the other on Juan Fernandez Island—and two babies were born, one named Atlantic and the other Pacific, after the oceans where they first saw life.

When the *Brooklyn* Saints arrived at Yerba Buena, the American flag already flew over California. They found employment wherever they could and began looking for a site to establish a colony. The new settlement was called New Hope, and some members, unaware of the decision of Brigham Young and the Twelve to settle in the Great Basin, apparently hoped that it would become the basis for a permanent Mormon settlement in the West.

The voyage of the *Brooklyn* did not foreshadow a great Mormon migration by sea nor a Mormon headquarters in California, but it was a symbol of a remarkable saga that had begun in that important year of 1846. By the end of the year thousands of Saints had fled Nauvoo and were making camps in the Great Plains; the Mormon Battalion had marched through the Southwest to California; the sick detachments as well as a party of southern Saints were wintering in the Mexican village of Pueblo; the *Brooklyn* Saints had arrived at Yerba Buena; and in the East other Mormons were making provision to sell their homes and move. All over America one objective dominated the thoughts of Latter-day Saints: to leave whatever they were doing, wherever they were, and join the Twelve to help create a new refuge for themselves and the Kingdom of God. In spirit all sang with William Clayton:

> We'll find the place which God for us prepared,
> Far away in the West,
> Where none shall come to hurt or make afraid;
> There the Saints will be blessed.

The Dissenters

Some, however, were not so sure. Though few in number, they illustrate the reality that diverse personalities and emotional influences remained that would lead even former close associates in several directions. Even as the Saints who remained loyal to the Twelve were looking toward a new gathering place in the West, some of those they had known best were creating rival groups elsewhere.

Sidney Rigdon, once appointed by revelation as spokesman for Joseph Smith, had rejected the Twelve and been excommunicated. In Pittsburgh he began publishing again the *Messenger and Advocate* in 1844 and established a rival organization called the Church of Christ. He was named "President of the Kingdom and the Church," but by 1847 his organization had almost disappeared.

A more successful leader was James J. Strang of Wisconsin, who had joined the Church only four months before the death of the Prophet. In August 1844 he presented a letter that, he claimed, had been written by Joseph Smith, appointing Strang as the Prophet's successor. The Twelve labeled it a forgery and excommunicated him, but the charismatic Strang gathered many believers and made a concerted effort to convert the rest of the Church to his claims. He was especially successful in the East, and finally established a headquarters on Beaver Island in Lake Michigan. He was even crowned king. By 1850, however, he had run into numerous economic and political difficulties, and in 1856 he was murdered by one of his own disaffected followers.

Most revealing of the misunderstandings of the time was the decision of the remaining members of Joseph Smith's family not to follow the Church west. William Smith, a member of the Council of the Twelve and the Prophet's only surviving brother, made his own claims to Church leadership and was finally excommunicated in 1845. For a while he was associated with James J. Strang, but later he began teaching that Joseph Smith's eldest son should, by right of lineage, inherit the presidency and that he, William, was to be a guardian and president pro tem until Joseph III was of age. His efforts at organization failed, and later he became nominally associated with the Reorganized Latter Day Saints.

There were others who refused to follow the leadership of

Brigham Young and the Twelve. William Marks, former stake president in Nauvoo, was excommunicated in 1845, joined the Strangites for a while, moved to a group headed by Charles Thomson, then attached himself in 1855 to another group headed by former apostle John E. Page. Jason W. Briggs also joined Strang but later claimed divine guidance that Joseph Smith III should become the leader. Zenos H. Gurley had spiritual experiences similar to those of Briggs, and the two men joined their small followings in 1852. All three of these men were instrumental in 1860 in bringing about a new organization that became known as the Reorganized Church of Jesus Christ of Latter Day Saints. At its head was Joseph Smith III, son of the Prophet, and its membership included the Prophet's widow Emma, who had since married Lewis A. Bidamon. Members of the new organization were soon dubbed by the Utah Saints the "Josephites." They, in turn, called the Utah Saints "Brighamites."

Although it was distressing to see even a few former associates abandoning the main group of Saints, none of these groups posed a serious threat to the leadership of Brigham Young and the Twelve. On the other hand, Church leaders were delighted when one famous dissenter returned. Oliver Cowdery, who had assisted Joseph Smith in translating the Book of Mormon and had shared many of his most sacred spiritual experiences, had been excommunicated in 1838. In 1848 he was practicing law in Wisconsin when Phineas H. Young brought him the greetings of the Twelve. He decided to return to the Church, and on October 24, 1848, he appeared at a conference in Kanesville, Iowa, where he bore witness of his earlier experiences and of the truthfulness of the Book of Mormon, and asked for readmittance to the Church. On November 12 he was rebaptized, and he began to lay plans to migrate to Salt Lake Valley with the rest of the Saints. His poor health, however, delayed his plans. On March 3, 1850, he died at the home of his friend and early Church associate, David Whitmer, who said he died "the happiest man I ever saw."

The Pioneer Company, 1847

The Saints in Winter Quarters and on the plains of Iowa waited out the winter of 1846-47 and laid plans for the momentous trek that would begin the following spring. It was decided that the vanguard company, including eight members of the Council of the

Brigham Young.   *Heber C. Kimball.*   *Willard Richards.*
Engraved by   *An early daguerreotype.*   *Engraved by*
Charles B. Hall from a   *(Church Archives)*   *Charles B. Hall from*
daguerreotype taken in   *Marsena Cannon daguerreotype.*
1855. (Church Archives)   *(Church Archives)*

Twelve, would consist only of able-bodied men who could travel fast and begin preparations for those to follow. As it turned out three women were included, so that the pioneer group consisted of 143 men, 3 women, and 2 children. They traveled in 73 wagons and took 93 horses, 52 mules, 66 oxen, 19 cows, 17 dogs, and some chickens. The pioneer company was fully provisioned to sustain itself for a year.

Plans for departure were carefully laid. A council in late February discussed the need for boats, seeds, maps, scientific instruments, and farm implements, and considered the location for a city as well as the necessity of irrigating crops in the arid West. In April the group began to rendezvous. Brigham Young made a final visit to Winter Quarters, where he met John Taylor, Parley P. Pratt, and Orson Hyde, who had just returned from a short mission to England. They brought money contributed to the cause by the English Saints, a map based on John C. Frémont's recent expedition to the Far West, and instruments for calculating latitude, elevation, temperature, and barometric pressure.

The westward trail was not, of course, totally unknown. For years westering adventurers and pioneers had been following what came to be known as the Oregon Trail, along the south side of the Platte River. The Saints, however, wanted to keep their distance in order to avoid clashes over grazing rights, water, and campsites, so they selected a new route on the north side of the river from

Winter Quarters to Fort Laramie. This segment of the journey took the vanguard company six weeks, from mid-April until June 1.

Because the pioneers were at first apprehensive of possible Indian danger, they formed a militia headed by Brigham Young and Stephen Markham. They also organized a night guard, traveled in close formation, and carried a cannon. Though they lost a few horses to Indians, they generally found them interested in trade and friendship.

The company suffered little unusual hardship, and the journey soon became almost leisurely. This seemed to nurture an attitude of flippancy and light-mindedness, which Brigham Young abhorred. On one occasion he roundly criticized the men for playing cards and dominoes and for boisterous dancing, urging them to conduct themselves in a way more befitting their serious mission. According to the camp diarist, there was some tearful repentance, but after that "no loud laughter was heard, no swearing, no quarreling, no profane language, no hard speeches to man or beast."[7]

William Clayton was an official camp journalist and was responsible for recording accurate mileage for later emigrants. For the first few days this meticulous record keeper monotonously counted the daily revolutions of a wagon wheel and calculated the mileage from that. Three days into the journey, however, he proposed a mechanical odometer, and on May 10 Brigham Young

A pioneer odometer. (Church Archives)

---

[7]William Clayton, *William Clayton's Journal* (Salt Lake City: Clayton Family Association, 1921), p. 201.

assigned Orson Pratt to design such a device. It was constructed by Appleton Harmon, an experienced woodworker, and thereafter Elder Clayton could record the mileage with great ease and accuracy. West of Fort Laramie he marked the trail with signposts every ten miles.

At Fort Laramie the company halted for repairs, Brigham Young celebrated his forty-sixth birthday, and the camp was joined by a company of Mormon Battalionists and Mississippi Saints from Pueblo. The pioneers then followed the regular Oregon Trail, which took them to Jim Bridger's trading post, Fort Bridger, on the Black's Fork of the Green River. They made frequent contact with other travelers along the trail across the continent, including some at the crossing of the Platte, which could not be negotiated without a ferry. Anticipating this, the Mormon company had carried its own boat from Missouri. The Saints were able to cross with comparative ease, and the Missourians they met there paid $1.50 per wagon for the ferry. As the Saints went ahead, nine men remained behind to continue the lucrative ferry. The rest pushed on through South Pass, rafted across the Green River, and arrived at Fort Bridger early in July.

During the last week of June the vanguard company met Samuel Brannan, who had traveled east from California hoping to induce them to go on to San Francisco Bay. Brigham Young had already made up his mind, however, and California was not his final destination. The disappointed Brannan returned to the Bay area, where he shortly left the Church.

About the same time the company was joined by thirteen members of the sick detachment of the Mormon Battalion; the rest of the detachment was not far behind. After the group reached Salt Lake Valley the men were mustered out of the service and delegated Captain James Brown to go to California for their army pay. Brown accompanied Samuel Brannan back across the Sierra.

Meantime, the Saints were discussing settlement prospects in the Great Basin with everyone they met. Moses Harris was pessimistic because he thought timber was too scarce. To him, Cache Valley in the north was the best spot. On the other hand, Jim Bridger, who camped with them one night and advised them on the best routes, was most enthusiastic about the region around Utah Lake. He described a country filled with wild cherries, berries, timber, an abundance of fish, and plenty of good grass. The

Indians there, he said, "raise as good corn, wheat, and pumpkins as were ever raised in old Kentucky."[8] Only the frost discouraged him, and he felt that it might kill the corn. Miles Goodyear, whom they met after leaving Fort Bridger, already owned a trading post at the mouth of the Weber River, not far from the Great Salt Lake. He was most enthusiastic about the possibility of agricultural success.

The pioneer company arrived at Fort Bridger on July 7. Thereafter travel became more rugged, as they negotiated the mountain passes. They had received conflicting advice on which route to follow into the Salt Lake Valley but decided to follow the route blazed the year before by the ill-fated Donner-Reed party bound for California.

By the time they reached the valley, the pioneers had broken into three groups. Since crossing the Green River some of them had suffered from attacks of severe fever and delirium, which left them weak and listless. Brigham Young was struck with this same

Charles B. Hall engraving of the Salt Lake Valley in July 1847, after a painting by H.L.A. Culmer. (Church Archives)

---

[8]Clayton, *Journal*, p. 278.

"mountain fever" (probably induced by wood ticks) soon after meeting Miles Goodyear. As a result, the company divided and a small sick detachment lagged behind. After July 13 a third division, under the direction of Orson Pratt, moved ahead to chart the route and prepare a wagon road through Emigration Canyon.

On July 21 Orson Pratt and Erastus Snow suddenly caught their first glimpse of the magnificent Salt Lake Valley and the broad waters of the Great Salt Lake, which "glistened in the sunbeams." After having been enclosed in the mountains for so many days and then beholding such extensive scenery, wrote Elder Pratt, "we could not refrain from a shout of joy, which almost involuntarily escaped from our lips the moment this grand and lovely scenery was within our view."[9] The two men took a twelve-mile circuit into the valley, then returned to camp.

The following day, July 22, was one of exploring. A delegation from the advance company went northward to the hot springs and found soil of "most excellent quality," abundant water, and green, "very luxuriant" vegetation along the streams. In other places the vegetation was dry for want of moisture, and large crickets swarmed in the foothills. That night the advance party camped in the valley.

The next day Orson Pratt dedicated the land to the Lord, then instructed his men to begin plowing and planting in order to preserve the seed they had carried from Winter Quarters. Some, like William Clayton, were "happily disappointed" because the lack of timber and the apparent scarcity of rainfall seemed foreboding. The soil, however, was fertile; all it lacked was water. While plowmen prepared the ground for potatoes and turnips, another group began to dam up the stream and dig the all-important ditches. From this crude beginning the Latter-day Saints would become experts in irrigation technology. When Brigham Young reached the mouth of Emigration Canyon, the pioneer camp was a beehive of activity.

On July 24 Brigham Young and the rest of the sick detachment zigzagged back and forth across a stream and made their way to the canyon mouth along a road freshly cleared of underbrush. "We gazed with wonder and admiration upon the vast rich fertile valley," wrote Wilford Woodruff in his diary. "President

---

[9]*Historical Record* 9 (April 1890): 74.

Young expressed his full satisfaction in the appearance of the valley as a resting place for the Saints and was amply repaid for his journey." In later years Elder Woodruff recalled the Church leader's words: "This is the right place, drive on."

For the next few days various companies scouted other nearby areas, but by July 28 the majority of the company had concluded that the site already selected was the best the valley had to offer. That afternoon Brigham Young identified the location for a temple and approved a city plan, and in a meeting that evening the location was unanimously approved by the company.

This was only the beginning of the task of conveying thousands of Saints to the new place of refuge, which continued through 1847 and into succeeding years. By December 1847, more than two thousand had completed the journey, and several hundred had returned east to bring families and friends. In 1850 census takers counted 11,380 residents in the Great Salt Lake Valley and settlements to the north and south. More than seven thousand Saints still waited in the semipermanent way stations in Iowa. They would be helped by William Clayton's *Latter-day Saints' Emigrants' Guide,* published in 1848 after he had remeasured the pioneer trail with a new odometer. He was among those who returned to Winter Quarters in August 1847 with Brigham Young.

Kanesville, Iowa, 1847-53

In August 1847 all the apostles who were with the vanguard company returned to the Missouri River camps with 161 other men. Traveling east to join their families, they met the first of ten westward-moving companies organized by Elders Parley P. Pratt and John Taylor. The historic Mormon trek was under way.

Meantime, federal Indian agents were complaining that the Mormons at Winter Quarters were stripping the country of timber and wild game. To avoid further misunderstandings, the Saints evacuated the camps west of the river in the spring, and Miller's Hollow, renamed Kanesville in honor of Thomas L. Kane, became the new headquarters. As a staging area for the migrating Saints, the community reached its peak population of five thousand in 1852. Other campsites, at least thirty of which became the basis for permanent towns in Iowa, grew up in surrounding regions. Agriculture flourished, craftsmen pursued their trades, and schools were conducted. The principal newspaper was Orson Hyde's

Kanesville, or Council Bluffs, Iowa, in an engraving by Charles B. Hall.
(*Church Archives*)

Frontier Guardian, established in 1849.

Kanesville's chief business was serving Church migration. Three Mormon-operated ferries met the needs of those who wished to cross the Missouri River near the staging center. They also helped an estimated 140,000 other pioneers traveling to Oregon and the California gold fields between 1848 and 1852. As the final abandonment of Kanesville approached in 1853, the Saints sold their land and improvements to other American frontiersmen, as they had done in Mt. Pisgah. The Mormon way stations had provided six years of important service.

Early Mormon Settlements in Utah

As the Saints laid plans to build their new Zion in the valleys of the Great Basin, their first challenge was to select appropriate sites for settlement. Each new townsite was thoroughly investigated for its agricultural potential, the availability of water supplies and of wood for fuel and building purposes, and grazing lands for livestock. Most early settlements were located near the mouths of canyons, which provided easy access to timber in the mountains and streams coming from them.

The first homes in Salt Lake City were simple cabins built within a stockade. The original adobe fort was expanded twice in 1848 to make room for new arrivals; by that time families were beginning to occupy city lots.

Expansion beyond the original settlement began in 1848. Families located on every stream northward to the Weber, and others moved southeasterly in Salt Lake Valley. Also that year Captain James Brown received authorization to use $3,000 of the Mormon Battalion pay, which he had been delegated to collect, to purchase the claims of Miles Goodyear on the Weber River. This cleared the way for the founding of Brownsville, later renamed Ogden. In 1849 thirty settlers moved into Ute Indian country and established Fort Utah on the Provo River. That fall a dozen families pioneered Tooele Valley and 224 settlers accepted Ute Chief Walkara's invitation to settle in Sanpete Valley at a location soon named Manti.

In each of these locations the first arrivals lived for several months in crude dugouts or lean-tos while they laid out city plots, assigned the surrounding farmland, and began to build houses or cabins. Although some cabins were built of logs, timber was in short supply and many settlers used adobe bricks. Mud-and-straw adobe was also used for fences.

In all these areas natural resources were at a premium, but the Saints had their own system of resource development. Water, timber, and land were considered to be precious stewardships, and their use and distribution were regulated by bishops. The bishop distributed land according to each man's needs and abilities, and until the area was all assigned, newcomers were assured of property. These practices implemented Brigham Young's instructions of July 25, 1847, when he said that there would be no buying and selling of land—no speculating and no profit making on essential resources and commodities.

Supporting the infant farming communities were a number of basic industries that sprang up quickly in Salt Lake Valley and surrounding settlements. Gristmills, pit saws, and blacksmith shops were among the first established, for they were needed to produce the flour, timber, horseshoes, nails, and tools necessary to the pioneer communities. In addition, cabinetmakers, tanners, bootmakers, potters, and other skilled artisans soon appeared in every community.

In 1848 seagulls saved enough crops from invading hordes of crickets that the Saints were able to survive the winter. The Saints soon began to see this as a sign of Divine intervention in their behalf, and the seagull story has been immortalized in music, drama, sculpture, and painting as the great Mormon miracle. This bronze relief at the base of the famous Seagull monument was executed by Mahonri Young in 1913. (Church Internal Communications Department)

The Saints were also at the mercy of natural forces. Though the first winter was relatively mild, flour was scarce, vegetables were generally unavailable, and meat from the overworked cattle was tough. As spring arrived the settlers found themselves turning to the sego lily and other roots and greens to save them from hunger. In March they began to plant seeds for the 1848 harvest, which would be especially critical, since the Saints arriving late that summer would not bring surplus food.

But 1848 was a dry year, and late spring frosts damaged many crops. Late in May the black crickets observed in the foot-hills the year before descended in swarms upon the winter wheat and maturing spring crops. Efforts to drown, mash, or burn the invading horde seemed futile. On Lorenzo Young's farm, he wrote in his diary on May 29, they destroyed in one day "¾ of an acre of squashes, our flax, two acres of millet and our rye, and are now to work in our wheat. What will be the result we know not." The result was grim, but it would have been much worse had it not been for the flocks of seagulls from the islands of the Great Salt Lake that swept in and began gorging themselves on the crickets. The hungry gulls ate all they could, regurgitated the indigestible portions, then ate again and again. This continued for several weeks, and much of the crop was saved. Though the harvest was greatly reduced, the Saints were grateful for what was spared and for the proof that the untried soil of the valley could indeed produce crops.

The winter of 1848-49 was especially severe, and both settlers and livestock suffered heavily. Firewood was difficult to obtain and food supplies dwindled. Some turned to boiling rawhide for nourishment—"glue soup," it was called by one family. Those who had surplus shared with those who were less fortunate; and to prevent excess profit-making, voluntary controls were established on the price of such necessities as beef and flour. The colony survived, but empty stomachs, frostbitten feet, and an unfamiliar environment discouraged many pioneers. For some, California's milder climate became an increasingly attractive lure.

Money and the Gold Rush

Not long after the severe winter melted into spring, thousands of Americans rushing to the gold fields of California passed through the City of the Saints. The Saints were naturally interested, and "California fever" spread to some. Church leaders cautioned against going to the gold fields, lest overnight success and concern for worldly things interfere with the building of the Kingdom.

Although most members followed counsel and stayed away from the mines, the gold rush had an important impact on their well-being. It supplied them with scarce commercial goods at surprisingly low prices. Merchant companies, organized to haul goods to California, learned when they reached Salt Lake City that food, clothing, implements, and tools sent by ship had beaten them to the marketplace. Rather than take an even heavier loss in California, they sold their goods at devalued prices in the Salt Lake Valley. California pioneers were equally eager to sell cheaply things that burdened them. In addition, the Saints operated ferry-boats and blacksmith shops, turning handsome profits by providing these and other services. The gold rush of 1849 brought welcome hard cash into the Mormon commonwealth.

The Saints were influenced by the gold rush in other ways. A mint was established in Salt Lake City to process the gold dust brought in by travelers and returning members of the Mormon Battalion. And in 1849 Brigham Young called in several young men, mostly Mormon Battalion veterans, and sent them on a confidential mission to the gold fields of California. He did not want the Saints generally to rush for gold, but if these young men could bring back substantial amounts of dust, there would be gold for the mint to help establish an acceptable circulating medium in the territory. As it turned out, the returning gold missionaries brought little to show for their adventure when they returned—hard-won proof that Brigham Young was right in urging the body of Saints to stay home.

Political Patterns

Until Congress provided a territorial government for the Saints in 1850, they governed themselves, first through the ecclesiastical machinery of the high council and then through the provisional State of Deseret, created by the Council of Fifty.

Before the apostles returned to Winter Quarters in 1847 they organized a municipal high council in the Salt Lake Valley, which presided for the next fifteen months. With John Smith, uncle of Joseph Smith, at its head, the council drafted laws, collected taxes, regulated prices, and conducted other public business. In January 1849 the Council of Fifty assumed the high council's municipal functions. This group of leading men drafted a plan for territorial government, which they later changed to one for state government, and while waiting for federal approval, they established the provisional State of Deseret.

The State of Deseret was the civil government of the Great Basin settlements for two years. It organized counties, granted rights to natural resources, regulated trade and commerce, established the Nauvoo Legion as an official state militia, and fulfilled all functions of a regular government. Brigham Young and his counselors were elected, respectively, governor, chief justice, and secretary. Members of the Council of Fifty and others, most of whom were prominent churchmen, filled other state offices and selected ward bishops as local magistrates. Church and state were clearly welded together through the persons of the officers, a precedent that later would bring severe criticism from the larger society. To the Saints, however, this seemed a natural expression of their needs.

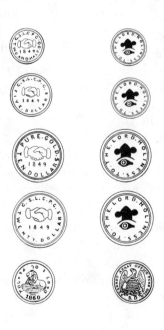

*Mormon gold coins, 1849
and 1860. Initials on the
earliest coins stand for
"Great Salt Lake
City Pure Gold." "Holiness
to the Lord" appears in the
Deseret alphabet on
the 1860 five-dollar coin.
(Charles B. Hall engraving,
Church Archives)*

Indian Relations

When the Mormon pioneers arrived in the Great Basin they confronted another problem—the people already there. Perhaps as many as twenty thousand native Americans of the Western Shoshoni, Ute, and Southern Paiute tribes inhabited the area that is now the state of Utah. The Indians generally existed by gathering and hunting, with little cultivation of the land. They were also traders and sometimes ranged as far as California to dispose of horses and other goods stolen in raids along the Old Spanish Trail. Differing customs and attitudes could well have led to continuing conflict, although the peculiar location of Salt Lake Valley helped alleviate the threat. The valley formed a natural buffer between lands frequented by the various tribes, although all ventured into it for salt. Mormon fencing, farming, and community building were not so great a threat there as they might have been in other places.

Within a week of the pioneers' arrival, Indians had visited camp to trade for guns, ammunition, and clothing. These visits became frequent, and at times larger numbers gathered. After a squabble among different bands over a stolen horse, the pioneers resolved to trade with the Indians only at their own encampment, and appointed two men to handle all commercial dealings. As an expression of benevolent service, a number of Mormon women provided clothing for the Indians of Deseret.

Encounters between the newcomers and older residents during the first years were generally peaceful, although during the winter of 1849-50 Indians threatened war against the LDS farmers of the Provo River settlement, Fort Utah. The state militia responded to the settlers' appeal, and in a two-day battle about forty Indians and one settler died. The confrontation effectively ended Indian resistance in Utah Valley and allowed the Saints to move out of their protective fort onto city lots and farms.

Lending assistance in the Fort Utah War was Captain Howard Stansbury, who arrived in August 1849 to conduct a government survey of the Great Salt Lake and Utah Lake. When the Saints first heard of Stansbury's expedition, they were apprehensive about its military and political implications, fearing another invasion of their rights. However, once the mission of the Army Corps of Engineers was made clear, Brigham Young cooperated fully and Albert Carrington, a Mormon, was hired by Stansbury to superintend the chain line. Stansbury's published report included the first accurate maps of the two valleys and much important scientific information about plant and animal life in the Great Salt Lake region.

Transplanting a Culture

The Saints brought with them to the Salt Lake Valley more than a concern for survival. They brought culture, and much of their time in these early years was spent attempting to rebuild what they had enjoyed in Nauvoo. As in most pioneering settlements, there was a cultural lag before education, social life, and the arts could become what they were before, but the Saints did what they could even while they were establishing their pioneer communities.

In their concern for education during the early months of settlement, the pioneers conducted rudimentary schools around campfires on the plains and in wagon boxes, tents, and dugouts. In addition, they continued to enjoy parties, dances, picnics, and holiday celebrations. Most important, they brought with them their religion, and the religious system they knew in Nauvoo was quickly reestablished. The high council, organized in part to take care of the affairs of the community, was the only priesthood quorum in the valley until the Twelve returned in the fall of 1848.

In Winter Quarters the Twelve had become convinced of the need for reorganizing the First Presidency, so, on December 27, 1847, in the log tabernacle near Kanesville, Brigham Young was sustained as President. Members in the Salt Lake Valley sustained the action in April 1848. The familiar organization was reestablished. In February 1849 the Salt Lake Stake was reorganized and nineteen wards were established.

Buildings for Church administration and worship were provided as quickly as possible, including a small adobe building constructed as a church office in 1848, and a Council House, completed in 1850, which served as an important meeting place for various groups. The temple block was the site for immediate construction of a brush-covered bowery used for religious worship; it was soon replaced by a larger one and then, in 1851, by the "old" tabernacle.

In beginning again in the West, the pioneers were rededicating themselves to the religious goal of establishing Zion. As a symbol of their renewed commitment, the first arrivals were re-baptized by immersion in water. Many of those who followed shared the same experience. The Twelve proposed this renewel of covenants, not with any feeling that the prior baptism lacked validity, but rather as a symbol of thanksgiving and rededication. Like the pilgrims of earlier generations, the Saints had abandoned homes and farms in many places for the rigors of an untamed wilderness. Claiming it as their promised land, they hoped to re-establish themselves as a modern Israel, guided by a prophet and committed to the belief that the society they were building would one day become an ensign to all nations.

CHAPTER 8

Establishing an Ensign, 1851-1856

On July 24, 1849, President Brigham Young attended an elaborate Pioneer Day celebration in Salt Lake City, the first celebration to commemorate the pioneers' arrival two years earlier. Bands played, a huge American flag was unfurled atop a hundred-foot liberty pole, bells rang, guns fired, an impressive parade was held, and when the Constitution of the United States was presented to the President he led the assembled throng in three successive shouts, "May it live forever!" Eight years later he attended another Pioneer Day celebration with several thousand Saints in Big Cottonwood Canyon. There he was informed that a major expedition of the United States Army was traveling to Utah, and he suspected a hostile intent. Between these two events, the Latter-day Saints worked feverishly in their new place of refuge to create a self-sufficient community that could never again be forced to move. They grew in numbers, established civil government, and spread Mormon communities throughout much of the Great Basin. But they also saw the unfortunate beginning of new misunderstandings between themselves and their American neighbors. It was a time of high hope and accomplishment as well as one of trial, dominated by the energetic leadership of the "great colonizer," Brigham Young.

Territorial Government for Utah: Organization and Seeds of Conflict

By 1851 more than 350 miles of Utah wilderness between Bear River in the north and the Virgin River in the south had been explored and settlements located along a 250-mile strip of the Wasatch Front sustaining a population of 15,000 Saints. The State of Deseret provided efficient government until 1850, when the territory was officially organized by the Congress of the United States.

When John M. Bernhisel was first sent to Washington to petition for territorial status, Colonel Thomas L. Kane astutely foresaw certain dangers and warned the Saints that they should press for full statehood. Only this, he argued, would assure them the right of self-government without interference from federally appointed officials who might not be sympathetic with their religious purposes. In 1849 he told them:

> You are better off without any government from the hands of Congress than with a Territorial government. The political intrigues of government officers will be against you. You can govern yourselves better than they can govern you. . . . You do not want corrupt political men from Washington strutting around you, with military epaulettes and dress, who will speculate out of you all they can. . . . You do not want two governments. You have a government now, which is firm and powerful, and you are under no obligations to the United States.[1]

The following year Brigham Young instructed Elder Bernhisel to apply for statehood, but the Territory of Utah already had been created by Congress. The question of statehood had become part of the larger American controversy over the status of slavery in the territories recently acquired from Mexico. After a heated debate that almost tore the nation apart, the dispute ended with the famous Compromise of 1850. California became a state, with a constitution prohibiting slavery, and the territories of New Mexico and Utah were organized with the understanding that they could decide the issue of slavery for themselves. Disappointed, the general assembly of Deseret nevertheless resolved in March 1851 to "cheerfully and cordially" accept territorial status. The new territorial legislature soon adopted all the laws of the provisional State of Deseret.

---

[1]Brigham Young, "Manuscript History," November 26, 1849.

Mormon community of Fillmore, Utah, 1855, showing the old Statehouse. In 1851 Fillmore was designated as the location of the territorial capital, and the legislature met there in 1855 and 1856. Jules Remy, one of many visitors to Utah in this period, published this engraving in his book, Journey to the Great Salt Lake.

As residents of a territory of the United States rather than a state, the Saints in Utah suddenly found themselves, as Thomas L. Kane had predicted, again under the threat of external political influence. As in the past, it would be impossible for them to avoid political conflict so long as their ideas and practices clashed with those of the men in power. They were unable to elect their own governor, judges, or executive officials, for these officers were appointed in Washington. They could send a delegate to Congress who could lobby, debate, and participate in committee work, but not vote. Happily for the Saints, some of the first territorial appointments were given to Church members. Brigham Young was appointed governor, Zerubbabel Snow became one of the three federal district judges, and Seth Blair and Joseph L. Heywood were made U.S. attorney and U.S. marshal, respectively. On the other hand, the chief justice for the territory, the second associate justice, the territorial secretary, and two Indian agents were all non-Mormon appointees.

The stay of the first gentile officials in Utah was both brief and controversial, sowing seeds of new misunderstanding. They did not arrive until late in August 1851, and the difficulties began almost immediately. At a special Church conference early in September Justice Perry Brocchus requested and received permission to speak to the Saints. He expressed friendship for the Mormons, but some of his remarks were uncomplimentary, especially to the women in attendance. President Young was visibly irritated, and in defending the Saints he sharply criticized Brocchus and other government officials. Two weeks later, when the legislature opened, a disagreement developed over control of the $24,000 congressional appropriation that the territorial secretary had brought. Judge Brocchus was disturbed because the legislature did not choose him as Utah's congressional delegate. Before the end of the month the two non-Mormon judges, the territorial secretary, and an Indian agent had become so dissatisfied that they left the territory, taking the $24,000 with them. The accusations they carried to Washington were only the beginning of a series of unfortunate and distorted reports that would again result in misunderstanding and tragedy.

With two of the three federal judges gone, the territorial legislature quickly filled the judicial vacuum by granting criminal jurisdiction to the territorial probate courts. This created a unique situation that illustrates the unusual relationship between the Church and civil government in early Utah.

The chief legislative and executive body of the counties was the county court, which consisted of the probate judge and three selectmen. The probate judge also presided over the county probate court, which had jurisdiction over estates, guardianship, and other civil affairs. When criminal jurisdiction was added, the power of the judge was significantly broadened. He now held concurrent jurisdiction with the federal district courts in all criminal matters, so that even when a federal court was in session, those accused of crimes could proceed through the local probate courts instead.

The legislature's action in granting such jurisdiction created a situation loaded with potential misunderstanding, even though it had been done in other territories. In most cases the county probate judge, who was appointed by the territorial legislature, was also a local bishop or other church leader. To unsympathetic outsiders it could easily appear that the church and local government were one and the same. In cases where a bishop presided over the court, for example, the same man held executive, legislative, and judicial power within the county, as well as strong ecclesiastical influence. In the minds of most Latter-day Saints this was both natural and desirable. To the gentiles, it appeared un-American.

As the settlement of the Great Basin proceeded, a close working relationship developed between the ecclesiastical units and local government. Before local government was officially organized, bishops as church officers directed the dispensing of land, building of roads, digging of ditches and canals, and other necessary projects. Even after civil government began to function, the county courts often used the Church to carry out important tasks. Bishops were the natural leaders and were often appointed as watermasters, herd ground overseers, and supervisors of roads and canyons. The Church was also often asked by the county court to assist in building schools, determining locations for roads, collecting certain taxes, and even in liquor control. The practical, beneficial result of this relationship was that the church and civil government worked closely together in the many tasks necessary for building new communities.

Some Utah gentiles were concerned with the unusual judicial authority given the probate courts. Whereas anti-Mormon federal judges were unwilling to grant citizenship to immigrating Latter-day Saints as long as the Church accepted the practice of plural marriage, the probate courts had the right to hear citizenship petitions and grant American citizenship. It also became apparent that many Saints distrusted the federal courts and did all they could to take their criminal cases to the probate courts. Ultimately, in 1874 the federal government removed the controversial jurisdiction by granting exclusive jurisdiction in both civil and criminal cases to the federal courts.

The Church helped promote order and justice in the Territory of Utah in another way. President Brigham Young and his counselors encouraged the Saints to avoid taking their personal disputes to courts of law. It seemed incongruous for a Saint to take his brother to court if the matter could be settled amicably some other way. Church leaders had little trust for most gentile lawyers, who seemed to them to value individual profit more than public well-being. As a result, church courts, especially bishops' courts, were often used to settle differences between members. They usually became courts of arbitration, and the Saints accepted the bishops' decisions. Church courts, relying more heavily upon an inherent sense of justice than upon technicalities growing out of legal precedent, gained such a reputation for fairness that non-Mormons sometimes took their claims there instead of to the territorial courts. In disagreements over property lines, ownership of livestock, and other matters that could be settled by arbitration, Church courts were often the most effective dispensers of justice in the territory.

Utah's territorial legislature met annually. Members of the legislature were usually Church leaders, elected by the people of the various counties. In some ways they viewed their political responsibilities as an extension of their church activity, for they were all engaged in building a political community conducive to the success of the Kingdom.

For a time, at least, the Council of Fifty had great influence on policy making. Working informally and behind the scenes, it functioned as a kind of coordinating council between the Church and the political institution. Many of its members were also members of the legislature, others served as lobbyists, and some became heads of territorial government agencies. To the Saints, it seemed natural that the elected leaders of the territory should be the "chief men of Israel," and that an unusual degree of political harmony should prevail. This very unity, however, led to conflict with gentile appointees who resented their own lack of influence.

After the runaway officials of 1851 left the territory, a feeling of accord between other federal appointees and the Church prevailed for about four years. Then two new federal judges, George Stiles and W. W. Drummond, became particularly irritated by the jurisdiction of the probate courts and the territorial marshal. Drummond, in particular, ridiculed some of the practices of the Saints, and he soon left the territory. Arriving in Washington in the spring of 1856, he leveled a number of charges against the Saints, including the false accusation that they had destroyed federal court records in Salt Lake City.

Malicious reports against the Saints were also directed to Washington by David Burr, the territorial surveyor general. He criticized the legislature's action in granting certain leading Saints exclusive control or stewardship over water sites, timber, and grazing lands. This was actually done to assure equitable distribution and use of these natural resources, but to Burr it ran counter to

American free enterprise and individualism. It may also have been illegal. The Saints also found themselves in conflict with Garland Hurt, a federally appointed Indian subagent. Brigham Young, as superintendent of Indian affairs, was his superior, but Hurt was suspicious of the Church's motives and worked to counteract Brigham Young's policies. The reports and accusations of these federal appointees unfortunately contributed to a misunderstanding that combined with political events to create the Utah War of 1857-58.

Expansion of Mormon Communities

The settlement of the Great Basin was a grand experiment in planned expansion. President Young was anxious for the Saints to occupy as much land as possible in order to provide for incoming converts. He also didn't want the Saints ever again to be driven from their homes because they were numerically overwhelmed by unsympathetic outsiders. Unlike most American colonizing activities, then, the unique Mormon commonwealth was the result of careful economic planning by Church leaders, authoritative direction in carrying out the plan, and the willing cooperation of members.

The chief economic activity of the Saints in Utah was agriculture, and in planning their settlements they chose areas most capable of sustaining farming. Brigham Young approved of mining for iron and coal, the raw products needed in building a new society, but opposed large-scale mining for precious metals. The boom and bust cycle of most mining would not provide the stability needed for permanent communities. Small-scale, family-oriented agriculture would offer the Saints steady employment and close proximity to each other. The major communities, of course, needed skilled artisans and craftsmen of all kinds, but the basic economy was necessarily agricultural.

The Saints considered a call to settle a new area as important as a call to serve on a proselyting mission. It was not uncommon for someone sitting in a conference meeting to suddenly hear himself called on a mission to locate a new community. This often meant leaving newly established homes and farms and starting over again in another strange and uninviting area. It was nevertheless a religious duty, and most Saints were willing to do as directed. They had the vision of being engaged in building the Kingdom and were willing to make more sacrifice if it was necessary to that

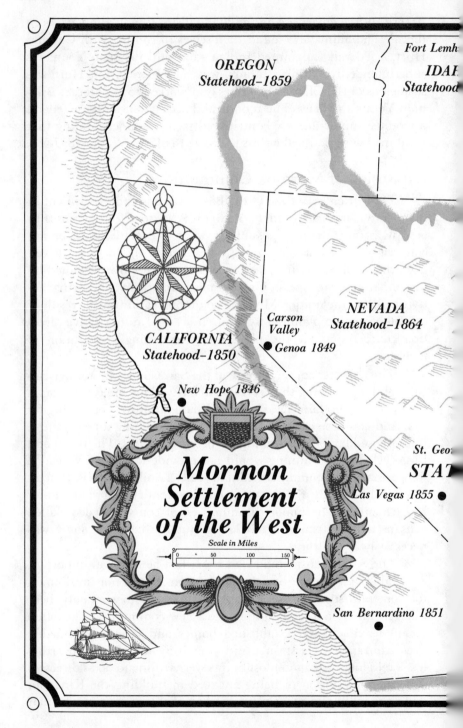

OREGON
Statehood–1859

Fort Lemh

IDAI
Statehood

NEVADA
Statehood–1864

Carson
Valley
Genoa 1849

CALIFORNIA
Statehood–1850

New Hope 1846

St. Geoi
STAT

Mormon
Settlement
of the West

Las Vegas 1855

Scale in Miles

0   50   100   150

San Bernardino 1851

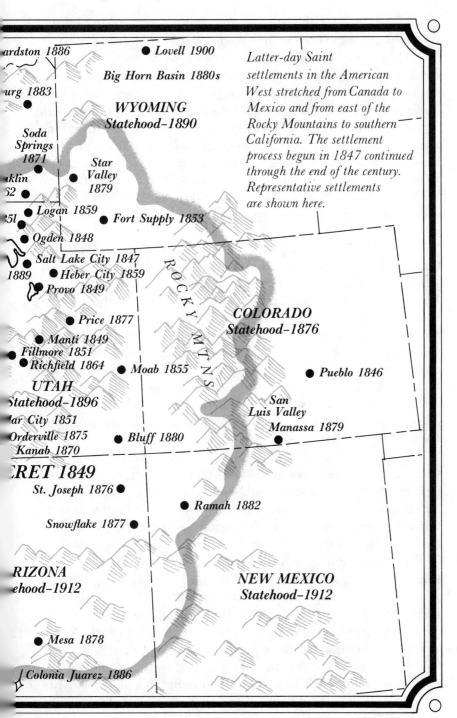

ardston 1886   ● Lovell 1900

                Big Horn Basin 1880s

urg 1883
    ●   **WYOMING**
                       Statehood-1890
  Soda
 Springs
  1871   Star
klin   Valley
62 ●   1879

5l   ● Logan 1859   ● Fort Supply 1853

   ● Ogden 1848

      ● Salt Lake City 1847
1889   ● Heber City 1859
    ● Provo 1849

        ● Price 1877   **COLORADO**
                               Statehood-1876
     ● Manti 1849
   ● Fillmore 1851
   ●Richfield 1864   ● Moab 1855

  UTAH   ● Pueblo 1846
Statehood-1896   San
ar City 1851   Luis Valley
Orderville 1875   ● Bluff 1880   Manassa 1879
 Kanab 1870   ●

RET 1849
   St. Joseph 1876 ●

                    ● Ramah 1882

  Snowflake 1877 ●

RIZONA   **NEW MEXICO**
ehood-1912   **Statehood-1912**

   ● Mesa 1878

 Colonia Juarez 1886

ROCKY MTNS

Latter-day Saint
settlements in the American
West stretched from Canada to
Mexico and from east of the
Rocky Mountains to southern
California. The settlement
process begun in 1847 continued
through the end of the century.
Representative settlements
are shown here.

goal. To appreciate the unusual colonizing success of the Latter-day Saints, it is essential to understand that kind of discipleship.

Until 1850 Mormon colonies were generally confined to the vicinity of Salt Lake City, Ogden, and Provo. During the winter of 1849-50, the Council of Fifty sent out the Southern Exploring Company, which led to the establishment of Parowan in southern Utah in 1851. That fall, about thirty-five men skilled in mining and manufacturing were called from Parowan to establish an "iron mission" about twenty miles further south. There they founded Cedar City, began mining the rich iron ore nearby, and in less than a year had a blast furnace in operation. By 1853 nearly all the sites recommended by the Southern Exploring Company had been settled.

But Brigham Young had a larger plan in mind. Parowan, Cedar City, and the other communities along the Wasatch Front were part of what is sometimes called the Mormon Corridor. President Young announced as early as 1849 that the Church would build a string of settlements from Salt Lake City to the Pacific Ocean. Although he was reluctant to send many Saints to California, he did want an outpost near Los Angeles that would serve as a reception and outfitting post for immigrants. He could then encourage them to come by ship from Europe to California, even though it meant going around Cape Horn. They could then migrate overland along a route almost completely controlled by the Saints.

In 1851 President Young called apostles Amasa Lyman and Charles C. Rich to lead a group to California to select a site for settlement. They purchased a ranch and founded the community of San Bernardino. Within four years 1,400 Mormon settlers lived in the area—many more than the President had anticipated—and they were cultivating 4,000 acres.

The colony provided a port of entry for converts from the Pacific missions, a gathering place for California Saints generally, and a rest and supply station for missionaries. In 1857 the San Bernardino colony was officially discontinued, partly because of the approach of federal troops to Utah and also because the colony was experiencing internal dissension and problems with non-Mormon neighbors. Brigham Young had come to doubt the wisdom of having such a large Mormon center in California. After the recall some Saints remained in San Bernardino, although the majority responded to counsel and eventually returned to Utah.

The expansion of Mormon settlements was influenced by work among the Indians. Soon after the founding of Cedar City, groups were sent to explore the Virgin and Santa Clara rivers of southern Utah, and in 1854 men were sent to work among the Indians of the region. The missionaries not only taught the Indians the gospel, but also tried to help them build homes and learn better agricultural methods. In the process they discovered that cotton could be grown in southern Utah, and in the late 1850s and early 1860s a "cotton mission" settled St. George and other colonies in Utah's Dixie.

During the 1850s several colonies developed beyond the perimeters of the Great Basin. In April 1855 missionaries were called to teach Indians in a number of areas, including present-day Oklahoma. Missionaries were also assigned to establish Indian missions at Las Vegas, at Elk Mountain near present-day Moab, Utah, and at Fort Limhi in Idaho. None of these missions proved very successful. Elk Mountain was abandoned the year it began, while Las Vegas and Fort Limhi ended when Brigham Young recalled the settlers in 1857. A small Mormon settlement also grew up in Carson Valley in western Nevada, but because serious friction developed with non-Mormon miners in the area, the settlement was recalled in 1857. In each of these cases, as well as in the case of San Bernardino, the impending Utah War provided an official reason for withdrawing the Saints. It is also clear that some of the settlements were having difficulties, they were too far from the central body of the Saints, and Brigham Young was impressed with the importance of maintaining strength in the central gathering place.

To supervise access to Utah from the east and to serve as supply stations for immigrants, two outposts were established along the Oregon Trail. Fort Bridger was originally owned by Jim Bridger, the famous mountain man and fur trader. It was here that Mormon pioneers often stopped to rest and purchase supplies before beginning the last hundred miles of their trip to Salt Lake Valley. Unable to purchase Ft. Bridger, colonists were sent out from Salt Lake City in 1853 to found Fort Supply, about twelve miles from Fort Bridger, and to do missionary work among the Indians. In 1855 the Church finally bought Fort Bridger and thus controlled that portion of the Oregon Trail. The two outposts pro-

William Henry Jackson's painting of Fort Bridger. (Photo courtesy Church Archives)

vided supplies for both Mormon and non-Mormon travelers. The Saints burned Fort Bridger and Fort Supply in October 1857 as part of their effort to slow down the U.S. Army advancing toward Salt Lake City.

Despite a few failures, the accomplishment of bringing tens of thousands of immigrants from America and Europe and successfully settling them in new communities is truly astounding. By 1857 more than fifty settlements had been established along the western slopes of the Wasatch Mountains and approximately forty more in other places, with a total of forty thousand Saints. Though the settlement pattern was interrupted in 1857-58, it continued afterward until the end of the nineteenth century when more than five hundred settlements had been established by the Saints in the Mountain West.

The planting of each Mormon colony followed a similar pattern. First, exploring parties were sent out to identify sites with the greatest potential. Next, Church authorities called a leader and other colonists, making sure that various skills were represented so the colonists could create a smoothly functioning community. The group met in Salt Lake City or another major center, then traveled together to its destination. The traveling company was organized in groups of tens, fifties, and one hundreds, with captains over each.

Upon arrival, the settlers dedicated the land and immediately began working. The planning was frequently done in priesthood meetings. Some colonists were assigned to work on the stockade that would provide a temporary home and protect them against the Indians, while others built dams, dug irrigation ditches and canals, planted crops, built roads, hauled timber, and erected houses. Until the first homes were finished, they often lived in wagons and makeshift dugouts.

A typical Mormon community in the West was carefully designed to encourage close-knit community life and religious activity. The town was laid off in square blocks separated by wide streets. The blocks varied from five to ten acres, but each was divided into equal lots of about an acre, and a community drawing was held to determine ownership. Each family had sufficient acreage in town for a garden, a small orchard, and sheds for poultry and livestock, but the main agricultural activity took place outside the village. The center square was set apart for a meetinghouse, and usually the first public building erected was a combination church and school.

On the outskirts of the village was a large area known as the Big Field. It was divided into plots of several acres, depending on the amount of land available, and again each family received a section by drawing lots. The Big Field was used mainly for raising grain and hay, and it was fenced cooperatively by the community. Outside the fenced area was a common pasture for livestock, and men and boys would usually be assigned to take turns as herdsmen.

One key to the success of the Mormon communities was their peculiar combination of private enterprise and economic cooperation. In most cases each family head was considered owner of the property he had been assigned, but it was understood the land was to be cultivated and not held for speculative purposes. The land was free, but it was for the benefit of all, and in some cases if the man did not use the land it was transferred to someone who would. (Technically, no one held legal title until after the federal land office was set up in Utah in 1869.) The grazing lands and timber and water resources were considered community property, and everyone had equal access to them. Even though certain individuals were given control of the canyons and could charge for the use of roads into them, this was only to compensate for the expenses involved in building and maintaining the roads, and the fees charged were not excessive. When new settlers joined a community they were given land and community resources on the same basis as the original settlers. Thus Mormon community building was an exercise in both cooperative planning and free enterprise, regulated for the benefit of all by the authority of the Church.

The Latter-day Saint farmer continually had the problems of nature to combat. After the difficulties of 1848 and 1849, harvests were generally good until 1855 and 1856, when natural disasters brought near-famine. Rocky Mountain locusts caused serious damage in earlier years, and during 1855 a grasshopper plague was more destructive than during any previous year. In addition, this was a hot year, which cut down available irrigation water and caused a late-season drought. In some areas as much as one-third to two-thirds of the crop was destroyed. Yet that same year 4,225 immigrants reached the Salt Lake Valley, more than any year since 1852. To add to the difficulties, an unusually severe winter in 1855-56 killed almost half the cattle in the territory, and during the next summer a damaging grasshopper invasion left another poor harvest.

Once again the organization and strength of the Church helped ward off utter starvation and disaster. Priesthood leaders instituted a rationing program and asked those with surplus to distribute it among the destitute. In addition, the Church inaugurated the practice of fast offerings, which has since become a fundamental practice among the Saints. During the winter of 1855-56 the Saints were asked to fast on the first Thursday of every month and to donate the food saved to the bishop's storehouse. These offerings were used for those most urgently in need.

Indian Affairs

The Saints had a special attitude toward the Indians, for the Book of Mormon bore record that the Indians were a chosen people of the house of Israel who ought to have the gospel. Brigham Young urged patience and kindliness toward the Indians and instructed the Saints to feed rather than fight them and to teach them peaceful agricultural pursuits. While this policy did not prevent some early skirmishes, or a small war in 1853-54, it was generally successful in maintaining peace.

One of the most serious difficulties arose over the Indian slave trade. Occasionally Indians voluntarily sold their own children into slavery to Mexican or other Indian traders, and often tribes raided each other for children and women to be sold. The Ute chief, Walker, was at first friendly with the Church, and even allowed himself to be baptized, but when differences on the slave trade became apparent, his amiability began to cool. The Saints were indignant about the slave trade but were unable to persuade the Indians it should stop. In 1852 the territorial legislature passed a law authorizing probate judges to purchase Indian women or children who had become slaves and assign them to suitable homes for care, protection, and education. Ironically, the Saints thus actually fostered a slave law in the territory, but its primary purpose was to liberate victims of Indian slavery.

The slave law angered the Indians, who saw it as interference with a profitable business. Slave traders encouraged them to resist the law and supplied them with arms. This became an important factor in the outbreak of the Walker War in July 1853, when the Utes attacked various Mormon settlements beginning at Springville. The intermittent fighting lasted until May 1854, when Brigham Young and Chief Walker arranged a peace settlement.

The Walker War was followed by renewed missionary activity among the Indians. Often the missionaries would take their families to live in Indian villages, help the Indians learn to farm, work with them in the fields, and teach them the gospel. They baptized many and directed scores of Indian children who went to live in Latter-day Saint homes. The missionaries also worked among white Mormons themselves to get them to show more charity and understanding toward the native Americans. An attempt was made to establish Indian farms in a few central and southern Utah counties where the Indians would be taught farming methods as well as the gospel. Some of these farms existed until the 1870s.

However charitable in intent, Mormon policies toward the Indians led to friction with the federal government. In 1853 John W. Gunnison, leader of a U.S. Topographical Survey unit, was killed in a tragic massacre, and since the Mormons were at peace with the Pahvants, some people accused the Saints of complicity in the affair. There was no basis to the charge. Moreover, certain federal Indian agents resented Mormon friendship with the Indians, for it undermined their own influence. Garland Hurt, for example, even though he cooperated briefly in the Indian farm experiment, disliked Mormon missionary activity, and especially disliked the distinction sometimes made by the Indians between "Mericat" and "Mormonee." His antagonistic reports to Washington caused the federal government to withhold part of the funds appropriated for territorial Indian programs.

Business and Financial Affairs among the Saints

Chief among Brigham Young's temporal goals for the Saints was the hope of economic self-sufficiency. As much as possible he wanted to end reliance upon outside interests and institutions for the needs of Mormon society. The plan called upon the Saints to develop their own manufacturing industries, largely as cooperative rather than private enterprise. Large sums of money needed to back these industries could not be obtained from the private sector, so the Church itself shouldered the principal responsibility. This meant that the Church needed a substantial source of income. In addition, it needed funds to support the building, administrative, colonization, and welfare activities that daily multiplied.

Although limited income was available from church properties and donations for special purposes such as the Perpetual Emigrating Fund, the basic source of funds was tithing. As a result, a tithing house, sometimes called the bishop's storehouse, sprang up in every community. About two-thirds of the tithing donated at local offices went to the General Tithing Office in Salt Lake City for general church needs; the rest was used at the discretion of local bishops.

In pioneer Utah tithing could be paid in several ways. Cash was always acceptable, but there was little available. Many people donated one day of labor in every ten toward various church projects. Most common, however, was payment of tithing "in kind." Pioneer farmers commonly brought chickens, eggs, cattle, vegetables, and goods they had manufactured themselves to the tithing houses. Uniform financial values were attached to these items, and the Church used them to pay its creditors as well as to distribute food and supplies to the Saints employed on its public works projects. The tithing house soon became a basic economic institution in every Mormon community. There local settlers would pay tithing, exchange one form of produce for another, and receive credit for surplus goods deposited. Tithing scrip was printed and issued to those who received credit, and this scrip, though not an official currency, became an important circulating medium in Utah in the 1850s. The tithing houses served almost every economic need in the community, even providing a postal system, since mail was taken in and forwarded by tithing labor. Through these activities the Church was thoroughly involved in the economic life of its members.

But the Church needed increased capital to finance public works, immigration, colonization, and development of industry. To meet this requirement, Brigham Young attempted in 1854 and 1855 to reinstitute the law of consecration, and by 1856 a large percentage of the family heads in the territory had deeded their property to the Church. The federal government failed to establish procedures for legal ownership of land, however, and it was not possible to put the consecration plan into effect.

The main hope for further economic development lay in industry, and in 1851-52 the Church commenced a systematic program to develop manufacturing. Such industry would provide work for the rapidly increasing population and help combat the high cost of importing eastern goods. The iron mission, for example, was designed to provide Utah ore to support the manufacture of iron products in the territory. That project, however, was

Deseret Store and Tithing Office, about 1868. Hotel Utah presently stands on the spot once occupied by this building. (Church Archives)

beset with such major difficulties—inadequate fuel and water, as well as the problems of the Utah War—that by 1859 it had closed.

Other manufacturing enterprises during the 1850s met similar fates. A pottery plant was abandoned in 1853, although a more successful private business was set up three years later. The attempt to establish a lead smelter at Las Vegas in 1856-57 also failed. In 1851 Elder John Taylor purchased machinery in Paris for a woolen factory, but it did not arrive in Utah until 1862, which meant that until then no major woolen factory existed among the Saints. Similarly, the effort to establish sugar manufacturing failed for technical reasons, although local farmers demonstrated they could grow sugar beets. More successful was establishment of a paper mill in the 1850s as part of the Church's public works program. This process required the continuous gathering of rags for conversion into paper, and for a time bishops sponsored extensive "get out the rags" campaigns. One faithful Saint was even called on a "rag mission" in 1861 and for three years traveled among the people collecting rags for the paper project.

The failure of these early manufacturing projects did not mean economic disaster for individual Mormons. Since these were cooperative Church-sponsored ventures, the losses were sustained primarily by the Church. These various manifestations of the search for economic self-sufficiency are important as an illustration of the Church's wide-ranging activities in attempting to build the Kingdom of God in the West. When one experiment failed, persistent leaders tried another, for they believed it was important to the Kingdom to promote both the spiritual and the economic well-being of the Saints.

Very early, the rapid influx of converts created a major surplus of labor in the territory; in response the Church inaugurated a Public Works Department in 1850. The new department had the dual advantage of being able to provide employment for immigrants as well as needed laborers for public building projects and experimental manufacturing enterprises. Supported by tithing funds, it kept between two hundred and five hundred men on its rolls. Several important projects were supported by the public works program. Of special significance was the Endowment House, finished in 1855, which provided the only place for the performance of temple ordinances until the completion of the St. George

Temple in 1877. Workers built a wall around Temple Square and helped with the temple itself. They labored in the sugar, wool, and paper manufacturing experiments, in a machine shop and foundry, and manufactured adobe bricks, the territory's major building material.

Church leaders also attempted to launch an overland freight business. They were displeased that unfriendly merchants controlled transportation of goods from the East and seemed to be reaping exorbitant profits. As early as 1852, Church spokesmen petitioned Congress for a coast-to-coast railroad that would run through Utah and reduce the cost of transportation. In 1856 Hiram Kimball, acting for the Church, received a contract for hauling mail from Independence, Missouri, to Salt Lake City; it was hoped he could also haul freight more cheaply than outside merchants. Then, in 1857, the Church organized the Brigham Young Express and Carrying Company, better known as the Y. X. Company, designed to operate between Salt Lake City and Independence. Forty settlements were planned along the route to act as supply stations. More than $100,000 was invested in the enterprise, but just as prospects looked hopeful, the federal government cancelled the mail contract, a chief source of revenue for the company. Antagonists criticizing Church action in Washington had succeeded not only in stopping the mail contract but also in inaugurating the Utah War.

Life among the Pioneer Saints

All was not work and worry for the Saints in pioneer Utah. On the contrary, visitors were often impressed by the good humor and enjoyment of life that marked every community. Singing, dancing, drama, and other wholesome recreation characterized Latter-day Saint life. The Nauvoo Brass Band, under William Pitt, was reinstituted in Salt Lake City, and later Domenico Ballo, an Italian immigrant, organized and conducted an even more famous band. Brigham Young himself regularly led the dancing at parties held by the Saints wherever he went. Holidays were times of special celebration, characterized by picnics, parades, dances, and good times in general. In 1852 the Deseret Dramatic Associaton was organized, and the following year the Social Hall in Salt Lake City was constructed. It became the center for dramatic productions in the Mormon capital until the beautiful Salt Lake Theatre was completed in 1861. Gentile visitors often observed that such social activities were accepted parts of the Mormon religion, remarking with interest that social events were always opened with prayer.

Nor did the Saints forget the importance of education, although during the earliest years their efforts were somewhat limited. During the first winter in Salt Lake City a single school class for children was taught in a tent; by 1854 schools had been established in every ward. Usually the first building erected in a new community was a combination school and church house, but before such buildings were ready, some classes were conducted in the homes of the teachers. The University of Deseret (later renamed the University of Utah) was created by the legislature of the State of Deseret in 1850, although it ceased operation temporarily after the first five years. The Deseret Agricultural and Manufacturing Society was also formed in 1856 to instruct farmers in better farming techniques. Educational opportunities were limited, but the difficulties of forming a new community did not cause the Saints to ignore them completely.

Serving as a substitute for adult education was the Polysophical Society, organized during the winter of 1852 by Lorenzo Snow, who wanted to encourage young men and women to cultivate literary talents. Begun in the Snow home, the society moved to public halls and then spawned similar organizations in Salt Lake City and surrounding settlements. A forerunner of the Mutual Improvement, or Retrenchment, Associations of the 1860s, this popular educational organization featured essays, debates, musical numbers, and other expressions of the heart and mind. It gradually ceased operation after Elder Snow moved to Brigham City during the religious retrenchment of 1856.

In general, social life centered around the ward. Ward socials, dances, and dramas, and even some music clubs, contributed to the feeling of community among the Saints.

Religious life also centered around the ward. By the end of the 1850s there were only four stakes in Utah, but each community had its ward. The wards began to assume a religious significance different from that of earlier periods of Church history. They varied in size and were without auxiliaries except for a few Sunday Schools for children. Nevertheless, the bishop assumed the religious leadership of the community, and the wards began to hold

Huge crowd gathered for groundbreaking ceremony for the Salt Lake Temple, February 14, 1853.
(Marsena Cannon photograph, Church Archives)

preaching meetings each Sunday as well as fast meetings one Thursday each month. In addition, block teaching was inaugurated and helped create a greater cohesiveness among ward members. This was basically an Aaronic Priesthood responsibility, but since the lesser priesthood was not well organized, bishops began to call Melchizedek Priesthood holders as acting teachers to visit each family monthly and exhort to good works.

In the 1850s general conferences of the Church held semiannually in Salt Lake City also acquired greater significance. From the beginning these conferences had been a time of religious instruction, but in the Great Basin, since the Saints often traveled for hundreds of miles to attend, they also became a time of reunion and socializing. The conference became one of the great symbols of Mormon unity as well as a cohesive force in building a sense of community. As one eastern correspondent good-naturedly observed, the general conference became "the post office, newspaper, legislature, Bible, almanac, temporal, spiritual, and social director of the people."[2]

The most controversial aspect of Latter-day Saint religious

_____
[2]*Harper's* 2 (December 4, 1858): 781.

and social life was the practice of plural marriage. Even though the doctrine had been privately taught and practiced by Joseph Smith and other Church leaders in Nauvoo, it was not announced publicly until August 29, 1852, at a conference in Salt Lake City. Elder Orson Pratt of the Council of the Twelve was chosen to give the first public sermon on plural marriage and he used his time to show why he believed the doctrine had come from God. Among other things, he said that it would provide the opportunity for the righteous Saints to raise up a numerous posterity in the true principles of the gospel. He added that the practice was protected by the U.S. Constitution, for it was a religious practice and the Constitution guaranteed freedom of religion. In later years some federal legislators and judges emphatically disagreed.

Actually, even though plural marriage became one of the major focal points for persecution against the Church, it played a relatively small role in the total life of most Mormon communities. Most Saints accepted it in principle but did not practice it. It was not only a complicated social problem, but also a heavy economic burden, especially in times of persecution. Exactly how many people married into plural marriage is impossible to determine, but probably between 10 and 15 percent of the families in pioneer Utah were involved. Local leaders were sometimes encouraged to take more than one wife in order to set the example, but apparently most men who married a second wife did not take another.

Nevertheless, plural marriage had some unusual social dimensions for the Saints. According to the accepted guidelines, a man had to receive the permission of both his first wife and the leaders of the Church to be sealed to a second wife, and permission depended upon his spiritual worthiness as well as his economic status. In practice, many plural families were successful, while others found difficulties. Often a first wife would actually select her husband's second wife; frequently she would be a sister or close friend. Sometimes a plural marriage was contracted without the first wife's permission. Whether or not both families lived in the same house varied; some families chose to live together while others lodged in separate homes. It is true that stresses sometimes arose, but it is also true that many of the wives lived together as affectionate, mutually helpful sisters. Most entered only out of a firm conviction that it was part of the restoration of the ancient gospel and that it would help ensure a large posterity and the blessings of eternal exaltation. Like the law of consecration, however, "the principle," as it was called, was something many avoided. When the Church officially stopped sanctioning plural marriage in 1890, an overwhelming majority of members sustained the change.

Perhaps the most dramatic religious event of the 1850s was the reformation of 1856-57. Sparked by the fiery preaching of Elder Jedediah M. Grant, a member of the First Presidency, the reform was an effort to persuade the Saints to renew their dedication to righteous living. The leaders, deeply concerned about what appeared to be signs of a moral and spiritual decay, traveled around the territory preaching repentance with unprecedented fervor. Members were called upon to repent and rededicate themselves fully to the work of the Lord and to seal this rededication with rebaptism.

Political problems, economic reverses of previous years, plus the evidence of moral laxity contributed to the apparent need for reformation. The zeal with which it was preached became at times almost excessive. The result, however, was that thousands of Saints rededicated themselves to the building of the Kingdom. All this may have accounted for the fact that the following year the Saints were emotionally prepared to confront the army of the United States en route to Utah. So thorough was the reformation that on December 30, 1856, the entire membership of the all-Mormon territorial legislature was rebaptized for the remission of their sins, and all were confirmed by the laying on of hands of the Twelve. "This was a new feature in the Legislature," wrote one member. "We believed if we could get the Spirit of God we could do business faster and better than with the spirit of the Devil, or the spirit of the World."[3]

Missionary Work and the Gathering

Regardless of the tremendous tasks the Saints faced in building a new community in the Mountain West, few things were more urgent than spreading the gospel and preparing for the gathering of the Saints. Even though it appeared that Europe, especially England, was the most fruitful field for converts outside North

---

[3]Wilford Woodruff, "Journal," December 30, 1856, Ms., Church Archives.

America, hopes for spreading the gospel worldwide were emphasized by the sending of missionaries to Latin America, the islands of the Pacific, India, Asia, and South Africa. The Church was hardly a world church, but the nascent spirit of worldwide influence was present. The missionaries took literally the prophecy of Daniel: the latter-day kingdom would begin as a stone cut out of a mountain, then would roll forth and eventually fill the whole earth. The Kingdom had been established in the tops of the mountains, and the Saints intended to start moving it toward its international destiny. In 1852, for example, of the 159 missionaries set apart—the most in a single year since 1844—only 22 were assigned to work within the United States.

Although most converts during this period came from England and Scandinavia, the work of the missionaries in other areas illustrates the scope of what the Saints were attempting. In 1851 the first elders arrived in India. These missionaries, originally British converts, began working among British citizens. Within a short time they had baptized several people, and when Brigham Young heard of their success, he called nine more elders to India. They arrived in April 1853 and spread throughout the subcontinent.

Although the British-born missionaries baptized several natives, neither they nor the American-born elders understood the native languages and customs of India well enough to succeed. Therefore, the missionaries worked primarily among British citizens at military bases, until they ran into trouble with chaplains of the Church of England; then they tried unsuccessfully to work among the natives. They translated the Book of Mormon into one of the Hindu tongues, but it was never printed. A number of the Caucasian converts immigrated to Utah.

At the same time Hosea Stout, a former police captain in Nauvoo, and two companions attempted to open a mission to China. The political situation of the country prevented them from venturing inland, so they remained in Hong Kong. They could find no one to teach them the native language, and the reception they received from the English-speaking people was generally hostile. After fifty-six days of almost total discouragement, they headed home. Wrote Elder Stout in his journal shortly before departure: "We feel that we have done all that God or man can require of us in this place. We have preached publickly and privately as long as any one would hear and often tried when no one would hear. . . . And thus it is this day we do not know of one person in this place to whome we can bear our testimony of the things of god or warn to flee the wrath to come."[4]

In South America, Elders Parley P. Pratt and Rufus Allen landed in Valparaiso, Chile, in 1851. They were hampered by a disruptive revolution and their lack of fluency in Spanish. Equally important, they could not use the standard missionary approach of working through families and friends, or preaching to large gatherings. These methods had worked well in England, but in South America Catholicism seemed to have an unbreakable hold on the social customs of the upper classes. The lower classes and pure-blooded Indians were uneducated and dominated by the land-owners, making communication difficult. As in both China and India, the missionaries were unprepared to cope with economic and social conditions vastly different from anything they had known, and they sailed for home in less than a year.

In northern Europe, and especially in England, success was phenomenal. The Scandinavian Mission, organized in 1850, baptized about a thousand converts each year during the decade, mostly in Denmark. About 25 percent of these emigrated to the United States. Missionary work was also opened in France, Italy, and Switzerland in 1850, although success there was minimal. In England, however, more than 15,000 British converts left for Utah between 1849 and 1857. In addition, several hundred emigrated from France, Italy, and Germany. Missionary work outside England and Scandinavia temporarily languished after missionaries were called home by Brigham Young in 1857 and 1858 because of the Utah War.

The migration of thousands of Saints to Zion demanded organization. When the first companies left England in 1840, they were assisted in their planning by the Council of the Twelve, but generally, once in America, they had to organize and arrange for their own supplies and transportation. In the next few years various attempts at organization were tried. In 1845 Reuben Hedlock, just released as British Mission president, organized the Mutual Benefit Association. Designed to bolster the economy of Nauvoo, it was actually a private business venture, though en-

---

[4]Brooks, *On the Mormon Frontier,* 2:482.

*Latter-day Saints emigrating from Europe frequently rode Mississippi
riverboats upstream from New Orleans to an outfitting post, where they would
prepare for the trek across the plains. (A Frederick Piercy engraving in
Linforth,* Route from Liverpool to Salt Lake City)

dorsed by the Church. At the same time it assisted the British
Saints and provided land and goods for them in America. This
commercial aspect of emigration did not last long, and Hedlock's
company was dissolved in 1846.

Following relocation of the Saints in the Great Basin, the
Church's involvement in emigration became more needful. In 1849
Church leaders were faced with the realization that some eight
thousand refugees from Nauvoo were still camped on the Great
Plains. A special call in conference brought $5,000 and several
yokes of oxen to help them to Utah. This was the beginning of the
Perpetual Emigration Fund (PEF), and the following year the Perpetual Emigrating Company, which administered funds and
supervised migration, was formally incorporated under the laws of
the State of Deseret.

The accomplishments of the new company have been recognized as unique in the history of immigration. PEF agents were
employed in England to charter ships and assemble and instruct
prospective emigrants. The agent was located in Liverpool; all applications went through him, and he informed the Saints when
they should arrive. Some emigrants could pay their own way completely; others needed some help from the fund, while others were
so poor their trip required total financing. The fund was maintained by donations of cash and property from the Saints in the

Great Basin as well as by the agreement that those who were helped would repay as soon as possible. Some, of course, did not repay their indebtedness—an irritant to Brigham Young, on whose shoulders rested the responsibility of raising sufficient funds. In 1856, for example, the indebtedness to the fund totaled $56,000, and the disgusted President declared, "I want to have you understand fully that I intend to put the screws upon you, and you who have owed for years, if you do not pay up now and help us, we will levy on your property and take every farthing you have on the earth."[5] This was simply rhetoric, for the debtors were never abused, even though the Church constantly tried to persuade them to repay.

The Liverpool PEF agent sometimes chartered ships exclusively for the Saints, but if this was not possible, he arranged to have the ship partitioned into separate sections for Mormons and non-Mormons. The emigrants were noted for their heavy luggage, having been encouraged to take tools and equipment with them, and some captains were heard to complain that their ships were an inch lower in the water than usual.

Once aboard ship, the Saints were usually organized into wards or branches, with a returning missionary presiding over each. The daily routine included morning prayer, cleaning the ship, religious classes, and evening prayers, with special religious services on Sunday. Charles Dickens said the captain of one such ship told him, "They came from various parts of England in small parties that had never seen one another before. Yet they had not been a couple of hours on board, when they established their own police, made their own regulations, and set their own watches at all the hatchways. Before nine o'clock, the ship was as orderly and as quiet as a man-of-war."[6]

Mormon emigrating companies shared the experiences of other groups plus some that were unusual. They saw romance and marriages, births and deaths, and burials at sea. At the same time, the Saints were missionary-minded and made many conversions at sea; on one occasion they even converted an entire ship's crew after a storm. Baptisms were sometimes performed in a large barrel filled with sea water, which had to be entered from a ladder. At

---

[5]*Journal of Discourses*, 3:6.
[6]Quoted in William Mulder and A. Russell Mortensen, *Among the Mormons* (Lincoln: University of Nebraska Press, 1958), p. 336.

other times a platform was suspended from the side of the ship and the convert was baptized in the ocean.

At first the emigrants sailed to New Orleans, where another PEF agent met them and booked passage up the Mississippi River to St. Louis. Then a third agent arranged transit up the Missouri River about 500 miles to an outfitting post, where a final agent prepared them for the overland journey to the Great Basin. Later, after the railroad reached St. Louis, when cholera was taking an unfortunate toll along the river, the Saints were routed to New York, Boston, or Philadelphia, whence they traveled by railroad to St. Louis and then continued on to the outfitting posts. The total journey usually required eight or nine months.

Even with donations from the Saints, the PEF found itself in financial difficulty, and Church leaders sought to cut costs. In 1855 Brigham Young revived a plan that had been considered once before but never instigated. The worthy poor were instructed to walk from the end of the railroad to Zion and to carry their possessions across the plains in handcarts. Some nineteen hundred European Saints volunteered, and they were divided into five companies for emigrating in 1856. Each group arriving at the railway terminus in Iowa City was outfitted with handcarts and supplies, along with a few wagons to carry heavier baggage. Then began one of the most heroic treks in the history of Mormon migration. The first three companies reached Salt Lake City safely and were greeted with joy and enthusiasm by the Saints. "As I gazed upon the scene," wrote Wilford Woodruff, "it looked to me like the first hoisting of the floodgates of deliverance to the oppressed millions. We can now say to the poor and honest in heart, come home to Zion, for the way is prepared."[7]

Joy soon turned to sorrow with the tragic experience of the Willie and Martin companies. When they arrived at the railroad terminus they found their handcarts not yet prepared. Some observers wisely suggested that they postpone crossing of the plains until the following year, as the season was getting late. Determined to join the Saints as soon as possible, however, they waited until their carts (some hastily made of green wood) were finished, then headed west. After reaching Wyoming they were caught in an early snowstorm.

---

[7]Wilford Woodruff to Orson Pratt, September 3, 1856, *Millennial Star* 18 (1856): 795.

Handcart pioneers at a campsite on the plains. (Painting by C. C. A. Christensen. From the Permanent Collection of Brigham Young University)

When leaders in Salt Lake City heard that a thousand Saints were still on the plains, they were shocked. October conference was about to convene, and Brigham Young quickly calculated what would be needed to rescue them. He and other leaders devoted their conference addresses to the task of delivering the handcart pioneers, exhorting the Saints in the valley to donate food, clothing, teams, and wagons for their relief. Even though the Saints had little surplus, their response was warm and overwhelming. On October 7 an advance group of twenty-seven men with sixteen mule teams was on its way eastward with provisions, and more were to follow. Both companies were rescued, though only after more than two hundred had frozen to death. The last group struggled into Salt Lake City at the end of November. In all, some eight thousand Saints arrived in Utah between 1856 and 1860, and just over three thousand had walked. But 1860 was the last year for handcarts.

When new immigrants arrived in Salt Lake City, they were usually met as they emerged from Emigration Canyon and escorted to a block appropriately named Emigration Square. After being greeted by President Young or some other Church leader, they were treated to a celebration feast by the wards of the city. Then they were placed with families or in campgrounds until they could be permanently located. Some were sent to distant settlements or assigned to help colonize new areas, while others were given land and work in the Salt Lake City area. The Public Works Department often provided temporary employment until the immigrants could be relocated. Such planning was an important key to the success of the entire colonization program. One gentile visitor to Salt Lake City was highly impressed with what he saw when an immigrant train rolled in. Presiding Bishop Edward Hunter was instructing other bishops in their responsibilities:

An emigrant train had just come in, and the bishops had to put six hundred persons in the way of growing their cabbages and building their homes. One bishop said he could take five bricklayers, another two carpenters, a third a tinman, a fourth seven or eight farm-servants, and so on through the whole bench. In a few minutes I saw that two hundred of these poor emigrants had been placed in the way of earning their daily bread.[8]

Salt Lake Temple stone quarry, Little Cottonwood Canyon. (C.W. Carter photograph, Church Archives)

[8]William Hepworth Dixon, *New America*, 2 vols. (London: Hurst and Blackett, 1867), 1:252-53.

By 1856, less than a decade after the first pioneers entered Salt Lake Valley, almost forty thousand Latter-day Saints had arrived in Utah. They had founded many communities, established a permanent agricultural society in a difficult environment, begun to develop a small industrial potential, created the basis for a more permanent religious community than anything they had yet known, sent numerous missionaries throughout the world, and organized a vast and successful program for immigration. To most Latter-day Saints the Great Basin Zion was becoming an ensign to the nations, a New Jerusalem from which the Kingdom would eventually roll forth to fill the world. When faced with serious problems and reverses, the Saints took them in stride, believing that strength can come through adversity. They also realized that misunderstanding with the rest of the nation, or with the federal government, could not be avoided even though they were trying to act as honorable and upright citizens. Nevertheless, they were amazed in July 1857, while celebrating their tenth anniversary in the Great Basin, to hear that an American army was approaching their place of refuge.

PART III

Defending the Kingdom, 1857–1896

This view of Temple Square and vicinity was taken in 1892, at the laying of the capstone of the Salt Lake Temple. It represents the near-completion of much of what the Saints were seeking in the latter half of the nineteenth century. (C. R. Savage photograph, Church Archives)

DURING THE LAST HALF of the nineteenth century the American people witnessed momentous events that changed the course of their nation's history. The same events were also of consequence for the Latter-day Saints and hold a key to an understanding of this period of their history.

In July 1854 fifteen hundred anti-slavery enthusiasts congregated at Jackson, Michigan, antagonized by congressional acceptance of the Kansas-Nebraska Act. The measure, engineered by Senator Stephen A. Douglas of Illinois, organized two new American territories and permitted the people of those territories to decide for themselves whether or not they would allow slavery. This grant of local option was called popular sovereignty, and it eliminated prohibitions against slavery in parts of the Louisiana Purchase north of 36° 30' north latitude. Lands considered closed to slavery since the Missouri Compromise of 1820 were now opened to that controversial institution.

Popular sovereignty angered abolitionists in both the Whig and the Democratic parties. The provision apparently meant that Congress had relinquished its right to prohibit slavery in the territories. In response, the Jackson convention adopted a free-soil platform and created a new political coalition called the Republican party. Over the next thirty-five years this new party constantly played the role of antagonist against the Mormons.

In 1856 the Republican party made an impressive showing at the polls in its first national election. The campaign that year turned upon a catchy phrase linking polygamy and slavery as "twin relics of barbarism." Four years later the nation elected a Republican president, Abraham Lincoln; and, fearful of what he might do to slavery, the South left the Union. Secession touched off the Civil War, for President Lincoln believed that no state had the constitutional authority to withdraw, and he felt obligated to prevent illegal acts with military force, if necessary.

Few Latter-day Saints left their isolated refuge in the Rocky Mountains to participate in the Civil War, but the dreadful battles caused them to remember Joseph Smith's 1832 prophecy on war and to wonder if they foreshadowed the Millennium, when the Kingdom of God would be fully established on the earth. The war was not that anticipated climax, yet important changes soon swept the nation and involved the Latter-day Saints in the reforming zeal of the postwar reconstruction era. The main objective of the radical Republican reformers was to restructure the South politically and socially, and though it was not achieved at that time, the goal was full civil and political rights for the freed Negroes. Among the other institutions challenged by the reformers was the Latter-day Saint practice of plural marriage. It was a Republican president who signed the first anti-polygamy bill in 1862 and Republican congressmen who spearheaded the political campaign against the Church that lasted until 1890.

While defending themselves against intrusions, the Saints in these years were influenced by other affairs in the expanding nation. In their mountain haven they found themselves peculiarly fitted to profit from the continuing westward movement. In the 1850s they provided goods and services for California-bound emigrants, and later sold agricultural products to adventurers in nearby mining towns. They profited from the unwanted presence of federal troops sent to Utah in 1857-58 and again during the Civil War.

Completion of the transcontinental railroad in 1869 changed economic patterns and institutions in the nation and among the Saints. For the United States, coast-to-coast travel and the more rapid shipment of goods between East and West generated an economic revolution. It increased settlement of the plains states, filled in other areas, and stimulated industrial development. For the Saints, it meant an end to their unrealized goal of economic self-sufficiency and fostered instead a strengthening of ties with the national economy. The Saints participated directly in constructing the railroad and profited through investments in related enterprises. The arrival of the iron horse also hastened immigration, an important element in their continuing efforts to build Zion in the tops of the mountains.

The half-century under territorial government in Utah was generally a time of defensiveness for the Saints. Very early they confronted an American army that they mistakenly thought was sent to drive them from their homes. The tone of their public preaching during these years was one of indignation toward their detractors. Their economic experiments were often designed to strengthen them against the growing gentile influence within the boundaries of their western commonwealth.

Through it all, the ultimate goal of the Saints continued to be building the Kingdom of God on earth in preparation for the coming Millennium, and if anything, their millennial expectation increased with the years. The Saints also continued their determination to create an ideal and exemplary community, a Zion that would convince impartial observers of the strength and goodness of the Latter-day Saint way of life.

As the century drew to a close, the Saints reached a compromise with the federal government that seemed satisfactory to all. The sanction of plural marriage was abandoned as church policy, and the long-sought goal of statehood, which meant local self-government without the interference of federal overseers, was finally achieved. Forty years of important accomplishments through a period of watchful defensiveness prepared the Saints and the Church for a new era of more rapid growth and a more friendly relationship with their American neighbors.

CHAPTER 9

In the National Spotlight, 1856-1863

Thirty miles southwest of Salt Lake City is the tiny settlement of Fairfield, with a population of scarcely twenty families. Just west of town is a military cemetery with eighty-four graves, almost incongruous against its isolated desert background. To the casual visitor it is hard to believe that this was once the location of the third largest city in Utah. The military base, Camp Floyd, housed three thousand American soldiers, and the satellite town of Fairfield accommodated seven thousand civilians. Today the cemetery stands as a desolate symbol of the unhappy consequences of misinformation, misunderstanding, and miscalculation.

The years between 1857 and 1863 were, indeed, years of tragic misunderstanding. The Mountain Meadows Massacre, which contributed to the distorted image of the Saints throughout the nation, was the result of imprudent words and actions by certain California-bound travelers and overzealous responses from a few Latter-day Saints. The wasteful military expedition to Utah in 1857 was the result of poor information and lack of investigation by the president of the United States, and the unfortunate soldiers spent a freezing winter in Wyoming because the Mormons misinterpreted their mission. Within ten short years after their exodus

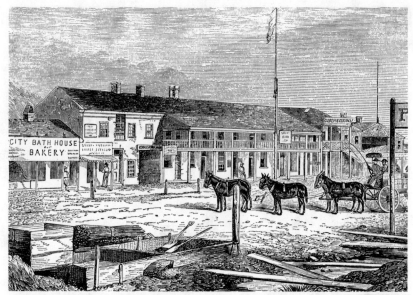

Evidence of new construction and varied economic activity can be seen in this portrayal of Salt Lake City's Main Street. The engraving appeared in Richard Burton's book, City of the Saints *(1861).*

from the United States, the Saints once again realized that their place of refuge was not a place of isolation, and their efforts to build the Kingdom would have to be conducted in the presence of others, under the watchful eye of the nation. Often that watchful eye was myopic, but a cure for its faulty vision was something the Saints were long in discovering.

The "Mormon Question" in National Politics

In the distorted reports that reached the American public in the 1850s, two themes stood out: the Mormon belief in plural marriage and the firm control of the government of the Territory of Utah by Church leaders. Both practices seemed to conflict with traditional American values. Many people considered plural marriage a violation of Christian morality; it seemed impossible to them that Mormon women who entered plural marriage accepted the principle without coercion, that good men could relish the thought of more than one wife, and that the reason for its practice was religion rather than depravity. Critics saw church influence in territorial affairs as the antithesis of American political pluralism, and they could not believe the system would produce anything but political tyranny. It was hardly surprising that the Mormon question entered national politics in the 1850s.

It was not, of course, a major question, but it was present, and the national political climate seemed right to consider it. This was the decade in which the so-called Know-Nothing party became temporarily important by spreading ill-founded rumors of a conspiracy by Catholics to take over America and by charging that immigrants threatened the American way of life. Even though the party never turned its attention officially to the Saints, the charges of murder and subversion that it made against Catholics and aliens sounded similar to the indictments others were making against the Saints. The fact that Mormon society consisted largely of immigrants made the charges even more plausible to those who sympathized with the Know-Nothings.

More significant was the decision to make the Mormon question part of the Republican party's platform in 1856. It was tied to the bitter national debate over slavery and popular sovereignty, which would soon divide the nation in civil war. Defenders of slavery had argued that states were sovereign and should be able to decide for themselves whether to be slave or free. When the opponents of slavery joined together in the Republican party with the goal of keeping slavery out of the territories, Mormonism was used as a bad example of what might happen under popular sovereignty. If popular sovereignty meant that the people of a territory could pass legislation protecting slavery, it also meant that the Latter-day Saints could practice their peculiar marriage system without congressional interference.

In 1856 a number of antipolygamy resolutions first appeared in Congress. That same year Utah made another bid for statehood, but it did not take the Mormon delegates long to discover that this was the wrong time politically. That same year the new Republican party entered its first national campaign and nominated the popular John C. Frémont as its presidential candidate. The party's official platform included a resolution that "it is both the right and the imperative duty of Congress to prohibit in the Territories those twin relics of barbarism—Polygamy and Slavery."

The Republicans lost the election, but the anti-Mormon activities of 1856 had an important effect. Forced to disclaim any partiality for the Saints, the new Democratic president, James

Buchanan, felt under obligation to do something to clear both himself and his party from any lingering suspicion that they supported the Mormons in Utah.

Buchanan Sends the Utah Expedition

Shortly after his inauguration in March 1857, President Buchanan appointed Alfred Cumming of Georgia governor of Utah, to replace Brigham Young. At the same time, in the mistaken belief that the Mormons were in rebellion against the government, Buchanan sent along a large military force to ensure the new governor's acceptance and authority.

The decision to send the Utah Expedition was based on misinformation fed to Buchanan by disgruntled federal officials who had left the territory. The most influential was W. W. Drummond, who had been appointed an associate justice of the Utah territorial supreme court in 1854. Almost immediately Drummond came in open conflict with the Saints. He first attacked the jurisdiction of the probate courts, which the Saints considered their most important legal defense against attacks from their enemies. In addition, he joined other federal appointees in writing letters to Washington decrying the Church. In March 1857 he wrote a letter of resignation that was probably the most important factor in forming the Buchanan administration's image of the Church. Buchanan did not realize that Drummond had an unsavory character long before he came to Utah and that, even as he was berating the Saints, his own conduct was far from exemplary. He had deserted his wife and children, for example, and had taken with him to Utah a prostitute who occasionally sat beside him in court. Even territorial chief justice John F. Kinney, another federal appointee, urged Drummond's removal from office because he was immoral and "entirely unworthy of a place upon the bench."

Drummond's letter charged that the Mormons looked to Brigham Young, and to him alone, for the law by which they should be governed, and considered no law of Congress binding. Further, he charged, there was a secret, oath-bound organization among all male members of the Church created to resist the laws of the land and acknowledge no law except the priesthood. He further charged the Church with murder, destruction of federal court records, harassment of federal officers, and slandering the federal government. He concluded by urging the president to appoint a governor who was not a member of the Church and to send with him sufficient military aid to enforce his rule.

The image created by Drummond and several others was sometimes so distorted as to be even ludicrous. Some charged that the Mormons were held virtually in bondage, unhappy with the rule of Brigham Young. They ignored the fact that each year a flood of immigrants poured into Utah, that only a trickle left, and that priesthood suppression certainly could not have held them if any large number wanted to leave. The Saints were charged with harassing federal officials, yet in most cases the appointment of these officials had been injudicious. The Mormons were accused of disloyalty to the government and of promoting separatism, yet an impartial observer would have seen that their very actions belied such charges. They constantly appealed for statehood, and each July 4 they celebrated Independence Day with an intense patriotism that would have been exemplary in any American community. They often criticized officers of the government, sometimes in severe language, but never criticized the Constitution or the form of government itself. Buchanan, however, did not look beyond the anti-Mormon reports that came to his desk. Twenty-five hundred officers and men were ordered to escort the new governor to the territory.

Buchanan blundered further; he failed to officially notify Brigham Young, governor of Utah Territory, that he was to be replaced or that a military expedition was on the way. When President Young learned of the approach of the troops, therefore, he acted on the assumption that they had no legal authority to enter the territory. As governor he must use the best means of opposing a group that the Saints firmly believed would become a hostile mob and would attempt to drive them from their homes again.

Buchanan issued his general orders on May 28, designating General William S. Harney as commander and ordering the troops to assemble at Fort Leavenworth, Kansas, to begin the march. It took time to make adequate preparations, for the troops needed thousands of cattle and enough equipment and supplies to fully outfit the expedition, and it was not an easy matter to take that many men across the Great Plains. Finally, on July 18 the first contingent left Fort Leavenworth.

Coincidentally, on that same date nearly six hundred miles to the west, four Latter-day Saints were leaving Fort Laramie on a hasty ride to Salt Lake City to inform the Saints that the expedition was on its way. Abraham O. Smoot, mayor of Salt Lake City, had taken the June mail to the states and along the way had noted signs of military activity and heavily laden government supply trains. At Independence he had talked to William H. Russell, a partner in the freighting firm of Russell, Majors, and Waddell, and learned that Russell's freight trains were to haul supplies to Salt Lake City for government troops. He also learned that the mail contract the Y.X. Company was depending upon had been cancelled. Heading west, Smoot and those with him disbanded the company stations and took the livestock with them. At Fort Laramie, Smoot, Porter Rockwell, and Judson Stoddard decided to push on to Salt Lake City as fast as possible.

On July 24 Brigham Young and twenty-five hundred Saints were camped in Big Cottonwood Canyon celebrating the tenth anniversary of the Saints' arrival in the valley. About noon the three weary travelers rode into camp and informed Brigham Young of the approaching army. President Young had been expecting something like this, and for weeks had been warning of the possibility of conflict. When the news came he was not surprised, but he waited until the celebration was over before he calmly announced it to the Saints that evening.

The reaction of the Saints was just what might be expected. With no official word of the expedition's purpose, it was easy for most of them to believe that once again hostile forces would attempt to drive them from their homes. Recalling the persecutions of earlier years, the settlers easily accepted the rumor that spread among them, and many feared the worst. The sermons of Church leaders and editorials in the *Deseret News* did little to allay their fears; for the next few months the spirit in Utah was one of indignant preparation for defense. The federal government, to be sure, was not bent on driving out the Mormons or even on beginning hostilities, though some of the soldiers harbored hatred of the Saints and were heard to brag of designs to permanently rid the country of these despised people. The expedition's only real purpose was to escort the governor and provide him with such aid as he called upon them to render, and Governor Cumming was not disposed to begin hostilities. But just as misunderstanding of the Mormon system led to sending the expedition in the first place, so the Mormons' lack of knowledge of the army's mission created apprehension and led to elaborate military preparations in Utah.

On August 1 word of the approaching army was circulated to all units of the Nauvoo Legion, and immediately they began quiet but definite preparations for defense. Latter-day Saints were advised to save their grain, for an ample supply of food would be essential. Church leaders called home colonists who had gone to San Bernardino, Carson Valley, and other scattered settlements in an effort to consolidate and strengthen the Saints should they have to defend themselves. Missionaries were also called home. Finally, patrols of the Utah militia were sent on the plains to protect, if necessary, the immigrants headed for Zion and to report on the progress of the federal troops. On one occasion two Mormon militiamen actually mingled with the troops, representing themselves as California immigrants. They heard firsthand the anti-Mormon braggadocio of some soldiers who claimed they were going to "scalp old Brigham." Although not reflecting the official instructions of the expedition, this attitude could only make the Mormons more apprehensive about the approaching confrontation.

In the meantime, the expedition plodded west. General Harney was detained in Kansas, and his replacement, General Albert Sidney Johnston, was unable to catch up with his troops until early November, after all hope of making it into Utah before winter had disappeared. On July 28, however, Captain Stewart Van Vliet was sent ahead to make whatever provisions were necessary to accommodate the troops in Utah. No one expected at that point that the Saints would forcefully resist.

Van Vliet arrived in Salt Lake City on September 7. He was the first official contact the Saints had with either the military or the government. The Mormons treated him kindly and with personal respect, but their attitude toward his approaching comrades was made clear.

The Saints' experience told them that the government had only evil designs against them, and the frustrated captain found it impossible to persuade them otherwise. The Saints informed him that they had made their last retreat and were now prepared to fight to defend their homes. Van Vliet attended Sunday services, heard emotional speeches, and saw the Saints raise their hands in a unanimous resolution to guard against any "invader." When he returned to the army, he was sobered, and he knew it was impossible to obtain supplies or any other form of help from the Mormons in Utah. He feared the possibility of conflict if the army proceeded too boldly, and advised that it should not push into Salt Lake City that season.

Captain Van Vliet's report demonstrated that as an astute and observant officer he understood what the Mormons were ready to do. Every person he interviewed told him the same thing—if the government should continue in its course, the Latter-day Saints were ready to burn their homes, destroy their crops, and make Utah a desert before the troops arrived. They would take to the mountains and there defy any power that came. Further, he predicted, the Saints would not resort to actual hostilities until the last possible moment. Rather, they would burn grass, cut up roads, and stampede army animals in an effort to delay the troops until

Alfred Cumming, who replaced Brigham Young as governor of the Territory of Utah in 1858. (Church Archives)

snowfall made it impossible for them to proceed. The lateness of the season, he said, would then make it dangerous for the troops to force their way in, for snow was already falling at Fort Bridger, and it would soon fill up the mountain passes.

Van Vliet's prediction was fully accurate. On September 15 Brigham Young issued a proclamation that declared martial law in the Territory of Utah and forbade the entry of armed forces. He ordered the Nauvoo Legion to make itself ready for the invasion, and in nearly every Utah community defensive preparations were accelerated. In a letter to bishops and other leaders in the territory, Brigham Young and Daniel H. Wells, commander of the Nauvoo Legion, gave some significant instructions that demonstrated the spirit of their preparations. They expected the "big fight" would take place in another year, and they were to be ready to lay to waste everything that would burn if hostilities actually occurred. They were to leave nothing for the army but, rather, were to "waste away our enemies and lose none."

Tragedy at Mountain Meadows

As if one source of trouble were not enough, 1857 brought a disaster that not only intensified national feelings against the Saints but was also a tragedy in its own right. The same week that Captain Van Vliet appeared in Salt Lake City to negotiate with the Saints, two hundred miles south an angry band of Indians and a few overzealous settlers murdered a company of emigrants on their way to California. Though the Church itself cannot be held responsible, the massacre at Mountain Meadows is nevertheless the most tragic slur on its history, for some members of the Church participated.

Exactly how the tragedy occurred is difficult to ascertain, but a few observations on the circumstances surrounding it may be made. The ill-fated Fancher company was only one of several groups of Americans migrating to California in search of new economic opportunities. It was not unusual that they should pass through Utah, and late in the season they took the southern route to avoid early snows in the Sierra Nevada. The Fancher company was the first to take this route in the 1857 season.

These emigrants arrived in Utah during a time of unusual tension and high emotion. Because of the approach of Johnston's Army, nearly every able-bodied man in the territory had been

mustered into the militia, and regular military drills were beginning. The Saints anticipated serious trouble, and they looked upon
all strangers with suspicion. Normal trading activities had ground
to a halt, for the Saints' efforts to preserve food meant that they
would not sell it to outsiders. This was especially hard on the emigrant companies of that year, and it angered them. In southern
Utah, priesthood leaders from Salt Lake City, especially Elder
George A. Smith, had preached the gospel of military preparedness
and the possibility of conflict. The feeling ran to extremes among
some of the local Saints, for Elder Smith noted in his report, even
before he knew of the massacre, "There was only one thing that I
dreaded and that was a spirit in the breasts of some to wish that
vengeance for the cruelties that had been inflicted upon us in the
States."[1] He realized that people were remembering the massacre
of the Saints in Missouri and the martyrdom of Joseph Smith, and
some could not resist the desire to avenge those acts. It would have
been a tense situation for any outside party, but when a group attached to the Fancher company, called the Missouri Wildcats,
were heard breathing threats against the Saints and boasting that
they had participated in the Missouri outrages, it was little wonder
the Mormons looked at them with more than disdain. Trouble
began as soon as the migrants passed Salt Lake City, and the feelings of hostility intensified as they traveled further south toward
Cedar City.

   Complicating the picture was the Indian problem in southern
Utah. The Saints had been cultivating good relations with the Indians, but the relationship was by no means perfect. The Walker
War had ended only three years earlier. In addition, the Indians
had few good feelings for the "Mericats," as they called non-
Mormon travelers in the territory. All this was complicated when
the pending invasion made it seem imperative to leaders that if
fighting should break out, they must have the Indians on their
side. Aware of the increasingly hostile feelings between the Saints
and the "Mericats," the Indians undoubtedly felt less restraint as
they began to raid emigrant companies, stealing their cattle and
supplies. They also threatened some of the small communities of
the Saints, and the settlers felt themselves risking danger if they

---

[1]As quoted in Juanita Brooks, *The Mountain Meadows Massacre* (Norman: University of
Oklahoma Press, 1962), p. 39.

acted too openly to restrain the Indians. The natives were especially hostile against the Fancher party, whom they accused of
poisoning their springs and of giving them poison meat.

The Fancher company stopped at Mountain Meadows, in an
area where settlers refused to sell them food. The migrants became
enraged and began to help themselves. The Indians, who had been
threatening for days, attacked the party on September 7 and laid
siege to the encampment for the rest of the week. John D. Lee, who
had been working with the Indians as a farmer, was unsuccessful in
his efforts to calm his wards and felt threatened himself if they
were stopped from raiding the wagon train. After a tense Sunday
meeting of officials at Cedar City on September 6, a messenger was
sent to Brigham Young asking for advice concerning the immigrant train. President Young sent word back immediately by the
same messenger, instructing the settlers of southern Utah not to
molest the party, and to avoid bloodshed.

But the message arrived too late. For reasons still not fully
known, the local leaders of the militia in southern Utah ordered
the destruction of the company, though the Indians were supposed
to do most of the work and receive the blame. John D. Lee was not
prone to that kind of violence, and he wept bitter tears when he
received his orders, but by the morning of September 11 he was
somehow convinced that this was what Brigham Young would
have wanted. Agreements were made with the Indians, and on
that tragic morning Lee and others decoyed the besieged emigrants from their encampment under the promise of protection. At
a prearranged signal, both Indians and white militia turned on the
company, and 120 people were slain. When some militiamen
refused to follow orders, the Indians did the work of destruction for
them. Only seventeen small children survived, and they were cared
for in nearby communities until friends or relatives could claim
them.

When the affair was reported to Brigham Young, he was told
simply that it was an Indian massacre. Only gradually did the
truth filter out from diverse and conflicting sources. A few local
Church officials, suspected of having ordered the massacre in their
capacities as militia leaders, were released from their church positions. Twenty years later, John D. Lee was tried and executed for
his part in the crime, but firm evidence against the others was so
hard to develop that they were never brought to justice.

When word of the tragedy reached the LDS settlements, there was only horror and disgust. None would condone the massacre, and even its perpetrators wept. There were even wider repercussions. Coming, as it did, while the Utah Expedition was marching toward the territory, the massacre added fuel to the already inflamed public opinion against the Saints. Brigham Young and the Church could not be held responsible, but the people outside the territory did not know that. Their only information came from the newspapers.

The Bloodless War

In the meantime, Johnston's Army, still without its leader, was pushing westward. The temporary commander did not as yet know the expedition's purpose. Mormon scouts hovered in the hills watching the movements of the troops and hearing wild threats from the soldiers about what they would do once they arrived in Utah. When the officers of the Nauvoo Legion learned that the army intended to disregard Governor Young's proclamation forbidding its entry into the territory, they decided to enforce the order. About eleven hundred men were sent to Echo Canyon, east of Salt Lake City, on the most direct route into the territory. At a narrow point in the ravine they built stone walls and dug trenches from which they planned to act as snipers. They also loosened huge boulders that could easily be sent crashing down on the moving columns, and constructed ditches and dams in the valley that could be opened to send water across the army's path. There was no doubt about Mormon determination.

The most colorful and daring activities of the Mormon militia were the exploits of Major Lot Smith and his "raiders" on the plains of Wyoming. They would have been almost comic in effect had the circumstances been less serious. On the night of October 5, Smith and twenty of his followers rode up to a wagon train carrying freight for the army. Smith noted as he rode into the light of the campfire that he could not see the end of his line of troops, which made it appear that he had more men behind him than was actually the case. The captain of the wagon train was duly impressed when he was ordered to evacuate his men from the wagons. After taking enough supplies to outfit themselves and after providing a group of Indians with some canvas, flour, and soap from the train, Smith and his men set torches to the wagons and rode off into the night, leaving them ablaze. In all, fifty-two wagons in two wagon trains were burned that night, and the oxen and cattle accompanying them were driven off.

Such exploits succeeded so well in delaying the progress of the army that when General Johnston finally joined his command in November, he realized that it was too late to enter the valley and they must winter at Fort Bridger. By this time the situation of the army was desperate. It took fifteen days to push thirty-five miles through storms and below-zero weather, cattle died by the hundreds, and the soldiers arrived at the fort only to discover that the Mormons had burned the wooden buildings. The stone walls were intact, however, and provided partial shelter for the winter, and the army had enough cattle and supplies to see it through. A major military engagement would have been impossible. Thus ended the only hostilities of the Utah War.

The Occupation

Back in the states the difficulties of the army were becoming known, and Buchanan was being severely criticized. He was chided in particular for sending the expedition without first thoroughly investigating the charges and for sending it so late in the season that it could not get through the mountains before snowfall. At this point Thomas L. Kane, a long-time and influential friend of the Saints, offered to go to Utah as a mediator, and his offer was gratefully accepted. It was a near-heroic journey for him. Unable to enter Utah through the mountains because of the heavy winter, he took a ship to Panama, crossed the isthmus, took another ship to southern California, and went overland through San Bernardino to Salt Lake City, arriving late in February 1858.

After persuading President Young that the Saints should let the new governor enter the territory unmolested, he traveled eastward through bitterly cold weather to Fort Bridger. Kane persuaded Governor Cumming to return with him to Salt Lake City without a military escort, assuring him that the Saints would accept him peacefully. When Cumming arrived he found that Kane was right, for he was treated with dignity and respect. He administered his office with tact and diplomacy and won the respect and confidence of the people. Equal tact on the part of the president of the United States nearly a year earlier might have

Thomas L. Kane,
friend of Brigham Young and the Mormons.
(Church Archives)

averted the unfortunate confrontation with the Saints altogether.

The Saints still did not completely trust the army. Recognizing that military resistance would ultimately end in tragedy, they decided to adopt, if necessary, a scorched-earth policy. Even before Governor Cumming arrived they had begun preparations for a move south. The Saints organized themselves magnificently. The settlers in southern Utah did not move, but groups were sent to explore possible settlement sites further south and west. Between the end of March and mid-May some thirty thousand settlers from Utah's northern towns moved south to the vicinity of Provo, leaving behind only enough men to care for fields and crops. If it appeared the army intended to occupy their homes, these men were to set fire to them. It was an extraordinary operation. As the Saints moved south they cached all the stone cut for the Salt Lake Temple and covered the foundations to make it resemble a plowed field. They boxed and carried with them twenty thousand bushels of tithing grain, as well as machinery, equipment, and all the Church records and books. The sight of thirty thousand people moving south was awesome, and the amazed Governor Cumming did all he could to persuade them to return to their homes. Brigham Young replied that if the troops were withdrawn from the territory, the people would stop moving, but that 99 percent of the people would rather spend the rest of their lives in the mountains than endure governmental oppression.

Meanwhile Colonel Kane traveled back to army headquarters at Fort Bridger and then, ill from the months of difficult
travel, continued eastward to report to President Buchanan. Before
Kane arrived, Buchanan had decided to send a peace commission
to the Saints, and in June the two commissioners, Ben McCullock
and Isaac Powell, arrived in Salt Lake City, carrying an offer of
pardon if the Saints would reaffirm their loyalty to the government. The Saints were indignant at the idea that they needed to
be pardoned, for they had never been disloyal, but they accepted it
in order to establish peace. Thus "Buchanan's blunder," as people
were beginning to call it, was effectively whitewashed by a pardon
that did not need to be issued, carried by a peace commission that
followed an army of occupation that never needed to be sent.

On June 26 the army entered Salt Lake City. The city was
quiet and deserted, except for those left behind to set the torch to it
if the army did not respect Johnston's pledge to leave their
property alone. That night the army camped on the banks of the
Jordan River, and soon General Johnston began to erect a
permanent base in Cedar Valley, west of Utah Lake. On June 30
the Saints were told they could go back to their homes. Brigham
Young himself led the return. The campaign had taken its toll,
and most of the Saints were beset with poverty and frustrated by
the confusing chain of circumstances that had interrupted their
plans for building Zion. As Leonard Arrington has summarized
the end of the Utah War:

A decade and more of achievement and social independence, in the face
of hostile nature and hostile humanity, had ended in poverty and disappointment. The picture of 30,000 pioneers trudging back to their
hard-won homes, farms, and orchards, with their skimpy and ragged suits
and dresses, driving their pigs and family cows, to the accompaniment of
jeers from "the cream of the United States Army" would live long in the
hearts and minds of the pioneer leaders. None would have dreamed that
within three years Babylon itself would be engulfed in a terrible fratricide
as the result of which the tables would be reversed: Soldiers would be
pulled out of Utah leaving to the Saints the spoils.[2]

Johnston's Army remained in Utah for three years, until it
was recalled because of the Civil War. The occupation meant
several things for the Saints. Their ten-year period of relative isola-

---

[2]Leonard J. Arrington, *Great Basin Kingdom* (Cambridge: Harvard University Press, 1958),
p. 194.

Campsite of Johnston's Army, October 29, 1858. (C. R. Savage and George Ottinger photograph, Church Archives)

tion was clearly at an end, for the army symbolized the growing numbers of gentiles who would come to live among them. The supporting community of some seven thousand people in Cedar Valley, in addition to the soldiers, proved a definite advantage to the economy of the Saints, who found a market there for agricultural and other goods. In addition, when the army finally abandoned Camp Floyd in 1861 it provided a windfall for the Saints, since some four million dollars worth of surplus goods were sold for a fraction of their value. The blessing was mixed, however, for all the vices of civilization were introduced and nurtured by the army and its satellite community.

The Saints and the Civil War

The retirement of Governor Cumming in 1861 was the result of a new tragedy in America: the outbreak of Civil War. Cumming was from Georgia, and when the southern states seceded from the Union, he felt it his duty to resign from his federally appointed position and return to his native state. The same was true of General Johnston, who joined the Southern Confederacy and was killed at the Battle of Shiloh in 1862.

The Saints viewed the Civil War with mixed emotions. They

were firm believers in the American Constitution, and in general supported the cause of a united nation. On the other hand, many of them believed that this was the beginning of the dissolution of the Union prophesied by Joseph Smith as early as 1832, which, he said, would spread bloodshed throughout the United States and would ultimately result in war being "poured out upon all nations."[3] To many of the Saints the Millennium was close at hand, and at that time, they expected, the Kingdom of God would be established and take precedence over all governments, including that of the United States. It was such religious considerations that made their attitude toward the war appear ambivalent.

Nevertheless the Saints had definite feelings about the political issues that divided North and South. Because of their own experiences with federal interference, they supported the idea of local sovereignty and therefore had some appreciation for the southern position. But they did not seriously consider supporting the southern Confederacy, and they repeatedly affirmed their loyalty to the Union. It was significant that when Brigham Young was given the privilege of sending the first message from Salt Lake City on the newly completed transcontinental telegraph in 1861, he chose to say to the president of the telegraph company, "Utah has not seceded, but is firm for the constitution and laws of our once happy country." Acting Governor Frank Fuller wired President Lincoln the same day: "Utah, whose citizens strenuously resist all imputations of disloyalty, congratulates the President upon completion of an enterprise which spans a continent."

The first opportunity the Mormons had to demonstrate their loyalty to Lincoln came in 1862. With the federal troops gone from Utah, the overland mail and telegraph needed protection. It was significant that the president wired Brigham Young, who was not then governor of the territory, and authorized him to raise a company of cavalry for ninety days' service along the southern Wyoming route. In response, a company of 120 men under the command of Major Lot Smith was raised to perform the service. Major Smith, along with Daniel H. Wells and Robert T. Burton, had only five years earlier led forces against the federal troops as officers in the territorial militia; now they were serving the government.

---

[3]D&C 87:3.

But the citizens of Utah went even further, for in 1862 they made their third attempt to gain full statehood in the Union. They chided their critics by pointing out that while many states were trying to leave the Union, they were trying to get in. The petition was denied. In the meantime, the people of Utah drafted a constitution for the proposed State of Deseret and elected a full slate of officers, with Brigham Young as governor. The "ghost-state" government continued to meet for several years. Many of its officers were members of the Council of Fifty, and since they were also members of the territorial legislature, the decisions they made as a "ghost" government of Deseret became law when they met as the official legislature. It was just such unusual political activity that continued to arouse suspicions in Washington.

The Mormon militia guarded the mail route for only a short time. In October 1862 Colonel Patrick Edward Connor arrived in Salt Lake City at the head of the Third California Volunteers. This group was ordered to take over the guard duty from the Mormons. The Saints were taken aback, first because this seemed to impugn their own ability, and second because the presence of Connor and his troops seemed to cast new doubt upon their loyalty. Connor believed the accusations of Mormon disloyalty and made it clear that one of his assignments was to keep them under surveillance. The Saints expected he would take his men to the post recently vacated by Johnston's Army, but instead he chose a site in the foothills directly east of Salt Lake City from which he could look down on the capital city. This new military post was named Camp Douglas (later Fort Douglas). As a military officer Connor led his troops well and was later acclaimed for a battle against the Indians on the Bear River--in reality a massacre of innocents-- but as an individual he joined with those who were doing all they could to force the Mormons to relinquish their influence in Utah and change their way of life.

In Washington, meanwhile, the first successful anti-Mormon legislation was passed in 1862. This was the Morrill Anti-Bigamy Act of 1862. Applying specifically to the Territory of Utah, it levied penalties against anyone practicing plural marriage, disincorporated the Church, and limited the value of real estate which it could hold to $50,000. Any amount of property above that figure could be confiscated by the government.

Abraham Lincoln signed the bill on July 8 but did not push

Barracks at Fort Douglas, several years after its founding. (Church Archives)

for its enforcement. He was fair-minded with regard to the Mormon question and tried to steer a middle ground between the Saints and their most vocal opponents. He expressed an attitude to one member that the Saints seemed to like. When he was a boy on a farm, he said, there was a great deal of timber that had to be cleared away. Occasionally they came to a log that was "too hard to split, too wet to burn, and too heavy to move," so they plowed around it. That, he said, is what he planned to do about the Mormons. "You go back and tell Brigham Young that if he will let me alone I will let him alone."[4] Through the remainder of the war this attitude won him the respect of the Saints, and they genuinely mourned his assassination in 1865.

Some of Lincoln's appointees were not so impartial. Governor Stephen S. Harding continued to accuse the Saints of disloyalty, despite their continued protests. When Harding and two federal judges attempted to set aside the powers of the probate courts and the territorial militia, the Saints finally petitioned the president for their removal. Attempting to be fair, Lincoln removed the governor, but to placate the gentiles he also removed the one judge

---

[4]This and other anecdotes are found in George U. Hubbard, "Abraham Lincoln as Seen by the Mormons," *Utah Historical Quarterly* 31 (Spring 1963): 91-108.

the Mormons considered their friend, John F. Kinney, and territorial secretary Frank Fuller. Harding's replacement, Governor James Duane Doty, promoted Lincoln's policy by showing genuine impartiality, and thus gained the Saints' friendship and support.

But the Church Goes On

Many histories are dominated by the stories of confrontations and stress and strain, and this has been equally true of the histories of the Saints. The entire nineteenth century, it seems, was a series of challenges from outside as well as from within the Church. The historian finds it necessary to dwell on these because they represent challenges to a people's goals and aspirations. But amidst all the troubles and excitement of the battles, life went on. Immigrants continued to arrive each year, although their numbers diminished during the Civil War. The handcart pioneers continued to arrive until 1860, eager and enthusiastic to join the Saints in a home they had never seen. During this era of problems, most of which were known to the immigrants before they left their native lands, the spirit of gathering to Zion remained firm. The converts fully believed that they were on the Lord's errand in trying to build a righteous kingdom in the West. The spirit is well illustrated in the "Handcart Song":

> Ye saints who dwell on Europe's shore
> Prepare yourselves for many more,
> To leave behind your native land,
> For sure God's judgments are at hand.
> For you must cross the raging main
> Before the promised land you gain
> And with the faithful make a start
> To cross the plains in your handcart.
>
> *Chorus:*
> For some must push and some must pull
> As we go marching up the hill;
> So merrily on our way we go
> Until we reach the Valley-o.[5]

The Saints continued to send missionaries abroad, even though in 1857 they were temporarily called back because of the

---

[5]Thomas E. Cheney, *Mormon Songs from the Rocky Mountains* (Austin, University of Texas Press, 1968), pp. 64-65.

LDS missionaries in Echo Canyon east of Salt Lake City, in 1867. (C. W. Carter photograph, Church Archives)

impending conflict with federal troops. In Europe some areas were left largely to the management of local leaders between 1858 and 1860. Swedish-born Carl Widerborg, for example, presided over the Scandinavian Mission during these two years, and in 1858 reported over a thousand baptisms. In 1860 Elders Amasa M. Lyman, Charles C. Rich, and George Q. Cannon of the Council of the Twelve were appointed as the presidency of the European Mission. The result was an impressive number of new converts and emigrants to America. As in earlier years, missionary work was most successful in England and in the Scandinavian countries. The missionaries were barred from France in 1864, and the French Mission was not reorganized until nearly fifty years later.

More than four hundred missionaries were sent out between 1855 and 1864, most of them going to European countries. The missionaries were responsible for paying their own way, and usually they would travel without purse or scrip, relying on the people they met for sustenance. Few missionaries had means to support themselves. Often they would leave wives and families at home, depending on the priesthood quorums to help care for their needs if the families could not provide. In 1857 seventy-six missionaries left from Salt Lake City and pushed handcarts east as far as Florence, Nebraska. If the converts could come west by handcart, why shouldn't the missionaries go east by them? One missionary wrote a song to sing along the way, which catches the spirit of the Latter-day Saint elder in the 1850s.

No purse no script, they bear with them, but cheerfully they start
And cross the plains a thousand miles, and draw with them a cart.
Ye nations list! The men of God, from Zion now they come,
Clothed with the Priesthood and the Power, they gather Israel home!

Chorus
Then cheer up ye Elders, you to the world will show,
That Israel must be gathered soon, their oxen are too slow.

. . . .

Some folks would ask, Why do you start with carts, come tell I pray?
We answer: When our Prophet speaks, the Elders all obey;
Since Brigham has the way laid out that's best for us, we'll try,
Stand off ye sympathetic fools, the handcarts now or die.[6]

And so the handcart missionaries proceeded faithfully, proclaiming the American Far West as the gathering place, a new place of refuge and strength for the Saints.

Not that the Saints in Utah were united on every question. There would always be those who disagreed, and some who would claim that they had been called of Heaven to instruct the leaders. Such a man was Joseph Morris, who wrote to Brigham Young in 1857 that he, Morris, had been called to be prophet, seer, and revelator to the Church. President Young decided that the best course was simply to ignore such claims. In 1860, however, Morris began promoting his revelations in earnest and a few people believed him. The following year Morris and seventeen followers were excommunicated, but this made little difference. Morris soon began to prophesy that the second coming of Christ would occur late in 1861. His followers joined him at a place called Kingston Fort near the Weber River to await the event. They took their leader's advice not to plant or harvest crops. Morris must have been unusually persuasive, for several times between December 1861 and February 1862 he announced specific dates for the advent of the Savior, and with each disappointment he would receive explanatory revelations and predict another date. Several hundred

---

[6]Cheney, *Mormon Songs from the Rocky Mountains,* p. 67.

persons remained loyal to him, even though his prophecies were unfulfilled and they were suffering shortages of food and inadequate housing. Finally, when one dissenter tried to leave the group with his property, he was caught and held prisoner by Morris and his followers. Chief Justice Kinney then issued a warrant for the arrest of Morris and some of his lieutenants, and when they refused to submit, a posse led by Robert T. Burton was sent to capture them. The unhappy result was that Morris, determined never to surrender, called his followers to take up arms and follow him even to death. Shots were fired and Morris and three of his followers were killed. The remainder went to settle at Soda Springs, Idaho, and later in Montana.

Visitors among the Saints

Although disgruntled politicians, businessmen, and others sought to undermine the image of the Church, other visitors to Utah were impressed quite differently. On the one hand, few critics were as opinionated as Mrs. Benjamin G. Ferris, who arrived with her husband in October 1852. Ferris had been appointed secretary of the territory, but in less than a year he and his wife were gone. Both published stinging denunciations of the Saints. In Mrs. Ferris's book, published in 1856, she could say

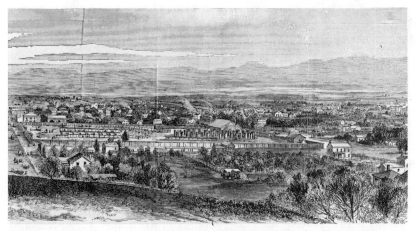

Salt Lake City, looking south down Main Street, 1865. On Temple Square the foundation of the temple, the old Tabernacle, and the pillars of the new Tabernacle can be seen. The Endowment House is on the northwest corner. The engraving is from a photograph by Savage and Ottinger. (Church Archives)

nothing kind about any of the Saints, but described the Mormon capital as full of "wretchedness, abominations, and crimes." An opposite point of view came from Elizabeth Cumming, wife of Governor Alfred Cumming. Like her husband, she took time to try to understand the Saints and developed great sympathy for them. In one candid letter she told her sister that although her husband did not like Mormonism, he liked the Mormons; their courage, intellect, and "admirable horsemanship" he had never seen equaled. She described the Church leaders as polished in their manners and able to conduct interesting conversations. The Mormon community, she said, was peaceable and well disposed. After several months in Utah she had never heard noise or oaths in the street and had seen only one Mormon man intoxicated. Of the women she said, "The Mormon ladies talk a great deal about their religion. They live it. They feel it. Every act almost of their lives is Mormonized. They talk most of their happiness in having found the only true gospel."[7]

Other visitors also came—some of special note in both America and Europe. In 1855 Jules Remy, a French botanist, and Julius Brenchley arrived in Salt Lake City for a month's stay. Remy published his observations in Europe in 1860, and while they were critical of the Mormons in some respects, in general they were more friendly than accounts by many Americans. He gave a particularly interesting description of an October conference meeting. The Saints were still meeting in the Bowery, and the travelers were invited to sit on the stand with Church leaders:

> Everywhere were to be seen rustic wagons, drawn by mules, oxen, or horses, going on fast or slow, and filled with Saints of both sexes, whose costume—varied without any attempt at show, picturesque in its simplicity—would have attracted the pencil of an artist. . . . At each meeting, the religious exercises began as soon as the president announced that the business of the day was to begin. Then the choristers and band belonging to the choir executed a piece of one of our greatest masters; and we feel bound to say that the Mormons have a feeling for sacred music, that their women sing with soul, and that the execution is in no notable degree surpassed by that which is heard either under the roof of Westminster, or the frescoes of the Sistine chapel. The music finished, the officiating priest extemporizes a prayer, often long enough, in which he returns thanks to God for his mercies, and makes known to him the wants of his people. At

---

[7]Letter reproduced in Mulder and Mortensen, *Among the Mormons*, pp. 303-15.

the end of the prayer all the faithful respond "Amen." Then the choir sing a hymn, after which one or more sermons follow.[8]

Another notable visitor was Richard Burton, a famous world traveler who arrived in 1860 and later published a book entitled *The City of the Saints.* It was sympathetic toward the Mormons and became the century's most widely read travel book about them.

One of the most instructive pieces of contemporary observation came from an ordinary soldier who arrived at Camp Floyd in 1858. His name has not been preserved, for he signed his letters to the Philadelphia *Daily Evening Bulletin* simply "Utah." But his observations on some aspects of Mormon society poignantly reveal the other side of their image. On the way to Camp Floyd, "Utah's" company passed through Provo Canyon, where they took a road the Saints had built. Without exception, the young soldier reported, it was the best piece of road he had seen since Fort Leavenworth. "The builders had great difficulties to overcome, but notwithstanding the narrowness of the passage, the hardness of the rock and the almost perpendicularity of the mountainsides, they succeeded in making a road fit at any time for a railroad track." There could be little better tribute to the pioneer skill and industry of the Saints. He described them as very friendly, and supported their criticism of Judge Drummond. As he traveled to Utah he was determined to reveal all the evils of the Mormon people he had heard so much about. After being among them for a while, however, he could only say: "Uncle Sam had not a more faithful, loyal, liberty-loving people within his proud domains than they; and from my association with them I am convinced that they are not liable to the charge of false pretense. Some of the more ignorant and bigoted of the soldiery are continually berating them, calling them all manner of hard names, and telling what they 'would have done if the Mormons hadn't caved in!' but the thinking and intelligent portion (a very small minority, I am sorry to say), appreciate their worth and treat them accordingly." Then, speaking of a local bishop for whom he sometimes worked on the side, "Utah" reported, "Last Sabbath I heard him preach one of the most eloquent and powerful sermons it has ever been my lot to listen to. . . . There was nothing of fanaticism or bigotry in his ad-

---

[8]Significant portions of this are reproduced in Mulder and Mortensen, *Among the Mormons,* pp. 279-80.

dress, but an earnest heart-stirring appeal to all to rally around the up raised standard of Jehovah, and fight the good fight. . . . And when he prayed it was not for the success of Mormonism or the glory of 'our Church,' but for all mankind, be they what they may. Had you heard him, you would have agreed with me that those who rant about the ignorance, bigotry and fanaticism of the Mormons are merely slanderers of the lowest grade."[9]

The few short years from 1856 to 1862 were indeed years of stress and trial for the Latter-day Saints. In their imperfections they sometimes made mistakes that marred the Church's public image and acceptance. The period was one of mutual misunderstanding and misinformation between the Saints in Utah and the government in Washington. As a result, the five years between 1857 and 1862 saw Brigham Young replaced as governor, the morality and loyalty of the Saints drawn into question nationwide, an army dispatched to Utah, thirty thousand Saints leaving and preparing to burn their homes if the invasion took place, a brutal massacre by a handful of overzealous Saints, and a second military unit occupying the territory at the beginning of the Civil War. Yet the Church not only survived but continued to grow. Its isolation, however, was ending, and ensuing years would see the Saints respond with redoubled efforts to build a kingdom that could not be shaken in either its spiritual or economic and political power.

[9]Harold D. Langley, ed., *To Utah With the Dragoons and Glimpses of Life in America and California* (Salt Lake City: University of Utah Press, 1974), pp. 91, 101-2.

CHAPTER 10

Challenges and Cooperatives, 1864-1872

A s the American Civil War drew to a close, the Latter-day Saints had reason for optimism that they could now work to build the Kingdom in relative peace. Abraham Lincoln had treated them impartially, and the Church was beginning to adopt economic policies designed to achieve a greater degree of self-sufficiency. The coming of the transcontinental railroad, however, brought important changes to Zion. It led the Saints into new economic experiments, was instrumental in introducing renewed political and judicial crusades against the Church, and was the catalyst for the outbreak of a rash of religious challenges in the heart of the Kingdom itself. Nevertheless, the inner strength and dynamics of the Church meant continued growth in numbers and a strengthening of its organization. Total membership in the decade following 1860 grew from approximately 80,000 to 110,000 and the number of missionaries almost doubled.

Continuing the Quest for Economic Self-Sufficiency

During the 1860s the Saints continued to work toward economic independence. The goal of Brigham Young's planning was a self-sufficiency based primarily on agriculture, supplemented by manufacturing and trade, and not on the speculative mining booms that characterized other western settlements. For this reason he vigorously opposed the efforts of Colonel Patrick E. Connor, who encouraged his soldiers to prospect for precious metals in the mountains near Salt Lake City. Ores bearing silver and gold were discovered southwest of the city in 1863, and Connor immediately tried to promote a mining boom in the territory. The *Daily Union Vedette,* an anti-Mormon newspaper founded by Connor, actively promoted Utah mining opportunities. It was Connor's avowed purpose to attract enough gentiles to overwhelm the Mormons at the ballot box and wrest control of the territory from them.

The colonel's efforts failed to spark the full-scale rush he anticipated or to attract many miners from more profitable areas. Most importantly, the opposition of Church leaders discouraged all but a few Latter-day Saints from joining the speculation. Connor himself remained in Utah after his military discharge in 1866 and became a respected business leader.

In the meantime, the Church continued efforts to strengthen its economic self-sufficiency, and selective mining was important to this plan. A mission sent to Minersville in 1859 produced large amounts of lead for use in molding bullets and mixing paint. Coal was also essential, and in 1860 settlers were sent to Coalville on a mining mission. This enterprise provided a substitute for scarce timber fuel and helped hundreds of men find employment.

One of the most ambitious missions designed to exploit and develop the natural resources of the region was the cotton mission begun in 1861. Brigham Young strongly believed that the southern area known as Utah's Dixie could produce enough cotton to supply cloth for all the Saints, with surplus for the eastern market. By 1864, however, it became clear that the experiment was floundering. Determined to make it succeed, Church leaders furnished thousands of dollars in cash, merchandise, tools, and equipment. They also provided the settlers of the St. George area with a cotton factory, which began operation in 1869. It seemed, however, that every problem imaginable conspired to hamper the cotton-growing enterprise. Poor soil, grasshopper and cricket plagues, alternating floods and drouth, and other problems caused some settlers to leave. Many of those who remained found other crops more profitable than cotton. Eventually it was alfalfa, not cotton, that revolutionized the agriculture of Dixie. It provided better feed for livestock and better nutrients for the soil, producing better grain when the crops were rotated.

In the meantime, about two hundred families were called between 1865 and 1867 to establish three communities along the Muddy River, a few miles southwest of St. George. These agricultural missionaries were supposed to produce cotton and other farm products, such as molasses and figs. They too had problems with the forces of nature, Indians, and malaria. These challenges were compounded in 1870 when a government survey placed their settlements just outside the Territory of Utah. The Nevada government promptly assessed the surprised settlers back taxes, demanding payment in specie. But hard money was scarce, and in 1871 Brigham Young advised the Mormon farmers to abandon their claims, which they did.

These activities were only part of a major effort of the early 1860s to develop the agricultural potential for Utah's southern colonies. At the same time a group of Swiss immigrants was called to raise grapes and other fruits at Santa Clara. They soon developed a flourishing business in dried fruits and wine. Since the Word of Wisdom was not yet considered a commandment among the Saints, the wine was sold in Utah as well as to outside settlements. It was also used for the sacrament service in many wards until the practice was officially ended near the end of the century.

Also intended to bolster the agricultural colonies of Utah's Dixie was the plan to use the Colorado River for shipping. In 1864 Anson Call received a call to locate a road from St. George to the Colorado River, build a settlement on the river, and establish a landing and warehouse. Call's Landing was founded in December 1865, about fifteen miles above the present site of Hoover Dam. According to the plan, ships steaming up the Colorado from a point 150 miles below Call's Landing would bring both immigrants and freight, which could travel via the Muddy River colonies to St. George and then to Salt Lake City. Little business was actually conducted on the route, and in 1869 the expensive enterprise was abandoned.

In their drive for self-sufficiency the Saints seemed indefatigable, and Brigham Young remained the incurable optimist. He began to decry the use of any items the Saints could not grow or manufacture themselves. "We can produce them or do without them," he exclaimed on one occasion. This attitude gave fresh em-

*The interior of the Provo Woolen Mills, taken some years after this
cooperative enterprise was established. (C. W. Carter photograph, Church
Archives)*

phasis to the nonuse of tobacco, another step toward more uniform
compliance with the Church's health code.

To further promote husbandry, the Deseret Agricultural and
Manufacturing Society was revitalized in the 1860s. It immediately encouraged self-sufficiency with such products as cane
sugar, molasses, flax, hemp, sheep, and silk. The society maintained its own experimental farm in Salt Lake City and went to
great lengths to provide agricultural information to settlers in
every Mormon town.

One of the organization's experiments was raising silkworms
in order to foster a Utah silk industry. This created an immediate

need for mulberry trees, since silkworms thrive on the leaves of this plant. In 1866 Brigham Young personally directed transplanting some one hundred thousand such trees in all parts of Utah. George D. Watt was called on a "silk mission" to spread the "gospel of silk" throughout the territory. Eventually the Women's Relief Society organized the Deseret Silk Association, and during the 1870s nearly 150 communities sponsored silk projects. In 1877 producers boasted of five million silkworms. Many fine silk dresses, handkerchiefs, and other items were produced, but eventually this industry, too, succumbed to external competition.

From one perspective, the history of these attempts at economic self-sufficiency was a history of almost impossible dreams and successive failures. From another, the failures generated positive by-products. St. George, Santa Clara, and other southern Utah settlements remained permanent communities for the Saints. Even though their economies developed in a different direction than planned, the towns in Mormon Dixie contributed to the widening of the physical perimeters of the Latter-day Saint commonwealth. Brigham Young's plan for building a western Zion was not always achieved in every detail, but without the vision the Saints would have achieved less. This was true of Brigham Young and his plan for building a western Zion. From another perspective the dream became a test of faith and a challenge to the Saints, who saw themselves as the people of God. The trials of pioneering the hot, desolate country surrounding St. George, at the expense of leaving well-established homes elsewhere, revealed the Saints' faith and inner strength. Critics may consider such dedication blind and self-demeaning, but the Kingdom could not be built without individual willingness to sacrifice personal ambitions because of faith in something larger than self.

The story of these settlements offers a rich treasure trove of pioneer tales, folklore, and songs that illuminate the pioneers' spirit, dedication, disappointments, and sense of humor. In October 1861 John Pulsipher was called to the cotton mission:

This news was very unexpected to me. Volunteers were called for at conference to go on this mission, but I did not think it meant me, for I had a good home, was well satisfied and had plenty to do.

But when Apostle Geo. A. Smith told me I was selected to go I saw the importance of the mission to sustain Israel in the mountains—we had need of a possession in a warmer climate, and I thot I might as well go as anybody. *Then the Spirit came upon me so that I felt to thank the Lord that I was worthy to go. . . .*[1]

Another missionary heard the news when he came home from a hard day's work. He dropped in his chair exclaiming, "I'll be damned if I'll go," but after sitting a few moments he stood up and he said to his family, "Well, if we are going to Dixie we had better start to get ready." A pioneer song written about 1870 jabs humorously at the hard life in St. George. One verse reads:

> The sun it is so scorching hot
> It makes the water siz, Sir,
> The reason why it is so hot
> Is just because it is, Sir.
> The wind like fury here does blow
> That when we plant or sow, Sir,
> We place one foot upon the seed
> And hold it till it grows, Sir.
>
> *Chorus:*
> Mesquite, soap root, prickly-pears and briars,
> St. George ere long will be a place that everyone admires.[2]

The quest for economic well-being included development of trade with western mining communities. In the 1860s products grown by the Saints were marketed in Colorado, Idaho, Montana, and Nevada. Commerce with outsiders was not particularly encouraged, but when Mormon farmers participated in it anyway, the Church helped them regulate prices to ensure the highest possible return for their produce. After general conference each April and October, the leading farmers were invited to a price convention in Salt Lake City, where each pledged to support the established prices, eliminating hurtful competition. Controlled by the priesthood, those conventions helped raise the standard of living for Latter-day Saint farm families. The Mormon price convention was succeeded in 1866 by the Utah Produce Company, an organization that regulated the marketing of surplus products.

Another aspect of the self-sufficiency program was the operation of Church team trains. John W. Young's unusual sermon on

---

[1]As quoted in [Juanita Brooks,] "The Cotton Mission," *Utah Historical Quarterly* 29 (July 1961): 207.

[2]Cheney, *Mormon Songs*, pp. 114-15.

"the science of Ox-teamology" at the general conference of October 1860 convinced the Saints of the feasibility of the new program. Every year but two between 1861 and 1868 the Church sent ox teams from Salt Lake City to the Missouri River. The teamsters, who were considered missionaries, sold Utah-produced goods and picked up emigrants. The result was a great savings to the Latter-day Saints, for transportation west was less expensive, food for the immigrants was provided from Utah rather than purchased in the East, and profits were made from goods sold. The Church trains brought more than sixteen thousand Europeans to Utah at a total cost of about $2.4 million. Most of the cost was met by voluntary donations of labor, teams, and supplies from the Saints. The enterprise was an outstanding example of the success of Church cooperative activity. The need for Church teams ended with the coming of the railroad in 1869.

Another example of Church cooperative enterprises was the Deseret Telegraph line. After the transcontinental telegraph was completed through Salt Lake City in 1861, the Church launched a program to construct auxiliary lines. Under priesthood direction, a five-hundred-mile system from north to south was completed in 1867, much of it by tithing labor, and in later years more lines were added. After its incorporation, the Deseret Telegraph Company was fully owned and controlled by the Church. The Kingdom was growing, and a worthwhile communications network aided materially by directly connecting settlements with headquarters.

Defensive Economy: The Challenge of the Railroad

The economy of the United States was changing in the years following the Civil War, and one of the most significant symbols of change was completion of the transcontinental railroad in 1869, marking both a transportation and an industrial revolution. Consumer goods, mail, and passengers could now go from coast to coast in days instead of weeks or months. As auxiliary lines expanded into all parts of the West, they revolutionized the marketing of cattle and farm products. In addition, the railroad contributed greatly to the growth of goods processing, oil production, manufacture of consumer goods, and, in general, rapid industrialization. The tracks from east and west were joined at Promontory Summit in Utah. This was an important symbol for

The end of isolation: A Mormon wagon train meeting newly completed Central Pacific Railroad near the Great Salt Lake. (Utah State Historical Society)

the Church, for just as the railroad brought change to America, it also brought significant change to the Saints in Utah and the West.

As Church leaders contemplated the pending arrival of the railroad, they anticipated new challenges to Mormon self-sufficiency and isolation as well as new opportunities for growth and profit. They would try to deal with both in appropriate ways.

Church leaders were apprehensive that the railroad would bring a flood of non-Mormons who would undermine Latter-day Saint principles and attempt to destroy the Mormon way of life. It appeared that the economic plan of the Saints was in jeopardy, for an influx of cheap goods from the East would undercut local agriculture and industry. While all this might help in some ways, it could leave many others unemployed and shatter Zion's self-sufficiency. The possibility also loomed that the railroad would stimulate a massive expansion of Utah mining. Church leaders had already rejected a mining economy as the basis for a permanent ideal society.

Despite these potential problems, Brigham Young and other leaders welcomed the railroad. It would stimulate immigration by making it easier and cheaper for converts to travel to Utah, even though the cash needed for fares would be difficult to raise. It would stimulate other economic activities which, if properly controlled, could greatly improve conditions in the Great Basin. Said President Brigham Young in 1867:

> Speaking of . . . this railroad, I am anxious to see it, and I say to the Congress of the United States, through our Delegate, to the Company, and to others, hurry up, hasten the work! We want to hear the iron horse puffing through this valley. What for? To bring our brethren and sisters here.[3]

The anticipated arrival of the railroad was one reason for organization of the School of the Prophets in 1867. This school was actually a confidential forum of leading high priests in the different communities who discussed religious doctrines, economic policies, and political problems. To some degree the central school in Salt Lake City assumed the functions of the Council of Fifty, which had led political and economic planning in the early years but had ceased to function.

Under the direction of the First Presidency, the School of the Prophets formulated plans to combat the potentially undesirable influence a rapid influx of non-Mormons might bring. One of the first acts was to sponsor a contract in the name of Brigham Young for construction of the railroad within the Territory of Utah. This would have the dual advantage of keeping out transient, possibly undesirable, workers and simultaneously providing employment and income for Latter-day Saint laborers. Contracts were signed with both the Union Pacific and the Central Pacific, and Mormon workers were either called or volunteered. Latter-day Saints thus helped build the track and joined in festive ceremonies at Promontory Summit on May 10, 1869. In effect, it was another cooperative church enterprise. The men worked in ward groups, specially called to represent the Church. It was probably the most unusual situation in the history of western railroad building, with workers generally adhering to Mormon standards: most of them refrained from swearing and drinking, there was no work on Sunday, and each man paid a faithful tithe.

Church leaders also initiated construction of a connecting network of railroads within Utah. The Utah Central, Utah Southern, and Utah Northern were all completed in the early 1870s. In each case the railroad was financed, at least in part, by

---

[3] *Journal of Discourses,* 12:54.

private individuals who were prominent Church leaders, and the profits came back to them. In reality, they acted in behalf of the Church, but since the Anti-Bigamy Act of 1862 had prohibited the Church from owning more than $50,000 worth of property, it was necessary for the leaders (particularly Brigham Young) to carry much church business in their private accounts.

Another potential threat related to the coming of the railroad concerned landholdings. Even though the Saints had occupied Utah for over twenty years, they could neither purchase nor homestead the land legally without a federal survey, and no federal land office existed in the territory. In 1869, completion of the railroad made a land office essential, if only to distribute land grants to the railroads. Anticipating possible conflicts of interest, the School of the Prophets set up a committee to work with governmental authorities and the settlers. Eventually most Mormon land titles were confirmed.

The newly defensive posture of the Kingdom was well illustrated at the October conference of 1868 when several leading brethren discussed the potential threat posed by the continuing influx of gentiles, and urged the Saints to new cooperation. Brigham Young reminded them that they were building both a spiritual and a temporal kingdom; then, in the rather forceful language appropriate to the day, he asked: "But if this is the Kingdom of God and if we are the Saints of God . . . are we not required to sustain ourselves and to manufacture that which we consume, to cease our bartering, trading, mingling, drinking, smoking, chewing and joining with all the filth of Babylon? . . . We want you henceforth to be a self-sustaining people. . . . What do you say brethren and sisters? All of you who say that we will be a self-sustaining people signify it by the show of your right hands." Everyone in the new Tabernacle raised his hand, and the renewed drive for economic cooperation among the Saints began. "Let us govern our wants by our necessities," he said toward the end of his address, "and we shall find that we are not compelled to spend our money for nought. Let us save our money to enter and pay for our land, to buy flocks of sheep and improve them, and to buy machinery and start more woolen factories. We have a good many now, and the people will sustain them."[4]

---

[4]*Journal of Discourses*, 12:284-89.

President George Q. Cannon emphasized the urgency of economic reform by declaring: "We are told—openly and without disguise, that when the railroad is completed there will be such a flood of so-called 'civilization' brought in here that every vestige of us, our church and institutions shall be completely obliterated. When we are told thus plainly and undisguisedly, would it not be folly, nay insanity, for us to sit still, fold our arms supinely and await the crash without making a single effort to ward it off?" Then, as if to foreshadow the coming struggles, he declared: "The question is, Will we sustain the Kingdom of God or will we not? Will we sustain the priesthood of God, or will we not? This power of which I have been speaking, or more properly, this antagonistic class in our midst, flatter themselves with the idea that when it comes to the test this people will desert their leaders and cleave to something else. This is an illusory hope. The Latter-day Saints know too well the source of their blessings."[5]

The result was a new cooperative movement, directed largely by the School of Prophets. The new movement stressed cooperative stores and factories rather than individual enterprise more emphatically than at any time since the days of Missouri. Nearly two hundred separate cooperatives were founded in the Mormon commonwealth.

The most controversial part of the plan was the proposition that Latter-day Saints should not trade with outsiders. If they were to keep the Kingdom from being too strongly influenced or controlled by non-Mormon merchants, they must support their own cooperative institutions. From 1868 until 1882 the Church encouraged members to boycott non-Mormon merchants and trade only with Mormon establishments. While this may seem harsh and unfriendly in retrospect, most Latter-day Saints genuinely felt that the gentiles posed a real and present danger to their economic well-being, and there was evidence that some outside merchants were trying to undermine the Church and its way of life. Many of the Saints had been driven from New York, Ohio, Missouri, and Illinois by unsympathetic neighbors. It is understandable that they did not want to be driven a fifth time, especially from a territory they considered peculiarly their own. At the very least, they felt justified in refusing to contribute to the profits of those among

---

[5] *Journal of Discourses,* 12:290-91, 297.

At right is one of many Mormon-owned stores that became part of the ZCMI chain during cooperative movement of the 1860s. John K. Trumbo, non-Mormon businessman who responded bitterly to Mormon economic policies, seems to be lampooning Brigham Young's religious-economic influence in sign above his door. (C. W. Carter photograph, Church Archives)

them whose activities threatened to destroy the Church's strength.

The Mormon program of cooperative buying and selling revolved around a parent company organized in October 1868 as Zion's Cooperative Mercantile Institution (ZCMI), originally a wholesale house. Its first supply of goods came from leading Mormon merchants, who were encouraged to subscribe their goods in exchange for cash or stock in the new company. Stock was widely sold to others in the territory, making the ownership of the company broadly based. When it began to make a profit, the company tithed its profits first and then distributed the rest to the stockholders. The feeling was that this would benefit the community as a whole, rather than a few private wholesalers.

Cooperative retail stores were soon established in nearly every community in the territory. The parent institution did not own these outlets, but they all purchased their goods from it, and it maintained control over prices. These retail outlets also absorbed the business of local Mormon storekeepers, paying either cash or stock, and they also sold stock widely. Brigham Young expressed sympathy for Mormon retailers who thus went out of business, but he explained that it was for the larger good of all. He encouraged those with money to invest in other kinds of agricultural or manufacturing activities.

While only partially successful, the cooperative program lasted about ten years and demonstrated Latter-day Saint determination to become self-sufficient. The cooperative enterprises were owned neither by the government nor by the Church. They were privately owned with a broad popular base, but were regulated by Church policy for the benefit of the entire community. They represented a unique departure from the traditional method of building communities through individual entrepreneurship and differed from the socialistic programs of government ownership that many were beginning to advocate in America. At the same time, the exclusiveness of the system created some suspicion and antagonism.

Both ZCMI and the local cooperatives expanded their operations by establishing cooperative manufacturing enterprises for boots, shoes, clothing, furniture, and other small items. They also promoted cooperative livestock herds and cooperative dairy activities. In addition, the various cooperatives shared their products with each other, widely distributing the benefits of their specialties.

Although ZCMI was an outstanding financial success and became a permanent retail institution, the various local outlets gradually declined as cooperatives. The controlling stock found its way into fewer and fewer hands, so the stores again assumed the flavor of limited individual enterprises. Finally, in 1882, President John Taylor opened the way for growth of more privately owned retail stores by officially declaring an end to exclusive Church support of local cooperatives.

Other cooperative activities inaugurated during this period of defensive economic activity included an iron works in southern Utah, various cooperative textile factories, and a bank (Bank of Deseret).

Some Saints objected to economic regulation by the Church, and the most extreme forms of objection led, as in earlier days, to apostasy. The most vigorous opposition to church leadership in economic affairs came from the Godbeites. The founders of this movement, William S. Godbe and E. L. T. Harrison, were already

Zion's Cooperative Mercantile Institution, Salt Lake City, in late 1870s. (C. R. Savage photograph, Church Archives)

dissatisfied with certain teachings. The Church's effort to control business in the territory helped strengthen their dissent and direct it toward apostasy and excommunication. Godbe and Harrison were joined by a few other businessmen and intellectuals who sided with non-Mormon businessmen in calling for a return to un-controlled free enterprise in the territory and lauded the economic value of mining. The outlet for their opinions was the *Utah Magazine,* founded in 1868, which was succeeded by the *Mormon Tribune* in 1870. Its name was soon changed to the *Salt Lake Tribune.* The Godbeite leaders were excommunicated in 1869, and the movement was short-lived, but the fact that it attracted some of the leading intellectual and business figures among the Saints demonstrates that there was some opposition to church policy in that turbulent era.

The Spiritual Kingdom: Growth and Development

Church economic activities were designed primarily to solid-ify the earthly Kingdom of God and help it grow. At the same time, growth and development were taking place in many other ways. Five new stakes were organized in Utah in 1868 and 1869, bringing the total to nine. Missionary work continued to expand as 417 new missionaries were sent out between 1865 and 1869, com-pared with 222 during the previous four-year period. New missions were opened in the Sandwich Islands (Hawaii), the Netherlands, and the Eastern States, though the latter was shortly closed.

The mission to Hawaii was of particular interest. It had been opened earlier, but the missionaries were called home in 1857 because of the Utah Expedition. Not long after that, the eccentric Walter Murray Gibson, a traveler and soldier of fortune, arrived in Salt Lake City and was converted to the Church. When he suggested that the Saints move to the islands of the East Indies, Brigham Young rejected the idea. But impressed with Gibson's enthusiasm, the President sent him alone to the Pacific to do missionary work.

Gibson arrived on the Hawaiian island of Lanai in July 1861. There he exceeded the bounds of his instructions and soon gained virtual control of the native Saints. He proclaimed himself "Chief President of the Islands of the Sea and of the Hawaiian Islands for The Church of Jesus Christ of Latter-day Saints," and soon began practices completely foreign to church policy. He gathered the Saints at a six-thousand-acre plantation and set up an elaborate hierarchical system. He sold priesthood offices (some of them offices not authorized in the Church, such as archbishop), wore a white robe, and even required the Saints to crawl in his presence. Apparently he planned eventually to unite all the Hawaiian Islands into one empire, with himself as king, by converting as many natives as possible and using his army to bring in the others.

Such unauthorized and irresponsible activity could not long go unchallenged, and some twenty-five native Saints finally wrote to headquarters in Salt Lake City. The result was that Elders Ezra T. Benson and Lorenzo Snow of the Council of the Twelve were sent to the islands, accompanied by Elders Joseph F. Smith, Alma L. Smith, and William W. Cluff. Confronting Gibson, who seemed to have solidly won most natives, the elders excommunicated him. Subsequently all the Saints who had followed Gibson deserted him. One incident that aided the elders occurred when two of them walked on a rock Gibson had identified as a sacred shrine, warning that anyone who walked on it would be struck dead. When they did not die, Gibson's prestige began to wane. Joseph F. Smith remained for a time as mission president, and under his direction the Church began to develop a plantation at Laie, which eventually became mission headquarters and the home of many Hawaiian Saints.

The Sunday Schools were also revitalized in the 1860s. The first Sunday School had been established in 1849 by Richard Ballantyne, but as the movement spread, each Sunday School was an independent unit with no central direction. This worked well, but by the 1860s Sunday School leaders were discussing the need for adopting a uniform system. In 1866 Elder George Q. Cannon began publishing the *Juvenile Instructor,* which eventually became the official Sunday School publication, and later that year a central, coordinating body known as the Parent Sunday School Union was formed. In 1872 a plan was finally developed. On August 2, Elder Cannon, a member of the Council of the Twelve, was selected as general superintendent of the Deseret Sunday School Union, as the organization was officially named. Intended mainly for the benefit of young people, it was not until the twentieth century that the Sunday School held adult classes on a churchwide basis.

During this era other auxiliaries were either revitalized or initiated. The Women's Relief Society was reorganized in 1867, when Eliza R. Snow, secretary of the Nauvoo Relief Society and local feminist leader, became the president and remained one of the most influential women in pioneer Utah. In a way, the new emphasis on Relief Society work was part of the reaction to the coming of the railroad, for in addition to aiding the poor, the sisters were asked to be frugal and avoid buying luxuries. They were to assist in the operation of cooperative stores and support home industry.

The Relief Societies also stimulated the organization of Retrenchment Societies among the young ladies. This movement actually began in 1869, when Brigham Young called together his wives and daughters and gave them instructions in economy and modest living. Concerned about the extravagance and vanity that seemed to be taking hold in the community, he wanted to bring about a reform and to have his own daughters set the example. The following year Mary Isabella Horne was assigned by President Young to assist Eliza R. Snow in forming Retrenchment Associations. Soon the movement became known as the Young Ladies' Mutual Improvement Association. Its members participated in all kinds of practical economic and cultural activities. In 1872 they began publication of the *Woman's Exponent,* which served as the organ for the dissemination of news, practical information, and

Four of the leading women of Zion (left to right): Zina D. H. Young, Bathsheba W. Smith, Emily P. Young, and Eliza R. Snow. (Church Archives)

editorials of the women's viewpoints throughout the territory.

Special emphasis was placed on fashions for two reasons. Brigham Young wanted the women to cease buying from outsiders in order to stimulate self-sufficiency, but he also wanted them to learn frugality. He decried the vanity and extravagance that led to showy dresses made of several yards of material. One 1872 sermon colorfully portrays some of his very practical instructions:

If I were a lady and had a piece of cloth to make me a dress, I would cut it so as to cover my person handsomely and neatly; and whether it was cut according to the fashion, or not, custom would soon make it beautiful. I would not have eighteen or twenty yards to drag behind me, so that if I had to turn around I would have to pick up my dress and throw it after me, or, just as a cow does when she kicks over the milk pail, throw out one foot to kick the dress out of the way. That is not becoming, beautiful or convenient—all such fashions are inconvenient. Take that cloth and cut you a skirt that will be modest and neat; that does not drag in the dirt nor show your garters; but cut it so that it will clear the ground when you walk.[6]

Later he reminded the young ladies they should dress neatly and plainly, trying to please the Lord, not "flaunting, flirting and

---

[6]Quoted in Mulder and Mortensen, *Among the Mormons*, p. 388.

gossiping, as a great many are, and thinking continually of their dresses and of this, that and the other that will minister to and gratify their vanity. Such women seldom think of their prayers."

The young men also began to organize themselves for purposes other than priesthood and work. Several independent mutual improvement and literary societies were created in various LDS communities. In 1875 Junius F. Wells was called by President Young to officially organize the young men. The Young Men's Mutual Improvement Association was inaugurated on June 10 in the Salt Lake City Thirteenth Ward, and within a year it too had become a churchwide movement.

The growing solidarity of the Church was, in part, symbolized by its building program. The most famous of the new edifices was the Salt Lake Tabernacle, begun in 1865 and sufficiently completed by October 1867 that it could accommodate the general conference. Finally dedicated in 1875, this unique structure was built largely under the direction of the Church's public works program. It became famous for its self-supporting dome, outstanding acoustics, and the fact that part of the construction was accomplished without metal nails. The original pipe organ, designed by Joseph H. Ridges, was built of native materials by Mormon craftsmen.

The first conference in the Tabernacle was in many ways a fitting representation of the faith, enthusiasm, and practical nature of the Saints. Word that it would be held in the new building created a special excitement, and crowds of people were lined up outside long before the doors were opened. When the conference began at 10:00 A.M. on October 6, 1867, there were still crowds outside unable to find seating. Several choirs sang at the conference services, which lasted four days. On Monday, October 7, President Brigham Young outlined some significant topics he wanted the speakers to deal with. One was the need to subscribe money to aid the Perpetual Emigration Fund. Education received attention, as the Saints were told to teach their children the ways of the Lord and to introduce scriptures into their schools. They were also told to introduce phonetics. Young ladies were encouraged to study arithmetic, bookkeeping, and other aspects of business so they could tend stores and operate the telegraph offices, freeing men to labor in the canyons, build houses, work farms, and more fully support their families. Five hundred teams were requested to haul rock from Little Cottonwood Canyon for the Salt Lake Temple, and the Saints were told that they could prolong their lives best by living frugally and temperately. In addition, 163 missionaries were called to establish settlements in southern Utah. This single day's preaching reveals the wide variety of concerns that characterized the lives of the Saints in the 1860s.

Brigham Young's emphasis on learning was complicated by the presence of many immigrants who did not speak English. In an attempt to simplify the learning of the English language, the board of regents of the University of Deseret had appointed a committee in 1853 to create a phonetic alphabet. The committee included Parley P. Pratt and Heber C. Kimball from among the General Authorities, and George D. Watt, a man skilled in shorthand, who transcribed many of the major addresses of Church leaders for the *Journal of Discourses*. Interest in using the new Deseret Alphabet of thirty-eight characters was revived in 1868. That year two readers were printed in the unique alphabet, and the following year Orson Pratt published part of the Book of Mormon using it. Public interest was not widespread, however, and the experiment soon ended.

This historic photograph, probably taken in the early 1870s, shows both the old and new tabernacles, as well as construction work taking place on the Salt Lake Temple. (C. W. Carter photograph, Church Archives)

The Non-Mormon Religious Challenge

The Latter-day Saints could hardly hope to create their own religious society without some challenge from other churches. They were becoming better known in the nation than they were in the days of Joseph Smith, and ministers and missionaries who were offended by Mormon teachings (or by what they thought were Mormon teachings) would continue to attempt to reform them.

One of the most-publicized challenges came from Dr. John P. Newman, chaplain of the United States Senate. In April 1870 he gave a sermon in Washington, D.C., against the practice of plural marriage, and in June he traveled to Utah, where he challenged Brigham Young to a debate. President Young refused to enter into such a public spectacle over what he considered a sacred religious practice, but after great pressure he allowed Elder Orson Pratt to debate Newman on the subject "Does the Bible sanction polygamy?" The well-publicized and well-attended debate was held in the Tabernacle and extended over three days, June 12, 13, and 14. As in most such debates, neither side convinced the other, and the followers of both were confirmed in their own opinions, but Elder Pratt's mastery of the scriptures and his knowledge of Hebrew stood him well against Newman and greatly surprised the Senate chaplain.

More important to the life of Utah was the fact that by the end of the 1860s other denominations were beginning to establish themselves in the territory. The Church made no effort to keep out other faiths and sometimes cooperated by letting them use Mormon chapels until they could build their own meeting places.

Among the first non-Mormons in Utah were Jews, some of whom came as merchants and businessmen as early as 1854. Strong friendships grew between the Jews and the Mormons, and more than once Brigham Young made Mormon church buildings available for Jewish religious services.

Roman Catholics came to Utah in 1862 as members of the California Volunteers. In 1866 when the Reverend Edward Kelly was looking for a place to celebrate mass, he was allowed to use the old tabernacle, and Brigham Young helped him obtain a clear title to land for a cathedral. Though the Catholics and the Latter-day Saints had little in common religiously, they maintained general good will. The Reverend Lawrence Scanlan arrived in Utah in

1873 and remained until his death in 1915, becoming bishop. He established parishes wherever possible, and on one occasion in 1873 was invited by Mormon leaders in St. George to use their tabernacle for worship. Fearful that some of the service would have to be omitted because it called for a choir singing in Latin, he learned to his surprise that the leader of the St. George Tabernacle choir had asked for the appropriate music, and in two weeks the choir would sing it in Latin. On May 18 a Catholic high mass was sung by a Mormon choir in the St. George Tabernacle, symbolizing the good will that existed between Father Scanlan and the Saints.

Other groups came to Utah with the express purpose of converting the Mormons. The first was the Reorganized Church of Jesus Christ of Latter Day Saints, headed by Joseph Smith III, who sent missionaries to Utah in 1863. Six years later two younger sons of the Prophet Joseph Smith, Alexander and David, also appeared as missionaries, though their mission was less successful. Eventually, a branch of the Reorganized Church was established in Salt Lake City.

In later years the Congregationalists, Episcopalians, Presbyterians, Methodists, Baptists, and Lutherans all came among the Saints. Each began with a small nucleus of its own members, primarily in Salt Lake City, Ogden, and some of the mining communities. In many cases these churches established mission schools with educational facilities sometimes better than those found in the LDS communities. One purpose of these schools was to draw the Mormon children and act as tools for pulling some away from the Church. The challenge presented by such schools eventually led the Saints to reemphasize excellence in their own schools and to pay more attention to the establishment of Church-sponsored academies (high schools) in their communities. The Church also began to support more fully the idea of free, tax-supported elementary schools, and in 1869 the first free public school in Utah was opened in American Fork.

The Judicial and Political Crusade Begins

In the late 1860s an intensified judicial and political crusade against the Church began. Though it presented serious difficulties to the efforts of the Saints to build the Kingdom, it at least served as a rallying point for increasing unity. By giving them little respite from external pressure, it kept them constantly reminded that God's people would always have differences with the outside world, and that sometimes they must sacrifice for the sake of those differences.

The political conflict manifested itself in many ways. One was the aftermath of the murder of two prominent gentiles in 1866: Newton Brassfield, who had won the affections of and married the wife of an absent LDS missionary, and King Robinson, a surgeon at Camp Douglas who had challenged some of the Saints on certain land titles. Both murders remained unsolved, but members of the gentile community made every effort to blame them on the Saints.

Another manifestation of conflict was the 1867-68 contest for a territorial delegate to Congress. In February 1867 William H. Hooper, the Mormon incumbent, defeated his challenger, William McGorty, by the resounding margin of 15,068 to 105. McGorty, however, challenged the election the following year before a congressional committee, claiming he had postponed the challenge beyond the legal ninety-day limit because of his fear of reprisal from the Saints. He charged that the election was improper because the people of Utah had an anti-republican form of government and because through the practice of plural marriage they were violating the laws of the United States. Hooper, he said, represented this illegality and had taken a secret religious oath that disqualified him. Actually, most such charges of secret oaths referred to the sacred endowment ceremonies, in which non-Mormons, of course, were not permitted to participate. To the uninformed and suspicious gentiles, participation in these ceremonies was interpreted as a secret conspiracy against the government. McGorty lost his appeal, but the case was significant, for it brought the Church and its practices officially to the attention of a congressional committee.

Such disagreements soon caused a new political alignment in Utah that placed the Saints on one side and the gentiles and a number of dissatisfied and apostate Mormons on the other. In 1870 the leaders of the apostate Godbeite movement joined prominent members of the gentile community to form the Liberal party, which would oppose not only Mormon marriage practices but also the Church's political and economic influence. In response, the Saints took what seemed to be the only reasonable alternative and formed their own party, the People's party. The Liberal party was not fully united, for some members, such as the Godbeites, were not eager to completely disrupt Mormon family relationships. In 1871, therefore, the most extreme anti-Mormon faction formed the Gentile League of Utah, with the avowed purpose of destroying Mormon theocracy.

While all this was taking place in Utah, renewed anti-Mormon sentiment was felt in the national capital. It may have been influenced by at least two things. One was the activities of anti-Mormon business and political leaders in Utah whose reports to Washington constantly placed the Saints in a bad light and whose suggestions for combating the Church were included in some proposed anti-Mormon legislation. At the same time, the campaign to eliminate plural marriage was probably connected with a general reform program inaugurated by Radical Republicans after the Civil War. The Radicals controlled Congress and, in their efforts to change the social structure of the South, passed legislation designed to promote civil and political rights for the blacks just freed from slavery. Some of the same Radicals who were working so hard to reform the South were among those who sought to reform the social structure of Utah.

Senator Benjamin F. Wade of Ohio had in 1864 authored the harsh Wade-Davis bill, which would have disfranchised all former southern Confederate officials and made it difficult for the southern states to return to full partnership in the American Union. The bill was vetoed by President Abraham Lincoln, but its intent was nevertheless carried out by later congresses. In 1866 this same Senator Wade introduced a bill in Congress designed to destroy polygamy and the power of the Church in Utah. Some of the more stringent provisions of the bill increased the territorial governor's power over the militia and authorized him to select the county probate judge. The measure left jury selection to the U.S. marshal and barred LDS leaders from performing marriages. The bill also forbade tax exemptions for the Church, made it legally impossible for the Church to regulate fellowship, and required the Church to make annual financial reports to the governor.

The bill failed but was soon followed by the Cragin Bill, which would have eliminated trial by jury in cases involving polygamy. In 1869 a different, though still unsuccessful, approach was made in the House of Representatives through the Ashley Bill, which proposed completely dismembering the Territory of Utah and dividing the area among surrounding states and territories. The Wade, Cragin, and Ashley bills all failed to pass, but they indicate some of the hostile sentiment that existed on the national level.

The legislation that came closest to passing was the Cullom Bill of 1870, which passed the House of Representatives but not the Senate. Less drastic than the Cragin Bill, it provided that all cases involving plural marriage should be prosecuted exclusively by federal judges and that juries would be selected by federally appointed marshals and attorneys. When news reached Utah that it had passed the House, three thousand Latter-day Saint women held a massive protest meeting in the Salt Lake Tabernacle, demonstrating to surprised people throughout the country that the women in Utah supported plural marriage. In addition, certain prominent newspapers and legislators saw its passage leading to possible civil war with the Mormons. They argued that such drastic measures were not needed. These voices of moderation helped finally to defeat the bill.

Another approach to the Mormon question was the effort of some members of Congress to establish female suffrage in Utah,

Photograph taken in 1892 shows many of the Utah women who were active in the suffrage movement about 1870. Seated on the front row, third from the right, is Susan B. Anthony, national women's rights leader. (Church Archives)

under the impression that if the women had the vote, they would destroy plural marriage at the ballot box. Utah's delegate to Congress gave the measure such enthusiastic support that its sponsors changed their minds and dropped it. Ironically, just at this time, February 12, 1870, the Utah legislature passed a women's suffrage bill, against the opposition of anti-Mormons in Utah. Seventeen years later the federal Congress itself outlawed women's suffrage in Utah as part of the effort to fight polygamy!

Even the new president of the United States, Ulysses S. Grant, and his vice-president, Schuyler Colfax, joined in denouncing Mormon practices. After he took office in 1869, Grant did not continue the conciliatory policy toward the Saints that had marked the administrations of Lincoln and Johnson. Strongly influenced by Colfax and by J. P. Newman, as well as his own sense of Victorian morality, Grant adopted a get-tough policy, reflected in the nature of those he appointed to office in Utah Territory.

General J. Wilson Shaffer, who had served the aims of the Radical-controlled government well in helping establish federal rule in the South, was appointed governor in 1870. "Never after me," he boasted, "shall it be said that Brigham Young is governor of Utah." Though he died within the year, his actions displayed his bias and contributed to a renewed tension between the Saints and federal officials. Shaffer's home became virtual headquarters for the anti-Mormon group that conspired to destroy the Church's power. He was influential in securing the removal of the territorial chief justice, Charles C. Wilson, which paved the way for Grant to appoint James B. McKean to that office. In addition, Shaffer effectively immobilized the Nauvoo Legion, the authorized territorial militia, when he appointed Patrick E. Connor as commander, ignoring the previous election of Daniel H. Wells to that position. Shaffer also suspended the annual musters of the militia, forcing the Nauvoo Legion into an inactivity, which continued until its official disbandment seventeen years later.

Simultaneously, starting in 1869, a new judicial crusade was begun by Associate Justices O. F. Strickland and C. M. Hawley, who attempted to strip the probate courts of their criminal jurisdiction. The major power in this crusade was Chief Justice McKean, who had earlier been identified with the Republican party in New York when it began its campaign against the "twin relics of barbarism," slavery and polygamy. The first "relic" had been eliminated, and McKean was sent to Utah by President Grant with instructions to root out the second by strictly enforcing the law.

McKean accepted this assignment with a sense of mission that was almost as great as the dedication of the Mormons themselves. His four-year tenure was a study in the conflict of value systems. The Saints firmly believed that the federal law against plural marriage was unconstitutional, for it violated their freedom to practice their religious faith. McKean, on the other hand, believed just as firmly that the law was right, that "the Mormon system" was wrong, and that he must pursue his goal with every means at his command. This sense of mission prompted him in 1872 to declare to Louis Dent, the president's brother-in-law, "Judge Dent, the mission which God has called upon me to perform in Utah, is as much above the duties of other courts and judges as the heavens are above the earth, and whenever or wherever I may find the Local or Federal laws obstructing or interfering therewith, by God's blessing I shall trample them under my feet."[7] To him it was not a matter of religion, but of upholding federal authority against "polygamic theocracy."

Ignoring the fact that he was subject to judicial procedures established by the territorial legislature, Judge McKean allowed the U.S. marshal to impanel juries. Indictments, convictions, and prison sentences soon multiplied. With his associate justices, he denied criminal jurisdiction to the probate courts. In addition, he took aim at the Mormons in the matter of naturalization of aliens by granting citizenship only if the applicants agreed to abide by the Anti-Bigamy Law of 1862. He even denied citizenship to people who had taken plural wives before the law was passed, as well as to some who, though they did not practice plural marriage, admitted they believed the principle was right.

McKean's major target was the entire Latter-day Saint system, but Mormonism's greatest symbol was Brigham Young. For his participation in plural marriage, President Young was indicted on a charge of adultery. While awaiting trial, he and several others were also indicted on a flimsy charge of murder, brought by an anti-Mormon acting United States district attorney, based on

---

[7]Edward W. Tullidge, *Life of Brigham Young* (New York: [n.p.], 1876), pp. 420-21.

nothing more than the testimony of a notorious gunman. He appeared in court on January 2, 1872, and was released on bail until the trial. McKean was undoubtedly pleased with the prospect for, he said, "A system is on trial in the person of Brigham Young."

The President of the Church was never brought to trial on this charge, for on April 15 some of McKean's judicial errors caught up with him. In an earlier case Paul Englebrecht, a local liquor dealer, had violated city ordinances by operating without a license. Acting under city law, officials had confiscated and destroyed his stock of liquor, and Englebrecht brought suit against them. Judge McKean allowed the jury to be impaneled by the United States marshal rather than by the territorial marshal as required by law. In this and other cases, such a method had excluded Mormons from juries. Englebrecht won his case, but it found its way to the Supreme Court, which ruled that the jury had been illegally drawn. The result was a stunning blow to Judge McKean, for it not only set aside the Englebrecht ruling, but it also released from custody about 130 prisoners who had been tried during the previous eighteen months before similar juries. The Supreme Court also quashed all other indictments pending, including the charges against Brigham Young.

Though a resounding rebuff to the career of Judge McKean, the Englebrecht case did not delay long the mounting pressure against the Church. By the early 1870s the Saints' economic and political activities were in open conflict with the ideas and ambitions of many non-Mormons in Utah as well as in the national government. In the next few years Judge McKean would be heard from again, and new federal legislation against the Mormons would pass, but the Saints themselves would show increased determination to stand firmly for the principles they believed were true and for the right to build an ideal community in the West that would be acceptable as the earthly manifestation of the Kingdom of God.

CHAPTER 11

Close of a Career, 1872-1877

Brigham Young was President of the Church for thirty years, longer than any other man in its history. Through Joseph Smith the gospel had been restored and the foundation laid for the establishment of the Kingdom of God on earth. "Brother Brigham," as he was affectionately called by the Saints, believed his task was to build on that foundation and to see that the gospel was carried to all nations. He directed the westward movement of the Church, inspired the establishment of more than 350 communities, promoted numerous economic and social programs designed to make the Saints self-sufficient, and led in firm defiance of all harmful external forces.

One of his greatest attributes as a leader was his confidence in the ultimate accomplishment of his goals and his willingness to try whatever programs seemed necessary to achieve them. At the same time, he seldom, if ever, pronounced his programs perfect—many of them were frankly experimental, and if they did not work, he tried something else. This constant looking forward with hope rather than backward with dismay was a trait that inspired and impressed both Saints and gentiles. During the last four years of President Young's life the Saints continued to suffer political hardships and saw important changes in their society. Politically, they were still governed by federal appointees, the majority of whom were antagonistic toward the Church and its doctrines, and they were the target of national legislation that resulted in new restrictions on political independence. Despite these problems they overcame the most severe effects of an economic depression, expanded their cultural and educational activities, established important new colonies, and dedicated their first temple in the Rocky Mountains. In addition, Brigham Young led a significant reform in Church government.

Confrontation in Education

A basic problem in the conflict between the Saints and the gentiles in Utah was simply misunderstanding, and it manifested itself not only in economic and political activities but also in education. In the 1870s a potential crisis that had been smoldering for two decades erupted.

In the early days of settlement the Saints made every effort to establish elementary schools in each ward. These were private schools, in which teachers' salaries were paid by tuition, with little subsidy from either the Church or the territorial government. Gradually, public schools were established throughout the territory, even though opposed by key Church leaders. With the growing influence of the gentiles, some members became fearful that non-Mormon teachers would be unsympathetic toward Church principles and might undermine the faith of the children. At the same time, scattered Protestant mission schools were beginning to provide better educational opportunities than the Mormon-controlled, poorly financed community schools, and a few Saints began to send their children to Protestant schools. The time was right for the Church to reevaluate its educational politics, and gradually Church leaders shifted their support to the free, tax-supported public schools.

This policy raised new questions. Church leaders became concerned with a movement that seemed to strike at their attempts to establish the Kingdom. The Saints believed that if they were to establish a righteous society, they must teach its principles in the public schools, at least as far as Bible reading would promote them. Some gentiles, on the other hand, objected to teaching religion in the schools. They reflected a contemporary movement in the United States to free public education from denominational influence, on the assumption that tax-supported schools as secular institutions of learning should not promote the viewpoint of any one religious group. Many people considered this as essential to a strict separation of church and state and at the heart of the American tradition. President Ulysses S. Grant supported this argument and in 1875 went so far as to recommend unsuccessfully that all church property in the nation be subject to taxation for the support of public schools. The Saints were dismayed at the suggestion, as were many American Catholics, who foresaw that such a policy could tax their extensive school system out of existence. In Utah, non-Mormons favored elimination of Bible teaching from schools not just because it was a national trend, but also because they thought it would help undermine Mormon influence.

A related issue was the hiring of teachers. By the 1870s many gentiles were teaching in the public schools. The Saints were concerned that their own influence in education would diminish in proportion to the number of non-Mormon teachers, while gentiles continued to resent the obvious Mormon dominance. In the early 1870s Governor George L. Woods, an avowed anti-Mormon, expressed the typical view by implying that the Church had usurped the government's function in education. "It is a violation of the fundamental doctrines upon which the Republic is founded," he said, "to permit any Church or people of any religious belief, to share any privileges which are not accorded, alike, to all." He argued that not even a majority had a right to control school revenues to suit their own religious faith, for governments were "not established for the benefit of majorities, but for the purpose of protecting minorities. Individual rights, and not collective rights, constitute the true foundations of all just governments."[1]

Even though they vividly remembered when the Saints themselves in other places were in the minority, Church leaders objected to such views. Nevertheless, they could point to significant differences now. As the majority, they had no intention of destroying any other religion or way of life, driving anyone from their midst, or destroying property. They believed, however, that they had the right to insist that the Bible be taught in the public schools and that teachers be selected from among their own

---

[1]As quoted in James R. Clark, "Church and State Relationships in Education in Utah" (Ed.D. thesis, Utah State University, 1958), pp. 209-10.

people. In 1877 Elder John Taylor was elected territorial superintendent of district schools, and he openly defended this position on public school teachers. "See that they are men and women who fear God and keep his commandments," he declared in a general conference in 1879. "We do not want men or women to teach the children of the Latter-day Saints who are not Latter-day Saints themselves. Hear it, you Elders of Israel and you school-trustees! We want none of these things."[2] The issue was not fully resolved because Saints and gentiles continued to see differently on the subject.

During these same years the need for better schools, especially for secondary schools, was becoming more apparent. Even though he had himself received little formal schooling, Brigham Young was convinced of the need for a broad, well-balanced education. He followed with interest the private Dusenberry School in Provo, founded by two brothers who were initially non-Mormons but soon joined the Church. This school was eventually absorbed by the University of Deseret; then, despite this help, it was discontinued in 1875 because of financial problems.

Brigham Young had commissioned John R. Park as early as 1871 to study educational systems in the eastern United States and several European countries. In 1873 preliminary plans were laid for establishment of a college. One of President Young's primary goals was to create a school that would train teachers for Latter-day Saint youth. In 1875, he selected a group of trustees and set aside some of his Provo property as the basis for a school, which became known as Brigham Young Academy, later Brigham Young University. BYA began operation in 1875, and later that year Karl G. Maeser, a German-born convert and educator, became principal. The academy's early students were mostly in the elementary grades, but in later years it became a secondary school, a teacher training college, and finally a university. President Young also founded Brigham Young College in Logan, which began operating in 1876 and continued until 1926.

These two schools exemplified Brigham Young's educational ideals and established a precedent for future church education. Both emphasized a broad, liberal arts education, high moral and ethical principles, and sound factual knowledge, and both made

---

[2] *Journal of Discourses*, 20:179.

"Brigham Young's Back Yard." This interesting scene was painted by Dan Weggeland, prominent Utah artist, in 1868, then copied by the artist himself in later years. Original Eagle Gate may be seen, spanning what is now State Street. To the left is schoolhouse built by Brigham Young for his children, and to the right is Beehive House, President Young's official residence. This 1915 copy is owned by the Historical Department of the Church. (Church Curator)

room in their curricula for the teaching of religion. President Young constantly advised the Saints to involve themselves in every field of learning, and on one occasion he emphasized his broad perspective by saying, " 'Shall I sit down and read the Bible, the Book of Mormon, and the Book of Covenants all the time?' says one. Yes, if you please, and when you have done, you may be nothing but a sectarian after all. It is your duty to know everything upon the face of the earth, in addition to reading those books."[3] The two schools he founded were forerunners of a more widely distributed academy movement that would characterize Church education during the rest of the century and the early part of the twentieth.

The Courts and Politics—a Never-ending Struggle

The judicial and political crusade against the Church seemed to heighten in the mid-1870s. Chief Justice James B. McKean was

---

[3] *Journal of Discourses,* 2:93-94.

not the only federal officer attempting to destroy plural marriage, but his court became a rallying point for all anti-Mormon activity. The most widely publicized case was that of Ann Eliza Webb Young, Brigham Young's last and youngest plural wife. In 1873, at the urging of some members of the gentile "Utah ring," she sued for divorce, charging neglect, cruel treatment, and desertion. The suit placed Judge McKean in a dilemma: he wished to embarrass President Young and force him to pay the costs and alimony requested, but if he granted the divorce he would be recognizing the marriage, thus admitting the legality of the very system of plural marriage he was trying to destroy. Despite this, the judge ordered President Young to pay $3,000 in court fees and a $500 monthly maintenance to Ann Eliza.

Acting upon his lawyers' advice, President Young declined to pay the fee, pending an appeal to a higher court. Because of this, the judge ordered him to face charges of contempt, but the President defended his right to the review. Should he lose the appeal he would pay, and although he did not intend to treat the order of the territorial supreme court with contempt, he wanted the benefit of the appeal. McKean, however, found him in contempt of court, fined him twenty-five dollars, and sentenced him to the penitentiary for one day.

The spectacle of the aging President of the Church being sent to prison was immediately publicized in the national press. So blatantly irresponsible were McKean's actions that many newspapers sympathized with Brigham Young. Five days later President Grant removed McKean from office. Other reasons prompted the unseating, including charges of judicial corruption and poor judgment, but the Ann Eliza Webb Young case probably contributed. At any rate, the man who seemed most to symbolize the challenge to Mormon autonomy was finally out of the territory.

During these years many federal officials, among them the president of the United States, were increasing their determination to alter some of the Church's political and social practices. All this was difficult for the Latter-day Saints to understand, for to them their marriage customs were a fulfillment of religious principle. Those who opposed polygamy, such as Ulysses S. Grant, although people of integrity and honor, could not understand the religious motivation behind the practice. They considered it an outright violation of federal law and morally reprehensible. President Grant stated to Congress in December 1871: "It is not with the religion of the self-styled Saints that we are now dealing, but with their practices. They will be protected in the worship of God according to the dictates of their consciences, but they will not be permitted to violate the laws, under the cloak of religion."[4] His desire to be fair is demonstrated by his recommendation that Congress legitimize all children born prior to a certain fixed date. But as he said in 1872, he wanted laws that would result in the "ultimate extinguishment of polygamy."[5]

It was to be expected, therefore, that Grant should appoint federal officers in the Territory of Utah who were sympathetic with his goals. Some of them, however, harassed the Saints beyond the limits of judicial propriety. Cyrus M. Hawley, judge of the Second Judicial District Court, in an obvious effort to discredit the Saints in 1872, charged that it was almost impossible to dispense justice in southern Utah because of the antagonism of the Mormons. His suggestion that a military post be established at Beaver was approved by the secretary of war in September 1873, and a military barracks, Fort Cameron, was soon constructed. The Saints of Beaver did not object to the presence of the troops, for it aided their commercial activities, but they did not see the need. Such occupation offensively implied that they were disorderly citizens. The fort was maintained until 1883, when the troops were withdrawn.

The Saints' antagonists were not without fault. It was soon disclosed that Judge Obed Strickland had actually purchased his office from his predecessor, and that Judge Cyrus Hawley was guilty of bigamy. It was also charged that McKean had been allowed to write editorials in the *Salt Lake Tribune* supporting his own judicial decisions. George C. Bates, United States district attorney, became so disgusted with the general nature of justice in Utah that he wrote President Grant:

Your entire administration of affairs in Utah, your special Message to Congress, and many of the most important appointments made by you here, have all been the result of misrepresentation, falsehood, and

---

[4]James D. Richardson, ed., *A Compilation of the Messages and Papers of the Presidents, 1789-1897*, 10 vols. (Washington: Government Printing Office, 1896-1899), 7:151.

[5]Richardson, *Messages and Papers of the Presidents*, 7:203.

misunderstanding on your part of the real condition of affairs in this territory. . . .

In other communications, soon to be made, in every instance accompanied by the evidence, I will demonstrate how other distinguished officers have bought their offices, how you were made a mere catspaw, by corrupt Senators and Representatives, to send officers here whom you would not have trusted among your horse blankets in the executive stable.[6]

Despite the ineptness of President Grant's appointments, when he visited the territory in 1875 he received a grand welcome. He was the first American president to visit Utah, and when he arrived, many territorial and Church officials, including President Brigham Young, courteously greeted him. Compliments were exchanged, and impressive crowds cheered him as his carriage moved along the streets. He arrived in Salt Lake City on a Sunday, and well-dressed Sunday School children, waving happily, lined the streets. It is said that he inquired whose children they were and was answered by the governor, "Mormon children," after which he was silent for a while, then quietly remarked, "I have been deceived."[7] The story may well be apocryphal, for after he returned to Washington he continued his attack on Mormon practices.

Congress Acts Once Again

In the meantime, the failure of McKean's judicial crusade reemphasized to the Utah gentiles the need for more national legislation if their attack on polygamic theocracy was to be successful.

A number of measures were introduced in Congress in 1873 aimed directly at Mormon practices. While these bills failed to pass, an 1874 bill sponsored by Representative Luke P. Poland of Vermont passed both houses of Congress and was signed by the president. The law abolished the controversial jurisdiction in both criminal and civil cases that had been given to the probate courts nearly twenty-five years earlier and also did away with the offices of territorial marshal and attorney general, whose powers had overlapped those of the United States marshal and district attorney.

The debates in the House of Representatives over the Poland

---

[6]*Millennial Star* 35 (1873): 241-43.
[7]Orson F. Whitney, *History of Utah*, 4 vols. (Salt Lake City: George Q. Cannon & Sons Co., 1892-1904), 2:778.

Bill were especially interesting, for among the participants was Elder George Q. Cannon, Utah's representative to Congress. Poland argued vehemently that federal officials simply were not able to exercise their authority in Utah because they were effectively supplanted by Mormon officials, becoming only figureheads. He was particularly irate that the territorial legislature was filled by Mormons, "controlled entirely by Brigham Young and the 'twelve apostles,' " and he was incensed that so many probate judges were Latter-day Saint bishops. Delegate Cannon ably defended Utah and made it clear that the main reason these courts held the unusual jurisdiction in the first place was that justice could not be obtained in the federal courts. He demonstrated the fairness of the probate courts by producing a list of eighty-four civil cases that had been tried in Salt Lake City involving Mormons and non-Mormons. Fifty-nine of these were decided in favor of non-Mormons or dissenting Mormons, while twenty-five were decided in favor of the Mormons. The courts had acted impartially. Elder Cannon then presented a justification of Utah's unique ecclesiastical situation that summarized the peculiar needs and attitudes of the Saints:

> Sir, there is probably no officer in the Utah Territory, if he belongs to the Mormon people, who does not hold some position in the Church. The Mormon people do not believe in salaried preachers; but they believe it to be the privilege of every worthy man of the organization to be an elder, and, when called upon, to make himself useful in preaching. Doubtless many gentlemen about me who have visited Utah Territory will recollect, if they passed a Sabbath there, that elders were very frequently called from the body of the congregation to preach from the stand without any preparation whatever. Bishops, probate judges, men of different vocations in the community, are thus called upon to speak to the people, so that if you say that a man must not exercise political functions in Utah because he is an officer in the church you exclude from all offices in the Territory every respectable Mormon.[8]

Despite his logic and eloquence, Elder Cannon's pleadings were in vain, and the long sought anti-Mormon legislation became a reality.

Prosecution and the Reynolds Case

As soon as the Poland Bill became law, the federal judiciary

---

[8]United States Congress, House, *Congressional Record*, 43 Cong., 1 sess., 1874, vol. 2, pt. 5:4471.

began criminal proceedings against plural marriage under the Anti-Bigamy Act of 1862. Like the American revolutionaries a century earlier, the Saints believed that a higher law compelled them to violate one they considered unjust, and one they believed would ultimately be declared unconstitutional.

The most significant case was that of George Reynolds. Church leaders hoped to use it to test the constitutionality of the law in the U.S. Supreme Court. Reynolds, private secretary to Brigham Young, was arrested in October 1874 and voluntarily gave evidence against himself. He was found guilty of bigamy and sentenced to pay a $500 fine and serve one year in prison. His conviction was overturned by the territorial supreme court, however, because the grand jury that indicted him had been illegally drawn. In October 1875 he was indicted a second time; his trial resulted in another guilty verdict, a $500 fine, and two years of hard labor. On July 6 the territorial supreme court upheld the conviction, and an appeal was quickly made to the United States Supreme Court.

Before the U.S. Supreme Court, Reynolds's attorney presented several technical arguments about the nature of the jury and the testimony that convicted Elder Reynolds, and argued that plural marriage was not intrinsically evil. It was, rather, part of the social and religious life of the area, and should be left alone as an exercise in freedom of religion. The court turned a deaf ear to all these arguments and ruled that polygamy constituted an offense against society. As such, said the court, it was a valid matter for legislation. With only one dissent, the lower court's decision was upheld. On January 6, 1879, therefore, the Anti-Bigamy Act of 1862 was affirmed as the constitutional law of the land.

Needless to say, the decision of the Supreme Court stunned Church leaders. Perhaps it was a kind providence that saved President Brigham Young from this disappointment by taking him from mortality two years earlier. The Church leaders who remained faced a cruel dilemma. Should they continue to preach and practice what they believed was a divine law, or should they now conform to the constitutional law of the land? It had taken many of them a long time to accept the principle of plural marriage in the first place, but they had sincerely and fully accepted it and were living it as the Lord's law. It would take another eleven years to become prepared for a revelation that ended church-sanctioned plural marriages.

The United Orders of Zion

During the last five years of his life, President Brigham Young continued to promote the economic independence of the Kingdom through an increased emphasis on cooperation. As before, the creeping impact of outside competition and other economic forces in the nation threatened the economic solidarity of the Saints. The railroad had made possible a booming development of mining, and inevitably the territory had become dependent on the prosperity of that industry. In addition, the railroad brought to Utah consumer goods that could often be sold less expensively than those produced in the territory. This was the condition when the United States was suddenly hit by the financial depression of 1873. The firm of Jay Cooke and Company overextended itself in building the Northern Pacific Railroad, and when its failure contributed to a national lack of confidence, many depositors began to withdraw their funds from the nation's banks. These institutions, in turn, began to call in their short-term loans to build up their reserves, but soon bank failures multiplied, the circulation of money slowed, and movements of some agricultural products were halted. Credit declined, people hoarded cash, consumer spending dropped, unemployment rose, and the panic was on.

In Utah, bank deposits dropped by more than 30 percent in a year; the mines closed, causing a decline in the business of stores; and shops and factories, the agricultural market, and two major banks failed. Despite their efforts at independence, the Saints in Zion were clearly affected by the economic rhythm of the nation.

This was proof enough to many Latter-day Saints that they were still too entangled in economic alliances with the world. Church leaders tried to soften the effects of the panic by reemphasizing home industry and reaffirming their teachings on unity and brotherly love. They also began to instruct the Saints in the United Order of Enoch. The willingness of many to accept the plan of a more advanced system of economic cooperation than had already been adopted was at least partly the result of their fear of the deepening panic of 1873.

The move into the United Order was not sudden; it had found expression in the cooperative movement of the late 1860s. "This cooperative movement," President Young declared in 1869,

A Brigham City manufacturing cooperative. Lorenzo Snow, founder of the town's cooperative movement, stands at the end on the right. (Church Archives)

"is only a stepping stone to what is called the Order of Enoch, but which is in reality the order of Heaven."[9] The next step, the actual establishment of United Orders throughout the territory, was inspired in part by the impressive success of the Brigham City Cooperative, which had weathered the disastrous panic of 1873. Lorenzo Snow had founded a cooperative mercantile establishment in 1864, and it soon branched out into some forty cooperative departments. Brooms, hats, molasses, furniture, a general store, a tannery, a woolen mill, sheep, milk cows, hogs, flax, all phases of the building trades, and specialized farms were all part of the Brigham City Cooperative. It was owned by approximately four hundred shareholders who represented nearly every family in this village of two thousand, and the profits from its activity were paid to shareholders in kind (goods and services) rather than cash. The panic left the cooperative almost untouched, and the reputation of Brigham City spread as far as England and impressed social reformers everywhere. It was reported later that Brigham Young had said that "Brother Snow has led the people along, and got them into the United Order without their knowing it."[10]

When Brigham Young took his annual winter trip to southern Utah in the winter of 1873-74, he began to preach the need for improving community economic efforts. He believed that half the labor necessary to make the people moderately comfortable under any other system would make them independently rich in an ideal cooperative society. He envisioned a society in which the people would make and raise all they needed to eat, drink, or wear, and still realize a surplus for sale to outsiders. Such a dream was, of course, idealistic, and no one knew better than Brigham Young that the ultimate ideal society would never be created in this world until people completely overcame every vestige of selfishness and were prepared for the millennial reign of Christ. But the ideal was worth striving for, and the economic problems of the territory provided the impetus for bold new experiments.

It was significant that this new economic program should emerge when other reform programs were attracting attention. The newly industrialized American society had recorded some incredible achievements, but it had also created economic inequality, some poverty, and some lack of opportunity for the rural and urban workers alike. In this setting political reformers were beginning to advocate stricter government controls to ensure a more even distribution of America's new wealth. The Latter-day Saints clearly opposed the idea of a socialist state in which all means of production and distribution would be owned outright by the federal government. The same problems that concerned the reformers, however, made the Saints willing to try to establish communities based on cooperation and equality, grounded in the religious belief that the earth's abundance belonged to God and that in building their ideal communities they were furthering the cause of the Kingdom of God on earth. Unlike many contemporary reformers who advocated a national system of state ownership, the Latter-day Saints were promoting community organization based on individual, voluntary association. Their communities would exist side-by-side with the larger society and would engage in trade with it, but they would also be economically self-sufficient

---

[10]As quoted by Lorenzo Snow in a sermon of April 21, 1878, *Journal of Discourses*, 19:347.

and not dependent upon the outside in times of emergency.

The cotton mission settlement at St. George was particularly in need of an economic boost in the winter of 1873-74, and it was there that Brigham Young organized the first United Order. Nearly three hundred people, most of the adults in the city, pledged their time, energy, ability, and property to the order and became subject to the direction of an elected board of management. In return for property, each person received a commensurate amount of stock. Stockholders pledged themselves to boost local manufacturing, stop importing goods, and deal only with members of the order. The order was also to be a spiritual union, and a long list of rules for Christian living was drawn up. Each person entered the order by being rebaptized and pledging to obey all the rules.

That winter Brigham Young established the order in about twenty communities in southern Utah, and the following spring he organized each settlement along his way to Salt Lake City. In all, about 150 United Orders were established, and most of them adopted constitutions similar to the pioneer model at St. George.

Under assignment, most other leaders of the Church preached economic reform and establishment of the new United Orders. In the general conference of October 1875, Elder George Q. Cannon reminded the Saints of one of their chief goals:

> We can see very plainly that we must be a self-sustaining people, that we must manufacture in our midst, to the greatest possible extent, that which we consume, that is necessary for our comfort and convenience. Unless we take this course, it is an impossibility that we can become the people that we design to be, and that God in his revelations had predicted we shall be. No people who are dependent upon others can become a great people. A people who are constantly producing for others to manufacture, never can become a great people. If we produce wool, and hides, and grain, and other things from the earth, and send them away to be manufactured, we shall constantly pay tribute to other people, and the object of the United Order is to stop this.[11]

Another equally fundamental reason for establishing the new system was to protect the Church from the internal schism that could be caused by the development of separate wealthy and poor classes among the Saints. In a pamphlet published in 1875 the First Presidency decried class distinctions and labeled them as a

---

[11]*Journal of Discourses*, 18:104-5.

primary reason behind the original cooperative movement:

> Years ago it was perceived that . . . a wealthy class was being rapidly formed in our midst whose interests, in the course of time, were likely to be diverse from those of the rest of the community. The growth of such a class was dangerous to our union; and most of all people, we stand in need of union and to have our interests identical. Then it was that the Saints were counseled to enter into co-operation.[12]

St. George represented one of four general types of United Orders. In communities following that pattern, members received wages and dividends depending upon the amount of labor and property they contributed. When problems naturally arose regarding fair distribution of benefits, many Saints decided that they were not ready to live the plan. Most experiments of this type lasted little more than a year, and the St. George order itself was dissolved in 1878.

A second type of United Order following the Brigham City plan was established in communities where a cooperative network already existed. This plan did not require members to consecrate all their economic property and labor to the order. Rather, it emphasized community ownership and operation of particular enterprises. In Hyrum, Utah, and Paris, Idaho, for example, the cooperative activity began with a general store, which used its profits to establish cooperative sawmills, blacksmith shops, tanneries, and herds. Under this pattern each person retained his own private property in addition to the stock he held in the cooperative businesses. The Brigham City order was disbanded in 1885. Several natural disasters, economic restrictions by federal officials, and the fact that Elder Snow was sentenced to the penitentiary for practicing polygamy made it difficult to operate.

A third variation on the United Order was designed for larger cities: Salt Lake City, Ogden, Provo, and Logan. Each ward was required to organize its own cooperative enterprise, and all ward members were expected to help finance it. For example, the Logan First Ward built a foundry and machine shop, while the Second Ward organized a woodworking shop, and the Third Ward managed a dairy. Like the Brigham City type, most of these co-ops lasted until the mid-1880s, when the federal government's anti-

---

[12]James R. Clark, ed., *Messages of the First Presidency of the Church of Jesus Christ of Latter-day Saints, 1837-1964*, 6 vols. (Salt Lake City: Bookcraft, 1965-1975), 2:268.

Deseret currency represents a number of important aspects of Mormon economy in nineteenth-century Utah, including the development of local cooperatives and the emphasis on home industry. (Church Archives)

polygamy activities combined with other problems to compel their abandonment. Most of the business activities were continued as private enterprises.

The best-known United Orders were those of the type established at Orderville, Utah. In most cases these were organized in small communities, ranging from 50 to 750 in size. Settlers retained no private economic property at all, shared equally in the community's production, and lived and ate together as a well-regulated family. This was the ultimate in economic cooperation, for no one could live in the community without becoming part of the order. This was also the closest the Saints came to the ideal communities established by the New Testament apostles among the Christians in Jerusalem and by the people of the Book of Mormon who "had all things common among them."

The experience at Orderville aptly illustrates both the achievements and the problems of such United Orders. The community was founded in 1875 by 24 families, consisting of 150 people, though within five years there were 700 people in the town. By cooperative labor they built all the apartment units, shops, bakeries, barns, and other buildings needed for a well-regulated community. Each family had its own apartment, but at first everyone ate together in a large dining room with the women taking turns at kitchen duty. They operated farms, orchards, dairies, livestock projects, and various manufacturing enterprises. They produced an excess of furniture and sold it to surrounding communities in exchange for funds for expansion. They wore the same kind of clothes, all manufactured at Orderville, and no member of the community could improve his situation unless all were likewise improved. The self-discipline and dedication to others that were required during the ten years the order functioned was indeed remarkable.

As might be expected, there were human problems that caused difficulty. The generous Saints were perhaps too ready to allow new members to join, and consequently, Orderville became too crowded for effective cooperation. In addition, the young people of the community became restless as they compared themselves with the youth of surrounding towns. As the whole region became more wealthy in the late 1870s, the old-fashioned jeans, shoes, and straw hats they wore, as well as their very small apartments, became objects of ridicule. In one instance the young men of Orderville became so enamoured with the new style of trousers worn by the boys of surrounding communities that they took to wearing out their own sturdy, "everlasting" jeans by placing them on the community grindstone! The result was that the community manufactured new trousers for all. In addition, natural disagreements crept in over the equitable distribution of goods and credits, and some people began to chafe under the rigid regulation necessary to keep the community going. When the accelerated anti-polygamy campaign of the 1880s drove many of their leaders into hiding or placed them in the penitentiary, they were counseled by Church authorities to dissolve the order.

How did people react to life in these cooperative communities that spanned a decade of Mormon history? Some complained of the regulation, of course. It was a tremendous exercise in self-sacrifice to accept total equality when some could probably obtain a better living on their own. Sometimes people left the communities. For the most part, those who worked to build Orderville looked back with genuine nostalgia for the happy feelings it gave them to live in a well-ordered Christian community.

Like so many other economic experiments of that age, the United Orders did not achieve all their economic goals, and most were abandoned by 1877. Others continued until the political problems of the 1880s forced their demise. Despite these apparent failures, the order accomplished some notable things. For the time being, at least, there were fewer imports, production increased, local investment was stimulated, and progress was made toward diminishing economic inequality among the Saints. The order promoted thrift and industry as well as more rapid development of local resources. For a while, and probably when it was most crucially needed to assist in the other goals of the Kingdom, the United Order helped the Saints maintain a degree of economic independence from the East. In addition, United Orders aided significantly in building the temples at St. George, Logan, Manti, and Salt Lake City, by furnishing both labor and materials.

The Settlements on the Little Colorado

While all this was happening, the Church was expanding the perimeters of its commonwealth. The most important area of expansion in the 1870s was along the Little Colorado River in Arizona, and the establishment of the Little Colorado colonies was a fitting close to the career of the "great colonizer," Brigham Young.

The Church had long been collecting data on northern Arizona, and as early as the 1850s Church explorers had penetrated the region. In addition, beginning in 1858 and extending until the early 1870s, Jacob Hamblin and a handful of his associates designated as Indian missionaries made periodic visits to the mesa villages of the Hopis. They became well acquainted with the deserts of northern Arizona, though they probably did not explore much of the Little Colorado. The Saints also knew of that country through close contact with John Wesley Powell and other government explorers. They cooperated with official surveyors and profited by an exchange of information.

In 1870 the Navajos, who had conducted intermittent raids along Utah's southern frontier since 1865, were pacified, enabling the Church to resume the southward movement, which had long been an important element of Brigham Young's design for a great Latter-day Saint commonwealth in the intermountain region. Settlements were established at Kanab, Pipe Springs, Paria, and Lee's Ferry between 1870 and 1873, and these soon served as the approach to Arizona.

Daniel P. McArthur, St. George Stake president, baptizing a Shivwits Indian, about 1875. Standing on the rock is Sheriff Augustus P. Hardy, who, along with Jacob Hamblin, helped establish the Santa Clara Indian Mission in 1854. (Church Archives)

The eventual settlement of the Saints in Arizona was the result of a much more ambitious plan conceived by Brigham Young and Thomas L. Kane, the long-time, important friend of the Mormons. The two men spent the winter of 1872-73 together in St. George and laid plans for a second gathering place for the Saints in Sonora Valley, Mexico. The settlements in Arizona were to form a connecting link between Utah and Mexico.

The first effort to colonize along the Little Colorado River was discouraging. In December 1872, an exploring company under the leadership of Bishop Lorenzo Roundy was sent into the region. His report, written in March, was perhaps too optimistic, and immediately about 250 missionaries were called to move south, as soon as weather permitted, under the leadership of Horton D. Haight. Only a little more than a hundred got underway before the mission was abandoned.

The first group crossed the Colorado River at Lee's Ferry (an outpost maintained by John D. Lee) on April 22, 1873. The party found little but discouragement. The arid, broken countryside was difficult to traverse, the river seemed to be drying up, and an advance exploring party that went 120 miles further upstream found the area a desert. A messenger was sent to the telegraph in southeastern Utah for instructions, but when no word came, the advance party turned back and the mission was abandoned.

At this point the amazing optimism of some of the Saints again became significant. Belatedly, Brigham Young had sent word to the struggling company of missionaries that they were to stay in Arizona, and he made clear his belief that no matter what the obstacles were, a company of determined Saints could establish a successful outpost. At the same time, other leaders proclaimed that such formidable, uninviting territory was actually a blessing, for there the Saints could settle without fear that anyone else would try to take it away. "If there be deserts in Arizona," said George Q. Cannon, "thank God for the deserts. . . . The worst places in the land we can probably get, and we must develop them. If we were to find a good country how long would it be before the wicked would want it and seek to strip us of our possessions?"[13] Even some of the unsuccessful missionaries were not certain the enterprise was a total failure. After one group inscribed on a rock "Arizona Mission Dead—1873," a more visionary writer countered by composing a poem that began, "Thou Fool, This Mission is not dead, it only sleeps," and went on to emphasize the lack of wisdom and understanding of those who despised this land, created by God. Saints of this persuasion looked upon the hardships as challenges and the mission as the will of God to further strengthen the Kingdom.

During the next two years more thorough exploring was undertaken by various groups of Saints, including missionaries to the Indians, and early in 1876 Lot Smith led the first successful Mormon settlement in the lower valley of the Little Colorado. That year four regular Mormon villages were founded, in addition to a community to support missionary work among the Indians in Arizona and another in New Mexico. As in earlier colonization activities, the Saints in Arizona built their villages by community cooperation, working together in building dams, constructing irrigation ditches, clearing the land, and harvesting their crops.

---

[13] *Journal of Discourses,* 16:143.

Lot Smith, prominent for activities in the Utah War and later important as a leader of pioneer Mormon settlements in Arizona. (Church Archives)

A second group of settlements was founded during the next two years along Silver Creek, a major tributary of the Little Colorado. Here other settlers had already attempted to establish farming and livestock communities, but several of their holdings eventually fell into Mormon hands. One group of LDS settlers departed from the normal pattern of the time and did not adopt the United Order. Under the leadership of William J. Flake, they were encouraged by Elder Erastus Snow of the Council of the Twelve, and the successful village was aptly named Snowflake. Eventually it became one of the major centers of Mormon settlement in Arizona. Finally, in 1879 and 1880 a third group of Latter-day Saint settlements was begun at St. Johns and the area near the headwaters of the Little Colorado. The basis for strong Mormon influence in Arizona had been laid.

But this activity did not result immediately in a push further south to Mexico—the Mexican colonies were established later and for different reasons. Historically, it demonstrates once again that in this period of Church history many significant achievements were often the result of even more ambitious dreams, and that without the dreams less would have been accomplished. In 1873 George Q. Cannon predicted that "the time must come when the

Latter-day Saints . . . will extend throughout all North and South America, and we shall establish the rule of righteous and good order throughout all these new countries."[14] Another hundred years would see the fulfillment of this prediction, but it would come through missionary work rather than colonization.

The St. George Temple

The last years of Brigham Young's life encompassed concerns beyond political problems and colonization ventures. Perhaps the most important symbol of the establishment of the Kingdom in the tops of the mountains was the building of temples. The site for the magnificent temple in Salt Lake City was chosen just four days after the Saints entered the valley, although actual construction did not begin until 1853. A large granite quarry in Little Cottonwood Canyon provided the building material, and especially after the Utah Expedition had left, ox teams were constantly engaged in hauling the stone to the temple site, where sometimes more than a hundred stonecutters were at work.

The first temple to be completed was at St. George, which became almost a second headquarters of the Church as President Young spent most of his winters there in his later years. The dedication shown in the building of earlier temples was fully matched in St. George, where ground was broken in November 1871. The Saints opened rock quarries, hauled timber eighty miles, and donated one day in ten as tithing labor. Some worked for a pittance in the quarry after walking five miles each day to work, then donated half their wages to the temple. Others donated food, clothing, and other goods to those who were working full time. The beautiful white structure was finally completed and dedicated on April 6, 1877. Sites for the Logan and Manti temples were dedicated the same year, and these temples were completed in 1884 and 1888 respectively.

The St. George Temple symbolized many things to the Saints. First, of course, it demonstrated their continued dedication to temple work; here the Saints began for the first time to perform endowments in behalf of the dead. In addition, no sealings in behalf of the dead had been performed since the days of Nauvoo, and

---

[14] *Journal of Discourses*, 16:144.

First temple to be completed in Utah was the St. George Temple, shown here in process of construction. Groundbreaking took place in 1871, and it was dedicated in 1877. The original spire was replaced later with a much taller one. In the early twentieth century the interior of the temple was redesigned to provide separate lecture rooms for the various stages of the endowment ceremony. The temple was rededicated in 1975 after another major interior renovation. (Church Archives)

it was in the St. George Temple that this practice was again inaugurated. That the work assuring the eternity of the family relationship was moving forward again after thirty years reflected the determination of Brigham Young and the Saints to carry out all that had been established through the Prophet Joseph Smith.

The temple also symbolized other things to Brigham Young. The dedication of the Saints in building it was exemplary, as was their craftsmanship. Like all the temples of the nineteenth century, it was a labor of love, a monument to the faith, and a striking example of the painstaking handwork of pioneer artisans. Equally important, the St. George Temple represented the self-sufficiency and independence of the Saints. Built entirely by the labor of the

Saints from native materials, it was a monument to President Young's great concern for the development of local industry and lack of dependence upon outside sources. Even the decorations were produced in Utah: the Provo Woolen Factory made carpet, the local sisters made rag carpets for the hallways, and fringe for the altars and pulpits was made from Utah-produced silk. Finally, the April general conference was held in St. George that year, and on April 6 the dedication of the temple took place with President Daniel H. Wells offering the prayer. This was to be President Brigham Young's last conference.

Administrative Reform

During these same years the General Authorities took time to examine how the administrative structure of the Church had

Typical church service in the new Ephraim, Utah, tabernacle in the early 1870s. In this important photograph today's Latter-day Saint will note a number of interesting differences between Church practices today and those of a century ago. The painting of murals in chapels was more commonplace; few young children attended preaching services; the sacrament was administered and distributed by mature men (possibly "acting" priests); and people offering public prayers often raised their hands in a worshipful attitude. (Church Archives)

developed since Nauvoo, and they found need for some changes. As the Church had grown the administrative burdens on President Young were becoming heavier, and he sought to relieve himself of some of them. In April 1873 he resigned the office of trustee-in-trust and named his first counselor, George A. Smith, to succeed him. At the same time a dozen men were named assistant trustees. In addition, he selected five men as counselors, besides the two counselors already serving in the First Presidency. The precedent for this had been set earlier by Joseph Smith, and as Brigham Young advanced in years he felt the need to do the same thing.

A more basic decision concerning Church leadership was the question of seniority among the presiding authorities. It had not been fully clarified, and by June 1875 it appeared that two apostles held positions within the Council of the Twelve contrary to President Young's understanding of seniority. Elders Orson Hyde and Orson Pratt had been excommunicated because of misunderstandings in the days of Joseph Smith, but both had been reinstated to their earlier positions in the Council of the Twelve, even though other men had been ordained and sustained in the meantime. With the full support of the Twelve, President Young ruled that seniority was to be held by those with the longest continuous position in the quorum. John Taylor, Wilford Woodruff, and George A. Smith were placed ahead of the other two as a result of this ruling, and thus the order of seniority was clearly defined and accepted by the leaders of the Church.

In the last year of his life President Young inaugurated changes directly affecting the operation of the Church on the local level. Membership growth in the Rocky Mountain stakes had created a need for a general reform of some practices, but they had been neglected amid the problems of colonization, economic planning, and political conflict. Before he left St. George for the last time in the spring of 1877, he reorganized the officers of the stake, then proceeded to do the same in other stakes. Some that had become too large and unmanageable were divided, increasing the number of stakes from eight to eighteen. Members of the Council of the Twelve who had been presiding in stakes were released from local positions. In addition, stake presidents were instructed to hold stake conferences each quarter and to begin to hold monthly priesthood meetings.

Priesthood quorums were also affected by the reform. Elders

quorums were instructed that they must be properly organized with ninety-six elders in each, even if it meant that two wards must join together to form a quorum. The quorums were encouraged to involve themselves in welfare services and to work closely with the United Orders then being established.

Equally important, the organization and administration of wards was tightened. In some areas acting bishops had been serving without having been ordained, and some bishops were serving without counselors. A *Circular of the First Presidency* issued July 11, 1877, directed that henceforth all bishops were to be ordained high priests, and they were to have two counselors who were high priests. It was also emphasized that bishops were the presiding high priests in their respective wards. Previously there had been some differences between bishops and priesthood quorum leaders about who was the presiding authority.

All this was significant representation of what had happened to the organization of the Church since the days of Nauvoo. The bishops' responsibilities had greatly expanded beyond their original economic functions, and the ward was becoming a fundamental part of the church administrative structure. Ward bishops also began to handle temple donations, and their responsibility to preside over priests quorums was reemphasized. Aaronic Priesthood quorums were clearly given ward status, something that had not been carefully defined before; many had functioned as stake units rather than as ward units. One of the most significant aspects of the developing organization was the emphasis placed on the ward as the primary local unit of church activity and the expanded role of bishops as heads of wards. These developments would be further augmented in the twentieth century, but by 1877 the ecclesiastical ward had come of age.

Another important move was the introduction of more youth into the Aaronic Priesthood. Brigham Young declared that the priesthood would be good training for young men and that they needed it much earlier than they had customarily been receiving it. No ages were set for receiving priesthood offices, but from that time young men began to receive the Aaronic Priesthood more frequently than before.

In the October 1877 conference, Elder George Q. Cannon commented on the significance of the reform:

I do not believe myself that President Young could have felt as happy, as I know he does feel, had he left the Church in the condition it was in when he commenced his labors last spring. I am convinced that it has added greatly to his satisfaction; it has been a fitting consumation to the labors of his long life that he should be spared to organize the Church throughout these valleys in the manner in which it now is organized.[15]

-    The closing years of President Young's life, then, were a fitting conclusion to a remarkable career. True to his reputation as a colonizer, he had directed the opening of new colonies in Arizona. Known for his excellence in planning and administration, he had devised and promoted new plans for economic cooperation for the Saints. Never one to resist change if he believed change was needed, he had encouraged the founding of auxiliaries as well as the further development of stake, ward, and priesthood organization. At the same time, he was convinced that he was only building the Kingdom upon the foundation that Joseph Smith had laid. On August 29, 1877, Brigham Young died. His last words were simply: "Joseph! Joseph! Joseph!"

---

[15] *Journal of Discourses*, 19:232.

CHAPTER 12

A Turbulent Decade, 1877-1887

Brigham Young was spared the shock of the Reynolds decision outlawing plural marriage, as well as the agony of deciding whether to continue or abandon the practice. His successor, John Taylor, was not so fortunate. During his leadership the Church continued to grow in numbers, expand its colonies, and refine its religious programs to meet the spiritual needs of the Saints, but it faced more intense legal challenges than ever before. For a time the Saints in both Utah and Idaho were disfranchised as new national legislation provided a more effective basis for legal attacks upon the Church, men and women alike among the Saints were jailed as criminals, Church leaders were imprisoned or went into hiding, and the President of the Church went into exile. The ten years after 1877 constituted a turbulent decade.

The Second Apostolic Presidency

President Brigham Young's death left no question, as there had been at the death of Joseph Smith, about who should lead the Church. It was clear that the duties of the First Presidency devolved upon the Council of the Twelve, and the only question was when a new First Presidency should be organized. The Twelve disagreed on whether this should be done immediately, and until a unanimous agreement could be reached the Twelve functioned as the presidency of the Church. It was clear, however, who should lead. Brigham Young's action in 1875 of clarifying the order of seniority among the Twelve had made John Taylor the senior member, and all agreed that he was rightfully President of the Twelve. This also made him presiding officer over the entire church. Daniel H. Wells and John W. Young, who had been Brigham Young's counselors but were not members of the Twelve, were sustained as counselors to the Twelve Apostles.

As a presidency, the Council of the Twelve continued the administrative reforms begun by Brigham Young and encouraged the expansion of church programs. The auxiliary programs received special attention. In 1878 a central committee was established in each county of Utah to direct the work of the Young Men's Mutual Improvement Association. Since stake organizations were not yet perfected, the county system seemed the most practical alternative. In 1880 the work had grown to such proportions that a general superintendency for the entire church was named from among the Twelve. Wilford Woodruff was superintendent and Joseph F. Smith and Moses Thatcher were his counselors. The Young Men's organizations were specifically instructed that they were not to intervene with priesthood functions—they were auxiliary organizations only. Their major responsibility concerned the cultural and recreational needs of the youth.

The women's organizations also received attention. The name of the Retrenchment Association was changed to the Young Ladies' Mutual Improvement Association by Eliza R. Snow, who had long been the principal leader of Latter-day Saint women. In 1878 she began organizing stake boards, and this reform proceeded rapidly during the next two years. Finally, in 1880, a churchwide organization was created, with Elmina S. Taylor as president. On the same day, Eliza R. Snow was made general president of the Relief Society, but she continued in an advisory role to the YLMIA under a new calling as "president of woman's work of the Church in all the world."

About this time a new auxiliary, the Primary Mutual Improvement Association, later known as the Primary Association, was founded for the benefit of the children. The first Primary was organized in Farmington, Utah, on August 11, 1878, by Aurelia S.

Rogers. Children in the community were taught both crafts and church doctrine, and each year a Primary Fair allowed them to display the results of their handiwork. In 1880 a churchwide organization was formed with Louie B. Felt as president.

Leaders of the Church made every effort to see that participation in these auxiliaries was encouraged. In 1878 a group of missionaries was called to assist the officers of the Deseret Sunday School Union to promote membership in that organization. The idea of sending out specially called missionaries had been used earlier to boost economic activities and was now applied to social and educational programs. The practice soon spread. In 1880 the Mutual Improvement Associations were divided into seven districts, and MIA missionaries were called to strengthen that program. These missionaries were to help stake leaders perfect the organization, encourage the establishment of libraries and reading rooms, and extend the circulation of the *Contributor,* the official MIA publication. The successful MIA missionary program continued for twenty-five years. The auxiliaries were soon extended to other areas. The first Relief Society and MIA in Denmark were organized at Copenhagen in 1879, and other groups were soon organized in the rest of Scandinavia.

While these organizations were being established to provide for the educational and social needs of the youth, elderly persons were not forgotten. As early as 1876 annual Old Folks excursions were being taken to various Utah canyons and to Black Rock Beach on the shores of the Great Salt Lake. In 1880, for example, the Old Folks of Salt Lake County conducted an excursion to American Fork, Utah, consisting of 600 persons, 405 of whom were more than seventy years of age.

One of the internal administrative problems facing the Twelve was the complicated estate of Brigham Young. Because the anti-bigamy law of 1862 had made it illegal for the Church to own property valued at more than $50,000, Brigham Young had found it necessary to mix many Church accounts with his own. His associates acted similarly. It was clear to those involved that most of Brigham Young's apparent wealth actually consisted of bonds and property he was holding for the Church, but after his death it was difficult to sort out the holdings accurately. It was finally determined that his estate was worth approximately $1,626,000 and that obligations of more than a million dollars to the Church plus other debts and executors' fees reduced the family's claim to $224,000. When seven of his dissatisfied heirs challenged this settlement, the matter was settled out of court in a compromise with the heirs in which the Church agreed to give them an additional $75,000. Because of the unfortunate restrictions of the law, the policy of mixing Church property into private accounts was not discontinued until the early twentieth century, but transfer of title from one administration to another during that period was accomplished with relative ease.

One interesting item included in Brigham Young's estate was the magnificent, though uncompleted, "Gardo House." Designed originally as a private home, it was also envisioned as an official residence for the President of the Church, where visiting dignitaries could be appropriately entertained. With the encouragement of the Twelve, Elder George Q. Cannon had suggested after 1877 that John Taylor make it his residence, and each time President Taylor had declined. In April 1879, Elder Cannon

The imposing Gardo House was built as an official residence for Church presidents. This view of South Temple Street in 1881 also shows Brigham Young's office, between his Lion House and Beehive House, his steepled, family schoolhouse, and a rear view of George A. Smith's residence and the adjacent Historian's Office. (Church Archives)

presented the matter to the general conference, which approved President Taylor's use of the mansion as a Mormon "White House." A man of simple tastes and not given to ostentation, President Taylor only reluctantly accepted the offer. This beautiful home was a fitting symbol of the amazing growth and progress of the Church against tremendous odds in the thirty-two years since its headquarters had moved to the Rocky Mountains. After President Taylor's death the home was rented, and then sold, to others. In 1925 it was razed to make way for a federal reserve bank building.

A more important symbol was the Year of Jubilee, celebrated in 1880. Following the ancient Hebrew custom of celebrating every fiftieth year as a jubilee, the April general conference became a jubilee conference. There President Taylor made some dramatic proposals, again suggested by Hebrew anniversary practices. Many individuals still owed money to the Perpetual Emigration Fund Company, but the indebtedness of the "worthy poor" was struck from the books. This amounted to $802,000, or half the total deficit. "The rich can always take care of themselves," explained President Taylor in the spirit of equity that characterized this pioneer period, "that is, so far as this world is concerned."[1] In addition, half the unpaid tithing was forgiven the poor on the same principle. President Taylor also proposed distributing a thousand head of cattle and five thousand sheep to the poor. Further, the Relief Society had been storing grain for years while a number of Saints had ignored similar advice and were without grain after a drouth in 1879. The Relief Society was asked to loan nearly 35,000 bushels to the less fortunate farmers, to be returned the next year without interest. All this was accepted, and President Taylor raised his voice in a dramatic exclamation: "It is the time of Jubilee!"

In a further expression of the jubilee spirit, members were asked to be generous with one another in their financial obligations. In an official circular President Taylor urged the well-to-do to forgive their debtors as much as they would desire if their circumstances were reversed, "thus doing unto others as you would that others should do unto you. . . . Free the worthy, debt-bound brother if you can. Let there be no rich among us from whose tables fall crumbs to feed a wounded Lazarus. . . . The Church of

---

[1]Roberts, *Life of John Taylor*, p. 334.

Christ has set us a worthy example, let us follow it, so that God may forgive our debts as we forgive our debtors."[2]

In the meantime, President Taylor became especially anxious that the First Presidency be reorganized so that the Church would be fully organized according to the accepted revelations. In October 1880 the Council of the Twelve discussed the matter for two days and came to a unanimous conclusion that it was the will of the Lord that this should happen. At the general conference of that month John Taylor was sustained President, with George Q. Cannon and Joseph F. Smith as his counselors.

Church Publications

Fifty years after its organization, The Church of Jesus Christ of Latter-day Saints was thriving, its purposes expressed in a multitude of activities designed to build the Kingdom. In some ways the publications of that period represented the variety of its concerns. Improvement and literary associations had been established in several wards, and some of these began to publish the works of their members. The *Amateur,* which appeared in Ogden in 1877, was an early effort. Two years later the first edition of the *Contributor* was issued. This periodical, edited by Junius F. Wells, became the official publication of the Mutual Improvement Associations and got its name from its announced purpose of encouraging young people to contribute their works for publication.

That same year the Sunday School began publishing readers for the children, and in 1884 it issued the *Deseret Sunday School Union Music Book.* This replaced the music cards previously used and provided a broader range of music for the fife and drum bands the Sunday Schools had begun to organize to develop youthful talents.

In 1882 Andrew Jenson, one of the most capable Church historians of that era, issued the first number of *Morgenstjernen,* later called the *Historical Record.* He later compiled numerous historical records and chronologies that became invaluable to the study and writing of Church history.

This period also saw renewed interest in publishing modern scriptures. The Book of Mormon was published in Swedish in 1878, although it first was issued from the press as a series of

---

[2] Roberts, *Life of John Taylor,* p. 337.

First Presidency, 1880-1887: President John Taylor, with George Q. Cannon, first counselor (left), and Joseph F. Smith, second counselor (right). (Church Archives)

pamphlets, then as a complete bound volume. In 1879 the first edition of the Doctrine and Covenants was issued with extensive cross-references and explanatory notes. Prepared by Elder Orson Pratt, who had divided the book into chapters and verses three years earlier, this new edition, published in England, was also the first to include 136 sections. This book was re-canonized by a vote at the general conference of 1880. At this same conference the Pearl of Great Price was formally accepted as scripture. Previously it had been used as a missionary tract, and Brigham Young and other leaders had quoted from it, but it had not been officially accepted as scripture. By October 1880 the Church officially had four standard works of scripture: the Bible, the Book of Mormon, the Doctrine and Covenants, and the Pearl of Great Price.

A New Look at Economics

In 1878, during the period of apostolic presidency, Church leaders established a new economic organization, Zion's Central Board of Trade, with John Taylor as president. The United Orders established under Brigham Young were failing, yet his objectives of economic independence for the Saints in Zion remained a vital hope. Mormon leaders sought a plan that would be less rigidly structured than the United Orders but that would promote cooperative economic activity for the benefit of all the Saints. As a result, boards of trade were created in each stake to function under the coordination of the central organization.

Council of the Twelve in the 1880s: Wilford Woodruff, Lorenzo Snow, Erastus Snow, Franklin D. Richards, Brigham Young, Jr., Albert Carrington, Moses Thatcher, Francis M. Lyman, John Henry Smith, George Teasdale, Heber J. Grant, John W. Taylor.

Unlike the cooperatives of the 1860s and the United Orders of the mid-1870s, the Board of Trade was not itself a business. Rather, it was a powerful coordinating agency that held considerable influence because of its direct association with the Church. It was designed to promote business activities that would benefit the entire territory, seek new markets, disseminate information to farmers and manufacturers, prevent competition harmful to home industry, and, when necessary, regulate wages and prices for community benefit. The board promoted a variety of economic activities. Through regulating competition, it actually began to increase private enterprise in the territory and work toward completion of a comprehensive plan of resource development. It seemed to strike a satisfactory balance, at least for a time, between the need to maintain private enterprise and initiative and the need for group economic planning. Unfortunately, it was forced to disband in 1885 as a result of the anti-Mormon raid that reached its peak that year.

Zion's Borders Expand

Even though Brigham Young was gone, his dream of expanding the Kingdom's perimeters was very much alive. During the next decade the settlements in Arizona expanded rapidly. On August 29, 1878, the Salt River Valley in western Wyoming, later called Star Valley, was dedicated by Elders Brigham Young, Jr., and Moses Thatcher of the Council of the Twelve as a new gathering place. In 1879 and 1880 Bunkerville and Mesquite, Nevada, were settled. The Saints were also expanding into Castle Valley in eastern Utah, as well as into the rugged San Juan River country of southeastern Utah. Beginning in 1878, they located settlements in south-central Colorado, populated by converts from the southern states and Saints from southern Utah. Between 1876 and 1879 at least one hundred new settlements were founded outside Utah and more than twenty within the territory.

All these colonies were part of the regular efforts of the Latter-day Saints to expand the borders of the Kingdom. In the mid-1880s they were expanded even further as a result of the mounting antipolygamy prosecution. The pressure had become so intense by 1884 that President John Taylor instructed Christopher Layton, president of the St. Joseph Stake in Arizona, to lead his people into Mexico, if necessary, to defend themselves against attacks of their persecutors. Once again the Saints sought a place of refuge, and this time it would be under the Mexican government. "Better for parts of families to remove and go where they can live in peace," he wrote, "than to be hauled to jail and either incarcerated in the territory with thieves and murderers and other vile characters, or sent to the American Siberia in Detroit to serve out a long term of imprisonment."[3]

President Taylor himself, along with several other Church officials, visited Mexico in 1885, and by the end of the year hundreds of colonists, mostly from Arizona and New Mexico, were pouring into the Mexican state of Chihuahua. Difficulties arose when the colonists were unable to purchase lands and the acting governor of Chihuahua ordered them expelled from the province. Apparently he was influenced by certain officials who believed the Mormons were part of a Yankee effort of conquest, and by anti-Mormon propaganda from the United States.

The beleaguered colonists met their new challenge with faith and action. Sunday, April 12, 1885, was set aside as a day of fasting and prayer, and the colonists were told by their leaders to plow and plant on their rented lands anyway. In the meantime, Elders Moses Thatcher and Brigham Young, Jr., of the Council of the Twelve made a hurried trip to Mexico City, where they met with President Porfirio Diaz and other officials. Surprised at the action of the acting governor, Diaz revoked the expulsion order and the Saints were allowed to remain in Mexico.

Settlement was not easy. The committees negotiating for land purchases seemed blocked at every turn, and the colonists continued to live in wagon boxes, tents, and caves. Early in 1886 the negotiations were successful, and on March 21 the happy colonists held a grand celebration and named their new settlement Colonia Juarez, in honor of a Mexican folk hero whose birthday was on that day. Late that spring their hopes were dashed again when they received word that an error had been made in describing the boundaries of their purchase, and their legal location was about two miles to the north. They were allowed to harvest their crops but were forced to move to the valley of the Piedras Verdes River, which was narrow and rocky, with poor soil and scarce

---

[3]As quoted in Thomas Cottam Romney, *The Mormon Colonies in Mexico* (Salt Lake City: Deseret Book Co., 1938), p. 52.

water. Chances for success seemed bleak. In the spring of 1887, the water level of the Piedras Verdes fell even lower. Then on May 7 an earthquake hit the region. Remembering the 1848 cricket plague in Utah, the Saints in the Piedras Verdes valley watched with despair as rocks tumbled from the mountains and forest fires burned for days. It soon became evident, however, that the earthquake had opened fissures that increased the river's water by a third. The Mexican colony was saved. As the colonists put it, "The Lord was in the earthquake."

In less than a decade more than three thousand Saints settled in Mexico. Three main settlements were established—Colonia Juarez, Colonia Dublan, and Colonia Diaz—and until 1895 George Teasdale, a member of the Council of the Twelve, presided over them. In that year a stake was organized, marking the success of the new place of refuge. Throughout this period the Latter-day Saint colonies in Mexico existed as an isolated center of American culture in a Mexican environment.

Even as some pushed south seeking refuge in Mexico, Charles Ora Card, president of Cache Stake in Logan, Utah, was instructed by John Taylor to seek out a place of "asylum and justice" in Canada. In September 1886 a small group of explorers

Townsite of Colonia Juarez, Mexico, looking northwest. (Church Archives)

went into Canada and identified the vicinity of Cardston, Alberta, as the northern gathering place. The following spring a number of settlers from Cache County arrived, and soon settlements spread. By 1895 the body of Saints in Canada was large enough to warrant a stake in Alberta, the first to be organized outside the United States. Both Canada and Mexico were important centers of gathering for the harassed Saints who chose to leave the United States rather than face prosecution and disruption of their families.

Missionary Work in a Time of Stress

Even as the Church devoted attention to expanding its colonies, it continued to augment its missionary activities—sometimes with impressive success and at other times in the face of serious obstacles.

In Latin America, the first proselyting efforts since Parley P. Pratt's failure in 1852 began in 1876. Meliton G. Trejo, a former Spanish army officer who had joined the Church in Salt Lake City, was one of a group of missionaries who went into northern Mexico that year. He and a fellow missionary, Daniel W. Jones, had translated portions of the Book of Mormon into Spanish. The group soon felt discouraged, although in 1877 other missionaries did make a few converts. A copy of the Book of Mormon left by the 1876 missionaries fell into the hands of Plotino C. Rhodacanaty, a Greek resident of Mexico City, who wrote President John Taylor asking for more information. Moses Thatcher of the Council of the Twelve and Elders Trejo and James Z. Stewart were quickly sent to Mexico City. There a small group already studying LDS literature became the basis for a mission. In April 1881 Elder Thatcher dedicated Mexico for the preaching of the gospel, and Elders Trejo and Stewart finished their translation of the Book of Mormon. Only a few missionaries were called to Mexico, but between 1879 and 1889, when the mission was closed, 242 converts were baptized. After that most of the branches collapsed and Juarez Stake remained the sole Latter-day Saint outpost in Mexico.

In New Zealand a branch was organized among the Maori people in 1883, and a native chief, Manihera, was ordained a priest and made president of the branch. At the same time, the number of missionaries in Europe continued to increase. In December 1884, Jacob Spori opened the Turkish Mission, which included the land of Palestine. Later Elder Spori and his companion, Joseph M. Tanner, preached to a small colony of Germans at Haifa, and on August 29, 1886, George Grau became the first person baptized in Palestine.

Because missionary activity was resulting in much immigration from Europe, the Mormon question created a minor international episode in the mid-1880s. As early as the 1850s Mormon immigration attracted the attention of those who opposed the Saints, and efforts were made to discourage foreign converts from flocking to Utah. In 1858 President James Buchanan even commented to Lord Clarendon, British secretary of foreign affairs, "I would thank you to keep your Mormons at home."[4] In 1879 both President Rutherford B. Hayes and Secretary of State William M. Evarts were convinced that they must try to halt Latter-day Saint immigration. On October 9 Evarts issued a proclamation to the American ambassadors in England, Germany, Norway, Sweden, and Denmark asking them to seek the aid of these governments in stopping any further Mormon departures to the United States. This was justified on the grounds that they were "potential violators" of the laws against polygamy.

The reaction in Europe was mixed. By this time considerable anti-Mormon sentiment colored public opinion, and distorted accounts of the Church in the American West were becoming widespread. Such things, however, could hardly justify a barrier against emigration, even though the Scandinavian countries promised to discourage it if they could. In England Secretary Evarts was ridiculed by the press. The *London Times,* for example, denounced the very idea of curtailing the emigration of those "who have contravened no law," and the *London Examiner* took him severely to task. Through it all the gathering to Utah continued uninterrupted, almost as if the debate had never happened.

Perhaps the most brutal treatment received by Mormon missionaries in this era occurred in the American South, which was still suffering the indignities of political reconstruction and seemed unwilling to tolerate any preventable outside influence. In this bitterly charged atmosphere Mormon missionaries were mistrusted not just because of the distorted image spread everywhere about them, but because to southern whites they represented an

---

[4]William Mulder, "Immigration and the 'Mormon Question': An International Episode," *Western Political Quarterly* 9 (June 1956): 416.

external intrusion. Also, after the Southern States Mission was organized in 1875, many converts emigrated from Tennessee, Arkansas, Georgia, Alabama, Mississippi, and Virginia, mostly to Colorado and Arizona, and these successes angered many local citizens. Irate mobs, encouraged by southern ministers and congregations, drove the missionaries from their communities, and many elders were tied to trees, severely beaten, and threatened with death if they returned.

On July 21, 1879, Joseph Standing, the presiding elder in the vicinity of Varnell's Station, Georgia, was shot to death by a mob. Surprisingly, his companion, Rudger Clawson, was allowed to leave the scene to secure help in removing the body. A coroner examined the body and gave a verdict of murder. Georgia state officials arrested three suspects, and these men were acquitted by the local jury despite the positive indentification and eye-witness testimony given by Elder Clawson.

The Standing murder proved to be only a precedent as persecution mounted. The most flagrant act was the 1884 massacre at Cane Creek in Tennessee. In that incident a mob interrupted religious services at the home of James Condor and demanded the surrender of the elders. Shooting ensued, and two missionaries, two investigators, and the leader of the mob were killed and a woman was crippled for life. The mission president had gone to Salt Lake City and had left the mission in charge of B. H. Roberts, soon to become a member of the First Council of the Seventy. Risking his own life, Elder Roberts went to Cane Creek in disguise, secured the bodies of the murdered elders, and sent them to Utah.

The Continuing Crusade

To many Saints, the 1879 Supreme Court decision in the Reynolds case was not only a shattering blow to their confidence in the ultimate protection of the law, but was also evidence that the forces of evil were infecting the highest offices in the land. To President John Taylor, his plural family was based on mutual love and respect as well as religious obligation. How, then, could he abandon wives who had already endured many hardships for the sake of religious principle, and what could he say to his children who would thus seem disowned? The seventy-year-old President had fought too long for the principle to immediately give it up, despite court decisions. His inward struggle must have been trau-

Elder B. H. Roberts in disguise. In 1884 he found it necessary to dress this way in order to enter the region of Cane Creek in Tennessee to obtain the bodies of two murdered missionaries. (Church Archives)

matic as he considered his courses of action, but the principle remained the law of God until revoked by Him. President Taylor could not advise the Saints to abandon it—he could only advise them to hide from the law, face prosecution, or flee to new gathering places outside the United States. His attitude was boldly expressed to a federal official in Utah shortly after the Reynolds decision. The United States Constitution forbade interference with religious affairs, he declared, and to the Saints marital relations were religious. "I do not believe that the Supreme Court of the United States . . . has any right to interfere with my religious views, and in doing it they are violating their most sacred obligations." Then, in a typical Mormon response to the common accusations of immorality among the Saints, he added,

> We acknowledge our children, we acknowledge our wives; we have no mistresses. We had no prostitution until it was introduced by monogamy, and I am told that these other diabolical deeds are following in its train. The courts have protected these people in their wicked practices. We repudiate all such things, and hence I consider that a system that will enable a man to carry out his professions, and that will enable him to acknowledge his wife or wives and acknowledge and provide for his children and wives, is much more honorable than that principle which violates its marital relations, and, whilst hypocritically professing to be true to its pledges, recklessly violates the same and tramples upon every principle of honor.[5]

These considerations counted little with any but the Saints. Instead, the crusade against them intensified. In September 1878 the *Boston Watchman*, a Baptist newspaper, proposed steps for a new anti-Mormon campaign, and these foreshadowed events of the next decade: Utah was to be prevented from becoming a state until polygamy was abandoned; Congress was to repeal women's suffrage in Utah; all those involved in plural marriage, including husbands, wives, and children, were to be disfranchised; and the public schools were to be "rescued" from Mormon control.

The following month two hundred non-Mormon women met in Salt Lake City and drafted an appeal to "the Christian Women of the United States," asking them to join in urging Congress to take stronger action against the Saints. Even Mrs. Rutherford B. Hayes, wife of the president of the United States, was enlisted in the crusade. A week later two thousand Latter-day Saint women held a counter-demonstration in the Salt Lake Theatre and passed a resolution endorsing plural marriage as a religious practice. It was soon made known to the public that Mormon wives and daughters fully supported their religion.

The attacks on polygamy came from every direction. Women and women's groups were often in the forefront; prominent re-

---

[5]*The Supreme Court Decision in the Reynolds Case: Interview between President John Taylor and O.J. Hollister*, reported by G.F. Gibbs (Salt Lake City: n.p., 1879), pp. 4, 7.

ligious groups throughout the country also joined the crusade, though none of them attacked with more bitterness than certain Protestant churchmen in Utah. Perhaps the most revealing evidence of the saturation of the American mind with anti-Mormon sentiment was the fact that every president of the United States in this era made the crusade a point of public discussion. The attitude of President Grant has already been described (see chapter 11). His successor, Rutherford B. Hayes, recognized that Utah had sufficient population for statehood, but he declared it would not happen "while the citizens of Utah in very considerable number uphold a practice which is condemned as a crime by the laws of all civilized communities." In 1880 he recommended to Congress that "the right to vote, hold office, and sit on juries in the Territory of Utah be confined to those who neither practice nor uphold polygamy." In his inaugural address of 1881 James A. Garfield said that by sanctioning polygamy the Church "offends the moral sense of manhood"; and the following December his successor, Chester A. Arthur, pledged to cooperate with Congress in any lawful measure designed to suppress the Mormon practice. In 1883, after twelve thousand Saints had been denied the vote in Utah, he was convinced that even more powerful weapons were needed in the battle, and he recommended elimination of the government of the Territory of Utah and "the assumption by the National Legislature of the entire political control of the Territory." Even Grover Cleveland, whose general attitude was lenient and conciliatory, discussed the Mormon issue at length in his first annual message to Congress in 1885 and recommended passage of a law that would prohibit immigration of Mormon converts into the United States.

It is clear that motives behind the crusade were mixed. Some people were simply seeking political advantage, while others were outraged at a system they did not understand and took little time to investigate. Some were seeking public attention or the money that follows the publication of popular books and articles. Still others were well-meaning reformers whose only objective was to require the Saints, as American citizens, to conform to the marriage practice they considered the foundation of Christian society. The clash between people who were otherwise men of good will displays one tragedy of the conflict. Another was in the lives of those families who suffered as a result of the raids of the 1880s.

The Edmunds Law

The mounting pressures finally resulted in congressional approval of the Edmunds Act of 1882. The new law provided punishment for both polygamy and unlawful cohabitation. Anyone who had a husband or wife living and then married another was guilty of polygamy and could be sentenced to a $500 fine and five years in prison. A person could be tried for both offenses at the same time. In addition, the law made it impossible for anyone practicing polygamy to perform jury service. It declared vacant all offices in the Territory of Utah connected with registration and election duties, and established a board of five commissioners, to be appointed by the president, to assume these functions. The law also disfranchised and barred from public office anyone guilty of polygamy or unlawful cohabitation. Finally, the Edmunds Act provided that children born of polygamist parents before January 1, 1883, were legitimate, and the president of the United States was authorized to grant amnesty to those who had entered into plural marriage, provided they complied with whatever conditions he should set. The long-awaited "teeth" for the old anti-bigamy act had been provided.

Federal commission appointed under the Edmunds Act of 1882 to supervise election procedures in Utah. These men attempted to be fair but firm in their execution of the law. (Church Archives)

The new law was put into effect almost immediately. The Utah Commission was appointed on June 16 and consisted of men who proved to be generally honest and fair, but who were determined to uphold the law. Their main function was to supervise all election procedures. The commission interpreted the law to mean that anyone who had ever practiced plural marriage could be excluded from voting. This meant that even a person who had lived in plural marriage before the 1862 law was passed but who for any reason was not then living it could be disfranchised. New registration and voting officials were appointed throughout the territory, and anyone wishing to vote was required to take a test oath affirming he was not in violation of the law. As a result, more than twelve thousand Saints in Utah were disfranchised in the first year of the commission's existence. In 1885, much to the relief of the Latter-day Saints, the U.S. Supreme Court declared the Utah test oath unconstitutional.

First to be prosecuted under the new law was Rudger Clawson. His case was also the first to be brought before Charles S. Zane, the newly appointed federal judge in Utah and the major judicial force in the final battle against plural marriage. In the Clawson trial of 1884 the nature of the two opposing forces was clearly revealed. Unlike many earlier federal officials, Judge Zane was recognized as a man whose personal integrity was above reproach. Numerous cases outside the realm of polygamy demonstrated his commitment to fair play and justice before the law. Now that the Edmunds law was in effect, however, he was adamant about its enforcement. He demonstrated great leniency toward those willing to comply with the law and agree to abandon plural marriage, but he felt the need for severity for those who refused to conform.

The twenty-seven-year-old Rudger Clawson, on the other hand, was equally determined to obey the law of God. Only the force of revelation would compel him to stop living the principle of plural marriage, and that revelation had not yet come. At his trial, he was convicted of both polygamy and unlawful cohabitation, but when Judge Zane allowed him to make a statement before being sentenced he only replied, "Your honor, I very much regret that the laws of my country should come in conflict with the laws of God; but whenever they do, I shall invariably choose the latter. If I did not so express myself, I should feel unworthy of the case I represent." Clawson's sincerity was self-evident, as was his bold-ness, but he was sentenced to pay an $800 fine and serve four years in prison. After three years, he was pardoned by President Grover Cleveland.

Thus the judicial crusade began, and it almost created a new way of life for many of the Saints. Otherwise law-abiding men sud-denly found themselves escaping to the underground—that is, go-ing into hiding, and frequently moving from place to place to escape the marshals who were hunting them. Hideouts were pre-pared in homes, barns, and fields to serve as way stations for the fleeing "cohabs," as they were nicknamed by their pursuers. Secret codes were invented that could be sent between towns to warn of approaching deputies, and Mormon spotters became proficient at detecting the hunters and spreading the alarm. Not to be outdone, the scores of federal officers brought into the territory to conduct this all-out raid disguised themselves as peddlers or census takers in order to gain entry into homes and hired their own spotters to question children, gossip with neighbors, and even invade the pri-vacy of homes. Ten- and twenty-dollar bounties were offered for every Latter-day Saint violator captured.

Even at its mildest the raid caused much distress. With hus-bands away, wives and children tended the farms, and often they, too, were forced to flee. Women were sometimes required to testify against their husbands, and some were sent to prison for refusing. Babies were born on the underground and wives and mothers suffered long periods of deprivation and fear. In all, between 1884 and 1893 more than a thousand judgments were secured for un-lawful cohabitation and thirty-one for polygamy. At least one man, Edward M. Dalton, was killed by a pursuing deputy in 1886, adding to the bitterness of the Saints against the federal marshals' relentlessness.

In the meantime, the Supreme Court slowly clarified the legal technicalities of prosecution for polygamy, as many cases originating in Utah reached it for review. The Reynolds case of 1879 upheld the constitutionality of the anti-bigamy law of 1862, though the court thought the sentence imposed was too severe, and remanded it to the lower court with instructions to lighten the penalty. In 1885 the test oath was declared unconstitutional, but in the same decision the court struck down the Latter-day Saint argu-ment that the Edmunds law was an ex post facto law and therefore unconstitutional. The Saints claimed they could not be prosecuted for marriages entered into prior to the passage of the law, but the court ruled that illegal cohabitation was a continuing violation, so that if it continued after the law was passed, a person could be prosecuted. Later the same year Angus M. Cannon was found guilty of cohabitation even though he had divided his large home into separate apartments after the Edmunds law was passed and had stopped living with his second wife in a marriage relationship. The court upheld the guilty verdict in a far-reaching decision that defined cohabiting as providing food and shelter on a regular basis for more than one woman. Such a decision made it tragically difficult even for Saints who tried to live the law but felt obligated to continue to care for their plural wives. In 1886, however, the court demonstrated more humane reason by overturning a particularly harsh decision of Judge Zane. The judge had developed a so-called segregation rule in which he assumed that the time a man lived in polygamy could be divided into years, months, or even weeks, and that each period of time thus constituted a separate offense, and the man could be tried for each offense. Another judge went even further and determined that offenses could be counted by days. When the case of Lorenzo Snow reached the Supreme Court in 1886, the court ruled cohabitation was "a continuous offense," and dividing it into segments for the sake of separate convictions was arbitrary and wrong. This was small satisfaction for the Saints, who felt they should not be tried at all.

Beyond the problems of legal prosecution, the crusade of the 1880s had important political ramifications. In 1880 George Q. Cannon was overwhelmingly reelected to a fifth term as Utah's delegate to Congress. Governor Eli H. Murray, however, verified that the Liberal party candidate, Allen G. Campbell, had been duly elected. His reasoning was that as a Mormon, George Q. Cannon was ineligible for citizenship. Even the anti-Mormon press denounced such blatant misuse of power, and Elder Cannon contested the matter in Washington and was eventually seated. In 1882, after the passage of the Edmunds Act, the case was heard again in the House of Representatives, and this time Elder Cannon lost. The House, however, did not vote to seat Campbell, and the seat remained vacant until the next election.

The unpopular Governor Eli Murray was finally recalled by President Grover Cleveland and replaced by Caleb B. West in

1886. One of the new governor's first acts was to visit Church leaders in the penitentiary and offer them amnesty if they would obey the federal law, that is, abandon their plural wives. They did not accept his offer, but his attitude developed better rapport than the leaders had experienced with many governors.

Prosecution was not limited to the Territory of Utah. The legislature of the Territory of Idaho also established a test oath that disfranchised the Saints, and an equally intense crusade was conducted by the federal marshals and judges there. In Arizona, too, the same thing happened, and when the prisons in these places became too crowded, the convicted "cohabs" were escorted to the federal penitentiary in Detroit, some two thousand miles away. This led to President Taylor's 1885 visit to the Saints in Arizona and his decision to advise them to flee to another country. After also visiting Mexico, President Taylor detoured to San Francisco on his way home. There he received word it would be unsafe for him to return to Salt Lake City, for the federal authorities had decided that he, too, should be arrested. But the aging Church President made up his mind his place was in Utah, and he arrived back in Salt Lake City on January 27, 1885. On February 1 he preached his last public sermon. Clearly indignant at what he considered judicial outrage, he criticized all that was taking place and explained his own refusal to willingly submit to arrest. He would submit to the law, he said, "if the law would only be a little more dignified," but until then he had no intention of being arrested. That night this prophet who had been with Joseph Smith at the time of his assassination disappeared from public view and, like so many of his followers, went into hiding on the underground.

The crusade disrupted many normal church activities, including the custom of holding general conference in Salt Lake City. Between 1884 and 1887 Church leaders considered it prudent to hold these meetings in Logan, Provo, and Coalville in order, if possible, to relieve those who attended from pressures of possible arrest. Federal officers, nevertheless, continued to show up at conference sites in the hope of apprehending fugitives, though they usually left empty handed. The conferences were sparsely attended by Church officials, for most were in hiding. Apostle Franklin D. Richards, immune from arrest, presided over some of them. Guidance to the conferences came in the form of general epistles, signed by President Taylor and his first counselor, George Q. Can-

JOHN TAYLOR.   **GEORGE Q. CANNON.**

To be Paid for the Arrest of John Taylor and George Q. Cannon.

The above Reward will be paid for the delivery to me, or for information that will lead to the arrest of

JOHN TAYLOR,

President of the Mormon Church, and

George Q. Cannon,

His Counselor; or

$500 will be paid for Cannon alone, and $300 for Taylor.

All Conferences or Letters kept strictly secret.

S. H. GILSON,

22 and 23 Wasatch Building, Salt Lake City.

Salt Lake City, Jan. 31, 1887.

Reward poster appeared in the late 1880s when President Taylor and many other General Authorities of the Church had gone underground in order to escape prosecution under the Edmunds-Tucker Act. (Church Archives)

non. Joseph F. Smith, the second counselor, was in Hawaii as a missionary. To the Saints, continuing to hold conferences even without their leaders bolstered their faith and eloquently testified of their continued opposition to any surrender to the government.

Meanwhile President Taylor moved from place to place and continued to direct the Church by writing letters. Hundreds of other Saints were also being pursued and hounded as the raids continued. As 1886 ended, nearly every settlement in Utah had been raided by federal marshals, hundreds of Saints had sought refuge in Mexico or Canada, and nearly all the leaders were in hiding. The situation was critical, and in the following year it would become even worse.

CHAPTER 13

The End of an Era, 1887-1896

In general conference on the morning of October 6, 1890, the Church approved an official declaration, usually called the Manifesto, which announced that plural marriage had been discontinued. In an atmosphere charged with both disappointment and faith, George Q. Cannon, first counselor to President Wilford Woodruff, explained why the long-resisted move had finally been made. His sermon was based on portions of a revelation given to Joseph Smith in 1841, after the Saints had failed to build the city and temple they had been commanded to erect in Jackson County:

> Verily, verily, I say unto you, that when I give a commandment to any of the sons of men to do a work unto my name, and those sons of men go with all their might and with all they have to perform that work, and cease not their diligence, and their enemies come upon them and hinder them from performing that work, behold, it behooveth me to require that work no more at the hands of those sons of men, but to accept of their offerings.[1]

The application to the principle of plural marriage was obvious. "It is on this basis," said President Cannon, "that President

---

[1]D&C 124:49.

Woodruff has felt himself justified in issuing this Manifesto."[2]

The Saints had fought to carry out the Lord's commandments, but as they entered the 1890s circumstances were changing. The Manifesto was only one of many events symbolizing the end of an important era and foreshadowing the adjustment of the Church to new challenges in the political and economic milieu of the twentieth century.

Another Change in Leadership.

Beginning in early 1885, President John Taylor remained on the underground for nearly two and a half years, separated from family and friends except for a few companions who shared his voluntary exile. His official residence, the "Gardo House," was continually watched and raided by United States officers bent upon his capture, but he was constantly on the move, accepting the hospitality proffered by trusted friends who felt honored at having the prophet beneath their roofs. So well kept was the secret of his whereabouts that squads of deputy marshals more than once approached the very house where he was staying, never suspecting how near they were to their objective. President Taylor's health began to fail in mid-1886, and on July 25, 1887, he died at his hiding place in Kaysville.

The death of President Taylor dissolved the First Presidency for the third time in the history of the Church, and again there was disagreement as to whether it should be reorganized immediately. As a result, the Twelve presided over the Church for another two years, with Wilford Woodruff as their President and therefore head of the Church.

Wilford Woodruff's first public appearance after the death of President Taylor was heartwarming. Accompanied by Elders Lorenzo Snow and Franklin D. Richards, he entered the Salt Lake Tabernacle just before a general conference meeting on the afternoon of Sunday, October 9, 1887. The white-haired leader was immediately greeted with warm applause, which did not subside until he arose from his seat and waved to the multitude. No attempt was made to arrest him, but since it was unwise to remain "off the underground" for long, he went into retirement again after the meeting.

---

[2]Full discourse is in *Deseret Weekly*, October 18, 1890.

First Presidency under Wilford Woodruff. President Woodruff retained the men who had been John Taylor's counselors, and this group led the Church during the early years of transition after the "Manifesto." (Church Archives)

At the general conference of April 1889, the First Presidency was reorganized. President Woodruff retained George Q. Cannon and Joseph F. Smith as counselors. He was concerned, however, that at some future time failure to organize the First Presidency could cause serious problems. After considerable thought and prayer he instructed Lorenzo Snow, President of the Twelve, and other leaders that it was the will of the Lord that in case of the death of a President, a new First Presidency should be organized without delay. This was the last time the Council of the Twelve would be left to preside for any extended period.

Edmunds-Tucker Law and National Politics, 1887-89

At the national level in 1887, it was clear to political leaders that the Latter-day Saints had no intention of changing their policies, despite intensified prosecution under the Edmunds law. They prepared a measure, therefore, that seemed designed to destroy the Church itself, eliminating both polygamy and the influence of the Church on Utah's political life. This legislation was the Edmunds-Tucker Act of 1887.

Throughout this period the Church maintained several influential lobbyists in the nation's capital to plead its cause. In 1887 LDS agents in Washington, D.C., included John T. Caine, Utah's delegate to Congress; John W. Young, a railroad promoter; Franklin S. Richards, the Church attorney; and George Ticknor Curtis, a non-Mormon attorney associated with Franklin Richards. These men were fully aware of the implications of the Edmunds-Tucker Bill and did all they could to block it. Their most novel plan was to persuade Congressman William L. Scott of Pennsylvania to sponsor an amendment that would give Utah time to draw up another constitution and apply for statehood before the law went into effect. The new constitution would outlaw polygamy in the new state. Mormon agents felt the only way to escape the perils of the forthcoming legislation was to persuade the public that plural marriage could be eliminated without it.

The Scott amendment failed to pass, and the Edmunds-Tucker Act went to President Grover Cleveland for approval. The president disliked its harsh provisions and was reluctant to sign it, especially if there was any chance the people of Utah would accept the spirit of the Scott amendment and present a petition for

statehood based on an anti-polygamy constitution. But he was
caught in a dilemma: if he signed the bill, he jeopardized his future negotiations with the Church; if he vetoed it, he would be in
trouble with both political parties, clearly endangering his own
political future. He finally allowed the bill to become law without
his signature.

In Utah, meanwhile, Church leaders debated the merits of
the Scott amendment. At first President John Taylor was adamant
in his refusal to consider it seriously. It would give the appearance,
he felt, that the Saints intended to surrender plural marriage, and
this he could not endorse unless God revoked the principle. He also
believed that the move was politically unwise, for congressmen
would be skeptical of a Mormon-supported anti-polygamy constitution and would reject it anyway.

The discussion continued and other leaders suggested that
there was a way to adopt such a constitution without denying their
religious principles. The constitution would outlaw polygamy in
Utah, but it would be up to Utah itself to define the term, and this
might be done in such a way that celestial marriage, at least, was
not part of the definition. Furthermore, even if the more limited
definition were not adopted, Utah courts would obviously be more
lenient in their prosecution of polygamy than the federal courts,
which were so tenaciously harassing the Saints. Home rule was the
objective of statehood, and it seemed as if an anti-polygamy constitution was the only way to get it. Such a constitution would not
force the Church to denounce the doctrine or abandon its practice
outside the state.

When Church leaders in Utah received word that the
Edmunds-Tucker Bill had passed, President Taylor took a second
look at the alternative proposal and decided to accept it if it would
mean a complete settlement of the issue as far as the government
was concerned. It would be clearly understood that the Church
was not abandoning its teaching, even though it would allow its
members to vote for a constitution outlawing polygamy. At the
end of June a constitutional convention in Utah drew up such a
document, and it was almost unanimously approved by the elec-
torate in August. It was presented to Congress that fall, but after
nearly two years it failed to pass. As President Taylor had
suspected earlier, national politicians would not accept a halfway
measure in their effort to curb polygamy. It was not surprising that

Utah's sixth attempt at achieving statehood had failed.

Partly in an effort to support the proposed constitution of 1887, Church leaders deemed it prudent to remain silent on the issue of plural marriage. Beginning in 1887, they rarely if ever discussed the principle in public discourse. They even counseled Church publications to refrain from the inclusion of discussions of plural marriage at that particularly crucial time, and the Endowment House on Temple Square was torn down in 1889. The battle for statehood was lost, however, and the cruel consequences of the Edmunds-Tucker Act were being felt. It would be only a short time before President Woodruff, as a result of his quest for divine guidance, would make the agonizing decision necessary to save the Church from virtual destruction.

What the Law Provided

The Edmunds-Tucker Act was aimed at plugging the loopholes its sponsors saw in the Edmunds law of 1882; beyond that, it also included provisions designed to destroy the Church as a political and economic entity. Its sponsors reasoned that only in this way could they eventually force the Church to abandon the principle of plural marriage rather than face temporal destruction and thus lose its power. Accordingly, the law officially dissolved The Church of Jesus Christ of Latter-day Saints as a legal corporation and directed the attorney general to institute proceedings to accomplish this end. It also required the Church to forfeit to the United States all property in excess of $50,000. The chief agency for immigration, the Perpetual Emigrating Fund Company, was dissolved and its property escheated, and the Nauvoo Legion or territorial militia was disbanded.

To assist directly in the prosecution of polygamy, the law required compulsory attendance of witnesses at trials and stipulated the legality of testimony from a legal wife against her husband. County probate judges in Utah were henceforth to be appointed by the president of the United States, for these local officers helped empanel juries.

Other provisions struck at political rights and Mormon influence in the public schools. Women's suffrage was abolished in Utah and a new test oath incorporated into election procedures. No one could vote, serve on a jury, or hold public office unless he signed an oath pledging obedience and support of anti-polygamy laws. Congress further ordered that territorial voting districts be redefined so that voting results could be more effectively controlled. The office of territorial superintendent of schools was eliminated, and schools were placed under the control of the federally appointed territorial supreme court and a court-appointed commissioner. In addition, the act required that all marriages be certified in the probate courts. Children born of plural marriages more than one year after the act was passed were disinherited.

In Hiding and in Prison for Conscience' Sake

Meanwhile, harassment by federal officials bent on arresting and imprisoning Mormon leaders continued. President Wilford Woodruff was one of those on the underground, and often used St. George as his headquarters. Not far from the town was the tiny, out-of-the-way settlement of Atkinville, inhabited mainly by members of the William Atkin family. This loyal family willingly accepted the apostle in their home when he fled to avoid arrest in St. George. If any strangers approached Atkinville, word would come rapidly through various lookouts and he would immediately depart for a nearby wilderness area where thick undergrowth would protect him. As long as President Woodruff remained in Atkinville young Will Thompson traveled to St. George, carrying messages back and forth. The eighty-year-old President remained busy writing letters and conferring with trusted members.

One of the most important arrests of the period was that of George Q. Cannon. As first counselor to President John Taylor, President Cannon went into hiding with the President in February 1885, and for an entire year federal marshals searched for them. In February 1886 a poster appeared offering a $300 reward for information leading to the arrest of President Taylor and $500 for President Cannon. Immediately the tempo of the hunt stepped up. On February 13 President Cannon was arrested in Nevada and returned to Utah for trial. On February 17, at a hearing conducted in Salt Lake City, he was required to post $45,000 bail in order to go free until the trial. When the case was called up for trial on March 17, he had again retired to the underground and the bail was forfeited. The search continued with another reward offered for his arrest. On September 17, 1888, when it appeared likely that a newly appointed judge would pronounce a more lenient

Prisoners for conscience' sake. When George Q. Cannon and other Saints were serving time in the territorial penitentiary for their refusal to abandon their religious principles, they sometimes had their pictures taken for posterity, showing them in prison garb. Elder Cannon is seated in the center of the photograph. (Church Archives)

sentence, he gave himself up. He was sentenced to 175 days in prison and a $450 fine. His entering prison, he said, had at least one good effect, for "it proves that the leading men are willing to suffer but not to concede." He was discharged from the Utah penitentiary on February 21, 1889.

As the most distinguished guest of the Utah penitentiary, President Cannon was able to transact a great deal of church and personal business, for his visitors were allowed to come and go freely. Among other things he supervised the Sunday Schools and finished writing a book on the life of Joseph Smith. In addition, the mere presence of a member of the First Presidency seemed to lift the spirits of other Latter-day Saint prisoners.

The "cohabs," as the Mormon prisoners were called, enjoyed an unusual fraternity. They held regular religious services, often with outside speakers and musical numbers, including on one occasion the Tabernacle Choir. Many kept prison journals and autograph books in which they recorded original prose and poetry reflecting their feelings. Poor verse as it may have been, it aptly represented the deep religious convictions of a proud people. One such verse, written in 1888, ran:

> Though confined in this prison, you are for a while
> Keep cheerful and greet all your friends with a smile,
> The time will soon come when we all will be free,
> And the judgments of God on the wicked we'll see.
> We will pity them then and remember how they
> Sought to take both our rights and our families away.[3]

The Utah Commission reported with some dismay in 1890 that the prisoners were regarded as martyrs and that in some instances when they were released they were met at the prison gates by brass bands, escorted to their homes in a parade, and "toasted, extolled, and feasted as though it were the conclusion of some brilliant and honorable achievement."[4]

Enforcement of Edmunds-Tucker Act

These arrests and imprisonments were no real threat to the Church, for they could be endured by the Saints without disrupting its ability to operate as a legal institution in its day-to-day business. Temple building, missionary work, welfare activities, publishing, and general administrative affairs could continue, though somewhat curtailed. What did hurt was the Church's inability to acquire and hold the funds necessary to do these things, and the destruction of the political rights of many of its members, which meant they would have no influence on public policy in the territories in which they resided.

Despite the law of 1862 that limited Church property holdings to $50,000, by 1887 the institution had acquired real and personal property worth possibly $3 million. There had simply been no way to enforce the restriction, which was generally thought to be unconstitutional. The Edmunds-Tucker Act changed this, for it called specifically for escheatment of Church property and the appointment of a receiver.

The Church would not part with its property lightly. Before the act was passed, the trustee-in-trust (President Taylor) and other General Authorities began a plan of action that they hoped

---

[3]Quoted in Gustive O. Larson, *The "Americanization" of Utah for Statehood* (San Marino: The Huntington Library, 1971), p. 199.

[4]Larson, *"Americanization" of Utah,* p. 186.

would keep Church property from government control if the proposed measure became law. As Brigham Young had done earlier, they asked several prominent individuals to take over certain properties in their private accounts, holding them in trust for the Church. Since legally these properties would appear to be private property, there would be no need to forfeit them. Included in the transfer was the Church Historian's Office, which was the actual headquarters of the Church at the time—the place where most Church business was transacted. Separate nonprofit associations were also organized to hold property, such as the three Utah temples. Stake ecclesiastical associations received local meeting-houses, tithing houses, and stock in community herds of livestock.

The most important of all these financial transactions concerned tithing property, which was consigned to the ecclesiastical associations of the stakes before the new law became effective. Included were cattle, horses, sheep, grain, furniture, building materials, dairy products, and other items valued at approximately $270,000. Much of this property was used by the stakes to help establish academies.

Frank H. Dyer, the U.S. marshal in Utah and an active opponent of the Church, was appointed federal receiver for the property of the Church and for the Perpetual Emigration Fund. Immediately he confiscated all property that had not been sold or turned over to private individuals or other associations, then rented back to the Church certain properties, such as the Temple Block in Salt Lake City. He next attempted to obtain the property already deeded to other people, arguing that this was actually Church property and therefore ought to be escheated. By the middle of 1888 more than $800,000 worth of property had been taken by the receiver, including a promisory note of $475,000 in cattle or cash to compensate for the tithing property turned over to the stake ecclesiastical associations.

Church leaders hoped to get their case before the United States Supreme Court, for they believed that the confiscation of property under the Edmunds-Tucker Act was unconstitutional. In January 1889 they succeeded. Their attorneys argued, among other things, that the escheatment clause violated the property rights and sanctity of contracts guaranteed by the Constitution. The Court disagreed, however, and in a 5 to 4 decision on May 19, 1890, upheld the constitutionality of all the government had done under the new law. The Saints were shocked by the decision, but there seemed to be little they could do to ward off the impending economic destruction of the Church.

This economic crusade was matched by the continuing political crusade. The Liberal party in Utah was hard at work in its effort to undercut the power of the Church, and in 1889 it gained political control of the city of Ogden. Then, in the municipal elections of 1890, the Liberals gained control of Salt Lake City government. Many loyal Latter-day Saint men, it will be recalled, were not permitted to vote, and Congress had annulled women's suffrage in Utah. And since it was impossible for new convert immigrants to obtain citizenship in the territorial courts, they too were unable to vote. The bitter attitude of at least one judge was displayed in his remark that an alien who was a member of the Church was "not a fit person to be made a citizen of the United States."

The Edmunds-Tucker Act provided for the disfranchisement of anyone convicted of polygamy or unwilling to pledge obedience to anti-polygamy laws. By 1890 some twelve thousand Utah citizens had been deprived of their right to vote. But this was not enough. In Idaho a test oath had been written by the territorial legislature that disfranchised practically all Latter-day Saints by requiring them to swear they did not believe in or belong to a church that believed in plural marriage. If they did not so swear, they would lose their voting rights. In 1888 a number of members in Idaho went so far as to have their names withdrawn from the records of the Church so they could legally vote. Their main objective was to defeat Fred T. Dubois, anti-Mormon federal marshal, who was running for territorial delegate to Congress. Their strategy did not work and Dubois was elected. While Utah Mormons looked on with a fearful eye, in February 1890 the Supreme Court of the United States upheld the constitutionality of the Idaho law.

The decision on the Idaho test oath encouraged Utah liberals to seek one just like it and thus disfranchise even more Latter-day Saints. A representative was sent to Washington and soon a new measure, the Cullom-Strubble Bill, was introduced. Its basic intent was to wrest political power from the hands of the Church in Utah, and to do it by disfranchising all its members.

Fifty years earlier Joseph Smith and Elias Higbee had gone to the nation's capital seeking federal intervention to help the Saints secure their property rights in Missouri. A few years later Brigham Young and Jesse C. Little had sought federal aid in the Church's move. In later years Mormon agents in Washington had pressed hard for Utah's right to become a state in the Union so the Saints in Utah could rule themselves. Now, in 1890, they were fighting for one of the basic rights of citizens in a free society—the right to vote in their own local elections. The only man left alive who had been a General Authority at the time of the first confrontation was Wilford Woodruff. It was fitting that he should preside at the time of this last, and very different, confrontation of the nineteenth century.

The Church quickly sent a delegation to Washington, headed by George Q. Cannon and intent on warding off the fearsome legislation. While this delegation was there, they received news that the Supreme Court had upheld the Edmunds-Tucker Act. The temporal strength of the Church had been dealt a crushing blow, and now, if the Cullom-Strubble Bill passed, its political influence would be equally devastated. In Utah the Saints organized a defense fund, which gathered contributions from the wards and stakes in support of what they considered one of the most pivotal battles they had yet waged in the American capital.

One of the men who labored hard to defeat the bill was Frank J. Cannon, son of George Q. Cannon. The younger man represented, in many ways, "Young Utah"—the second and third generation of Utah Saints, most of whom, although fully loyal to the Church and its ideals, had not entered plural marriage and were quite willing to pledge that they would not enter into it. They felt it blatantly unfair that those who had not violated the law should be disfranchised because of what others had done, yet this is what the bill would have achieved. Young Cannon pleaded:

> The young men of the Mormon faith have accepted the special conditions imposed by the Government. They are giving every reasonable pledge that they will not disobey the laws of Congress relating to polygamy; and will not aid or abet others in disobeying such laws. It is a poor reward that this bill proposes to bestow—to inflict the same political deprivation on the men who are obeying the law as have been imposed upon offenders.[5]

---

[5]Whitney, *History of Utah*, 3:732.

The Utah delegation to Washington met with little encouragement, and returned to Salt Lake City confident that nothing short of a declaration by the Church that plural marriage had ended would prevent approval of the Cullom-Strubble Bill or assure statehood for Utah. President Woodruff had already been thinking about this possibility for months, discussing it with Church leaders and others and praying more earnestly than he had ever prayed in his life. On September 25, 1890, having received divine assurance, he issued the Manifesto. It was apparent that only this action forestalled passage of the bill.

President Woodruff's Revelation and the Manifesto

The Manifesto was not simply a political document. In many ways it represented other deep-rooted religious principles, some of which were much more important to the Saints than the principle of plural marriage. One of these was millennialism. The Latter-day Saints firmly believed that through Joseph Smith the Kingdom of God had been established in preparation for the second coming of Christ and the establishment of the Millennium. In preparation for that event, they had tried to establish a political as well as an ecclesiastical kingdom. The political kingdom (as represented by the Council of Fifty) was no longer functioning, but to allow the spiritual kingdom, the Church, to be destroyed would be, in President Woodruff's opinion, the great failure of all. Obviously, the Church must be preserved to meet the Savior when he came, even if it meant withdrawing approval of plural marriage. In this sense, preparation for the Millennium was a factor in producing the Manifesto. President Woodruff did not pretend to know when the Millennium would arrive, though he believed it was imminent and that it would result in the political ascendancy of the Kingdom of God over all the earth, with Christ at its head. He was careful to avoid the unwise speculation of some Saints that these apocalyptic events would come in 1890, but on December 31, 1889, he wrote in his diary:

> Thus ends the year 1889 and the word of the Prophet Joseph Smith is beginning to be fulfilled that the whole nation would turn against Zion and make war upon the Saints. The nation has never been filled so full of lies against the Saints as today. 1890 will be an important year with the Latter Day Saints and the American nation.

A second essential principle to the Latter-day Saints was

revelation. Despite any political or economic pressure that could be mustered, Church leaders would clearly not have accepted the momentous decision on plural marriage had they not been assured that it came by revelation. How President Woodruff received the revelation, and how he let it be known, is an essential part of the history of the Manifesto.

Early in September 1890 President Woodruff made a trip to California, where he met with Isaac Trumbo and other political and business leaders, and then returned to Salt Lake City on September 21. There is no record of what they discussed, but clearly the problems of the Church weighed heavily on the President's mind, and he was concerned with the views of these men on Utah's chance for statehood, as well as the possibility of easing the Church's political and financial burdens. Immediately after his return he met with his counselors and members of the Council of the Twelve to discuss the policies that he now knew he must follow. "In broken and contrite spirit," he told them, he had sought the will of the Lord, and it had been revealed to him that the Church must relinquish the practice of plural marriage. There was a long and serious discussion in which some of the brethren at first resisted the inevitable, but one by one they acknowledged his decision as revelation. That same day, September 24, the Manifesto was issued to the press in the form of a reply to recent accusations that polygamous marriages were still being performed. Authorization for plural marriage had already been withdrawn, but this was the first official announcement that the Church would now fully conform to the law of the land. When questioned later, President Woodruff made it clear that the prohibition would apply throughout the Church, even in places where the law did not forbid the practice, and it would therefore be uniform Church policy. On September 25 he made the following poignant entry in his journal:

> I have arrived at a point in the history of my life as the President of the Church of Jesus Christ of Latter-day Saints where I am in the necessity of acting for the Temporal Salvation of the Church. The United States government has taken a stand and passed laws to destroy the Latter-day Saints upon the subject of polygamy or patriarchal order of marriage. And after praying to the Lord and feeling inspired by his spirit I have issued the following proclamation. . . .

The Manifesto was simply an official declaration that the

Church had already halted the teaching of plural marriage and was not allowing anyone to enter into the practice. In it President Woodruff said he intended to submit to the laws of the land and that there "is nothing in my teaching to the Church or in those of my associates, during the time specified, which can be reasonably construed to include or encourage polygamy and when any elder of the church has used language which appeared to convey such teaching he has been promptly reproved."

About two weeks later, on October 6, 1890, the Manifesto was presented to a general conference and approved. This action helped convince skeptics that the membership at large had accepted the new position. A few Church members, of course, would not accept the change, just as a few have always opposed new ideas or programs as they have been introduced, but most Saints readily accepted the new direction. At the same time, a few die-hard opponents of the Church accused the Saints of insincerity and continued their attacks, but for the most part the Manifesto was accepted in good faith and the path toward statehood and home rule was cleared. The Manifesto was finally incorporated into the Doctrine and Covenants in 1908.

President Woodruff on the Nature of Revelation

The Manifesto was a significant watershed in the history of the Latter-day Saints, and President Woodruff and his associates declared that this change in policy came by revelation. Yet a few members could not accept it as revelation, for it seemed to contradict an earlier command. These few were not even persuaded by President Cannon's powerful sermon on October 6 reminding them the Lord had said through Joseph Smith that He would not require the Saints to fulfill a command that became impossible because of persecution from their enemies. Yet the very principle of continuing revelation, which is one of the foundations of the Latter-day Saint faith, meant that changing circumstances would inevitably require new instructions. Joseph Smith once remarked that "that which is wrong under one circumstance, may be, and often is, right under another."[6] Continued revelation has always been a keystone of Church policy. The Saints in all ages have heard sermons about the importance of following the *living*

---

[6]Joseph Smith, *History of the Church*, 5:135.

prophets, and this was the essential principle involved in accepting the Manifesto. As President Woodruff told a group of Saints in Logan in 1891:

> The Lord showed me by vision and revelation exactly what would take place if we did not stop this practice. . . . He has told me exactly what to do, and what the result would be if we did not do it. I have been called upon by friends outside of the Church and urged to take some steps with regard to this matter. They knew the course which the government was determined to take. . . . I saw exactly what would come to pass if there was not something done. I have had this spirit upon me for a long time. But I want to say this: I should have let all the temples go out of our hands; I should have gone to prison myself, and let every other man go there, had not the God of heaven commanded me to do what I did do; and when the hour came that I was commanded to do that, it was all clear to me.[7]

Aftermath and Statehood

Issuance of the Manifesto left some problems unresolved, but in general the atmosphere changed and the Church entered a new era of cooperation and understanding. One question was the status of those who became plural wives before the Manifesto; it was generally understood that husbands would not be required to reject them or their children. Even though some enemies of the Church were skeptical of the Saints' sincerity, most federal officials demonstrated faith in their intentions and leniency in administering the laws. Judge Zane, for example, who earlier had been extremely harsh, demonstrated that his only concern was in upholding the law, not in punishing the Saints or destroying the Church. He was lenient with those who were now brought before his court and charged with polygamy, and he even signed a petition asking that an official pardon be given to members. Such action antagonized some anti-Mormons, but it heralded the approach of a new era of understanding. In one instance Judge James C. Miner heard the case of a Saint indicted on two counts of polygamy and asked him if he accepted the Manifesto and considered it valid. When the defendant said yes, the judge dismissed the case with a fine of six cents. In January 1893 retiring President Benjamin Harrison issued amnesty to all the Saints who had been in compliance with the law since 1890, and in September 1894 President Grover Cleveland issued a more general amnesty.

---

[7]*Deseret Evening News,* November 7, 1891.

Statehood for Utah was finally achieved in 1896. This photograph of the interior of the Tabernacle was taken a year later, when the Church and the state celebrated the first anniversary of statehood. (Church Archives)

At the same time, the quest for statehood continued. Before this could be achieved, the Church political party in Utah had to be eliminated. The only way to do this convincingly was to divide the Saints along national party lines. Accordingly, in June 1891 the People's party was formally dissolved. Two years later the Liberal party disbanded. So serious were Church leaders about the Saints aligning themselves with both national parties that they even preached it in stake conferences. Traditionally the Saints leaned toward the Democratic party, for the Republicans had been blamed for most anti-Mormon legislation. When it seemed, therefore, that the balance in Utah might favor the Democrats so heavily that it would appear as another Church party, the leaders encouraged some members to join the Republicans.

At the same time, national Republican party leaders looked with increasing favor on Utah statehood, and the Democrats, once thought to be the friends of the Mormons, seemed to be dragging their feet. Church leaders were forming increasingly close friendships with Republican political leaders and businessmen, and it was due to a series of astute political moves by Republicans in Congress that the Utah enabling act was finally passed in 1894. It was signed by the Democratic president, Grover Cleveland, on July 16. Utahns immediately started writing a constitution that specifically prohibited plural marriage and ensured the complete separation of church and state. On January 4, 1896, Utah became a state, nearly fifty years after Brigham Young first began to seek that goal.

Inevitably, there were disagreements and some misunderstandings within the Church over political matters. In 1892, Elder Moses Thatcher of the Council of the Twelve, Elder B. H. Roberts of the First Council of Seventy, and Charles W. Penrose of the Salt Lake Stake presidency campaigned openly for the Democratic party, assuming that their church positions did not prohibit them from participating, as individuals, in partisan politics. The prevailing opinion among the leaders was that it would be unwise for such high officials to take to the political stump at that time. After being soundly reprimanded, the three brethren in question confessed themselves in error.

In 1895 the matter came up again when Elder Thatcher accepted the nomination of the Democratic party for senator from Utah and B. H. Roberts agreed to be candidate for congressman. Again they were disciplined for having accepted the nominations without prior consultation with Church leaders. This did not mean that they could not be active in their respective political parties, President Woodruff explained in a public statement of October 19, but simply that they must get proper permission before running for office.

Neither man was elected, and the following year the General Authorities issued a formal statement, known as the "political rule of the Church." Designed to avoid similar controversies in the future, it reaffirmed that before accepting any position that would interfere with the discharge of his ecclesiastical duties, a leading Church official should apply to proper authorities to determine whether he could function adequately in both positions. "To maintain proper discipline and order in the church," the announcement read, "we deem this absolutely necessary." The document was signed by all General Authorities except two. One was in Europe and the other, Elder Moses Thatcher, refused to sign. Because of his disharmony on this and other matters, Elder Thatcher's name was not presented with the other authorities sustained in the general conferences of 1896, and on November 19 he was officially dropped from the Twelve.

Church Activity in a Still Troubled Time

The Manifesto was issued partly to enable the Church to resume its normal activity, but other affairs had not been ignored in the meantime. Missionary work continued to expand, new stakes and wards were organized, auxiliary programs were augmented and refined, and increasing attention was paid to education.

Perhaps no President has been known for his devotion to missionary work more than Wilford Woodruff, and during his administration this Church activity was not neglected. Between 1890 and 1900, for example, 6,125 missionaries were called and set apart, nearly triple the number of the previous decade. Between 1888 and the end of the century eleven new missions were opened.

Much of the new missionary activity centered in the South Pacific. In Samoa a mission was formally organized in June 1888. The mission president, Elder Joseph H. Dean, had been proselyting in Hawaii, where he had gone to escape prosecution under the Edmunds-Tucker Act. Upon arrival with his family in Samoa, he was received by Samuela Monoa, a Latter-day Saint from Hawaii, who helped him become acquainted and served as an interpreter. By the end of the year thirty-five people had been baptized, a meetinghouse constructed, and a Sunday School and Relief Society organized. Missionary work has been continuous in Samoa since then.

Missionaries were sent to Tonga in 1891. The elders quickly erected a mission home and purchased a thirteen-foot boat for travel among the various islands. Their success was limited, and the mission closed in 1897, not to reopen until 1917. At the same time, other elders were finding greater success among the Maori people of New Zealand and the Australians. Both areas were part of the Australasian Mission, but in 1898 the two were organized into separate jurisdictions.

Though immigration into Utah was declining in the 1890s and most immigrants still came from Europe, a number of converts from the South Pacific also wanted to emigrate. In 1894, for example, seven Maoris left New Zealand with a group of missionaries returning home, the beginning of a small but steady migration.

An effort by Pacific islanders to establish themselves in Utah was one of the most unusual colonizing experiments in Church history. This was the colony of Iosepa, in western Utah's Skull Valley. In 1889 the Church purchased a 1,290-acre ranch in this arid valley for the benefit of Hawaiian Saints who wanted to be near the Salt Lake Temple. The name, Iosepa, was the Hawaiian word for Joseph, and the settlement was named in honor of Joseph F. Smith, who had been prominent in spreading the gospel in the Hawaiian Islands. It must have seemed strange indeed to see these Hawaiian settlers begin stock raising and farming in an environment so different from their tropical island home. But with the aid of the Church they survived, and by the time the colony was abandoned, they were beginning to show a profit. They had many problems in adjusting; several people became discouraged, and in the end a plague of leprosy struck the settlement. The experiment ended in 1917 after the Church announced it would build a temple in Hawaii and offered to assist those interested in returning to their native land. Today the tiny, lonesome graveyard of the Hawaiian Saints with its toppled and deteriorating markers seems paradoxical in its Utah desert setting. It is a fitting though pathetic reminder of the faith and determination of one group of Polynesian Saints, as well as lingering evidence of international efforts in the nineteenth century.

It this same period, missionary work began in California in 1892 and reopened in the eastern United States in 1893. In Asia, missionary work began in Turkey about 1885, under the direction of Jacob Spori, though it proceeded very slowly. The same year the first converts in Russia were baptized by a traveling elder from the Scandinavian Mission. Russia was officially dedicated for preaching the gospel in 1903 by Elder Francis M. Lyman, but since then missionaries have been unable to work in that country. In no area of the Near East did missionary work take hold permanently, but the efforts represented the Church's continuing interest in expanding its work worldwide.

The Church continued to make converts in its organized European missions, and many continued to emigrate. In general, however, the flow to Utah declined in the 1890s, dropping to half that of the previous decade. One reason was the dissolution of the Perpetual Emigration Fund Company under the Edmunds-Tucker Law, which made it more difficult for the European Saints to find the means to leave their homeland. Another reason was that the Church itself began to change its attitude toward immigration. The colonization era was over, and economic opportunities for immigrants in Utah were becoming more limited. The original purpose of immigration, filling the region with Latter-day Saints so that the Kingdom could not be shaken loose again, had been fulfilled. By the end of the decade Church leaders were beginning to encourage the Saints abroad to realize that emigration would not solve their economic problems. In 1898 President George Q. Cannon remarked in October conference that they had been counseling the Saints in other lands to "remain quiet for a while; to not be anxious to break up their homes to gather to Zion." With changing times and changing needs, this and other policies of the Church were also changing. Henceforth more attention would be paid to building Zion in other lands and in the hearts of the Saints, as the closing of the pioneer era foreshadowed greater efforts at internationalization.

To strengthen Zion in the wards and branches, the Church continually reassessed its auxiliary programs. In 1889 annual conferences were begun in Salt Lake City for Relief Society and Primary workers. This considerably reduced the load of general officers in these auxiliaries who earlier had tried to visit the stakes and wards regularly to give instructions. Representatives from the stakes could now carry the instructions back from the conferences.

The Sunday School was particularly active in the search for new and better ways to accomplish its mission of teaching the gospel. Sunday School missionaries continued to work in the stakes to create new interest. In November 1892 Brigham Young Academy opened a Sunday School normal training class, taught by the faculty but directed by the Deseret Sunday School Union board. By the end of the year nearly 150 Sunday School workers had been called to take this teacher training course, and they responded as if they had been called on missions. In 1894 the Sunday School also began to establish model Sunday Schools, which were conducted by prominent educators and served as examples to other Sunday School workers. To help support all these new efforts, in 1891 the auxiliary began an annual "Nickel Day" in the Sunday Schools,

A Utah schoolroom of the late nineteenth century. (Church Archives)

with members invited to make voluntary contributions of five cents or more. In later years "Nickel Day" became "Dime Sunday," and for years this annual collection was an important Sunday School tradition. In 1893 the Sunday School Union board began holding Sunday School conferences in each stake to better coordinate and promote the work. With these and other innovations, the auxiliaries helped provide continued spiritual instruction and growth.

At the same time the Church was expanding its programs of formal, week-day education, both religious and secular. Under the Edmunds-Tucker Act the funds appropriated from the Church were redirected to strengthen the tax-supported public schools in Utah, where religious education would, of course, be excluded. As religious instruction was eliminated from the schools and Utah's children attended public schools in larger numbers, the Church soon began to hold religion classes in various ward meeting houses after school, where the religious training could take place without violating separation of church and state. In addition, academies or high schools were founded by the Church in most larger settlements. Between 1888 and 1891 at least thirty-one academies were started in Utah, Idaho, Arizona, Canada, and Mexico, and in 1907 and 1909 two more were begun in Colorado and Wyoming. Under the direction of a Church board of education, appointed in 1888, these academies were financed partly by the Church and partly by local stakes. Some began as elementary schools, but most soon became secondary schools and emphasized classical and vocational education as well as religious instruction.

Most symbolic of the Church's spiritual strength as the pioneer period closed was completion of the Salt Lake Temple. After forty years of construction, it was officially dedicated on April 6, 1893, though daily dedicatory services were held until

Salt Lake Temple, dedicated in 1893, forty years after Brigham Young broke ground. This photograph of the Celestial Room was taken in 1911 and published the following year, along with photographs of other rooms of the temple, in James E. Talmage's The House of the Lord. *(C. R. Savage Company photograph, Church Archives)*

April 18 in order to accommodate the crowds wanting to attend. Special services were held later for children under eight, and it was ultimately estimated that more than seventy-five thousand people attended the programs.

Among other things, the completion of the Salt Lake Temple represented the Saints' renewed determination to seek after the names of their dead ancestors and perform vicarious saving ordinances in their behalf. At the same time, the nature of the sealing ordinances was clarified by President Woodruff. Since the days of Joseph Smith the Saints had performed vicarious baptism in behalf of their dead loved ones. In addition, it was the custom for members to have themselves and their families sealed to prominent Church leaders under what was known as the law of adoption. By 1893 about thirteen thousand such adoptions in behalf of the dead had taken place. Members believed that by having themselves and their immediate progenitors adopted to prominent priesthood leaders, they would be assured in the next life of being attached to families holding the priesthood. The doctrine relating to missionary work in the spirit world had not yet been fully expounded. This would come during Joseph F. Smith's administration.

By 1894 Church leaders had given the doctrine a great deal of reconsideration. In the April general conference President Woodruff announced that he had received a revelation on the subject, and this revelation ended adoption in favor of the more understandable practice of vicariously sealing family groups together. In announcing the new revelation President Woodruff emphasized the importance of every man being adopted or sealed to his own father, and so on back, "not to Wilford Woodruff, nor to any man outside the lineage of his fathers. That is the will of God to this people." If this should be done faithfully, he declared, the Saints would be doing "exactly what God said when he declared He would send Elijah the prophet in the last day."[8]

The results of the new revelation were impressive. Previously little genealogical work had been done among the Saints and few sealing ordinances had been performed beyond two or three generations. Now President Woodruff told them to trace their

---

[8]*Deseret Evening News*, April 21, 1894.

genealogies as far as they could and perform the appropriate sealings to "run this chain through as far as you can get it." The
following month the Genealogical Society of Utah was formed
under the Church's sponsorship, providing powerful stimulus to
genealogical work. In the nineteenth century much of the Church's
energy was absorbed by colonization, community building, and
strengthening the temporal roots of Zion, but in the twentieth
century a consuming dedication to genealogical research and
temple work would replace some of their earlier concerns.

In this period of reevaluation and change, Church leaders
also examined other long-standing practices. The custom of holding a special fast day and meeting on the first Thursday of each
month, for example, was beginning to interfere with employment
of Saints who could no longer drop their work in the middle of the
week. Accordingly, in 1896 the First Presidency issued instructions
that henceforth fast day would be observed on the first Sunday of
each month.

Another nineteenth century practice that was reexamined
was rebaptism. For many years it had been common for members

*Until dedication of the new Church Office Building in 1917, the old Church
Historian's Office served as a headquarters building. It also housed the
Genealogical Society of Utah, formed in 1894. Pictured here in the upper
story genealogical library are, left to right, Nephi Anderson, Lillian
Cameron, Joseph Christensen, Joseph Fielding Smith, and Bertha Emery.
(Church Archives)*

to rededicate themselves to building up the Kingdom through re-baptism. This practice was not considered essential to salvation, but was a symbol of rededication. On other occasions the Saints were baptized as a symbolic gesture related to blessings for their health, entry into the United Order, preparation for marriage, and even for going to the temple if they had not been there for some time. So common, in fact, was rebaptism that printed forms introduced in 1877 for ward membership records contained columns for recording it, and these forms were not replaced until 1900.

In 1893 the First Presidency instructed stake presidents not to require rebaptism for Saints wishing to attend the Salt Lake Temple dedication, for "the Lord will forgive sins if we forsake them." In 1897 the practice was discontinued altogether. As explained by President George Q. Cannon, the possibility of frequent rebaptism led many people to think of it as an easy way to obtain constant forgiveness of their sins. "It is repentance from sin that will save you," he reminded them, "not rebaptism."[9]

An Economic Era Also Ends

As the nineteenth century ended, long-standing temporal policies were disappearing and changing conditions were suggesting new directions for the future. Economically, the Church had ended its boycott of gentile merchants in 1882, opening retailing and manufacturing in Utah to private enterprise more widely than before. This meant that the Church would have less direct control over the region's economy, even though most of the proliferating businesses were owned and operated by individual Latter-day Saints. Most Church-owned concerns were sold to private interests or adopted the competitive policies of private enterprise. As Church cooperatives disappeared, the economy of "Mormon Country" was characterized increasingly by a competitive economic system. Just as the elimination of polygamy and the alignment with national political parties had brought the Saints closer to the mainstream of American social and political life, so these economic changes foreshadowed their rapid assimilation into the national economic system. This did not mean that the Church divorced itself completely from business enterprise. Rather, the few businesses it retained were operated independently as income-

---

[9]*Conference Report*, October 1897, p. 68.

producing ventures rather than as shared community cooperatives.

At the same time, the Church consciously promoted establishment of certain basic industries in the region and even, in some cases, loaned money to help them become established. This included beet sugar manufacturing, salt refining, hydroelectric power, and certain mining and transportation facilities.

Even while the Church promoted the region's well-being, its own financial situation was distressing. In 1894 its escheated personal property was returned and in 1896 the real estate came back, but it was less than what had been confiscated and did not greatly aid in settling the debts. In addition to the damage done by escheatment in the first place, the Church was hurt by the drop in tithing income when members felt it would only be confiscated by the government receiver and therefore saw no purpose in donating their income to that source. Probably the nationwide depression of the 1890s also contributed to the loss of income. At the same time, the Church attempted to aid the families of those in prison, maintained a large defense fund for legal expenses, and faced the costs of finishing the Salt Lake Temple, expanding the educational program, and assisting in the development of industry. It had to operate on credit, and by 1898 the total debt amounted to more than $1,250,000. President Woodruff attempted to relieve the debt by issuing bonds and selling them to eastern financiers, but these negotiations fell through. It would remain for his successors, Lorenzo Snow and Joseph F. Smith, to find more successful ways of removing heavy financial burdens.

In a very real sense the year 1896 was both a culmination and a new beginning for the Church. The long struggle for statehood and home rule in Utah was ended. Plural marriage and the need for direct political involvement were now history; economic exclusivism and cooperative experimentalism were left behind. At the same time, important doctrines and practices were being clarified and a variety of programs expanded to provide greater spiritual and moral direction to the lives of the Saints. Despite all the changes, the Church had not lost sight of its major goals and the reason for existence. The 1890s saw a reaffirmation of the faith that the Kingdom of God had indeed been restored to earth through Joseph Smith, that divine priesthood authority existed within the Church, that the destiny of the Church was still guided by revelation, and that the fundamental principles received through Joseph

World Room in the Manti Temple, which was dedicated in 1888. Logan Temple, dedicated four years earlier, was first to include in its original plans separate rooms for each stage of the sacred temple ceremony. It soon became the practice to commission prominent artists to paint murals in some of the rooms of the temples to represent what those rooms symbolized. Near the end of the century a number of artists were sent to Europe for the express purpose of improving their skills and, upon their return, painting temple murals. This impressive mural in the Manti Temple was completed in 1948 by Minerva Tiechert, whose paintings also grace many chapels and mission homes in the Church. It symbolizes the people of the world in many times and places, and in the background may be seen the peaceful valley where the temple itself is located. Temple mural art was once one of the distinctive art forms of Mormonism, and within the walls of these temples are the works of some of the Church's most distinguished artists, as well as a few important non-Mormon artists. The Los Angeles Temple, completed in 1956, was the last to be designed according to the traditional pattern and the last to include extensive murals. (Church Archives)

Smith, the Book of Mormon, and the other scriptures were true. In doubling their efforts at missionary work and augmenting their dedication to genealogical and temple work, the Saints also demonstrated their basic faith that the gospel was for both the living and the dead, and that priesthood authority provided the means to save both. In the years to come they would continue their accommodation to the realities of the world around them, as well as their efforts to remain a "peculiar people," even while sharing their religious peculiarities with all who would listen.

PART *IV*

A
New Era,
1897–1938

Church Office Building (now called the Church Administration Building), completed in 1917, symbolized the transition of the Church from the problems of the nineteenth century to the security and prestige of the twentieth. (Church Archives)

AS THE TWENTIETH CENTURY dawned on New Year's day, 1901, the venerable Lorenzo Snow attended a special service in the Mormon Tabernacle in Salt Lake City and presented a greeting to the world. The gentle, white-bearded prophet had lived through the entirety of Mormon history and now, eight months before his death, he looked forward to the new century as an era of dramatic possibilities.

"The lessons of the past century should have prepared us for the duties and glories of the opening era. It ought to be the age of peace, of greater progress, of the universal adoption of the golden rule. The barbarism of the past should be buried. War with its horrors should be a memory. The aim of nations should be fraternity and mutual greatness. The welfare of humanity should be studied instead of the enrichment of a race or the extension of an empire."[1]

President Snow's hope for universal peace and brotherhood reflected the Saints' continuing faith in the eventual establishment of the Millennium. But that was not to come within the immediate future. Instead, the first forty years of the new age saw the tempo of war accelerate around the world and new evidences of political corruption, greed, poverty, and social injustice appear.

The President's comment on the "enrichment of a race or the extension of an empire" was an oblique reference to the Spanish-American war recently ended, a war for an American empire justified in part by ill-perceived concepts of racial superiority. But the United States was not alone in its imperialistic ambitions, and by the outbreak of World War I in 1914, Western powers had extended their influence to nearly all parts of the earth. After the war most world leaders banded together in the League of Nations, hoping to create a force for peace. The United States, however, refused to cooperate for fear of undermining its own sovereignty, and while this was not the only reason for the league's failure, it did contribute. By the end of the 1930s war threatened again to engulf the world as Germany, Italy, Japan, and the USSR attempted to expand their political perimeters.

The progress that Lorenzo Snow hoped for was in many ways achieved. While mankind did not find the way to peace or to the alleviation of all

---

[1]Deseret Evening News, *January 1, 1901.*

social ills, the world did see amazing scientific and technological achievements. The radio, the automobile, and the airplane all brought the people of the world closer together. In medicine, improved anesthesia, better drugs, and new surgical developments prolonged life and improved health. Scientists registered significant attainments in chemistry, electronics, and atomic science, which had great potential for human happiness as well as potential for tragedy.

As far as the Latter-day Saints were concerned, world movements became more and more a part of their history. Although always influenced by the forces around them, they felt the nature of that influence change in subtle and important ways. In the nineteenth century they had attempted to build the Kingdom somewhat apart from the political forces that seemed to be working against them. In the first four decades of the twentieth century they abandoned separatism and became more directly involved in the broader political and economic life of the world around them, especially in that of the United States. Their willing participation in America's wars, as well as their encouragement of non-American Saints to be loyal to their own countries, demonstrated that building the Kingdom was basically nonpolitical. They were influenced by and contributed to certain reform movements that swept America, particularly those, like prohibition, with direct application to church principles. They became active participants in American economic and political life, and a number of prominent Latter-day Saints made important contributions to the American scene while helping to create a positive image for the Church in the minds of their constituents. One was Reed Smoot, a member of the Council of the Twelve who served in the United States Senate for thirty years. As chairman of the powerful Senate Finance Committee, he had great influence on American economic policy and was co-author of the controversial Smoot-Hawley Tariff of 1930. Another was J. Reuben Clark, Jr., a prominent international lawyer who held several important federal offices. After serving on international claims commissions and arbitration boards and as undersecretary of state and ambassador to Mexico, he retired from public service in 1933 when he was called into the First Presidency.

Other prominent Latter-day Saints in government during this period included James H. Moyle, assistant secretary of the treasury from 1917 to 1921; Edgar B. Brossard, member and then chairman of the United States Tariff Commission; William H. King, senator from 1917 to 1941; and William Spry, commissioner of public lands from 1921 to 1929. In addition, the man who was President of the Church from 1918 to 1945, Heber J. Grant, was a successful, respected American businessman. These individuals represented the new reality that Mormonism was more a part of American political and economic life than ever before.

Even as the Saints were moving toward greater integration with the broader society, they attempted to remain aloof from the sins and destructive forces in that society. Their objective was to influence the world with the gospel, and to do so, they must remain in the world though not of it. Between 1900 and 1940 membership grew from 268,300 to 862,000 and the number of missionaries in the field increased to more than 2,000. The Church took advantage of new technological advances to enhance its programs. It continued to adjust its internal organization to meet the needs of a growing membership, and began to lay special emphasis upon the importance of building up the Church throughout the world, rather than emigrating to Zion. Stakes were organized outside the Mountain West and new missions were opened.

The Church also confronted the challenge of new scientific thought. With respected scientists listed among its General Authorities, it assured its members that scientific truth would never really conflict with fundamentals of the gospel. Finally, the economic forces that produced the great depression of the 1930s caused the Church to adopt a new program of economic security for the Saints that became one of its most publicized features.

As the last prophet of the nineteenth century looked forward in 1901 to the new era, he concluded his message with a moving summary of the Saints' real objective for the world:

"I hope and look for grand events to occur in the Twentieth Century. At its auspicious dawn, I lift my hands and invoke the blessings of heaven upon the inhabitants of the earth. May the sunshine from above smile upon you. May the treasures of the ground and the fruits of the soil be brought forth freely for your good. May the light of truth chase darkness

from your souls. May righteousness increase and iniquity diminish as the years of the century roll on. May justice triumph and corruption be stamped out. And may virtue and chastity and honor prevail, until evil shall be overcome and the earth shall be cleansed from wickedness. Let these sentiments, as the voice of the 'Mormons' in the mountains of Utah, go forth to the whole world, and let all people know that our wish and our mission are for the blessing and salvation of the entire human race. May the Twentieth Century prove the happiest as it will be the grandest of all the ages of time, and may God be glorified in the victory that is coming over sin and sorrow and misery and death. Peace be unto you all!"

CHAPTER 14

A Time of Transition, 1897-1907

T he celebration of statehood was barely forgotten when a second public observance attracted the attention of the Saints in Utah. This was the Pioneer Jubilee of July 20-24, 1897—in one sense a symbolic rite of passage from the old order to the new— and it presented two significant themes. One looked back and honored Utah's pioneers, while the other marched forward from 1847, applauding progress. These same themes would reveal themselves continuously in the coming years.

The pattern of Church history in the twentieth century reflected the changing status of the Church itself. No longer would Church history display such things as immigration, the rigors of carving new settlements out of uninhabited areas, the possibility of being continually driven from place to place, conflict with federal authority, and imprisonment for the sake of conscience. Instead, the Church found itself dealing with the problems created by a rapidly growing population, educational concerns, the need for more social and cultural programs, and constant consideration of necessary administrative reforms. While these concerns differed from the adventures of the nineteenth century, they were neverthe-less as significant to the progress and development of the

Kingdom. The early years of the twentieth century reflected these new patterns.

The turn of the century was a time of transition; the pioneering past gone, new challenges lay ahead. In 1897 only a few of the founding fathers of Mormonism remained. President Wilford Woodruff died September 2, 1898, and Lorenzo Snow became president eleven days later. In another three years, on October 10, 1901, President Snow passed away and his place was taken by Joseph F. Smith. Presidents Woodruff and Snow were the last of the first generation of Mormon leaders. Other positions of leadership were already being filled by sons and grandsons of earlier stalwarts. Between October 1897 and 1907 eleven new apostles, two new members of the First Council of the Seventy, a new Presiding Bishop, and three Presiding Bishop's counselors would be chosen; of the whole group, only one was born before the Saints migrated to Utah. In addition, four auxiliaries would have new general presidencies.

At least six important themes may be identified as a new generation of leaders helped guide the Church into the twentieth century. First, and of particular significance under the new political detente achieved at Utah statehood, was a series of challenges to the Saints' political integrity. At least three times during the following decade their status as patriotic, law-abiding citizens was tested. Next, out of a past that had been discredited in the public mind, the Saints were newly awakened to their heritage of sacrifice and honor and began to place new emphasis on placing this creditable inheritance before the world. Third, the burden of financial indebtedness and the obligations of economic development received special attention. A fourth area of concern was the Church's contribution to family life and education. A fifth important thrust involved a revitalized effort to carry the gospel to all the world. Finally, the Church was concerned with perfecting the Saints and launched a significant reform movement that affected both its priesthood and its auxiliary programs.

The Saints and American Politics

The agreements that led to statehood anticipated that in the future the Church would refrain from direct involvement in political affairs. This did not mean that individual leaders could not participate, but only that they would not exercise their influence as if they were speaking for the Church. It was also assumed that the Saints would demonstrate their political loyalty to the American system by upholding the laws against plural marriage. The Spanish-American War gave the Saints an opportunity to demonstrate a supportive attitude toward America in wartime, and the struggles over seating two General Authorities in Congress brought to light several political questions left dangling since 1896. In a sense, each of these events was a test of the Saints' political adaptability as they emerged into a new era.

In 1898 the United States declared war on Spain, culminating a months' long campaign promoted by American expansionists and certain journalists. The brutal treatment of Spanish political prisoners and others in Cuba was one of the most publicized complaints, but it was also clear that many expansionists hoped for war in order to grab the Philippines and other Spanish possessions for the United States. When it appeared that Spain was responsible for sinking the American battleship *Maine* in Havana Harbor, the popular clamor practically pushed America into war.

Although the Spanish-American War was generally popular, there were some Americans who decried it as evidence of American imperialism. In Utah, too, there were various opinions. The Church-owned *Deseret News* criticized the idea of American militarism, and Joseph F. Smith told a Salt Lake Stake conference he deplored the war spirit. Nevertheless, most Church leaders felt it important to stand with the American government, and for this reason they supported the war.

It soon appeared that Brigham Young, Jr., a member of the Council of the Twelve, held a minority view. He counseled young men against enlistment and preached in the Tabernacle against the call for volunteers. The First Presidency requested him to stop his personal campaign against the war, which he did, and on April 28 they issued a formal statement in support of the war effort. Utah's volunteer quota was 500 men—a number that brought immediate comparison with the Mormon Battalion—and the response of the whole state to the war effort was positive. Official encouragement from the Church and the speed with which Utah's volunteer units were filled demonstrated that the Latter-day Saints in Utah were loyal to the American government and would support its military efforts. If former critics doubted Mormon patriotism, this response should have helped persuade them.

Mormon volunteers who participated in the Spanish-American War.
(*Church Archives*)

As the Church worked to disengage itself from direct involvement in matters of politics and government, members were urged
to exercise their freedom in political activities and to put principle
ahead of party in electing good men to public office. "I do not care
whether a man is a Republican or a Democrat," said Wilford
Woodruff in 1897, "but it is your duty to unite in electing good
men to govern. . . . unite together within your party lines and appoint good men."[1]

In this spirit, in 1898 Elder B. H. Roberts obtained permission from the First Presidency to seek the Democratic nomination for a seat in the House of Representatives. Elder Roberts had
entered into plural marriage before the Manifesto and was still living with his plural wives. By informal agreement arranged after
the Manifesto, it was assumed—though not written into law—that
in such cases men would not be punished so long as they entered
into no new plural marriages. Most Utah political leaders felt that
polygamy was therefore a dead issue and that Elder Roberts would

------

[1]*Conference Report*, October 1897, p. 71.

be accepted as a law-abiding citizen, as entitled to election as anyone else. The contest became an important test of that assumption.

Elder Roberts won both the nomination and the election, but the nature of his opposition was unexpected. Protestant ministers in Utah accused him and the Church of a breach of faith on the issue of polygamy, and after he was elected they promoted a nationwide campaign against him. Numerous protests were sent to Washington, including a petition claiming seven million signatures. Having failed to prevent his election, his opponents were determined to keep him from being seated.

For six weeks after Elder Roberts presented himself in Washington, a specially appointed committee investigated the charges against him. In the end the House voted 268 to 50 not to seat him. His place was later filled by William H. King, a Democrat and a monogamous Mormon. It is significant that after 1890 Elder Roberts was never accused in the courts of violating the laws against polygamy, but his expulsion from the House of Representatives demonstrated that the nation at large was still wary of Latter-day Saint motives and that the Church had not yet completed the transition to widespread public acceptance.

Four years after the Roberts case another General Authority, Reed Smoot of the Council of the Twelve, was elected to the United States Senate as a Republican from Utah. Even though Elder Smoot could categorically deny any involvement with plural marriage, he spent nearly five years defending the legality of his election in a Senate investigation that once again exposed the Church, its leaders, and its doctrines to the scrutiny of the American public.

Prior to Elder Smoot's election the Church had made every effort to calm the continuing tempest over polygamy. In response to a national campaign for anti-polygamy amendments to the American Constitution, President Lorenzo Snow issued a statement in 1900 reaffirming the Church ban and declaring that any Latter-day Saint who contracted an unlawful marriage must "bear his own burden." At the same time, leaders made a quiet effort to have repealed a territorial unlawful cohabitation law that had been inadvertently codified into state law. Even though there was general agreement that former plural marriages contracted before the Manifesto could be continued, it was still possible for anti-

Mormons to bring embarrassing action under that law whenever they wished. When opponents of the Church interpreted this move as a step toward reinitiating the practice, Church leaders attempted to quiet the agitation by publicly approving Governor Heber M. Wells's veto of the legislation that would have repealed the law.

A more pervasive problem was politics. A general, though unwritten, understanding provided for dividing important public offices somewhat equally between Mormons and friendly non-Mormons, but a few influential opponents of the Church felt left out. Their irritation led to the formation of the hostile American party, which dominated Salt Lake City's municipal government from 1905 to 1911. They charged that too much Church involvement still persisted in politics. The Church's position that Latter-day Saint voters should place a candidate's personal qualifications above party label had subtle implications that contributed to this feeling. Joseph F. Smith, first counselor in the First Presidency, advised the Saints that before voting they should "get the word of the Lord as to who is the right man."[2] Even though the President of the Church still avoided taking an official stand on individual candidates, such statements along with the obvious personal interest Church leaders took in public issues gave partisans grounds for charging that Mormon leaders had not abandoned their involvement in political affairs.

Prominent Latter-day Saints were optimistic that these potential sources of conflict were only minor difficulties and that the Church was entering a new era of public acceptance. It was in this optimistic setting that Elder Reed Smoot announced his candidacy for the Senate in May 1902. Immediately there was a wave of opposition from the Salt Lake Ministerial Association, protesting it as a violation of the principle of separation of church and state. But on January 20, 1903, the Republican-dominated Utah legislature overwhelmingly elected him.

By the time Senator Smoot reached Washington, a number of protests were already there. The Senate voted to seat him, but the Committee on Privileges was given the responsibility of conducting a full investigation of the charges. The hearings opened in

---

[2]*Conference Report,* October 1900, p. 48.

January 1904, and in the next thirty months over three thousand printed pages of testimony accumulated.

Objections to Senator Smoot took many forms. The extreme charge that he had plural wives and was therefore a lawbreaker was easily refuted. More serious was the accusation that he belonged to a self-perpetuating fifteen-member ruling body that controlled Utah's elections and economy. Church leaders, including Elder Smoot, were also charged with secretly continuing to preach and permit plural marriages. In addition, he was accused of taking a secret pledge of disloyalty to the American government.

Senator Smoot's opposition was indeed impressive. Attorney Robert W. Tayler called as witnesses not only leading sectarian ministers and missionaries but also important Church leaders, who were subjected to rigorous cross-examination. Tayler was effectively assisted by Fred T. Dubois, Idaho's leading crusader against the Mormons, and Frank J. Cannon, who had once helped fight for the Mormon cause but who was now politically embittered against the Church. Senator Smoot, on the other hand, had competent attorneys helping him, as well as a Church-appointed task force whose able spokesman was James E. Talmage. Smoot had the backing of several influential senators on the committee.

In reply to the charges against him, Senator Smoot emphasized the legality of his election and said he could be unseated only if he had been convicted of violating the law against polygamy or if he had taken an unpatriotic oath. Neither of these conditions existed. The hearings gave Elder Smoot's defenders opportunity to counter charges of Church control of politics by explaining the internal operations of the Church. Witnesses on his behalf asserted that the Church operated by common consent at all levels and that its members had their free agency in all things.

In December 1903 the First Presidency issued a statement clarifying the use of the term "Kingdom of God" and denying that the Church constituted a political kingdom. When the "political rule of the Church," which required leaders to get permission before they ran for public office, was questioned, Church witnesses replied that this was merely a reasonable housekeeping regulation and that the Church had made no attempt to control state elections. With regard to plural marriage, a church census was displayed that showed that in 1902 there were only 897 polygamous families, as compared with 2,451 families twelve years

IN 1950.

First Man—Who's the elderly looking Senator?
Second Man—That's Senator Smoot, the grand old man from Utah. They're
still taking his seat away from him.

This cartoon, friendly in spirit, was published in the Washington Herald
*during three-year investigation concerning the seating of Reed Smoot in the
United States Senate. (Church Archives)*

earlier. This was clear evidence that the practice was dying out.

Perhaps the most dramatic point in the investigation was when President Joseph F. Smith appeared as a witness. He testified regarding the nature of revelation and church doctrine, free agency in the Church, and the discontinuance of polygamy. He had no firsthand knowledge, he reported, of any plural marriages being performed since 1890, for he had neither witnessed, performed, nor authorized any.

In response to questions concerning what statements or literature could be considered church doctrine, President Smith asserted that authoritative doctrine could be found only in the standard works and that any other writings or speeches were not binding. This was intended to satisfy the public that Latter-day Saints were free agents and not bound by some dictatorial system to accept every declaration that came along from high church officials.

In the end, Senator Smoot retained his seat, despite the majority committee report which recommended his expulsion. He went on to serve a distinguished thirty-year career in the Senate, becoming highly respected among his colleagues for his personal integrity and hard work. He was most influential in economic affairs, especially as chairman of the Senate Finance Committee.

Additional Consequences of the Smoot Hearings

The Smoot hearings were important because they once again exposed the Church to national scrutiny, but they also had significant consequences within the Church. In 1904, for example, President Smith responded to charges of continuing polygamy with a new "Official Statement" denying that any marriage violating the law had taken place "with the sanction, consent or knowledge of the Church," and declaring that any known transgressors would be excommunicated. This statement, sometimes called a "second manifesto," was a clear public signal that further plural marriages, even outside the United States (in Mexico and Canada), would be ended, even though they were not technically in violation of the law.

It was true that a few Church authorities had adopted a literal interpretation of the Manifesto, in spite of President Woodruff's statement that it applied everywhere, and had continued to perform plural marriages outside Utah. This was without official sanction from the First Presidency, but the new declaration was a definite indication that the practice must stop. Even then, two apostles, John W. Taylor and Matthias F. Cowley, could not accept this interpretation of the Manifesto. In October 1905 they finally submitted letters of resignation, and at the following April conference they were dropped from the Council of the Twelve.

Another result of the Smoot hearings was that President Smith directed that President Woodruff's 1890 Manifesto be published in the Doctrine and Covenants. This satisfied critics who had pointed out that this book of scripture contained the revelation authorizing plural marriage but no revelation terminating it.

Finally, in 1907 the First Presidency published *An Address: The Church of Jesus Christ of Latter-day Saints to the World.* Prepared with the help of an eight-member study committee, this sixteen-

First Presidency and Council of the Twelve, September 1898. Front row, left to right: Brigham Young, Jr., Franklin D. Richards, President Lorenzo Snow, George Q. Cannon (first counselor), Joseph F. Smith (second counselor), Anthon H. Lund. Back row: Matthias F. Cowley, Abraham O. Woodruff, George Teasdale, Francis M. Lyman, John Henry Smith, Heber J. Grant, Abraham H. Cannon, Marriner W. Merrill. When Lorenzo Snow became President of the Church in September, a vacancy was left in the Council of the Twelve, which was filled the following month by Rudger Clawson. (Church Archives)

page document was an important reply to the charges made in Washington during the previous four years. Written in a conciliatory spirit, the address restated the basic religious beliefs of the Church and affirmed that it had no intention of dominating the state, was politically loyal, and had abandoned plural marriage. It was adopted unanimously by the general conference of April 1907. The difficult problems of political transition were not totally resolved, but at least the Church was making progress in eliminating public misunderstandings.

Creating a New Image

Throughout the nineteenth century the Church and its members were presented to the public in popular magazines and novels that stressed the sensational. Many readers gained their only conception of Mormonism from articles condemning polygamy or criticizing the leaders as autocrats and denouncing the Church as un-American. The image changed little during the decade of the Roberts and Smoot investigations, though some members received positive recognition for their practical accomplishments in economics and education. The tone of periodical literature seemed to be moving from hostility toward neutrality, but fictional accounts retained the proven format of money-making sensationalism. The literature was often lurid, combining sensualism and violence, and it even found its way into the European press. Missionaries almost anywhere in the Western world might encounter people who said they had "read *all* about Mormonism."

More favorable comments were volunteered on occasion by people who took time to observe the Saints seriously. To encourage and promote the spread of positive statements, Church leaders often referred to them in public speeches, and Church magazines often cited them. The *Improvement Era,* for example, was understandably pleased in 1904 when G. P. Putnam's Sons published *Scientific Aspects of Mormonism* by BYU Professor N. L. Nelson. According to the *Era,* it was the first friendly book written by a Mormon to be published by a prominent eastern house. More directly, non-Mormon Charles Ellis wrote a pamphlet in 1899 entitled *Mormons and Mormonism: Why They Have Been Opposed, Maligned and Persecuted.* The pamphlet was eventually reprinted by the Church for missionary use.

To counteract the generally negative image still being promoted, a program was established for disseminating information to tourists. Heretofore visitors to Utah commonly received their information from cab drivers who made storytelling a profitable business. As early as 1898 Benjamin Goddard suggested the need for a local missionary program aimed at visitors, and in 1901 LeRoi C. Snow discussed the suggestion with the general board of the YMMIA. The matter soon reached the First Council of the Seventy, and, with the approval of the First Presidency, the Seventies established a Bureau of Information and Church Literature on Temple Square. It opened on August 4, 1902, in a small octagonal building measuring about twenty feet across, costing less than six hundred dollars.

Staffed with about two dozen volunteers, the bureau distributed Articles of Faith cards and thousands of free tracts. By the end of the year 150,000 tourists had heard the Mormon story from the Mormons themselves. So pleased were Church leaders that in 1903 they authorized the opening of a branch center at the Saltair resort on the Great Salt Lake, and the following year a new $9,000 building was provided for the bureau on Temple Square.

The new information center became a significant force in building good will toward the Latter-day Saints. Eastern newspaper editors were among the thousands who went away impressed and so reported to their readers. In addition, the free guided tours of Temple Square helped promote the fame of the Tabernacle organ and the Salt Lake Tabernacle Choir. In the summer of 1906 daily recitals on the enlarged and rebuilt organ were begun and soon became a regular feature offered to tourists. By the late 1920s annual visitors numbered two hundred thousand; today they number in the millions.

Recapturing the Past

The improvement in public image was accompanied by a concern that Church members be given a better appreciation of their heritage. This was expressed in part by numerous historical celebrations in which members participated during these years, as well as formation of a number of historical organizations in the 1890s. These included the Genealogical Society of Utah (1894), the Utah Society of the Sons of the American Revolution (1895), the Utah State Historical Society (1897), and the Sons and Daughters of the Utah Pioneers (1898), later organized separately.

By the turn of the century the work of the Church Historian's Office was becoming increasingly important. In 1900 Anthon H. Lund was named Church Historian. The following year he was called to the First Presidency, and in 1902 four men already working on historical assignments were named assistant Church historians: Andrew Jenson, Orson F. Whitney, A. Milton Musser, and B. H. Roberts. Andrew Jenson was an avid compiler of historical sketches, manuscript histories, and chronologies, and in 1899 he brought out a second edition of his popular *Church Chronology*. Unlike the first edition, this volume was sponsored by the Church and its sale was urged through circular letters to local authorities. In May 1901 President Joseph F. Smith appointed B. H. Roberts to edit Joseph Smith's *History of the Church* for republication. Meanwhile, Elder Roberts's own study of the Missouri persecutions was compiled from a series of *Contributor* articles of fifteen years earlier and issued as a book in 1900. Orson F. Whitney was also making an important contribution with his well-known four-volume *History of Utah*, published comercially between 1892 and 1904, and John Henry Evans published a popular *History of the Church* for the youth in 1905. This spurt of historical activity represented an important commitment to helping the Saints become acquainted with their heritage.

The Church was also interested in recording contemporary history, and around the turn of the century a major program was inaugurated to improve record keeping. Instructions were sent to wards and stakes detailing the kinds of records that should be kept. Individual members were encouraged to trace their priesthood authority and keep their own record of ordinances and ordinations. Missionaries were instructed to keep diaries, and members who owned pioneer diaries or manuscripts were urged to lend them to the Church for copying or to donate them for safekeeping. "We want to make you all historians," said Andrew Jenson.

In 1903 President Joseph F. Smith began to authorize the purchase of Church historic sites. Two of these acquisitions, the Solomon Mack homestead in Vermont and Carthage Jail in Illinois, marked the beginning and the end of the life of Joseph Smith the Prophet. Purchase of a twenty-five-acre parcel adjacent to the Independence Temple lot in Missouri underscored continuing Latter-day Saint interest in the Center Place of Zion. Along with the opening of the first Bureau of Information in 1902, these purchases marked the beginning of a new educational and proselyting thrust through the management and interpretation of historic sites.

Because the birthplace of the Prophet held special significance for the Latter-day Saints, Junius F. Wells was asked to direct the construction of a memorial cottage around the hearthstone of the original Mack family home. He also supervised the hauling of fifty tons of native stone for an impressive granite monument on the site. The memorial's thirty-eight-and-one-half-foot central spire, a foot for each year of Joseph Smith's life, was described by the quarryman as "the largest polished shaft in America." Donations from members helped pay for the project, and both the cottage and the monument were completed for the hundredth anniversary of Joseph Smith's birth, December 23, 1905. Church leaders did not intend to reconstruct the historic setting in which Joseph Smith was born. Rather, the spot became an impressive memorial to the young man from New England whom Saints around the world revered as the founder of their faith.

Church Finance in a Time of Transition

At the turn of the century the Church was still concerned about its heavy financial indebtedness. In response to this economic concern, in 1899 President Snow initiated a retrenchment policy designed to help balance income and expenditures. The Church stopped borrowing for investments, consolidated its debts through a million-dollar bond issue, sold its controlling interest in a number of businesses, and launched a major campaign that stressed a new dedication to the principle of tithe paying—"the Lord's law of revenue."

Remembering the failure of his predecessor to sell Church bonds in the East, President Lorenzo Snow determined that the Church should borrow money "among ourselves" rather than "go into the world." Two local bond issues of $500,000 were both purchased quickly. President Snow also established an annual "sinking fund" which would accumulate until the debt was paid. Half the bonds were redeemed in December 1903 and the balance three years later.

To help relieve financial pressures, the Church continued to reduce its involvement in business investments, though it did retain control of some businesses and a minority interest in other enterprises it had promoted. In addition, in 1899 the Church regained control of the daily *Deseret News* and reinstated Charles W. Penrose as editor. Subscriptions increased by nearly seven thousand in one year and the newspaper business became profitable. The Deseret News Bookstore, predecessor of the Deseret Book Company, was purchased a year later from the Cannon family. The Church also began a new business in 1905 when President Smith encouraged formation of the Beneficial Life Insurance Company. Within five years this enterprise became a major Utah financial institution, with the Church holding controlling interest.

During this period of returning prosperity special emphasis was laid not only on getting the Church out of debt but also on the evils of individual indebtedness. The simple formula, "get out of debt," was stressed again and again. In addition, Church leaders advocated a diversified regional economy, although they reemphasized the value of agriculture as a vocation. They warned the Saints against flocking to overcrowded cities where day laborers and office workers were severely affected by times of depression and unemployment.

At the same time many young families were leaving Utah cities and marginal farmlands after becoming discouraged with the urban job market or poor agricultural prospects. They headed for new colonies in the Big Horn Basin, Wyoming; Alberta, Canada; Grande Ronde Valley, Oregon; and southern Arizona. "The days of colonizing by his people are by no means past," said Elder Abraham O. Woodruff, who until his death in 1904 directed the final organized Mormon settlement efforts. The Saints cautioned against joining the outward movement too hurriedly, without the counsel of local priesthood leaders, and those who did leave were urged to gather in designated colonies. The strength of the Church lay partly in its communities, and if the Saints became too scattered, the sense of community could diminish.

The Church's unsettled financial conditions during the raid and the depression of the 1890s had led to a great decline in tithe paying. In 1899, therefore, Church leaders saw the opportunity to achieve a spiritual reform and simultaneously help deliver the Church from financial bondage. At the April conference no fewer than seven speakers mentioned the subject, although official inauguration of the reform was announced by President Snow in May.

The aged Mormon leader was on a preaching tour in southern Utah, where a severe drouth was causing great concern for the future. At a special conference in St. George he suddenly preached on a topic he had seldom mentioned before. "The Lord requires me to say something to you," he said. "The word of the Lord to you is not anything new; it is simply this: The time has now come for every Latter-day Saint . . . to do the will of the Lord and pay his tithing in full." He then made a dramatic promise to the people of southern Utah that if they would pay an honest tithe they would be blessed with rain and a satisfactory harvest.

This began the reform. Journeying northward, President Snow preached tithing everywhere, and in June the annual conference of the Mutual Improvement Association voted to accept the new emphasis as "the present word and will of the Lord unto us."

The tithing reform caught hold throughout the Church. Southern Utah got its rain and a reasonable harvest. For the next two years general conferences resounded with the tithing message, and local priesthood leaders soon reported satisfying progress. The percentage of full tithe payers rose dramatically, and President Snow remarked with satisfaction that it was "a reformation . . . that is perfectly marvelous."

Also changing was the ratio of cash to tithing paid in kind. Cash accounted for two-thirds of the tithing receipts in 1901, a significant change from 1890 when about two-thirds was paid in produce and livestock.

An increase in the payment of tithing plus better returns on business investments made it possible for the Church to wrest itself free from debt. It was a proud day for President Joseph F. Smith when he could announce in general conference in April 1907, "Today the Church of Jesus Christ of Latter-day Saints owes not a dollar that it cannot pay at once. At last we are in a position that we can pay as we go."

Social and Humanitarian Concerns

The turn of the century ushered in a complex period in America often called the Progressive Era. Progressives were concerned with reform in American politics, economic life, and

Riverdale Ward, Weber Stake, early twentieth century. This little rock chapel was typical of chapels in many Mormon communities in the nineteenth and early twentieth centuries. (Church Archives)

social institutions, and generally believed that both national and local governments must broaden the scope of their activities to bring about needed reform. In the social realm, reformers looked with dismay at the evils of crowded cities which seemed to foster poverty, crime, ill health, and general lack of opportunity for the underprivileged.

The Church, too, was concerned with the social ills of society in the changing world of the early twentieth century. In general, however, it did not counsel its members to become involved with the active reform groups that were attracting national followings, though some prominent members did participate. The ideal was to work on improving individuals who would then improve society. Later the Church would espouse a few nationally organized reform movements such as prohibition and the anti-cigarette movement, but in the first few years of the new century its social and humanitarian efforts were concerned with emergency welfare and health care, family relationships, and wholesome activities for youth.

The humanitarian impulse of the Church was demonstrated in 1906 when it sent shipments of food and supplies to aid those left homeless in the huge San Francisco earthquake and fire of 1906. The Relief Society sent flour, and wards contributed food, clothing, and quilts, some of which were collected at benefit concerts. Members also contributed aid to the families of 200 miners killed in eastern Utah's Scofield mine explosion of 1900, and when word came of famine in China the Relief Society contributed a carload of flour. The Latter-day Saints were at last in a position to look beyond their own needs in times of tragedy and misfortune.

Health care was a traditional concern of the Latter-day Saints. It was most visibly expressed during this period in the construction of the Groves LDS Hospital in Salt Lake City. It was built with a donation of $25,000 from the estate of Dr. William S. Groves, a $10,000 donation from the Fifteenth Ward in Salt Lake City, and the balance of $175,000 from general church funds. Opened in 1905, it was the first modern hospital built by the Church and served many families in the Intermountain West. At the same time, the Church counseled its members on personal health care, warning them against unproven patent medicines and other products of medical quackery.

One of the most debated questions of the day was that of vaccination for smallpox, and after a mild epidemic in 1900-1901 it became a major public issue in Utah. When school children were required by the State Board of Health to be vaccinated, strong protests arose throughout the state. The Church became involved because the *Deseret News* took an editorial stand against compulsory vaccination. The First Presidency, however, issued a statement recommending voluntary vaccination, and this approach eventually became Utah law.

The general life-style of the time was of special concern, for changing conditions seemed to pose threats to the family life so important to Mormon culture. Young people had more leisure, and many who left the farms and headed for the cities found themselves in a new and unfamiliar environment that led to many forms of self-indulgence. In addition, the worldly trend toward small families, often achieved by birth control or abortion, worried Church leaders. This led to many sermons and much advice in the early twentieth century that sounds little different from that heard in the last quarter of the century. Youth were encouraged to dress modestly, marry within the Church, and avoid any temptation to postpone the responsibilities of marriage and children. Parents were reminded that teaching the gospel was primarily *their* responsibility, not that of the auxiliaries, and they were encouraged to set aside regular times for family activity.

In addition, the Church paid increasing attention to sponsoring appropriate youth activities. The ward was the center of the Mormon community, and ward recreation committees began to plan youth activities more regularly than before. Leaders urged young people to remain aloof from Sunday sports, pool halls, card games, and non-LDS dance halls, and actively encouraged wholesome activities such as theatricals, picnics, concerts, dances, team sports, music, and properly chaperoned excursions. Summer youth conferences and field days organized by the MIA included excursions to recreation resorts. Church-sponsored activity for the youth had come a long way from the Retrenchment Associations of a quarter of a century earlier.

Educational Adjustments

An expanded commitment to education, both secular and religious, characterized these years of transition, as funds for Church schools became the fastest growing portion of the Church budget. It had become compulsory for Utah children to attend schools; as a result, free public elementary schools had become available in most communities. The Church then moved out of the elementary school program, and its academies began to offer high school training. Public high schools were beginning to grow in Utah, but for several years the academies offered the only secondary training available in many communities.

As the Church moved out of elementary education, the religion class program was expanded. Often these classes were held in public school buildings. In 1905, in response to criticism, the First Presidency advised that they move elsewhere. Not all members enthusiastically supported religion classes, saying they duplicated the Primary, but by 1908 some thirty thousand Latter-day Saint students were enrolled in religion classes.

At the college level, the greatest need was for the training of teachers. The Church was especially concerned that its own young people be trained as teachers so they could take their place in the public schools and retain some Latter-day Saint influence on training of youth. Brigham Young Academy at Provo, therefore, began to move slowly in the direction of providing a better normal course (teacher training) as it advanced from a secondary school curriculum to higher education. In addition, the Brigham Young College at Logan and the Latter-day Saints' College in Salt Lake City also began to teach college courses, though all three remained basically secondary schools. The Salt Lake school expanded its offerings in 1902 and became one of the largest schools of business in the intermountain area. Under a new name, Latter-day Saints' University, and with a new campus on part of the block east of Temple Square, it served as the principal Church-owned institution of higher education until 1907, when that honor went to the school that specialized in teacher education—Brigham Young University.

In the realm of teacher training, the new century opened with a contest between the University of Utah and Brigham Young Academy. Some University of Utah supporters believed the academy should not compete with the state university, and even suggested that it be closed. A series of discussions between Church leaders and university officials were held in 1900 and 1901. Because of financial difficulties, for a time Church leaders seemed almost persuaded to close the Provo academy. In the end, the Church decided to maintain its position, and in 1903 the name of the academy was changed to Brigham Young University. The Church remained in the business of teacher education and soon expanded into other college- and university-level education.

Expanding Horizons: The Church's Worldwide Mission

As the pioneer era ended with the turn of the century, President Lorenzo Snow became particularly concerned with the work of the apostles. He felt they were spending too much time dealing with affairs just as easily handled by local officers. It was the business of the apostles and the seventies, he said, "by the appointment of the Almighty, to look after the interests of the world," and he instructed local leaders to depend less upon the top authorities. The commission given the apostles was to see that the gospel was preached throughout the world, in preparation for the approaching Millennium.

Under President Snow's prodding, the Twelve began to expand their horizons. An early step was the opening of a mission in Japan in 1901, under the direction of Elder Heber J. Grant and a few handpicked associates. "The Lord has not revealed to me that they will succeed," said the President at a farewell reception, "but he has shown me positively that it is their duty to go." The enthusiasm of the missionaries was soon dampened as they grappled with a new and difficult language and a culture they did not understand, but at least the mission was a beginning in a renewed effort to fill the earth with the gospel. Elder Grant soon returned, but one of the missionaries accompanying him, Alma O. Taylor, remained in Japan for nine years and translated the Book of Mormon into Japanese.

This was the only new mission established in these early years of the new century, but it did not exhaust the possibilities. "The eyes of the Twelve have been roaming over the habitable globe," said Brigham Young, Jr., in 1901, "and they have looked upon Turkey, Austria, Russia, and especially South America. . . . As Brother Heber J. Grant has gone, so others will go when the Spirit indicates the place and the time."[3] The mission to Mexico was reopened in 1901 as an anticipated first step into Latin America, and two years later Mormon elders returned to South Africa after an absence of nearly forty years. But in these areas, too, there were difficulties and little success. In Mexico, Elder Ammon M. Tenney was able to reestablish several former branches.

At the same time, the Church strengthened established missions by contributing funds for meetinghouses and mission headquarters. This helped ensure permanent branches and supported the policy of discouraging emigration to Utah. "We desire it distinctly understood," said President Smith in 1903, "that 'Mormonism,' as it is called, has come to the world to stay."

The missionary force declined slightly in the first few years of the century, and the nature of the missionaries changed. It was becoming more common in the late nineteenth century for young, unmarried men to be called, and by the 1890s they formed the bulk of the missionaries. The first lady missionaries were called in 1898. They were relatively few in number, 27 out of 866 missionaries called in 1902, but it quickly became apparent to mission presidents that the sisters were as effective in the work as the elders.

---

[3]*Conference Report*, October 1901, p. 66.

*Sunday School conducted by missionaries in Sapporo, Japan, about 1907.
Seated in the foreground are Elders Justus B. Seely and J. Preston Cutler.
(Church Archives)*

Most of the new missionaries were better prepared than their
predecessors. Before being called they were carefully interviewed,
to identify health problems and to attest to spiritual preparation,
and after 1899 increasing numbers of them had taken the special
missionary training courses offered at six academies and colleges in
Utah and Arizona.

The missionaries were introduced to proselyting techniques
that differed in some ways from those used by their fathers and
grandfathers. They no longer relied as heavily on street meetings
or on traveling without purse or scrip, because legal restrictions
had arisen against both. On the other hand, they distributed literature as their fathers had done, relying principally on a new series of
tracts, *Rays of Living Light*, written by Charles W. Penrose. The
effectiveness of missionary work varied greatly from place to place.
In the United States the greatest success was in the Midwest; in
Europe, it was in Great Britain and Scandinavia.

Administrative Adjustments and Refinements

In his message admonishing the apostles to remember their

calling as "special witnesses unto the nations of the earth," Lorenzo Snow gave a parallel charge to local presiding officers.
Henceforth they would receive less help from the General Authorities. They were urged to "be lively" in their own "wonderful
responsibility" of working with the Saints, a timely plea in an age
when "reform" was on every tongue. The reawakening soon
extended from the highest to the lowest priesthood offices and into
the auxiliaries.

Despite his interest in relieving General Authorities of peripheral responsibilities, President Joseph F. Smith considered the
Patriarch to the Church an exception. In order to enhance the
prestige and importance of that position, beginning in 1902 Patriarch John Smith was invited to address the general conference.
In addition, his name was added to the fifteen General Authorities
customarily sustained as "prophets, seers, and revelators." President Smith encouraged the Patriarch to travel among the Saints
and believed such action was necessary to give the office the primal
position outlined in the Doctrine and Covenants.

The general move to decentralize priesthood responsibility
had direct implications at the local level, where leaders were given
increased responsibilities. In the process, many former bishoprics
and stake presidencies were released and nineteen new stakes were
created. Thirteen of the new stakes were carved from long-
established units that had become so large they were unwieldy.
Some had memberships of from ten to twenty thousand. The
average stake after the reshaping consisted of five or six thousand
members and about ten wards. Similar action was taken at the
ward level. But the reform went further than mere reorganization.
More clearly than before, stake presidents and ward bishops were
identified as the key links in the jurisdictional chain between
members and General Authorities, and members were counseled to
go to these local officers before taking their problems higher.
Decentralization thus enhanced the importance of local priesthood
leaders. At the same time, bishoprics and quorum presidencies
were given advice on how to function more effectively. They were
to hold regular preparation meetings. They were reminded that
they were administrators, not preachers, and should not make
unauthorized, authoritarian doctrinal pronouncements. Stake high
councils also felt the impact of the reform movement as President
Snow prodded them to go beyond their traditional roles as priest-

hood courts. Soon high councilors were undertaking regular monthly speaking assignments to the wards, a practice that has continued to the present.

These administrative reforms had the desired effect of involving more Saints in local church affairs. Reports from the stakes indicated increased attendance at church, but, more importantly, smaller units allowed bishops and other leaders to give closer attention to individual needs. In October 1907 Elder Francis M. Lyman, president of the Council of the Twelve, reported that decentralization had succeeded and local officers were doing such an effective job of handling affairs in the fifty-five stakes of Zion that appeals to the First Presidency were becoming rare. Though decentralization tended to place members another step from central leaders, the growth in membership made it necessary. It also had the advantage of bringing into activity many more people, enhancing spirituality, and providing important leadership experience to thousands. This attitude toward decentralized responsibility became a permanent feature of church administration.

The organization of new stakes and wards and the slowed pace of construction during the preceding two decades created a pressing need for many new meeting places, and an expanded building program soon characterized the twentieth-century direction of the Church. Church architects introduced some changes in meetinghouse design, began using concrete and steel, and experimented with a variety of styles. Sunday School officers requested that ward meetinghouses include partitioned classrooms in basements or annexes, rather than the curtained dividers commonly used, and ward recreation committees stressed the need for amusement halls. The Relief Societies, meanwhile, continued to build separate halls for their own meetings and granaries for their wheat storage program. In the early years of the twentieth century building proceeded at an unprecedented rate.

Auxiliary Reform

The reform in the auxiliaries started with what Elder Francis M. Lyman called "the re-baptism of Mutual Improvement." Beginning in 1897 the Young Men's Mutual Improvement Association, recognizing the need for many local units to awaken from comparative lethargy, revitalized its program in such a way that other auxiliaries took note and the general reform movement soon became all-inclusive.

In general, the auxiliary reformation exhibited three common trends, though the degree differed from one organization to the other. One tendency was the greater application of contemporary educational methods, as other auxiliaries followed the lead of the Sunday School in structured gospel education. Next, an increasing reliance on central planning developed, strengthening the auxiliaries' general hierarchy. This did not lessen local responsibility, but rechanneled it along lines more clearly determined by general officers. Finally, the auxiliaries began developing a common curriculum based on the standard works and Church history rather than on secular subject matter. In a sense, though each auxiliary maintained separate functions, the result of these common trends was to soften the distinctions between them.

Profiting from the experiences of the Sunday School, by 1903 the Mutual Improvement Associations and the Primary had incorporated graded classwork or departments into their programs. They developed better recruitment policies and demonstrated a new awareness of the need for teacher training activities. There was also an increased use of officers' handbooks, uniform curricula, and centrally prepared lessons. In these matters the authority of the general auxiliary officers was enhanced and the local organizations were drawn more tightly under their direction.

The reform of the young men's organization included several innovations. The MIA missionary program was abandoned after 1903 because local workers were relying too heavily on the missionaries to perform their own administrative duties. A new training program for local leaders had been introduced in 1900. This was the annual stake convention, held jointly each fall with the young women's leaders. The YMMIA developed a religious course of study that replaced the greater variety of topics, both secular and religious, that had been taught earlier. They also began holding opening exercises at each weekly meeting in conjunction with the young women. These and other changes were indicative of the greater degree of churchwide uniformity in the YMMIA. In addition, this organization introduced a new magazine in 1897: the *Improvement Era*. As the official organ of the YMMIA, it consisted of a format designed to uplift young men and inform them on important subjects relating to the gospel and current

*Mutual Improvement Association missionaries, 1899-1900. Seated near the
bottom of the picture are J. Golden Kimball and Heber J. Grant.
(Church Archives)*

affairs. The editor was Joseph F. Smith, whose "Editor's Table"
provided a forum for opinions on pressing religious and social
questions. Associate editor B. H. Roberts's running history of the
Spanish American War and other features kept readers abreast of
world affairs.

    The Young Women's MIA was naturally affected by what
happened to the Young Men, but in 1896 and again in 1902 its
officers soundly rejected a proposal that the two organizations be
merged. They accepted joint preliminary exercises, conferences,
training sessions, and meeting times, but the young ladies wanted
to maintain their independence in other areas. Consolidation, they
said, was too reminiscent of a dating bureau. Reforms in the
YWMIA were similar to those in the young men's organization
and consisted of more uniform direction from the top, a graded
instruction program, and continuation of the *Young Women's
Journal,* which was founded in 1889. The curriculum offered by the
young women included literature, history, physical culture,

physiology, and ethics. Its attractively illustrated journal offered practical help on the arts of homemaking, such as recipes, home furnishings, and sewing, and included mind-expanding features such as poetry, fiction, articles on literature and the arts, and travel features.

The Sunday School also published its own journal, the *Juvenile Instructor,* which was purchased from the Cannon family in 1900. It had been owned and edited by George Q. Cannon since its founding, albeit specifically for the benefit of the Sunday School. As part of the reform movement, the Sunday School attempted to increase its membership and improve the quality of teaching. In some wards it seemed at cross purposes with the MIA, as both vied for the best teachers. The Sunday School, long the leader in adapting educational methods to religious instruction, adopted a system of effectively grouping children in classes by age group, and in 1902 this became standard practice churchwide. About the same time the Sunday School adopted uniform courses of study, based on outlines published by the general officers. A new program of teacher training was introduced in 1902. Stakes began to hold stake "union meetings"—training sessions for teachers under the new stake boards, organized along departmental lines. The most significant innovation, however, was the parents' class, introduced churchwide in 1906 after a successful two-year experiment in Weber and other stakes. Organized initially around discussions of child-rearing, the classes became immediately popular and were the beginning of a regular adult program in the Sunday Schools.

The reform in the Primary was clearly influenced by what was happening in the other auxiliaries and imposed greater uniformity in the Primary programs. This included a strengthening of the central board, graded classwork, and introduction of a uniform, churchwide curriculum. The Primary also developed its own magazine, the *Children's Friend,* which first appeared in January 1902. Originally a magazine for the benefit of Primary teachers, it soon added a section for parents. Once it was in the homes, parents began to pressure Primary leaders to make it useful for children as well. In 1905 the magazine announced its intention to include children among its readers.

The introduction of the Parents' Department in the *Children's Friend* in 1903 was part of a broader program intended to strengthen ties between the auxiliary and the home. Earlier many wards had instituted special mothers' meetings to coordinate teaching between the Primary and the home. These changes demonstrate the Church's involvement in the widespread national interest in child development and its continued commitment to home and family.

The new attention to revitalizing organizations naturally created a few administrative conflicts. The Primary, for example, felt that the week-day religion classes competed with it and proposed an amalgamation. This was not approved. In 1903 the Primary also proposed that it be merged with the MIA. With the upper age-limit for Primary and the lower age-limit for MIA both set at fourteen, some Primary leaders felt the organization functioned as a junior class of the MIA. Certainly it was a "feeder" to the MIA membership, and President Louie B. Felt, at least, believed the organizations would function better if joined. The idea of integrating a junior MIA, however, did not appeal to the leaders of the YMMIA and the YWMIA, and though they cooperated in other things, the proposed merger did not take place.

In 1901 Bathsheba W. Smith became president of the Relief Society and directed the ensuing reforms in that organization. These changes were not as sweeping as those in the other auxiliaries, and the Relief Society tended to retain greater independence of action. The Relief Society existed not just to serve its members and build their spiritual well-being, but also to render public service. It was affiliated with the National Council of Women and participated in such national activities as the women's rights movement. Its quasi-official magazine, the *Woman's Exponent,* reported regularly on national women's activities and other public affairs. After 1900 the activities of the Relief Society turned gradually away from national crusades, though it was still very much involved in local public activities affecting the Saints' well-being.

The Relief Society's reforms were all associated with the Church's changing needs. It attempted to revitalize itself by bringing in younger women and developing new programs to meet their needs. These efforts had encouraging results. In 1905 the Relief Society established an employment bureau to aid the young women who were flocking to cities seeking work. In educational efforts in 1902 the society launched its first eight-month course in nursing, designed to help its members more fully assist the needy sick. The course continued until 1920, with many stakes sending representatives to the successive training sessions. Another new program of 1902 was the mother's class, which became a feature of all the Relief Societies in the Church. Structured to assist in child training, this innovation became the first uniform classwork offered in regular Relief Society meetings and was the forerunner of a broader curriculum that appeared a few years later.

The Relief Society also continued some important older programs. Wheat storage, for example, received continued emphasis and included flour and beans. Another agricultural carry-over from the nineteenth century was the continuation of efforts to raise silkworms. In addition, Latter-day Saint women continued to participate in a few public movements, such as the Mother's Congresses and the peace movement.

Revitalizing the Priesthood Quorums

The priesthood quorums were not immune to the reforming spirit of the age. President Smith looked forward to the time when the priesthood would completely fulfill its proper function and eliminate the need for auxiliaries. At the time the quorums hardly seemed capable of assuming such responsibility, for even though they displayed remarkable brotherhood, they were characterized by a disappointing lack of activity. The key word in reform was "activation," and the major goal as announced by Elder Abraham O. Woodruff in 1900 was "a renewal of interest in all the quorums."

According to Church leaders, only about half of those who had received the priesthood were actively magnifying their callings, and they believed that at least one reason for priesthood inactivity was the growing popularity of fraternal lodges. They complained that membership in such organizations interfered with week-night priesthood meetings and that lodge dues sometimes took precedence over church contributions. In urging priesthood holders not to affiliate with these lodges, Church leaders pointed out that they tended to divide the allegiance of the brethren. The Saints were reminded that "everything necessary for their salvation, both temporal and spiritual," including brotherhood, was to be found within the Kingdom of God. In some cases local auxiliaries excluded members of these societies from leadership positions. Some leaders also questioned the affiliation of some members in

Coalville Tabernacle, dedicated in 1899, is representative of the numerous
fine pieces of architecture erected by the Church in the late nineteenth century.
These distinctive buildings added a special flavor to their communities and
some still stand to help remind the Saints of their heritage. Though
unfinished at the time, this building was the site of the October 1886 general
conference.

radical labor unions, though it was primarily the compulsory nature of certain union memberships that disturbed them.

One way to stimulate activity among the young men of the
Aaronic Priesthood was to encourage them in their obligations to
visit families in the ward. Beginning in 1902 Presiding Bishop
William B. Preston authorized bishops to call Melchizedek Priesthood holders to accompany each priest or teacher on his rounds.
These older men were dubbed "acting priests" and "acting
teachers," for they were acting in the revealed duties of the lesser
priesthood, but they were charged as tutors of the young men. In
earlier years the older men had, themselves, performed these
duties, but now that young men were regularly being ordained to
the priesthood it was important to train them in their duties. This
was only the beginning of a major priesthood reform that

blossomed during the last decade of Joseph F. Smith's presidency.

By 1907, then, the Church had begun to take on a new aura, both publicly and internally. While it was still not widely praised, it had demonstrated its accommodation to some American norms by proving that it had indeed abandoned its misunderstood marriage practices and that its people were loyal to country. Some of its leaders were beginning to gain impressive public acceptance, and Senator Reed Smoot, a member of the Council of the Twelve, was beginning a distinguished career of public service. Economically the Church had shaped its involvement in business to the pattern of the broader American society and, most importantly, was out of debt. In addition, it was anxiously devoting itself to spreading the gospel worldwide, improving its image in the public eye, discovering and promoting its inspiring heritage, and reforming all its programs to meet the challenges of growth and other modern problems.

In 1906 President Joseph F. Smith looked optimistically at the current reforms and the possibility that one day every priesthood council would fully magnify its responsibility. "When that day shall come," he told the Saints, "there will not be so much necessity for work that is now being done by the auxiliary organizations, because it will be done by the regular quorums of the Priesthood. The Lord . . . has made provision in the Church whereby every need may be met and satisfied through the regular organizations of the Priesthood." In the spirit of this hope, the next decade would witness continued internal reform as well as growth and progress in spiritual and economic affairs.

CHAPTER 15

Consolidating for Growth, 1908-1918

At the close of the hearings over the seating of Utah Senator Reed Smoot, President Joseph F. Smith left Salt Lake City for a working vacation in Europe. In part, he took the trip to relax after the strain and harassment of the Senate inquiry, which had visibly fatigued him. He invited his close friend Charles W. Nibley (soon to be named Presiding Bishop) to join a small group of family members for the tour. Wherever they went President Smith met with the Saints in special conferences and shared with them his personal warmth and his insights into gospel topics.

Four years later, in 1910, President Smith returned to Europe and again met with members and missionaries in several countries. He was the first President of the Church to visit Europe while in office, and his personal concern with Church affairs there reflected an increasingly significant attempt to build up permanent organizations outside the American West. During his presidency he also made several visits to the Hawaiian Islands and visited Canada and Mexico. Everywhere he encouraged the faithful to remain in their homelands, even though the full program of the Church was not yet available to them. His intent was to move toward that goal as rapidly as possible, and his travels gave emphasis to the hope for broadening Church influence in the twentieth century.

Economic Policy in a Decade of Prosperity

The last decade of Joseph F. Smith's presidency was one of general prosperity for the United States. This prosperity was shared by the Church, both in its active involvement in business enterprise and in its expenditures for buildings and other improvements.

Most members still lived in Utah, Idaho, and Arizona, where agriculture remained the mainstay of the economy. Sugar was Utah's most viable agricultural industry, and stable prices enabled Mormon sugar beet farmers to reap generous profits. The Church's relationship with this industry typified its new attitude toward economic affairs. The key was no longer cooperative self-sufficiency but, rather, economic cooperation with the world, in which gentile capital was turned to good purposes under commercial arrangements only indirectly involving Church members. The Utah-Idaho Sugar Company, formed in 1907 through the merger of several companies, vigorously expanded its ability to process sugar by establishing many new factories. Church leaders continued to hold influential positions in the new company, even though the Church remained a minority stockholder. Mormon farmers provided most of the raw products, but the key to success was the combination of church and private funding. Most of the investment capital was contributed by Henry O. Havemeyer of the American Sugar Refining Company.

One of the most sharply debated investments was Hotel Utah, an elegant hotel in downtown Salt Lake City promoted directly by the Church. The hotel had been built with space for several small businesses designed to help the area around Temple Square and the Church offices remain a vital part of the city's business district. The Church hoped to attract influential men to that part of town, where they would be close to Temple Square and could be more easily introduced to the Church and its programs.

Some persons criticized the First Presidency for the venture, especially when the Hotel Operating Company, which leased the facility from the Church-backed Utah Hotel Company, opened a bar. Shortly after the hotel opened for business President Smith defended church involvement at the October 1911 general conference. He explained the financial arrangements that made it possible and reminded the congregation that he had worked hard in an unsuccessful attempt to influence Salt Lake City voters to declare the city dry. But since it was not dry, visitors expected "something to wet up with," and if they couldn't get it at Hotel Utah they would stay elsewhere. He also reminded Church members of Joseph Smith's revelation authorizing construction of the Nauvoo House—a hotel to entertain important visitors to the Mormon capital of the early 1840s. This explanation satisfied most members, and Hotel Utah soon became widely known for its first-rate accommodations.

Construction of the Hotel Utah also represented a shift away from President Lorenzo Snow's policy of selling controlling interest in church-founded businesses. After the payment of its bonds released the Church from debt in 1907, the prosperous times that had made this possible made it clear that a conservative investment policy could create a reliable income for the Church in addition to its increasing tithing receipts. The Church resumed control of the Provo Woolen Mills, became the major stockholder in Beneficial Life Insurance Company, and reacquired control of Utah-Idaho Sugar Company in 1914, when federal trustbusters dissolved the Havemeyer monopoly. The Trustee-in-Trust reacquired about one-fourth of the ZCMI stock and maintained its control of the Salt Lake Theatre, Zion's Savings Bank & Trust Company, *Deseret News,* and Deseret News Bookstore, while continuing to hold stock in several other companies. In 1919 the Deseret Sunday School Union Bookstore was merged with the Deseret News Bookstore, and the combined facilities became Deseret Book Company.

The greatest benefit to the Church of such commercial ventures was the realization of income that could be expended to support other important purposes. Some of the Church's income helped subsidize charitable institutions, such as hospitals. In 1913 a wing was added to the Groves' Latter-day Saints Hospital in Salt Lake City, doubling its capacity to 250 beds. In 1915 the Thomas D. Dee Memorial Hospital in Ogden was purchased, an institution that the local stakes had operated for three years.

New Building Programs

From the early years of the Church, the affairs of the First Presidency, the Presiding Bishopric, the Church Historian, and later the auxiliary organizations had been conducted from small, scattered offices. After Utah statehood was achieved, authorities began seriously to consider the need for Church buildings rather than offices. A Central Women's Building was among the first to gain approval. A site was approved in 1901, but later Church leaders decided to consolidate in one building the offices of the women's organizations, the Primary, the Presiding Bishopric, and Young Men's MIA. This move represented closer priesthood super-

"Bishop's Block," Salt Lake City, about 1909. This photograph suggests transition taking place in Utah and the Church at beginning of the twentieth century. Old Deseret Store and Tithing Office, formerly located on the corner, is in last stages of demolition, while behind it the Bishop's Building nears completion. The new building housed the Presiding Bishopric and Church auxiliaries, and the modern architecture suggests the strength and permanence the Church had achieved by this time. In the first stages of construction is the Deseret Gymnasium. New streetcar tracks surround the statue of Brigham Young, sculpted by Cyrus E. Dallin. It was placed at this intersection in 1897, a symbol of the unity between the past and the present. (Utah State Historical Society)

vision of the Relief Society and Young Women's MIA but disappointed those who had contributed toward the separate women's auxiliary building. In 1910 the new Bishop's Building, as the combined facility was called, was completed and dedicated on the block immediately east of the Salt Lake Temple. The same year a recreational facility, the Deseret Gymnasium, was also completed on that block.

Seven years later the five-story Church Office Building was completed at 47 East South Temple. It housed the First Presidency, the Church Historian, and the Genealogical Society library and for the first time provided central offices for the Council of the Twelve, the First Council of the Seventy, and the Patriarch to the Church. To some members the handsome Grecian Ionic-style granite structure with native marble and fine wood interiors seemed unnecessarily lavish, yet it was a symbol of the Church's newfound prosperity and increasing acceptance in the world, and it allowed General Authorities to conduct their affairs in a dignified setting. The attic and basement storage areas provided much-needed archival space for historical records, which had been housed previously in facilities without fire protection.

To make room for these and other new buildings, it had been necessary to raze the old Deseret Store and other structures related to the Presiding Bishop's Office. The removal of the tithing barns and warehouses was particularly significant, for in 1908 the Church ended its general policy of receiving tithing in kind. Cash rather than home produce was rapidly becoming the medium of exchange, and when this change was announced, more than three-fourths of all tithing was being paid in cash. The transition that had begun in the early 1890s was virtually complete.

The change in economic patterns also affected local building programs. Bishop's tithing offices and granaries in local wards fell into disuse, and the bishops were provided offices in ward meetinghouses. Separate Relief Society halls were no longer built, and ward recreation halls were increasingly incorporated into the consolidated ward buildings. For twenty years architects had been experimenting with different styles for ward meetinghouses, and in 1910 the first truly modern Latter-day Saint buildings were constructed. They were largely the work of Harold W. Burton and Hyrum C. Pope, who introduced to the Church the prairie-style architecture of Frank Lloyd Wright, a noticeable contrast to the earlier mixture of Gothic and Classical design. These two men were also selected as architects for new temples in Canada and Hawaii.

The decision to build these first temples outside the continental United States reflected a number of important trends: the acceptance of modern architectural design; the end of a period of indebtedness, which allowed church funds to be committed to such projects; and the de-emphasis on gathering to the Great Basin. Joseph F. Smith had discussed the prospects of a temple in Europe during his travels, but the membership there was not yet strong enough. In Alberta and Hawaii, on the other hand, membership was sufficient to justify temples that would serve broad areas in the American Northwest and in the Pacific. A site for a temple at Cardston was dedicated in July 1913 and construction began soon afterward. President Smith dedicated a site at Laie, on the island of Oahu, during his visit to the Hawaiian Islands in June 1915.

Continuing Challenges to the Public Image

One characteristic of the Progressive Era in the early twentieth century was a public reexamination of most of America's basic economic, political, and social institutions. Especially active were the so-called muckrakers, who spared no efforts in the press to ferret out embarrassing information about illegal and otherwise corrupt business and political practices. Though they often did considerable good in providing the impetus for important reform legislation, such as the Pure Food and Drug Act of 1906, they also produced a great deal of sensationalist literature based on distortion and exaggeration. In this climate the Church, still not widely popular, could hardly escape renewed criticism and a revival of many old charges.

The most direct attack came in the years 1910 and 1911 in such popular magazines as *Pearsons, Everybody's Magazine, McClure's,* and *Cosmopolitan.* Though primarily intending to discredit Senator Reed Smoot, who was easily reelected by the Utah legislature in January 1911, the muckrakers also attacked the Church and continued their articles well beyond the election. A *Cosmopolitan* series entitled "The Viper on the Hearth," by Alfred Henry Lewis, accused the Church of laying plans to subvert the family structure of America and take over the country both politically and economically. It was so vicious that both author and publisher were

This anti-Mormon illustration was one of many in a series of attacks on the Church published in Cosmopolitan Magazine *in 1911. Seldom since then has the Church been the brunt of such distorted imagery in the public press.*

censured by their colleagues. Nevertheless, many newspapers picked up the themes of polygamous living and Mormon domination of politics and economics and joined the dissonant chorus. The net effect was the spread of considerable misinformation about Latter-day Saint life and the reinforcement of negative images of the Church in the United States.

Reports from the magazine campaign in the American muckraking press hit Great Britain during a time of social unrest there. Many conservative political and religious leaders were speaking out against the erosion of Victorian moral standards, and in this they had the sympathy of Latter-day Saints, who themselves denounced trends toward smaller families, abortion, unchastity, and increasing divorce. Ironically, certain crusaders decided to let Mormonism represent the evils of immoral living, and rumors of the survival of plural marriage became a central theme in their lectures, rallies, movies, and novels. A typical plot in the popular novels of Winifred Graham (Cory), for example, followed the trials of the naive British heroine who at the last moment would be rescued from the deceit of a crafty American missionary.

The anti-Mormon crusade in England attracted little general

support except in certain regions in the north and in East Anglia, but emotions in those areas were aroused to such an extent that anti-Mormon rallies turned to violence. Chapels in Birkenhead and Nuneaton were pelted with rocks and mud, a branch leader was tarred and feathered, and missionaries were harassed and asked to leave town. The missionaries were also expelled from Germany and rumors circulated that other European nations were considering sanctions against proselyting.

These hindrances to missionary work had temporary adverse effects. In England, baptisms since 1900 had been double those of the previous decade, with only a 25 percent increase in missionaries. During the renewed anti-Mormon agitation, while the number of missionaries dropped by a third, convert baptisms slid from 963 in 1910 to a low of 363 in 1912.

Church leaders were not reluctant to respond. In Europe the mission president, Rudger Clawson, answered the agitators with letters to sympathetic newspapers. The London *Evening Times* published a response from the First Presidency, in which Church teachings were outlined and policies on emigration and plural marriage explained. Responses were also published in American newspapers, and the April 1911 general conference approved an official statement which received wide circulation in pamphlet form.

A persistent rumor was that plural marriages were continuing in the Church. The First Presidency reminded stake presidents and bishops in 1910 and again four years later of their obligation to try offenders for their membership, since a few Latter-day Saints continued to support the fundamentalist interpretation. Problems continued with the two members of the Council of the Twelve who had resigned from office in 1905; Elder Matthias Cowley was disfellowshipped and Elder John W. Taylor excommunicated. (Both men were later restored to full membership, Elder Cowley in 1936 and Elder Taylor, posthumously, in 1965.) These actions and similar ecclesiastical sanctions at the local level helped demonstrate the Church's continuing commitment to sustaining the law.

At the height of the anti-Mormon magazine crusade the Tabernacle Choir accepted an invitation to sing at the American Land and Irrigation Exposition in New York City in 1911. On behalf of the choir, George D. Pyper arranged four dozen additional concerts in twenty-five cities in the Midwest and East. Critics of the Church circulated flyers and attempted to prevent the appearances in larger cities, but only in Buffalo, New York, were they successful. Elsewhere, the 200-voice "New York Chorus" led by Evan Stephens was received with unabashed praise. The choir sang for ten days at Madison Square Garden and on the return trip presented a special concert in the East Room of the White House for President and Mrs. William Howard Taft and invited guests. Music critics were generally pleased with the quality of these western voices, and their positive comments helped remold the popular image of the Latter-day Saints.

Other efforts that helped counter misinformation included a series of articles on Church history written for *Americana,* a magazine of history, by Elder B. H. Roberts. He initiated the series to correct information published earlier in the magazine, and so pleased were the editors that they invited him to prepare a more thorough explanation of the Church's origins. The magazine devoted much of its space between 1909 and 1915 to the articles, which were later revised, expanded, and republished in book form during the Church centennial as the six-volume *Comprehensive History of the Church.* In April 1911 *Colliers* printed a letter from former President Theodore Roosevelt refuting allegations on Mormon polygamy and charges of secret political deals, and applauding the strength of Mormon families and their adherence to high standards. These comments, and an investigation in Great Britain instigated by Home Minister Winston Churchill to quell unfounded reports there, added voices of influence to the Latter-day Saint plea for a fair hearing and were indicative of better times ahead for the Church in the popular press.

Adjustments in Church Programs

Continuing a process begun earlier, a number of changes characterized the priesthood and auxiliary programs in the last decade of President Smith's administration, demonstrating an increasing concern with the application of spiritual principles in daily life. In its auxiliary programs the Church gave less attention to secular subjects now being taught in the new public high schools and more attention to inculcating higher religious and moral principles into the lives of its members.

One change was seen in the activities of the Melchizedek Priesthood quorums. By 1905 only about one-fourth of the full-time missionaries held the office of seventy; five years later the figure was less than 18 percent. This reflected a trend begun earlier to call younger men on missions and not to ordain them seventies for this service. Nevertheless, the seventies were still looked upon as potential missionaries and those not tied down with obligations were still recommended for missionary work.

Increasingly the seventies were becoming part of stake and ward activities. They were encouraged to serve as home teachers and home missionaries, though the emphasis continued to be on preparation for missionary service. With this in mind the First Council of the Seventy inaugurated a "new movement" focused on gospel study. Beginning in November 1907 seventies quorums began holding weekly meetings on Sunday mornings to study a special manual, *The Seventies Course in Theology,* prepared by Elder B. H. Roberts. Because these meetings conflicted with Sunday School in most wards, bishops were instructed to release seventies from Sunday School work wherever possible. The new program was launched with a general conference of seventies—the first since 1844—and the *Improvement Era* began carrying monthly helps in a special seventies column.

The "new movement" quickly proved successful and led to a general revival of Melchizedek Priesthood activity. Traditional summer vacations from priesthood meetings were eliminated in most stakes, quorum members attended their meetings more faithfully, and the systematic approach to gospel study created lively discussions. The First Presidency soon appointed a Priesthood Committee on Outlines to prepare lesson manuals for all other priesthood quorums. These were introduced in 1909. At that time the seventies agreed to move their meeting back to the traditional Monday night so that the priesthood quorums could meet together in an opening exercise before separating for quorum instruction. The *Improvement Era* was designated the official organ for the priesthood quorums as well as for the Young Men's MIA. In 1914 all Melchizedek Priesthood quorums began studying the same lesson manual. Soon afterward enrollment procedures were simplified so that a person moving into a ward was no longer required to present a written recommend from his former priesthood leader before he could be added to quorum rolls.

The Aaronic Priesthood was also revitalized in an effort to stimulate young men to greater activity and more effectively train them as leaders. It was becoming general policy to ordain them to various offices at specific ages, though as late as 1907 President Joseph F. Smith still felt that their training could be improved. He expressed his concern in April conference:

> The bishops should take especial charge of the lesser priesthood, and train them in the duties of their callings—the priests, teachers and deacons. Our young men should be looked after. The boys, as soon as is prudent, should be called to take part in the lesser priesthood. If it were possible to grade them, from the deacon to the priest, and from the priest upward through all the offices that will eventually devolve upon them, it would be one of the best things that could be done.[1]

In this spirit, Church leaders began more clearly to identify duties for each office so that young men could grow through greater activity. Deacons, for example, were invited to assist in caring for ward cemeteries and meetinghouse grounds, act as ushers, distribute special notices, pump organs at meetings, chop wood for widows, collect fast offerings, and so on. Similar lists gave teachers and priests appropriate opportunities for service. At the same time bishops began a more systematic advancement program. This built up the teachers and priests quorums and greatly reduced the number of over-age deacons in the wards.

The general reform had a direct impact on ward teaching. Districts were reduced in size and more adults were called as ward teachers. Regular visits—summer months included—were stressed and reporting procedures were standardized. These changes increased the ratio of families visited each month from 20 percent in 1911 to 54 percent four years later and 70 percent by 1921.

The net effect of the entire priesthood revitalization movement was to enhance the educational role of priesthood quorums and multiply the number of priesthood-sponsored activities. This pursuit of gospel knowledge and better performance of priesthood duties gave the quorums a new vitality. It was this spark that priesthood leaders had found lacking earlier when they compared quorum work with the activities of auxiliary organizations.

The revival in the Young Men's MIA launched just before the turn of the century had given that organization new responsibility in religious education. Now priesthood quorums were involved in the same work, and both priesthood and the YMMIA

---

[1] *Improvement Era* 10 (May 1907): 545.

were invading a field long dominated by the Sunday School. In effect, the multiplication of programs for studying the gospel created a need for a closer correlation between organizations and led General Authorities to sponsor a series of coordination studies that would continue over the next half century.

One of the most significant results of the priesthood reform movement was the decision to eliminate theological studies from the Mutual Improvement Associations. The youth auxiliaries turned increasingly to music, drama, sports, dance, and other activities, and away from doctrinal classes. The ward recreation committee, which had functioned as an agent of the bishop in controlling amusements within ward boundaries, became an MIA committee, and the MIAs took up the task of providing wholesome entertainment and recreational activities for ward members of all ages.

Week-day programs designed for twelve- and thirteen-year-olds were also reexamined. These age groups had been the responsibility of the Primary Association and religion classes, but many young people in these transitional years attended MIA meetings under an arrangement that allowed them that option. In 1911 the MIA adopted the program of the Boy Scouts of America and two years later tried the national Campfire Girls program. These innovations firmly committed the MIA to serving boys and girls of twelve and thirteen. Scouting met Church needs adequately, but after a year's trial the girls' program was dropped in favor of the Beehive class, an adaptation of the Campfire Girls. The Primary, meantime, dropped its classes for these age groups. These adjustments brought Church programs into closer correlation with secular educational trends, which were eliminating the eight-year elementary schools in favor of junior high schools catering to the special needs of the early teens.

The Relief Society was the last auxiliary to adopt standardized lessons after the Sunday School curriculum pattern, and that decision became effective in 1914. For twelve years the Relief Society had offered a mothers' class, though the lessons on child rearing were prepared independently in each stake to meet local interests and needs. Occasional lectures on other topics paved the way for a definite educational offering, organized around a four-week lesson format, that filled a vacuum created when the Young Women's MIA dropped its study of secular subject matter. The

In 1911 the Church adopted the Boy Scout movement as an official part of its program. (Church Archives)

new lessons were published first in a monthly *Bulletin* and, commencing in 1915, in the *Relief Society Magazine*, which replaced the independently owned *Woman's Exponent* as the official Relief Society organ. Under the new class schedule one week in each month was set aside for a work and business meeting, another for theology lessons and testimony bearing, a third for genealogy and literature or art, and a fourth for home economics. This pattern in Relief Society classwork has continued, with some variations, since that time.

Other evidences of uniformity appeared in the women's auxiliary between 1914 and 1916. Stake board and union meetings were introduced, ward Relief Society meetings were moved to a uniform Tuesday schedule, a *Circular of Instructions* was issued, record books were made uniform, and visiting teachers were provided with standard messages. At the same time, the Relief Society did not forget its concern for the charitable needs of members. In 1913 it opened a boarding home for working girls who came to Salt Lake City from rural areas with no relatives or friends to take them in. This home continued for nearly eight years until it was replaced by the Young Women's Mutual Improvement Association's boardinghouse in the Beehive House. The Relief Society also operated an employment office, adoption services, and a clearing house for Latter-day Saint transients.

The inclusion of a regular genealogy lesson in the Relief Society curriculum in 1914 and an optional course along similar lines as much as seven years earlier signaled a broadening interest in educating members in genealogical research. The initiative in this educational effort centered in the women's committee of the Genealogical Society. Beginning about 1907 this committee sponsored a series of lessons on genealogy taught by Susa Young Gates at the Lion House. This led to written lessons, which were published in 1912, but in the meantime, requests for the classes came from many stakes outside the Salt Lake area. The society sponsored union meetings or conventions in several locations to fill the need.

In 1909 Joseph Fielding Smith, secretary of the Genealogical Society, and Bishop Joseph Christensen visited genealogical societies in the eastern United States to study their libraries and programs. In a report of their findings to Genealogical Society president Anthon H. Lund they suggested the need for a magazine, and this proposal was approved. Launched in 1910 as a quarterly, the *Utah Genealogical and Historical Magazine* published articles on research helps, family pedigrees, and local history. The publication, which continued until 1940, was important to the public image of the society, which claimed 667 members and a library of about sixteen hundred books. Another boost given the work of the society was the designation in 1912 of an annual Genealogy Sunday. Sacrament meetings in all the wards considered the doctrinal basis of genealogical and temple work, and the practice continued through the 1930s as a reminder to the Saints of their obligations. All these efforts increased activities in genealogical research, and in the temples several endowment sessions were scheduled each day, where before only one had been conducted.

Elaborations on Doctrine

Publication of a genealogical magazine and of articles on related subjects in other Church magazines, scriptural studies in auxiliary classes, discussions on man's place in the world, and articles on Joseph Smith and the Book of Abraham, all helped create a

growing interest among members in theological discussions on the
plan of salvation. It was appropriate that in this setting two important doctrinal statements illuminated and amplified some important teachings of the Church.

The first was in an official doctrinal exposition issued on June
20, 1916, by the First Presidency and the Council of the Twelve.
The precise circumstances leading to the statement are not known,
but a contributing factor may have been a widely circulated anti-
Mormon pamphlet that misrepresented official Church doctrine
on the identities of Jesus and Adam. Furthermore, some confusion
existed among the Saints over the use of the term "Father" in
scripture, especially in view of the Latter-day Saint teaching that
Jesus Christ was the Creator of the earth and the Jehovah of the
Old Testament.

In their exposition, "The Father and the Son," the General
Authorities noted that the term "father" was used in four different
ways in scripture: referring to God as the literal parent of the
spirits of all men, to Jesus as Creator or Father of the earth, to
Jesus as the father of those who abide in his gospel, and to Jesus as
one invested with the authority of the Father while on earth.
Widely published as an authoritative pronouncement on doctrine,
this clarifying statement has taken its place among the important
documents of the Church. To help lessen confusion over the nature
of the Godhead, the "Lectures on Faith," which contained ideas on
the Holy Ghost no longer consistent with Church understanding,
were eliminated from the Doctrine and Covenants after 1921.

A second important doctrinal statement came in a document
entitled "Vision of the Redemption of the Dead." On October 3,
1918, just six weeks before his death, President Joseph F. Smith
was sitting in his room pondering the scriptures related to the
atonement of Christ. He turned to Peter's discussion and was especially impressed with those verses which told of the Savior preaching to the "spirits in prison" during the three days that his physical body lay in the tomb. "For this cause was the gospel preached
also to them that are dead," he read, "that they might be judged
according to men in the flesh, but live according to God in the
spirit."[2] Then, said President Smith, "As I pondered over these
things which are written, the eyes of my understanding were

---

[2]See 1 Peter 3:18-20; 4:6.

opened, and the Spirit of the Lord rested upon me, and I saw the hosts of the dead, both small and great."

In the manifestation that followed, President Smith saw the Savior during his visit to the spirits of the dead. He perceived that the Savior did not himself preach to those who had rejected the truth during their earthly lives, but organized missionaries from among the spirits of the righteous. President Smith was also given to understand that since that time missionary work had continually been conducted in the spirit world and that faithful elders of the modern era who had died were participating in that important work. He had the experience recorded on the last day of October; it was submitted to the other General Authorities, who unanimously accepted it. It was published in the December 1918 issue of the *Improvement Era,* giving the Saints new insight into the nature of missionary activities in the spirit world and a fresh incentive to do temple work on behalf of the dead. In April 1976 it was added to the Pearl of Great Price.

The Challenge of Secular Education

During the last years of President Smith's administration, the Church continued to adjust to the complex challenges of secular education. With the continued growth of public schools, it became increasingly clear that members could no longer afford to support two competing systems. By 1910 the Church had largely vacated the field of elementary education. Its basic concern was that students receive religious instruction along with their secular training, and this was provided for elementary school students in religion classes and the Primary.

The Church continued to operate its academies in various stakes, and in Utah these academies accommodated about half the secondary school students. An amendment to the Utah Constitution in 1911, however, paved the way for better financing of a statewide public high school system, and the Church soon began to reevaluate its policy. It was unwilling to give up the academies until an alternative way could be found to provide religious instruction. The result was a new experiment in religious education that would have far-reaching consequences for the Church.

In 1912 Church leaders persuaded the Granite School District in Salt Lake City to approve the establishment of an experimental LDS seminary near Granite High School. There religious instruction would be offered to high school students on a voluntary basis, with "released time" being granted by the school. If successful, such seminaries could provide religious training for LDS students at a fraction of the cost of maintaining regular church schools. Seminary classes began that fall and by the end of the decade had spread to other schools.

As the seminary program continued, the Church worked in close cooperation with state education officials, and in January 1916 the state board of education granted limited high school credit for released-time classes in Bible history and literature. This provided an important boon to seminary enrollment.

In the meantime, the state superintendent of public instruction discussed state concerns with the Church board of education and urged the Church to withdraw completely from secondary schools. The money saved, he suggested, could be used to establish good normal schools for teacher training, a seriously growing need in the state of Utah.

The Church was already sympathetic with the idea of better teacher training and especially concerned that public school teachers be well prepared in their academic subjects and also in tune with the spiritual and moral ideals of the Church. As a result, as the Church considered the elimination of its Utah academies, it designated several for continuation, not as high schools but as teacher training institutions. In the years 1916-18 Dixie, Snow, and Weber academies became normal schools and joined Brigham Young University, Brigham Young College at Logan, and the Latter-day Saint University in Salt Lake City in offering some college courses along with high school work.

Brigham Young University's expanding program in teacher training led the Church board of education to designate it as the official Church normal school. BYU officials also wanted to become the official Church university, and in anticipation of this, they were already planning a new administration building: the $100,000 Karl G. Maeser Memorial Building soon to be erected on a new campus on Temple Hill in Provo. They were competing for the honor with Latter-day Saints University in Salt Lake City, which early in the century had added three new buildings and had expanded its offerings in business, mechanical arts, and domestic sciences. Church leaders ultimately reasoned that there was no need to compete with the University of Utah in Salt Lake City, and BYU was named as the major Church school. The Latter-day Saint University soon dropped all except its commercial, business, and music courses, and these later were separated in order to create the LDS Business College and the McCune School of Music. Brigham Young College at Logan, meanwhile, de-emphasized its teacher training to specialize in liberal arts and "practical subjects"; the Provo school began to concentrate heavily on becoming an excellent college for the training of teachers.

The adjustments to a secular school system for Utah were not made without criticism. The president of the Presbyterian West-minster College in Salt Lake City, for example, disapproved of the close cooperation between church and state during this transitional period. He particularly disliked the decision to train Utah school teachers at the University of Utah and Mormon schools, and preferred that the state import well-trained teachers. For im-mediate needs, however, this was impractical.

President George H. Brimhall immediately launched a concerted effort to enlarge Brigham Young University and enhance its prestige. Within a year enrollment doubled, and fund-raising campaigns moved toward construction of the planned new building. More significantly he added to the faculty four professors who had received their training at Harvard, Chicago, Cornell, and the University of California. Henry Peterson became head of the education department, his brother Joseph taught psychology, Ralph Chamberlin headed biology, and his brother William taught ancient languages and philosophy. These men actively worked to enhance the image of BYU by providing greater in-tellectual challenges to students.

The new teachers were encouraged in their activities by the university administration, but soon questions were raised about their religious orthodoxy. The result was an important reflection of the uncomfortable problems often faced when religious teachings appear to conflict with the learning of the secular world. At the heart of the issue were two important trends in secular learning: "higher criticism" and the teaching of the theory of organic evolu-tion. Higher criticism was an approach to Bible study that went beyond simply trying to determine the accuracy of the text. Scholars also asked where the authors of the texts acquired their ideas in the first place, and the role that tradition, environment, and other influences may have had on the development of their writings. For some people this raised questions about the inspiration and literal truth of the scriptures.

All four men taught openly the theory of organic evolution and accepted the principles of higher criticism; to them these ideas did not conflict with the fundamentals of the gospel. They were not the first such teachers at BYU, but their effectiveness stirred up unusual interest among the students and caused concern among many people in the community. The controversy came to a head when stake presidents began complaining that students were becoming disturbed, and the professors were charged with raising doubts concerning the historical accuracy of certain portions of the Old Testament.

Horace H. Cummings, Church superintendent of schools, initially supported the professors, but he concluded late in 1910 that the matter should be brought before the Church board of education. He visited the campus and encouraged the teachers to avoid dogmatic presentations of views that some students found inharmonious with their understanding of the gospel. His report was followed by an investigation by the board, a hearing at which the teachers were quizzed on the charges against them, and a final decision to dismiss the men. Undoubtedly the professors had presented their views too dogmatically, and it was difficult for many students to distinguish between fact and opinion.

The real issue, it seems, was not the validity of the theory of evolution, but the dogmatism with which it was taught. Officially the Church took no position on the question, but authorities felt that it simply should not be taught as doctrine on BYU campus. In April 1911 President Joseph F. Smith explained the decision in an editorial. "In reaching the conclusion that evolution would best be left out of discussions in our Church schools," he said, "we are deciding a question of propriety and not undertaking to say how much of evolution is true or how much false." He also warned against speculation on the manner of the creation, for too much erudite speculation could, he felt, lead to a "theological scholastic aristocracy in the Church, and we should therefore not enjoy the brotherhood that now is, or should be common to rich and poor, learned and unlearned among the Saints."[3] Those able to harmo-

---

[3]*Instructor* 46 (April 1911): 209.

nize in their own minds scientific findings with Church teachings were free to do so, but they were not to push their view upon students who were unprepared for the challenge and could not perceive the harmony.

During these same years the Church turned to some of its best-trained minds for help in explaining the gospel to members. A number of capable scholars produced studies that survived the period to become important Church works. One was James E. Talmage, whose book *A Study of the Articles of Faith* was published in 1899 under the auspices of the First Presidency. It has gone through more than fifty editions and still stands as one of the most widely read doctrinal works in the Church. Talmage also published other works, such as *The House of the Lord* (1912) and *Jesus the Christ* (1915), which remain well known. Other important books of the period included John A. Widtsoe's *A Rational Theology* (1915) and David O. McKay's *Ancient Apostles* (1918), both originally prepared as lesson manuals. These men were avid students of the gospel as well as the learning of the world; their books, approved for general Church reading, demonstrated an ability to combine the best of both these areas.

Political Issues in the Progressive Era

In its 1907 "Address to the World" the Church affirmed its

The Maori Agricultural College, near Hastings, New Zealand, represented the Church's continuing interest in education for its members in the early twentieth century. (Church Archives)

commitment "to the doctrine of the separation of church and state; the non-interference of church authority in political matters; and the absolute freedom and independence of the individual in the performance of his political duties."[4] The Church was clearly committed to the elimination of ecclesiastical influence in political affairs, but in the next half dozen years some political issues arose that it found difficult to avoid. In some cases it was simply because Church leaders, as individuals, felt strongly enough to speak out, while in other cases it seemed that certain fundamental principles were involved.

One problem was the continuing political influence of the anti-Mormon American party, which still controlled the politics of Salt Lake City. So long as that party made politics a religious issue, some Church leaders could hardly avoid it. In 1911, however, the party's strength collapsed, and about the same time the *Salt Lake Tribune* discontinued its harsh editorial voice against the Church and against Senator Reed Smoot. The most open surviving political hostility was at an end.

Another issue centered around President Joseph F. Smith's personal endorsement of William Howard Taft as the Republican candidate for the American presidency in 1912. It was a mild endorsement at best, but critics reacted strongly. Their main complaint was that his endorsement had been printed in Church publications and would therefore unduly influence members who gave special credence to the political statements of their leaders made in a religious context. President Smith quickly issued a second statement emphasizing that his published editorial was merely an expression of his personal views. The discussion carried over into the general conference of October 1912, when various leaders expressed views concerning the importance of exercising freedom in political judgments but also of relying on prayer to help make those judgments.

One of the most intense political issues of the Progressive Era was prohibition, and here the Church faced a dilemma. There was no question that it opposed the sale and use of alcoholic beverages, but there was a question as to which of three governmental approaches, if any, it should support: a national prohibition

---

[4]The entire "Address to the World" may be found in Clark, *Messages of the First Presidency,* 4:143-55.

amendment, state prohibition laws, or state laws that allowed local option for each community. Both President Smith and Senator Smoot initially supported local option. They were aware that if the Church officially campaigned for a statewide prohibition law, it would run the risk of alienating many of the senator's supporters in his own party and perhaps of losing his seat in the Senate. In addition, when the Church had so recently been accused of controlling politics to its own ends, they did not want it to appear that a prohibition law was simply another religious bill being pushed through the state legislature. With the support of Senator Smoot, therefore, a state prohibition bill was defeated in 1909, and later Governor William Spry, a valiant member of the Church, vetoed similar bills.

Not all Church leaders agreed, however, and some of them, acting as individual citizens, did all they could to bring about total prohibition. Elder Heber J. Grant, especially, was active in the movement, and he was supported in his campaign by Elders George Albert Smith and David O. McKay. In 1911 a local option bill passed and these men joined in urging all Utah communities to eliminate liquor, which to them was only a first step toward mandatory statewide prohibition.

In 1916 President Smith threw the full support of the Church behind statewide prohibition. By then he had reached the conclusion that the question was of national import and one in which the Church must participate. Prohibition now appeared as planks in both national party platforms. General conference speakers pleaded for passage, the MIA adopted a theme calling for state and national prohibition, and the *Improvement Era* lent direct support to the campaign. In August 1917 Utah became the forty-first "dry" state in the Union under a bill signed by the state's first non-Mormon governor, Democrat Simon Bamberger. In 1919 the national prohibition amendment passed. Although they had disagreed on the methods for achieving that result, Church officials were uniformly pleased with the outcome of the prohibition movement. It had been an exercise in both political liberty and brotherhood in pursuit of a common cause.

War and the Saints Abroad

Church involvement in political questions centered in the Mountain West. But as membership increased outside the United

States, Latter-day Saints became increasingly affected by international affairs. Two significant upheavals, the Mexican revolution of 1911-12 and the World War of 1914-18, directly touched members living in other countries and prompted discussion of the Church's attitude toward war.

Latter-day Saint colonies in Mexico were prospering, and a full program of activities was being carried out in the Juarez Stake. Their peace was disrupted, however, with the outbreak of a revolution against the Mexican dictator Porfirio Diaz in 1910, and for the next seven years the political situation remained unsettled. Revolutionary forces under Francisco I. Madero sought military support from the American government and from Latter-day Saint colonists, who were mostly American citizens. But the United States maintained a noninterventionist attitude, and when Church officials declared their intention to remain neutral, the Saints were threatened, robbed, and expelled from their homes and farms, and several were killed.

In 1912, with little advance notice, the Saints were suddenly forced to leave Mexico. Women and children left first on a train for El Paso, Texas, and nearby border towns, and the men followed on horseback shortly afterward. A few Saints disagreed with the decision to leave and returned to their homes in Chihuahua, but most became permanent exiles in the United States. The U.S. Congress granted emergency supplies for all American refugees, and the First Presidency asked Elder Anthony W. Ivins of the Council of the Twelve, a former stake president in Mexico, to handle resettlement plans for the Saints. The Juarez Stake was officially disorganized, freeing officers and members to find new homes elsewhere.

Eventually fewer than half of the Saints returned to their homes in Chihuahua, and none of them were able to reclaim their property in Sonora, though they did receive payment from the Mexican government. A new Mexican constitution adopted in 1917 required that all ministers be native-born Mexicans. This interfered with the reestablishment of missionary work and prevented the return of missionaries as presiding officers in the native branches around Mexico City. During the revolution, mission president Rey L. Pratt maintained contact with local priesthood officers through correspondence. He visited them in 1916 and reorganized the branches under Mexican leaders. American missionaries entered the country in small numbers after 1921, but when the constitution began to be rigidly enforced five years later, they were again deported and the mission business was conducted by mail from headquarters in Los Angeles.

The expulsion of the Latter-day Saints from Mexico was purely political in nature, even though the official Church position was one of neutrality. At the same time, pressures building up in Europe would soon involve members of the Church on both sides of an international conflict. In this case neutrality was no longer possible.

In August 1914 Germany and Austria-Hungary declared war on Serbia, Russia, and France. Britain entered the war that same month when Germany invaded Belgium, but the American president, Woodrow Wilson, declared impartiality in the conflict; his decision to keep the country out of war aided in his successful campaign for reelection in 1916. Church officials in the United States supported their government's decision and urged members to do likewise. At the October 1914 general conference members joined in a special prayer for peace. But American trade with the Allies angered the German government, and submarine attacks on ships carrying American goods and passengers finally brought the United States into the war in 1917.

Missionaries had been evacuated from western Europe in 1914 at the first outbreak of hostilities. Some people were disappointed when the elders, who had presided in branches, left their flocks, but the Church continued to function under local leadership and with native missionaries. The president of the Swiss-German Mission remained in Switzerland during the war, keeping in touch with the Saints by mail and through *Der Stern.* This mission magazine was sent to German members serving in the armed forces of their nation, and until it was restricted by the German government in 1916, it kept members informed of Church news. German membership actually increased from about seventy-five hundred to eight thousand during the war.

A pertinent question raised by the conflict was the attitude of the Church toward members in Germany who fought against the Allied forces. Were these Saints justified in supporting the German monarch in his aggression? In a classic statement reflecting the perplexities of war, President Joseph F. Smith said yes. "Their leaders are to blame, not the people. Those who embrace the gospel are innocent of these things and they ought to be respected by the Latter-day Saints everywhere."[5] As an expression of that respect, American members were encouraged by the First Presidency in 1915 to contribute to a Zion's Emergency War Fund to aid needy members in Europe. The German Saints themselves lent moral support to their branch members in the armed forces by writing letters and sending packages to the soldiers. About seventy-five Saints died in service to the German government.

Latter-day Saints in the United States exhibited a similar patriotism. Church leaders felt it particularly crucial that members support the war effort so critics would not accuse the Church of disloyalty. With the encouragement of the Church, members in Utah oversubscribed their quotas for enlistments, and more than twenty-four thousand donned the uniform of their country. Of these, 544 were killed in service. Latter-day Saints at home contributed generously to the Red Cross and surpassed the goals set for the purchase of Liberty bonds. The Church and its auxiliaries alone bought $1.4 million in bonds, and the Relief Society sold its store of more than two hundred thousand bushels of wheat to the government for wartime use.

One unfortunate problem in the United States was the bitter prejudice sometimes expressed toward German immigrants. The Church looked toward all men as brothers, and President Smith encouraged members in the United States to accept such immigrants on that basis. In his opening address at the April 1917 general conference, as the distinct possibility of American entry into the war loomed, he also spoke on the spirit that Latter-day Saints should manifest in war: "the spirit of humanity, of love, and of peace-making, that even though they may be called into action they will not demolish, override and destroy the principles which we believe in . . . ; peace and good will toward all mankind, though we may be brought into action with the enemy." He encouraged soldiers to serve as "ministers of life and not of death; . . . in the spirit of defending the liberties of mankind rather than for the purpose of destroying the enemy."

The peace the Saints worked and prayed for was achieved in the armistice of November 11, 1918. Eight days later, and only six days after his eightieth birthday, President Joseph F. Smith died.

---

[5]*Conference Report*, April 1917, p. 11.

Though an epidemic of influenza prevented the Church from honoring him with a public funeral, thousands showed their respect as a private funeral cortege proceeded along the city streets to the cemetery. Respected by the Saints, President Smith had endured a life of much public hostility against him and the Church but had lived to see that attitude mellow. He had presided over an important period of transition and had led the Church in marshalling its resources and revitalizing its programs for the challenges ahead.

CHAPTER 16

Change and Continuity in the Postwar Decade, 1919-1930

The Latter-day Saints considered themselves a "peculiar people," and some interesting aspects of their faith were well represented by the man who headed the Church on its hundredth anniversary. Heber Jeddy Grant was born in 1856, a son of Jedediah M. Grant, counselor to Brigham Young, and Rachel R. Ivins. But according to the faith of the Saints he was really the son of Joseph Smith, founder of the Church. His mother had been sealed by proxy to the Prophet and thus, according to Church doctrine, would be the Prophet's wife for eternity. She had married Jedediah Grant for time only, and their only son would thus become the son of the Prophet in eternity. In the minds of the Saints, there was something fittingly symbolic in having a son of the founding prophet serve as the living prophet a hundred years after the Church was organized.

President Grant had other qualities that represented important developments in the history of the Latter-day Saints. He was the first President of the Church born after the exodus from Nauvoo, and thus clearly represented a new generation of Church leadership. Before the Manifesto he had married three women and personally experienced the difficult times involved in changing from the old ways to the new. A successful businessman, he had been instrumental in getting the beet sugar industry on a firm footing in Utah and Idaho, representing the transition from old economics to the new which came with the turn of the century. Politically he was a Democrat, even though most of his associates were Republicans, but he constantly refused to impose his politics on members, demonstrating the Church's efforts to separate itself from partisanship in the twentieth century. At the beginning of the century he had opened missionary work in Japan, foreshadowing the Church's increasing international commitment in the new era. He was literally a man of two centuries who knew he was leading a dynamic church that was becoming more widely appreciated as the new century progressed. But in 1920 he was hardly prepared for the reception he received when he spoke to the Knife and Fork Club of Kansas City, Missouri. He arrived thinking that he would be called upon to defend his faith before critics. Instead, he heard nothing but praise and admiration for the Church.

Between 1918 and 1930 membership grew from less than 500,000 to more than 630,000. The number of organized stakes

President Heber J. Grant inaugurates broadcasting on the Deseret News radio station (later KSL), May 6, 1922. (Church Archives)

increased from 79 to 104, yet 20 percent of the membership still lived outside the stakes, compared with 18 percent in 1919. Progress was also seen in the continuing attention given the roles of priesthood auxiliaries, changes in the educational program, adjustments in the missionary program, temple construction, and new directions in public relations.

Continuity accompanied change and progress, and President Grant was again the perfect symbol. The traditional emphasis on temperance, sobriety, thrift, tithe paying, and setting an example of Christian living were continued, even enhanced, during his years. The peculiar Latter-day Saint doctrines of priesthood authority, salvation for the dead, and the importance of the restoration of the gospel through Joseph Smith continued to be emphasized. Missionary work was stepped up dramatically. President Grant's commitment to spreading the gospel to all the world was illustrated in a conference address in 1927: "I want to emphasize that we as a people have one supreme thing to do and that is to call upon the world to repent of sin, to come to God. And it is our duty above all others to go forth and proclaim the gospel of the Lord Jesus Christ, the restoration again to the earth of the plan of life and salvation. . . . We have in very deed the pearl of great price."[1]

As President Grant began his administration in 1918, the Church was entering a new era of prosperity and popularity. Bankruptcy and the attacks of politicians and muckrakers were generally things of the past. Early leaders, to be sure, had looked with trepidation at such a time: would it become too easy to be a Latter-day Saint? Would the lack of hardship diminish the unity and faith that had been the result of adversity? In 1918 a Protestant minister described the subtle new challenge as well as anyone. Though opposed to the Church, he was part of the new generation that recognized that Mormonism was no real threat to American institutions, though it possessed elements of great power. He believed that the Church's spiritual strength was waning, and that if Americans would simply stop opposing it, it would die a natural death. "The way to oppose Mormonism is not to throw mud upon it," he said. "A campaign of detraction only helps it grow. The thing to do is to treat it with candor and fairness. . . . It

---

[1]*Conference Report*, April 1927, pp. 175-76.

must fall of its own weight if it is to fall at all."[2] By the end of its first century, it showed no signs of falling.

The Dispersion of Modern Israel: A Beginning

In the decade following World War I America continued the trend toward urbanism that had begun shortly after the Civil War. By 1930 over 56 percent of the population lived in cities, and though the rest lived in areas designated as rural, only 25 percent of all Americans lived on farms. The farming areas were the hardest hit by the postwar agricultural depression; even though the 1920s was a decade of general prosperity, farmers remained in a state of comparative depression.

All this had an impact upon the Latter-day Saints. In 1920, 76 percent of all members still lived in Utah or the surrounding inter-mountain states. These were still largely rural areas, and 79 percent of the stakes were predominately rural in their economic orientation. The agricultural depression of the early 1920s was hard on the rural Saints, and many families from Utah, Idaho, Nevada, Arizona, and Wyoming headed toward the urban areas of those states or toward the West Coast in search of work. Some leaders, including President Grant, were still imbued with the Jeffersonian ideal of the nobility of agriculture as a way of life, and they looked with misgiving upon the social problems created by the city. They urged members to stay on the farm if they could rather than seek so-called easy jobs in the city, but at the same time they put no religious sanctions upon the idea of moving. Between 1920 and 1930 the percentage of members living in the intermountain region dropped from 76.1 to 72.3, while the percentage on the West Coast increased from 2.6 to 6.2. This change was a small but significant indication of an important trend.

At the same time two shifts in policy culminated in the 1920s. One was official discouragement of all immigration from abroad. Saints in Europe were still eager to migrate to Utah, for members were few in their homelands, and opportunities to mingle with the Saints and marry in the faith were extremely limited. Church leaders were nevertheless reluctant to encourage them to make a move they might later regret. Work opportunities in Utah were

---

[2]As quoted in Roberts, *Comprehensive History of the Church,* 6:551.

limited, and assimilation into the new society would be more difficult than in the days when the state was being filled with immigrants. Immigration had been discouraged since before the turn of the century, but the dream of a better life in America persisted. In a statement issued on October 18, 1921, the First Presidency urged the missionaries to stop preaching emigration. The Saints, they said, could be more useful to the Church by strengthening the Kingdom in their own lands, rather than sacrificing to emigrate to Zion where "their hopes will not be realized." The gathering definitely had "great meaning in our history," the Presidency said, "but we must realize that times and conditions change and that therefore the application of the principles and teachings must change."[3] The Saints in Europe were promised that one day temples would be built in their homelands so temple work could be accomplished without uprooting them.

Even in America there was no effort to encourage the Saints in the mission field to move to Utah, or to encourage Utah Saints to stay at home. In 1922, for example, the president of the Central States Mission reported he had made an extra effort to persuade the Saints to remain and help build up the Church where they lived rather than "move to the stakes of Zion, where through their inability to obtain employment they might get discouraged or even apostatize." In 1921 the Saints in the area of Santa Monica, California, wrote President Grant asking about the truth of rumors that the leaders were opposed to Mormons' moving to California. When he visited them in October, President Grant announced that permanent settlement in these areas was in full accord with church policy.

By the 1920s, then, the Church was implementing a policy of expanding Zion's borders by encouraging the Saints to build up the Church wherever they were. It was the beginning also of a modern dispersion of Israel. The gathering of former years had emphasized the importance of strengthening Zion in Utah, but that need had been fulfilled. No longer were young Latter-day Saints reluctant to leave the mountains in search of opportunity elsewhere. The reality of this change was emphasized in 1923 when the first stake outside the intermountain region was created in Los

---

[3]This document is included in Douglas Dexter Alder, "The German-speaking Immigration to Utah, 1850-1950," Master's thesis, University of Utah, 1959, pp. 114-18.

Angeles, California. In 1927 the second and third such stakes came into being in Hollywood and San Francisco. For the time being the dispersion was chiefly toward the West Coast, though there was also evidence it was moving east. In 1934 there were enough Saints in New York City and surrounding areas to create a stake in the state where the Church was originally organized.

Continuing Organizational Reform: Study and Implementation

The administrative changes of the 1920s, like those of most other periods, reflected both changing needs and growth in numbers. A primary effort was to continue to strengthen the priesthood.

The 1920s saw additional studies of the Church's growing programs and implementation of many needed changes tending to strengthen the priesthood and further define the proper roles of the auxiliaries. The Social Welfare Department of the Relief Society was established in 1919 to help handle problems of unwed mothers and adoption. In 1921 the Relief Society implemented a new monthly lesson sequence that included theology, literature, social service, and a business and work meeting. Mutual Improvement Association programs were gradually developed for youths who were seventeen to twenty-one years old, and were adopted church-wide in 1921 as the M-Men and Gleaner programs. In 1922 the Primary Association completed its Primary Children's Hospital in Salt Lake City, evidence of the Church's increasing commitment to social welfare concerns. This hospital eventually became one of America's major pediatric clinics.

In the meantime, special studies were made on the needs of Church organization. A general Church Correlation Committee had been organized in 1908 to coordinate the activities and curricula of the various organizations. In 1920 this committee was combined with the Social Advisory Committee of the General Boards. The combined committee was asked by the First Presidency and the Council of the Twelve to review the relationship between the priesthood and the auxiliaries with emphasis on eliminating gaps and overlaps. In April 1921 it submitted an extensive report that recommended a number of far-reaching changes, some of which were similar to recommendations made by another Committee of Correlation and Adjustment as early as

After completion of the Primary Children's Hospital, the Primary "penny parade" became a tradition among children of the Church. Birthday pennies helped care for children in the hospital. (Church Archives)

1907. The committee identified an overlapping of theological instruction and suggested that all such instruction in the ward become the responsibility of the Sunday School. The Primary and the MIA were to be responsible for organizing recreation, the Relief Society was to assist the bishop in social welfare programs, and the Church School System was to continue to operate daily religion classes. In addition, new correlation committees were to be set up at the ward, stake, and general levels to assess needs and coordinate programs.

After more than a year of study the First Presidency decided not to implement some of the most sweeping recommendations of the committee, particularly the plans for exclusive Sunday School control of theological instruction and for correlation committees. However, many of the ideas in its report so clearly reflected problems in local church administration that in 1923, the year after the release of the committee, the First Presidency sent circular letters to stakes making some very pointed suggestions. Auxiliary organizations were not to become independent entities but were to operate under the direct supervision of stake and ward authorities. Stake presidencies and bishoprics were advised to hold monthly planning meetings with their respective stake and ward officers. This suggestion was generally followed, and the idea became institutionalized in the 1960s with the official organization of ward and stake councils. The MIAs were assigned sole responsibility for recreation, and training its teachers was the duty of each auxiliary. Aaronic Priesthood quorums were instructed to work toward better preparation of missionaries.

As a direct result of the correlation committee's study, the Young Women's Mutual Improvement Association became wholly an activity program and began to sponsor, among other things, a summer camp program for girls. The MIA magazines were combined in 1929 into one, the *Improvement Era*, ending forty years of independent operation of the *Young Woman's Journal*. That same year the week-day religion classes for children, which seemed to compete with the Primary, were eliminated. In addition, more men and boys than ever before were active in the priesthood, especially in ward teaching.

The major thrust of reform was to strengthen the priesthood, but this centered in encouraging priesthood activities such as ward teaching rather than in the gospel instruction. Despite the First Presidency's rejection of some features of the correlation report, the idea that the Sunday School be given sole responsibility for gospel teaching did not die. Some persons still felt there was too much duplication when the priesthood, MIA, and Sunday School all sought to give weekly gospel lessons.

A new study committee consisting of Elders David O. McKay, Stephen L Richards, and Joseph Fielding Smith of the Council of the Twelve recommended that the teaching of the gospel take place in a unified Sunday morning meeting that would include the priesthood quorums. In October 1927 the First Presidency announced the adoption of a unified Sunday School program, with priesthood business being handled in a monthly quorum meeting. Having tried for twenty years to get priesthood holders to accept the idea of a separate Sunday priesthood meeting, to permit effective weekly coordination of Aaronic Priesthood activities, the Presiding Bishopric sent a letter urging bishops to hold weekly Aaronic Priesthood and ward teacher meetings a half hour before Sunday School and to include five minutes of gospel instruction. These instructions were rescinded in December, and by 1928 the Sunday School had become the teaching arm of the priesthood for theological and doctrinal instruction. A separate weekly priesthood meeting was scheduled each Tuesday night in connection with MIA; this session was designated, for a time, as the Priesthood-MIA.

Despite such changes, the ideals of correlation were not achieved in this decade. The auxiliaries had not become helps of the priesthood as intended; rather, they were influences tending to mold the priesthood into their own pattern of organization. In addition, the plans did not always meet the needs of outlying, scattered branches. Study committees continued to work on ways to improve coordination. The 1930s would see a permanent reinauguration of weekly priesthood meetings and the end of the unified Sunday School.

Changes in Education

The Church also reevaluated its secular education program in the postwar decade. Educational costs were soaring, and the advisability of continuing all the academies and colleges, which accounted for the major portion of the Church budget, was seriously considered. Horace Cummings, superintendent of Church Schools, had reported in 1918 that federal funds were aiding Utah schools, and Church schools would have an even more difficult time competing successfully. He referred to the recent Smith-Hughes Act, which provided funds, to be matched by the state, for vocational education. Utah had accepted $35,000, but even this comparatively modest amount was an important stimulus to the public schools.

In 1919 the Council of the Twelve authorized several significant changes in the administration of the school system. A member of the Council of the Twelve, David O. McKay, was made Church commissioner of education, for the first time placing a General Authority in direct charge of the education program. This was part of an over-all effort to centralize the direction of church activities, and it had important consequences for education by involving the Twelve more directly. Stephen L Richards and Richard R. Lyman, also members of the Twelve, became assistant commissioners.

By the 1920s the seminary movement had proved itself and become a permanent part of the Church educational program. This is the Payson, Utah, seminary, January 13, 1926. (Church Archives)

By 1920 it was clear that the seminary program, begun as an experiment in 1912 at Granite High School, was succeeding. About twenty seminaries were in operation by then. It was equally clear that the Church lacked sufficient funds to expand or improve its academies, especially when it was realized that there were enough public high schools to accommodate the needs of all Latter-day Saint youth in the intermountain area. Accordingly, in 1920 the Church commissioner of education recommended that eight academies be eliminated. By 1924 all academies except the one at Colonia Juarez, Mexico, had been closed or turned over to the states to be operated as secondary schools. At the same time, the seminary program was expanded so that week-day religious instruction could continue to supplement the secular education of its youth. Between 1922 and 1932, seminary enrollment increased from 4,976 to 29,427. At a much smaller cost per student, many more were being reached than could have been reached through the academy program.

The new seminaries were successful partly because of the willingness of school boards to grant released time to students for the purpose of taking private religious instruction and their willingness to grant high school credit. Ironically, the school board of Salt Lake City refused to grant either released time or credit, and in the city of the Church's headquarters students were required to take their seminary training either before or after school. As a result, seminary enrollment in Salt Lake City in the 1920s was only about 10 percent, compared with an average of 70 percent in released-time areas.

In 1930 the state high school inspector raised questions about the constitutionality of the released-time program. It violated the principle of separation of church and state, he said, because public school buses were used by pupils who also attended religious classes, and seminary teachers were sometimes being used by the public schools to supervise study periods, assist in registration, and even conduct some regular high school classes. The following year the state board of education ordered total disassociation of seminaries and their facilities from the schools. At the same time, the board rejected a resolution that would have denied credit for seminary work. In later years attempts to challenge the system in the courts continued, but a judicious and complete separation of the seminaries from the public schools helped avoid legal action.

In the 1920s the Church reevaluated its college program for reasons similar to those which led to elimination of the academies. Besides Brigham Young University, the Church still operated Brigham Young College at Logan, Dixie College at St. George, Weber College at Ogden, Snow College at Ephraim, all in Utah, and Ricks College at Rexburg, Idaho. These schools generally offered secondary training, but were strengthening their programs in post-high-school work. The major need in the intermountain area was the training of school teachers. Therefore, in 1920, at the same time that he recommended abandonment of the academies, the Church commissioner of education proposed that each of these colleges be authorized to establish a two-year normal course for the training of teachers. He recommended further that one institution in the Church system should develop a complete college course leading to a four-year degree, and that this institution should be Brigham Young University. These proposals were accepted, and these Church schools got their real start as institutions of higher education.

Because the state of Utah was also moving into the junior college field, it became necessary to resolve the pressing question of whether the Church should continue to operate a competing system. Church colleges seemed like an unneeded expense when

Ricks College in Rexburg, Idaho, was one of the few Church academies that survived as a junior college. This is the gymnasium building on the Ricks campus as it appeared sometime after 1913. (Church Archives)

equivalent education was becoming available at public cost. In 1926 the Church board of education explored the issue in great detail. There was considerable disagreement among board members, but in the end it was recognized that the Church must ultimately withdraw. Immediate action was taken with regard to Brigham Young College, which held its last commencement in May 1926. Buildings of the college were turned over to the City of Logan to house a public high school. Two years later the Church made known that it favored establishment of junior colleges by the state of Utah, and in 1930 it announced its decision to turn its Utah colleges over to the state. The transition was completed in 1933, though in the transfer the Church stipulated that if the state should ever cease operating educational facilities on any of the properties, they should be returned to the Church. In Idaho, the Church seriously considered turning Ricks College over to the state. When the offer was rejected, the Church decided to continue operation of the school.

The centralization of college-level programs at Ricks and BYU left a gap in religious instruction, which was filled by the institutes of religion. By 1926 the seminary program for high school students had been in operation fourteen years and demonstrated the effectiveness of a released-time approach. With the decision to eliminate the Church-supported network of junior colleges came the inauguration of religious training centers adjacent to college campuses. The first institute of religion was opened for students at the University of Idaho at Moscow in 1926. From the beginning the program had four goals: religious instruction, student counseling, social activities, and worship. The experiment in Idaho gradually won student acceptance, and soon faculties were appointed and buildings provided adjacent to other campuses attended by numbers of Latter-day Saint students.

Missionary Work

With some exceptions, between five hundred and seven hundred missionaries were sent out each year during the 1920s. In some areas, of course, missionary work was difficult. In England, for example, distorted images and vicious stories and accusations persisted. An anti-Mormon film, *Trapped by the Mormons,* portrayed

In 1922 a film entitled Trapped by the Mormons *was produced in England and circulated widely, contributing to the negative image of the Church. It was later rereleased as* The Mormon Peril. (*Utah State Historical Society*)

the missionaries as mesmeric villains who would stop at nothing to delude the fair young women of England and lure them away to Utah. Missionaries were still sometimes harassed and beaten, yet in this decade LDS membership in Europe increased by about four thousand, in addition to those who emigrated.

Times were difficult for the Saints in Europe for reasons other than persecution. The tragedies of World War I had left devastation and poverty. To aid needy members in Europe, Zion's Emergency War Fund was organized, and in 1919 the Church also purchased food from the American Expeditionary Force in France. Wishing to escape poverty, and still clinging to the tradition of gathering to Zion in America, many European Saints ignored the admonitions of the 1920s against emigration. The years between 1922 and 1930 saw the greatest German LDS emigration in the Church's history—except for the period immediately after World War II. The decade also saw substantial numbers of British Saints emigrate to Utah, as well as some from other countries. Members distant from the Church's population center could not easily shake off the ideal of gathering that had been instilled in them for three or four generations. Despite this exodus, by 1930 there were about 29,000 Saints scattered throughout Europe. During this time a number of missions were reorganized or divided, and a new mission was opened in Czechoslovakia.

In Latin America the Church was having different kinds of difficulties. Rey L. Pratt continued as president of the Mexican Mission, but after 1913, political problems in Mexico kept him and other American missionaries from returning to live in the country. He kept in touch with native leaders, however, through letters and rare personal visits until his death in 1931. In 1919 he was sent to El Paso, Texas, where he set up a headquarters in exile for the mission and established a number of branches in American border towns with large Spanish-speaking populations.

Political conditions calmed enough in 1922 to allow American missionaries to enter Mexico again, though President Pratt was never able to take up residence there. The returning elders found local members had done a great deal of proselyting on their own, and the Church was growing. In 1926, however, the government began to enforce the constitutional provision against foreign-born ministers and the American missionaries were required to withdraw again. Despite these political difficulties, the membership in Mexico grew from 2,300 to 4,700 Saints in the 1920s.

There were few members elsewhere in Latin America, though in 1925 the South American Mission was officially opened. This resulted from an invitation to work with German immigrants in Argentina, rather than optimism that missionary work among the Spanish-speaking people would prosper. After World War I the Friedrichs and Hoppe families, who had joined the Church in Germany, migrated to Argentina. They soon began to share the gospel with other German families and in 1924 wrote the First Presidency asking for elders to assist in missionary work and other Church activities. Their request was favorably received and in 1925 Elder Melvin J. Ballard of the Council of the Twelve was sent to Argentina as president of the new South American Mission. Rulon S. Wells and Rey L. Pratt of the First Council of the Seventy accompanied him. Elder Wells spoke German and Elder Pratt was fluent in Spanish. Their success was limited, although they did baptize some German people already converted by Wilhelm Friedrichs and others. They departed after six months, leaving a German convert, Reinhold Stoof, in charge. Elder Stoof visited southern Brazil in 1927 and later assigned permanent missionaries among the German colonies there. The Church had virtually no success among the Spanish-speaking population in this period. By 1930 there were 751 members in Argentina and Brazil, practically all German-speaking. Only after World War II would there be substantial expansion in South America.

In Asia, the work of the Church was not going well at all. In 1924 President Grant decided to close the mission he had opened in Japan in 1901. Linguistic and cultural differences seemed to be at the heart of the problem. By the time the mission closed only 174 converts had been baptized. Despite the closing, the handful of active Japanese Saints made every effort to maintain an organization. A month after the closing, Elder Fujiya Nara of Tokyo and a few others organized the Japan Mutual Improvement Association, and on January 1, 1925, they began publishing a small magazine for the Japanese Saints. It continued sporadically until 1929. When Nara went to Manchuria in 1933, he was replaced as Church leader in Japan by Taken Fujiwara, who had attended BYU in 1927 at the invitation of President Franklin S. Harris. The Church in Asia continued to dwindle, though a few Saints remained active during World War II and were there to begin meeting with the many LDS servicemen who arrived in 1945.

In spite of its problems abroad, the Church was prospering in North America, where its membership in the 1920s increased by nearly 25 percent. At the same time at least one aspect of the missionary program was being reevaluated. Heretofore most missionaries were either from the seventies quorums or were ordained seventies when they received their calls. In 1900, for example, 92 percent of all missionaries were seventies. The percentage began to decline as the century progressed, but the multiplication of seventies created some difficulties. When they returned home there was little need for missionaries in the wards and stakes, since stake mission programs had not yet been established. Yet their priesthood office was basically a missionary calling. It seemed to many that the seventies were becoming too numerous, with little to do. In 1927 the General Authorities began to reduce the number of seventies, and thereafter most missionaries were drawn from the ranks of the young, unmarried elders.

An important assurance of the Church's worldwide interests came in 1920 and 1921 when David O. McKay of the Council of the Twelve traveled nearly 56,000 miles, on assignment by the First Presidency, in a worldwide survey of missions. On this tour he dedicated China for the preaching of the gospel. In Hawaii he was so impressed by a group of small children at a flag-raising ceremony at Laie that he was moved to predict that this location would eventually become an important religious and educational center for the Church. He visited many other areas in the South Seas and Asia, as well as India, Egypt, and Palestine, and returned home via Europe. In many places he was the first General Authority the Saints had ever seen. After that, visits of General Authorities to the missions became more frequent.

Other Church Activities: Spirituality and Public Relations

The Saints' continuing devotion to the sacred priesthood ordinances for themselves and their dead was demonstrated in this era by the dedication of three new temples. The Hawaii Temple, smaller and less costly than the others, was dedicated in 1919. Four years later a million-dollar temple was completed at Cardston, Alberta, Canada; and a temple in Mesa, Arizona, was dedicated in 1927. Architecturally each of these temples represented a distinct

Elder David O. McKay's world tour in 1920-21 symbolized the growing worldwide commitment of the Church. Here he and Elder Hugh J. Cannon are pictured with a group of Maori Saints in April 1921. (McKay Scrapbooks, Church Archives)

departure from the four Utah temples of the nineteenth century. None had spires or assembly rooms, and each was characterized by simple though elegant exteriors reflecting design concepts borrowed from mesoamerica and the work of Frank Lloyd Wright. The Alberta Temple, especially, has been praised as one of the finest examples of the adaptation of Church architecture to modern design. It was planned by Hyrum C. Pope and Harold Burton, who were selected in an architectural competition in 1913.

The modern trend in Church architecture evident in the design of these three international temples and in many meetinghouses of the 1910s disappeared in the 1920s in favor of a return to classical and colonial lines. Under Colonel Willard Young, Church architect, plans for ward and stake buildings in this period were standardized. This was the beginning of the so-called alphabet plans in which chapels, recreation halls, Relief Society rooms, Scout rooms, classrooms, and bishops' offices were combined under one roof in several basic patterns. Wards needing a new building were provided with an existing plan, which was frequently copied churchwide. The revival of colonial designs for Mormon meetinghouses seemed to mark a recognition of the Church's New England heritage, although in returning to more traditional concepts in religious architecture, designers departed from a trend that had begun to create a more modern image in meetinghouses.

The colonial revival in architecture was paralleled by further purchases and development of historic sites and monuments, primarily in the region of Mormon origins. In 1926 the Church purchased and began to improve the Peter Whitmer, Sr., farm, where the Church was organized, and in 1929 it purchased the Hill Cumorah. Here a monument to the Angel Moroni was erected in 1935, and two years later a bureau of information was established. In 1927 the Church cooperated with the Utah State legislature in erecting a monument to the Mormon Battalion on the grounds of the Utah State Capitol. The Church continued its efforts to preserve its heritage and to use that heritage both to build appreciation and to make converts.

To reach the world with its message, the Church did not hesitate to take advantage of the technology developing in the early twentieth century. In 1913, for example, Church leaders

Commemorating the pioneer heritage, the first This Is the Place monument was dedicated in Diamond Jubilee celebration in 1922. Standing near the monument are President Heber J. Grant and Lorenzo Zobieski Young, last survivor of the original pioneer company of July 1847. (Church Archives)

commended the release of a film entitled *One Hundred Years of Mormonism.* Not produced by the Church, it was nevertheless sympathetic. A grandson of Brigham Young even played the part of his illustrious progenitor. The film countered the impressions commonly gained by filmgoers of a depraved people under a despotic church government. Another developing medium was radio, first heard by members in the early 1920s. The Church was quick to see its advantages. In March 1922, experimental transmission demonstrated a listening radius from Salt Lake City of a thousand miles, and the *Improvement Era* speculated that in three years the voice of President Grant would be heard simultaneously by congregations in every part of the region. A Church-owned radio station, the forerunner of KSL, was dedicated in 1922, and two years later general conferences were first broadcast. Later that year plans were instituted for a regular Sunday evening program. In 1925 the Tabernacle Choir began broadcasting some of its performances, and four years later it began weekly network broadcasts.

Despite stepped-up efforts at public relations, the Church's image in America did not become fully positive during the 1920s. Some journalists still looked for the sensational and others were still unfriendly. Some writers pointed to the exodus from Utah as evidence the Church was beginning to lose its younger generation. Others played up the fact that certain people claiming allegiance to Mormonism still practiced polygamy. So-called Fundamentalists still insisted that they were right in performing new plural marriages. When they were discovered, they were cut off from the Church, but the publicity naturally linked them in the public mind with the Church. The First Presidency responded to the continuing criticism by emphasizing that the practice was restricted to an overzealous clique. In 1924 another official statement denounced as disloyal those who entered into new polygamous marriages, but the question continued to plague the Church for years.

A curious public was also interested in the new financial position of the Church, and while some applauded, others criticized it as a great wealth-gathering institution. On the other hand, the Church's conservative financial policies as well as the influence of Reed Smoot in the U.S. Senate helped it gain greater respectability among businessmen of the nation. Heber J. Grant was acknowledged as an astute business leader and was often invited to

address important conventions of business and public officials. In
the 1930s the changing public image would become predominantly positive.

The Church and Public Issues

Whether it wanted to or not, the Church could not avoid having its name associated with political issues. It remained dedicated
to the separation of church and state, of course, and President
Grant was adamant that members in the United States should be
active in political parties of their choice. As individuals, Church
leaders did not hesitate to speak out on issues of public importance, although they tried to separate their own opinions from
any official Church position. At the same time, there were a
number of issues that Church leaders believed went beyond
politics. On matters in which the Church held a vested moral
concern, it took sides.

One question on which the Church did not take sides but
which affected its national public image was the League of Nations
controversy. In 1919 the president of the United States, Woodrow
Wilson, was attempting to persuade the American people that the
only way to keep the peace just won in the Great World War was
to join the League of Nations. Senator Reed Smoot disagreed and
joined the powerful group of Republican "reservationists" who
were attempting to block the president's program. The Church became involved when Elder Smoot went so far as to suggest that
even the Book of Mormon opposed the idea of the League of Nations. His attitude became a matter of public comment in many
parts of the country. In Utah the debate raged heavily, with Brigham H. Roberts, a member of the First Council of the Seventy,
avidly supporting the League and declaring that Mormon scripture supported the idea. Unfortunately, as the debate intensified in
Utah, much was said by people on both sides that implied their
personal position was the Church position. It was apparent that
most Church leaders supported the League, though a few were outspokenly against it. Finally, on September 21, President Heber J.
Grant spoke at a quarterly conference of the Salt Lake Stake and
made his own declaration on the issue. He endorsed the League of
Nations but made it abundantly clear he was doing so as an individual, not as a church leader. This issue should not divide the
Church, he emphasized, and neither side represented an official

Church position. He also made it clear that latter-day scriptures were not to be used on either side of the argument. In the end, American membership in the League of Nations was blocked in the United States Senate.

More important than the controversy itself was the fact that subsequent events proved that President Grant did not allow differences of opinion on political matters to change his assessment of any of the discussants as religious leaders. He became a great friend and admirer of Reed Smoot. He called another League opponent, Charles W. Nibley, to be his counselor in 1925, and two others, J. Reuben Clark, Jr., and David O. McKay, to be counselors in 1933 and 1934. In the modern world, he declared, it was to be expected that men of integrity and strong will would be found on both sides of certain political issues, but this did not diminish their ability to function as brothers in the priesthood.

Other issues were of a different nature. The Church endorsed prohibition because it seemed consistent with the Word of Wisdom. President Grant, in fact, was one of the Church's strongest advocates of the Word of Wisdom, and preaching of this doctrine was significantly intensified during his administration. The prohibition amendment passed in 1919. With national prohibition, however, came the evils of bootlegging and its attendant corruption and violence. Pressure for repeal came from all sides. The Church stood steadfastly against it, but its opinion would not prevail.

The year 1930 was the centennial of the Church, and the general conference that convened in April was especially important. To highlight the occasion, a number of special events took place. The Salt Lake Temple was officially illuminated by floodlights. In the conference meeting of April 6, members participated in the "Hosanna Shout," usually reserved for temple dedications. Elder B. H. Roberts presented his six-volume *Comprehensive History,* covering the first century of the Church, to the conference. A memorable pageant, *Message of the Ages,* was presented throughout conference week. These and other activities represented appreciation for past progress and optimism for the future.

The Church had come a long way in a hundred years and had seen many changes. Each change was designed to better equip it to improve the lives of the Saints and proclaim the restored gospel throughout the world. The Church could not claim perfec-

The Hill Cumorah, purchased early in the twentieth century by the Church, became an important tourist attraction by the 1940s. (Church Archives)

tion, for its people were not perfect, and it would continue to examine and adapt its programs to strengthen them spiritually. One economic problem of immediate importance was scarcely recognized at the centennial conference. The world was in the first stages of the Great Depression, and the Saints would be as deeply affected as anyone. In the 1930s, in response to the problems of that depression, they would welcome a major new program that would carry the Church in an important new direction.

CHAPTER 17

The Church and the Great Depression, 1930-1938

As President Heber J. Grant led the Church into its second century, he faced the problem of guiding it through severe economic distress. The Great Depression threatened the financial well-being of many Latter-day Saints. The Church's response was the Security Plan of 1936, later known as the Church Welfare Plan, designed to restore economic confidence. The depression was only one of several forces that seemed to threaten the Saints' ability to live gospel principles, yet the 1930s saw continuing change and progress in programs. Leaders placed renewed emphasis on education, missionary work, welfare work, and the Word of Wisdom. Translation of the Book of Mormon into Braille and additional languages and increasing use of the radio helped expand the scope of missionary activity. Continuing efforts to preserve historic sites built appreciation for the past. The implementation of the Security Plan and greater public awareness of the high ideals of the Latter-day Saints helped reverse earlier ill will. It was a time of constant internal adjustment to meet the challenges of the world.

The Church Responds to the Great Depression

In ·the 1920s many farmers in the United States endured

serious financial depression. One result was increasing migration from country to city as the unemployed sought jobs. On the other hand, American businessmen saw a period of sustained economic growth. There were more jobs, higher incomes, and the growth of what seemed permanent economic well-being. At the same time, the rapidly growing economy encouraged stock market speculation and highly extended credit. During these years Church leaders strongly counseled against the bondage of debt and condemned waste, extravagance, and speculation. They urged members to be industrious, frugal, and to live within their means.

Then came the dark days of the depression. Following the stock market crash in October 1929, previously wealthy men became poverty stricken. Fortunes were wiped out. Factories, businesses, and banks closed their doors. Industrial expansion ceased and agricultural markets dried up. During 1929 and 1930 national farm income, already low from the failure to recover from the

Planning welfare activities in the Church, April 1939. Before he became a General Authority, Harold B. Lee (left) was responsible for managing the welfare program. Here he meets with other men involved in welfare planning. Standing is Henry D. Moyle, who also later became an apostle; seated are three members of the Council of the Twelve, Elders Albert E. Bowen, Melvin J. Ballard, and John A. Widtsoe. (Church Archives)

postwar collapse in 1921, dropped 15 to 20 percent, followed by another drop of 20 percent during 1932 and 1933.

As business adjusted to depressed conditions and agriculture reduced its labor force, millions were thrown out of work. The number of Americans unemployed increased from 1,499,000 in 1929 to 12,634,000 in 1933, encompassing over one-fourth of the labor force. During the 1920s many had lived extravagantly, failing to provide for hard times. When they lost their jobs during the 1930s, they had money for neither rent nor food. Breadlines formed; want, hunger, and despondency became widespread. To alleviate some of the widespread suffering and distress, the federal government instituted numerous programs for the unemployed and destitute, pouring millions of dollars into make-work projects and other ameliorative measures.

With the depression worsening and no promise of respite, Church leaders began considering the Church's role in providing relief and ending the economic crisis. They realized that temporal and spiritual well-being were intimately related. Accordingly, the 1931 annual conference offered much practical and familiar advice: keep out of debt, patronize home industry, pay tithes and offerings. Elder George F. Richards of the Council of the Twelve reminded the Saints of their responsibility to give fast offerings for the poor. He said that if members had lived fully the law of tithing and fast offering, they would have no need for government relief. To the question, "Can the depression be cured?" Church authorities responded affirmatively, stressing that "despondency and pessimism will never better the situation." They emphasized that prosperity would return when selfishness, strife, and bitterness were discarded and genuine brotherhood was established in economic relations.

Recognizing that much of the Mormons' economic achievement in the past had come from their willingness to work together, authorities urged cooperation among the Saints. They felt that "every person who wants work should be able to find it" and directed priesthood quorums to assume responsibility for helping their members find employment. The Presiding Bishop urged each ward bishop to appoint a ward employment committee composed of a high priest, a seventy, an elder, and a representative from the Relief Society, to function in conjunction with a proposed stake employment committee.

Early in the depression, Church leaders disapproved of spending money to provide food, clothing, and shelter as outright gifts, believing that efforts would be more wisely directed toward providing work for the unemployed. As a result, government programs providing relief in the form of a dole aroused considerable concern. Church authorities received reports of some able-bodied Latter-day Saints on government relief who had sufficient cattle, hay, and chickens to provide for their own needs. President J. Reuben Clark, Jr., remarked that "the thought [among the Latter-day Saints] that we should get all we can from the government because everybody else is getting it, is unworthy of us as American citizens. It will debauch us."[1]

Federal work relief programs, on the other hand, received full Church support. But as early as 1933, the First Presidency began to fear that these programs would be curtailed, placing a considerable burden on Church relief organizations and an increasing reliance upon the dole. They did not know how long government aid would last or how sufficient it would be. They began, therefore, urging members to prepare to shoulder the burden of providing for their own welfare. "The cries of those in distress must be hushed by our bounty. The words of the Lord require this from us. A feeling of common humanity bids it from us. . . . If we shall fully observe that law, the Lord will pour out His richest blessings upon us; we shall be better and happier than ever before in our history; and peace and prosperity will come to us."[2]

In 1933 the First Presidency began to plan a more comprehensive Church relief program by requesting each stake president to conduct a survey, indicating resources available, areas of need, and employment opportunities. "The Lord will not hold us guiltless if we shall permit any of our people to go hungry, or to be cold, unclad, or unhoused during the approaching winter," the message emphasized. "Particularly he will consider us gravely blameful if those who have heretofore paid their tithes and offerings to the Church when they had employment, shall now be permitted to suffer when the general adversity has robbed them of their means of livelihood."[3]

---

[1]*Conference Report*, October 1933, p. 102.
[2]"A Message from the First Presidency Concerning Preparation for Relief Measures," in Clark, *Messages of the First Presidency*, 5:333.
[3]Clark, *Messages of the First Presidency*, 5:331.

Results from the survey enabled the First Presidency to issue instructions for relief work during the coming year. The brethren were especially impressed that no new organization needed to be established. Under direction of the priesthood, and properly coordinated by bishops and stake presidents, the organizations already established could function successfully as relief agencies. The First Presidency urged the leaders of wards and stakes to develop private, community enterprises in which able-bodied members could find employment. They were careful to stress that relief should not be extended as a handout, except to the worthy sick, infirm, or disabled. Faithful Saints were "independent, self-respecting and self-reliant" and did not desire aid. Each bishop and stake president was directed to provide the less fortunate in their wards and stakes with food supplies and other materials.

In these ways Church authorities delegated responsibility for providing relief to local units without at first setting up a coordinated program. Each stake acted independently in aiding members within its boundaries. Left to their own resources, many stakes and wards devised truly innovative programs. For example, Pioneer Stake in Salt Lake City, with more than half of its adult members unemployed in 1932, instituted a program to provide wood, blankets, quilts, clothing, and canned food to its estimated 2,500 needy. It also found jobs in private industry for more than seventy-five men upon recommendations from their bishops. Other unemployed members were put to work renovating chapels, cutting wood, and helping farmers harvest crops. In order to store goods that were donated to the stake, leaders rented the Bamberger Electric Train Company warehouse in Salt Lake City at a cost of $100 per year. A portion of goods from the warehouse was given to the needy and the rest sold to members who could afford to pay. The receipts were placed in a fund to purchase items the stake could not produce for itself. At one point, Harold B. Lee, president of the stake, even obtained permission to keep tithing revenues within the stake, making it almost entirely self-sufficient.

Other stakes experimented with different programs for taking care of their poor and unemployed, with varying degrees of success. Between September 1931 and June 1932, ten Salt Lake City stakes distributed a total of $177,438 for relief. By 1935, however, it appeared that many local wards had fallen short of earlier expectations, and about the same time, the federal government announced its intention to shift the burden of relief to the states and localities. That year a churchwide survey to ascertain actual relief conditions showed that almost 18 percent of the membership (88,460 persons) were receiving either church or government relief. Further study revealed that between 11,500 and 16,500 of these persons did not actually need this relief.

Alarmed that many active members depended upon government handouts, and concerned that the government might soon discontinue its program, the First Presidency decided to act immediately. After studying the experimental plans devised by various stakes, the General Authorities formulated the Security Plan and formally launched it during the April 1936 conference. They urged that all members endeavor to make themselves independent and self-supporting, that the destitute and unfortunate be provided for through collective effort within the Church, and that immediate steps be taken by the wards and stakes to lay in stores of food, fuel, and clothing for the winter in order that those who were worthy of charity would not suffer or become public charges. In October President Grant clearly stated the program's objective: "Our primary purpose in organizing the Church Security Plan was

An LDS Relief Society president in 1938 picks up a welfare order from a bishop's storehouse in Salt Lake City. (Church Archives)

to set up a system under which the curse of idleness will be done away with, the evils of the dole abolished, and independence, industry, thrift, and self-respect be once more established among our people. The aim of the Church is to help the people help themselves. Work is to be re-enthroned as the ruling principle in the lives of our Church members."[4]

Called to head the expanded welfare program was Harold B. Lee. It was a momentous assignment, one that took him completely by surprise. As he recalled thirty years later,

> There I was, just a young man in my thirties. My experience had been limited. I was born in a little country town in Idaho. I had hardly been outside the boundaries of the states of Utah and Idaho. And now to put me in a position where I was to reach out to the entire membership of the Church, worldwide, was one of the most staggering contemplations that I could imagine. How could I do it with my limited understanding?

The young stake president sought inspiration during a walk and private prayer in Rotary Park in Salt Lake City. In particular he was concerned with what kind of new organization should be set up. Then, he said, it came to him: " 'There is no new organization necessary to take care of the needs of this people. All that is necessary is to put the priesthood of God to work. There is nothing else that you need as a substitute.' "[5]

The Security Plan, designated the Welfare Plan at the April 1938 conference, was organized on that assumption. It was not a new philosophy; it simply revived the idea of a bishop's storehouse and adapted it to the needs of members in a new age. It functioned through regular priesthood channels, becoming part of the Church's long-time effort to strengthen the priesthood. Priesthood leaders received important new assignments, but no new auxiliary was established.

A general welfare committee, headed by Elder Lee and supervised by the First Presidency and the Presiding Bishopric, was responsible for formulating plans and directing operations. Each stake established an executive coordinating committee that exercised authority over the wards. Presidents of adjoining stakes formed councils to cooperate on a regional basis.

Priesthood quorums and Relief Societies within the wards

---

[4]Quoted in Henry D. Moyle, "Some Practical Phases of Church Security," *Improvement Era* 40 (June 1939): 354.
[5]*Conference Report*, October 1972, p. 124.

were charged with carrying out details of the program. The bishop had the responsibility of discovering where need existed. He appointed special committees from among the quorums and the Relief Society to study the problems of needy families, determine the extent of their economic distress, provide for their immediate needs, and then plan cooperatively for their permanent rehabilitation.

Each ward gave attention first to emergency cases. Women in the Relief Society sewed quilts and clothing and organized canned foods for distribution to the needy. Priesthood quorums leased land and obtained farming equipment to provide gainful employment for the needy as well as help them produce food for themselves. In some cases an exchange system was worked out between wards so that surpluses of one item might be traded for something more urgently needed.

To help employable members become self-supporting, bishops appointed special employment committees and work directors. The Church Welfare Committee also established special employment offices. One particularly innovative scheme involved vocational education for unskilled workers. Under this program apprentices were placed in businesses to learn new trades. After a training period they were qualified to be placed in commercially operated institutions. The Church also cooperated with school authorities in conducting training classes in bricklaying, carpentry, plumbing, and other trades.

There were not enough jobs to go around, however, so new projects had to be developed. Each priesthood quorum had the responsibility of organizing and maintaining at least one project for unemployed members of that quorum. These make-work projects included constructing homes and church buildings, sewing, repairing clothing and shoes, manufacturing furniture, logging, producing cement blocks, mining coal, and refining molasses. Those employed on such projects received work receipts that could be presented to the storehouse where goods could be drawn on the basis of need.

The mainstay of the welfare program was agriculture. As long as there was idle land there seemed no need for idle people. Contrary to the federal policy of attempting to create scarcity in order to raise farm prices, Church leaders believed an abundance of farm produce offered the best means of alleviating distress. On

Zion Park Stake Welfare Store House and Cannery, in the 1930s.
(*Church Archives*)

both purchased and donated land stakes and wards took up farming programs as community enterprises. As the welfare program
enlarged, it came to include an unpaid agricultural committee
that assisted private farmers in solving production problems.

During the first summer of its operation the welfare program
made impressive strides toward accomplishing its goal. Nearly
fifteen thousand needy Saints were transferred from government to
church relief and more than one thousand were placed in jobs.
Sufficient food, clothing, and fuel were collected to provide for
practically all needy families through the coming winter.

The welfare program provided immediate and positive publicity for the Church. Some journalists published exaggerated reports of its effectiveness. Its detractors, on the other hand, showed
that Utah was still high on the list of states receiving government
aid. Even though the goal of complete self-sufficiency was not
reached, after two years the results were impressive. By 1938 approximately twenty-two thousand Latter-day Saints had been
taken off federal relief rolls and more than thirty thousand others
had received some kind of aid. Private employment had been
found for an additional twenty-four hundred.

With the effectiveness of the welfare program established in
the minds of the General Authorities, it was decided early in 1937
to continue it in order to enable every able-bodied member to be-

come self-sustaining. That same year several leaders began speaking of the imminence of a more severe depression than the one the country was passing through. On September 19, 1937, the First Presidency asked members to observe a special fast and give the monetary equivalent toward construction of a regional warehouse for storage of the just-harvested bumper crops. The welfare program soon became a permanent part of the program of the Church.

The Word of Wisdom

Perhaps no doctrine was preached more enthusiastically by President Grant or stressed more in Church literature during his administration than the Word of Wisdom. Since the days of Joseph Smith, the revelation the Prophet received in 1833 (D&C 89) had been revered as the Lord's instructions regarding health. Members had been particularly enjoined to refrain from the use of tea, coffee, alcoholic beverages, and tobacco. It had been stressed more firmly in some periods than others, usually during times of spiritual reform, but until President Grant's administration it was not compulsory for advancement in the priesthood or entrance to the temples. Some Church leaders had urged this, and many local leaders had required it, and in the early 1930s it became a standard requirement for church advancement and temple recommends.

In the fall of 1930 the Church set up its first Word of Wisdom exhibit at the International Hygiene Exhibition at Dresden, Germany. Another exhibit was displayed in 1931 at the June Conference of the MIA in Salt Lake City. Lectures, charts, posters, pamphlets, pictures, models, motion pictures, and apparatus for conducting chemical, physiological, and mental tests portrayed the Church's renewed commitment to this principle of health. In addition, the *Improvement Era* began a no-liquor and no-tobacco column, and two members of the Council of the Twelve, John A. Widtsoe and Joseph F. Merrill, began producing literature on the subject. As might be expected, some members went to extremes and began denouncing many other items not specifically noted in the Word of Wisdom, but the major emphasis was on health and the general importance of proper diet. Abstinence from tea, coffee, alcohol, and tobacco were, and still are, required for faithful membership, but they were only symbols of the Saints' commitment to the broader principles of physical and spiritual well-being.

In 1932 Franklin D. Roosevelt ran for president of the United States on a platform that included repeal of the prohibition amendment. Although they had no desire to involve the Church in political controversy, the First Presidency and the Council of the Twelve maintained strong opposition to repeal. Since prohibition was to them a moral issue, it was of great consequence. "The ground already gained ought not to be surrendered," the First Presidency declared. "Liquor has always been and it will continue to be the intimate ally of crime."

The advocates of repeal argued that prohibition had created a situation worse than before. The law was not rigidly enforced, which made it a mockery, and simply because it was forbidden, many young people tried liquor. Speakeasies, bootleggers, and corruption of public officials were becoming all too common. Church leaders believed that these things could be overcome and that force of law should be used to eliminate liquor traffic. To the chagrin of President Grant, however, in 1933 Utah became the thirty-sixth state to ratify the repeal amendment, thus putting it into law. Though many of the Saints had been persuaded by proponents of repeal, the outcome was, from the Church's standpoint, not wholly negative: at least this was evidence to its critics that the Church did not control politics in Utah. After repeal the Church redoubled its emphasis on the Word of Wisdom.

In other political activities the Church continued to demonstrate that its leaders could hold different political views and retain love and harmony as brethren in the gospel. President Grant, for example, was an outspoken critic of the New Deal, as was his counselor J. Reuben Clark, Jr. But B. H. Roberts, a member of the First Council of the Seventy, was an open admirer of Roosevelt and the direction he was taking of involving the federal government more deeply in social and economic affairs. Utahns generally voted Democratic in that decade, and Reed Smoot, the long-time senator, was defeated at the polls in the Roosevelt landslide of 1932. In 1936 President Grant openly endorsed Alf Landon, the Republican candidate for president, though he quickly made it clear that he was speaking for himself and did not intend to commit Church members. In the ensuing election Roosevelt handily carried Utah and the nation.

The New Image

By the 1930s the Church had acquired a new and more favorable public image. It had been steadily improving since the
turn of the century, but in that decade the total number of positive
articles in American periodicals for the first time exceeded those
with a negative viewpoint. Favorable reports frequently appeared
as writers became increasingly aware of the positive aspects of
Mormon doctrine and practices, and as readers caught up in the
problems of the depression followed with great interest the outcome of the welfare program. Such widely read periodicals as *Life,*

*The First Presidency, 1934-45: President Heber J. Grant and counselors
David O. McKay and J. Reuben Clark, Jr. (Church Archives)*

Saturday Evening Post, Time, Newsweek, Nation, National Geographic, and the New York *Times* devoted considerable space to the welfare program. *Nation,* for example, complimented it as the "only project organized solely to free Americans from the burden of government relief, and advertised as such." *Life* published two pages of illustrations dealing with welfare projects and a full-page photograph of President Grant. *Catholic Worker* suggested, "It is a bitter tea that we must swallow," but that Catholics could learn a few lessons in charity from the Latter-day Saints.

A few periodicals paid attention to the Word of Wisdom. *Horizon* in New York published an article reprinted in *Health Digest* in 1936 praising the Mormon health code as "the greatest experiment in correct eating and correct living ever conducted." The new public image of the Church was also spread by the continuing broadcasts of the Tabernacle Choir.

Education and the Secular Challenge

Meantime, the work of the Church went on, and one of its most expensive continuing programs was education. The depression was cutting heavily into Church income and the leaders were therefore cautious about new expansion, but where necessary it was allowed. No institutions were closed, other than those that the Church had already determined to close or turn over to the states, and no teachers were released because of the depression. There was, however, a necessary retrenchment of teacher salaries.

After the Church turned its Utah colleges over to the state in 1933, the only remaining institutions of advanced learning that it operated were Brigham Young University in Provo, Ricks College in Rexburg, Idaho, and the LDS Business College and the McCune School of Music in Salt Lake City. In 1935 Dr. M. Lynn Bennion became supervisor of the seminary system, and through his efforts the curriculum was revised and student-centered instruction enhanced. The programs of the institutes of religion were expanded, with institutes being opened at most major colleges in the Mountain West where substantial numbers of Latter-day Saints attended. The first institute outside the Mountain West got its start in 1935 at the University of Southern California. Elder John A. Widtsoe of the Council of the Twelve had been invited to give a course on religion at the university, and while there he held meetings with Latter-day Saint students. A regular, full-time

By the 1930s the Church had committed itself to providing institutes of religion adjacent to college campuses. This is the interior of the Pocatello, Idaho, institute, October 1929. (Church Archives)

institute of religion was established several years later.

Even where there were no regular institute programs the Church was interested in the welfare of its college students. At several universities it authorized establishment of Deseret Clubs designed to bring students together on both a social and religious basis. These clubs were forerunners for many institute programs. At the same time a fraternity-type organization, Lambda Delta Sigma, was founded in 1936 by Dr. Lowell L. Bennion at the institute of religion adjacent to the University of Utah. The organization was designed to bring Latter-day Saint students together in a group that would compete with the attraction of the Greek-letter fraternities and sororities and would sponsor uplifting social activities as well as provide outlets for service. The organization spread rapidly to fifteen different campuses within the next ten years.

Now that the Church was fully committed to an expansion of its religious education programs at both the high school and college level, the need for excellent teachers and for writers to prepare manuals increased. Most teachers were trained at Utah institutions, and there were few high quality study materials available outside the scriptures themselves. Some Church leaders and educators became concerned with the possibility of excessive educational in-breeding. They wondered if a few Latter-day Saint teachers should have the advantage of studying under important scholars outside the Mountain West in order to become familiar with current insights and knowledge. Biblical studies, for example, was an especially important academic field, and it was felt LDS teachers should be aware of the new discoveries and new ideas about biblical interpretation.

Other persons challenged the idea that Mormon educators should draw on the learning of the world. Higher criticism and other developments in secular learning, they felt, could raise doubts about the validity of the scriptures. They were not impressed by the argument that a man with a firm testimony would not be hurt by the learning of the world and that a broad, well-disciplined education in which he had been challenged at every turn would make him a better teacher. The idea was pushed, however, by Dr. Adam S. Bennion, Church commissioner of education, and Joseph F. Merrill, who succeeded him in 1928. They were strongly supported by John A. Widtsoe of the Council of the Twelve. The result was that in the late 1920s and early 1930s a few Latter-day Saint teachers were encouraged to continue their education at prestigious institutions elsewhere, such as the University of Chicago, and were given leaves of absence to do so. They were encouraged to study religious subjects, and some of them received divinity degrees from the University of Chicago. It was an unusual calling, completely unanticipated by some, but one that demonstrated the Church's continuing interest in gaining knowledge from every available source.

The challenge of secularism in religious education was indeed a real one. The scientific method discounted experiences that could not be tested and demonstrated; therefore, the element of inspiration and revelation in the writing and interpretation of the scriptures was increasingly challenged. On the other hand, the new methodology was producing important information that Church teachers could not ignore if they were to respond intelligently to students' questions.

The theory that received the widest publicity in the 1920s and early 1930s was that of organic evolution. Church leaders did not take an official stand on any specific theories regarding evolution (and there were many), except to reaffirm that the Church would always accept the basic truth that man was created by God, that Adam was the parent of the human race, and that the destiny of man would be worked out according to the plan of God, which included the reality of the atonement of the Savior. Individually, some Church leaders went further. In 1930, for example, Elder James E. Talmage of the Council of the Twelve gave an important radio address, later reprinted and widely circulated, entitled "The Earth and Man." An internationally known scientist, Elder Talmage demonstrated in this address his own ability to reconcile the truths made known both by scientific investigation and by revelation. Church leaders recognized the value of the pursuit of secular knowledge. Their principal concern was that teachers refrain from propounding theories as if they were proven truths and teaching with such dogmatism that they could disturb the faith of youth.

The Mission of the Church Goes On

Important as such learning and discussion may have been to the intellectual climate of the Church, it did not receive the principal energy of Church efforts. As in earlier years, missionary work continued as a major concern.

In Europe, one of the most interesting challenges to Church growth came in Germany. About fifteen thousand Saints lived in Germany in the 1930s, and after the Nazi party came to power under Adolf Hitler in 1933, there was natural confusion about what direction they should take. Some, impressed with the Church's teaching that people should be loyal to their existing governments, felt comfortable sympathizing with the Nazi regime. Others did not. Under the regime, the Church suffered increasing political pressure as its activities were hampered or forbidden. The Boy Scout program, for example, had to be eliminated in favor of the Hitler Youth program, and missionaries found it difficult to obtain funds from America. By 1939 they were not allowed to distribute certain pieces of Church literature, particularly those with religious ideas that ran counter to Nazi propaganda.

Meantime the European missionary program was augmented by local missionaries serving on a part-time basis, even before the stake missionary program got going well in the United States.

Especially noteworthy was the German-Austrian Mission, where at one point there were 138 missionaries from the United States and 152 local missionaries. During the decade membership increased in all of Europe by only a thousand, partly due to the continuing emigration of the Saints.

Several new missions were opened in this decade. The Japanese Mission, closed in 1924, was reopened in 1936 with headquarters in Hawaii, though missionaries did not actually return to Japan until after World War II. Eight new missions were opened in Europe and the United States, and the Book of Mormon was published in Czech, Armenian, and Portuguese during those years and translated, though not published, into Hungarian. It was also translated into Braille.

Within the stakes, this decade saw the beginning of stake missionary programs. As with so many activities eventually adopted churchwide, this program had its beginning at the local level when leaders in some newly formed stakes outside the intermoun-

Council of the Twelve, April 1931. Seated, left to right: Rudger Clawson, Reed Smoot, George Albert Smith, George F. Richards, Orson F. Whitney, David O. McKay. Standing: Joseph Fielding Smith, James E. Talmage, Stephen L Richards, Richard R. Lyman, Melvin J. Ballard, John A. Widtsoe. (Church Archives)

tain region organized efforts to preach to their non-Mormon neighbors. Heretofore most stakes were in regions densely populated by the Mormons, and the need for local missionaries had not become apparent. The Mormon dispersion of the 1920s and 1930s, however, brought a new perspective to the whole church.

Utah stakes soon caught the spirit, and in 1934 Elder J. Golden Kimball of the First Council of the Seventy reported hundreds of converts had been made through the efforts of local missionaries in Los Angeles, Maricopa, Liberty, Salt Lake, Granite, East Jordan, and other stakes. He emphasized that all who held the office of seventy had a particular duty to preach the gospel and admonished local seventies they must be willing to serve as stake missionaries. At the general conference of April 1936, it was announced that supervision of stake missions was being assigned to the First Council of the Seventy and that each stake was to organize a mission immediately.

By the end of 1937 missions had been organized in 105 of the 118 stakes, and 1,757 converts had been baptized. In addition, 2,756 members had been reactivated and one ward reported an overall 50 percent increase in the activity of its members as a result of home missionary work. A powerful new stimulus had been added to the missionary program.

Missionary work was also enhanced by the increased use of radio, which by the 1930s was common in almost every home in America. In 1931 missionaries in the Eastern States Mission delivered more than 212 radio sermons in thickly populated areas, at no cost to the Church.

In the 1930s the Church also continued its efforts to preserve historical landmarks and perpetuate its heritage. In 1933 the Relief Society unveiled a monument at Nauvoo marking the site of the Joseph Smith store, where the Relief Society was organized in 1842. The Winter Quarters monument was one of the most impressive markers erected in this era. Designed to honor the memory of the hundreds of Saints who suffered and died during the winter following the exodus from Nauvoo, it was dedicated on September 20, 1936, at the cemetery located in Florence, Nebraska.

In 1937 the Church purchased eighty-eight acres of the original farm of Martin Harris, one of the witnesses to the Book of Mormon. That same year Wilford C. Wood purchased the original temple site at Nauvoo for the Church. Later he purchased about

The Church's interest in historic sites was symbolized in 1930 when these prominent leaders were part of a caravan along the Mormon Trail to Independence Rock, Wyoming. Left to right: Oscar A. Kirkham, B. H. Roberts, George Albert Smith, Andrew Jenson, John D. Giles. (*Church Archives*)

one-fourth of the original temple block and several homes of leading members.

Probably the best-known activity connected with these historic sites is the annual pageant at the Hill Cumorah, *America's Witness for Christ*. Pageants and programs had been presented periodically since the early days of the twentieth century at the site where the Prophet Joseph Smith received the gold plates from the Angel Moroni. In 1935 President Don B. Colton of the Eastern States Mission met with Professor E. H. Eastmond of Brigham Young University to discuss the possibility of a continuing, Church-sponsored production. They asked Elder Harold I. Hansen, a missionary, to direct the pageant in 1937; under his direction, the production became an annual presentation and was constantly enlarged and improved. Later Elder Hansen joined the Department of Dramatic Arts at Brigham Young University, and BYU students began participating with missionaries and local members in New York in staging the widely acclaimed production.

The first decade of Mormonism's second century, then, was a decade of new beginnings. Welfare work, the stake missionary program, a dramatic new effort at public relations—all represented fresh approaches to the Church's continuing commitment to its traditional values. Very shortly, however, its hopes for world peace would again be dashed and its members involved on both sides of another worldwide conflict.

PART V

The Gospel in All Nations, 1939-1976

New Church Office Building, completed in 1972, symbolizes on its facade the worldwide scope of the Church. (Internal Communications Department of the Church)

OUTWARDLY, THE HISTORY of the Church between 1939 and 1976 was characterized by two things: growth and internationalization. These years were marked by many internal problems and issues and frequent social and political confrontations with the larger society, but all this seemed transitory compared with the continuing challenge of administering a rapidly growing organization, accommodating programs to suit diverse cultures, and carrying out a determination to expand even further. The trend toward greater international involvement was seen in the 1940s and '50s, but it flowered in the 1960s and '70s.

Statistics for the period provide an important key to what was happening. In 1940 membership was approximately 862,600; thirty-five years later it was approaching 3.5 million. The greatest burst came in the 1960s, and the most dramatic areas of growth were outside North America. In that decade the Church's total population increased by 173 percent, though in North America it increased by only 145 percent. In South America, on the other hand, there was a growth of 964 percent (from 9,750 to 93,875), in Central America 930 percent, in Asia 502 percent, in Great Britain 527 percent (compared to only 284 percent in Europe generally), and in Australia, 354 percent. In 1940 some 77 percent of the members lived in the United States, but although the numbers of U.S. members increased substantially during the next two decades, the percentage dropped during the 1960s to 68 percent. Mormonism was still an American religion as far as most of its population was concerned, but the ratio of Americans was decreasing and the Church's cultural perspective was clearly beginning to change.

The full import of these figures is seen most clearly in the constant decline in the percentage of members living in the mission field as contrasted with membership in the stakes. Between 1900 and 1930 it climbed from 12 percent to a high of 20 percent, but then it began to drop, so that by 1973 it was nearly back down to 12 percent. This reflected no drop in membership in these areas, but an important effort, especially after World War II, to organize stakes wherever possible.

This trend is probably a better indicator of strength than growth in membership, for stakes are established only where there are sufficient numbers of trained local leaders and sufficient membership within a reasonable distance to assure that the full program of the Church can operate without constant outside supervision. Organization of a stake is a sign of local growth and maturity. In 1958 the first stake outside North America was organized (in Auckland, New Zealand), and by the 1970s stakes were functioning in Europe, South America, Australia, South Africa, the Pacific, and parts of Asia. In 1940 there were only 134 stakes in the entire church, an average of less than one new stake per year for all its history. At the close of 1975 there were more than 700, and they were being organized at a rate of more than thirty per year.

In these decades the Church continued to feel the influence of events and forces in the larger society. The Great Depression gave impetus to the welfare program, and the aftermath of World War II helped demonstrate its effectiveness. In addition, the Church became involved in a number of social and political issues that had important consequences.

In the 1950s and 1960s the threat of Communist expansion distressed Church leaders as it did other American political and business leaders, and Latter-day Saint officials were outspoken in their warnings against the Communist system. Disagreement surfaced over what methods a Saint might appropriately use to put his concern into action. The Church was also affected, especially in the 1960s, by America's racial problems, and in the 1960s and '70s it took open stands on other politically explosive social issues, such as birth control, abortion, pornography, and Sunday closing laws. In none of these was there total agreement among members, but the leaders felt an obligation to use whatever influence they had to promote the moral well-being of the society in which they lived.

The changing culture of youth was of special concern. In the United States, especially, many young people were disillusioned with the world their parents had created and began to seriously question the traditional values and institutions of their society. Many youths met the postwar world with cynicism as they contrasted the affluence of their parents with the poverty around them.

The apparent selfish acquisitiveness of modern society and the seeming complacency of the older generation led some young people to "drop out" in their search for new traditions and values. Known as the "beat generation," they congregated in large cities to share their rebellion in new musical sounds, verse, and life-styles that suggested to their worried elders not only nonconformity, but also irresponsibility. The Church faced the continuing challenge of seeing that its young members were headed in proper directions and kept uplifting goals in mind.

The postwar world offered a life of neither peace nor abundance, even though it was one in which science and technology provided modern tools for enriching the life of all mankind. People had not learned to share either the human or natural resources of the earth in ways that would uplift and ennoble man. The Church continued to maintain that only the gospel of Christ would bring peace, true brotherhood, and well-being to the people of the world. But with a membership representing less than one-tenth of one percent of the world's population, it had little impact, even in countries where its growth was most dramatic. Further, it had made no inroads into the vast territories of China, Russia, India, and many other countries, where over half the world's population was located. Looked at from this perspective, the mission the Church conceived for itself was awesome.

Still only a tiny stone cut out of a huge mountain, the Church had scarcely begun to roll forth to fill the world. The Latter-day Saints, nevertheless, still dreamed of filling the world, and many acted as if accomplishing that dream was their most urgent task. "Lengthen your stride," the Saints around the world were told in the 1970s. The Church must inform "all nations, kindreds, tongues and people" of the restoration of the gospel and the coming Millennium. With more than twenty-three thousand missionaries in the field in early 1976, it was clear that this historic Mormon sense of mission continued as the heart of its vitality.

CHAPTER 18

The Church and World War II, 1939-1950

By the end of the 1930s the earth again faced the specter of international war. Again the Church withdrew its missionaries from most of the world and retrenched its programs, and again the tragedy of war found members on both sides of the conflict. In the end, however, the clouds of war were brightened by a few silver linings, as Mormon servicemen helped introduce the gospel into various parts of the world, and as welfare activities among the Saints in war-torn Europe helped demonstrate that the brotherhood of the gospel was stronger than the politics of international conflict.

War and Response

In 1938 the threat of war hung over Europe. The expansionism of Germany and Italy under Adolph Hitler and Benito Mussolini had gone unchecked by the League of Nations and individual governments. After Hitler attacked Poland in September 1939, England and France honored their commitments to defend Polish independence, and war soon engulfed all of Europe.

The Church was paying close attention to world affairs. Like most religious groups, it looked with aversion at the prospect of another world conflagration, and its leaders condemned the use of war for expanding national boundaries. Throughout the crucial year of 1939 they continually warned the Saints not to be blinded by the various arguments used to justify wars of aggression. "God will not forgive betrayal of his children by those who rule over them," declared President J. Reuben Clark, Jr.

In 1939 Elder Joseph Fielding Smith of the Council of the Twelve was sent on a tour of the European missions. At the same time President Clark, a former undersecretary of state, was in daily contact with the U.S. State Department, and through his efforts Church leaders were kept constantly aware of changing European conditions. Their concern was two-fold: the welfare of the Saints in Europe and the well-being of the American missionaries in the countries threatened by war.

On August 24, 1939, just a week before Hitler invaded Poland, the First Presidency instructed Elder Smith to evacuate the missionaries from Germany, France, and England. At first the intention was to distribute them among the neutral nations of Europe. These nations, however, soon made it clear they would prefer to have all foreigners leave their borders, and as a result all missionaries were returned to the United States.

In the meantime, Japanese expansionism brought war to Asia and was threatening the Pacific. In 1940, therefore, missionaries were also withdrawn from the South Pacific and South Africa. Evacuation was carried out as swiftly as possible. One group of missionaries in Tahiti would have been delayed for six months if they had waited for regular commercial transportation, so they chartered a hundred-foot motorized schooner and made the fifteen-day voyage to Hawaii. By the end of 1940 full-time missionary work had ceased everywhere except in North and South America and in Hawaii.

In closing the missions of the world, the First Presidency charged the mission presidents to keep in touch with local leaders and members as much as possible. For the duration of hostilities communications between Church leaders and the Saints in most war-affected areas were cut off, and local leaders struggled to hold the members together without direction from any higher authorities.

On December 7, 1941, the Japanese attacked the American naval base at Pearl Harbor, Hawaii. Immediately the United

States and Japan were at war, and since Japan was an ally of Germany, the commitment of the U.S. government, and that of her allies, became worldwide.

Before United States entrance into the war, the popular sentiment was isolationist. Most citizens looked with revulsion at the aggressions of Germany, Italy, and Japan, but felt that the United States should remain uninvolved. Only after 1939 was President Franklin D. Roosevelt able to gain enough congressional support to begin to strengthen the armed forces and to provide economic aid to England through a lend-lease agreement. Unlike many Americans, he believed that unless the United States came to the aid of England, it, too, would ultimately be threatened by war. As German submarine warfare increased the threat to U.S. shipping, American isolationist sentiment became less and less pronounced.

The utterances of Church leaders from 1939 to 1941 demonstrated that they, too, were anxious that the United States remain neutral. President Clark was especially outspoken on the issue. "We would not settle it now by joining the conflict," he counseled in 1939. "This is one of those questions which can be settled only by the parties themselves by themselves."[1] The United States' role, he believed, was to be that of peacemaker, but this could not be achieved by intervention, even to protect neutral rights. Rather, America must demonstrate love for humanity, justice, and fair-mindedness before she could exercise her influence for peace. Other leaders echoed similar feelings.

The issue was frustrating. On the one hand, Church members could not submit complacently to any force that sought to destroy private property or undermine individual liberty and freedom of worship. On the other hand, there were Latter-day Saints in every country on both sides of the conflict, and revelation dictated that they should all be subject to their own sovereignties. The reconciliation of these concerns had never been, nor ever would be, easy.

When the United States entered the conflict, General Authorities quickly put behind them any isolationist tendencies and urged wholehearted support for the nation's war efforts. The official position necessarily became one similar to that of President Joseph F. Smith during World War I. Members were encouraged

---

[1]"In Time of War," *Improvement Era* 42 (November 1939): 657.

to retain a spirit of humanity, love, and peacemaking. Latter-day Saint servicemen were told to look upon themselves as ministers of life rather than death; they were fighting to defend liberties rather than to destroy enemies. To Saints who were citizens of enemy countries, Church leaders could only say that as innocent pawns of war, they had no recourse but to support the government to which they owed allegiance. In a special message delivered on April 6, 1942, the First Presidency declared:

> On each side they believe they are fighting for home, and country, and freedom. On each side, our brethren pray to the same God, in the same name, for victory. Both sides cannot be wholly right; perhaps neither is without wrong. God will work out in His own due time and in His own sovereign way the justice and right of the conflict, but He will not hold the innocent instrumentalities of the war, our brethren in arms, responsible for the conflict.[2]

The war brought many difficulties for the Church. Almost all communication with war-affected areas ceased during the six years of conflict. In addition, activities in America were curtailed. Travel was especially difficult. Automobiles were no longer readily available, and gasoline and tires were strictly rationed. To discourage travel, large Church-sponsored gatherings were curtailed. The general conference of April 1942 was closed to the general membership and confined to approximately 500 priesthood leaders. This policy continued for the duration of the war. In addition, the Relief Society postponed the elaborate centennial celebration scheduled to take place in Salt Lake City in April 1942. Instead, special commemorations were held in wards and branches. Because of paper shortages, publication of instruction manuals and other materials was severely limited. Food rationing led the national government to promote "victory gardens," but many Saints were a jump ahead of others, for the Church had long been urging them to grow their own food and to store a year's supply. The Saints who had followed this advice before the crisis could hardly be accused of hoarding after the war created a scarcity in food supply.

Mormon Servicemen

As the war approached, thousands of Latter-day Saint youths

---

[2]Clark, *Messages of the First Presidency,* 6:159.

During World War II Latter-day Saint servicemen made efforts to continue church attendance wherever and whenever possible. These signs on the island of Okinawa were typical of the kind of advertising seen along roads in many places in the world. (Church Archives)

in the United States found themselves in the armed forces, and by the end of the war nearly 100,000 young Mormon men and women had either been inducted or had enlisted. Previously there had been no continuing program of maintaining contact with those in the service, but such a program began in May 1941. Elder Hugh B. Brown, a former Canadian army officer, was appointed Church-Army coordinator, assigned to visit military installations and confer with Mormon servicemen, local leaders, and military officials. As a result of these visits he received information on the religious and social needs of servicemen, which subsequently led to a new program.

In the fall of 1943, acting upon Elder Brown's recommendations, the LDS Servicemen's Committee was organized. It was headed by Elder Harold B. Lee, who had been appointed to the Council of the Twelve two years earlier. The committee was responsible for providing Church programs and guidelines to Latter-day Saints in the service and for securing government cooperation in appointing LDS chaplains for all branches of the armed forces. Through the work of the committee the government was persuaded to increase the number of Mormon chaplains, and by the end of the war some servicemen were even allowed to have "LDS," rather than "Protestant," stamped on their identification tags.

A special publications program was especially important to the success of the servicemen's program. The committee published pocket-sized editions of the Book of Mormon and *Principles of the Gospel* and made them available to all members of the armed forces. Bishops and branch presidents were instructed to send the name and address of each person in the service to Church headquarters so he could receive the *Improvement Era* and the "Church News" section of the *Deseret News*. Late in the war the Church also published a servicemen's edition of the "Church News." Special homes were established near a number of military bases in the United States where military personnel could relax and socialize when off duty.

The greatest challenge was to maintain contact with and provide religious activities for all LDS servicemen. For this purpose the General Authorities authorized setting apart worthy elders, usually returned missionaries, as group leaders. These men had authority to hold meetings, administer the sacrament, and, under certain circumstances, baptize converts. These group leaders appeared on every battlefront and aboard many ships, helping to make the Church a vital force in the lives of many even in the midst of battle. But the absence of group leaders did not deter many enterprising young Latter-day Saints from holding their own meetings, administering the sacrament, and, regardless of military rank, enjoying the brotherhood and spiritual uplift of the gospel. In addition, forty-five Latter-day Saint chaplains served in the U.S. forces.

The appointment of Latter-day Saint chaplains was at first complicated by the fact that chaplains corps required men with three years of ministerial service, yet the Church had no professional ministry. The rule was soon interpreted, however, so that Latter-day Saints who had filled two-year missions and were employed full time as seminary teachers could qualify. Originally the Saints were restricted to twenty-four chaplains, due to a quota system based on World War I figures, but this number was subsequently raised to thirty-four. By the end of the war the quota was revised, and the Mormons were authorized 1.07 percent of the total number of chaplains, or a total of ninety-one, but rapid demobilization soon followed and the actual number did not increase.

Latter-day Saint chaplains saw duty in all major theaters of war. Officially they were considered Protestant chaplains, and they performed all such duties. Whenever possible, they also met and counseled with Mormon servicemen, though in most cases this was done on their own time, beyond their regular assignments. They generally achieved outstanding service records and played an important role in the servicemen's program.

World War II was filled with the hate, horror, and brutality characteristic of any war, but out of it also came dramatic and faith-promoting events that have become part of the tradition of the Saints. Missionary-minded, young servicemen on military bases, aboard ships, or even in trenches studied their pocket editions of the Book of Mormon and *Principles of the Gospel* and discussed religion with their buddies. Even though the difficulties of war led some Latter-day Saints to forget the high standards they had been taught, many servicemen became converted in battle, and many non-Mormons joined the Church as a result of their friends' examples and teachings. These military missionaries frequently bore testimony of the power of the priesthood as they witnessed the preservation of life or the comforting of the wounded through the laying on of hands. Nor was it uncommon for a young Latter-day Saint soldier feeling lonely to suddenly hear someone whistle the familiar tune "Come, Come Ye Saints," a refrain that gave sure notice of a kindred soul.

The war in Europe finally ended on May 8, 1945. Latter-day Saints rejoiced with other people of the war-racked nations, and as a symbol of this joy President Heber J. Grant turned on the exterior floodlights of the Salt Lake Temple, which had been darkened during the war. On August 14 Japan surrendered and the remaining thousands of Latter-day Saint servicemen scattered around the globe soon returned home—some to school, many to families, and others to mission calls, sometimes to countries where they had lately been fighting. On September 4 the Church sponsored a mass meeting of all faiths in the Salt Lake Tabernacle to give thanks for the return of peace to the earth. The excitement was dimmed only by the threat of an even more devastating future conflict fought with one of the most awesome developments of the war just past, the atomic bomb.

A Change of Leadership

On May 14, 1945, President Heber J. Grant died. He was succeeded by George Albert Smith, whose family had distinguished itself in Church service for four generations. His great-grandfather was John Smith, the Prophet Joseph's uncle, who served as Church Patriarch and as president of three stakes. His grandfather, George A. Smith (after whom he was named), had been ordained an apostle in the days of Joseph Smith and was an outstanding missionary, colonizer, and counselor to Brigham Young. His father, John Henry Smith, was also an apostle and a counselor to President Joseph F. Smith. Born in 1870, George Albert Smith became a member of the Council of the Twelve in 1903. He was active in public life as well as in the Church and worked both in government and business. Especially interested in youth, he won many awards for his contributions to scouting. Noted for his interest in other people, his greatest concern in life was sharing the gospel.

Reestablishing Contact and Reopening Missions in Europe

With the war over, Church leaders in America were eager to reestablish contact with the Saints in Europe, resume missionary proselyting, and provide badly needed welfare supplies to destitute members. On January 14, 1946, it was announced that Ezra Taft Benson of the Council of the Twelve had been appointed to preside over the European Mission. His main task was to reestablish missionary work, but he was also assigned to organize distribution of welfare food, clothing, and bedding.

Elder Benson left immediately for what proved to be an arduous but rewarding ten months in Europe. He arrived in England in February and by December had traveled sixty thousand miles. Transportation and communications had been seriously disrupted, and he found it difficult to place telephone calls from London to many missions on the continent. Some countries, such as Holland, Poland, and Czechoslovakia, could not be contacted by phone at all. Traveling on the continent, his party was often delayed by bombed-out bridges and damaged highways. Little groups of Saints often waited for hours past the appointed meeting time in expectation of his arrival. Such problems only added to the exhilaration of the European Saints as they anticipated renewed contact with apostles and prophets from America.

Elder Benson was gratified at the spirit he felt among the members, most of whom had remained loyal to the Church. Some practices had been slightly altered during the six years of isolation, and a few unauthorized doctrinal interpretations had crept in, but most branches had remained intact and local leaders were anxious to begin gaining strength under the direction of newly appointed mission leaders.

In April 1946 a letter from Elder Benson was read at general conference in Salt Lake City. In it he declared that "nowhere in all the world do members live and sustain their leaders more whole-heartedly than here," and that "never were there more sincere expressions of gratitude and such spirit" than in the meetings he had just completed in the war-torn European nations. Perhaps the spirit of the gospel was no more tenderly expressed than in a report he made of his first meeting in Karlsruhe, Germany, where the Saints had been waiting two hours for his arrival:

> And then for the first time in my life, I saw almost an entire audience in tears as we walked up onto the platform, and they realized that at last, after six or seven long years, representatives from Zion, as they put it, had finally come back among them. Then as the meeting closed, prolonged at their request, they insisted that we go to the door and shake hands with each one of them as we left the bombed-out building. And we noted that many of them, after they had passed through the line, went back and came through a second and third time, so happy were they to grasp our hands. As I looked into their upturned faces, pale, thin, many of these Saints dressed in rags, some of them barefooted, I could see the light of faith in their eyes as they bore testimony to the divinity of this great latter-day work, and expressed their gratitude for the blessings of the Lord.
>
> That is what a testimony does. We saw it in many countries. I say there is no greater faith, to my knowledge, anywhere in the Church than we found among those good people in Europe.[3]

Elder Benson discovered that during the war some European branches had organized their own local missionary activity; in some cases they seemed more effective at teaching converts than had been the full-time missionaries. Still, it was essential that regular missionary work be reestablished and new mission presi-

---

[3] *Improvement Era* 50 (May 1947): 293-94.

dents be appointed. Beginning in 1946 the Church engaged in a concerted effort to send missionaries to all parts of the world from which they had previously been withdrawn. Many of the new missionaries were fresh from military service. By the end of 1946 there were 2,294 in the field, including 311 in Europe. By 1950 the Church counted more than five thousand missionaries, with twelve hundred in Europe. In late 1946 and early 1947 mission presidents began to arrive again from the United States. While local leaders had carried on well during the war, it was important that they now receive direction from men more directly familiar with the general programs of the Church.

Aid to European Saints

After six years of war, conditions in some areas of Europe bordered on destitution. Marauding armies had destroyed or stolen much of worth, and recent crop failures had left thousands hungry and vagrant. Fuel supplies and clothing were meager, and many European Saints found themselves without homes. The period after the war was as much a test of their faith as the war itself had been.

Even before Church aid arrived from the United States, some members organized their own welfare programs, and these helped demonstrate what brotherhood across national boundaries really meant. Swedish Saints, for example, sent assistance to their brethren and sisters in Norway and Denmark, while the Danish Saints supplied food and clothing to Norway and Holland. The Swiss Mission also forwarded food and funds to Belgium, Holland, and Germany. Later the Saints in the Netherlands sent carloads of potatoes to members in Germany, and the Saints in Canada sent them large quantities of wheat.

Official arrangements for Church shipments of goods to Europe began with the visit of President George Albert Smith to President Harry S. Truman in November 1945. Pleased at the Church's willingness to ship food and clothing to Europe, the American president asked how long it would take to get it ready. He was surprised when President Smith informed him that the supplies were waiting. The Church leader then had a chance to inform President Truman of some aspects of the welfare program, begun nearly ten years earlier during times of distress in America, and of the Relief Society, which had over two thousand home-

President George Albert Smith meets with U.S. President Harry S. Truman immediately after World War II. (Church Archives)

made quilts ready to ship. All the Church needed was a pledge of cooperation and help from the government in arranging transportation, and this the nation's president readily gave.

After Elder Benson's arrival in Europe he immediately began making arrangements for the receipt and distribution of welfare goods. The major burden for this would eventually fall on the newly appointed mission presidents, but by March 14, 1946, he was able to cable Church headquarters to have the first shipments sent. They would be distributed first to the areas in greatest distress. Military authorities were amazed at the promptness with which the goods were shipped. Later some mission presidents estimated that as many as 88 percent of the Saints in some districts were clothed with goods shipped from America.

There were some problems in the distribution of welfare supplies. In West Germany the new mission president found in 1947 that some local authorities objected to goods being imported unless they were distributed to the people at large rather than just to Latter-day Saints. The president was finally able to persuade them that if it had not been for the American Saints these goods would not be there at all, and distribution to members was fully justified.

He did, nevertheless, demonstrate Mormon good will by sharing some of the goods with nonmembers.

The influx of welfare goods created some interesting situations and provided opportunity for important cooperative work. West German Mission president Jean Wunderlich and his wife spent a major portion of their first year in Europe dealing with welfare distribution problems. When it was discovered that American clothes were generally too small for the German women, they held fashion shows throughout the mission demonstrating clothing that had been remodeled or even reconstructed by combining two pieces. Knitted clothing was often unraveled to provide yarn for making other clothing, or if sweaters could not be used, the sleeves were sometimes refashioned into stockings. Button-sorting parties matched the thousands of buttons that came with the goods, and when it was discovered that there were many men's shoes that could not be matched into pairs, they were donated to a German

Elder Ezra Taft Benson (left) inspects cartons of welfare supplies stacked in warehouse of International Red Cross at Geneva, Switzerland, prior to distribution in Germany and Austria after World War II. (Church Archives)

hospital treating former soldiers who had lost one leg through amputation.

Welfare aid to European Saints continued for two years. In 1947 alone the Church shipped 149,600 pounds of food and clothing to seven missions and helped 6,872 people. By the end of the crisis approximately 140 railroad carloads valued at about two million dollars had been shipped. The European Saints were helped, and church brotherhood worldwide was enhanced.

Revitalizing Other Church Programs

During the war, missionary work continued outside the war zones but at a reduced tempo. Much of the usual missionary manpower had been diverted into military service or was committed to maintaining vital industries and agriculture at home. Nevertheless, during the 1940s converts accounted for 19 percent of Church growth, a drop of only one percent from the depression years of the 1930s.

The effectiveness of missionary work in this decade was enhanced by several experimental missionary approaches in teaching the gospel. One of the earliest was the "Message of Mormonism," which LeGrand Richards left behind when he completed a term as president of the Southern States Mission in 1937. This mimeographed outline was borrowed by other missions, used by teachers in Church schools, copied by stake missionaries, and finally expanded and published in 1950 as *A Marvelous Work and a Wonder.*

The interest in systematic proselyting plans continued and in the late 1940s led to development of a number of other approaches. Some of these were prepared by missionaries who felt the inadequacy of traditional methods. They organized lesson presentations around certain themes and incorporated well-known salesmanship techniques. Some plans proved so effective that mission presidents adopted them for the use of all the missionaries. In the Northwestern States Mission, for example, Elder Richard L. Anderson developed a plan that was accepted for the mission in 1948. Its effectiveness was demonstrated when baptisms jumped from 158 during the first six months of the year to 348 during the last half. In the Great Lakes Mission Elder Willard A. Aston, second counselor to President Carl C. Burton, developed a plan based on seven lessons, presented as sample dialogues. The increase in convert baptisms was impressive. These and other plans were so successful that other missions soon began using them.

None of the plans had the official backing of the Church, for they were still experimental in nature. In fact, some mission presidents resisted reliance on memorized dialogue because they felt it hindered the spontaneous promptings of the Spirit. Nevertheless, the systematic approach soon won a closer look from Church leaders and in the 1950s led to a standardized presentation in missions worldwide.

Meantime, with the close of hostilities in the two theaters of war, missionary work expanded. Shortly after Elder Benson began reconstructing the European missions, Elder Matthew Cowley of the Council of the Twelve arrived in the newly established Pacific Mission. His responsibility was to direct missionary efforts in Hawaii, the Central Pacific, Tonga, Tahiti, New Zealand, and Australia. That same year the Book of Mormon was published in Tongan, enhancing missionary possibilities in that island country. In 1947 Elder Cowley announced the long-awaited reopening of the Japanese Mission, and in 1949 he witnessed entrance of the first modern missionaries into Hong Kong. The Pacific soon became one of the most important areas of growth in the Church.

Missionary work in Latin America received a boost in August 1946, when a former Argentina Mission president, Frederick S. Williams, was given a party in Salt Lake City by some returned missionaries. Some members of the group, concerned over the need for more proselyting efforts in South America, obtained an appointment with the First Presidency. As spokesman, President Williams explained to them much of the political and social structure of South America and the opportunity for preaching the gospel more widely. The First Presidency treated the group with great courtesy and interest, and President Williams was invited to put his message in writing. Eight months later he was called to organize and become the first president of the new Uruguay Mission.[4]

There were problems in the twentieth century, however, as the affairs of the world increasingly imposed upon and affected Church programs. In the United States, Congress proposed, but

---

[4]From a tape-recorded presentation at the Uruguay Mission reunion, April 7, 1972, Church Archives.

Idaho Falls Temple, dedicated September 23, 1945. (Church Archives)

did not adopt, a universal military training program that would have required all young men to serve a term in the armed forces. In 1948, as it became increasingly clear that the United States had long-range military commitments to the United Nations, the Selective Service program was reinstituted. Once again the Church and the government competed for the services of young men, but the Church stressed that it would not encourage its young men to avoid whatever military service was required. For another twelve years, until the end of the Viet Nam conflict, military training and service affected the potential of the full-time missionary program.

In the United States, missionary work among the American Indians increased. From the early years of the Church, missionaries had been teaching the gospel to native Americans, but in 1943 the first formal mission opened to teach the Zuni and Navajo people. Six years later the mission was extended to all tribes in the area and renamed the Southwest Indian Mission. Elder Spencer W. Kimball directed this expansion in the years after 1945. Elder Matthew Cowley and President Antoine R. Ivins of the First Council of the Seventy were appointed to serve with him on a new Indian Relations Committee. By 1951 Indian missionary work had been organized in all the stakes where Indians lived or visited as mobile groups, and by the end of the year nearly 2,500 Indians had been baptized.

The decade of the 1940s was a time of reassessment and transition for other programs. Especially significant was the expansion of the number of General Authorities, symbolizing the continuing need to adjust the administrative structure to supervise a growing organization. In April 1941 five men were selected to become Assistants to the Council of the Twelve. President J. Reuben Clark, Jr., made the announcement during the process of sustaining leaders in general conference:

The rapid growth of the Church in recent times, the constantly increasing establishment of new Wards and Stakes, the ever widening geographical area covered by Wards and Stakes, the steadily pressing necessity for increasing our missions in numbers and efficiency that the Gospel may be brought to all men, the continual multiplying of Church interests and activities calling for more rigid and frequent observation, supervision, and direction—all have built up an apostolic service of the greatest magnitude.

The First Presidency and the Twelve feel that to meet adequately their great responsibilities and to carry on efficiently this service for the Lord, they should have some help.

Accordingly it has been decided to appoint Assistants to the Twelve, who shall be High Priests, who shall be set apart to act under the direction of the Twelve in the performance of such work as the First Presidency and the Twelve may place upon them.[5]

Seated comfortably in the audience was Marion G. Romney, president of the Bonneville Stake in Salt Lake City, who was shocked to hear his name listed first among the five to be sustained. As he recalled it later, "I hadn't heard about it; nobody else had heard about it. I didn't hear the other four names."[6] The other four were Thomas E. McKay, Clifford E. Young, Alma Sonne, and Nicholas G. Smith. The number of Assistants to the Twelve would later be significantly expanded, and, beginning in the 1960s, other important administrative changes would clearly reflect the growing needs of the Church. During the 1940s sixty-one new stakes were organized, many of them in California.

Among other programs, the seminary and institute systems

---

[5]*Conference Report*, April 1941, pp. 94-95.
[6]Marion G. Romney, oral history interviews by James B. Allen, 1972-73, Typescript, Interview 2, p. 16, Oral History Program, Archives, Historical Department of The Church of Jesus Christ of Latter-day Saints.

and other educational programs grew during the 1940s, in spite of the war. Between 1940 and 1951 thirty-nine new seminaries were opened and five new institute buildings were erected. In 1949 Ricks College became a four-year college. In that same year the First Presidency expanded the board of education to include all members of the Council of the Twelve, giving all these top leaders permanent and direct influence on educational policies. The commitment to education was further dramatized in 1950 by the completion of a two-million-dollar science building on the Brigham Young University campus.

Genealogical activity received special stimulus during the decade. The Genealogical Society of Utah began broadening its program of microfilming important documents and records around the world to make them accessible for study in a central location. Beginning with early county records of Tennessee, the society sent microfilmers to the southern, eastern, and New England states. After the war it extended these operations to Great Britain, Holland, Switzerland, Italy, Germany, Finland, and the Scandinavian countries. In 1944, while celebrating its fiftieth anniversary, the society was reincorporated as The Genealogical Society of The Church of Jesus Christ of Latter-day Saints.

The building program was also vigorously pushed after the war. In 1945 the Idaho Falls Temple, delayed because of shortages in building supplies, was dedicated. During the decade members constructed approximately 450 new chapels, and 400 more were nearing completion in 1950. Many of these reflected a new architectural style characterized by a plain, stucco finish with lack of decoration. It was both an attempt to find an international style and a reflection of the austerity of the war years. President Smith also initiated a program of beautifying and improving older chapels; as part of that program the Salt Lake Tabernacle was renovated with a fresh coat of paint, a new roof, and additional organ pipes.

Finally, the pioneer heritage of the Latter-day Saints received wide publicity in this decade in connection with two significant events. One was the 1947 centennial celebration of the settlement of the Great Salt Lake Valley. Special parades and celebrations were held throughout Utah and beyond, and the dramatic musical production *Promised Valley* made its first appearance. Written and composed by Arnold Sundgaard and Crawford Gates, it has been

Celebrating the centennial of the arrival of the Mormon pioneers in the Salt Lake Valley, the Sons of the Utah Pioneers retraced their steps in 1947 by covering their automobiles to give them the appearance of covered wagons. Here they are camped near Independence Rock, a familiar landmark to their forefathers. (Church Archives)

performed regularly since then in Salt Lake City and other stakes of the Church. The year 1947 also saw completion and dedication of the huge "This Is the Place" monument at the mouth of Emigration Canyon. Sculpted by Mahonri M. Young, the artist-grandson of Brigham Young, this imposing work commemorates many early explorers and trappers who passed through the region prior to its settlement. Its focal point is a group of statues representing Brigham Young, Wilford Woodruff, and Heber C. Kimball.

A second important monument to the Latter-day Saint heritage was a twelve-foot marble statue of Brigham Young, also by Mahonri Young, which was unveiled in the rotunda of the United States Capitol in Washington, D. C., in 1950. More than a thousand people attended the ceremony, and Vice-President Alben W. Barkley honored Brigham Young as a "man of God" and an "advocate of justice and democracy." Congress also recognized his importance and the positive significance of the Latter-day Saint contribution to American history when it authorized permanent placement of the figure in Statuary Hall and called Brigham Young one of Utah's "most eminent citizens, illustrious for his leadership as a colonizer." This was, indeed, a far cry from what national leaders were saying a hundred years earlier.

These events represented a century of achievement and increasing public acceptance, but, like the centennial celebration of 1930, they also represented new beginnings. The 1940s had been a decade of war and recovery. The period after the war was one of revitalization and recommitment. The vitality of the Church's welfare system was demonstrated in its program of aid to Europe. Education, missionary work, genealogical activity, and temple work were all stimulated and expanded in the postwar years. This activity, however, was only preliminary to the decade of the 1950s in which the Church made dramatic strides in every direction and laid the groundwork for genuinely becoming an international faith. In the early evening of his eighty-first birthday, April 4, 1951, President George Albert Smith died quietly in his home. He was succeeded by David O. McKay, who would lead the Church through the next two decades of remarkable growth.

CHAPTER 19

Foundations for Expansion, 1951-1959

David O. McKay was seventy-seven years old when members of the Church sustained him as their ninth President. An educator by profession, he became a school principal in Huntsville, Utah, at age twenty. He later attended the University of Utah, where he graduated from a three-year teacher education program, and thus was the first President of the Church to hold a college degree. He taught at Weber Stake Academy and became principal of that institution in 1902. This early commitment to education was still strong when, during his administration, the Church's educational program began an unprecedented expansion. President McKay's background also seemed well suited for the new internationalism of the Church, a second theme prominent during the 1950s. From 1897 to 1899 he fulfilled a mission in Scotland, and in 1920-21, as a young apostle, he traveled around the world for the Church. Thirty years later, as President, he toured all the European missions and announced that for the first time temple building would soon begin in Europe. In 1953 he dedicated temple sites in England and Switzerland, and during the next two years he traveled extensively to Europe, Africa, Latin America, and the South Pacific, announcing the decision to build a temple in New

President David O. McKay. (Church Archives)

Zealand in 1955. As the most widely traveled of all the Presidents and as a man thoroughly dedicated to a broad understanding of the world around him, President McKay was an appropriate leader for the Church in the postwar world.

A Social Profile of the Saints at Mid-Century

The growth of Church population in the first decade of President McKay's leadership was impressive. Membership expanded from about 1,100,000 in 1950 to 1,693,000 in 1960, and the number of organized stakes increased from 180 to 319 in the same decade. Such growth reflected, in part, the general increase in religious interest that followed World War II. In the United States, 63 percent of the population claimed some religious affiliation in 1958, more than at any previous time in American history. From 1952 to 1960, the Protestant Episcopal and Roman Catholic churches each grew by 39 percent, and the LDS Church followed closely with 38 percent.

This renewed American religiosity was exemplified by the popularity of such revivalists as Dr. Billy Graham, the fact that President Dwight D. Eisenhower opened his cabinet meetings with prayer, the addition of the words "under God" to the pledge of allegiance to the flag, and the fact that religious music, such as the Tabernacle Choir's performance of "Battle Hymn of the Republic," became national hits. There were also undercurrents of discontent with traditional religious and moral values in the 1950s, but the general tone of the period seemed to provide fertile ground for acceptance of religious faith.

Statistics compiled at the beginning of the decade revealed some interesting aspects of Latter-day Saint culture in mid-century America. The relatively high birthrate gave Mormons a youthful profile. In the Church 42.8 percent of the population was under twenty, while in the United States only 33.5 percent was in that age group. The median years of school completed by Latter-day Saints twenty years old and over was 12.2, while in the country as a whole it was 10.8. Statistics further demonstrated that 62 percent of Mormon families owned or were buying their own homes, compared with 55 percent in the nation. With respect to occupations, more Latter-day Saints were reported as farmers, 23.30 percent, than any other occupation. Next came craftsmen, foremen, and related workers, 18.91 percent; clerical and sales workers, 10.38

percent; and operatives, such as miners, factory workers, etc., 9.98 percent.

Though the Mormons had not moved away from agricultural life as rapidly as the rest of the nation, they were clearly caught up in the affairs of the complex, mobile, industrial society. But the values traditionally associated with the yeoman farmer—hard work, thrift, stability, reward for individual effort, home ownership, avoidance of debt, and private ownership of property— were still Mormon ideals. Not that others ignored them, but in a society where the welfare state seemed to be growing rapidly and traditional moral values seemed to be breaking down, the old, trusted standards were of special concern to Mormon leaders. The far-reaching challenge was to maintain them in the increasingly complex society of the new age. The Saints were participants in the world, but sought to maintain their own sense of community as a religious people.

Internationalization: The Asian Missions

With the steady growth of the Church, the time was not far off when Mormonism would truly be an international faith. In 1950 some 7.7 percent of the members lived outside North America; in 1960 this had changed to 10.4 percent. Asia, the Pacific, Australia, and Latin America saw the opening of new missions and augmentation of missionary activity, foreshadowing even more substantial growth in the decades to come.

Perhaps the most impressive example of expansion was in east Asia, where the Church finally succeeded in making important inroads. In 1950 only 439 members lived in the Orient. By 1960, some 7,400 members were organized in 51 branches. Though still not great, these numbers represented a new and permanent commitment to Asia.

The task of building the Church in Asia was not easy. In China, for example, the Communist party concluded a twenty-year civil war in 1949 by taking control of the mainland and driving the Nationalist government to the island of Taiwan. At this point the same kind of "iron curtain" that blocked entrance to European Communist countries descended around China. The Church opened a Chinese Mission in 1949 with headquarters in the British crown colony of Hong Kong, but lack of access to the mainland made it impossible to work among the vast majority of the Chinese people. The outbreak of the Korean conflict in 1950 forced the withdrawal of all missionaries and the final closing of the mission in 1953.

Shortly before World War II Hilton A. Robertson visited Japan to look after the needs of the Church there. Based on this activity, American military occupation officials allowed the Church to reopen its Japanese mission in 1948. Latter-day Saint servicemen had already helped prepare the way, and the conversion of Tatsui Sato was an impressive example of how the gospel could bridge the gulf between former enemies. Sato, who lived in Marumi village, already had strong faith in the Christian Bible and could speak English. One day late in 1945, while visiting with friends in a tea shop, he invited three American soldiers into the shop to warm themselves. The villagers were astonished when the soldiers politely declined cups of warm tea. One of them, Ray Hanks, explained to the gracious host, "Our church teaches us that our bodies are a very sacred gift from God, and that we should take special care of our health." In the conversation that followed, the Americans were able to explain much about the gospel, and when they returned to the village they brought a copy of the Book of Mormon and began holding study classes with the Sato family. Tatsui Sato was impressed as he read and reread the book, studied with the soldiers, and prayed. Soon more soldiers came, and a small Sunday School was begun in the Sato home. This continued for several months. Tatsui Sato and his wife became converted to the truthfulness of the gospel and the authenticity of the Book of Mormon. On July 7, 1946, the experience culminated in the baptism of the Sato family. The serviceman who baptized Chiyo Sato, Tatsui's wife, was twenty-one-year-old Boyd K. Packer, who in later years became a member of the Council of the Twelve.

The baptism of Brother Sato and his family began a new era for the Church in Asia. In the next few years many missionaries were sent to Japan, building sites were purchased in Tokyo and Yokohama, and in 1955 the Japanese Mission was divided into the Northern Far East and the Southern Far East missions.

Establishment of the Church in Korea was basically a product of the baptism of Dr. Kim Ho Jik and of the Korean conflict. As a Ph.D. candidate at Cornell University, Dr. Kim had been converted by a fellow graduate student, Dr. Oliver Wayman. Upon his return to Korea, where he was vice-minister of education, he was an active missionary. At the same time, many Latter-day Saint servicemen in Korea—both returned missionaries and others who had been called into military service before they could serve on missions—gave their time and money to share the gospel with the Korean people. In January 1952 they began offering both English language classes and gospel investigator sessions in the port city of Pusan. A few baptisms resulted. In 1954 Elder Harold B. Lee of the Council of the Twelve visited the country and was impressed with the work of Dr. Kim and of the Mormon chaplains and servicemen. In 1955 Korea was dedicated for missionary work by President Joseph Fielding Smith of the Council of the Twelve. The first regular missionaries came from among the American elders laboring in Japan, and a separate Korean Mission was organized in 1962.

The foundations for the expansion of the Church in the Philippines, Okinawa, and other Pacific islands were similar. World War II brought into these areas Mormon servicemen who were faithful in conducting their own church activities and living exemplary lives, and their work laid the foundation for regular missionary activity.

Missionary activity in Korea began when LDS servicemen from the United States found themselves stationed in that country. Here six servicemen pose with Korean converts at baptismal ceremonies, 1953. (Photograph courtesy Spencer W. Palmer)

Missionary Work

The postwar surge of missionary activity contributed a larger share of the membership increase than usual for the twentieth century. Between 1950 and 1960, the 177,000 converts accounted for 30 percent of the growth of the Church, while converts had made up only 20 percent of the increase in the previous two decades. The number of full-time missionaries in the field during the 1950s rose from 5,000 to nearly 6,000, with a temporary drop during the Korean conflict. At the same time, the desire and ability of members to go on missions surged upward. In 1950 the total number of full-time missionaries equaled approximately 26 percent of all male members between the ages of twenty and twenty-four, higher than ever before in the twentieth century, and by 1960, following a drop during the Korean conflict, it was up to nearly 28 percent.

At the same time an important administrative change improved supervision of missionary work. For years the responsibility had been divided among the Missionary Appointment Committee; Mission Home Committee; Radio, Publicity, and Mission Literature Committee; Indian Relations Committee; and the stake missionary program, under the direction of the First Council of the Seventy. To eliminate this unwieldy diffusion of responsibility, all missionary functions were consolidated in 1954 under the newly formed Missionary Committee, with Joseph Fielding Smith as chairman.

Church leaders meanwhile were so impressed with the effectiveness of experimental lesson plans during the late 1940s that in 1951 the Church Radio, Publicity, and Missionary Literature Committee, headed by Gordon B. Hinckley, decided to develop a churchwide plan. In 1952 the committee introduced a *Systematic Program for Teaching the Gospel,* which consisted of introductory material addressed to the missionary and seven lessons in dialogue form. Essentially it was the same plan developed by Elder Willard A. Aston in the Great Lakes Mission, with some modification and expansion of the introductory material.

Use of the new plan gradually spread to most of the missions, although it was generally understood that it was still experimental in nature and could be modified as experience dictated. By 1955 the Church was also distributing flannelboard material to all missions to visually supplement the standard lessons, and by 1958 the First Presidency wrote that the new program had become "something of a standard plan" of proselyting. There was still a tendency, however, for some missions to produce new and different plans, and the First Presidency expressed a desire that a single plan be adopted in order to make it easier to train missionaries in the mission home. They asked for criticism and suggestions regarding the authorized plan and indicated that a new publication would be made soon. In the 1960s these experimental efforts culminated in the *Uniform Plan for Teaching Investigators,* which was officially adopted churchwide. It too changed as experience demonstrated the need for further refinement. Like the earlier proselyting approaches, the uniform plan was meant to provide a systematic approach so that the basic principles could be explained clearly and effectively to the investigator, but the missionary was urged to be sensitive to different needs and responsive to the promptings of the Spirit.

Another new program of the 1950s was the effort to organize a special mission to the Jewish people in the United States. Latter-day Saint doctrine had always emphasized the importance of the Israelite heritage and the eventual gathering of all the scattered tribes of Israel. The Saints felt a special kinship with the Jews and had long been interested in finding ways to reach them. At the same time, most members did not understand modern Jewish religion and culture and therefore found it difficult to communicate. While different degrees of orthodoxy existed within the Jewish faith, orthodox Jews retained many Old Testament customs, forms, and traditions that helped them maintain a religious identity as tightly knit as that of the Saints themselves. Perhaps for this reason efforts to proselyte among the Jewish people had met with little success over the years.

One of the most avid missionaries was Elder LeGrand Richards, who became a member of the Council of the Twelve in 1952. In 1955 he published a book, *Israel! Do You Know?*, which was an effort to show the Jewish people the relationship between their heritage and the faith of the Mormons. That same year a special Jewish Mission was opened on a trial basis in Los Angeles. Soon other stakes in California, Utah, and a few other areas had similar programs. Each mission provided its own teaching plan based on an opening approach that directly linked the Mormons to the

Jews. By September 1958, some fifty stake missionaries were involved in the Jewish Mission in southern California.

At the same time, some members in southern California attempted to promote better Mormon understanding of the Jewish people. Called "Understanding Israel," the program taught young Latter-day Saints various aspects of Jewish culture, including modern Israeli folk-dancing. While not part of the Jewish Mission, the "Understanding Israel" program nevertheless came in contact with it, and eventually a broader effort to promote understanding was brought into the Jewish Mission.

There was considerable disagreement both among the missionary groups and within the leadership of the Church as to whether the specially directed Jewish program was satisfactory. The result of four years of effort seemed to suggest that it was not, although some Jews were converted, and finally in 1959 the First Presidency sent a circular to all stake and mission presidents directing that all Jewish missions be dissolved. Henceforth, proselyting among Jews would be a regular part of stake missions, but no missionaries were to confine themselves to work exclusively among the Jewish people. Members were warned not to promote discussions relating to pro- or anti-semitism, for some missionaries had apparently been unwise in making statements with controversial social and political implications. Some of the special missionaries had also been overzealous in their interpretation of the fulfillment of biblical prophecy and had made statements that were not church doctrine and could prove embarrassing. They were warned by the First Presidency of the "unwisdom of any attempt to set dates and times, for the fulfillment is in the unfathomable wisdom of the Lord. It is well to teach all people to be prepared for the fulfillment of prophecy, and leave all else to Him."[1]

Missionary Work and the Korean War

One of the greatest hindrances to the over-all missionary effort in the early 1950s was the Korean conflict. As the young men of the Church in the United States found themselves being drafted into the armed forces, the missionary corps dropped from 4,847 in 1951 to a low of 2,189 in 1953. To partially fill the gap, the First Presidency called upon the seventies quorums in 1951 to provide

---

[1] First Presidency, Circular Letter, March 2, 1959, Church Archives.

1,000 full-time missionaries. The need was urgent not only to fill the ranks of proselyting missionaries but also to help fellowship new members and provide leadership in small, isolated branches. Such a call required unusual sacrifice, for the seventies were usually men who had already been on missions, were married and had families, and were becoming settled in their occupations. Nevertheless, with the aid of families, friends, and priesthood quorums, many seventies accepted the challenge and filled short-term missions.

Another emergency innovation was the calling of young women under the age of twenty-three, the minimum age for lady missionaries at that time. On January 19, 1953, the First Presidency informed stake presidents of the need for stenographers and other office help in the missions and suggested that a few properly trained women who were at least twenty-one could be called. The response to this stenographic missionary assignment was so generous that by July all needs were met and permission to call women under twenty-three was suspended, though the regular program of calling sister missionaries to proselyte continued.

The most complicated wartime issue was obtaining draft exemptions for missionaries. Between 1950 and 1952, the United States increased the size of its armed forces from 1.4 to 3.6 million. The Church did not intend to keep young men from military service altogether, but it made every effort to make it clear that the missionaries were full-time ministers during the two years of missionary service and that they would be willing to serve their time in the armed forces when they returned. The problem was complicated in areas heavily dominated by Latter-day Saints when many local draft boards found themselves unable to both meet their quotas and allow many draft deferments for missionaries. Both the military and the Church were trying to draw from the same pool. The Church did place some restrictions on the calling of missionaries. For example, it did not call young men who had received notices to report for preinduction physical examinations, and in January 1950 the First Presidency required that all prospective missionaries receive prior clearance from draft boards.

As the military action continued, President Stephen L Richards conducted negotiations with various state and local Selective Service officials, as well as with General Lewis Hershey, director of Selective Service for the United States, to develop a plan for getting more young Latter-day Saints into the mission field. Hershey seemed favorable to such a plan if the manpower pools that local draft boards were attempting to maintain could be preserved. The Church worked out its proposal and, after clearing with Selective Service officials, in July 1953 the First Presidency introduced the quota system. Under this arrangement each ward in the United States could call only one man in 1953 and perhaps two the following year. By 1955 the crisis was over and the quota system was dropped.

Servicemen's Program

As more and more young men were called into the armed forces during the Korean conflict, Church leaders responded by revitalizing the servicemen's program. In August 1950 local leaders were again instructed to carefully maintain regular contact with men and women in the armed services and to be sure that a

Council of the Twelve, October 1953. Seated: Joseph Fielding Smith, Harold B. Lee, Spencer W. Kimball, Ezra Taft Benson, Mark E. Petersen, Matthew Cowley. Standing: Henry D. Moyle, Delbert L. Stapley, Marion G. Romney, LeGrand Richards, Adam S. Bennion, Richard L. Evans. (Church Archives)

pamphlet, *So You Are Going into Military Service,* was given to all prospective enlistees. In 1951 a new *Servicemen's Directory* was printed and distributed. Throughout the decade the Church continued to promote religious activities for servicemen, organizing special branches and holding servicemen's conferences. The servicemen themselves contributed to the stability of the Church in many areas by strengthening local branches and missionary work, helping build chapels, and, in some cases, providing additional leadership. In 1960 it was estimated that about fifteen thousand Latter-day Saints were still on active duty in the armed services of the United States.

The Building Program as a Symbol of Growth

The growth of the Church in this decade was no better illustrated than in the building program. The Latter-day Saints erected and dedicated 1,350 chapels, schools, and welfare buildings between 1946 and 1955, at an average cost of $90,000 each, and the chapels built in that period constituted more than half of all chapels then in use. In 1955 alone the Church spent $18,700,000 (which amounted to over half the total church budget) on buildings from its general funds. Another $11,300,000 was contributed directly by members. In July 1955 Wendell B. Mendenhall was selected to head the new Church Building Committee, serving also as special consultant to the committee selected to supervise completion of a new college and temple in New Zealand.

The building program in the South Pacific expanded more rapidly than in any other place and represented an attempt to provide needed facilities for a strengthened membership. In 1950 the members in Tonga participated in the beginnings of the labor-missionary program. The Liahona School was under construction, but volunteer laborers were unable to complete it because they lacked the skills needed for the most technical tasks. At that point the president of the Tonga Mission decided to call young men on missions to work until the school was finished and to receive special training from the building supervisor. The Church provided housing while local members provided food, and the school was soon completed. This work-training program spread to other parts of Tonga, and·in 1951 to New Zealand, where another school was under construction. The labor missionary approach soon became institutionalized and in the 1950s contributed to dozens of buildings, including chapels, schools, the Church College of Hawaii, and the New Zealand Temple. The benefits of the program were seen not only in construction of many fine buildings but also in the training of young men. Many learned new skills and trades and prepared themselves spiritually to contribute more fully to their various branches. Because of the success of the program in the South Pacific, it was extended throughout the Church during at least part of the 1960s.

Modern Temple Building

The Church erected four new temples in the 1950s. The most elaborate was the four million dollar building at Los Angeles, California, dedicated March 11, 1956, by President David O. McKay. The massive four-story building had a center spire rising 268 feet above the ground, topped by a gilded statue representing the Angel Moroni. The grounds were gracefully landscaped with a large variety of plants, including palm trees and other tropical foliage, and additional small palm trees were planted atop the annex. It was a dramatic reminder of Brigham Young's prediction in 1853 when, speaking of the Salt Lake Temple, he said: "Now do not any of you apostatize because it will have six towers, and

New Zealand Temple opened for public visits prior to its dedication in April 1958. (Church Archives)

Joseph only built one. . . . The time will come when there will be one in the center of Temples we shall build, and on top, groves and fish ponds."[2]

The other three temples constructed in the 1950s were outside the United States, reflecting the new international trend of the Church. In 1955 President McKay dedicated the first European temple, near Bern, Switzerland. Three years later he dedicated a temple near London, England, as well as one in New Zealand. In 1960 plans were announced for a temple in Oakland, California; it was completed in 1964.

Reflection on the changes in temple design that developed in the 1950s is relevant to an understanding of the dynamics of Mormonism. The Los Angeles Temple was the last to be designed with separate rooms for each stage of the endowment ceremony. Another innovation in that temple was the introduction of modern teaching devices. In all subsequent temples tape recordings and motion pictures have replaced some of the live actors in an effort to make the presentation more efficient and more adaptable to different languages. The Swiss, London, and New Zealand temples each consisted of only one ordinance room in addition to the Celestial Room. This smaller plan provided a less expensive way to construct temples and made it possible to build more temples throughout the world.

The Involvement of Youth

In the 1950s the Church became increasingly concerned with the winds of social change that tended to sweep many youth from traditional moorings and into a spirit of rebellion against the values and institutions of their society. The changes in the youth programs reflected efforts to keep the youth rooted in the Latter-day Saint tradition by giving them a greater sense of involvement. In 1950, for example, responsibility for the girls program was transferred from the Presiding Bishopric to the Young Women's Mutual Improvement Association. The MIA responded by sponsoring more musical and recreational programs, and in 1954 a huge regional conference in southern California featured music, dance, and drama festivals. Preparation included local activity in all the wards of the region and involved many young people in

---

[2] *Journal of Discourses,* 1:133.

long hours of planning and practice, under church sponsorship. This program exemplified the different direction the Church was attempting to lead its youth.

For young men, a slight but significant change was made in 1954 when the Presiding Bishopric announced that henceforth worthy boys could be ordained to the office of teacher at age fourteen and to the office of priest at sixteen. Fourteen-year-old boys, they explained, were restless as deacons, and because they did not want to be grouped with the younger boys in deacons quorums, their activity lessened. The earlier advancement was designed to give them a feeling of increased responsibility in the higher quorum. In lowering the age of ordination to the office of priest, young men were placed under the direct guidance of the ward bishop, who was president of the priests quorum, for three years, from ages sixteen to nineteen. The Church also continued its involvement in the Boy Scout program, and in 1955 the "Duty to God" award was established. To achieve this special recognition, a Scout was required to demonstrate unusual achievement in his religious activity as well as in the regular scouting program.

In the 1950s the Church had a higher proportion of boys enrolled in scouting than did any other religious group in America. In 1952 it adopted the national Cub Scout program, with the Primary Association directed to supervise it. The result was that all kinds of scouting activity became even more a part of traditional Mormon family life. Women in every ward were mustered into service as den mothers, and fathers found themselves on outings as well as regularly helping their Cub Scout sons carve model racing cars for the annual "pinewood derby."

When combined with the regular activities connected with Sunday School, the Aaronic Priesthood, and the seminaries, the broadened youth program of the 1950s helped large numbers retain a religious commitment that seemed unusual in the context of contemporary society.

The Commitment to Education

The decade of the fifties was also a time of growth and innovation in the educational program of the Church. Seminary enrollment jumped 220 percent (from 28,600 to 81,400) while enrollment in the institutes of religion increased 150 percent (4,300 to 10,200). The church's financial commitment was also increasing; in 1949 education absorbed 15.8 percent of the total church expenditures; in 1958, the last year such figures were published, it took 21.3 percent.

A far-reaching innovation was the early-morning seminary program, inaugurated churchwide because of the persistence of leaders in southern California. Nonreleased-time programs had not succeeded in other areas of the Church. Nevertheless, eleven California stake presidents met in April 1950 with Church Commissioner of Education Franklin L. West and urged introduction of a seminary program in their region. The plan was approved on a trial basis and Ray L. Jones was appointed to direct it.

When surveys were made among parents and students of every ward, the results could have been discouraging. A multitude of problems was raised: members were widely scattered; comparatively few Latter-day Saint students attended any one school; the California released-time law permitted only one hour per week and then ordinarily only for grades four through six; seminary could not be held at noon because lunch hours were staggered; texts and reference works would be expensive; if chapels were used for seminary, there would be transportation problems, for few chapels were within walking distance of the schools; and if early-morning seminaries were held, they would have to begin at 7:00 A.M. or earlier in order to accommodate schools that began at 8:15. In spite of such discouragement, six pilot classes with 198 students were opened in September 1950. They soon demonstrated that with proper organization and pioneer-type enthusiasm, an early-morning program could be successful. Teachers were drawn from the ranks of professional men, housewives, public school teachers, and others; transportation was provided through car pools; and with parental cooperation and urging, students began attending seminary classes each day before regular school hours. The program spread so rapidly that within a decade nearly 30 percent of all seminary students were enrolled in nonreleased-time programs.

Another important development was the Indian seminary. It began in Brigham City, Utah, where in 1949 the United States government opened an off-reservation dormitory school, the Intermountain Indian School. Six Latter-day Saints were among the first six hundred students to arrive, and local leaders immediately began planning for the religious needs of these students and those who would follow. J. Edwin Baird and Boyd K. Packer, both local officials, were placed in charge, and Elder Packer, then a teacher in the seminary at Brigham City, was soon assigned to develop a religious education program for all Latter-day Saint Indian students. In 1955 he became a general supervisor for the seminaries, and three years later he and A. Theodore Tuttle began a survey of all Indian schools in the United States. Their completed report was submitted to the Church Board of Education in 1958 and approved. Under their direction an effort was begun to provide religious instruction for all LDS students at the major Indian schools. In 1959 Elder Baird was appointed full-time director of the program, and by 1966 nearly 10,000 students were enrolled in Indian seminaries at some 200 schools.

In the South Pacific, limited educational opportunities persuaded Church leaders that they should build and maintain schools that offered academic training in secular subjects as well as religious education. New or enlarged schools included Mapusaga High School in American Samoa; the Church College of Western Samoa and the Pesaga Elementary School with shared facilities at Pesaga; schools in Sauniatu and on the island of Savai'i in Western Samoa; the Liahona High School in Tonga; and the Church College of New Zealand. Schools had been conducted in some of these areas for many years, but in every case they were mission schools, operated under the direction of the mission president and taught by full-time missionaries. By 1957 it was clear that the educational programs in the Pacific were too extensive to continue under mission operation, and in July of that year the Pacific board of education was established to centralize control. Under the direction of this new board the changeover to professionally trained teachers began, and the transition was nearly complete by 1959. The last mission school to close was the one at Vailu'utai, discontinued in 1963 after sixty-five years of operation.

All these schools were either elementary or secondary schools, though they sometimes carried the name "college." Their expansion was a clear indication of the responsibility felt by the Saints to provide basic education for their young people in the islands. But the Church College of Hawaii was of special importance, for it was established to provide the benefits of higher education to young people from all areas of the Pacific.

The story of that institution began at least as early as 1921 when David O. McKay attended a flag-raising ceremony at the mission school and was deeply impressed with the need for an institution of higher learning. From then until after he became President of the Church he held this vision in his mind. In 1951 a special advisory committee appointed by him recommended that the school be located at Laie, near the temple, that it be a boarding school, and that it emphasize vocational training. The First Presidency officially announced on July 21, 1954, that a college would be established in Hawaii. There was considerable controversy over the location, with many local Saints preferring the Honolulu area, but in the long run President McKay's early experience seemed to favor Laie. By the end of 1958 the new campus was completed and dedicated, and in 1959 the college received accreditation for its two-year program. In 1961 it received four-year accreditation.

The Church also expanded its educational programs in Mexico. A school had been operated there since 1887, but only in the 1950s did the program begin to expand into areas outside the Church's own colonies. By then more than 6,000 Saints lived in Mexico and it was apparent that less than 60 percent of their school-age children had the advantage of an elementary education. In October 1957 the First Presidency appointed a committee to study educational needs in Mexico, and the committee recommended that a number of primary schools be organized throughout the country. Even though branch buildings were used at first, the Church moved quickly to construct separate school buildings. In 1959 the committee submitted to the First Presidency a more detailed report that observed that the Mexican government had indicated a desperate need for more schools, especially in urban areas, and that private schools were encouraged. There would be 2,085 Latter-day Saint students available for grades one through eight in the fall of 1959, and the committee recommended the establishment of twelve to fifteen elementary schools. In January 1960 the First Presidency approved the plan, and the following September five primary schools were organized. From its beginning the school system drew upon Mexican citizens for its teachers and administrators.

Indian Placement

The Indian student placement program was another educational innovation of the 1950s with far-reaching consequences.

After World War II the federal government expanded its day schools and boarding schools to many reservations. The dropout rate was high, and cultural differences as well as lack of support from parents made it difficult for many Indian children to achieve. It was inevitable that the Church, with its special concern for the descendants of the people of the Book of Mormon, would develop a program for the growing number of Indian children within its ranks.

Officially, the Indian placement program was initiated in the 1950s. But it was actually one of those many important programs that had their beginnings at the grass roots and then, after their feasibility had been demonstrated, were adopted and expanded by the Church. This program went back to 1947 when Golden Buchanan, a member of the Sevier Stake presidency and resident of Richfield, Utah, was touched by the predicament of transient Indian workers in county sugar beet fields. He was especially concerned that members of his stake seemed to have no concern for the workers' personal welfare. After he expressed his feelings forcefully at a stake conference, a member of his stake told him of a particular Indian girl, Helen John, who spoke English and who had the job of bargaining with the farmers on behalf of the Indian workers. Helen wanted an education and indicated that she was willing to pitch a tent in a backyard if only she could stay and go to school. Buchanan went out to visit Helen. It was late in the fall, and he reported the visit this way:

> You never saw a muddier girl. It was snowing and all the Indians had gone home except a few that were staying to dig out the remaining beets that were frozen in the snow. There were Helen, Helen's older sister Bertha, and Lois Begay. Bertha didn't speak English at all and Lois had been to school only one or two years. These three girls were living in a tent way out in the field in six to eight inches of snow. They were as muddy as could be from the waist down. They were all three typical Indian girls with long hair. Mrs. Avery introduced me to the girls and we talked. Helen said, "I am just going to stay. I am not going home. I am going to get an education."[3]

Touched by such an expression, Buchanan wrote to Elder

---

[3]As quoted in Clarence R. Bishop, "Indian Placement: A History of the Indian Student Placement Program of the Church of Jesus Christ of Latter-day Saints" (M.A. thesis, Brigham Young University, 1967), p. 32, from an interview with Golden Buchanan, October 13, 1966.

Spencer W. Kimball of the Council of the Twelve. Two days later he was surprised by a personal visit from the apostle, who asked the Buchanans if they would consider taking Helen into their home while she went to school. After a night to think it over, the Buchanans accepted the challenge, and by January 1948 Helen was settled with them. Two of her friends were placed in the homes of other Richfield families.

From this beginning the program spread, although slowly, so that by 1953 sixty-eight Indian students were living in foster homes while attending school. In the meantime, Buchanan became acquainted with Miles Jensen of Gunnison Stake, who was already deeply involved with the Indian people because of his responsibility to coordinate and recruit migrant laborers for the Gunnison (Utah) Sugar Company. The Jensen family was one of those persuaded by Buchanan to take in foster children, and in June 1948 Elder Jensen received an assignment to be coordinator of Indian affairs for the Church, under the direction of the Indian Relations Committee headed by Spencer W. Kimball. The placement

An Indian family visits with the host family that has taken an Indian child into its home during the school year as part of the Indian placement program. (Church Archives)

of Indian children in foster homes was still not officially promoted by the Church, but Buchanan and Jensen were active throughout southern Utah in personally encouraging it. Jensen assumed full responsibility in 1951 when Buchanan was appointed president of the Southwest Indian Mission. By the fall of 1951 Indian student placements had extended to Idaho, Oregon, and southern California.

Even though the Church did not officially participate in the experimental program, Elder Kimball kept close to it and reported on it to other Church leaders. But it was with difficulty that some Caucasian members accepted the full implications of Indian placement. In April 1954 Elder Kimball began his general conference address by commenting with pleasure on the large number of Saints from various minority groups who were attending the conference, then quoted from an anonymous letter received from an ostensible member, which complained of Indians being allowed to talk in church, go to the temple, and otherwise participate intimately with other Church members.

If Mrs. Anonymous were the only one who felt that way! However, from many places and different directions I hear intolerant expressions. While there is an ever-increasing number of people who are kind and willing to accept the minority groups as they come into the Church, there are still many who speak in disparaging terms, who priestlike and Levite-like pass by on the other side of the street. . . .

In the letter quoted, there is the suggestion of a superior race! From the dawn of history we have seen so-called superior races go down from the heights to the depths in a long parade of exits. . . . Is the implication of Mrs. Anonymous justified that the white race or the American people is superior? . . .

The Lord would have eliminated bigotry and class distinction. He talked to the Samaritan woman at the well, healed the centurion's kin, and blessed the child of the Canaanitish woman. . . .

And now, Mrs. Anonymous, when the Lord has made all flesh equal; when he has accepted both the Gentiles and Israel; when he finds no difference between them, who are we to find a difference and to exclude from the Church and its activities and blessings the lowly Indian?

In July 1954, members having caught the vision, the Church officially inaugurated the Indian student placement program, with the full expectation that children placed in white foster homes would find genuine love and understanding. Seven stakes in southern Utah were asked to begin the official program, with foster families participating on a strictly voluntary basis. Since Indian families were generally without financial means to provide even the necessary food, clothing, and transportation, the foster families must be willing to shoulder such expenses. In addition, the First Presidency made it clear that "if an Indian child is taken into a home he comes not as a mere guest, nor as a servant, . . . he or she may enter the home as a welcomed member of the household to enjoy the spiritual and cultural atmosphere of the home, and to be given such schooling in the public schools as may be afforded to him."[4]

Under Utah law, the program had to be supervised by a licensed agency, and with the cooperation of the State Department of Public Welfare, the Relief Society was so licensed. Miles Jensen continued as a caseworker and supervisor, and Golden Buchanan, president of the Southwest Indian Mission, assumed responsibility for selecting participating students, who were required to be members of the Church. After passing physical examinations and receiving various immunization shots, the Indian students were introduced to their foster families. By 1956, 242 students were enrolled in the program. Ten years later the number had grown to 1,569. The program had expanded to many states and Canada and included students from sixty-four tribes.

Inevitably, there were problems. Some Indian children found the educational, cultural, and social challenges overwhelming and dropped out of school. Some white families were unable to adapt to foster children. And Indian families themselves were torn by mixed emotions as their children left home each fall. Some members and a few over-enthusiastic missionaries attempted to place children in foster homes without going through proper channels. It became necessary for the First Presidency to warn the Saints that such independent action could not be condoned, for it disregarded the law and jeopardized the well-being of the Indian children.

Equally serious were complaints that began to come from the U.S. Bureau of Indian Affairs and other sources about the operation of some parts of the program. Critics suggested that in some cases the program was used for proselyting and to encourage mass baptisms on the reservations, that it tended to alienate the affec-

[4]Stephen L Richards and J. Reuben Clark, Jr., to the presidents of seven southern Utah stakes, August 10, 1954, as quoted in Bishop, "Indian Placement," p. 43.

tion of children from their parents, that it deprived parents of the responsibility of training their own children, that it often took children from reservations when adequate education was available in their own communities, and that some of the caseworkers used in the program were not competent. An early response to such criticism came in a special meeting at Kanab, Utah, in March 1957, when representatives of the Church met with officials from state and federal welfare services. As a result, new guidelines were adopted that kept Church representatives in closer contact with state and federal agencies, provided better evaluation procedures, and gave increased attention to the relationship between the foster children and their natural parents. It was recognized that as long as the mission president and missionaries were responsible for selecting children for the program, it could well appear that it was a proselyting tool rather than a legitimate exercise in secular education. The student selection process had to be the responsibility of the professional staff.

The long-range effectiveness of the student placement program is difficult to assess, but it is clear that placing Indian children in white homes throughout Utah and other areas not only helped hundreds of children but also contributed to breaking down racial prejudice. In 1967 the annual dropout rate was no higher than that in off-reservation boarding schools and students often returned to the program after a year on the reservation. Educational attainment varied greatly, but in 1967 more than 80 percent of the program's graduates had received post-high-school training, and a large number had served missions.

Higher Education

As the Church expanded its commitment to higher education in the 1950s, a movement toward administrative consolidation became apparent. This change of direction was best illustrated at Ricks College in Rexburg, Idaho. In 1954 the school received the highest accreditation possible for a four-year college, but in that same year it was cut back to a two-year school. The First Presidency had given consideration to the overall development of the Church school system and concluded that Ricks would be of more service and "have greater destiny as an integral and permanent part of the school system by being a first class junior college

than by continuing as a relatively small four-year college."[5] The
First Presidency urged all Latter-day Saint students in the area to
obtain their first two years of college at Ricks, then transfer to
BYU, the senior university in the Unified Church School System.

Three years later the thirteen stake presidencies in the college
area were called together to hear a plan for moving the college to
Idaho Falls. The proposal was made by Dr. Ernest L. Wilkinson,
president of BYU and administrator of the Unified Church School
System. The surprised and dismayed local leaders asked for time to
prepare a response. Their reaction was presented to the President
of the Church and the Church board of education soon afterward,
and in July 1957 the Idaho leaders were informed by President
McKay that the school would remain in Rexburg.

In November 1958, Elders Marion G. Romney and Hugh B.
Brown of the Council of the Twelve announced to the leaders of
the two Rexburg stakes that the board of education had decided
after all to move the school to Idaho Falls. This reversal was based
upon the need to provide educational service for a greater number
of students near home. Idaho Falls, a larger community and able
to provide more student employment, was also closer for more
students.

A local "Committee of 1,000" countered with its own publication in February 1959, emphasizing the history and tradition of
the college in Rexburg and noting that with modern transportation, the twenty-eight miles between Rexburg and Idaho Falls was
not a significant distance for students. Arguments developed a
degree of heat, and the distraught president of the college, Dr.
John R. Clarke, found himself pulled in two directions. The controversy continued until 1961, when the First Presidency finally
announced three new buildings would be constructed on the Ricks
campus in Rexburg, which meant the college would remain where
it was.

The growth of Brigham Young University in this decade and
the unification of the school system were evidence of the gradual
development of a master plan for church education. Dr. Wilkinson, a noted Washington, D.C., attorney, had been selected to

---

[5]Letter of the First Presidency, April 7, 1954, as quoted in Harvey L. Taylor, "The Story of
the LDS Church Schools," 2 vols., typed Ms., prepared for the Church Commissioner of
Education, 1971, 2:183, in Church Archives.

head Brigham Young University in 1950 and was inaugurated in 1951. Almost immediately he launched a program of expansion. His well-designed, forceful presentations were influential in persuading the board of trustees that new buildings and facilities as well as new faculty members were needed at the university. In the ensuing decade enrollment more than doubled, from 4,584 to 10,445. The number of full-time faculty members increased from 196 to 502. By 1961 new buildings completed included a fieldhouse, an engineering laboratory building, a student service center, three classroom and office buildings, a plant science laboratory, a student health center, an industrial education building, several student resident halls, an alumni house, and a motion picture studio. This was only the beginning of the physical expansion at BYU.

The first doctorates were awarded in 1960, and an honors program was inaugurated that year. In 1963 an Indian education program was established. In 1961 a language training institution was started, forerunner of the Language Training Mission established in 1963 to prepare missionaries for foreign service. Under Wilkinson's guidance Brigham Young University became the largest church-related university in America.

The move toward consolidation of the Church's educational institutions began in 1952 when LDS Business College in Salt Lake City was placed under the administrative direction of Brigham Young University. In July 1953 all of the educational institutions were combined under one administration, except those still under the Pacific board of education, and President Wilkinson was named administrator of the Unified Church School System. The position of commissioner of education, which directed seminaries and institutes, was discontinued. William E. Berrett was appointed vice-president of Brigham Young University and vice-administrator of the school system with responsibility for religious education. The seminaries and institutes came directly under his jurisdiction. This arrangement continued until the appointment of Neal A. Maxwell as commissioner of education in 1970.

As part of the expansion of the school system, efforts were made to get ward members more directly involved in promoting seminary and institute enrollment. One such step was the organization of ward education committees in 1957. These committees were especially effective in the areas where nonreleased-time or early-morning seminaries were held. They were responsible for encouraging enrollment, organizing transportation pools, and supporting the seminary classes in other appropriate ways. In addition, they were instructed to maintain contact with college-age students and to encourage attendance either at a Church college or at a college where an institute of religion was established. By the end of the decade it was clear the efforts of these committees had helped substantially improve the percentage of young people enrolled in Church education programs. These committees continued to function until 1968, when the new correlation program began.

With the rapid growth in enrollments at colleges and universities, increasing attention was given to the church activity of LDS college students. Often those living away from home were not absorbed into wards and stakes in their college communities. Branches had been organized at BYU and other schools with large

Brigham Young University campus, about 1963. In the early twentieth century the campus began to move from downtown Provo to "Temple Hill." The first building to be completed in the new location was the Karl G. Maeser Building, seen in the front center of this view, which was dedicated in 1911. (Brigham Young University Archives)

Mormon student populations, but they still did not seem to provide the full range of training and activity needed. In other cases, students overcrowded the wards in college areas, dominating the classes and seemingly relegating older residents to the background.

With these problems in mind, administrators of the school system recommended the organization of student wards. In 1956 the first student stake was organized on the Brigham Young University campus. Campus wards were later organized at every location where the number of students justified it. Generally they were supervised by the local stakes, but in Rexburg and at the larger institutions of religion, such as those in Salt Lake City and Logan, Utah, and Pocatello, Idaho, student stakes were also created.

President Wilkinson often remarked that the organization of student wards and stakes was the most important thing to happen during his administration. In terms of the spiritual well-being of the students, he may well have been correct. Immediately students found themselves involved in every aspect of local church administration. Usually a professor or someone from the community served as bishop, but often mature students were called as counselors. Students became ward clerks, presidents of Relief Societies and MIAs, and even, in many cases, members of stake high councils. The student wards demonstrated a certain flexibility in church organization; the Mutual Improvement Association and the Relief Society, for example, were modified to meet students' special needs.

The results were outstanding, especially with regard to Relief Society, which traditionally had been considered an organization for the more mature women of the ward. In the college setting young women met in Relief Society on Sunday morning at the same time the men attended priesthood meeting. Thousands of young women suddenly found themselves not only involved in, but also excited about, the program of religious instruction, cultural training, social relations, and homemaking that the Relief Society sponsored. The spiritual growth of young people under the new program was phenomenal, and in temple marriages and attendance at meetings, as well as most other statistical measurements, student wards led the Church.

The growth of the school system promised to receive an important boost in 1954 when the Utah legislature authorized the governor to turn over three junior colleges—Dixie, Snow, and Weber—to the Church. The state was in financial difficulty, and to many people this seemed to be a logical solution to the problem. The Church had given the colleges in question to the state in the 1930s, with the provision that if the state should cease to operate them, the property would return to the Church. Seizing on this opportunity, Governor J. Bracken Lee urged the transfer, but a citizens' reaction put the matter on the ballot as a referendum in the next election. The Church stated its willingness to take the schools and operate them on a sound financial basis, but in the referendum a majority of Utah citizens voted against the proposition, and the schools continued under state sponsorship.

Secularism, Stress, and the Public Image

As the Church continued to grow in the twentieth century, it met stresses and strains both from within and from the secular world. University students came face to face with highly potent discussions of the theory of evolution, higher criticism, and other modern approaches to the scriptures, and scientific theories concerning the origin of the earth and the ancestry of the American Indian. To some observers, these seemed to challenge certain assumptions of traditional Latter-day Saint literalism. The result was stress within the university community, since the traditional function of a university was to teach students to think independently—even to question traditional kinds of authority in their independent quest for truth. Although this approach tended to disturb some students, Church universities and institutes of religion attempted to employ a class of teachers who could deal with such problems in a well-informed and non-dogmatic, yet faithful and constructive, way and help students over such religious-secular hurdles.

One nationally recognized scholar, not a Latter-day Saint, expressed in 1957 great admiration for an education program that was trying to cope with such stresses and strains, as well as confidence that the Church was still a vital force in the lives of its members. He met with a group of mature Latter-day Saint students who were studying in the social sciences and humanities at one eastern university and asked them what they really thought about the future of the Church as it more frequently confronted these challenges. "The result," he reported, "was more persuasive than any analysis could possibly be." Rather than responding dogmatically without awareness of the implications of their statements, the students discussed the questions intelligently and demonstrated great flexibility in an atmosphere of faith—an ability to distinguish passing tradition from the essential elements of the faith and thus reorient themselves to changing circumstances. He wrote:

> They demonstrated that Mormonism was meaningful to them, who were in some way Mormondom's young elite—those sent to bring learning and higher degrees to Utah. Their testimony must be admitted as eloquent.
>
> Strains, yes; conflict, perhaps; but strains and conflict are both signs and sources of vitality. The fact is that the Church of Jesus Christ of Latter-day Saints is still a vital institution. Conflict and strain have not been sufficient to prevent its orderly functioning over the last many decades. It may not be so well adapted or prepared to meet new problems as it was in times in the past; yet all transitions and all reorientations are difficult. That its values still provide a meaningful context to great numbers of its adherents cannot be denied. Its flexibility in the past and its viability under the most adverse conditions do not augur badly for its future.[6]

Such was one scholar's image of the Latter-day Saints, but there were other, more general, images of the Mormons being created in the 1950s. In national periodicals, for example, the 1950s saw a generally favorable public image. The Church was praised for its continuing activities in the welfare program. Successful Mormon businessmen were often favorably publicized, and frequently their church affiliation was pointed out. The continuing national broadcasts of the Tabernacle Choir also contributed to a positive image. The choir achieved special recognition for its successful tour of Europe in 1955 and a tour of the eastern United States in 1958. In 1959 it received the "Grammy" award from the record industry for its recording of the famous Civil War song "Battle Hymn of the Republic," and after the 1950s Mormon Tabernacle Choir records, including sacred and secular music, sold widely. In addition, in 1953 the Church began to televise its general conferences so that certain sessions could be seen in many

---

[6]Thomas F. O' Dea, *The Mormons* (Chicago: University of Chicago Press, 1957), p. 263.

parts of the United States. All this enhanced the image of Mormonism.

Political Affairs

Because of its predominance in Utah and its growing influence in the United States, the Church continued to become involved in public issues. This involvement came about in at least two ways. On the one hand, whenever individual leaders participated in political life, people asked if their views were endorsed by the Church. The leaders always affirmed that they were acting according to their individual persuasions and did not claim official church backing. But often if the individual was a General Authority, the respect members had for him helped lend considerable weight to his views. On the other hand, the Church found itself directly involved in consideration of some public policies, such as the disposition of Utah's junior colleges that had formerly belonged to the Church.

An example of the involvement of a leading Latter-day Saint in public affairs came in 1952 when Elder Ezra Taft Benson of the Council of the Twelve was appointed secretary of agriculture by the newly elected president of the United States, Dwight D. Eisenhower. Elder Benson, whose professional career before he became a General Authority had been in agricultural marketing, remained in the cabinet during the eight years of Eisenhower's administration.

As secretary of agriculture, Elder Benson gained respect for his integrity and energy. He had long been opposed to farm subsidies and crop controls, feeling that the American economy, including farmers, would operate best without government intervention and regulation. Though sometimes the object of criticism, he remained loyal to his principles and was successful in bringing about several significant reforms. In his first news conference, two weeks after taking office, he said that he believed in some price supports, as insurance against farm disaster, but that they should be flexible in order to help adjust each crop to the demands of the natural market. When Secretary Benson's specific proposals were sent to Congress by the president in 1954, the agricultural committees of both the Senate and House voted against them, but the entire body of Congress approved them. In 1956, as the result of Secretary Benson's advice, President Eisenhower vetoed programs

During the Eisenhower administration Elder Ezra Taft Benson of the Council of the Twelve served as Secretary of Agriculture. (U.S.D.A. photograph, Benson Papers, Church Archives)

that would have reversed the earlier legislation. Throughout his term in office Elder Benson worked vigorously for fewer government controls and an expansion of markets. When he left office in January 1961, he was highly respected, even by those who had opposed his views.

Other leaders also spoke out on national political affairs. One was President J. Reuben Clark, Jr., a former undersecretary of state, former American ambassador to Mexico, and since 1933 a member of the First Presidency. He was particularly vocal in the 1950s in his opposition to American involvement in the United Nations—and for the same reasons that he was opposed in 1919 to contemplated American entry into the League of Nations. In the same spirit as Elder Benson, when President Clark delivered an attack on the United Nations in 1952, in a speech entitled "Our Dwindling Sovereignty," he made it abundantly clear that he was speaking only for himself and not in behalf of the Church. Three months earlier he discussed the forthcoming speech with President McKay, recognizing that it would be controversial. President McKay saw no objection in his airing his personal views in that manner; and when he gave the speech President Clark declared, "For what I shall say tonight I am solely responsible."

Another Church leader who spoke out frequently on political affairs was Hugh B. Brown, who became an Assistant to the Twelve in 1953, a member of the Council of the Twelve in 1958, and who served as a member of the First Presidency from 1961 to 1970. A former Democratic candidate for U.S. senator, Elder Brown frequently spoke out in favor of the United Nations as well as some of the social welfare activities of the federal government. Although he credited Democratic leadership with much beneficial legislation in the twentieth century, his major emphasis when speaking to Church members was on political balance and toleration. On May 31, 1968, he declared at the Brigham Young University commencement exercises: "Strive to develop a maturity of mind and emotion and a depth of spirit which enables you to differ with others on matters of politics without calling into question the integrity of those with whom you differ. Allow within the bounds of your definition of religious orthodoxy variations of political beliefs. Do not have the temerity to dogmatize in issues where the Lord has seen fit to be silent."

It was to be expected that some people, both members and nonmembers, would either misinterpret or misconstrue for their own purposes the political views of such brethren. Because Church leaders who were active in politics seemed to lean toward one party or the other, some people were persuaded that in some way Latter-day Saint doctrines were more compatible with that party and that faithful Saints should adhere to it. Nothing could have been more contrary to the actual position of the leaders generally, who were constantly refusing to endorse candidates and were reminding members that the Church would not take an official stand on political issues, with a few exceptions on matters that seemed to affect fundamental gospel principles. There were Church leaders active in both principal American parties; their political differences did not keep them from maintaining genuine gospel brotherhood with the rest of their brethren.

Perhaps the feeling of the brethren with regard to members and their participation in politics was best characterized in a statement by President McKay during general conference in October 1952:

Twice, during the conference, reference has been made to the fact that we are approaching a general election, in which tension becomes high; sometimes feelings are engendered; often false reports are made; and innocent people are misjudged.

Recently we heard that in one meeting, for example, it was stated authoritatively by somebody that two members of the General Authorities had said that the General Authorities of the Church had held a meeting and had decided to favor one of the leading political parties over the other, here in this state, particularly. . . .

This report is not true, and I take this opportunity here, publicly, to renounce such a report as without foundation in fact.

In the Church, there are members who favor the Democratic party. There are other members who sincerely believe and advocate the principles and ideals of the Republican party. The First Presidency, Council of the Twelve, and other officers who constitute the General Authorities of the Church preside over members of both political parties.

. . . The welfare of all members of the Church is equally considered by the President, his Counselors, and the General Authorities. Both political parties will be treated impartially.[7]

The decade of the 1950s was an important time of transition for the Church. As the postwar world presented new challenges and opportunities, the Church grew rapidly and augmented its programs. New directions in missionary work, youth programs, temple activity, and educational programs as well as a renewed emphasis on building up the Church outside America laid the foundation for the two most dramatic developments of the 1960s and 1970s: genuine internationalism and major administrative developments that would help the Church accommodate both internationalism and growth.

[7]*Conference Report*, October 1952, pp. 129-30.

CHAPTER 20

Correlating the Worldwide Church, 1960-1973

Change and growth were coming more rapidly than ever before as the Church entered the 1960s. Still expanding worldwide, the Church in ten years would add more than a million people. Administratively it had long outgrown the simple ecclesiastical structure established in the days of Joseph Smith, and by the 1960s there were actually three kinds of organizations operating within the Church. One was the regular ecclesiastical system, with its well-designed chain of priesthood authority. Another consisted of the auxiliaries—the Relief Society, Sunday School, Mutual Improvement Associations, and Primary—each of which had its own general board and officers, published its own manuals, held its own conferences, determined its own courses of study, and published its own magazine. Efforts begun as early as 1908 to more effectively coordinate their specific goals and activities still had not been completely achieved.

A third type of organization included the multitude of professional services that were necessary to carry out the normal functions of the Church, and that would continue to burgeon. The educational arm of the Church was one such service, and by the 1970s it would spread worldwide. Other important programs that demanded professional staffs included legal services, the building department (which included architects and other professions associated with the building trades), communications, accounting, and many more. Thousands of people were employed full time—not as church officers but rather, much like civil servants in government, to carry out the essential day-to-day tasks without which the modern church could not function completely. None of these professional staffs operated independently of church direction, but as the work of some increased, the need for examining the interrelationship among them became apparent. By 1973 all church functions had been impressively though not completely correlated under a unique administrative system that clearly had the priesthood as its central force. The achievement of this organizational realignment was one of the principal themes of the Church's history for a dozen or so years after 1960.

Three Modern Prophets

From 1960 to 1973 three different men presided over the Church, but a distinct unity can be seen in the thrust of their administrations. David O. McKay presided until his death at age ninety-six in January 1970. As a young apostle he had been appointed in 1908 to the General Priesthood Committee on Outlines, the first group to seriously consider ways to correlate the entire church program. He was directly involved in all subsequent correlation attempts, and it was not unexpected that a major correlation effort would be conducted during the final decade of his presidency.

Joseph Fielding Smith became President of the Church at age ninety-three, on January 23, 1970. He was perhaps the most prolific writer on doctrinal subjects the Church had yet produced, and his numerous books and articles were widely read. In 1921 he became Church Historian, and in 1934 he was named president of the Genealogical Society. He also served as president of the Salt Lake Temple, chairman of the General Church Melchizedek Priesthood Committee, member of the Church Board of Education, chairman of the Church Committee on Publications, President of the Council of the Twelve, and after 1965 a counselor to President McKay. As President of the Church, he oversaw implementation of many administrative procedures recommended by the studies and experiences of the 1960s. Despite his advanced age,

President David O. McKay, known for his love of horses, often visited his family farm at Huntsville, Utah. (Church Archives)

President Smith proved that he was still vigorous mentally and physically. In addition, his kindly leadership demonstrated that he was, indeed, a generous, loving prophet whose basic concern was the well-being of all the Saints.

A few of the important decisions made during President Smith's administration were the reorganization of the educational program, the organization of the Historical Department, the revamping of the publications program, organization of the Social Services Department, and the inauguration of a training program for bishops. In addition, he created fourteen new missions, expanded the teacher development program churchwide, continued an active schedule of speaking at public meetings, and presided over the first area general conference in 1972. He kept up a remarkable pace, and many who had been critical of a system that allowed aged men to govern had ample reason to change their minds.

The Church was going through a metamorphosis, and President Smith proved capable of responding to the challenge. As an apostle he undoubtedly reflected the misgivings of some members about certain aspects of the rapid expansion when, in August 1962, he wrote in his journal: "Our spending everywhere is to me alarming. . . . We are constantly creating stakes in Europe, the islands of the Pacific, and on the American continent. I wonder if we have forgotten the commandment to gather. To come to Zion."[1] Eight years later, as President of the Church, he not only approved the organization of far-flung stakes but also presided over the conference in Manchester, England, the first general conference held outside the United States. At this significant meeting he declared:

> We are members of a world church. . . .
> The day is long since past when informed people think of us as a strange group in the tops of the Rocky Mountains in America. . . . we are coming of age as a church and as a people. We have attained the stature and strength that are enabling us to fulfill the commission given us by the Lord through the Prophet Joseph Smith that we should carry the glad tidings of the restoration to every nation and to all people. . . .
> Thus the church is not an American church except in America. In Canada it is a Canadian church; in Australia it is an Australian church; and in Great Britain it is a British church. It is a world church; the gospel is for all men.[2]

President Smith was a living example of the Church's changing outlook. The challenge was for other American Saints to gain the same perspective.

Harold B. Lee became President July 7, 1972, and served until his death on December 26, 1973. He was a man uniquely suited to encourage correlation, for he had never been fearful of innovation so long as it was carried out under the clear direction of priesthood authority. His first general Church assignment was to establish the welfare program in 1936, and after he became a member of the Council of the Twelve in 1948 he continued at the head of the program. In 1948 he was appointed by the First Presidency to head a committee of apostles assigned to recommend

---

[1] Joseph Fielding Smith, Jr., and John J Stewart, *The Life of Joseph Fielding Smith* (Salt Lake City: Bookcraft, 1972), pp. 325-26.
[2] "To the Saints in Great Britain," *Ensign* 1 (September 1971): 2-3.

changes in the work of the priesthood and auxiliaries—another effort at correlation. His committee's recommendations were not adopted, for they included organizational changes that President George Albert Smith did not think the Church was prepared for, but he remained vitally interested in the problem of effective coordination of all church units.

Elder Lee had other qualifications for leadership. A teacher by profession, he was concerned not only with the problems of youth but also with the need for constant improvement in both religious and secular training. Before becoming a General Authority he had served Salt Lake City as a city councilman and the Church as a stake president. Although he was the eleventh President of the Church, he was only the second—Heber J. Grant was the first—to have previously served as a stake president.

Achievements in Correlation

The goal of achieving effective coordination among all units of the modern church was complex and difficult, but in March 1960 the effort was renewed. Harold B. Lee, chairman of the Melchizedek Priesthood Committee, was assigned to conduct a study of church curriculum. He, in turn, appointed Antone K. Romney, dean of the College of Education at Brigham Young University, to head a committee that would make a historical survey of the auxiliaries and correlation efforts.

By March 1961 the report was complete. Dean Romney's committee recommended some far-reaching changes in church organization. Although this report—like earlier ones—was not implemented, the committee was instructed to take another look at the problem to see if correlation could be accomplished within the existing structure of the Church. On July 10 it made another report, which was ultimately adopted by the General Priesthood Committee.

The first public announcement of the new correlation effort came from Elder Lee at a general priesthood meeting on September 30, 1961. He described the formation of an all-Church Coordinating Council consisting of himself as chairman, three additional members of the Council of the Twelve, the Presiding Bishop, the auxiliary heads, and representatives from the Melchizedek Priesthood Committee and the education system. In addition, each of the three members of the Council of the Twelve would preside over one of three new age-group committees: child, youth, and adult. These committees would be responsible for instructional programs relating to their respective groups. Their ultimate goal was to consolidate and simplify all church curricula, publications, meetings, and other activities.

The make-up of the Coordinating Council changed from time to time, but Elder Lee remained at the head until he became president in 1972. The council's executive committee was called the Correlation Committee, though eventually all plans went to the First Presidency and the Council of the Twelve for approval. These authorities actually functioned as the ultimate correlation committee as far as final decision-making was concerned.

The three age-group committees went to work with vigor, but the task of creating a fully coordinated curriculum was highly complicated and ran into opposition from almost every group affected. Originally it was hoped that correlated courses would be ready by 1963, but deadlines were constantly postponed. One reason was that committees sometimes presented plans calling for a restructuring of church organizations. The Correlation Committee would reject them, since its commission was to work within the existing organizational structure.

Gradually the efforts at correlation began to affect every program. The first major innovation was home teaching, inaugurated churchwide in 1964. Actually, it was a redefining of the old ward teaching program that gave the priesthood increased responsibilities. Priesthood quorums rather than the bishop became responsible for supervision of home teaching, and priesthood holders were instructed that their responsibility was no longer simply to make a monthly visit. Rather, they were to become personally acquainted with all family members and make visits whenever necessary to contribute to their spiritual welfare and church activity. Significantly, the traditional monthly lessons were eliminated so that home teachers were more responsible to use their own initiative in determining what was best for the families concerned.

The Correlation Committee also determined that priesthood responsibility fell into four major categories: missionary work, genealogy, welfare, and home teaching. Accordingly, four committees were organized to deal with these responsibilities.

By the mid-1960s the wide sweep of correlation was beginning to visibly affect ward organization and activities. In 1963 each ward was instructed to set up a home teaching committee, which later became known as the priesthood executive committee. Consisting of the bishopric and priesthood leaders, this agency planned, coordinated, and directed ward priesthood activities. Each ward was instructed to organize a ward council, which met monthly. Comprised of the priesthood executive committee and the heads of the auxiliaries, it was designed to coordinate ward functions and discuss better ways to focus on the individual and determine which organization or combination of organizations could best assist those who needed help. This local aspect of correlation was designed to assure that no one would ever be lost because of lack of interest or concern on the part of the local members.

The correlation of activities at the local level was relatively easy compared with achieving full coordination in the higher echelons. Some auxiliaries, for example, continued to send out instructions to stake and ward workers without clearing them through the

President Joseph Fielding Smith at general conference converses with Harold B. Lee, who succeeded him as President. (Church Archives)

Correlation Committee. In addition, the reporting procedures tended to emphasize the independence of the auxiliaries, for each had its own system. These problems were partially solved in 1967 when all ward reports were consolidated into one set of forms, which were then routed through the stake president to the Presiding Bishop's Office, rather than through auxiliary heads to general auxiliary executives. In 1965 the *Priesthood Bulletin* was inaugurated, designed for distribution to all leaders. All organizations and committees were supposed to send their instructions through that correlated and unified publication.

One aspect of correlation that directly affected every member was the family home evening program, formally launched in 1965. The Church had frequently advised families to spend at least one night each week together, but now special home evening manuals provided suggested lessons and activities. Families were urged to be flexible and to plan those activities best suited to bring them together. Recognizing that church-sponsored events sometimes stood in the way of achieving this ideal, leaders soon requested that Monday night be left free of all other church activities for family home evening. One of the most successful of all innovations during this period, the Monday family home evening caught on throughout the Church and by the 1970s was an important and viable tradition. In some areas where the Latter-day Saints enjoyed a numerical majority, town and school administrators even scheduled athletic and community activities to avoid family night.

Administrative Reforms Under the Correlation Program

The increasing pace of correlation accompanied a steady growth in church population and a proliferation of wards and stakes. The burden on the General Authorities was becoming excessive, especially since they were still trying to visit stake conferences at least twice a year. As early as 1961 it was decided that members of the First Council of the Seventy would be ordained to the office of high priest so that when they attended conferences they could perform ordinations to that office and carry out other duties assigned them by the Council of the Twelve. In 1965 President McKay received further help by appointing two additional counselors in the First Presidency, Joseph Fielding Smith and Thorpe B. Isaacson.

In 1967 the position of Regional Representative of the Twelve was created. Initially sixty-nine men were called, but the number soon expanded. Each Regional Representative was assigned to regularly visit a certain number of stakes. He was not to preside at stake conferences, but he would act as an adviser to the stakes and as liaison officer between stake presidents and the Council of the Twelve. In 1972 a number of Mission Representatives were appointed with the same responsibility toward missions; in January 1974 they became Regional Representatives of the Twelve, as the function of this office was extended to include the missions.

But correlation was not complete. In 1970 a bishops' training program was inaugurated under the direction of the Presiding Bishopric. The following year a churchwide teacher development program was adopted that included a basic eleven-week course plus a correlated in-service training program for all teachers. Developed by professional Latter-day Saint educators, the program focused on basic principles to help teachers better reach and change the lives of individuals.

Elder Lee and his associates were still not satisfied that members had really grasped the concept that the directing influence in all church activity should be the priesthood and that the auxiliaries were in reality only helps to the priesthood in carrying out its proper function. In 1973, when Elder Lee was President of the Church, a major step was taken by combining the Mutual Improvement Associations and the priesthood. This plan had been envisioned as early as 1928 but never fully implemented.

The Aaronic Priesthood MIA, as it was called, retained the same age-group divisions, but henceforth the deacons quorum adviser served as the Scoutmaster, and the other Aaronic Priesthood advisers assumed responsibility for the same groups in the former MIA program. The young women were divided into corresponding groups, with a young woman appointed to supervise each group. In 1974 the name Mutual Improvement Association was dropped, and the two groups became known simply as the Aaronic Priesthood and the Young Women. Now that all youth activities were under the direction of the priesthood, the century-old tradition of having a separate auxiliary known as the Mutual Improvement Association was ended.

At the same time the interests of unmarried men and women

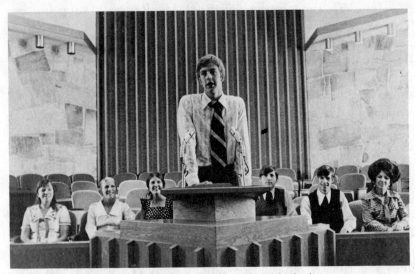

*Youth speaker in one of the modern chapels—typical of what was seen
regularly in meetings throughout the Church in the mid-twentieth century,
and a significant change from the typical Church meeting of a hundred years
earlier. (Church Archives)*

ages twenty-six and over became the concern of the Melchizedek
Priesthood MIA. Through stake and regional organizations they
participated in dances and other cultural activities and found
broader opportunities to become acquainted with Saints their own
age who shared common interests.

By the 1970s correlation was also changing other traditions.
In 1971, for example, the athletic and dance programs were re-
gionalized. In place of all-church athletic tournaments and dance
festivals, each region was instructed to conduct its own events. This
was designed to stimulate greater local participation and minimize
expenses and logistical problems involved in annual treks to Salt
Lake City. Another program developed under instructions from
the Correlation Committee affected college students. In the late
1960s the Latter-day Saints Student Association (LDSSA) was organized. Its purpose was to upgrade spiritual and social activities
for LDS students as well as to coordinate activities between
students and non-student young adults.

Adjustments in Central Services

The idea of more fully coordinating the various programs was beginning to affect the whole structure of the Church, including the top-level professional and administrative functions. The Church was becoming more deeply involved in a variety of social services, but responsibility for them tended to overlap. Accordingly, leaders began to look seriously at the need for restructuring the responsibility of various administrative units and at their own involvement in administrative affairs.

One of the first steps in the restructuring process came in 1969 when Indian student placement, child adoption, and youth guidance programs were combined in a unified social service program. In 1971, health, social, and welfare services were involved in a major reorganization under the Presiding Bishopric. Both the Social Services and Health Services became licensed corporations, and Social Services became responsible for programs relating to the American Indians. The Health Services Corporation took control of all Church-owned hospitals and such activities as nurses' training programs and training in preventive medicine for members in underdeveloped areas. In 1971 Health Services also inaugurated, for the first time in Church history, a health missionary program in which young adults were sent to underdeveloped countries to teach basic principles of nutrition and health care to members. While this was a far cry from the original scope of correlation, it indicates that the idea of better integrating and directing programs was affecting all church services by the 1970s.

Publications, too, were restructured under the principle of correlation. In December 1970, the last issues of the traditional magazines came off the presses. In their place three new magazines began publication in January 1971, designed to carry articles and instructions pertaining to the three basic age groups: the *Friend* for children, the *New Era* for youth, and the *Ensign* for adults. Regional publications had already been stopped, and a unified international magazine was begun in 1967. Translated into many languages, it included selected articles from the other Church magazines.

Publishing for a worldwide church presented serious problems of translation and distribution. Leaders were especially concerned with lesson manuals, which often were not published in non-English editions. Even when available they were usually written from the perspective of American culture; the examples used and issues raised simply were not always relevent in other cultures.

Health missionaries working with a family in Patzicha, Guatemala.
(*Church Internal Communications Department*)

Writing committees were instructed to use universal examples as
much as possible and to eliminate references that were unique to
the American culture.

In 1965 the Translation Department was organized, and in
1967 it was combined with the Distribution Department. Soon distribution centers were established in several places in Europe,
North and South America, the Pacific, and Asia to assist in getting
Church literature to the wards and branches as quickly as possible.

With such rapid expansion of services and the resulting
growth of administrative responsibility, leaders also recognized the
need for independent, professional examination of the Church's
administrative structure. In 1971 they employed two well-known
business consulting firms to make in-depth studies of internal
operations of the Church. These were Cresap, McCormack, and
Paget, Inc., of New York, and Safeway Stores, Inc., of Oakland,
California. By August 1971 both companies had completed their
studies and submitted comprehensive reports and recommendations. Many of these recommendations were soon adopted.

The Cresap report pointed to the obvious problem that the
General Authorities had become burdened with too much time
spent on administrative and operating responsibilities. It recom-

mended that most administrative functions be turned over to full-time managing directors, thus freeing the General Authorities, and especially the apostles, to attend to their roles as spiritual leaders and policy makers. Both studies recommended creation of two new departments: External Communications (later changed to Public Communications), for matters of public relations; and Internal Communications, to solve the serious problems involved in getting materials out to members. Both departments were organized and functioning in 1972.

The Department of Internal Communications would have the greatest effect on general church administration and correlation. Elder J. Thomas Fyans was named managing director, and designated members of the Council of the Twelve acted as advisers. The three apostles first named as advisers, Elders Gordon B. Hinckley, Thomas S. Monson, and Boyd K. Packer, had been chairmen of the three age-group correlation committees and were also advisers to the auxiliary organizations. The old Correlation Committee was dissolved, and its functions became part of the responsibility of Internal Communications. Elder Fyans was given full responsibility for planning, preparing, translating, printing, and distributing all communications, instructional materials, and periodicals for members worldwide. Translation and distribution services, the magazines, editorial services, and curriculum planning were brought together under Internal Communications.

The most effective steps toward genuine correlation of curricula were taken through the Division of Instructional Materials. An elaborate instructional development program was set up to create teaching materials for all organizations. It was directed by full-time professional educators, with each sub-committee manned by individual writers and researchers who were called to devote their church service time to these assignments. Elder Fyans's office received requests from priesthood or auxiliary organizations, established priorities, and directed the preparation of long-range plans. It was also responsible for eliminating duplication of effort and unnecessary overlapping, and insured that all materials approved for publication conformed to church doctrine, standards, and procedures.

The original correlation concept had thus, in the 1970s, become largely the responsibility of the director of instructional materials, who had the staff and authority to carry it out. By 1974 control of the writing of manuals had been completely removed from the auxiliaries. A further refinement came in that year when the correlation section was made into a separate division of the Department of Internal Communications, with the idea that it could more objectively review the materials produced by the Division of Instructional Materials as well as those written for the magazines.

In the spirit of the Cresap Report, other agencies were restructured in the early 1970s to relieve General Authorities from day-to-day administrative responsibilities and turn the growing work load over to professional, full-time staffs. One was the Church Historian's office. When he became President of the Church in 1970, Joseph Fielding Smith had been Church Historian for forty-nine years. He was succeeded in that position by Elder Howard W. Hunter of the Council of the Twelve. It was becoming increasingly clear, however, that the administration of the vast archives of the Church was becoming complex and that there was a rapidly growing need to do more research and writing in the field of Church history. The staff must be enlarged and more professional help was clearly needed.

Under President Smith's direction, the Church Historian's Office was reorganized in January 1972 as the Historical Department of the Church, with three major divisions. The Church Archives, under the direction of Earl L. Olson, was responsible for acquiring, storing, and managing documents and records relating to Church history. The Church Library, under Donald T. Schmidt, was responsible for acquiring and making available to Church authorities as well as to the public printed materials pertaining to the Church. The History Division, under Leonard J. Arrington as Church Historian, was responsible for writing and publishing Church history. The new department was under the general direction of a managing director, Elder Alvin R. Dyer (later Elder Joseph Anderson), and it soon began to provide vastly expanded historical services. Later the library and archives were combined into one division, and a new division, under Church Curator Florence Jacobsen, was added to look after historical buildings, artifacts, and paintings.

These were only some of the changes brought into the administrative structure during the era of correlation which, symbolically at least, came to a close with the death of President Harold B. Lee. Not every objective had been achieved, and there would still be problems of coordination, but the machinery created thus far now seemed to need a time for testing and perfecting, rather than replacement with any new machinery. Spencer W. Kimball remarked in 1974 in his first general conference after becoming President of the Church: "I anticipate no major changes in the immediate future, but do hope to give increased emphasis to some of the programs already established. This is a day of consolidating our efforts, and firming up our programs, and reaffirming our policies."

Church Growth Around the World

The need for such far-reaching refinements in administration was in large part a reflection of the Church's growth; its continuing expansion in every field during the 1960s was impressive. Over a million members were added, bringing total membership to more than 2,800,000; 206 new stakes were organized; 2,158 chapels were completed, many of them outside the United States. Sixty-nine school buildings were constructed in South America, Mexico, and the Pacific; and 81 new institute of religion and 113 seminary buildings were erected in the United States. The Church began broadcasting around the world from a new shortwave radio transmitter, participated in several international fairs, and opened dozens of new missions.

Tabernacle Choir performs at a general conference in the Tabernacle in Salt Lake City. (Church Archives)

Just as the 1950s had witnessed a surge of growth in the Pacific, the 1960s became a special era of growth for Latin America and Asia. Latin American Saints increased in numbers from 18,700 to 135,000 in ten years. The first Latin American stake was organized in Mexico in 1961. By the end of 1973 there were seven stakes in Mexico, nine in Brazil, three in Argentina, and one each in Chile, Peru, Uruguay, and Guatemala. Much of the growth came as the missionaries expanded their activities outside the major cities into underdeveloped rural areas.

Expansion in Latin America was not free from problems. Missionary work was often hampered when it became difficult to obtain or renew visas, not just because of occasional religious intolerance but also because of the concern of certain governments that foreign missionaries might prove subversive. In some countries it also became difficult to import church literature, and partly for that reason printing centers were eventually established in Sao Paulo and Mexico City, along with translation and distribution centers.

The growth in Latin America necessitated further expansion of church education in the area. It was the Church's policy to establish schools only where local school systems did not provide adequate opportunity for basic education. In 1963 two elementary schools were organized in Chile. A large educational complex, including an elementary and secondary school as well as a normal school for training teachers, was dedicated in Mexico City in 1968. By 1972 more than 11,000 students were enrolled in LDS elementary and secondary schools in Bolivia, Chile, Mexico, Peru, and Paraguay. Home-study seminary programs were also beginning to function in all countries where the Church was located.

Other programs were extended to Latin America because of the special needs of some Saints there. In the 1970s some of the first agricultural missionaries went to Guatemala and other areas, in an effort to improve the farming skills of rural members. In 1972 Brigham Young University began sending students and faculty on "Project Mexico" to help teach agricultural skills. Many of the first health missionaries also went to Latin America; they gave instruction in sanitation, nutrition, and preventive medicine.

There were other informal, unofficial ways in which some North American Saints began to assist Latin American members in various self-help projects. In eastern Guatemala, Cordell Anderson, a former missionary, established a large agricultural project that provided employment for many members. Another program, AYUDA, was founded in 1968 as a nonprofit venture by a group of former missionaries from the United States. In 1969 the group opened a medical clinic in Cunen, Guatemala, where volunteers, including doctors, dentists, nurses, educators, builders, and other professional people, gave from two weeks to twelve months of voluntary, unpaid assistance.

In Asia membership rose from 5,100 to 25,900 in the 1960s. The first Asian stake was organized in Tokyo in 1970. Singapore, Indonesia, Viet Nam, and other areas were dedicated for preaching the gospel, several new missions were opened, and the Book of Mormon was published in Chinese and Korean. In 1968 the Language Training Mission at the Church College of Hawaii began to offer training in various Asian and Pacific languages to better prepare missionaries for work in those countries.

An impressive event occurred in 1965 when 166 Japanese Saints conducted an excursion to the Hawaiian Temple. In order to make the trip they had to raise some $600 per couple—for some, nearly the equivalent of a year's salary. Under the direction of the mission president they had sponsored fund-raising projects, patterned after such practices in America, but the difference in cultures was revealed when some Japanese Saints at first wondered if such fund raising was honorable or Christian. The Saints also worked at genealogical research and submitted to the temple at least three family group sheets each so they would have opportunity to do considerable temple work for Japanese people. In the meantime, Tatsui Sato was authorized to go to Hawaii, where he spent six months translating the audio tapes of the temple ceremony into Japanese. "Project Temple," as it was called, reached its inspiring climax in July 1965 when the group arrived in Hawaii and participated in baptism, endowment, and sealing rites. Other excursions in later years strengthened the local leadership of the Church in Japan.

The worldwide growth resulted in another important innovation in 1971. On August 27 the first area general conference convened in Manchester, England, with President Joseph Fielding Smith presiding. It had become manifestly impossible for members around the world to attend general conferences in Salt Lake City, so the General Authorities decided to take the conferences to the members. Another area conference was held in Mexico in 1972. These were the forerunners of a series of area conferences in Europe, Latin America, the Pacific, and Asia in subsequent years. For the first time many members had the opportunity to see and be instructed by the prophet and other General Authorities. The resulting spiritual uplift in those areas was evidence of the Church's worldwide unity.

Missionary Work

The growth in the 1960s was in part a reflection of a renewed emphasis on missionary work. A new six-lesson missionary plan was introduced in 1961. The eligible age for young men to accept mission calls was lowered from twenty to nineteen, and the slogan "Every Member a Missionary" was introduced as an ideal. Families were encouraged to invite friends and neighbors to hear the missionaries, and special emphasis was placed on what young people could do among their friends. All these suggestions resulted in an increase in the number of group meetings attended by missionaries, for members were more enthusiastically sharing the responsibility of finding investigators. One mission president reported that his missionaries were now spending 90 percent of their time actually teaching rather than searching for contacts.

On June 27, 1961, and continuing for a week, the first world seminar for mission presidents was held in Salt Lake City. There they were instructed in new programs and techniques and were told that missionary work must be a cooperative program between full-time and part-time missionaries as well as the auxiliary organizations. They were also introduced to the new proselyting plan, *A Uniform System for Teaching the Gospel*, in which many of the principles and techniques found in earlier plans were refined.

The result of this renewed missionary emphasis was a rapid increase in the number of full-time missionaries, as well as the number of convert baptisms per missionary. The surge of baptisms lasted until about 1965, then declined, though it remained unusually high compared with earlier years; it began climbing again in 1968.

Certain aspects of the missionary program distressed some members and began to create a negative image in the public press. In their enthusiasm for making records, some mission presidents established goals and promoted them in ways that encouraged young missionaries to baptize people before they were truly converted. There appear to have been instances in which young boys were proselyted simply by putting them on athletic teams and telling them that they must be baptized in order to join. Attempts were made to prevent such abuses when they were discovered. Meanwhile, stories of too-rapid conversions, in what some people called "baseball baptisms," offended some members and created unnecessary problems for branches that were suddenly made responsible for so-called members who really did not know what the Church was all about. By the mid-1960s, leaders were strongly cautioning against such proselyting techniques and were placing special emphasis on the importance of converting whole families. The number of conversions declined for a time but the staying power of the converts increased.

By 1965 the goal of twelve thousand missionaries was reached, and the number continued to climb. As part of the effort to relieve General Authorities from burdensome routine activities, instructions were issued in 1970 that in the future stake presidents would be responsible for setting apart missionaries before they went into the field. By the end of 1973 more than sixteen thousand missionaries were in the field.

The Church also expanded bureaus of information as part of the missionary effort. The Mormon Pavilion at the world's fair in New York City in 1964 and 1965 attracted thousands of visitors and resulted in many important missionary contacts. This was followed by similar pavilions at other expositions, such as those in San Antonio, Texas (1968); Osaka, Japan (1970); and Spokane, Washington (1974). Visitors centers were expanded at many temples, and those at Church historic sites were reoriented to include films, slide presentations, and more informative literature.

Other Signs of Change and Growth

Change and growth were seen in every phase of church activity in this era. New temples were dedicated in Oakland, California, and in Provo and Ogden, Utah. Reporting systems also reflected church growth. In 1968 the Church Historian's Office authorized the submission of reports in languages other than English, and it was announced that membership records would soon be transferred to a computer system. That same year the auditing began for all membership records prior to transfer to the au-

Inside the Granite Mountain vaults, constructed by the Church to preserve many permanent records. (Church Internal Communications Department)

tomated program. Genealogical and temple records were already being automated, and by the 1970s the records of individual financial contributions were computerized. The Church was taking full advantage of modern technology to make its record keeping as simple and accurate as possible.

In 1966 the Church officially dedicated a huge record vault that had been carved into a granite cliff in Little Cottonwood Canyon, near Salt Lake City. It was to be used primarily for the storage of vital documents and film records of the Genealogical Society, and the peculiar structure and location contributed to proper temperature and humidity control.

In 1972 a new prospective elders program was inaugurated, designed to more effectively influence the lives of male members over the age of thirteen. Instead of being placed in senior Aaronic Priesthood programs when they became adults, men over the age of nineteen were assigned to the elders quorums even though they may not have been ordained. This meant that the elders were directly responsible for activating and fellowshipping all men over the age of nineteen who still held the lesser priesthood, though ideally young men were to be ordained to the office of elder when they reached that age.

Perhaps the most visible symbol of the growing church was the twenty-eight-story Church Office Building, which was completed in 1972. That fall administrative units that had been housed throughout the Salt Lake area began moving in. The First Presidency, Council of the Twelve, and most General Authorities retained offices in the old Church Office Building, but most of the professional services and administrative units were now housed in the towering new structure. Huge cast-stone representations of the world's hemispheres on the building's wings symbolized the worldwide nature of the Church.

In the field of education, programs spread to many places, particularly to Latin America. In 1964 the Pacific board of education was discontinued and the Pacific schools became part of the Unified Church School System. The following year Harvey L. Taylor became administrator of that system when it was separated, at least temporarily, from Brigham Young University. At the same time, discussions continued concerning the feasibility of establishing a chain of two-year junior colleges. Enrollment was expanding so rapidly at BYU that many members feared their children could not get in, and by 1970 enrollment there had been limited to 25,000.

It was soon determined that expansion would come only in seminaries and institutes and in areas where secular learning facilities were not otherwise available. It seemed a useless expenditure of funds to create new junior colleges that would only duplicate other colleges, especially when institutes of religion were expanding so rapidly. In 1970 Church colleges enrolled 32,900 students, while nearly 200,000 Latter-day Saints attended other institutions around the world, and nearly 50,000 of these were enrolled in institutes of religion.

In 1970 a major change in the administration of church education occurred when the office of commissioner of education was reestablished and Neal A. Maxwell was appointed to the post. The commissioner was made responsible for all phases of church education, including Brigham Young University, though the university and the colleges would each have its own president. Commissioner Maxwell announced in January 1971 a unified admissions system for the Church's colleges. In looking at the basic needs in church education, he had suggested that many young people, especially in the less advantaged areas of the world, should be encouraged to go into technical and vocational training, and it was suggested that the Church schools would develop increasingly competent programs in those fields. In 1972 a team of experts from BYU was sent on an extensive tour of Asia to survey the educational needs of that region and make appropriate recommendations.

Social and Cultural Activities

Latter-day Saints became increasingly involved in a variety of social and cultural affairs, and as the Church grew, these activities became better known to the public. The annual dance festivals sponsored by the Mutual Improvement Associations were major events in the Mountain West and included young people who had previously participated in local festivals. In 1970 both a youth symphony and youth chorus were organized in Salt Lake City, symbolizing the Church's encouragement to interested youth everywhere to participate in similar activities. The annual Hill Cumorah pageant continued to draw capacity crowds and became known as one of the outstanding theatrical spectacles in the region. Members in other areas promoted local pageants, such as *The Mormon Miracle* in Manti, Utah, which expressed the Church's story in music and drama and achieved wide publicity. *Promised Valley*, the musical drama initially presented in Salt Lake City in 1947, became an annual production in the 1960s and attracted thousands of visitors. In 1970 alone, an estimated 118,000 persons viewed it, and in 1972 the old Lyric Theater in Salt Lake City was renovated under Church sponsorship and became the Promised Valley Playhouse. Here this drama and other productions appropriate as family entertainment were presented.

One of the outstanding cultural developments of the period was the Polynesian Cultural Center in Hawaii, dedicated in 1963. Students at the Church College of Hawaii represented nearly every group of Polynesian people and the Cultural Center, developed under Church sponsorship, provided employment for these students as they gave visiting tourists an authentic feeling for their

President Spencer W. Kimball and First Counselor N. Eldon Tanner enjoy a tour of the Polynesian Cultural Center, a cultural attraction sponsored by the Church in Hawaii. (Church Internal Communications Department)

native cultures. Almost immediately it became a major tourist attraction in Hawaii.

A different kind of cultural activity came in 1962 with the founding of Nauvoo Restoration, Incorporated. This private foundation had the full backing and partial financial support of the Church and was eventually taken fully under the auspices of the Church. Its objective was to make an authentic restoration of part of the city of Nauvoo as it appeared in the mid-1840s. The restoration would become an important cultural attraction in Illinois, reminding visitors of the Mormon contribution to the Midwest as well as telling the general story of the Latter-day Saints.

These and other cultural developments were all enhanced by the fact that a growing number of highly trained, professional Latter-day Saints in many fields were dedicated to achieving excellence in portraying the story of the Saints. In 1968 Brigham Young University sponsored its first annual Mormon Festival of Art, which placed emphasis on Mormon contributions in music and the visual arts. In literature, *Brigham Young University Studies*, founded in the 1950s and revitalized in the 1960s, provided an outlet for LDS writers who were beginning to produce works of literary and scholarly importance in many fields.

Outside the official sponsorship of the Church, private individuals were also concerned with what they could contribute to a greater understanding of the LDS heritage. This was especially true in the 1960s in the field of history. Leonard J. Arrington's *Great Basin Kingdom* (published in 1958) was among the first of several important new studies that gained wide acceptance because of their scholarly, balanced presentation and new insights into the history of the Church. A number of Latter-day Saints and other interested historians formed the Mormon History Association, designed to promote scholarly research and writing. LDS history increasingly became the subject of articles in national journals and scholarly sessions at national historical conventions. There were other outlets for published treatments of LDS culture, as a growing number of journals in various fields accepted Church-oriented articles, and a number of independent periodicals, such as *Dialogue: A Journal of Mormon Thought*, devoted their pages to various literary, historical and other scholarly assessments of Latter-day Saint life.

The Church and Public Policy

In the United States, the Saints, already predominant in Utah and parts of other intermountain states, were becoming more visible throughout the nation. In the 1960s there was more commentary on the involvement of the Church and its leaders in public affairs than in any period since 1920. An unusual number of public issues arose in which the Church seemed to have a direct interest, and for that reason the 1960s was not only a period of growth and correlation but also one of controversy and some public criticism.

It began during the presidential campaign of 1960 when, as in earlier years, the public press seemed insistent upon interpreting the political statements of the President of the Church as somehow reflecting church policy rather than private opinion. When the Republican candidate, Richard M. Nixon, visited Salt Lake City, President David O. McKay was heard to tell him "we hope you are successful." This comment was quickly picked up in the national press and interpreted as an official endorsement. To many people this interpretation seemed logical, since Elder Ezra Taft

Benson was still serving in the Republican Eisenhower cabinet. President McKay, however, quickly clarified his statement by declaring that he was speaking "as a personal voter and as a Republican," but certainly not for the Church as a whole.

More controversial than the endorsement of candidates was the debate over what methods should be employed to combat the growth of communism. It was clear that the spread of communism posed a threat to the American economic and political system, and that Communists were involved in various subversive activities in the United States. At the same time many Americans were disturbed by the activities of certain anti-Communist groups that seemed to go too far in making unproven accusations and defaming the character of other Americans by implying they were involved in subversive activities.

All this directly affected the Church. President McKay affirmed that it was unalterably opposed to the Communist system, and the Saints would do well to actively oppose its spread. At the same time a number of well-known Saints became nationally prominent for their outspoken stands on the issue and their apparent friendship with and endorsement of certain groups—groups that tended to oppose any program that would in any way extend the power and influence of the federal government. Some members interpreted these actions as official church endorsement of conservative political causes. In some areas members indiscreetly began to use chapels to promote their personal political causes. In response the First Presidency continually issued statements reiterating that the Church took no position on partisan politics, prohibiting the use of church buildings for political purposes, and making it clear that even though the Church opposed communism, the First Presidency could not condone the methods sometimes employed by some individuals and groups.

In spite of its efforts to remain aloof from partisan politics, the Church did take sides on a few significant political issues in the 1960s. One was liquor by the drink, which had obvious moral implications as far as the Church was concerned. The issue came before Utahns in 1968, and the Church not only stood publicly against the sale of liquor by the drink but openly used its priesthood organization to distribute literature and circulate petitions. Even here, opposition to the Church stand was not construed to mean disloyalty to the Church, though it was clear that on this issue the Church was taking sides.

The First Presidency also supported Sunday closing laws, upheld the spirit of civil rights legislation (although it did not take sides on specific bills), and favored the protection of state right-to-work laws. In each case Church leaders felt a moral obligation to take a stand, though they were occasionally criticized for "dabbling in politics."

The most delicate public issue involving the Church in the 1960s was civil rights. In the United States this was the decade in which racial strife reached a peak as black citizens demanded an end to racial discrimination in every form. Prejudice and the tradition of segregation led to violence in many parts of the country, though in the end considerable constructive legislation provided a legal basis for an end to discrimination in housing, education, employment opportunity, and all other public aspects of American life. In the turmoil every institution in America was reexamined, and for the first time many people became aware of the Church's stand with regard to the priesthood. It had been the policy since the early days of the Church not to ordain blacks to the priesthood. This was interpreted by some people in the 1960s as a sign of racial prejudice and discrimination, and the Church quickly came under fire in many national periodicals and from civil rights groups. In the late 1960s protest rallies were held in Salt Lake City, and delegates from many civil rights groups sought audiences with Church leaders in an effort to get them to change the policy. Brigham Young University athletic teams were picketed and harangued while on road trips, and at some games anti-Mormon riots broke out. A few schools severed athletic relations with BYU.

The Church's response was that it could not change the policy without divine instructions to do so. Church leaders reminded critics that the issue was a matter of religious faith and that those who did not share that faith should not attempt to dictate policy to the Church. Anyway, the priesthood policy had nothing to do with the position of individual members on the matter of civil rights; the Saints were duty-bound to support the principle of full civil rights for all people. In 1963 President Hugh B. Brown of the First Presidency declared in October general conference,

. . . we believe that all men are the children of the same God, and that it is a moral evil for any person or group of persons to deny any human being the right to gainful employment, to full educational opportunity, and to

New Church Office Building, completed in 1972. (Church Internal Communications Department)

every privilege of citizenship, just as it is a moral evil to deny him the right to worship according to the dictates of his own conscience. . . .

We call upon all men, everywhere, both within and outside the Church, to commit themselves to the establishment of full civil equality for all of God's children.

On December 15, 1969, partly because protests still continued, the First Presidency issued another official statement. It said, "We believe the Negro, as well as those of other races, should have his full constitutional privileges as a member of society, and we hope that members of the Church everywhere will do their part as citizens to see these rights are held inviolate."[4]

The period from 1960 to 1973, then, was a period of significant development. The Church's growth was impressive, its internationalism was more clearly apparent, and its efforts at correlation had achieved much of what leaders had been seeking for sixty years. Correlation had also resulted in important innovations in church administration. The Church's public image had suffered

---

[4]These comments are published in *Conference Report*, October 1963, p. 91, and *Improvement Era* 73 (February 1970): 70.

because of the overzealousness of some of its missionaries as well as its involvement in public affairs. It could no more avoid public issues now than it could in the days of Joseph Smith and Brigham Young, but most were only passing questions, and by the 1970s new issues would affect public awareness. New challenges would also face the Saints, as the next few years became a time of consolidation rather than innovation and yet one of even greater determination to extend the gospel worldwide.

CHAPTER 21

"Lengthening Our Stride," 1973-1976

O n Saturday, December 6, 1975, President Spencer W. Kimball, then eighty years old, was at the Logan Temple early in the morning to conduct a solemn assembly for stake and ward priesthood leaders. The assembly lasted all morning, and then the vigorous President traveled to the Salt Lake Temple for another solemn assembly in the afternoon and still another that night. The leaders heard no new policy or doctrine, but they were challenged by the President to demonstrate increased spirituality in the days ahead—a rededication to living Latter-day Saint principles. Because the signs of spiritual and moral corruption were increasing in the world, they were told, the Saints must be examples of righteous living. The traditional message that they were to be in the world but not of it was seldom more meaningful than when expressed by the living prophet in these impressive and sacred assemblies.

A Modern Prophet and His Message

President Kimball's personal schedule that day was grueling, though little different from his usual pace since becoming President of the Church. Both his schedule and his message symbolized a new vitality that seemed to spread throughout the Church as he

President Spencer W. Kimball visits the Mesa Temple on the occasion of its rededication. It was the first temple to be completely renovated and rededicated. Left to right: President Kimball, Temple President C. Bryant Whiting, President N. Eldon Tanner (first counselor to President Kimball), President Marion G. Romney (second counselor), and President Ezra Taft Benson of the Council of the Twelve. (Church Internal Communications Department)

assumed leadership. His personal vigor was contagious, and it brought a visible new commitment to principles he had taught and exemplified through his years as a General Authority.

Often in his teaching President Kimball had stressed the vital importance of personal moral cleanliness and chastity. These qualities received special consideration, along with renewed emphasis on the principles of repentance and forgiveness. His 1973 book, *The Miracle of Forgiveness,* was a best seller among the Saints. He emphasized many other aspects of Christian living: honest dealing with one's fellowmen, exemplary personal grooming, strong opposition to pornography and other degrading influences in the literature and theaters of the world. All of this was not surprising in a leader of the Church. Most urgent in President Kimball's mind was a new drive to expand the missionary force. "If I need a title for what I desire to say this morning," he told a seminar for Regional and Mission Representatives on October 3,

1974, "I think it would be 'Lengthening Our Stride.' " That theme expressed the major thrust of the first years of his administration.

President Kimball was born in Salt Lake City in 1895, but grew up in Arizona. He was educated at the University of Arizona and Brigham Young University and then worked in the real estate business in Arizona. In 1938 he became president of Mount Graham Stake, and in 1943 he was called to the Council of the Twelve.

President Kimball's remarkable will to survive was well illustrated in a series of miraculous recoveries from illness. As a young boy he nearly drowned. At age thirteen he lay near death for weeks with typhoid fever, which was followed by a serious case of smallpox. After he was called to the Council of the Twelve he suffered a series of heart attacks, and then, in 1957, he developed a malignancy of the throat and vocal chords. He lost one chord and part of another, as well as his voice. He was required to learn to speak again, this time in a softer, less audible tone. After he became president a special miniature microphone was constructed for him to better amplify his voice for radio and television audiences. After all this, at age seventy-nine he was able to inform the news media that he was in sound health and felt vigorous. His subsequent activities, in which he set a pace of physical, spiritual, and mental activity that much younger men found difficult to follow, demonstrated the truth of the comment of Harold B. Lee that Spencer W. Kimball was "no ordinary man."

Newly chosen as leader of the Church, President Kimball immediately set the tone of vigor that reflected his personality. "We would not have had it thus," he humbly declared when he was sustained on April 6, 1974, "but now the only thing for us to do is press forward firmly." He told the Regional Representatives that the time had come to "change our sights and raise our goals," and he asked the Church to do just that.

Missionary work received an immediate boost. In general and area conferences President Kimball called for more young people from every land to accept mission calls. In April 1974 he declared to the Regional Representatives: "The question is frequently asked: Should every young man fill a mission? And the answer has been given by the Lord. It is 'Yes.' Every young man should fill a mission." Within two years more than twenty-two thousand full-time missionaries were in the field.

Council of the Twelve, mid-1975. Seated: President Ezra Taft Benson,
Mark E. Petersen, Delbert L. Stapley, LeGrand Richards, Hugh B. Brown,
Howard W. Hunter. Standing: Gordon B. Hinckley, Thomas S. Monson,
Boyd K. Packer, Marvin J. Ashton, Bruce R. McConkie, L. Tom Perry.

Not only did he want more missionaries; he wanted them better prepared. "I am asking that we start earlier and train our missionaries better in every branch and every ward in the world," he told the Regional Representatives. The missionaries must be physically, mentally, and spiritually well, and leaders were challenged anew to do all within their power to see that they were prepared. Even as he was issuing these challenges, several stakes were experimenting with their own missionary training program, instructing prospective missionaries and letting them give the missionary lessons in the homes of interested members as well as nonmembers.

The Church lengthened its stride in other programs. Near Washington, D.C., the largest temple was completed in 1974, and in November President Kimball presided at ten dedicatory services. That same year it was announced that two older temples, in St. George, Utah, and in Mesa, Arizona, would be adapted to the use of film and recorded sound presentations. The necessary renovations made it appropriate to rededicate the temples, and on

April 15, 1975, the Mesa Temple was rededicated. The St. George Temple rededication followed in November. In 1975 President Kimball announced plans for a new temple in São Paulo, Brazil; one in Tokyo, Japan; and a third in Seattle, Washington. In April 1976 a temple was announced for Mexico City.

Area general conferences became regular occurrences. In August 1974 President Kimball presided over a conference in Stockholm, Sweden, where 4500 Saints from Denmark, Norway, Sweden, and Finland gathered to hear him and other General Authorities. In February and March 1975 conferences were held in Argentina and Brazil, and in August conferences took place in the Philippines, Hong Kong, Taiwan, Japan, and Korea. In February and March 1976 there were conferences in Australia, New Zealand, Samoa, Fiji, Tonga, and Tahiti. In June area conferences would be held in England and Scotland, and in July and August in France, Finland, Denmark, Germany, and the Netherlands.

Area conferences were all part of what President Kimball called "a great new adventure in taking the whole program of the

One of the area conferences in 1975 was held in Hong Kong, China. These conferences symbolized the worldwide nature of the Church in the latter twentieth century. (Church Internal Communications Department)

Church out to the people of the whole world."[1] In each conference there were inspiring calls to greater service by President Kimball, messages from other General Authorities, and outstanding cultural programs by the people of the region involved. At every conference many attended who had sacrificed and saved for months, sometimes under great personal hardship, to share the spiritual richness of the occasion.

In education, the Church continued to extend its seminary and institute programs worldwide and, where necessary and feasible, to expand its elementary and secondary schools. At the same time, the Church College of Hawaii was merged with BYU in 1974 and became the Brigham Young University—Hawaii Campus. At BYU itself the new J. Reuben Clark, Jr., School of Law was dedicated in September 1975.

Continuing Change in the Growing Church

Though no new major programs were announced, a number of important administrative changes symbolized the continued growth and the problems associated with directing the Church. Continuing the spirit of correlation, in June 1974 it was announced that annual churchwide conferences would no longer be held for the Primary, Sunday School, and Relief Society. The traditional June Conference for youth leaders was also discontinued, and in the future the instructions and cultural activities associated with these meetings would be conducted on a regional and local level. Also in 1974 the names of stakes and missions were changed to reflect their geographic locations. Each of them now carried the name of a city and a state or country and could be identified alphabetically by this location title. The former New Zealand North Mission, for example, headquartered in Auckland, was changed to the New Zealand Auckland Mission, and the former Sharon Stake in Orem, Utah, was changed to the Orem Utah Sharon Stake. Although some traditionalists regarded a uniform nomenclature unnecessary, there were more than 700 stakes and nearly 140 missions by the end of 1975, and Church leaders believed a more convenient and understandable system of designation was necessary.

Early in 1976 a basic administrative change was instituted in

[1]"Church News" (section of *Deseret News*), July 12, 1975.

the correlation program. A new Correlation Executive Committee was appointed, consisting of five members of the Council of the Twelve. A new Correlation Department was organized, separate from the Department of Internal Communications and headed by Elder Neal A. Maxwell, Assistant to the Twelve. The Department of Internal Communications would continue to prepare instructional materials and supervise all Church publications, and the new department would be responsible for long-range planning, review of published materials, and evaluation of Church programs.

In May 1975 a new supervisory program was announced for the Church outside North America. Not since the nineteenth century had it been customary for General Authorities to live away from Salt Lake City. Now, however, six supervisory areas were established, and an Assistant to the Twelve was appointed to reside in each, to give supervision over the stakes and missions in his area. Soon afterward the missions in the United States and Canada were divided into twelve areas, with a member of the Council of the Twelve acting as adviser to each and another General Authority directly supervising. These men continued to live in Salt Lake City but were responsible, through mission presidents, for intensifying and improving proselyting activity and leadership training. These supervisory changes were necessary in a church faced with the increasingly serious challenge of maintaining unified direction in rapidly growing areas throughout the world.

One of the most significant administrative developments was introduced at the general conference in October 1975 when President Kimball announced the reorganization of the First Quorum of the Seventy. This quorum had not been filled since the Saints left Nauvoo. According to early practice the First Council of the Seventy was to preside over the first quorum, but since the days of Joseph Smith, Church leaders had never felt an urgent need to organize the quorum. Now, with a burgeoning church creating a need for more top-level supervision, it was decided to recall the first quorum into being. Three men were sustained at the October conference as members of that quorum, to serve as General Authorities. Four more were sustained in April 1976, and the conference was informed that members of this quorum would function with the same authority as Assistants to the Twelve. Others would be called as the need arose.

In the fall of 1974 it was announced that the Church would

Temple near Washington, D.C., dedicated in 1974, presents an imposing image from certain vantage points outside the American capital city. (Church Internal Communications Department)

divest itself of the fifteen hospitals it had been operating for many years in Utah, Idaho, and Wyoming. It was felt the Church could more wisely spend its money on the health needs of members around the world rather than in a few intermountain states. The hospitals were turned over to a nonchurch, nonprofit corporation, Intermountain Health Care, Inc. Other Church-sponsored health services were soon expanded. More health services missionaries, for example, were called to augment the 120 already serving on Indian reservations in the United States and among members in twenty foreign countries.

Another sign of growth came when President Kimball announced that, as President of the Church, he no longer had time to act as board chairman of various businesses in which the Church held substantial interest. Traditionally the President had been chairman of the boards of these corporations, but President Kimball decided the increasing press of ecclesiastical business would interfere with his performance of such duties. His lengthening stride was in the direction of more vigorous church activity, and he left the business world in other hands. His counselors and other General Authorities remained as chairman and board members for such corporations as ZCMI, Hotel Utah, Utah-Idaho Sugar Company, Beneficial Life Insurance Company, Zion's Security Corporation (the Church's holding company for real estate), Deseret Management Corporation (a holding company for Church-owned corporations), Bonneville International (a holding company for church broadcasting facilities), Deseret Book Company, Deseret Press, and Deseret News.

The First Presidency and Council of the Twelve also enlarged the canon of Latter-day Saint scripture. Two additions to the Pearl of Great Price were accepted in the general conference of April 1976. One was Joseph Smith's vision of the celestial kingdom, received in the Kirtland Temple on January 21, 1836. It dealt with the salvation of those who died without hearing the gospel. The other was President Joseph F. Smith's 1918 vision of the redemption of the dead. These were the first additions to the scriptures in seventy years.

Some Continuing Problems of Public Relations

The Church was not without its problems in this modern time. Often the problems simply represented the complications of growth. Building projects, for example, came into conflict with the burgeoning interests of historic preservation in the 1960s and 1970s. Once programs had outgrown an older chapel or tabernacle—a common occurrence in areas where there had been a ward since the nineteenth century—there was need for an updated facility. In many instances the older building was razed without hesitation and a new one built. There were cases, however, in which public sentiment for a historic building was strong enough to demand action to spare it. A number of them were placed on the National Register of Historic Sites, because of their representation of the pioneer heritage. Heber City's 1889 Wasatch Stake Tabernacle was such a case, and in 1965 the Church turned that building over to the city and the Wasatch County chapter of the Utah State Historical Society for preservation as a public theater and lecture facility.

The most prominent controversy concerned the Coalville (Utah) Tabernacle, on which construction had begun in 1879. The building was razed in March 1970 after a struggle that brought

The Bountiful (Utah) Tabernacle, dedicated in 1863, is impressive example of nineteenth century LDS architecture. In 1975 it was designated for preservation by the First Presidency. (Utah State Historical Society)

national attention. In the years that followed that event, the tensions that arose each time a building was considered for demolition were eased by a more careful consideration of each case.

Politically, the Church became embroiled in the debate over the equal rights amendment when it appeared before the Utah legislature. Though President Kimball took no official stand, the "Church News" section of the *Deseret News* editorialized against it, and Barbara B. Smith, president of the Relief Society, made public statements opposing its ratification. The amendment would have provided a national guarantee against discrimination in any form on the basis of sex, but those against it felt that it was not needed, that it could lead to abusive extremes, and that its proper objectives could be achieved under existing legislation. Some members supported the amendment, just as others opposed it, but the Utah legislature did not give its approval.

Another potential problem affected Brigham Young University as well as all other privately endowed schools in the United States. Federal anti-discrimination laws had prohibited any sort of discrimination in employment or admission practices for schools receiving federal aid in any form. Although Brigham Young University did not accept direct federal aid to support teachers' salaries, it was affected because many students were beneficiaries of federally guaranteed student loans, many were supported by veterans' benefits, and a number of research projects were sponsored by federal funds.

The university did not challenge the law itself, but university and church officials became deeply concerned with interpretations of the law by administrators in the U.S. Department of Health, Education, and Welfare, whose long list of rules seemed at times to go beyond the intent of the law and would have made it difficult, if not impossible, for the Church to promote its own standards on campus. Many of these bureaucratic rules seemed unconstitutional infringements upon the rights of private universities. In October 1975 BYU president Dallin H. Oaks publicly announced that the university intended to contest them. As provided by law, a notice of noncompliance was published in Utah newspapers. President Oaks, himself a noted constitutional lawyer, and other church attorneys prepared to try to persuade the federal bureaucracy to change six of the rules and, if that failed, to contest their constitutionality in the courts. There was no sign that this would lead

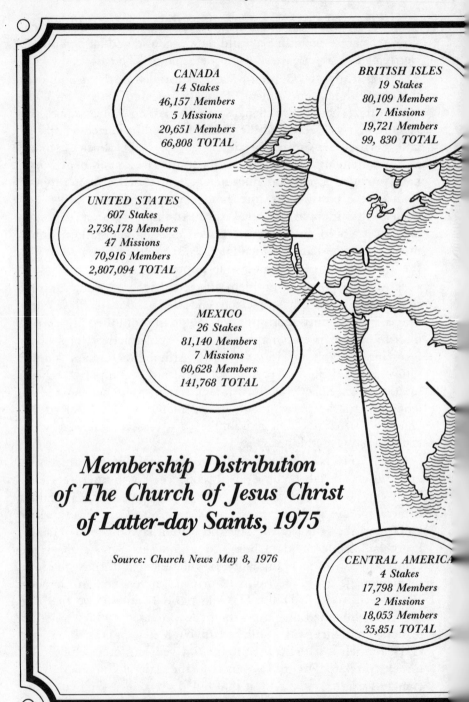

CANADA
14 Stakes
46,157 Members
5 Missions
20,651 Members
66,808 TOTAL

BRITISH ISLES
19 Stakes
80,109 Members
7 Missions
19,721 Members
99, 830 TOTAL

UNITED STATES
607 Stakes
2,736,178 Members
47 Missions
70,916 Members
2,807,094 TOTAL

MEXICO
26 Stakes
81,140 Members
7 Missions
60,628 Members
141,768 TOTAL

Membership Distribution of The Church of Jesus Christ of Latter-day Saints, 1975

Source: Church News May 8, 1976

CENTRAL AMERICA
4 Stakes
17,798 Members
2 Missions
18,053 Members
35,851 TOTAL

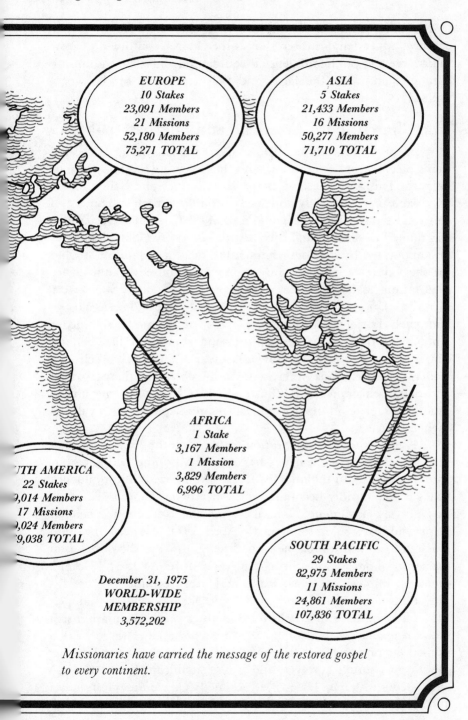

EUROPE
10 Stakes
23,091 Members
21 Missions
52,180 Members
75,271 TOTAL

ASIA
5 Stakes
21,433 Members
16 Missions
50,277 Members
71,710 TOTAL

AFRICA
1 Stake
3,167 Members
1 Mission
3,829 Members
6,996 TOTAL

..UTH AMERICA
22 Stakes
..,014 Members
..17 Missions
..,024 Members
..9,038 TOTAL

December 31, 1975
WORLD-WIDE
MEMBERSHIP
3,572,202

SOUTH PACIFIC
29 Stakes
82,975 Members
11 Missions
24,861 Members
107,836 TOTAL

Missionaries have carried the message of the restored gospel to every continent.

to the unfortunate confrontations that characterized an earlier century, but it demonstrated that as the Church continued to grow in prestige and public influence it could not avoid some continuing entanglement with the legal and political forces of the world around it.

The Church: Both American and International

In the United States, 1975 marked the beginning of the nation's bicentennial celebration, and the Church was happy to participate. This was the land of the Restoration, and Saints in the U.S. were urged to study and speak proudly of their religious and cultural heritage. Elder L. Tom Perry of the Council of the Twelve was named to the national Bicentennial Advisory Council and was also appointed by President Kimball to head a committee to plan for the Church's contribution to the two-hundredth anniversary celebration. Stakes and wards throughout the United States were asked to plan appropriate projects of a patriotic and civic nature, and each Latter-day Saint was asked to donate a significant amount of time to a community service project. The general conference of October 1975 saw a number of patriotic speeches by General Authorities as America entered its bicentennial period. In addition, speakers observed that Latter-day Saints in every nation should take pride in their own heritage and demonstrate loyalty to their countries.

The bicentennial celebration emphasized the American background which was clearly part of the Mormon heritage, but church activities in the mid-1970s also emphasized that in modern times it was rapidly becoming an international church. The tone was set by President Kimball when he addressed Regional Representatives at a seminar in April 1974. "Where the land masses of the world are," he said, "there, also, are the population masses to whom we must bring the gospel of Jesus Christ." Despite national animosities, wars, fears, and other commotion, he displayed optimism that the message would one day be delivered.

The countries that held most of the world's population still had not opened their doors to the missionaries, and there was no immediate prospect that they would. The Church was probing for every opportunity, however, and it was significant that America's ambassador-at-large, David M. Kennedy, a valiant churchman and former U.S. cabinet member, had been appointed an interna-

The Christus *by Bertel Thorvaldsen is the central point of the Visitors Center on Temple Square in Salt Lake City. It reminds all visitors of the central focus of the LDS faith. (Church Archives)*

tional representative of the First Presidency with the responsibility of establishing friendly relations with all countries and discovering ways for the missionaries to operate. In June 1975 President Kimball placed the responsibility squarely on the members when he called for a churchwide prayer campaign, in which members would join in "a serious, continuous petition to the Lord." There were two things the Saints should ask for: that the Church could obtain all the missionaries needed to "cover the world as with a blanket," and that when the Church was ready to carry the gospel to inaccessible nations, the gates would be opened.

The 22,000 missionaries who were already in the field represented many nations, and the Church was becoming genuinely international. Every day somewhere in the world missionaries met again with families they had been visiting perhaps for only a few short weeks and bore solemn witness that the authority to baptize for the remission of sins had been given to the Prophet Joseph Smith by John the Baptist. Then, after a short discussion, one of the missionaries would ask, "Will you and your family follow the Savior by keeping the Father's commandment to repent and be baptized by those holding proper authority?" Sometimes they were rejected, but frequently the family was ready to accept the challenge, and the number of Latter-day Saints increased.

The idea of filling the entire world with the message of the restored gospel of Jesus Christ still seemed remote, but the determination of the missionaries and of President Kimball made that remoteness a secondary consideration. As the modern prophet told the Regional Representatives in April 1975: "Sometimes it seems impossible, but again remember the little stone cut out of the mountain without hands which was destined to roll forth and fill the whole earth. It has gone a long way but it must go farther."

The list of works below identifies some of the most valuable books, articles, graduate theses and dissertations, and reference volumes for a comprehensive study of LDS Church history. It is not a complete bibliography, but it is intended to help the reader pursue further the topics discussed in this book as well as to indicate the principal sources we consulted. Because we have identified only direct quotations with footnotes within the narrative, this listing is intended in part to express our debt to other historians.

Preceding the separate chapter bibliographies are sections titled General Works, Biography and Autobiography, Collected Works, and Bibliographies and Historiography. Included in these sections are sources covering a broader period than any one chapter or section and works helpful in other ways not directly related to the chronological framework of the chapters. Works identified with full bibliographic citation in these general sections are listed by shortened title in the separate chapter bibliographies. Many of the works cited contain bibliographies of their subjects.

GENERAL WORKS

Broad Surveys

The most extensive overview of Church history published to date, B. H. Roberts's *A Comprehensive History of The Church of Jesus Christ of Latter-day Saints, Century I,* 6 vols. (Salt Lake City: The Church of Jesus Christ of Latter-day Saints, 1930), though nearly half a century old, remains a valuable resource for information and commentary. Readers should also watch for the appearance of an up-to-date, comprehensive history in sixteen volumes now in preparation under the general editorship of Church Historian Leonard J. Arrington. This series, "The History of the Latter-day Saints, 1830-1980," will be published by Deseret Book Company in cooperation with the Historical Department of the Church in observance of the Church's sesquicentennial anniversary. The authors selected to write these histories and the periods or topics they will cover are as follows: Richard L. Bushman, Introduction and Background to 1830; Milton V. Backman, Jr., The Ohio Experience to 1838; Max H. Parkin, The Missouri Experience to 1839; T. Edgar Lyon, The Illinois Period, 1839-1846; Reed C. Durham, Jr., The Crossing of the Plains;

Eugene E. Campbell, The Early Pioneer Period, 1847-1869; Charles S. Peterson, The Later Pioneer Period, 1869-1900; Thomas G. Alexander, The Early Twentieth Century, 1900-1930; Richard O. Cowan, The Church from 1930 to 1950; James B. Allen, The Contemporary Church, 1950 to 1980; Douglas F. Tobler, A History of the Latter-day Saints in Europe; Lanier Britsch, A History of the Latter-day Saints in Asia and the Pacific; F. LaMond Tullis, A History of the Latter-day Saints in Mexico, Central America, and South America; S. George Ellsworth, A History of the Expansion of the Faith; Davis Bitton, A Social and Cultural History of the Church, 1830 to 1900; and John L. Sorenson, A Social and Cultural History of the Church, 1900 to 1980. When published, these studies will be available separately or as a complete set and will represent a major contribution to scholarly research in Latter-day Saint history.

Most of the shorter, one-volume overviews now available have been written for use as textbooks. Joseph Fielding Smith's *Essentials in Church History,* 26th ed. (Salt Lake City: Deseret Book Co., 1973), was first published in 1922 for use in Melchizedek Priesthood quorums and has since become a standard reference for general use. Another widely published volume is William E. Berrett, *The Restored Church: A Brief History of the Growth and Doctrines of The Church . . . ,* 14th ed. (Salt Lake City: Deseret Book Co., 1969). First published in shorter form in 1936, it was combined with Berrett's *Doctrines of the Restored Church* in 1944 and has been translated into several languages for use as a text in Church seminaries. College-level texts include a pair of books, one by Ivan J. Barrett, *Joseph Smith and the Restoration: A History of the Church to 1846,* 2nd ed. (Provo, Utah: Brigham Young University Press, Young House, 1973), and the other by Russell R. Rich, *Ensign to the Nations: A History of the Church from 1846 to the Present* (Provo: Brigham Young University Publications, 1972); and the brief narrative and topical overview by James B. Allen and Richard O. Cowan, *Mormonism in the Twentieth Century,* 2nd. ed. (Provo: Brigham Young University Press, 1967). A sympathetic account written for the popular market is Robert R. Mullen, *The Latter-day Saints: The Mormons, Yesterday and Today* (Garden City, N.Y.: Doubleday, 1966), which has been published in English, German, Japanese, and Danish editions. Another writer's interpretation, emphasizing the early years, is Carl Carmer, *The Farm Boy and the Angel* (Garden City, N.Y.: Doubleday, 1970).

The common background through 1844 is interpreted from a somewhat different point of view in the first chapters of a one-volume history of the Reorganized Church of Jesus Christ of Latter Day Saints: Inez Smith Davis, *The Story of the Church,* 7th ed. (Independence: Herald Publishing House, 1964). Two books often cited by non-Mormon writers but unreliable in their presentations are T. B. H. Stenhouse, *The Rocky Mountain Saints* (New York: D. Appleton & Co., 1873), and William A. Linn, *The Story of the Mormons, from the Date of Their Origin to the Year 1901* (New York: Macmillan, 1902). A newer, journalistic account focusing on current affairs is Wallace Turner, *The Mormon Establishment* (Boston: Houghton Mifflin, 1966).

Specialized Histories

Many of the general histories of the Church adopt a political framework for events, especially of the nineteenth century. Several recent interpretations of political history are listed in the chapter bibliographies. Broader studies include the unpublished work of JoAnn (Jan) B. Shipps, "The Mormons in Politics: The First Hundred Years" (Ph.D. diss., University of Colorado, 1965); and the highly interpretive *Quest for Empire: The Political Kingdom of God and the Council of Fifty in Mormon History* (East Lansing: Michigan State University Press, 1967), by Klaus J. Hansen.

The standard monograph on nineteenth-century economic programs, and a book extremely valuable to us in our work, is Leonard J. Arrington, *Great Basin Kingdom: An Economic History of the Latter-day Saints, 1830-1900* (Cambridge: Harvard University Press, 1958). No comparable study exists for twentieth-century activities, nor has the social and cultural history of the Saints received comprehensive treatment. A useful introduction to Mormon values and social institutions is Thomas F. O'Dea, *The Mormons* (Chicago: University of Chicago Press, 1957), an insightful interpretation by a Catholic sociologist. These important books by Hansen, Arrington, and O'Dea are available in paperback editions.

The gathering of the Saints to central settlement sites and the story of that nineteenth-century migration from all parts of the world form the basis of many books and articles. General studies include the successful literary account by Wallace Stegner, *The Gathering of Zion: The Story of the Mormon Trail*, American Trail Series (New York: McGraw-Hill Book Co., 1964), and Gustive O. Larson, *Prelude to the Kingdom: Mormon Desert Conquest; A Chapter in American Cooperative Experience* (Francestown, N.H.: Marshall Jones Co., 1947).

The early migration from Great Britain is recounted in P.A.M. Taylor, *Expectations Westward: The Mormons and the Emigration of Their British Converts in the Nineteenth Century* (Edinburgh and London: Oliver & Boyd, 1965). Articles by Taylor preceding his book include "Why Did British Mormons Emigrate?" *Utah Historical Quarterly* 22 (July 1954): 249-70; "Mormons and Gentiles on the Atlantic," ibid., 24 (July 1956): 195-214; and "The Mormon Crossing of the United States, 1840-1870," ibid., 25 (October 1957): 319-38. Immigrant contributions in Utah are discussed in Frederick S. Buchanan, "Scots among the Mormons," ibid., 36 (Fall 1968): 328-52.

Another part of the story is told in the valuable work of William Mulder, *Homeward to Zion: The Mormon Migration from Scandinavia* (Minneapolis: University of Minnesota Press, 1957). Also useful are his analysis, "Mormonism's 'Gathering': An American Doctrine with a Difference," *Church History* 23 (September 1954): 248-64; and "Utah's Ugly Ducklings: A Profile of the Scandinavian Immigrant," *Utah Historical Quarterly* 23 (July 1955): 233-60. An important unpublished study is Douglas D. Alder, "The German-speaking Migration to Utah, 1850-1950" (M.A. thesis, University of Utah, 1959).

Important primary sources on the migration include James Linforth, ed., *Route from Liverpool to Great Salt Lake Valley, Illustrated . . . from Sketches made by Frederick Piercy . . .* (Liverpool: Franklin D. Richards; and London: Latter-day Saint Book Depot, 1855), available most recently in an edition edited by Fawn M. Brodie (Cambridge: Belknap Press, Harvard University Press, 1962), and William Clayton, *The Latter-day Saints' Emigrants' Guide . . . from Council Bluffs to the Valley of the Great Salt Lake . . .* (St. Louis: Missouri Republican Steam Power Press and Chambers & Knapp, 1848), reproduced as an addendum to Roberts, *Comprehensive History of the Church*, vol. 3. The earliest extant journal of a transatlantic voyage by Mormons is published with an introduction and editing by James B. Allen and Thomas G. Alexander, *Manchester Mormons: The Journal of William Clayton, 1840 to 1842* (Santa Barbara and Salt Lake City: Peregrine Smith, 1974).

Additional sources on Latter-day Saint migration are listed in appropriate chapter bibliographies.

The Church in the American West

Much information on the Saints as pioneers and settlers in the western United States is contained in books written with a secular focus. Especially useful are histories of Utah in the territorial period, 1847 to 1896, when Mormon activities often dominated. A widely recognized study is Nels Anderson, *Desert Saints: The Mormon Frontier in Utah* (Chicago: University of Chicago Press, 1942), also available in paperback. Another useful source is Milton R. Hunter, *Brigham Young the Colonizer* (1940; 4th ed. rev., Santa Barbara and Salt Lake City: Peregrine Smith, 1973). An overview of the period to 1877 is Ray B. West, Jr., *Kingdom of the Saints: The Story of Brigham Young and the Mormons* (New York: Viking Press, 1957.) A geographer's assessment of settlement is D. W. Meinig, "The Mormon Culture Region: Strategies and Patterns in the Geography of the American West, 1847-1964," *Annals of the Association of American Geographers* 55 (June 1965): 191-220.

Comprehensive histories of territorial Utah include the early standard, Hubert Howe Bancroft, *History of Utah*, 1540-1886 (1889; reprint ed., Salt Lake City: Bookcraft, 1964); the historical and biographical work of Orson F. Whitney, *History of Utah*, 4 vols. (Salt Lake City: George Q. Cannon & Sons Co., 1892-1904); and the one-volume survey of Levi Edgar Young, *The Founding of Utah* (New York: Charles Scribner's Sons, 1923). A pair of books concentrating on the early migration and settlements are Leland H. Creer, *Founding of an Empire: The Exploration and Colonization of Utah, 1776-1856* (Salt Lake City: Bookcraft, 1947), and Andrew Love Neff, *History of Utah, 1847-1869,* ed. Leland H. Creer (Salt Lake City: Deseret News Press, 1940).

Textbooks include the selective summary of Gustive O. Larson, *Outline History of Utah and the Mormons* (Salt Lake City: Deseret Book Company, 1958), and the comprehensive junior high school text by S. George Ellsworth, *Utah's Heritage* (Santa Barbara and Salt Lake City: Peregrine

Smith, 1972). An older but still useful short survey is Orson F. Whitney, *Popular History of Utah* (Salt Lake City: Deseret News, 1916). A new college-level, topical treatment is David E. Miller, Eugene E. Campbell, and Thomas G. Alexander, eds., *Utah: A Cooperative History,* forthcoming from Brigham Young University Press. Also scheduled for 1976 publication is Charles S. Peterson's interpretive Utah history for the Bicentennial series of the American Association for State and Local History, "The States and the Nation" (New York: W. W. Norton). The *Deseret News* staff produced *Deseret, 1776-1976: A Bicentennial Illustrated History of Utah* (Salt Lake City: Deseret News Publishing Co., 1975), as a commemoration of the state's accomplishments. All of these Utah histories deal somewhat with the Church's involvement in community affairs. Many histories of other states tell the story of the Latter-day Saints within their borders, particularly those of Ohio, Missouri, Illinois, Iowa, Nebraska, Nevada, Arizona, Idaho, and Wyoming.

Mission Histories

The limitations imposed by the size of this present book have prevented us from using very much material on the Church in the missions. An indication of the spread of membership can be seen in Dean R. Louder, "A Distributional and Diffusionary Analysis of the Mormon Church, 1850-1970" (Ph.D. diss., University of Washington, 1972); and the patterns of missionary service in Gordon Irving, "Numerical Strength and Geographical Distribution of the LDS Missionary Force, 1830-1974," *Task Papers in LDS History,* No. 1 (Salt Lake City: Historical Department of The Church of Jesus Christ of Latter-day Saints, 1975).

A careful study for a limited period is S. George Ellsworth, "A History of Mormon Missions in the United States and Canada, 1830-1860" (Ph.D. diss., University of California, Berkeley, 1951). Also useful is Barbara Joan McFarlane Higdon, "The Role of Preaching in the Early Latter Day Saint Church, 1830-1846" (Ph.D. diss., University of Missouri, 1961).

For the history of the Church in most missions and countries, the reader must consult graduate theses and dissertations. The most useful of these are listed below, with abbreviation of the name of the Church when it appears in the title. In addition to those listed above, North and South American mission histories include Lamar C. Berrett, "History of the Southern States Mission, 1831-1861" (M.S. thesis, Brigham Young University, 1960); Eugene E. Campbell, "A History of The Church . . . in California, 1846-1946" (Ph.D. diss., University of Southern California, 1952); Melvin S. Tagg, "A History of the Church . . . in Canada, 1830-1963" (M.S. thesis, Brigham Young University, 1963); John DeLon Peterson, "History of the Mormon Missionary Movement in South America to 1940" (M.A. thesis, University of Utah, 1962); and other sources on Canada and Mexico cited in the bibliography for chap. 12. Others are David Kay Flake, "A History of the Mormon Missionary

Work with the Hopi, Navaho, and Zuni Indians" (M.A. thesis, Brigham Young University, 1965), and Arnold Harrison Green, "A Survey of the Latter-day Saint Proselyting Efforts of the Jewish People" (M.A. thesis, Brigham Young University, 1967).

Published histories of the Church in Europe are Richard L. Evans, *A Century of Mormonism in Great Britain: A Brief Summary* . . . (Salt Lake City: Deseret News Press, 1937); Andrew Jenson, *History of the Scandinavian Mission* (Salt Lake City: Deseret News Press, 1927); and Gilbert W. Scharffs, *Mormonism in Germany: A History of the Church* . . . *in Germany* (Salt Lake City: Deseret Book Co., 1970). Unpublished studies include: A. Dean Wengreen, "A History of the Church . . . in Sweden, 1850-1905" (Ph.D. diss. Brigham Young University, 1968); Curtis B. Hunsaker, "History of the Norwegian Mission from 1851 to 1960" (M.A. thesis, Brigham Young University, 1965); Marius A. Christensen, "History of the Danish Mission of the Church . . . " (M.A. thesis, Brigham Young University, 1966); Keith C. Warner, "History of the Netherlands Mission of the Church . . . , 1861-1866" (M.A. thesis, Brigham Young University, 1967); and Gary R. Chard, "A History of the French Mission of the Church . . . , 1850-1960" (M.A. thesis, Utah State University, 1965).

The Church in southern Europe and the Middle East is examined in Ralph L. Cottrell, Jr., "A History of the Discontinued Mediterranean Missions of the Church . . ." (M.S. thesis, Brigham Young University, 1963), and Rao H. Lindsay, "A History of the Missionary Activities of the Church . . . in the Near East, 1884-1929" (M.A. thesis, Brigham Young University, 1958).

For the Pacific area see Comfort Margaret Bock, "The Church . . . in the Hawaiian Islands" (M.A. thesis, University of Hawaii, 1941); John Douglas Hawkes, "A History of the Church . . . in Australia to 1900" (M.A. thesis, Brigham Young University, 1965); and Brian W. Hunt, "History of The Church . . . in New Zealand" (M.A. thesis, Brigham Young University, 1971).

The Church in Asia is outlined in Spencer J. Palmer, *The Church Encounters Asia* (Salt Lake City: Deseret Book Co., 1970), and in R. Lanier Britsch, "Early Latter-day Saint Missions to South and East Asia" (Ph.D. diss., Claremont Graduate School and University Center, 1968). Specific missions are examined in Britsch, "A History of the Missionary Activity of the Church . . . in India, 1849-1856" (M.A. thesis, Brigham Young University, 1964); Don W. Marsh, comp., *"The Light of the Sun": Japan and the Saints* (Tokyo: Japan Mission, 1968); Murray L. Nichols, "History of the Japan Mission of the Church . . . , 1901-1924" (M.A. thesis, Brigham Young University, 1958); and Lowell E. Call, "Latter-day Saint Servicemen in the Philippine Islands: A Historical Study of Their Religious Activities and Influences Resulting in the Official Organization of the Church . . . in the Philippines" (M.A. thesis, Brigham Young University, 1955).

Church Government and Organizations

No single volume presents an adequate administrative history of the

Church, but much information has been accumulated in studies of priesthood and auxiliary organization activities. The theses of Michael Quinn and Kent Dunford cited in the bibliography for chap. 3 should be consulted for details on development of the governing hierarchy and priesthood organization. Another broad study is the dissertation of Neil Coleman listed in the bibliography for chap. 16. An earlier treatment is Wesley P. Lloyd, "The Rise and Development of Lay Leadership in the Latter-day Saint Movement" (Ph.D. diss., University of Chicago, 1937). Authoritative statements on administrative practices are collected in John A. Widtsoe, comp., *Priesthood and Church Government* (Salt Lake City: Deseret Book Co., 1939). Members of the First Presidency and Council of the Twelve from 1832 to 1970 are ranked by seniority in a study by Reed C. Durham, Jr., and Steven H. Heath, *Succession in the Church* (Salt Lake City: Bookcraft, Inc., 1970). Jay R. Lowe, "A Study of the General Conferences of the Church . . . , 1830-1901" (Ph.D. diss., Brigham Young University, 1972), sketches in the outlines of successive conferences.

General studies of specific offices in the Church are Thomas Jay Kemp, *The Office of the Patriarch to the Church in the Church of Jesus Christ of Latter-day Saints* (Stamford, Conn.: Thomas J. Kemp, 1972), and James N. Baumgarten, "The Role and Function of the Seventies in Latter-day Saint Church History" (M.A. thesis, Brigham Young University, 1960). Studies narrower in scope are included in appropriate chapter bibliographies.

The story of auxiliary organizations is told in books and articles, usually prepared by the organization itself and often in commemoration of an anniversary. Few of the studies are comprehensive and many need updating.

The most recent history of the Church's oldest auxiliary is Relief Society, *History of the Relief Society, 1842-1966* (Salt Lake City: General Board of Relief Society, 1967). This is essentially a reworking and updating of the organization's *A Centenary of Relief Society, 1842-1942* (Salt Lake City: General Board of Relief Society, 1942).

The published *Jubilee History of Latter-day Saint Sunday Schools, 1849-1899* (Salt Lake City: Deseret Sunday School Union, 1900) must be supplemented with articles prepared by officers of the organization. A good general account is A. Hamer Reiser, "Latter-day Saint Sunday Schools," *Improvement Era* 38 (April 1935): 241, 262-63. More detailed is the "Sunday School Centennial Edition, 1849-1949," *Instructor* 84 (December 1949), an entire issue devoted to a chronology of Sunday School history and short histories of various Sunday School activities. This issue culminated a year-long series, J. N. Washburn, " 'Ye Have Need That One Teach You': A History of the Sunday Schools of the Church . . . ," *Instructor* 84 (January through November 1949).

A study that looks at both Mutual Improvement Associations in the early twentieth century is Scott Kenney, "The Mutual Improvement Associations: A Preliminary History, 1900-1950," *Task Papers in LDS History*, No. 6 (Salt Lake City: Historical Department of The Church of Jesus

Christ of Latter-day Saints, 1976). The organizations themselves have prepared separate histories of the young women's and young men's programs. The early years of the YWMIA are narrated in Susa Young Gates, *History of the Young Ladies Mutual Improvement Association* (Salt Lake City: Deseret News Press, 1911). The story is continued in an undigested topical account by Marba C. Josephson, *History of the YWMIA* (Salt Lake City: Young Women's Mutual Improvement Association of The Church . . . , 1955), and is illustrated with photographs in [Young Women's Mutual Improvement Association], *A Century of Sisterhood: Chronological Collage, 1869-1969* (Salt Lake City: Young Women's Mutual Improvement Association, 1969). A brief summary is Clarissa A. Beesley, "The Young Women's Mutual Improvement Association," *Improvement Era* 38 (April 1935): 243, 264-66, 271.

The most comprehensive treatment of the Young Men's MIA is in the unpublished work of two graduate students, Leon M. Strong, "A History of the Young Men's Mutual Improvement Association, 1877-1938" (M.S. thesis, Brigham Young University, 1939), and John Kent Williams, "A History of the Young Men's Mutual Improvement Association, 1939 to 1974" (M.A. thesis, Brigham Young University, 1976). A note on origins is Henry W. Naisbitt, " 'Polysophical' and 'Mutual,' " *Improvement Era* 2 (August 1899): 741-47. Useful especially for what they reveal about the periods in which they were written are Edward H. Anderson, "The Past of Mutual Improvement," ibid., 1 (November and December 1897): 1-10, 85-93; Junius F. Wells, "Historic Sketch of the Y.M.M.I.A., First Period," ibid., 8 (June 1925): 712-29; and Richard R. Lyman, "The Young Men's Mutual Improvement Association," ibid., 28 (April 1935): 242, 253, 259-62.

For the early years of the Primary Association see Aurelia S. Rogers, *Life Sketches of Orson Spencer and Others, and History of Primary Work* (Salt Lake City: George Q. Cannon & Sons, 1898). A more recent but brief account is Marion Belnap Kerr, "The Primary Association Yesterday and Today," *Improvement Era* 38 (April 1935): 244-72. Helping to fill the gap in Primary history is Conrad Afton Harward, "A History of the Growth and Development of the Primary Association of the LDS Church from 1878 to 1928" (M.A. thesis, Brigham Young University, 1976).

Several preliminary studies have looked at Church departments and other programs. Early historical activities are traced in Charles P. Adams and Gustive O. Larson, "A Study of the LDS Church Historian's Office, 1830-1900," *Utah Historical Quarterly* 40 (Fall 1972): 370-88, while current projects are noted in Ronald K. Esplin and Max J. Evans, "Preserving Mormon Manuscripts: Historical Activities of the LDS Church," *Manuscripts* 27 (Summer 1975): 166-67.

On the Genealogical Department see Merrill S. Lofthouse, "A Glance Backward: Historical Sketch of the Genealogical Society," *Improvement Era* 72 (July 1969): 14-17; his "A History of the Genealogical Society of The Church . . . to 1970" (M.A. thesis, Brigham Young University, 1971); and William R. Bruce, "The Utah Genealogical Society" (M.A.

thesis, University of Chicago Graduate Library School, 1956).

Among the studies of music in the Church are J. Spencer Cornwall, *A Century of Singing: The Salt Lake Mormon Tabernacle Choir* (Salt Lake City: Deseret Book Co., 1958), and Ruth Alene Thomson Symons, "The Song of the Righteous: An Historical and Literary Analysis of the Latter-day Saint Hymnal, 1835-1871" (Ph.D. diss., Brigham Young University, 1971). A recent discussion is contained in articles in a special theme issue of *Dialogue: A Journal of Mormon Thought* 10 (Spring 1975), edited by Rowan Taylor and Walter Whipple.

An overview of Church newspapers is Harrison R. Merrill, "The Latter-day Saint Press, 1830-1930" (M.S. thesis, Columbia University, 1930). A history of the Church-owned *Deseret News* is Wendell J. Ashton, *Voice in the West: Biography of a Pioneer Newspaper* (New York: Duell, Sloan & Pearce, 1950). Combining this and other journalistic ventures are the studies by Monte B. McLaws, "Early Mormon Journalism and the Deseret News, 1830-1898" (Ph.D. diss., University of Missouri, 1970), which has been revised for publication in the Brigham Young University Press series Studies in Mormon History, and Loy D. Banks, "Latter Day Saint Journalism" (M.A. thesis, University of Missouri, 1948).

Early temples of the Church are described in James E. Talmage, *The House of the Lord: A Study of Holy Sanctuaries, Ancient and Modern* (1912; reprinted with additions; Salt Lake City: Deseret Book Co., 1976). Basic details on recent temples are noted in a brief appendix; for further information see special features in temple dedication issues of Church magazines. Many of the older temples have also been studied individually in master's theses (several are listed in our chapter bibliographies). Less useful is the collection of miscellany in N. B. Lundwall, comp., *Temples of the Most High* (Salt Lake City: Bookcraft, 1952).

Education

Students in pursuit of graduate degrees in history and education have completed a large number of theses and dissertations on aspects of the Church educational program. A general survey of doctrinal and philosophical underpinnings is Wendell O. Rich, "Certain Basic Concepts in the Educational Philosophy of The Church . . . , 1830-1930" (Ph.D. diss., Utah State Agricultural College, 1954). Related studies are the intriguing work of James R. Harris, "A Comparison of the Educational Thought of Joseph Smith with That of Certain Contemporary Educators" (Ph.D. diss., Brigham Young University, 1965), and an examination of continuing themes (he finds no significant changes) in Royal R. Meservy, "A Historical Study of Changes in Policy of Higher Education in the Church" (Ed.D. diss., University of California, Los Angeles, 1966). An excellent study of school and society is James R. Clark, "Church and State Relationships in Education in Utah" (Ed.D., Utah State University, 1958).

A standard reference is the concise history by M. Lynn Bennion, "The Origin, Growth, and Extension of the Educational Program of the Mormon Church in Utah" (Ph.D. diss., University of California,

Berkeley, 1935), widely available in published form as *Mormonism and Education* (Salt Lake City: [Church] Department of Education, 1939). More recent information, including highlights in the history of each Church school, is compiled in Harvey L. Taylor, "The Story of LDS Church Schools," 2 vols., typed Ms., prepared for the Church Commissioner of Education, 1971, in Church Archives. A narrative overview of the period 1951-64 is Leon R. Hartshorn, "Mormon Education in the Bold Years" (Ph.D. diss., Stanford University, 1965). A specialized education program is traced in Lawrence G. Coates, "A History of Indian Education by the Mormons, 1830-1900" (Ph.D. diss., Ball State University, 1969).

On specific schools see Ernest L. Wilkinson, ed., *Brigham Young University: The First One Hundred Years,* 4 vols. (Provo: Brigham Young University Press, 1975-76); Jerry C. Roundy, "Ricks College: A Struggle for Survival," (Ph.D. diss., Brigham Young University, 1975); Arnold Kent Garr, "A History of Brigham Young College, Logan, Utah" (M.A. thesis, Utah State University, 1973); and other material narrower in scope listed in chapter bibliographies.

Public Image

The image of the Church in periodicals, novels, and other popular media has recently attracted the attention of several qualified researchers. General overviews are Richard O. Cowan, "Mormonism in National Periodicals" (Ph.D. diss., Stanford University, 1961); Dennis L. Lythgoe, "The Changing Image of Mormonism in Periodical Literature" (Ph.D. diss., University of Utah, 1969); and Jan Shipps, "From Satyr to Saint: American Attitudes toward the Mormons, 1860-1960" (paper presented at the Chicago meeting of the Organization of American Historians, April 1973), copy in office of the Church Historian.

Concentrating on the public image in the nineteenth century are Gail Farr Casterline, " 'In the Toils,' or 'Onward for Zion': Images of the Mormon Woman, 1852-1890" (M.A. thesis, Utah State University, 1974); and two published essays: David Brion Davis, "Some Themes of Counter-Subversion: An Analysis of Anti-Masonic, Anti-Catholic, and Anti-Mormon Literature," *Mississippi Valley Historical Review* 47 (September 1970): 205-24, and D. L. Ashliman, "The Image of Utah and the Mormons in Nineteenth-Century Germany," *Utah Historical Quarterly* 35 (Summer 1967): 209-27.

Specializing in the image of the Saints in fiction are Neal Lambert, "Saints, Sinners and Scribes: A Look at the Mormons in Fiction," ibid., 36 (Winter 1968): 63-76; Lambert and Richard H. Cracroft, "Through Gentile Eyes: A Hundred Years of the Mormons in Fiction," *New Era* 2 (March 1972): 14-19; Leonard J. Arrington and Jon Haupt, "Intolerable Zion: The Image of Mormonism in Nineteenth Century American Literature," *Western Humanities Review* 22 (Summer 1968): 243-60; Arrington and Haupt, "Community and Isolation: Some Aspects of 'Mormon Westerns,' " *Western American Literature* 8 (Spring and Summer 1973): 15-31;

and Arrington, "Mormonism: Views from Without and Within," *Brigham Young University Studies* 14 (Winter 1974): 140-54.

BIOGRAPHY AND AUTOBIOGRAPHY

Biographical studies of Latter-day Saints are numerous, though few are professionally done and many give only a selective look at the life of the individual. The titles listed below represent a small portion of those available in libraries of Latter-day Saint history. Many of these works contain background information useful in understanding Church history.

Collective Biography

For the essential details on prominent Latter-day Saints in the nineteenth and early twentieth centuries the standard references are Andrew Jenson, *Latter-day Saint Biographical Encyclopedia: A Compilation of Biographical Sketches of Prominent Men and Women in The Church . . . ,* 4 vols. (Salt Lake City: Andrew Jenson History Co., 1901-1936), now available in a reprint edition (Salt Lake City: Western Epics, 1971); and Frank Esshom, *Pioneers and Prominent Men of Utah* (Salt Lake City: Utah Pioneers Book Publishing Co., 1913).

Chapter-length biographies are presented in Preston Nibley, *The Presidents of the Church,* 13th ed. rev. (Salt Lake City: Deseret Book Co., 1974). Personal glimpses into the lives of men serving in five different First Presidencies are captured in Joseph Anderson, *Prophets I Have Known: Joseph Anderson Shares Life's Experiences* (Salt Lake City: Deseret Book Co., 1973). Miscellaneous facts and anecdotes are compiled in Emerson R. West, *Profiles of the Presidents,* rev. ed. (Salt Lake City: Deseret Book Co., 1974). Other Church leaders are introduced by the brief personality portraits in Lawrence R. Flake, *Mighty Men of Zion: General Authorities of the Last Dispensation* (Salt Lake City: Karl D. Butler, 1974). A scholarly study in group biography is D. Michael Quinn, "Organizational Development and Social Origins of the Mormon Hierarchy, 1832-1932: A Prosopographical Study" (M.A. thesis, University of Utah, 1973).

Specialized collections of biographies include Augusta Joyce Crocheron, *Representative Women of Deseret: A Book of Biographical Sketches . . .* (Salt Lake City: J. C. Graham & Co., 1884); Edward W. Tullidge, *Women in Mormondom* (1877; reprint ed., Salt Lake City: n.p., 1966), which is presented in a framework expounding Tullidge's own interpretations of Mormon theology; Claire Augusta Noall, *Guardians of the Hearth: Utah's Pioneer Midwives and Women Doctors* (Bountiful: Horizon Publishers, 1974), a collection of articles first published in *Improvement Era* and *Utah Historical Quarterly;* and Gene Allred Sessions, *Latter-day Patriots: Nine Mormon Families and Their Revolutionary War Heritage* (Salt Lake City: Deseret Book Co., in cooperation with the Historical Department of The Church . . . , 1975), readable accounts following selected families through several generations.

An interest in women's studies is beginning to produce new biographical and historical works on the role of Latter-day Saint women in society. Among the first to appear was Leonard J. Arrington, "Blessed Damozels: Women in Mormon History," *Dialogue: A Journal in Mormon Thought* 6 (Summer 1971): 22-31, one of several pieces in a special issue on women edited by Claudia Lauper Bushman and Laurel Thatcher Ulrich. Others include Maureen Ursenbach Beecher, "Under the Sunbonnets: Mormon Women with Faces," *Task Papers in LDS History*, no. 4 (Salt Lake City: Historical Department of The Church . . . , 1975); her "Three Women and the Life of the Mind," *Utah Historical Quarterly* 43 (Winter 1975): 26-40; Jill Mulvay, "The Two Miss Cooks: Pioneer Professionals for Utah Schools," ibid., 43 (Fall 1975): 396-409; and Beecher, "The Eliza Enigma: The Life and Legend of Eliza R. Snow," *Essays in the American West 1974-75*, Charles Redd Monographs in Western History, no. 6 (Provo: Brigham Young University Press, 1976), pp. 29-46.

Biographies of Church Presidents

Book-length biographies on all deceased Church Presidents have been published, with the greatest interest focusing on the lives of Joseph Smith and Brigham Young. Though no completely satisfactory biography exists on either of these men, much useful information has been published and new biographies are presently being prepared for publication.

For many Latter-day Saints the most satisfying history of the first President is John Henry Evans, *Joseph Smith, An American Prophet* (New York: Macmillan Company, 1933). This was reprinted by Deseret Book Company in 1946 for the Mormon market and conveys a generally positive assessment of the Prophet, as does Daryl Chase, *Joseph the Prophet, As He Lives in the Hearts of His People* (Salt Lake City: Deseret Book Co., 1944.)

The most analytical biography is Fawn M. Brodie, *No Man Knows My History: The Life of Joseph Smith, the Mormon Prophet* (1945; 2nd ed. rev., New York: Alfred A. Knopf, 1971). It has been accepted by many national historians in the United States as the standard biography of the Prophet, but because of Brodie's assumptions about the nature of Joseph Smith's experiences, and her nonuse of important primary source material in the Church Archives, the book is not highly regarded by Mormon historians. Most useful as assessments of the book's place in historical literature are the careful essays of Marvin S. Hill, "Brodie Revisited: A Reappraisal," *Dialogue: A Journal of Mormon Thought* 7 (Winter 1972): 72-84, and "Secular or Sectarian History? A Critique of 'No Man Knows My History,'" *Church History* 43 (March 1974): 78-96. Earlier reactions, less useful to the scholar, are Hugh Nibley, *No, Ma'am, That's Not History: A Brief Review* . . . (Salt Lake City: Bookcraft, 1946), and a book-length alternative approach prepared at the request of Church leaders, John A. Widtsoe, *Joseph Smith: Seeker After Truth, Prophet of God* (Salt Lake City: Deseret News Press, 1951).

Another widely read study is Preston Nibley, ed., *History of Joseph*

Smith by His Mother, Lucy Mack Smith (Salt Lake City: Bookcraft, 1954). This edition is based on the "Utah" version, issued in 1902 by the *Improvement Era*. It differs in certain respects from the original work, first published as Lucy Smith, *Biographical Sketches of Joseph Smith the Prophet and His Progenitors for Many Generations* (Liverpool: S. W. Richards for Orson Pratt, 1853), which has been reprinted by Herald Publishing House (Independence, Mo., 1969) and by Arno Press (New York, 1969), and which is being prepared for republication alongside parallel manuscript versions by Richard L. Anderson and Dean C. Jessee. Readers of the work should consult Anderson's "The Reliability of the Early History of Lucy and Joseph Smith," *Dialogue: A Journal of Mormon Thought* 4 (Summer 1969): 13-28.

Drawn from Lucy Mack Smith's account and from Joseph Smith, *History of the Church*, is Preston Nibley, *Joseph Smith, the Prophet* (Salt Lake City: Deseret News Press, 1944). Another detailed study by a prominent Latter-day Saint is George Q. Cannon, *Life of Joseph Smith* (Salt Lake City: Deseret News Press, 1907). The work by Edward W. Tullidge, *Life of Joseph Smith the Prophet* (New York: Tullidge & Crandall, 1878), was discredited by Church leaders in Tullidge's day (see John Taylor's comments in James R. Clark, *Messages of the First Presidency*, 2:315-30). Incidents from the Prophet's life are compiled in Hyrum L. Andrus, *Joseph Smith, the Man and the Seer* (Salt Lake City: Deseret Book Company, 1960); the recollections of associates are in Hyrum L. Andrus and Helen Mae Andrus, *They Knew the Prophet* (Salt Lake City: Bookcraft, 1974).

General histories of the nineteenth century Church understandably pay close attention to the public life of Joseph Smith and Brigham Young. President Young's activities are followed especially in the works mentioned earlier by Ray B. West (*Kingdom of the Saints*) and Milton R. Hunter (*Brigham Young the Colonizer*). Biographical treatments likewise mingle institutional and personal history. One of the more successful studies is the well-written, though skeptical, biography by Norris R. Werner, *Brigham Young* (New York: Harcourt, Brace & Co., 1925). Preston Nibley, *Brigham Young, the Man and His Work* (Salt Lake City: Deseret News Press, 1936), lacks historical interpretation and is built around numerous direct quotations.

Besides these two standard treatments there is a recent study, based heavily upon biased newspaper reports, by Stanley P. Hirshson, *The Lion of the Lord: A Biography of Brigham Young* (New York: Alfred A. Knopf, 1969); the much less satisfactory older biographies by Edward H. Anderson, *The Life of Brigham Young* (Salt Lake City: George Q. Cannon & Sons, 1893); and Edward W. Tullidge, *Life of Brigham Young; or, Utah and Her Founders* (New York: Tullidge & Crandall, 1876). Family members have written admiring tributes: Susa Young Gates, in collaboration with Leah D. Widtsoe, *The Life Story of Brigham Young* (New York: Macmillan Company, 1930); S. Dilworth Young, *"Here is Brigham": Brigham Young, the Years to 1844* (Salt Lake City: Bookcraft, 1964); and Clarissa Young Spencer with Mabel Harmer, *Brigham Young at Home* (Salt Lake City:

Deseret Book Co., 1940), first published as *One Who Was Valiant* (Caldwell, Ida.: Caxton Printers, 1940).

Other Presidents have been eulogized in books selective in their coverage and often prepared by family members or close associates. Not all of these studies were intended as full biographies; some are extracted from first-person documents and many others merely recapitulate events that highlighted the leader's life in Church service, but with little analysis. Quite comprehensive is B. H. Roberts, *The Life of John Taylor, Third President of the Church* . . . (1892; reprinted, Salt Lake City: Bookcraft, 1963). First-person diary entries are welded together in Matthias F. Cowley, *Wilford Woodruff, Fourth President of the Church* . . . : *History of His Life and Labors as Recorded in His Daily Journals* (Salt Lake City: Deseret News, 1909). The documentary approach is also used in Eliza R. Snow Smith, *Biography and Family Record of Lorenzo Snow, One of the Twelve Apostles of The Church* . . . (1884; reprinted, Salt Lake City: Zion's Book Store, 1975); while a more thorough treatment is Thomas C. Romney, *The Life of Lorenzo Snow: Fifth President of The Church* . . . (Salt Lake City: Nicholas G. Morgan, Sr., 1955). A lengthy section on ancestors introduces the fairly complete biography in Joseph Fielding Smith, *Life of Joseph F. Smith* (Salt Lake City: Deseret Book Co., 1938). A brief account is Bryant Hinckley, *Heber J. Grant: Highlights in the Life of a Great Leader* (Salt Lake City: Deseret Book Co., 1951). Published sketches of the eighth President in Church magazines should be supplemented by reference to a recent study by Glen R. Stubbs, "A Biography of George Albert Smith, 1870 to 1951" (Ph.D. diss., Brigham Young University, 1974). Selected episodes in David O. McKay's life are recounted by a sister in Jeannette McKay Morrell, *Highlights in the Life of President David O. McKay* (Salt Lake City: Deseret Book Co., 1966). A brief background report on the next President by Joseph F. McConkie, *True and Faithful: The Life Story of Joseph Fielding Smith* (Salt Lake City: Bookcraft, 1971), has been supplanted by the work of Joseph Fielding Smith, Jr., and John J Stewart, *The Life of Joseph Fielding Smith, Tenth President of the Church* . . . (Salt Lake City: Deseret Book Co., 1972). Brief sketches on the life of President Harold B. Lee are published in the August and November 1972 issues of the *Ensign;* and of President Spencer W. Kimball in the March 1974 issue of that magazine. Biographies of these men in the latest edition of Preston Nibley's *Presidents of the Church* should also be consulted.

Other Biographies

Only a few of the many other biographies of Latter-day Saints can be listed here. Two classic autobiographies are Parley P. Pratt, ed., *Autobiography of Parley Parker Pratt* (first published in 1874; 3rd ed., 1938; reprinted, Salt Lake City: Deseret Book Co., 1961), and Annie Clark Tanner, *A Mormon Mother: An Autobiography,* Utah, the Mormons, and the West Series, No. 1 (1941; rev. ed., Salt Lake City: Tanner Trust Fund, University of Utah Library, 1973). Other important biographies include the classic by Juanita Brooks, *John D. Lee: Zealot, Pioneer Builder, Scapegoat,*

Western Frontiersmen Series, vol. 9, (1961; rev. ed., Glendale, Calif.: Arthur H. Clark Company, 1972); Harold Schindler, *Orrin Porter Rockwell: Man of God, Son of Thunder* (Salt Lake City: University of Utah Press, 1966); Andrew Karl Larson, *Erastus Snow: The Life of a Missionary and Pioneer for the Early Mormon Church* (Salt Lake City: University of Utah Press, 1971); Leonard J. Arrington, *Charles C. Rich: Mormon General and Western Frontiersman,* Studies in Mormon History, vol. 1 (Provo: Brigham Young University Press, 1974); and Eugene E. Campbell and Richard D. Poll, *Hugh B. Brown: His Life and Thought* (Salt Lake City: Bookcraft, Inc., 1975).

Articles useful for their biographical contributions include Frederick G. Williams III, "Frederick Granger Williams of the First Presidency of the Church," *Brigham Young University Studies* 12 (Spring 1972): 243-61; Paul Edwards, "The Sweet Singer of Israel: David Hyrum Smith," ibid., 12 (Winter 1972): 171-84; Steven Pratt, "Eleanor McLean and the Murder of Parley P. Pratt," ibid., 15 (Winter 1975): 225-56; Paul L. Anderson, "William Harrison Folsom: Pioneer Architect," *Utah Historical Quarterly* 43 (Summer 1975): 240-59; Leonard J. Arrington and Richard Jensen, "Pioneer Portraits: Lorenzo Hill Hatch," *Idaho Yesterdays* 17 (Summer 1973): 2-8; and Ray C. Hillam, comp., "J. Reuben Clark, Jr.: Diplomat and Statesman," a collection of essays by various authors, *Brigham Young University Studies* 13 (Spring 1973): 231-456.

We have listed published diaries at appropriate points in the chapter bibliographies.

COLLECTED WORKS

Useful for general reference are a number of publications in which essays, sermons, statistics, and important documents are collected. We list a few of the most valuable here.

Articles and Essays

The most important sources for articles are the professional journals, usually issued quarterly, from which we have cited many titles throughout this bibliography. Nine of the most important essays in Mormon history and two previously unpublished ones are collected in Marvin S. Hill and James B. Allen, *Mormonism and American Culture,* Interpretations of American History Series (New York: Harper & Row, 1972). Thirteen new articles on topics spanning the history of the Church are published in Mark F. McKiernan, Alma R. Blair, Paul M. Edwards, eds., *The Restoration Movement: Essays in Mormon History* (Lawrence, Kans.: Coronado Press, 1973). Most of the articles in these two books are cited separately in appropriate chapter bibliographies; exceptions are three essays broad in coverage: Leonard J. Arrington and D. Michael Quinn, "The Latter-day Saints in the Far West, 1847-1900," in *Restoration Movement,* pp. 257-71; Davis Bitton, "Early Mormon Lifestyles; or, the Saints as Human Beings," in ibid., pp. 273-306; and James B. Allen, "The Mormon Search for Community in the Modern World," ibid., pp. 307-40.

Useful for background information are the articles by Leonard J. Arrington and Thomas G. Alexander in *A Dependent Commonwealth: Utah's Economy from Statehood to the Great Depression,* ed. Dean May, Charles Redd Monographs in Western History, no. 4 (Provo: Brigham Young University Press, 1974). We have also used Clark Knowlton, ed., *Social Accommodation in Utah,* American West Center Occasional Papers (Salt Lake City: American West Center, University of Utah, 1975).

Lesson booklets issued monthly by the Daughters of Utah Pioneers, Salt Lake City, often contain information on nineteenth-century Church activities and biographical information on early Latter-day Saints. These are collected into annual volumes, compiled by Kate B. Carter: *Heart Throbs of the West,* 12 vols. (1939-51); *Treasures of Pioneer History,* 6 vols. (1952-57); and *Our Pioneer Heritage,* 18 vols. to date (1958-75).

Sermons

A vast resource for talks given by early Church leaders is the serial publication issued by British Mission officials from transcriptions provided by George D. Watt and many other reporters, *Journal of Discourses . . . ,* 26 vols. (London: Latter-day Saints' Book Depot, 1854-1886), available in a 1967 reprint edition. An effort to continue this series is *Deseret Discourses: Bridging the Gap between the Journal of Discourses and Conference Reports, 1889-   ,* 3 vols. to date (Provo: David C. Martin, 1975-   ). Issued semiannually in 1880 and the years since 1898 is the *Conference Report* of general conferences of the Church. Older volumes have been reprinted by Hawkes Publishing, Inc. (Salt Lake City, 1974-   ). The series now includes reports of the area general conferences published separately. The discourses of many individual authorities have also been published in convenient compilations.

Reference Works

A basic work of reference for the Mormon historian is Andrew Jenson, *The Historical Record: A Monthly Periodical Devoted Exclusively to Historical, Biographical, Chronological, and Statistical Matters,* 9 vols. (Salt Lake City, 1882-1890). Jenson's *Encyclopedic History of The Church . . .* (Salt Lake City: Deseret News Publishing Co., 1941) contains detailed information drawn from the manuscript histories of wards, branches, stakes, missions, and mission conferences that are on file in the Church Archives. Useful for dating events in the Church is Jenson's *Church Chronology: A Record of Important Events . . .* (1886; 2nd ed. rev., Salt Lake City: Deseret News Press, 1914), which compiles under one cover the 2nd edition (1889) and two supplements (covering 1899-1905 and 1906-1913) with indexes. A modern reference work updated annually is *Deseret News Church Almanac* (Salt Lake City: Deseret News, 1974-   ). This work includes a selective chronology, data on current and former General Authorities, and information on Church departments, stakes and missions, missionaries, historic sites, temples, publications, schools, and other useful material.

Published Documents

Only a small portion of the vast collection of documents housed in

the Church Archives has been published. The principal source for the period through 1846 is Joseph Smith, *History of the Church of Jesus Christ of
Latter-day Saints. Period I: History of Joseph Smith, the Prophet,* and . . . *Period II:
From the Manuscript History of Brigham Young and Other Original Documents,* ed.
B. H. Roberts, 7 vols. (Salt Lake City: published by the Church, 1902-
1932). Sometimes referred to as the "Documentary History," it is more
properly cited by the short title, *History of the Church,* the pattern we have
adopted in this book. Joseph Smith's history was first published in serial
form in early Church newspapers. For the story behind the history and
the men involved in compiling it, see Dean C. Jessee, "The Writing of Joseph Smith's History," *Brigham Young University Studies* 11 (Summer 1971):
439-73.

The documentary pattern is also followed in [Joseph Smith III,
Herman C. Smith, and F. Henry Edwards, eds. and comps.,] *The History of
the Reorganized Church of Jesus Christ of Latter Day Saints,* 6 vols. to date (Independence, Mo.: Herald House Publishers, 1967-   ). The record of the
first Church historian, "The Book of John Whitmer; Kept by Commandment," is published in Heman C. Smith, ed., "Church History," *Journal of
History* (Lamoni, Iowa) 1 (January, April, and July 1908): 43-63, 135-52,
292-305.

Official circulars, letters, and other documents are published in
James B. Člark, ed., *Messages of the First Presidency of the Church . . . ,* 6 vols.
(Salt Lake City: Bookcraft, 1965-75). A variety of published and
unpublished material is brought together in William E. Berrett and Alma
P. Burton, comps., *Readings in L.D.S. Church History, from Original Manu-
scripts,* 3 vols. (Salt Lake City: Deseret Book Co., 1953-58). Information re-
lating to programs of the modern church is collected in Richard O.
Cowan and Wilson K. Andersen, *The Living Church: The Unfolding of the
Program and Organization of The Church . . . during the Twentieth Century* (Provo:
Brigham Young University Printing Service, 1974). Many personal ac-
counts of value are included in William Mulder and A. Russell
Mortensen, eds., *Among the Mormons: Historic Accounts by Contemporary Ob-
servers* (New York: Alfred A. Knopf, 1958; and Lincoln: University of
Nebraska Press, 1973). The period from the origin of the Church through
the martyrdom is included in selections compiled by Keith C. Huntress,
ed., *Murder of an American Prophet: . . . Materials for Analysis* (San Francisco:
Chandler Publishing Co., 1960). Documents also appear from time to
time in James B. Allen, ed., "The Historian's Corner," a regular feature of
Brigham Young University Studies.

To make the resources of the Church Archives more widely avail-
able, a new series of published documents has been launched by the His-
torical Department of the Church. The first to appear is Dean C. Jessee,
Letters of Brigham Young to His Sons, Mormon Heritage Series, vol. 1 (Salt
Lake City: Deseret Book Co., 1974). A good introduction to the book is
Jessee's "The Writings of Brigham Young," *Western Historical Quarterly* 4
(July 1973): 273-94. The Church Archives staff is also preparing registers
describing important collections of unpublished papers.

BIBLIOGRAPHIES AND HISTORIOGRAPHY

Important guides to further reading and research are included in most of the general surveys listed in this bibliography; and detailed bibliographies on specialized topics are included in the monographs, theses, and dissertations. Essays identifying the most important works are Thomas G. Alexander and James B. Allen, eds., "The Mormons in the Mountain West: A Selected Bibliography," *Arizona and the West* 9 (Winter 1967): 365-84; Marvin S. Hill, "The Historiography of Mormonism," *Church History* 27 (December 1959): 418-26; and P.A.M. Taylor, "Recent Writing on Utah and the Mormons," *Arizona and the West* 4 (Autumn 1962): 249-60. A discussion and listing of dissertations is Leonard J. Arrington, "Scholarly Studies of Mormonism in the Twentieth Century," *Dialogue: A Journal of Mormon Thought* 1 (Spring 1966): 15-32.

Comprehensive bibliographies, listing both historical and other types of studies, include *A Catalogue of Theses and Dissertations Concerning The Church . . . , Mormonism, and Utah* (complete to January 1970), compiled by the College of Religious Instruction at Brigham Young University (Provo: College of Religious Instruction, 1971), and Peter Crawley, "A Bibliography of the Church . . . in New York, Ohio, and Missouri," *Brigham Young University Studies* 12 (Summer 1972): 465-537. An excellent selection of book, article, and graduate studies titles is in David J. Whittaker, comp., *Early Mormon History: A Selected Bibliography, 1771-1847,* mimeographed (Los Angeles: David J. Whittaker, 1973).

For current publications, the most helpful are the annual listing, "Mormon Bibliography," compiled by Chad J. Flake for *Brigham Young University Studies,* and the three compilations a year by Ralph W. Hansen, ed., "Among the Mormons: A Survey of Current Literature," in *Dialogue: A Journal of Mormon Thought.* Still awaiting publication at University of Utah Press is Chad J. Flake and Dale L. Morgan, eds., *Mormon Bibliography, 1830-1930,* a union catalog of about ten thousand publications by and about the Latter-day Saints. Forthcoming from Brigham Young University Press is Davis Bitton, ed., *Guide to Mormon Diaries and Autobiographies,* a descriptive listing of nearly three thousand items.

Early critiques of the way Mormon history has been written and with suggestions for correcting imbalances include the survey by Marvin Hill noted earlier in this section and essays by Leonard J. Arrington, "The Search for Truth and Meaning in Mormon History," *Dialogue: A Journal of Mormon Thought* 3 (Summer 1968): 55-66; Robert B. Flanders, "Writing the Mormon Past," ibid., 1 (Autumn 1966): 47-61; and Fawn M. Brodie, *Can We Manipulate the Past?* (Salt Lake City: Center for Studies of the American West, 1970), reviewed by Marvin S. Hill, "The Manipulation of History," in *Dialogue: A Journal of Mormon Thought* 5 (Autumn 1970): 96-99.

Continuing the discussion are Leonard J. Arrington, "Centrifugal Tendencies in L.D.S. History," in Truman Madsen and Charles Tate, Jr., eds., *To the Glory of God: Mormon Essays on Great Issues* (Salt Lake City: Deseret Book Co., 1972), pp. 165-77; Richard L. Bushman, "The Historians and Mormon Nauvoo," *Dialogue: A Journal of Mormon Thought* 5 (Spring 1970): 51-61; and Robert Flanders, "Some Reflections on the New Mormon History," ibid., 9 (Spring 1974): 34-42. Offering suggestions for making religion and naturalistic history compatible are Richard L. Bushman, "Faithful History," ibid., 4 (Winter 1969): 11-25; and Richard D. Poll, "God and Man in History," ibid., 7 (Spring 1972): 101-9. Paul M. Edwards, "The Irony of Mormon History," *Utah Historical Quarterly* 41 (Autumn 1973): 393-409, comments further on the question. A literary approach is suggested in Robert A. Rees, " 'Truth Is the Daughter of Time': Notes Toward an Imaginative Mormon History," ibid., 6 (Autumn-Winter 1971): 15-22.

Other comments on Mormon historiography are Moses Rischin, "The New Mormon History," *American West* 6 (March 1969): 49; and Rodman W. Paul, "The Mormons as a Theme in Western Historical Writing," *Journal of American History* 54 (December 1967): 511-23.

CHAPTER BIBLIOGRAPHIES

CHAPTER 1
The Religious Setting for the Restoration

Most general histories of the Church comment on the religious setting of the Restoration. From them, and from the specialized studies mentioned below, we have prepared the brief overview contained in this introductory chapter.

Among the general Church histories commenting on this period are Barrett, *Joseph Smith and the Restoration*, chaps. 1-2; Roberts, *Comprehensive History of the Church*, vol. 1, chaps. 1-5; and Joseph Fielding Smith, *Essentials in Church History*, chaps. 3-6.

For more detail on major religious trends, the reader should consult standard histories such as Sydney E. Ahlstrom, *A Religious History of the American People* (New Haven and London: Yale University Press, 1972), parts 1-4; Edwin Scott Gaustad, *A Religious History of America* (New York: Harper & Row, 1966), chaps. 5-12; or Clifton E. Olmstead, *History of Religion in the United States* (Englewood Cliffs, N.J.: Prentice-Hall, 1960), chaps. 1-17. Much information important to Latter-day Saint history is conveniently summarized in Milton V. Backman, Jr., *American Religions and the Rise of Mormonism*, rev. ed. (Salt Lake City: Deseret Book Co., 1970).

Additional insights on the social origins of Mormonism are in Whitney R. Cross, *The Burned-over District: The Social and Intellectual History of Enthusiastic Religion in Western New York, 1800-1850* (New York: Cornell University Press, 1950; and New York: Harper & Row, 1965), chaps. 1-8; Marvin S. Hill, "The Role of Christian Primitivism in the Origin and Development of the Mormon Kingdom, 1830-1844" (Ph.D. diss., University of Chicago, 1968), chaps. 1-2; Hill, "Quest for Refuge: An Hypothesis as to the Social Origins and Nature of the Mormon Political Kingdom," *Journal of Mormon History* 2 (1975): 3-20; Laurence M. Yorgason, "Some Demographic Aspects of One Hundred Early Mormon Converts, 1830-1837" (M.A. thesis, Brigham Young University, 1974); and Yorgason, "Preview on a Study of the Social and Geographical Origins of Early Mormon Converts, 1830-1845," *Brigham Young University Studies* 10 (Spring 1970): 279-82.

On the revivals, see general histories listed above and the biographies of Joseph Smith named in the General Bibliography. For recent discussion, see Wesley P. Walters and Richard L. Bushman, "Roundtable: The Question of the Palmyra Revival," *Dialogue: A Journal of Mormon Thought* 4 (Spring 1969): 59-100; and Peter Crawley, "A Comment on Joseph Smith's Account of His First Vision and the 1820 Revival," ibid., 6 (Spring 1971): 106-7. A good summary is Milton V. Backman, Jr., *Joseph*

Smith's First Vision: The First Vision in Its Historical Context (Salt Lake City: Bookcraft, 1971), chaps. 1-4, which is supplemented by Backman's "Awakenings in the Burned-over District: New Light on the Historical Setting of the First Vision," *Brigham Young University Studies* 9 (Spring 1969): 301-20.

A number of articles listed below (chap. 2) are also useful to a study of religious backgrounds and the origins of the Church.

Biographical information and documents pertaining to the Prophet's ancestors are in Richard Lloyd Anderson, *Joseph Smith's New England Heritage: Influences of Grandfathers Solomon Mack and Asael Smith* (Salt Lake City: Deseret Book Co., 1971); and in the many biographies of the Prophet. Also pertinent is Reed C. Durham, Jr., "Joseph Smith's Own Story of a Serious Childhood Illness," *Brigham Young University Studies* 10 (Summer 1970): 480-82; Richard L. Anderson, "Joseph Smith's Home Environment," *Ensign* 1 (July 1971): 56-59; and James B. Allen, "Joseph Smith as a Young Man," *New Era* 1 (January 1971): 19-23.

CHAPTER 2
The Restoration Commences, 1820-1839

The New York period in Church history, the years between the First Vision and the Prophet's move to Ohio, has attracted renewed interest among historians. Though the traditional outlines of the story remain unchanged and can be found in all standard histories, much new information is available as historians have studied previously unexamined documents and asked new questions of the familiar sources.

Earlier treatments of the material covered here may be found in Roberts, *Comprehensive History of the Church*, vol. 1, chaps. 5-19; Joseph Smith, *History of the Church*, vol. 1, chaps. 1-11; Joseph Fielding Smith, *Essentials in Church History*, chaps. 7-14; and Barrett, *Joseph Smith and the Restoration*, chaps. 3-8. To supplement these, we have drawn liberally from the excellent specialized studies listed below.

A concise overview of the entire period is Larry C. Porter, "The Church in New York and Pennsylvania, 1816-1831," in McKiernan et al., *Restoration Movement*, pp. 27-61. For greater detail on the people involved and the historic sites, see Porter's "A Study of the Origins of The Church . . . in the States of New York and Pennsylvania, 1816-1831" (Ph.D. diss., Brigham Young University, 1971).

Several early documents on the First Vision were first examined and described by Paul R. Cheesman, "An Analysis of the Accounts Relating Joseph Smith's Early Visions" (M.R.E. thesis, Brigham Young University, 1965). More easily accessible is Backman, *Joseph Smith's First Vision*, which we used also in chapter 1, and Dean C. Jessee, "The Early Accounts of Joseph Smith's First Vision," *Brigham Young University Studies* 9 (Spring 1969): 275-94. James B. Allen presents a convenient summary and analysis in "Eight Contemporary Accounts of Joseph Smith's First Vision: What Do We Learn from Them?" *Improvement Era* 73 (April 1970): 4-13, and examines public knowledge of the vision in "The Significance of Joseph Smith's First Vision in Mormon Thought," *Dialogue: A Journal of Mormon Thought* 1 (Autumn 1966): 28-45. A related study is Richard L. Anderson, "Circumstantial Confirmation of the First Vision Through Reminiscences," *Brigham Young University Studies* 9 (Spring 1969): 373-404. On the minister who is thought to have influenced Joseph Smith's search for religion see Larry C. Porter, "Reverend George Lane: Good 'Gifts,' Much 'Grace,' and Marked 'Usefulness,' " ibid., pp. 321-40.

Very early in Church history, writers began taking sides as critics or defenders of Joseph Smith and Mormonism, and only more recently have histories taken a more religiously neutral and scholarly tone. Historians now are trying to understand and assess the historical evidence used by both detractors and defenders. A good introduction is James B. Allen and Leonard J. Arrington, "Mormon Origins in New York: An Introductory Analysis," *Brigham Young University Studies* 9 (Spring 1969): 241-74. See also Marvin S. Hill, "The Historiography of Mormonism," *Church History* 28 (December 1959): 418-26. Discussion of specific issues can be found in Brodie, *No Man Knows My History,* pp. 427-41; Hill, "Secular or Sectarian History? A Critique of 'No Man Knows My History,' " *Church History* 43 (March 1974): 78-96; Hill, "Joseph Smith's New York Reputation Reappraised," *Brigham Young University Studies* 10 (Spring 1970): 283-314, which we found particularly useful; Leonard J. Arrington, "James Gordon Bennett's 1831 Report on 'The Mormonites,' " ibid., pp. 353-64; and Jan Shipps, "The Prophet Puzzle: Suggestions Leading toward a More Comprehensive Interpretation of Joseph Smith," *Journal of Mormon History* 1 (1974): 3-20. Also pertinent are Backman's study on the First Vision cited above; Richard L. Anderson, "The Reliability of the Early History of Lucy and Joseph Smith"; and Hugh Nibley, *The Myth Makers* (Salt Lake City: Bookcraft, 1961).

Another approach to Mormon origins seeks to understand Church history in a broad historical context. Two important early essays of this kind by non-Mormon historians are David Brion Davis, "The New England Origins of Mormonism," *New England Quarterly* 27 (June 1953): 148-53, and Mario S. DePillis, "The Quest for Religious Authority and the Rise of Mormonism," *Dialogue: A Journal of Mormon Thought* 1 (Spring 1966): 68-88. Both have been reprinted in Hill and Allen, *Mormonism and American Culture,* pp. 13-28 and 29-34. Continuing the discussion are Klaus J. Hansen, "Mormonism and American Culture: Some Tentative Hypotheses"; McKiernan et al., *Restoration Movement,* pp. 1-26; Marvin S. Hill, "Quest for Refuge: An Hypothesis as to the Social Origins and Nature of the Mormon Political Kingdom," *Journal of Mormon History* 2 (1975): 3-20; Mario DePillis, "The Social Sources of Mormonism," *Church History* 37 (March 1968): 50-79; and Hansen, "The Millennium, the West, and Race in the Antebellum Mind," *Western Historical Quarterly* 3 (October 1972): 373-90.

New information on events leading to the publication of the Book of Mormon can be found in four articles in the Spring 1970 issue of *Brigham*

Young University Studies: Russell R. Rich, "Where Were the Moroni Visits?" 10:255-58; Dean C. Jessee, "The Original Book of Mormon Manuscript," pp. 259-78; Russell R. Rich, "The Dogberry Papers and the Book of Mormon," pp. 315-19; and Stanley B. Kimball, "The Anthon Transcript: People, Primary Sources, and Problems," pp. 325-52. Another useful study is Richard P. Howard, *Restoration Scriptures: A Study of Their Textual Development* (Independence, Mo.: Herald Publishing House, 1969), chaps. 1-4. On the internal consistency of the Book of Mormon, see Francis Kirkham, *A New Witness for Christ in America,* vol. 1: *The Book of Mormon* (1942; 4th ed., Salt Lake City: Published by the Author, 1967); Paul Cheesman, *The Keystone of Mormonism: Little Known Truths about the Book of Mormon* (Salt Lake City: Deseret Book Co., 1973); and books by Hugh Nibley: *An Approach to the Book of Mormon,* 2nd ed. (Salt Lake City: Deseret Book Co., 1964), and *Since Cumorah: The Book of Mormon in the Modern World* (Salt Lake City: Deseret Book Co., 1967).

The restoration of priesthood is described in Roberts, *Comprehensive History,* vol. 1, chap. 15, and Richard L. Anderson, "The Second Witness of Priesthood Restoration," *Improvement Era* (September 1968): 15-24; and in two sources noted earlier: Porter, "The Church in New York and Pennsylvania," and Hill, "The Role of Christian Primitivism."

On the organization of the Church, we have supplemented standard sources with Carter E. Grant, "Peter Whitmer's Log House," *Improvement Era* 62 (May 1959): 349, 365-66, 369; Larry C. Porter, "The Colesville Branch and the Coming Forth of the Book of Mormon," *Brigham Young University Studies* 19 (Spring 1970): 365-86; and two sources mentioned earlier: Porter, "The Church in New York and Pennsylvania," chap. 6; and Yorgason, "Some Demographic Aspects of the One Hundred Early Mormon Converts." An important letter is reproduced in D. Michael Quinn, "The First Months of Mormonism: A Contemporary View by Rev. Diedrich Willers," *New York History* 54 (July 1973): 317-33.

Additional information on early missionary work can be found in the dissertations of Porter, Hill, and DePillis mentioned earlier; in Richard L. Anderson, "The Impact of the First Preaching in Ohio," *Brigham Young University Studies* 11 (Summer 1971): 474-96; and in Warren A. Jennings, "The First Mormon Mission to the Indians," *Kansas Historical Quarterly* 38 (Autumn 1971): 288-99. Useful on doctrine is Marvin S. Hill, "The Shaping of the Mormon Mind in New England and New York," *Brigham Young University Studies* 9 (Spring 1969): 351-72. Preliminary comments on identifying locations are in T. Edgar Lyon, "How Authentic Are Mormon Historic Sites in Vermont and New York?" ibid., pp. 341-50.

CHAPTER 3
Unfolding Latter-day Zion, 1831-1836

In the early 1830s important events were transpiring in both Kirtland, Ohio, and Jackson County, Missouri. We combine the familiar stories from these two places in this chapter. For more information on these eventful years the reader may consult Roberts, *Comprehensive History of the Church*, vol. 1, chaps. 19-31; Joseph Fielding Smith, *Essentials in Church History*, chaps. 15-21; Barrett, *Joseph Smith and the Restoration*, chaps. 9-17; and Joseph Smith, *History of the Church*, vol. 1, chaps. 12-35, and vol. 2, chaps. 1-30.

Descriptions of the two gathering places are in Robert L. Layton, "Kirtland: A Perspective on Time and Place," *Brigham Young University Studies* 11 (Summer 1971): 423-38, an excellent treatise on the geographical setting; Richard L. Anderson, "Jackson County in Early Mormon Descriptions," *Missouri Historical Review* 65 (April 1971): 270-93, based on travel accounts; and Anderson's "New Data for Revising the Missouri 'Documentary History,'" *Brigham Young University Studies* 14 (Summer 1974): 488-501. Also of interest is Max H. Parkin, "The Courthouse Mentioned in the Revelation on Zion," ibid., pp. 451-57.

For a survey of Church history in Ohio see Milton V. Backman, Jr., "The Quest for a Restoration: The Birth of Mormonism in Ohio," *Brigham Young University Studies* 12 (Summer 1972): 346-64, and the comprehensive summary by Max H. Parkin, "Kirtland, a Stronghold for the Kingdom," in McKiernan et al., *The Restoration Movement*, pp. 63-98. Parkin's article is based on his topical study, "The Nature and Causes of External and Internal Conflict of the Mormons in Ohio between 1830 and 1838" (M.A. thesis, University of Utah, 1966). An expansion of chapter 7 of that thesis is "Mormon Political Involvement in Ohio," *Brigham Young University Studies* 9 (Summer 1969): 484-502. Another interpretation is in Robert Kent Fielding's well-researched analysis, "The Growth of the Mormon Church in Kirtland, Ohio" (Ph.D. diss., University of Indiana, 1957). Anne B. Prusha, "A History of Kirtland, Ohio" (M.A. thesis, Kent State University, 1971), is a political town history with a Midwestern perspective.

Personal glimpses into Mormon life are in Dean C. Jessee, ed., "The Kirtland Diary of Wilford Woodruff," *Brigham Young University Studies* 12 (Summer 1972): 365-99, and Leonard J. Arrington, ed., "Oliver Cowdery's Kirtland, Ohio, 'Sketch Book,'" ibid., pp. 410-26.

Narratives of the Missouri experience, besides those in general histories, include Warren A. Jennings, "The Expulsion of the Mormons from Jackson County, Missouri," *Missouri Historical Review* 64 (October 1969): 41-63, which is drawn from chap. 5 of his "Zion Is Fled: The Expulsion of the Mormons from Jackson County, Missouri" (Ph.D. diss., University of Florida, 1962). Important essays seeking to understand the Missouri problems are Jennings, "The City in the Garden: Social Conflict in Jackson County, Missouri," in McKiernan et al., *Restoration Movement*, pp. 99-119; Richard L. Bushman, "Mormon Persecutions in Missouri, 1833," *Brigham Young University Studies* 3 (Autumn 1960): 11-20; and R. J. Robertson, Jr., "The Mormon Experience in Missouri, 1803-1839," *Missouri Historical Review* 68 (April and July 1974): 280-98 and 393-415. An important survey of the Latter-day Saint image is David Brion Davis, "Some

Themes of Counter-Subversion: An Analysis of Anti-Masonic, Anti-Catholic, and Anti-Mormon Literature," *Mississippi Valley Historical Review* 47 (September 1970): 205-24, which has been reprinted in Hill and Allen, *Mormonism and American Culture*, pp. 59-73. Events are given a religious interpretation in B. H. Roberts, *The Missouri Persecutions* (1900; reprinted, Salt Lake City: Bookcraft, 1965), and are placed in a theological framework in Alvin R. Dyer, *The Refiner's Fire: The Significance of Events Transpiring in Missouri*, 3rd ed. rev. (Salt Lake City: Deseret Book Co., 1972).

One aspect of the conflict is examined in Warren A. Jennings, "Factors in the Destruction of the Mormon Press in Missouri, 1833," *Utah Historical Quarterly* 35 (Winter 1967): 56-76, drawn from chap. 4 of his dissertation. Useful for background reading is Donnie D. Bellamy, "Free Blacks in Antebellum Missouri, 1820-1860," *Missouri Historical Review* 67 (January 1973): 198-226. The race issue and its implications are traced beyond this period in Stephen Taggart, *Mormonism's Negro Policy: Social and Historical Origins* (Salt Lake City: University of Utah Press, 1970), and in Lester Bush, Jr., "Mormonism's Negro Doctrine: An Historical Overview," *Dialogue: A Journal of Mormon Thought* 8 (Spring 1973): 11-68.

We have followed Peter Crawley and Richard L. Anderson, "The Political and Social Realities of Zion's Camp," *Brigham Young University Studies* 14 (Summer 1974): 406-20, for our account of the attempt to reinstate the Saints on their Jackson County lands. An earlier study is Warren A. Jennings, "The Army of Israel Marches into Missouri," *Missouri Historical Review* 62 (January 1968): 107-35, from chap. 7 of his dissertation. Additional detail is in Wilburn D. Talbot, "Zion's Camp" (M.A. thesis, Brigham Young University, 1973).

Selected aspects of the conflict and comments on economic activities are in T. Edgar Lyon, "Independence, Missouri, and the Mormons, 1827-1833," *Brigham Young University Studies* 13 (Autumn 1972): 10-19. Basic economic studies are Leonard J. Arrington's careful analysis, "Early Mormon Communitarianism: The Law of Consecration and Stewardship," *Western Humanities Review* 7 (Autumn 1953): 341-69, and his *Great Basin Kingdom*, chap. 1. Differing assessments on the law of consecration and economic policies are Mario S. DePillis, "The Development of Mormon Communitarianism, 1826-1846" (Ph.D. diss., Yale University, 1960), and R. Kent Fielding, "The Mormon Economy in Kirtland, Ohio," *Utah Historical Quarterly* 27 (October 1959): 331-56, which draws from his dissertation.

Much work yet remains to be done on the administrative history of the Church. We have drawn from Joseph Smith, *History of the Church*, in the chapters noted above, and D. Michael Quinn, "The Evolution of the Presiding Quorums of the LDS Church," *Journal of Mormon History* 1 (1974): 21-38, based on chap. 1 of his "Organizational Development and Social Origins of the Mormon Hierarchy, 1832-1932: A Prosopographical Study" (M.A. thesis, University of Utah, 1973). Another unpublished study is C. Kent Dunford, "The Historical Development of Priesthood Organization and Government in the Church of Jesus Christ of Latter-day Saints from 1830-1844" (M.A. thesis, Brigham Young University, 1967). Studies of the life of an important early leader include the early standard biography of Daryl Chase, "Sidney Rigdon, Early Mormon" (M.A. thesis, University of Chicago, 1931), and the more recent one by F. Mark McKiernan, *The Voice of One Crying in the Wilderness: Sidney Rigdon, Religious Reformer, 1793-1876* (Lawrence, Kans.: Coronado Press, 1971).

On varied Church activities we found helpful Davis Bitton, "Kirtland as a Center of Missionary Activity, 1830-1838," *Brigham Young University Studies* 11 (Summer 1971): 497-516; F. Mark McKiernan, "The Conversion of Sidney Rigdon to Mormonism," *Dialogue: A Journal of Mormon Thought* 5 (Summer 1970): 71-78; a chapter on the Kirtland School in John A. Patrick, "The School of the Prophets: Its Development and Influence in Utah Territory" (M.A. thesis, Brigham Young University, 1970); and Louis C. Zucker, "Joseph Smith as a Student of Hebrew," *Dialogue: A Journal of Mormon Thought* 3 (Summer 1968): 41-55. On the Kirtland Temple, see Talmage, *House of the Lord,* chap. 5; Lauritz G. Peterson, "The Kirtland Temple," *Brigham Young University Studies* 12 (Summer 1972): 400-409; Laurel B. Blank Andrew, "The Nineteenth-century Temple Architecture of the Latter-day Saints" (Ph.D. diss., University of Michigan, 1973); and Clarence L. Fields, "History of the Kirtland Temple" (M.S. thesis, Brigham Young University, 1963).

Joseph Smith's revision of the Bible is described in Robert J. Matthews, *"A Plainer Translation": Joseph Smith's Translation of the Bible; A History and Commentary* (Provo: Brigham Young University Press, 1975), and in Howard, *Restoration Scriptures,* chaps. 5-9. E. D. Howe, *Mormonism Unvailed* [*sic*] (Painesville, N.Y.: E. D. Howe, 1834), raised the question of Joseph Smith's reputation in New York (see the writings on detractors and defenders in our bibliography for chap. 2) and introduced the Spaulding-Rigdon theory of the origin of the Book of Mormon. This theory has long been discredited by writers, among them George Reynolds, *The Myth of the "Manuscript Found"; or, The Absurdities of the "Spaulding Story"* (Salt Lake City: Juvenile Instructor Office, 1883); Brodie, *No Man Knows My History,* pp. 442-56; and Kirkham, *New Witness for Christ,* 1:299-336. It is discussed in its historical context in Arrington and Allen, "Mormon Origins in New York: An Introductory Analysis," pp. 245-48; and the document itself has been published as *The "Manuscript Found": Manuscript Story, by Rev. Solomon Spaulding, Deceased* (Salt Lake City: Deseret News Co., 1886).

The development of the Doctrine and Covenants is treated briefly in most general histories and in many commentaries on that scripture. Detailed historical treatises are in Howard, *Restoration Scriptures,* chaps. 10-11; and John W. Fitzgerald, "A Study of the Doctrine and Covenants, 1833-1921" (M.S. thesis, Brigham Young University, 1940). See also Earl E. Olson, "The Chronology of the Ohio Revelations," *Brigham Young University Studies* 11 (Summer 1971): 329-49.

The history of the Book of Abraham is described in Jay M. Todd, *The Saga of the Book of Abraham* (Salt Lake City: Deseret Book Co., 1969), and Walter L. Whipple, "The St. Louis Museum and the Two Egyptian

Mummies and Papyri," *Brigham Young University Studies* 10 (Autumn 1969): 57-64. Numerous articles on the internal historical evidences of the Book of Abraham and on the Joseph Smith Egyptian papyri have been published since the Church acquired several papyrus fragments in late 1967. For the principal ones see *Brigham Young University Studies,* issues of Winter, Spring, and Autumn 1968, Summer 1969, Summer 1970, Winter 1971, and Summer 1971; and *Dialogue: A Journal of Mormon Thought,* a special issue, Summer 1968, and articles in Autumn 1968 and Summer 1969. Also see Hugh Nibley, "A New Look at the Pearl of Great Price" (in 22 installments), *Improvement Era* 71-73 (January 1968-May 1970), and his *The Message of the Joseph Smith Papyri: An Egyptian Endowment* (Salt Lake City: Deseret Book Co., 1975).

Studies on specific LDS teachings originating in this period are Leonard J. Arrington, "An Economic Interpretation of the 'Word of Wisdom,' " *Brigham Young University Studies* 1 (Winter 1959): 37-49; Edward T. Jones, "The Theology of Thomas Dick and Its Possible Relationship to That of Joseph Smith" (M.A. thesis, Brigham Young University, 1969); Robert J. Matthews, "The 'New Translation' of the Bible, 1830-33: Doctrinal Development during the Kirtland Era," *Brigham Young University Studies* 11 (Summer 1971): 400-423; Gordon Irving, "The Mormons and the Bible in the 1830s," ibid., 13 (Summer 1973): 473-88, which is based on his "Mormonism and the Bible, 1832-1838" (B.A. thesis, University of Utah, 1972); Russel B. Swensen, "The Influence of the New Testament upon Latter-day Saint Eschatology from 1830-1846" (M.A. thesis, University of Chicago, 1931); and Edward Allen Warner, "Mormon Theodemocracy: Theocratic and Democratic Elements in Early Latter-day Saint Ideology, 1827-1846" (Ph.D. diss., University of Iowa, 1973). Chap. 3 of Louis G. Reinwand, "An Interpretative Study of Mormon Millennialism during the Nineteenth Century with Emphasis on Millennial Developments in Utah" (M.A. thesis, Brigham Young University, 1971), briefly summarizes the years 1830-44.

CHAPTER 4
The Saints on the Move, 1836-1839

The last years in Ohio and Missouri have been portrayed by historians as years of conflict. This chapter and the sources from which it has been drawn reflect that theme. The essential story is told in general surveys such as B. H. Roberts, *Comprehensive History of the Church,* vol. 1, chaps. 32-39, and Joseph Fielding Smith, *Essentials in Church History,* chaps. 22-26; in the documents collected in Joseph Smith, *History of the Church,* vol. 2, chaps. 31-36, and vol. 3, chaps. 1-22; and in Barrett's lively textbook, *Joseph Smith and the Restoration,* chaps. 18-21.

New insights on the traditional story and, in some cases, studies of new subtopics have appeared in recent years to aid our understanding of this period. These include a number of articles published in special summer issues of *Brigham Young University Studies,* 1972, 1973, and 1974. Two graduate studies of particular relevance are those by Parkin (cited in the bibliography for chap. 3), and Leland H. Gentry, "A History of the Latter-day Saints in Northern Missouri from 1836 to 1839" (Ph.D. diss., Brigham Young University, 1965).

Events at key places in northern Missouri are discussed in Floyd C. Shoemaker, "Clay County," *Missouri Historical Review* 52 (October 1957): 25-34; Robert J. Matthews, "Adam-ondi-Ahman," *Brigham Young University Studies* 13 (Autumn 1972): 27-35; Leland H. Gentry, "Adam-ondi-Ahman: A Brief Historical Survey," ibid., 13 (Summer 1973): 553-76; Dyer, *Refiner's Fire,* pp. 136-324; and F. Mark McKiernan, "Mormonism on the Defensive: Far West," in McKiernan et al., *Restoration Movement,* pp. 121-40.

A discussion of certain strains is in Willis Thornton, "Gentile and Saint at Kirtland," *Ohio State Archaeological and Historical Quarterly* 63 (January 1954): 8-33. Davis Bitton examines the neglected years after Joseph Smith's departure in "The Waning of Mormon Kirtland," *Brigham Young University Studies* 12 (Summer 1972): 455-64.

A combination of historical and economic research techniques has produced significant reinterpretations of Latter-day Saint financial affairs in Ohio, reported in D. Paul Sampson and Larry T. Wimmer, "The Kirtland Safety Society: The Stock Ledger Book and the Bank Failure," ibid., pp. 427-36; Scott H. Partridge, "The Failure of the Kirtland Safety Society," ibid., pp. 437-54; and an important paper, still unpublished, by Marvin S. Hill, Larry T. Wimmer, and Keith C. Rooker, "The Kirtland Economy Revisited: A Market Place Critique of Sectarian Economics," delivered as a part of the Charles Redd Center for Western Studies lecture series, Brigham Young University, January 15, 1975. Other treatments are D. A. Dudley, "Bank Born of Revelation: The Kirtland Safety Society Anti-Banking Co.," *Journal of Economic History* 30 (December 1971): 848-53, and the analyses by Fielding and Parkin cited in the bibliography for chap. 3.

Supplementing the sources listed above on the Missouri difficulties are the following articles in *Brigham Young University Studies:* Peter Crawley, "Two Rare Missouri Documents," 14 (Summer 1974): 502-27, which reproduces the *Evening and the Morning Star* Extra of February 1834 and Sidney Rigdon's July 4, 1838, oration; F. Mark McKiernan, "Sidney Rigdon's Missouri Speeches," 11 (Autumn 1970): 90-92; Leland H. Gentry, "The Danite Band of 1838," 14 (Summer 1974): 421-50; Paul C. Richards, "Missouri Persecutions: Petitions for Redress," 13 (Summer 1973): 520-43; Eliza R. Snow, "Letter from Missouri," ibid., pp. 544-52; Reed C. Durham, Jr., "The Election Day Battle at Gallatin," 13 (Autumn 1972): 36-61; and Alma Blair, "The Haun's Mill Massacre," ibid., pp. 62-67. Also pertinent are Monte B. McLaws, "The Attempted Assassination of Missouri's Ex-Governor, Lilburn W. Boggs," *Missouri Historical Review* 60 (October 1965): 50-62, and Schindler, *Orrin Porter Rockwell,* chap. 2.

On the final months in Missouri see Gregory Maynard, "Alexander

Doniphan: Man of Justice," *Brigham Young University Studies* 13 (Summer 1973): 462-72, and Leonard J. Arrington, "Church Leaders in Liberty Jail," ibid., 13 (Autumn 1972): 20-26. That Nauvoo was not the only place of refuge for exiles from western and northern Missouri is pointed out in Stanley B. Kimball, "The Saints and St. Louis, 1831-1857: An Oasis of Tolerance and Security," ibid., 13 (Summer 1973): 489-519.

CHAPTER 5
Building the City Beautiful, 1839-1842

Several detailed studies are available on the Church at Nauvoo to supplement the information given in general surveys of Church history. Historians have dealt thoroughly with Nauvoo's political and economic life, less adequately with social and religious activities. Most histories of this period focus on events in Nauvoo, and except for the British Mission say little of the Church outside the central gathering place.

In the general histories, the early Nauvoo period is described in Roberts, *Comprehensive History of the Church,* vol. 2, chaps. 40-49; Joseph Fielding Smith, *Essentials in Church History,* chaps. 27-32; Barrett, *Joseph Smith and the Restoration,* chaps. 22-26; and Joseph Smith, *History of the Church,* vol. 3, chaps. 18, 23-28; vol. 4; and vol. 5, chaps. 1-12.

Two recent monographs are especially useful: Robert B. Flanders, *Nauvoo: Kingdom on the Mississippi* (Urbana: University of Illinois Press, 1965), analyzes political and economic life in depth, while David E. Miller and Della S. Miller, *Nauvoo: The City of Joseph* (Santa Barbara and Salt Lake City: Peregrine Smith, 1974), offers a narrative survey, with useful sections on land purchases, religious activities, and the operations of city government. Of the older works, B. H. Roberts, *The Rise and Fall of Nauvoo* (1900; reprint, Salt Lake City: Bookcraft, 1965), is a narrative of political activities and persecutions written for youth; and E. Cecil McGavin, *Nauvoo the Beautiful* (Salt Lake City: Stevens & Wallis, 1946), focuses on personal suffering in a sentimental presentation. A brief overview is found in Stanley B. Kimball, "The Mormons in Illinois, 1838-1846: A Special Introduction," *Journal of the Illinois State Historical Society* 64 (Spring 1971): 4-21. Samuel W. Taylor, *Nightfall at Nauvoo* (New York: Macmillan Company, 1971), is a fictionalized account.

On the British Mission and emigration, see James B. Allen and Malcolm R. Thorp, "The Mission of the Twelve to England, 1840-41: Mormon Apostles and the Working Classes," *Brigham Young University Studies* 15 (Summer 1975): 499-526; and relevant sections of Allen and Alexander, *Manchester Mormons;* P.A.M. Taylor, *Expectations Westward;* and Flanders, *Nauvoo: Kingdom on the Mississippi.*

Government in Nauvoo is discussed in the monographs by Flanders and the Millers and in two articles by James L. Kimball, Jr., "The Nauvoo Charter: A Reinterpretation," *Journal of the Illinois State Historical Society* 64 (Spring 1971): 66-78, and "A Wall to Defend Zion: The Nauvoo Charter," *Brigham Young University Studies* 15 (Summer 1975): 491-97, both of which draw from Kimball's "A Study of the Nauvoo Charter, 1840-1845" (M.A. thesis, University of Iowa, 1966). On the city militia, see Hamilton Gardner, "The Nauvoo Legion, 1840-1845: A Unique Military Organization," *Journal of the Illinois State Historical Society* 65 (Summer 1961): 181-97, a concise chronicle of the Legion's legal basis, activities, and uniqueness, and John Sweeney, Jr., "A History of the Nauvoo Legion in Illinois" (M.A. thesis, Brigham Young University, 1974), a year-by-year account with lists of officers and charts of organization.

Economic life in Nauvoo receives adequate treatment in Flanders and the Millers. Additional insights are in Arrington, *Great Basin Kingdom,* pp. 3-35; and M. Hamblin Cannon, ed., "Bankruptcy Proceedings against Joseph Smith in Illinois," *Pacific Historical Review* 14 (December 1945): 424-33, and 15 (June 1946): 214-15.

For other aspects of Nauvoo society, see Paul Thomas Smith, "A Historical Study of the Nauvoo, Illinois, Public School System, 1841-1845" (M.E. field study, Brigham Young University, 1969); Kenneth W. Godfrey, "Some Thoughts Regarding an Unwritten History of Nauvoo," *Brigham Young University Studies* 15 (Summer 1975): 417-24, a brief sampling from firsthand sources for a social history; Godfrey, "Joseph Smith and the Masons," *Journal of the Illinois State Historical Society* 64 (Spring 1971): 79-90; James C. Bilderback, "Masonry and Mormonism, Nauvoo, Illinois, 1841-1847" (M.A. thesis, State University of Iowa, 1937); and E. Cecil McGavin, *"Mormonism" and Masonry* (Salt Lake City: Deseret News Press, 1935).

The personal lives of the Saints at Nauvoo can be sampled in three articles in the Summer 1975 issue of *Brigham Young University Studies:* Maureen Ursenbach, ed., "Eliza R. Snow's Nauvoo Journal," 15:391-416; Ronald K. Esplin, ed., "Sickness and Faith: Nauvoo Letters [of John and Leonora Taylor]," pp. 425-34; and Stanley B. Kimball, "Heber C. Kimball and Family: The Nauvoo Years," pp. 447-79. Other personal views are in Warren A. Jennings, ed., "Two Iowa Postmasters View Nauvoo: Anti-Mormon Letters to the Governor of Missouri," ibid., 11 (Spring 1971): 275-92; Eudocia Baldwin Marsh, "Mormons in Hancock County: A Reminiscence," ed. Douglas L. Wilson and Rodney O. Davis, *Journal of the Illinois State Historical Society* 64 (Spring 1971): 22-65; and Maureen Ursenbach Beecher, "Letters from the Frontier: Commerce, Nauvoo, and Salt Lake City," *Journal of Mormon History* 2 (1975): 35-52.

Our treatment of Church organization and doctrine draws from Miller and Miller, *Nauvoo: City of Joseph,* chap. 3; Joseph Smith, *History of the Church,* vols. 4-5; and two useful articles by T. Edgar Lyon: "Nauvoo and the Council of the Twelve," in McKiernan et al., *The Restoration Movement,* pp. 167-205, and "Doctrinal Development of the Church during the Nauvoo Sojourn, 1839-1846," *Brigham Young University Studies* 15 (Summer 1975): 435-46.

For information on the Nauvoo Temple beyond that in histories of the period, see Stanley B. Kimball, "The Nauvoo Temple" *Improvement Era* 66 (November 1963): 974-84, for a physical description; Virginia S. Harrington and J. C. Harrington, *Rediscovery of the Nauvoo Temple: Report on the Archaeological Excavation* (Salt Lake City: Nauvoo Restoration, Inc., 1971); and for detail on the construction, Don F. Colvin, "A Historical Study of the Mormon Temple at Nauvoo, Illinois" (M.S. thesis, Brigham Young University, 1962).

CHAPTER 6
Difficult Days: Nauvoo, 1842-1845

The specialized studies on the Nauvoo period by Flanders, Miller and Miller, and Roberts listed earlier contain much information on developments leading to the death of Joseph Smith. The political strains, the martyrdom itself, and the question of succession also receive substantial treatment in general Church histories.

For the basic outlines of the story, consult the above works and Roberts, *Comprehensive History of the Church,* vol. 2, chaps. 50-69; Joseph Fielding Smith, *Essentials in Church History,* chaps. 31-36; Barrett, *Joseph Smith and the Restoration,* chaps. 27-30; and Joseph Smith, *History of the Church,* vol. 5, chaps. 13-28; vol. 6; and vol. 7, chaps. 1-37.

An important interpretive study is Klaus J. Hansen, *Quest for Empire: The Political Kingdom of God and the Council of Fifty in Mormon History* (East Lansing: Michigan State University Press, 1967). Further discussion on selected political themes is Hansen's "The Political Kingdom of God as a Cause for Mormon-Gentile Conflict," *Brigham Young University Studies* 2 (Spring-Summer 1960): 241-60, which is reprinted in Hill and Allen, *Mormonism and American Culture,* pp. 112-26; a more recent study by Hansen, "The Metamorphosis of the Kingdom of God," *Dialogue: A Journal of Mormon Thought* 1 (Autumn 1966): 63-83; and two articles by Robert B. Flanders, "The Kingdom of God in Illinois: Politics in Utopia," ibid., 5 (Spring 1970): 26-36; and "Dream and Nightmare: Nauvoo Revisited," in McKiernan et al., *The Restoration Movement,* pp. 141-66. Alternative interpretations are presented in Marvin S. Hill, "Quest for Refuge," cited in the bibliography for chap. 1, and George R. Gayler, "The Mormons and Politics in Illinois: 1839-1844," *Journal of the Illinois State Historical Society* 49 (Spring 1956): 48-66. Kenneth W. Godfrey presents a topical analysis in "Causes of Mormon—Non-Mormon Conflict in Hancock County, Illinois, 1839-1846" (Ph.D. diss., Brigham Young University, 1967), and a summary of political events in "The Road to Carthage Led West," *Brigham Young University Studies* 8 (Winter 1968): 204-15.

Detailed information on the search for a place of refuge is in Lewis Clark Christian, "A Study of Mormon Knowledge of the American Far West Prior to the Exodus (1830-February 1846)" (M.A. thesis, Brigham Young University, 1972).

On the 1844 campaign see Richard D. Poll, "Joseph Smith and the Presidency, 1844," *Dialogue: A Journal of Mormon Thought* 3 (Autumn 1968): 17-21, and Martin B. Hickman, "The Political Legacy of Joseph Smith," ibid., pp. 22-27, which introduces a reprint of Joseph Smith's *Views of the*

Powers and Policy of the Government of the United States, ibid., pp. 28-36. Additional comments on the issues are in James B. Allen, "The American Presidency and the Mormons," *Ensign* 2 (October 1972): 46-56.

A thorough study of legal questions is Dallin H. Oaks, "The Suppression of the Nauvoo Expositor," *Utah Law Review* 9 (Winter 1965): 862-903. Thomas G. Alexander, "The Church and the Law," *Dialogue: A Journal of Mormon Thought* 1 (Summer 1966): 123-28, comments on Oaks. An earlier interpretation is George R. Gayler, "The 'Expositor' Affair, Prelude to the Downfall of Joseph Smith," *Northwest Missouri State College Studies* 25 (February 1961): 3-15.

Two views of the Illinois governor's role are Keith Huntress, "Governor Thomas Ford and the Murderers of Joseph Smith," *Dialogue: A Journal of Mormon Thought* 4 (Summer 1969): 41-52; and George R. Gayler, "Governor Ford and the Death of Joseph and Hyrum Smith," *Journal of the Illinois State Historical Society* 50 (Winter 1957): 391-411. Useful for background is David Grimsted, "Rioting in Its Jacksonian Setting," *American Historical Review* 77 (April 1972): 361-97. Documents on the Nauvoo and earlier periods are collected in Huntress, *Murder of an American Prophet.*

Events following the martyrdom can be traced in general histories. Also useful are Durham and Heath, *Succession in the Church,* chap. 4, and Davis Bitton, "Mormons in Texas: The Ill-fated Lyman Wight Colony, 1844-1858," *Arizona and the West* 11 (Spring 1969): 5-26. Dallin H. Oaks and Marvin S. Hill, *Carthage Conspiracy: The Trial of the Accused Assassins of Joseph Smith* (Urbana: University of Illinois Press, 1975), is a balanced study of legal affairs. An important primary source for the late Nauvoo and early Utah periods is Juanita Brooks, ed., *On the Mormon Frontier: The Diary of Hosea Stout, 1844-1861,* 2 vols. (Salt Lake City: University of Utah Press and Utah State Historical Society, 1964).

CHAPTER 7
Exodus to a New Zion, 1846-1850

The migration of the Saints to the Great Basin has captured the attention of many historians, and the story has been told with detail in most general histories of the Church and in histories of Utah. The reader should also consult specialized studies on the Mormon migration and settlement. A number of these are listed in our General Bibliography.

Of special value in the preparation of this chapter were Leland H. Creer, *Founding of an Empire,* chaps. 9-13, and Leonard J. Arrington, *Great Basin Kingdom,* chaps. 2-3. For the story of the trek see also Roberts, *Comprehensive History of the Church,* vol. 3, chaps. 70-91; Joseph Fielding Smith, *Essentials in Church History,* chaps. 37-41; and Rich, *Ensign to the Nations,* chaps. 1-8. Useful documentary collections are Joseph Smith, *History of the Church,* vol. 7, chaps. 38-41, and Elden J. Watson, ed., *Manuscript History of Brigham Young, 1846-1847* (Salt Lake City: Elden J. Watson, 1971).

For the early years in the Great Basin, see Ellsworth, *Utah's Heritage,* chaps. 9-12; Dale L. Morgan, *The Great Salt Lake* (1947; reprint, Albuquerque: University of New Mexico Press, 1973), chaps. 10-12; Hansen, *Quest for Empire,* chap. 7; and Preston Nibley, *Exodus to Greatness: The Story of the Mormon Migration* (Salt Lake City: Deseret News Press, 1947).

Although the patterns of historical interpretation for this period were set years ago, several special studies, mostly articles, deserve mention.

For the evacuation of Nauvoo, see the histories cited in our reading list for chapters 5 and 6, and Andrew Jenson, "The Battle of Nauvoo," *Historical Record* 8 (June 1889): 845-47. The early stages of the trek are outlined in Stanley B. Kimball, "The Iowa Trek of 1846," *Ensign* 2 (June 1972): 36-45, and William J. Petersen, "The Mormon Trail of 1846," *Palimpsest* 47 (September 1966): 353-67.

For a scholarly analysis of the Mormon Battalion, see John F. Yurtinus, "A Ram in the Thicket: A History of the Mormon Battalion in the Mexican War" (Ph.D. diss., Brigham Young University, 1975). The march is logged on small-scale maps in Charles S. Peterson, John F. Yurtinus, David E. Atkinson, and A. Kent Powell, *Mormon Battalion Trail Guide* (Salt Lake City: Utah State Historical Society, 1972). Probing important aspects of the topic are W. Ray Luce, "The Mormon Battalion: A Historical Accident?" *Utah Historical Quarterly* 42 (Winter 1974): 27-38; Eugene E. Campbell, "Authority Conflicts in the Mormon Battalion," *Brigham Young University Studies* 8 (Winter 1968): 127-42; and Hamilton Gardner, "The Command and Staff of the Mormon Battalion in the Mexican War," *Utah Historical Quarterly* 29 (October 1952): 331-52. Daniel Tyler, *A Concise History of the Mormon Battalion in the Mexican War, 1846-47* (1881; reprint, Chicago: Rio Grande Press, 1964), is a standard reference.

Eugene E. Campbell, "A History of The Church of Jesus Christ of Latter-day Saints in California, 1846-1946" (Ph.D. diss., University of Southern California, 1952), presents useful histories of the *Brooklyn* Saints (chap. 2), the Mormon Battalion (chap. 3), and Mormons and the Gold Rush (chap. 4). The Mississippi Saints and Battalion sick detachment are carefully followed in Leroy R. Hafen and Frank M. Young, "The Mormon Settlement at Pueblo, Colorado, during the Mexican War," *Colorado Magazine* 9 (July 1932): 121-36, and in LaMar C. Barrett, "History of the Southern States Mission, 1831-1861" (M.S. thesis, Brigham Young University, 1960), part 5.

On dissenters, see the helpful overview in Russell Rich, *Those Who Would Be Leaders (Offshoots of Mormonism),* 2nd ed. (Provo: Brigham Young University Extension Publications, 1967). The standard reference on James J. Strang is Milo M. Quaife, *The Kingdom of Saint James: A Narrative of James J. Strang, the Beaver Island Mormon King* (Lansing, Mich.: National newer studies are Doyle C. Fitzpatrick, *The King Strang Story: A Vindication of James J. Strang, the Beaver Island Mormon King* (Lansing Mich.: National Heritage, 1970); Klaus J. Hansen, "The Making of King Strang: A Reexamination," *Michigan History* 46 (September 1962): 201-29; and William D. Russell, "King James Strang: Joseph Smith's Successor?" in McKiernan et al., *The Restoration Movement,* pp. 231-56. Two sympathetic views of another group are Alma R. Blair, "The Reorganized Church of Jesus Christ of Latter Day Saints: Moderate Mormons," in ibid., pp. 207-30; and Richard P. Howard, "The Reorganized Church in Illinois, 1852-1882: Search for Identity," *Dialogue: A Journal of Mormon Thought* 5 (Spring 1970): 63-75.

Scholars have consistently slighted the story of the Missouri River settlements. A brief introduction is Ernest W. Shumway, "History of Winter Quarters, Nebraska, 1846-1848" (M.S. thesis, Brigham Young University, 1953), from which is drawn Shumway's "Winter Quarters, Nebraska, 1846-1848," *Nebraska History* 35 (June 1954): 115-25. For settlement sites, see Clyde B. Aitchison, "The Mormon Settlements in the Missouri Valley," *Quarterly of the Oregon Historical Society* 8 (September 1907): 276-89, and Charles H. Babbitt, *Early Days at Council Bluffs* (Washington, D.C.: Press of Byron S. Adams, 1916). Also useful is Robert A. Trennert, Jr., "The Mormons and the Office of Indian Affairs: The Conflict over Winter Quarters, 1846-1848," *Nebraska History* 53 (Fall 1972): 381-400. Comments on political affairs in Iowa and early Utah are in James Keith Melville, *Conflict and Compromise: The Mormons in Mid-Nineteenth-Century American Politics* (Provo: Brigham Young University Press, 1975), parts 1 and 2.

For background on western wagon roads, see Merrill J. Mattes, *The Great Platte River Road: The Covered Wagon Mainline via Fort Kearny to Fort Laramie* (Lincoln: Nebraska State Historical Society, 1969). The story of the pioneer journey is well-told in general histories, but see Guy E. Stringham, "The Pioneer Roadometer," *Utah Historical Quarterly* 42 (Summer 1974): 258-77, for a new point of view on a minor detail. The standard account of the 1847 trek is *William Clayton's Journal: A Daily Record of the Journey of the Original Company* . . . (Salt Lake City: Clayton Family Association, 1921). Another published diary of the journey is Leland H. Creer, ed., "Journey to Zion: From the Journal of Erastus Snow," *Utah Humanities Review* 2 (April and July 1948): 107-28, 264-84.

To supplement basic studies on the early Utah period, see Leonard J. Arrington, "Coin and Currency in Early Utah," *Utah Historical Quarterly* 20 (January 1952): 56-76; William Hartley, "Mormons, Crickets, and Gulls: A New Look at an Old Story," ibid., 38 (Summer 1970): 224-39; Lawrence L. Linford, "Establishing and Maintaining Land Ownership in Utah Prior to 1869," ibid., 42 (Spring 1974): 126-43; and Richard H. Jackson, "Righteousness and Environmental Change: The Mormons and the Environment," in Thomas G. Alexander, ed., *Essays on the American West, 1973-74,* Charles Redd Monographs in Western History, No. 5 (Provo: Brigham Young University Press, 1975), pp. 21-42.

Background on the Latter-day Saint role in government for the Great Basin before 1850 can be gleaned from Dale L. Morgan's excellent "The State of Deseret," *Utah Historical Quarterly* 8 (April, July, October 1940): 65-239; Hansen, *Quest for Empire,* chaps. 6-7; Leland H. Creer, "The Evolution of Government in Early Utah," *Utah Historical Quarterly* 27

(January 1958): 23-44; and Gwynn W. Barrett, "Dr. John M. Bernhisel: Mormon Elder in Congress," ibid., 36 (Spring 1968): 143-67.

One aspect of the cultural transplanting is discussed in Robert Winter, "Architecture on the Frontier: The Mormon Experiment," *Pacific Historical Review* 43 (February 1974): 50-60.

CHAPTER 8
Establishing an Ensign, 1851-1856

Basic sources for this chapter include the standard histories of the Church, histories of Utah, and several specialized studies. Useful as introductions to the period are Ellsworth, *Utah's Heritage,* chap. 13, and Larson, *Outline History of Utah and the Mormons,* chap. 15. The story is fleshed out in Nels Anderson, *Desert Saints,* chaps. 5-6; and the settlement story and economic policy are detailed in Arrington, *Great Basin Kingdom,* chaps. 4-5. A fuller general discussion is in Roberts, *Comprehensive History of the Church,* vol. 3, chaps. 92-93, and vol. 4, chaps. 94-99. Much data not contained elsewhere is in Hunter, *Brigham Young the Colonizer,* chaps. 9-34. Information in Rich, *Ensign to the Nations,* chaps. 9-13, should be compared with other sources. The period is summarized in Joseph Fielding Smith, *Essentials in Church History,* chap. 42; and useful background information is in Bancroft, *History of Utah,* chaps. 17-18, and Whitney, *History of Utah,* vol. 1, chaps. 23-27.

Specialized studies on the Church and territorial government include: James B. Allen, "Ecclesiastical Influence on Local Government in the Territory of Utah," *Arizona and the West* 8 (Spring 1966): 35-48; Melville, *Conflict and Compromise,* part 3; P.A.M. Taylor, "Early Mormon Loyalty and the Leadership of Brigham Young," *Utah Historical Quarterly* 30 (Spring 1962): 102-32; Hansen, *Quest for Empire,* chaps. 7-8; James R. Clark, "The Kingdom of God, the Council of Fifty, and the State of Deseret," *Utah Historical Quarterly* 26 (April 1958): 130-48. Also see D. Michael Quinn, "The Flag of the Kingdom of God," *Brigham Young University Studies* 14 (Autumn 1973): 105-14.

The settlement process has received thorough treatment in the basic references noted above and in two standard monographs: Joel E. Ricks, *Forms and Methods of Early Mormon Settlement in Utah and Surrounding Region, 1847 to 1877* (Logan: Utah State University Press, 1964), and Lowry Nelson, *The Mormon Village: A Pattern and Technique of Land Settlement* (Salt Lake City: University of Utah Press, 1952). On Mormon outposts, see Joseph S. Wood, "The Mormon Settlement in San Bernardino, 1851-1857" (Ph.D. diss., University of Utah, 1968), and the recent work of Eugene E. Campbell, "Brigham Young's Outer Cordon: A Reappraisal," *Utah Historical Quarterly* 41 (Summer 1973): 220-53 (also published in Thomas Alexander, ed., *Essays on the American West, 1972-73,* Charles Redd Monographs in Western History, no. 3 [Provo: Brigham Young University Press, 1974], pp. 105-36; Fred R. Gowans, "Fort Bridger and the Mormons," *Utah Historical Quarterly* 42 (Winter 1974): 49-67; and Gowans and Campbell, *Fort Bridger: Island in the Wilderness* (Provo, Utah: Brigham Young University Press, 1975). A new assessment of Mormon contributions is Leonard J. Arrington and Dean May, " 'A Different Mode of Life': Irrigation and Society in Nineteenth-Century Utah," *Agricultural History* 49 (January 1975): 3-20.

Indian relations are summarized in a fine interpretive article by Charles S. Peterson, "Jacob Hamblin, Apostle to the Lamanites, and the Indian Mission," *Journal of Mormon History* 2 (1975): 21-34, and Leonard J. Arrington, "The Mormons and the Indians: A Review and Evaluation," *The Record* (Friends of the Library, Washington State University, Pullman) 31 (1970): 5-29. Other studies include Peterson's "The Hopis and the Mormons, 1858-1873," *Utah Historical Quarterly* 39 (Spring 1971): 179-93; Charles E. Dibble, "The Mormon Mission to the Shoshoni Indians," *Utah Humanities Review* 1 (January, April, and July 1947): 53-73, 166-77, and 279-93; the broad overview by Lawrence G. Coates, "Mormons and Social Change among the Shoshoni, 1853-1900," *Idaho Yesterdays* 15 (Winter 1972): 3-11; and a study of the mission at Limhi by John D. Nash, "The Salmon River Mission of 1855," ibid., 11 (Spring 1967): 22-31. An important firsthand account is Thomas D. Brown, *Journal of the Southern [Utah] Indian Mission: Diary of Thomas D. Brown*, ed. Juanita Brooks, Western Text Society Series, No. 4 (Logan: Utah State University Press, 1972).

On religious life in the early 1850s we have profited from discussions with William G. Hartley and Dale Beecher, who have done task papers for the Church Historical Department on priesthood activities and the role of bishops. A basic statistical analysis is Stanley S. Ivins, "Notes on Mormon Polygamy," *Western Humanities Review* 10 (Summer 1956): 229-39, which has been reprinted twice: in *Utah Historical Quarterly* 35 (Fall 1967): 309-21, and in Hill and Allen, *Mormonism and American Culture,* pp. 101-11. On the movement for spiritual uplift see Gustive O. Larson, "The Mormon Reformation," *Utah Historical Quarterly* 26 (January 1958): 45-63, and Howard C. Searle, "The Mormon Reformation of 1856-1857" (M.S. thesis, Brigham Young University, 1956).

Convenient sources on specific missions are R. Lanier Britsch, "Church Beginnings in China," *Brigham Young University Studies* 10 (Winter 1970): 161-72; Britsch's "The Latter-day Saint Mission to India, 1851-1856," ibid., 12 (Spring 1972): 262-77; Evans, *A Century of Mormonism in Great Britain;* and Jenson, *History of the Scandinavian Mission.* We have also profited from a compilation of missionary statistics and a research paper, "Missionaries and Proselyting," by Gordon Irving of the Church Historical Department.

On migration, we have supplemented general histories with Robert Flanders's account of the Mutual Benefit Association in *Nauvoo: Kingdom on the Mississippi,* pp. 78-86; and the useful summary by William G. Hartley, "Coming to Zion: Saga of the Gathering," *Ensign* 5 (July 1975): 14-18. LeRoy R. Hafen, "Handcarts to Utah, 1856-1860," *Utah Historical Quarterly* 24 (October 1956): 309-17, is a convenient summary of the main themes of his and Ann W. Hafen's *Handcarts to Zion: The Story of a Unique Western Migration, 1856-1860 . . . ,* The Far West and the Rockies Historical Series, vol. 14 (Glendale, Calif.: Arthur H. Clark Co., 1960). The handcart diary of Archie Walters is reproduced in William J. Peterson, "The Handcart Experiment," *Palimpsest* 48 (September 1966): 368-84. The story of Mormon migration is also told in Larson, *Prelude to the Kingdom,* chaps. 11-22; Mulder, *Homeward to Zion;* and Taylor, *Expectations Westward.*

CHAPTER 9
In the National Spotlight, 1856-1863

These troublesome years have received careful attention in the political histories covering the Utah War period and in a number of specialized works. Still reliable is the account in Roberts, *Comprehensive History of the Church,* vol. 4, chaps. 100-120; vol. 5, chaps. 121-27. Additional insights into the social and economic life can be found in Anderson, *Desert Saints,* chaps. 7-8, and Arrington, *Great Basin Kingdom,* chaps. 6-7. Roberts is summarized in Joseph Fielding Smith, *Essentials in Church History,* chaps. 43-45; and the story is given a secular setting in Bancroft, *History of Utah,* chaps. 18-22. See also Whitney, *History of Utah,* vol. 1, chaps. 28-32, and vol. 2, chaps. 1-4.

For an analysis of the way Latter-day Saints were depicted in popular novels of the time, see Leonard J. Arrington and Jon Haupt, "The Missouri and Illinois Mormons in Ante-Bellum Fiction," *Dialogue: A Journal of Mormon Thought* 5 (Spring 1970): 37-50. The political effect of this image is traced in Richard D. Poll, "The Mormon Question Enters National Politics, 1850-1856," *Utah Historical Quarterly* 25 (April 1957): 117-31, and in Richard D. Draper, "Babylon in Zion: The L.D.S. Concept of Zion as a Cause for Mormon-Gentile Conflict, 1846-1857" (M.A. thesis, Arizona State University, 1974).

On the Utah expedition, the best account is Norman F. Furniss, *The Mormon Conflict, 1850-1859* (New Haven: Yale University Press, 1960). Supporting documents are collected in LeRoy R. Hafen and Ann W. Hafen, eds., *The Utah Expedition, 1857-58: A Documentary Account . . .* (Glendale, Calif.: Arthur H. Clark Co., 1958). Additional insights are in Leonard J. Arrington, "Mormon Finance and the Utah War," *Utah Historical Quarterly* 20 (July 1952): 219-37, and William F. Mackinnon, "The Buchanan Spoils System and the Utah Expedition: Careers of W.M.F. Magraw and John M. Hockaday," ibid., 31 (Spring 1963): 127-50. For the reaction of the *Deseret News* see A. R. Mortensen, "A Local Paper Reports on the Utah War," ibid., 25 (October 1957): 297-318. Among several published diaries is one of a Mormon soldier: Hamilton Gardner, ed., "A Territorial Militiaman in the Utah War: Journal of Newton Tuttle," ibid., 22 (October 1954): 297-320.

The thorough research of Juanita Brooks, *The Mountain Meadows Massacre* (1950; new ed., Norman: University of Oklahoma Press, 1962), has made this balanced account the standard on the subject. Also of interest are the speech of Juanita Brooks and the response by Ralph R. Rea at the dedication of a monument to the victims: "An Historical Epilogue," *Utah Historical Quarterly* 24 (January 1956): 71-77.

For studies of two personalities who played key roles in the Utah War, see Charles S. Peterson, " 'A Mighty Man was Brother Lot': A Portrait of Lot Smith, Mormon Frontiersman," *Western Historical Quarterly* 1 (October 1970): 393-414; and Albert L. Zobell, "Thomas L. Kane, Ambassador to the Mormons," *Utah Humanities Review* 1 (October 1947): 320-46. The aftermath of the military arrival is studied in Thomas G. Alexander and Leonard J. Arrington, "Camp in the Sagebrush: Camp Floyd, Utah, 1858-1861," *Utah Historical Quarterly* 34 (Winter 1966): 3-21; and Davis Bitton, "The Cradlebaugh Court (1859): A Study in Early Mormon-Gentile Misunderstanding," in Knowlton, *Social Accommodation in Utah,* pp. 71-97.

On the Civil War period we found useful the overviews by Gustive O. Larson, "Utah and the Civil War," ibid., 33 (Winter 1965): 55-57, and Ray C. Colton, *The Civil War in the Western Territories: Arizona, Colorado, New Mexico, and Utah* (Norman: University of Oklahoma, 1959), pp. 180-90. Of interest is George U. Hubbard, "Abraham Lincoln as Seen by the Mormons," *Utah Historical Quarterly* 31 (Spring 1963): 91-108.

Recent investigations of Joseph Morris and his schism include C. LeRoy Anderson and Larry J. Halford, "The Mormons and the Morrisite War," *Montana, the Magazine of Western History* 24 (October 1974): 42-53; Halford's "Mormons and Morrisites: A Study in the Sociology of Conflict" (Ph.D. diss., University of Montana, 1972); and M. Hamlin Cannon, "The Morrisite War: Insurrection by a Self-Styled Prophet," *American West* 7 (November 1970): 4-9 and 62.

The accounts of visitors who observed Latter-day Saint society in these years include the biased accounts of Benjamin G. Ferris, *Utah and the Mormons: . . .* (1854; reprint, New York: AMS Press, 1971), and his wife, *The Mormons at Home: . . .* (1856; reprint, New York: AMS Press, 1971); the delightful observations of Elizabeth Randall Cumming, "The Governor's Lady: A Letter from Camp Scott, 1857," ed., A. R. Mortensen, *Utah Historical Quarterly* 22 (April 1954): 165-73; the descriptions of world travelers Jules Rémy and Julius Brenchley, *A Journey to Great-Salt-Lake City,* 2 vols. (1861; reprint, New York: AMS Press, 1971), and Richard F. Burton, *The City of the Saints and Across the Rocky Mountains to California,* ed. by Fawn M. Brodie (1861; New York: Alfred A. Knopf, 1963); and the letters collected in Harold D. Langley, ed., *To Utah with the Dragoons and Glimpses of Life in Arizona and California, 1858-1859* (Salt Lake City: University of Utah Press, 1974).

CHAPTER 10
Challenges and Cooperatives, 1864-1872

This important period of economic and cultural adjustment has been thoroughly examined with respect to political and economic activities, less thoroughly concerning religious and cultural developments. Several recent publications, however, have added considerably to our understanding of these years surrounding the completion of the transcontinental railroad.

The best survey of economic activities is Arrington, *Great Basin Kingdom*, chaps. 7-10. Thorough political treatments are in Whitney, *History of Utah*, vol. 2, chaps. 5-23, and Roberts, *Comprehensive History of the Church*, vol. 5, chaps. 129-41. Still useful is information in Bancroft, *History of Utah*, chaps. 22-24, and Neff, *History of Utah*, chaps. 26-33. For brief surveys see Nels Anderson, *Desert Saints*, chaps. 9-11, and Joseph Fielding Smith, *Essentials in Church History*, chaps. 46-47.

For background on the quest for economic self-sufficiency see Leonard J. Arrington, "Abundance from the Earth: The Beginnings of Commercial Mining in Utah," *Utah Historical Quarterly* 31 (Summer 1963): 192-219, and his "The Deseret Agricultural and Manufacturing Society in Pioneer Utah," ibid., 24 (April 1956): 165-70. The southern Utah-Nevada economic experiments are described in a local history, Andrew Karl Larson, *"I Was Called to Dixie": The Virgin River Basin, Unique Experiences in Mormon Pioneering* (Salt Lake City: The Deseret News Press, 1961); in a special issue of *Utah Historical Quarterly*, edited by Juanita Brooks, "Utah's Dixie: The Cotton Mission," 29 (July 1961): 193-302; in L. A. Fleming, "The Settlements on the Muddy, 1865 to 1871: 'A Godforsaken Place,' " ibid., 35 (Spring 1967): 147-72; and in Leonard J. Arrington, "Mormon Trade on the Colorado River, 1864-1867," *Arizona and the West* 8 (Autumn 1966): 239-50.

Important to an understanding of the defensive economic programs are Robert G. Athearn, "Opening the Gates of Zion: Utah and the Coming of the Union Pacific Railroad," *Utah Historical Quarterly* 36 (Fall 1968): 291-314; John R. Patrick, "The School of the Prophets: Its Development and Influence in Utah Territory" (M.A. thesis, Brigham Young University, 1970); and Leonard J. Arrington, "The Transcontinental Railroad and the Development of the West," *Utah Historical Quarterly* 37 (Winter 1969): 3-15, and other articles in this special issue, "The Last Spike Is Driven." A related question is discussed in Gustive O. Larson, "Land Contest in Early Utah," ibid., 29 (October 1961): 3-25, and in a more recent study, Lawrence R. Linford, "Establishing and Maintaining Land Ownership in Utah Prior to 1869," ibid., 42 (Spring 1974): 126-43. Also useful on the 1860s and '70s is Kenneth J. Davies, "The Secularization of the Utah Labor Movement," in Knowlton, *Social Accommodation in Utah*, pp. 19-64.

Schismatic groups are considered in Bancroft, *History of Utah*, chap. 23, and the group of greatest interest to this period in Grant H. Palmer, "The Godbeite Movement: A Dissent against Temporal Control" (M.A. thesis, Brigham Young University, 1968). A religious interpretation of the Godbeites is set forth in two articles by Ronald W. Walker, "The Commencement of the Godbeite Protest: Another View," *Utah Historical*

Quarterly 42 (Summer 1974): 216-44, and "The Stenhouses and the Making of a Mormon Image," *Journal of Mormon History* 1 (1974): 51-72. The Godbeites are placed in a broader context in Davis Bitton, "Mormonism's Encounter with Spiritualism," ibid., pp. 39-50.

We have followed the traditional interpretation set forth by assistant Church historian Andrew Jenson, "Walter Murray Gibson: A Sketch of His Life in Two Chapters," *Improvement Era* 4 (November and December 1900): 5-13 and 86-95; graduate student Frank W. McGhie, "The Life and Intrigues of Walter Murray Gibson" (M.S. thesis, Brigham Young University, 1958), chaps. 7-9; and writer Samuel W. Taylor, "Walter Murray Gibson: Great Mormon Rascal," *American West* 1 (Spring 1964): 18-27. This view has been challenged by Gwynn Barrett, "Walter Murray Gibson: The Shepherd Saint of Lanai Revisited," *Utah Historical Quarterly* 40 (Spring 1972): 142-62; but the older interpretation is sustained in an unpublished 1975 study by R. Lanier Britsch, "Another Visit with Walter Murray Gibson," to which we have had access.

For information on the auxiliaries we have used the standard histories of those organizations listed in our General Bibliography. The history of an important Salt Lake City landmark is told in Stewart L. Grow, *A Tabernacle in the Desert* (Salt Lake City: Deseret Book Co., 1958). An educational innovation is described in "The Deseret Alphabet," *Utah Historical Quarterly* 12 (January and April 1944): 99-102; S. George Ellsworth, "The Deseret Alphabet," *American West* 19 (November 1973): 10-11; and S. S. Ivins, "The Deseret Alphabet," *Utah Humanities Review* 1 (July 1947): 223-39.

On the non-Mormon challenge see Robert D. Hatch, "The Pratt-Newman Debate" (M.S. thesis, Brigham Young University, 1960), and Robert Joseph Dwyer, *The Gentile Comes to Utah: A Study in Religious and Social Conflict (1862-1890)* (1941; 2nd ed. rev., Salt Lake City: Western Epics, 1971). A related article is C. Merrill Hough, "Two School Systems in Conflict: 1867-1890," *Utah Historical Quarterly* 28 (April 1960): 112-28. Juanita Brooks tells the story of another religious group among the Mormons in *History of the Jews in Utah and Idaho* (Salt Lake City: Western Epics, 1973).

For the beginnings of the crusade against Mormonism, we have supplemented general histories with the detailed account in Gustive O. Larson, *The "Americanization" of Utah for Statehood* (San Marino, Calif.: Huntington Library, 1971), chaps. 2-3, and with the discussions of Hansen, *Quest for Empire*, chaps. 7-9, and S. George Ellsworth, "Utah's Struggle for Statehood," *Utah Historical Quarterly* 31 (Winter 1963): 60-69. Useful articles include Howard R. Lamar, "Political Patterns in New Mexico and Utah Territories, 1850-1900," ibid., 28 (October 1960): 363-87; Thomas G. Alexander, "An Experiment in Progressive Legislation: The Granting of Woman Suffrage in Utah in 1870," ibid., 38 (Winter 1970): 20-30; James B. Allen, "The Unusual Jurisdiction of County Probate Courts in the Territory of Utah," ibid., 36 (Spring 1968): 132-42;

and Jay E. Powell, "Fairness in the Salt Lake County Probate Court," ibid., 38 (Summer 1970): 256-62.

CHAPTER 11
Close of a Career, 1872-1877

Most of the themes that dominated the last years of Brigham Young's life have been examined in specialized studies that we have listed below. Of the general works, Joseph Fielding Smith, *Essentials in Church History,* chaps. 47-48, presents a concise survey of the period, while Roberts, *Comprehensive History of the Church,* vol. 5, chaps. 142-46, offers a more detailed treatment. Other standard sources are Whitney, *History of Utah,* vol. 2, chaps. 24-30, and Bancroft, *History of Utah,* chaps. 24, 26-28. Rich, *Ensign to the Nations,* chap. 16, summarizes Brigham Young's life.

For information on Latter-day Saint educational policies and programs we have drawn from the excellent work of James R. Clark, "Church and State Relationships in Education in Utah" (Ed.D. diss., Utah State University, 1958); the new multivolume history prepared under the direction of Ernest L. Wilkinson, ed., *Brigham Young University: The First One Hundred Years,* vol. 1, chaps. 2-3; the pioneering work of Stanley S. Ivins, "Free Schools Come to Utah," *Utah Historical Quarterly* 22 (October 1954): 321-42; and the analysis of C. Merrill Hough, "Two School Systems in Conflict, 1867-1890," ibid., 28 (April 1960): 112-28.

The judicial and political crusade against the Saints is given most thorough examination in Larson, *The "Americanization" of Utah,* chaps. 3-4, and in the works of Roberts and Whitney noted above. Legal actions are traced in Thomas G. Alexander, "Federal Authority versus Polygamic Theocracy: James B. McKean and the Mormons, 1870-1875," *Dialogue: A Journal of Mormon Thought* 1 (Autumn 1966): 85-100. The involvement of journalists is told in O. N. Malmquist, *The First 100 Years: A History of "The Salt Lake Tribune," 1871-1971* (Salt Lake City: Utah State Historical Society, 1971), chaps. 1-4; and the influence of two Godbeite protestors in Walker, "The Stenhouses and the Making of a Mormon Image," listed in the bibliography for chap. 10, along with articles by Allen and Powell on the role of probate courts.

For the section on the United Orders we have relied heavily on Arrington, *Great Basin Kingdom,* chaps. 10-11. An excellent new book that traces the movement from its beginning is Leonard J. Arrington, Dean L. May, and Feramorz Fox, *Building the City of God: Community and Cooperation Among the Mormons* (Salt Lake City: Deseret Book Co., 1976). Four articles in *Utah Historical Quarterly* examine the order in individual communities: Mark A. Pendleton, "The Orderville United Order of Zion," 7 (October 1939): 141-59; Leonard J. Arrington, "Cooperative Community in the North: Brigham City, Utah," 33 (Summer 1965): 198-217; Feramorz Y. Fox, "Experiment in Utopia: The United Order of Richfield, 1874-1877," 32 (Fall 1964): 355-80; and P. T. Reilly, "Kanab United Order: The President's Nephew and the Bishop," 42 (Spring 1974): 144-64. An important enterprise is described in Arrington's "The Provo Woolen Mills: Utah's First Large Manufacturing Establishment," ibid., 21 (April 1953): 97-116; and a sympathetic travel account by Mrs. Thomas L. [Elizabeth Wood] Kane is *Twelve Mormon Homes Visited in Succession on a Journey Through Utah to Arizona,* ed. Everett L. Cooley, Utah, the Mormons, and the West Series, vol. 4 (Salt Lake City: Tanner Trust Fund, University of Utah Library, 1975), which was first published in 1874.

The history of the Arizona Mormon settlements is assessed in Charles S. Peterson, *Take Up Your Mission: Mormon Colonizing along the Little Colorado River, 1870-1900* (Tucson: University of Arizona Press, 1973).

On temple design and construction see David S. Andrew and Laurel B. Blank, "The Four Mormon Temples in Utah," *Journal of the Society of Architectural Historians* 30 (March 1971): 51-65, and Kirk M. Curtis, "History of the St. George Temple" (M.S. thesis, Brigham Young University, 1964).

CHAPTER 12
A Turbulent Decade: Expansion, Crusades, and the Underground, 1877-1887

The history of this decade is told in some detail in Roberts, *Comprehensive History of the Church,* vol. 5, chaps. 147-52, and vol. 6, chaps. 153-65. Briefer accounts are in Rich, *Ensign to the Nation,* chaps. 17-18, and Joseph Fielding Smith, *Essentials in Church History,* chaps. 49-50. Two standard state histories also contain useful data: Bancroft, *History of Utah,* chaps. 25-28, and Whitney, *History of Utah,* vol. 3, chaps. 1-21.

On the transfer of authority following Brigham Young's death, see the useful outline in Durham and Heath, *Succession in the Church,* chap. 6, and a discussion of the principle of succession in John Taylor, *Succession in the Priesthood* (Salt Lake City: Deseret News Press, 1902).

Until adequate histories of the auxiliaries are available, reference must be to the published works listed in the General Bibliography.

Church-related economic events are detailed in Leonard J. Arrington, "The Settlement of the Brigham Young Estate, 1877-1879," *Pacific Historical Review* 21 (February 1952): 1-20, and his "Zion's Board of Trade: A Third United Order," *Western Humanities Review* 5 (January 1951): 1-20. The economic impact of Church construction programs is outlined in Arrington and Melvin A. Larkin, "The Logan Tabernacle and Temple," *Utah Historical Quarterly* 41 (Summer 1972): 301-14.

The expansion of settlement is summarized with detail in Richard Sherlock, "Mormon Migration and Settlement after 1875," *Journal of Mormon History* 2 (1975): 53-68. The drama of opening a route into extreme southeastern Utah is told in David S. Miller, *Hole-in-the-Rock: An Epic in the Colonization of the Great American West* (Salt Lake City: University of Utah Press, 1959), and the story of Arizona settlement in Peterson, *Take Up Your Mission.*

On the thrust beyond United States borders, we found most useful the excellent study of B. Carmon Hardy, "The Mormon Colonies of Northern Mexico: A History, 1885-1912" (Ph.D. diss., Wayne State University, 1963), and of Archie G. Wilcox, "Founding of the Mormon Community in Alberta" (M.A. thesis, University of Alberta, 1950). Also useful are Nelle S. Hatch, *Colonia Juarez: An Intimate Account of a Mormon Village* (Salt Lake City: Deseret Book Co., 1954), and Thomas C. Romney, *The Mormon Colonies in Mexico* (Salt Lake City: Deseret Book Co., 1938). Other studies of the northern frontier include the fine article by Lawrence B. Lee, "The Mormons Come to Canada, 1887-1902," *Pacific Northwest Quarterly* 59 (January 1968): 11-22, and Melvin S. Tagg, *A History of the Mormon Church in Canada* (Lethbridge, Alberta: Lethbridge Herald Co., 1968). A proposal for Pacific expansion is described in Sandra T. Caruthers, "Anodyne for Expansion: Meiji Japan, the Mormons, and Charles LeGendre," *Pacific Historical Review* 38 (May 1969): 129-39.

Useful on immigration is William Mulder, "Immigration and the 'Mormon Question': An International Episode," *Western Political Quarterly* 9 (June 1956): 416-33, as well as other titles by Mulder and P.A.M. Taylor listed in the General Bibliography.

The Church in the American South is discussed in William Whiteridge Hatch, *There Is No Law: A History of Mormon Civil Relations in the Southern States, 1865-1905* (New York: Vantage Press, 1968), a published M.S. thesis (Utah State University, 1965).

The history of federal legislation and legal prosecution against the Saints forms a central part of Larson's monograph, *The "Americanization" of Utah*. See chapters 4-10 of that book and Richard D. Poll, "The Political Reconstruction of Utah Territory, 1866-1890," *Pacific Historical Review* 27 (May 1958): 111-26, for information on the crusade. Larson's "An Industrial Home for Polygamous Wives," *Utah Historical Quarterly* 38 (Summer 1970): 263-75, is also pertinent.

An article on legal aspects of the crusade, Orma Linford, "The Mormons and the Law: The Polygamy Cases," *Utah Law Review* 9 (Winter 1964 and Summer 1965): 308-70 and 543-91, is critiqued in Thomas G. Alexander, "The Church and the Law," *Dialogue: A Journal of Mormon Thought* 1 (Summer 1966): 123-28. An excellent study of the judge behind the prosecutions is Alexander's "Charles S. Zane, Apostle of the New Era," *Utah Historical Quarterly* 34 (Fall 1966): 290-314. See also Leonard J. Arrington, ed., "Crusade Against Theocracy: The Reminiscences of Judge Jacob Smith Boreman of Utah, 1872-1877," *Huntington Library Quarterly* 24 (November 1960): 1-45, and M. Paul Holsinger, "Senator George Graham Vest and the 'Menace' of Mormonism, 1882-1887," *Missouri Historical Review* 65 (October 1970): 23-36. An examination of the crusade on moral grounds is Charles A. Cannon, "The Awesome Power of Sex: The Polemical Campaign against Mormon Polygamy," *Pacific Historical Review* 43 (February 1974): 61-82.

For the political actions against Latter-day Saints in Idaho, see Merle W. Wells, "The Idaho Anti-Mormon Test Oath, 1884-1892," *Pacific*

Historical Review 24 (August 1955): 235-52, and the studies concerning Fred T. Dubois listed in the bibliography for chap. 14.

CHAPTER 13
The End of an Era, 1887-1896

This pivotal decade in Church history is traditionally examined in terms of church-state relationships. The story is told with breadth of detail in Roberts, *Comprehensive History of the Church,* vol. 6, chaps. 166-75; in Whitney, *History of Utah,* vol. 3, chaps. 22-27; and briefly in other standard surveys.

The reader will find useful a recent treatment of the Mormon question in national politics, Larson, *The "Americanization" of Utah,* chaps. 11-14; Richard Poll's article listed in our bibliography for chap. 12; and his "The Americanism of Utah," *Utah Historical Quarterly* 44 (Winter 1976): 76-93. Other excellent analyses are Howard R. Lamar, "Statehood for Utah: A Different Path," ibid., 39 (Fall 1971): 307-27, and Ellsworth's article in our listing for chap. 10. A fresh look at the personalities involved is E. Leo Lyman, "The Saints in Politics: The Mormon Question for Utah Statehood, 1887-1894," paper presented in October 1975 at the Western History Association annual meeting in Tulsa, Oklahoma (copy in possession of the authors). The economic effects of the raid are dealt with in Arrington, *Great Basin Kingdom,* chap. 12; while M. Hamlin Cannon, ed., "The Prison Diary of a Mormon Apostle," *Pacific Historical Review* 16 (November 1947): 393-409, preserves the 1888 account kept by George Q. Cannon.

Interpretations of events in the late 1880s are Henry J. Wolfinger, "A Reexamination of the Woodruff Manifesto in the Light of Utah Constitutional History," *Utah Historical Quarterly* 39 (Fall 1971): 328-49; Kenneth W. Godfrey, "The Coming of the Manifesto," *Dialogue: A Journal of Mormon Thought* 5 (Autumn 1970): 11-25; and Gordon C. Thomasson, "The Manifesto Was a Victory," ibid., 6 (Spring 1971): 37-45. A significant study of millennial expectations and the Manifesto is Thomas G. Alexander, "Wilford Woodruff and the Changing Nature of Mormon Religious Experience," presidential address, Mormon History Association, April 1975, to be published during 1976 in *Church History.* Comments on events in the late nineteenth and early twentieth centuries by a participant are preserved in James Henry Moyle, *Mormon Democrat: The Religious and Political Memoirs of James Henry Moyle,* ed. Gene A. Sessions (Salt Lake City: James Moyle Genealogical and Historical Association, 1975).

The involvement of Church leaders in the Utah statehood movement is analyzed in E. Leo Lyman, "Isaac Trumbo and the Politics of Utah Statehood," *Utah Historical Quarterly* 41 (Spring 1973): 128-49. Jean Bickmore White has studied the activities of the constitutional convention itself in two articles, "The Making of the Convention President: The Political Education of John Henry Smith," ibid., 39 (Fall 1971): 350-69; and "Woman's Place Is in the Constitution: The Struggle for Equal

Rights in Utah in 1895," ibid., 42 (Fall 1974): 344-69. For applications of the Church's "Political Rule" see J. D. Williams, "Separation of Church and State in Mormon Theory and Practice," *Dialogue: A Journal of Mormon Thought* 1 (Summer 1966): 30-54.

Activities within the Church are less well examined for this period than the ᵖublic life of Mormonism, but the sketchy information in general histories is supplemented by a number of recent studies. On the experimental immigrant colony in western Utah see Leonard J. Arrington, "The L.D.S. Hawaiian Colony at Skull Valley," *Improvement Era* 57 (May 1954): 314-15, and Dennis A. Atkin, "A History of Iosepa, the Utah Polynesian Colony" (M.A. thesis, Brigham Young University, 1958). Auxiliary programs are described in the several histories of those organizations listed in our General Bibliography. On educational programs see the article on free schools by Ivins listed with our sources for chap. 11; D. Michael Quinn, "Utah's Educational Innovation: LDS Religion Classes, 1890-1929," *Utah Historical Quarterly* 43 (Fall 1975): 379-89; and his "The Brief Career of Young University at Salt Lake City," ibid., 41 (Winter 1973): 69-89.

Some Latter-day Saint religious practices are discussed in Gordon I. Irving, "The Law of Adoption: One Phase of the Development of the Mormon Concept of Salvation, 1830-1900," *Brigham Young University Studies* 14 (Spring 1974): 291-314, and Arthur Dean Wengreen, "The Origin and History of the Fast Day in The Church of Jesus Christ of Latter-day Saints, 1830-1896" (M.A. thesis, Brigham Young University, 1955).

The transition in Latter-day Saint economic policies in the post-Manifesto era is examined in Arrington, *Great Basin Kingdom*, chap. 13. An important Church-supported industry is described in Arrington's *Beet Sugar in the West: A History of the Utah-Idaho Sugar Company, 1891-1966* (Seattle: University of Washington Press, 1966); and LDS welfare activities are discussed in his "Utah and the Depression of the 1890s," *Utah Historical Quarterly* 29 (January 1961): 2-18.

CHAPTER 14
A Time of Transition, 1897-1907

The period of adjustment that bridged the centuries remains relatively unstudied by historians, except for attention to the political story. The decade following statehood for Utah, like much of the twentieth century, must be reconstructed from a sampling of contemporary records and too few historical studies. The most complete survey is Roberts, *Comprehensive History of the Church*, vol. 6, chaps. 174-81. Also useful as a guide are James B. Allen and Richard O. Cowan, *Mormonism in the Twentieth Century*, 2nd ed. (Provo: Brigham Young University Press, 1967), chaps. 2, 6, 10, and Allen's unpublished "A Growing Church in a Changing World: A Course of Study in the History of the LDS Church Since 1896" (typescript, prepared for the Church Department of Education, 1962).

Events connected with the fiftieth anniversary celebration of Mormon arrival in the Great Basin are recited in Horace Whitney, "A Jubilee Review," *Improvement Era* 1 (December 1897): 65-76, and Spencer Clawson, "The Pioneer Monument," ibid., 3 (October 1900): 881-85.

Supplementing Cowley's life of Wilford Woodruff and Romney's biography of Lorenzo Snow (both listed in our General Bibliography) are Franklin D. Richards, "Wilford Woodruff," *Improvement Era* 1 (October 1898): 865-80, and Nephi Anderson, "Life and Character Sketch of Lorenzo Snow . . .," ibid., 2 (June 1899): 561-70. The continuity between administrations is demonstrated in Joseph F. Smith, "The Last Days of President Snow," *Juvenile Instructor* 36 (November 15, 1901): 688-91; and the mechanics of the transfer of authority are outlined in Durham and Heath, *Succession in the Church,* chaps. 8-9. A basic source on the years after 1901 is *Life of Joseph F. Smith* by his son, Joseph Fielding Smith, which is listed in our General Bibliography.

Several article-length studies have added considerably to our understanding of the Latter-day Saint role in American political life. Surveying the transitional years is Jan Shipps, "Utah Comes of Age Politically: A Study of the State's Politics in the Early Years of the Twentieth Century," *Utah Historical Quarterly* 35 (Spring 1967): 91-111. Attitudes toward war are analyzed in D. Michael Quinn, "The Mormon Church and the Spanish-American War: An End to Selective Pacifism," *Pacific Historical Review* 43 (August 1974): 342-66, and in Robert Jeffrey Stott, "Mormonism and War: An Interpretative Analysis of Selected Mormon Thought regarding Seven American Wars" (M.A. thesis, Brigham Young University, 1974), chap. 4.

A careful study of "The B. H. Roberts Case of 1898-1900," by Davis Bitton, appears in *Utah Historical Quarterly* 25 (January 1957): 27-46. The public life of Roberts is examined in D. Craig Mikkelsen, "The Politics of B. H. Roberts," *Dialogue: A Journal of Mormon Thought* 9 (Summer 1974): 25-43. A study of detractor A. T. Schroeder is David Brudnoy, "Of Sinners and Saints: Theodore Schroeder, Brigham Roberts, and Reed Smoot," *Journal of Church and State* 14 (Spring 1972): 261-78.

T. Edgar Lyon, "Religious Activities and Development in Utah, 1847-1910," *Utah Historical Quarterly* 35 (Fall 1967): 292-306, is helpful in understanding the setting for ministerial opposition to the election of Roberts and of Senator Reed Smoot. On the latter's fight for his seat, see M. Paul Holsinger, "For God and the American Home: The Attempt to Unseat Senator Reed Smoot, 1903-1907," *Pacific Northwest Quarterly* 60 (July 1969): 154-60. Smoot's career is summarized in Milton R. Merrill, "Reed Smoot, Apostle in Politics" (Ph.D. diss., Columbia University, 1950). His contributions in Washington are analyzed in Thomas G. Alexander, "Reed Smoot and the Development of Western Land Policy, 1905-1920," *Arizona and the West* 13 (Autumn 1971): 245-64, and Alexander, "Reed Smoot, the L.D.S. Church, and Progressive Legislation, 1903-1933," *Dialogue: A Journal of Mormon Thought* 7 (Spring 1972):47-56.

On the opponents of Smoot, see the journalistic treatment in Malm-

quist, *The First 100 Years,* chaps. 13-20, and two portraits by M. Paul Hol-
singer: "J.C. Burrows and the Fight against Mormonism, 1903-1907,"
Michigan History 52 (Fall 1968): 181-95, and "Philander C. Knox and the
Crusade against Mormonism, 1904-1907," *Western Pennsylvania History
Magazine* 51 (January 1969): 47-56. An important political antagonist is
studied in Jay R. Lowe, "Fred T. Dubois, Foe of the Mormons: A Study
of the Role of Fred T. Dubois in the Senate Investigation of the Hon.
Reed Smoot and the Mormon Church, 1903-1907" (M.A. thesis, Brigham
Young University, 1960); Merle W. Wells, "Fred T. Dubois and the Idaho
Progressives, 1900-1914," *Idaho Yesterdays* 3 (Summer 1960): 24-31; and
Leo William Graff, "The Senatorial Career of Fred T. Dubois of Idaho,
1890-1907" (Ph.D. diss., University of Idaho, 1968). The official Church
response, the *Address . . . to the World,* was first published as a supplement to
the April 1907 *Conference Report* and appears also in *Improvement Era* 10
(May 1907): 481-95, and in Clark, *Messages of the First Presidency,* 4:142-55.
Also see the studies on plural marriage by Hilton and Jessee that are cited
in the bibliography for chap. 17.

   Information on the public image of the Church can be found in the
Holsinger articles cited above and in studies by Lambert, Cracroft,
Lythgoe, and Shipps, all noted in the General Bibliography.

   Supplementing Roberts on historic sites are "Bureau of Information
and Church Literature," *Improvement Era* 5 (September 1902): 899-901; Junius F. Wells, "The Birthplace of the Prophet Joseph Smith," *Contributor*
16 (February 1895): 203-11; and Susa Young Gates, "Memorial Monument Dedication," *Improvement Era* 9 (February and March 1906): 308-19
and 375-89.

   Financial affairs are previewed in Arrington, *Great Basin Kingdom,*
chap. 13, and in Roberts, *Comprehensive History of the Church,* vol. 6, chap.
180. Useful background is Arrington, "The Commercialization of Utah's
Economy: Trends and Developments from Statehood to 1910," in Arrington and Alexander, *A Dependent Commonwealth,* pp. 3-34. Two Church-
supported enterprises are chronicled in Ron Pedersen, "Beneficial Life Insurance Company," and Bradley Earl Morris, "The Involvement of the
L.D.S. Church in Hospital Building and Operation," both unpublished
papers (1972; copies in possession of Leonard J. Arrington). The tithing
reform is described in LeRoi C. Snow, "The Lord's Way Out of Bondage
. . .," *Improvement Era* 41 (July 1938): 400-401, 439-42, which is reprinted in
Berrett and Burton, *Readings in LDS Church History,* 3:258-66, as "Lorenzo
Snow and the Law of Tithing," and in sermons published in *Conference
Report,* 1899-1901.

   An important statement on social problems of the time is [Joseph F.
Smith,] "Editor's Table: Attitude of the Church Towards Reform-
Political Parties," *Improvement Era* 2 (February 1899): 310-12. Instances of
humanitarian concern are retold in Allen Kent Powell, "Tragedy at
Scofield," *Utah Historical Quarterly* 41 (Spring 1973): 182-94, and in
William G. Hartley, "That Terrible Wednesday: The Saints in the San
Francisco Earthquake," article accepted for publication in *New Era.* A

preliminary study of the smallpox issue is Annette Randall (Haws), "The Vaccination Controversy in Utah, 1900-1901" (unpublished article, 1971, in files of Leonard J. Arrington).

Church educational programs are well documented. Most of the sources listed in the General Bibliography comment on this period. An important contemporary statement of Church attitudes is Karl G. Maeser, *School and Fireside* ([Provo:] Skelton & Co., 1898). The writings of a BYU professor are analyzed in Davis Bitton, "N.L. Nelson and the Mormon Point of View," *Brigham Young University Studies* 13 (Winter 1973): 157-71.

In our treatment of missionary work we have supplemented standard sources listed earlier with reports from mission presidents published in *Conference Report* for this period and documents in Clark, *Messages of the First Presidency*, vol. 4. Heber J. Grant's diary and letters for 1901-1902 are extracted in Gordon A. Madsen, comp., *A Japanese Journal* (Salt Lake City: n.p., 1970). See also Murray L. Nichols, "History of the Japan Mission of the LDS Church, 1901-1924" (M.A. thesis, Brigham Young University, 1958). Attempts between 1889 and 1928 to establish a gathering place in Palestine are traced in Rao H. Lindsay, "The Dream of a Mormon Colony in the Near East," *Dialogue: A Journal of Mormon Thought* 1 (Winter 1966): 50-67.

We have drawn from the works listed in our General Bibliography for information on the auxiliaries. Priesthood activities are described in William G. Hartley, "The Priesthood Reform Movement, 1908-1922," *Brigham Young University Studies* 13 (Winter 1973): 137-56, and in general conference talks and *Improvement Era* articles of the period.

CHAPTER 15
Consolidating for Growth, 1908-1918

During the last decade of Joseph F. Smith's presidency, Church programs underwent significant adjustment, and the focus of Latter-day Saint history turns perceptively inward to follow institutional developments. The outlines of the story can be found in Roberts, *Comprehensive History of the Church*, vol. 6, chaps. 179-83. Much-distilled summaries are in Joseph Fielding Smith, *Essentials in Church History*, chap. 53, and Rich, *Ensign to the Nations*, chap. 21. The overviews by Allen and Cowan, identified in the bibliography for chap. 14, capture the highlights of the period, as does Joseph Fielding Smith's *Life of Joseph F. Smith*, chaps. 34-36 and 40.

Useful statistical and financial reports spanning the decade are in *Improvement Era* 13 (May 1910): 657-59; and 19 (May 1916): 653-54. Background reading for Church economic activities is Thomas G. Alexander, "The Burgeoning of Utah's Economy, 1910-1918," published in Arrington and Alexander, *A Dependent Commonwealth*, pp. 35-56. A new Church publishing venture is described briefly in "New Home of Zion's Printing and Publishing Company at Independence, Jackson Co., Missouri," *Liahona: The Elders' Journal* 13 (November 2, 1915): 289-91. A detailed description of the Administration Building by the architect, J.D.C. Young, is "The Latter-day Saint Church Headquarters Building," *Utah Genealogical and Historical Magazine* 8 (April 1917): 57-60. Meetinghouse design is characterized in a very good survey, Allen D. Roberts, "Religious Architecture of the LDS Church: Influences and Changes Since 1847," *Utah Historical Quarterly* 43 (Summer 1975): 301-27.

To supplement B. H. Roberts's treatment of the magazine crusade (*Comprehensive History of the Church*, vol. 6, chap. 179), we have drawn from studies of the Mormon image in periodical literature by Shipps and Lythgoe, and from Jan Shipps and Sandra Davidson, "The Public Image of Senator Reed Smoot, 1902-1932," unpublished paper read at Reed Smoot Symposium at Brigham Young University, March 19, 1974. Also useful is Malmquist, *The First 100 Years*, chaps. 20-23. Theodore Roosevelt's reaction to the anti-Mormon magazine campaign, Isaac Russel, ed., "Mr. Roosevelt to the 'Mormons,' " *Colliers*, April 15, 1911, is reprinted in *Improvement Era* 14 (June 1911): 712-18. European opposition is described in the thorough study by Malcolm R. Thorp, " 'The Mormon Peril': The Crusade against the Saints in Britain, 1910-1914," *Journal of Mormon History* 2 (1975): 69-88, and in a contemporary report by George F. Richards, "Why Are 'Mormon' Missionaries Expelled from Germany?" *Improvement Era* 13 (September 1910): 1004-7. The Tabernacle Choir tour is chronicled in J. Spencer Cornwall, *A Century of Singing*, chap. 8.

Priesthood activities can be traced in Baumgarten's thesis on the seventies, listed in the General Bibliography, and in Hartley's study of "The Priestood Reform Movement, 1908-1922," cited above (chap. 14). We also benefited from a student research paper by Gary L. Phelps, "The Effects of the 'Reform Movement, 1908-1922,' on Home Teaching" (Paper for History 665, Brigham Young University, August 1974; copy in possession of James B. Allen), and from a study of "Priesthood Programs of the Twentieth Century," by Richard O. Cowan of Brigham Young University and other members of a task committee under the direction of Dean C. Jessee of the Church Historical Department.

Histories of the auxiliaries cited in the General Bibliography furnished information on activities in those organizations. Bruce D. Blumell of the Church Historical Department has shared insights from his research into the history of the Genealogical Society.

The "Doctrinal Exposition on the Father and the Son" appears in *Improvement Era* 19 (August 1916): 934-42, and has been published as well in Talmage, *Articles of Faith*, pp. 465-73, and in Clark, *Messages of the First Presidency*, 5:26-33. President Smith's "Vision of the Redemption of the Dead" is in ibid., 5:102-6, and in the "Classics in Mormon Thought Series" in *Ensign* 1 (November 1971): 66-70.

On Church educational programs, consult sources listed in the General Bibliography and Quinn's article on religion classes cited in the listing for chap. 13. The controversy over scientific modernism is examined in Wilkinson, *Brigham Young University*, vol. 1, chaps. 13-14, and Mark K. Allen, *The History of Psychology at Brigham Young University* (Provo:

Brigham Young University Psychology Department, 1975), chaps. 5-7. The issue is placed in broader historical perspective in Duane E. Jeffrey, "Seers, Savants, and Evolution: The Uncomfortable Interface," *Dialogue: A Journal of Mormon Thought* 8 (Autumn-Winter 1973): 41-75.

Discussions of political issues in the Progressive Era are found in Shipps's article cited with sources for chap. 14, and in Reuben Joseph Snow, "The American Party in Utah: A Study of Political Party Struggles during the Early Years of Statehood" (M.A. thesis, University of Utah, 1963). See also comments on William Howard Taft's candidacy in Joseph F. Smith, "The Presidential Election," *Improvement Era* 15 (October 1912): 1120-21.

Latter-day Saint involvement in the prohibition movement is treated in Larry E. Nelson, "Utah Goes Dry," *Utah Historical Quarterly* 41 (Fall 1973): 340-57, and in Bruce T. Dyer, "A Study of the Forces Leading to the Adoption of Prohibition in Utah in 1917" (M.S. thesis, Brigham Young University, 1958).

Effects of the Mexican Revolution on Mormon colonists are recounted in the histories by Hardy, Hatch, and Romney listed in our bibliography for chap. 12, and in Joseph Flake Boone, "The Roles of the Church of Jesus Christ of Latter-day Saints in Relation to the United States Military, 1900-1975" (Ph.D. diss., Brigham Young University, 1975), chap. 3; B. Carmon Hardy, "Cultural 'Encystment' as a Cause of the Mormon Exodus from Mexico in 1912," *Pacific Historical Review* 34 (November 1965): 439-54; and Karl E. Young, *The Long Hot Summer of 1912* (Provo: Brigham Young University Press, 1967).

B. H. Roberts devotes two chapters to LDS participation in World War I, *Comprehensive History of the Church*, vol. 6, chaps. 182-83. For details not included in Roberts, consult chap. 4 of Boone's dissertation. General attitudes toward the war are discussed in chap. 5 of the excellent study by Stott cited in our bibliography for chap. 14. Its impact on the Saints in one European country is described in Scharffs, *Mormonism in Germany*, chap. 5.

CHAPTER 16
Change and Continuity in the Postwar Decade, 1919-1930

The early years of Heber J. Grant's presidency marked the beginning of a dispersion of Church membership beyond the concentration in the Rocky Mountain West. As the Church approached its centennial, important growth was recorded in membership and adjustments in programs. Roberts covers this period in *Comprehensive History of the Church*, vol. 6, chaps. 184-89. It is also treated briefly in Allen and Cowan, *Mormonism in the Twentieth Century*, especially chaps. 3, 9-10, and 14; in Joseph Fielding Smith, *Essentials in Church History*, chap. 54; and in Rich, *Ensign to the Nations*, chap. 22.

Helpful in charting growth patterns in the decade after World War I are appropriate sections in Dean R. Louder, "A Distributional and

Diffusionary Analysis of the Mormon Church, 1850-1970," and the analysis in D. W. Meinig, "The Mormon Culture Region: Strategies and Patterns in the Geography of the American West, 1847-1962," both cited in the General Bibliography. The movement to the West Coast is identified in Eugene Campbell, "History of the Church of Jesus Christ of Latter-day Saints in California, 1846-1946" (Ph.D. diss., University of Southern California, 1952), chaps. 9-10.

Especially helpful to us in understanding the coordination of priesthood and auxiliary activities is the study of "Priesthood Programs of the Twentieth Century" by Cowan and Jessee noted earlier (chap. 15). The history assembled by them supplements standard auxiliary histories and studies such as Neil K. Coleman, "A Study of the Church of Jesus Christ of Latter-day Saints as an Administrative System, Its Structure and Maintenance" (Ph.D. diss., New York University, 1967); Vernon L. Israelsen, "Changes in the Numbers and the Priesthood Affiliation of the Men Used as Ward Teachers in the Church . . ., 1920 to 1935" (M.S. thesis, Brigham Young University, 1937); and Hartley's article on priesthood reform listed with sources for chap. 14. Information on the end of the religion class program is in Quinn's article cited in the bibliography for chap. 13.

Developments in Church education are traced in the literature cited in the General Bibliography. A new program begun in this period is discussed in Leonard J. Arrington, "The Founding of the LDS Institutes of Religion," *Dialogue: A Journal of Mormon Thought* 2 (Summer 1967): 137-47, and in Gary A. Anderson, "A Historical Survey of the Full-time Institutes of Religion of the Church . . ., 1926-1966" (Ed.D. diss., Brigham Young University, 1968).

Additional information on missionary activities is in John D. Peterson's thesis on the "Mormon Missionary Movement in South America to 1940" and in three articles in *Brigham Young University Studies:* Dale F. Beecher, "Rey L. Pratt and the Mexican Mission," 15 (Spring 1975): 293-307; R. Lanier Britsch, "The Closing of the Early Japan Mission," 15 (Winter 1975): 171-90; and J. Christopher Conkling, "Members Without a Church: Japanese Mormons in Japan from 1924 to 1948," ibid., pp. 191-214.

Supplementing Lundwall and Talmage on temples is an unpublished paper by Paul Anderson, "Harold William Burton, Mormon Architect," typescript in possession of Leonard J. Arrington.

Histories of Church use of the electronic media are Heber G. Wolsey, "The History of Radio Station KSL from 1922 to Television" (Ph.D. diss., Michigan State University, 1967), and David Jacobs, "The History of Motion Pictures Produced by the Church . . . " (M.A. thesis, Brigham Young University, 1967). We found the dissertations by Cowan and Lythgoe, which are listed in the General Bibliography, especially helpful in our assessment of the Latter-day Saint public image in the 1920s.

On public issues of interest to the Church see Dan E. Jones, "Utah

Politics, 1926-1932" (Ph.D. diss., University of Utah, 1968); James B. Allen, "Personal Faith and Public Policy: Some Timely Observations on the League of Nations Controversy in Utah," *Brigham Young University Studies* 14 (Autumn 1973): 77-98; Larry E. Nelson, "Problems of Prohibition Enforcement in Utah, 1917-1933" (M.S. thesis, University of Utah, 1970); and John S. H. Smith, "Cigarette Prohibition in Utah, 1921-23," *Utah Historical Quarterly* 41 (Autumn 1973): 358-72. An interpretation of intellectual conflicts within the Church is Ephraim Edward Ericksen, *Psychological and Ethical Aspects of Mormon Group Life* (1922; reprint ed., Salt Lake City: University of Utah Press, 1975).

CHAPTER 17
The Church and the Great Depression, 1930-1938

This period has not been assessed thoroughly by scholars, and thus very little secondary literature exists from which to write a general survey. Allen and Cowan, *Mormonism in the Twentieth Century,* chap. 3 and topical chapters, touches upon it briefly, while Rich, *Ensign to the Nations,* chap. 22, and Joseph Fielding Smith, *Essentials in Church History,* chap. 54, review highlights of the depression years. We have benefited greatly from the investigations of Betty Barton, a research fellow with the Church Historical Department. Her work on the early years of the welfare plan is incorporated in an important section in this chapter. Many of the sources cited below are contemporary expressions published in Church periodicals.

Statements on the effects of the Great Depression on Latter-day Saints can be found in J. H. Paul, "Land Poor!" *Improvement Era* 35 (January 1931): 135-36; Joseph F. Merrill, "Can the Depression Be Cured?" ibid., 36 (November 1932): 5-6; and Lowry Nelson, "The Next Hundred Years," ibid., 36 (December 1932): 71-73, 117. For early reactions by Church leaders, consult *Conference Report,* October 1932; First Presidency, "An Important Message on Relief," *Deseret News,* April 7, 1936 (reprinted in Clark, *Messages of the First Presidency,* 6:9-13); and "A Message from the First Presidency Concerning Preparation for Relief Measures," July 1933, in Clark, *Messages of the First Presidency,* 5:330-34.

Useful histories are Leonard J. Arrington and Wayne K. Hinton, "Origin of the Welfare Plan of The Church of Jesus Christ of Latter-day Saints," *Brigham Young University Studies* 5 (Winter 1964): 67-85, and Paul C. Child, "Physical Beginnings of the Church Welfare Program," ibid., 14 (Spring 1974): 383-85. Early guides to the program are Henry D. Moyle, "Some Practical Phases of Church Security," *Improvement Era* 40 (June 1937): 354-55, 390, and Albert E. Bowen, *The Church Welfare Plan* (Salt Lake City: Deseret Sunday School Union, 1946). Operations are also explained in a pamphlet, *What Is the "Mormon" Security Program* (Independence, Mo.: Zion's Printing and Publishing Co., [ca. 1930]).

New emphasis on observance of the Word of Wisdom and opposition to the prohibition repeal movement are revealed in several contemporary statements. See First Presidency and the Twelve, "Prohibition: How We Stand," *Improvement Era* 35 (September 1932): 642 (reproduced in Clark, *Messages of the First Presidency*, 5:308-10); Mutual Improvement Associations, "In the Name of Temperance . . .," *Improvement Era* 36 (October 1933): 707; and James H. Wallis, "President Grant: Defender of the Word of Wisdom," ibid., 39 (November 1936): 696-98. On related activities see John A. Widtsoe, "The First Word of Wisdom Exhibit," ibid., 34 (November 1930): 13-14, 41, and George Albert Smith, Jr., "Word of Wisdom Exhibit," ibid., 34 (September 1931): 648-49, 673.

President Grant's lengthy statement to the April 1931 general conference countering Fundamentalist teachings on plural marriage is reproduced in Clark, *Messages of the First Presidency*, 5:292-303. For a fuller discussion on this question see Jerold A. Hilton, "Polygamy in Utah and Surrounding Area Since the Manifesto of 1890" (M.A. thesis, Brigham Young University, 1965); Dean C. Jessee, "A Comparative Study and Evaluation of the Latter-day Saint and 'Fundamentalist' Views Pertaining to the Practice of Plural Marriage" (M.A. thesis, Brigham Young University, 1959); and Lyle O. Wright, "Origins and Development of the Church of the Firstborn of the Fulness of Times" (M.S. thesis, Brigham Young University, 1963). A brief published overview of dissenting groups is Clair L. Wyatt, *"Some That Trouble You": Subcultures in Mormonism* (Salt Lake City: Bookcraft, 1974).

For our treatment of Church education we have again drawn from many histories, published and unpublished. Consult the General Bibliography for titles. On the issue of higher criticism, see the studies by Wilkinson and Jeffrey listed in our bibliography for chap. 14, and Russel B. Swensen, "Mormons at the University of Chicago Divinity School," *Dialogue: A Journal of Mormon Thought* 7 (Summer 1972): 37-47.

Church programs are examined in the general surveys listed above and in histories of the missions. We have also found useful John A. Widtsoe, "The Japanese Mission in Action," *Improvement Era* 42 (February 1939): 88-89, 125-27, and Joseph M. Dixon, "Mormons in the Third Reich: 1933-1945," *Dialogue: A Journal of Mormon Thought* 7 (Autumn-Winter 1971): 70-78.

CHAPTER 18
The Church and World War II, 1939-1950

This period, during which Church programs were dramatically curtailed by the world war, is outlined in the surveys by Joseph Fielding Smith, *Essentials in Church History*, chaps. 54-55; Rich, *Ensign to the Nations*, chaps. 22-23; and Allen and Cowan, *Mormonism in the Twentieth Century*, chap. 4. Documents pertaining to the period are collected in Berrett and Burton, *Readings in LDS Church History*, vol. 3. Beyond these sources, very little secondary literature is available on the period.

Contemporary Latter-day Saint expressions supportive of the isolationist viewpoint are J. Reuben Clark, Jr., "In Time of War," *Improvement*

Era 42 (November 1939): 656-57, 693-703; First Presidency, "Editorial: Comment on War," ibid., p. 672 (reproduced in Clark, *Messages of the First Presidency,* 6:92-93); and First Presidency, "To a World at War," *Improvement Era* 43 (December 1940): 712 (reprinted in Clark, *Messages of the First Presidency,* 6:115-17).

After Pearl Harbor, Church leaders threw their support behind the war effort in official statements read to the general conference by J. Reuben Clark, Jr., "Message of the First Presidency to the Church," *Improvement Era* 45 (May 1942): 272-73, 343-50, and David O. McKay, "The Church's Part in Defense: Message from the First Presidency," ibid., p. 274. These are also published in Clark, *Messages of the First Presidency,* 6:148-63 and 163-65. Other contemporary statements are John A. Widtsoe, "Evidences and Reconciliations, 48: Should a Soldier Love His Enemy?" *Improvement Era* 45 (April 1942): 225, and David O. McKay, "The Church and the Present War," ibid., (May 1942): 276, 340-42. We have also drawn from Lowell E. Call, "Latter-day Saint Servicemen in the Philippine Islands" (M.A. thesis, Brigham Young University, 1955); Richard T. Maher, "For God and Country: Mormon Chaplains during World War II" (M.A. thesis, Brigham Young University, 1975); and Campbell and Poll, *Hugh B. Brown: His Life and Thought,* chap. 11.

Supplementing the biographical sketches in the general histories is Preston Nibley, "George Albert Smith's First Mission," *Improvement Era* 48 (April, June, and August 1947): 206-8, 245, 358-59, 511-12.

On the subject of reopening the European missions we have used Frederick W. Babbel, "Europe's Valiant Saints Forge Ahead," *Improvement Era* 49 (October 1946): 622-23, 664-67, and Babbel, *On Wings of Faith* (Salt Lake City: Bookcraft, 1972). Additional firsthand accounts of postwar Europe are preserved in the typewritten transcripts of interviews conducted under the Oral History Program of the Church Historical Department, including interviews with Jean Wunderlich, Scott Taggart, A. Heimer Reiser, and others identified in the *Guide to the Oral History Program . . ., 1975* (Salt Lake City: Historical Department of The Church . . ., 1975).

The task of aiding the Saints is reported in "The Church Welfare Program Helps European Saints," *Improvement Era* 48 (December 1945): 747; Arthur Gaeth, "The Saints in Central Europe," ibid., 49 (March 1946): 148, 185; Henry D. Moyle, "Ten Years of Church Welfare," ibid., (April 1946): 207-9, 244-55; and Alma Stone, "The Church in Europe," ibid., 51 (July 1948): 426.

Other Church programs are described in Milton R. Hunter, "Unparalleled Growth Marks All Phases of Church Endeavor," *Deseret News,* Church News section, December 12, 1951. New missions are described in "The China Mission," *Improvement Era* 52 (December 1949): 784, 863, and Albert L. Zobell, Jr., "Uruguay: New Mission Field," ibid., 51 (January 1948): 47-48. An official statement on Selective Service, December 14, 1945, is "Letter of the First Presidency Concerning Military Training," ibid., 49 (February 1946): 76-77 (reprinted in Clark, *Messages of the First*

Presidency, 6:239-42).

We have benefited from McBride's study of LDS higher education and from other studies on education listed in the General Bibliography. Other events of interest to the Church are described in Albert L. Zobell, Jr., "The Temple at Idaho Falls," *Improvement Era* 50 (September 1947): 569; David O. McKay, "The Meaning of 'This Is the Place' Monument," ibid., 573, 601; and Charles W. Whitman, "The History of the Hill Cumorah Pageant, 1937-1964" (M.A. thesis, University of Minnesota, 1967). Davis Bitton, "The 'Ritualization' of Mormon History," *Utah Historical Quarterly* 43 (Winter 1975): 67-85, describes how parades, pageants, historic sites, and other activities function as an expression of a people's celebration of their heritage.

CHAPTER 19
Foundations for Expansion, 1951-1959

The years of postwar growth after David O. McKay became President of the Church have not yet been studied in any detail by historians. This chapter, then, reflects some preliminary findings based on sketchy overviews in a few general histories and a sampling of unpublished sources. Helpful introductions to the period include Allen and Cowan, *Mormonism in the Twentieth Century,* chap. 5 and topical chapters, especially chaps. 8, 10-15, and Larson, *Outline History of Utah and the Mormons,* chap. 25. President McKay's administration is summarized in Joseph Fielding Smith, *Essentials in Church History,* chap. 56, and Rich, *Ensign to the Nations,* chap. 24. For documents consult Cowan and Anderson, *The Living Church.* Besides these sources we have depended upon materials compiled in the "Journal History of the Church" and upon various other unpublished resources in the Church Archives.

Information on the social profile of the mid-century Saints is drawn from John A. Widtsoe, "How Is Church Membership Divided as to Ages?" *Improvement Era* 55 (February 1952): 78-79; Widtsoe, "What Are the Occupations of Latter-day Saints?" ibid. (March 1952): 142-43, 167; Widtsoe, "Are Latter-day Saints Homeowners?" ibid. (April 1952): 222-23; "What Are the Educational Attainments of the Latter-day Saints?" ibid. (May 1952): 310-11; and two unpublished reports found in the Church Archives: Howard C. Nielson, "Membership of the Church . . . by Areas" (Salt Lake City, 1971), and Daniel H. Ludlow, "A Study Comparing the Recent Growth of the Church . . . with Other Selected Christian Groups in the United States" (prepared for Institute of Mormon Studies, Brigham Young University, ca. 1963).

On the Asian missions see the overview by Spencer J. Palmer, *The Church Encounters Asia,* and the recent analysis by Paul V. Hyer, "Revolution and Mormonism in Asia: What the Church Might Offer a Changing Society," *Dialogue: A Journal of Mormon Thought* 7 (Spring 1972): 88-93. Copies of selected missionary teaching plans are on file at the Church Historical Department. A study of one approach is Arnold H. Green, "A

Survey of Latter-day Proselyting Efforts to the Jewish People" (M.A. thesis, Brigham Young University, 1967).

The expansion of physical facilities in one part of the world is told in David W. Cummings, *Mighty Missionary of the Pacific: The Building Program of the Church . . . : Its History, Scope, and Significance* (Salt Lake City: Bookcraft, 1961). This study and Harvey Taylor's "Story of L.D.S. Church Schools" were useful in writing the sections on educational expansion and administrative reorganization, as were other sources listed in the General Bibliography. A study extending through the late 1950s is Reuben D. Law, *The Founding and Early Development of the Church College of Hawaii* (St. George, Utah: Dixie College Press, 1972).

Helpful on the Indian Student Placement Program are Spencer W. Kimball, "The Expanded Indian Program," an October 1956 conference talk, in *Improvement Era* 59 (December 1956): 937-40, and Clarence R. Bishop, "Indian Placement: A History of the Indian Student Placement Program of the Church . . ." (M.S.W. thesis, University of Utah, 1967).

Public affairs in this period are discussed in O'Dea, *The Mormons;* Ezra Taft Benson, *Crossfire: The Eight Years with Eisenhower* (Garden City, N.Y.: Doubleday, 1962); Edward L. Schapsmeier and Frederick H. Schapsmeier, *Ezra Taft Benson and the Politics of Agriculture: The Eisenhower Years, 1953-1961* (Danville, Ill.: Interstate Printers and Publishers, 1975); and Stan A. Taylor, "[J. Reuben] Clark and the United Nations," *Brigham Young University Studies* 13 (Spring 1973): 415-25, which is one of nine essays in this special issue, "J. Reuben Clark, Jr.: Diplomat and Statesman," compiled by Ray C. Hillam.

CHAPTER 20
Correlation in the Worldwide Church, 1960-1973

The significant developments of the 1960s and early 1970s are just beginning to be examined by historians, but the period has produced a rich store of commentary by those who have lived through these eventful years. Although no general survey has been written, the period can be approached through appropriate sections in the biographies of Presidents McKay, Smith, and Lee listed in the General Bibliography and in the sketches in Preston Nibley's *Presidents of the Church.* We have drawn from "Journal History of the Church" and from numerous articles in Church periodicals, and have gleaned statistical information from the *Deseret News 1975 Church Almanac.*

Background on correlation in this and earlier periods can be found in Jerry J Rose, "The Correlation Program of the Church . . . during the Twentieth Century" (M.A. thesis, Brigham Young University, 1973). Contemporary statements include Harold B. Lee, "New Plan of Coordination Explained," *Improvement Era* 65 (January 1962): 34-37, and numerous other references that are listed in *Index to Periodicals of the Church . . ., 1961-1970* (Salt Lake City: The Church . . ., 1972). A convenient summary is John P. Fugal, comp., *A Review of Priesthood Correlation* (Provo:

Brigham Young University Press, 1968). We have also depended heavily upon research reports based on preliminary investigations in primary sources; these were prepared for us by Bruce D. Blumell of the Church Historical Department and Robert G. Mouritsen of the Department of Seminaries and Institutes. Many of the committees and programs mentioned in the text have generated guides, manuals, and handbooks that give information on their activities.

The meaning of Church growth outside North America is explored in John Sorenson, "Mormon World View and American Culture," *Dialogue: A Journal of Mormon Thought* 8 (Summer 1973): 17-29, and is examined in relation to an area of particularly rapid growth in LaMond F. Tullis, "Three Myths about Mormons in Latin America," ibid., 7 (Spring 1972): 79-87, and Tullis, "Politics and Society: Anglo-American Mormons in a Revolutionary Land," *Brigham Young University Studies* 13 (Winter 1973): 126-34. Reports on Asian growth are in Desmond L. Anderson, "Meeting the Challenges of the Latter-day Saints in Vietnam," ibid., 10 (Winter 1970): 186-96; and Seiji Katanuma, "The Church in Japan," ibid., 14 (Autumn 1973): 16-28.

Further information on Church education can be found in Wilkinson, *Brigham Young University,* vol. 3, and Taylor, "The Story of L.D.S. Church Schools."

The flowering of historical studies, represented by the numerous recently published articles and books cited in this bibliography, was accompanied by a parallel increase in published discussion of related aspects of Latter-day Saint life. The articles listed below sample that exchange of viewpoints on the place of the Latter-day Saint professional in the modern world.

On the life of the mind, stimulating historical surveys are Davis Bitton, "Anti-Intellectualism in Mormon History," *Dialogue: A Journal of Mormon Thought* 1 (Autumn 1966): 111-34, with comments by James B. Allen, "Thoughts on Anti-Intellectualism: A Response," ibid., pp. 134-40; Leonard J. Arrington, "The Intellectual Tradition of the Latter-day Saints," ibid., 4 (Spring 1969): 13-26; and Arrington, "The Intellectual Tradition of Mormon Utah," *Proceedings of the Utah Academy of Sciences, Arts, and Letters,* vol. 45, part 2 (1968): 1-20. On the application of reason to Latter-day Saint life, see Lowell L. Bennion, "The Uses of the Mind in Religion," *Brigham Young University Studies* 14 (Autumn 1973): 47-55, and Richard D. Poll, "What the Church Means to People Like Me," *Dialogue: A Journal of Mormon Thought* 2 (Winter 1967): 107-17.

The philosophical basis of education in the Church is examined in certain of the historical works cited earlier, particularly James R. Clark's dissertation on "Church and State Relationships," chaps. 1-5, and James R. Harris's dissertation on the "Educational Thought of Joseph Smith." For recent essays see Hugh Nibley, "Educating the Saints: A Brigham Young Mosaic," *Brigham Young University Studies* 11 (Autumn 1970): 61-87; Robert K. Thomas, "Academic Responsibility," ibid., 11 (Spring 1971): 293-303; and Arthur H. King, "The Idea of a Mormon University," ibid.,

13 (Winter 1973): 115-25.

With regard to the Church and the arts, an introductory overview growing out of the Mormon Festival of Arts is a collection of essays and artistic reproductions in Lorin F. Wheelwright and Lael J. Woodbury, eds., *Mormon Arts, Volume 1* (Provo: Brigham Young University Press, 1972). Assessments of the state of music in the Church are Lowell M. Durham, "On Mormon Music and Musicians," *Dialogue: A Journal of Mormon Thought* 3 (Summer 1968): 19-40, and Reid Nibley, "Thoughts on Music in the Church," *Ensign* 2 (February 1972): 13.

Lael J. Woodbury has commented on the prospects of "A New Mormon Theatre" in *Brigham Young University Studies* 10 (Autumn 1969): 85-94, and on "Mormonism and the Commercial Theatre" in ibid., 12 (Winter 1972): 234-40.

On another subfield in the arts a good introduction is James L. Haseltine, "Mormons and the Visual Arts," *Dialogue: A Journal of Mormon Thought* 1 (Summer 1966): 17-29. A brief commentary is Maida Rust Winters, "Art and the Church," ibid., 3 (Autumn 1968): 93-96; and an examination of sponsored works, Monte B. DeGraw, "A Study of Representative Examples of Art Works Fostered by the Mormon Church, with an Analysis of the Aesthetic Values of These Works" (M.S. thesis, Brigham Young University, 1959). Biographical approaches are Wayne K. Hinton, "Mahonri Young and the Church: A View of Mormonism and Art," *Dialogue: A Journal of Mormon Thought* 7 (Winter 1972): 35-43, and Richard L. Jensen, "The Mormon Years of the Borglum Family," accepted for publication in *Idaho Yesterdays*, 1976.

A historical overview of Church architecture is Allen D. Roberts, "Religious Architecture of the LDS Church," listed in the chap. 15 bibliography, while contemporary viewpoints are aired in Ronald Molen, Franklin T. Ferguson, Albert L. Christensen, and Paul G. Salisbury, "The Lamps of Mormon Architecture: A Discussion," *Dialogue: A Journal of Mormon Thought* 3 (Spring 1968): 17-26, and Donald Bergsma, "The Temple as a Symbol," ibid., pp. 27-28.

There has been a recent upsurge of interest in various aspects of LDS literature. A book of readings containing representative examples of many literary forms is Richard H. Cracroft and Neal E. Lambert, comps., *A Believing People: Literature of the Latter-day Saints* (Provo: Brigham Young University Press, 1974). Nine articles discussing "Mormonism and Literature," plus examples of fiction and poetry, are in a special issue of *Dialogue: A Journal of Mormon Thought* 4 (Autumn 1969): 11-80, assembled by guest editors Karl Keller and Robert A. Rees. Another commentary is Samuel W. Taylor, "Peculiar People, Positive Thinkers, and the Prospect of Mormon Literature," ibid., 2 (Summer 1967): 17-31. Focusing on specific works are R. A. Christmas, "The Autobiography of Parley P. Pratt: Some Literary, Historical, and Critical Reflections," ibid., 1 (Spring 1966): 33-43, and Thomas D. Schwartz, "Bayard Taylor's 'The Prophet': Mormonism as Literary Taboo," *Brigham Young University Studies* 14 (Winter 1974): 235-47.

The reawakening of interest in Latter-day Saint literature has led to proposals such as that of Douglas Wilson, "Prospects for the Study of the Book of Mormon as a Work of American Literature," *Dialogue: A Journal of Mormon Thought* 3 (Spring 1968): 29-41, one application of which is Robert E. Nichols, Jr., "Beowulf and Nephi: A Literary View of the Book of Mormon," ibid., 4 (Autumn 1969): 40-47. A form of literary investigation seeking internal evidences to support the historicity of scripture is presented in John A. Tvednes, "Hebraisms in the Book of Mormon: A Preliminary Survey," *Brigham Young University Studies* 11 (Autumn 1970): 50-60, and John W. Welch, "Chiasmus in the Book of Mormon," ibid., 10 (Autumn 1969): 69-84.

A reexamination of an approach to Latter-day Saint life and beliefs by American humorists is in articles by Richard H. Cracroft in *Brigham Young University Studies:* "The Gentile Blasphemer: Mark Twain, Holy Scripture, and the Book of Mormon," 11 (Winter 1971): 119-40, and "Distorting Polygamy for Fun and Profit: Artemus Ward and Mark Twain among the Mormons," 14 (Winter 1974): 272-88. Glimpses of humor among the Latter-day Saints themselves are in Ronald W. Walker, "The 'Keep-A-Pitchinin,' or, the Mormon Pioneer was Human," ibid., 14 (Spring 1974): 331-44, and Davis Bitton, *Wit and Whimsy in Mormon History* (Salt Lake City: Deseret Book, 1974).

Years of collecting from the oral tradition of the Saints are evident in the articles and stories in Austin Fife and Alta Fife, *Saints of Sage and Saddle: Folklore among the Mormons* (Bloomington: Indiana University Press, 1956); Folklore Society of Utah, comp., *Lore of Faith and Folly*, ed. Thomas E. Cheney et al. (Salt Lake City: University of Utah Press, 1971); Cheney, *Mormon Songs of the Rocky Mountains: A Compilation of Mormon Folksong* (Austin: University of Texas Press, 1968); and Cheney, *The Golden Legacy: A Folk History of J. Golden Kimball*, rev. ed. (Salt Lake City: Peregrine Smith, 1974).

Although the social sciences have contributed less general commentary than the arts and letters, a few examples can be listed. On the Latter-day Saint interest in prehistory and historic archaeology, see Michael Coe, "Mormons and Archaeology: An Outside View," *Dialogue: A Journal of Mormon Thought* 8 (Spring 1973): 40-48, and Dee Green, "Mormon Archaeology in the 1970s: A New Decade, a New Approach," ibid., pp. 49-55. From other fields see Robert D. Hunt and K.H. Blacker, "Mormons and Psychiatry," ibid., 3 (Winter 1968): 13-24; the collaboration of psychologist Gary L. Bunker and historian Davis Bitton in "Phrenology among the Mormons," ibid., 9 (Spring 1974): 43-61; and "Mesmerism and Mormonism," *Brigham Young University Studies* 15 (Winter 1975): 146-70.

The modern Latter-day Saint family is examined in Harold T. Christensen, "Stress Points in Mormon Family Culture," *Dialogue: A Journal of Mormon Thought* 7 (Winter 1972): 11-19, and in special theme sections of two publications: "Women, Family, Home," from talks given in Relief Society conference, *Ensign* 2 (February 1972): 47-74, and "The

Mormon Family in the Modern World," a series of ten articles, *Dialogue: A Journal of Mormon Thought* 2 (Autumn 1967): 41-108.

The subject of the Church and public policy can be approached through articles by Dennis L. Lythgoe, "The Changing Image of Mormonism," ibid., 3 (Winter 1968): 45-58; Thomas F. O'Dea, "Sources of Strain in Mormon History Reconsidered," in Hill and Allen, *Mormonism and American Culture*, pp. 147-67; and Leonard J. Arrington, "Crisis in Identity: Mormon Responses in the Nineteenth and Twentieth Centuries," in the same work, pp. 168-84. Also relevant are many of the articles in a special issue, "Mormons in the Secular City," *Dialogue: A Journal of Mormon Thought* 3 (Autumn 1968): 39-108.

Several political issues of the 1960s have attracted comment. For example, see Dennis L. Lythgoe, "The 1968 Presidential Decline of George Romney: Mormonism or Politics?" *Brigham Young University Studies* 11 (Spring 1971): 219-40, on a prominent Latter-day Saint's campaign for the U.S. presidency, and four articles on "The Church and Collective Bargaining in American Society," *Dialogue: A Journal of Mormon Thought* 3 (Summer 1968): 106-33, in a "Roundtable" discussion by Garth L. Mangum, Vernon H. Jensen, H. George Frederickson, Alden J. Stevens, Richard B. Wirthlin, and Bruce D. Merrill, and a response by Ken W. Dyal in "Letters to the Editors," ibid., 3 (Autumn 1968): 11-14. The relationship of church and state in Utah during the 1960s is discussed in Frank H. Jonas, ed., *Politics in the American West* (Salt Lake City: University of Utah Press, 1969), pp. 327-80. An issue of global concern is discussed by Ray C. Hillam, Eugene England, and John L. Sorenson, in "Roundtable: Vietnam," *Dialogue: A Journal of Mormon Thought* 2 (Winter 1970): 65-100. Gordon C. Thomasson, ed., *War, Conscription, Conscience, and Mormonism* (Santa Barbara: Mormon Heritage, 1971), reproduces miscellaneous articles and documents on Mormon attitudes toward war in the Vietnam years.

Attitudes on race relations are discussed in two articles by Armand L. Mauss: "Mormonism and Secular Attitudes towards Negroes," *Pacific Sociological Review* 9 (Fall 1966): 91-99, and "Mormonism and the Negro: Faith, Folklore, and Civil Rights," *Dialogue: A Journal of Mormon Thought* 2 (Winter 1967): 19-39, and in Brian Walton, "A University Dilemma: B.Y.U. and Blacks," ibid., 6 (Spring 1971): 31-36. Historical perspective is contributed in the studies by Taggart and Bush cited in the bibliography for chap. 3. Commenting on Bush's article are Gordon C. Thomasson, "Lester Bush's Historical Overview: Other Perspectives," *Dialogue: A Journal of Mormon Thought* 8 (Spring 1973): 69-72; Hugh Nibley, "The Best Possible Test," ibid., pp. 73-77; and Eugene England, "The Mormon Cross," ibid., pp. 78-86. For the First Presidency statement of December 15, 1969, on blacks and the priesthood see "Letter of First Presidency Clarifies Church's Position on the Negro," *Improvement Era* 73 (February 1970): 70-71. The letter was also published in Church News (section of *Deseret News*) January 10, 1970.

CHAPTER 21
"Lengthening Our Stride," 1973-1976

The most convenient chronology of recent events in Church history is the annual "Year in Review" section published in the *Deseret News Church Almanac.* Filling in details of these happenings are accounts in the *Ensign,* the Church News section of the *Deseret News,* and other newspaper and magazine articles compiled in the "Journal History of the Church" under the direction of the Church Historian. We have found this last-named compilation of special value in summarizing recent developments.

Biographical information on President Spencer W. Kimball can be found in Preston Nibley's *Presidents of the Church* (13th ed., rev.); Boyd K. Packer, "President Spencer W. Kimball: No Ordinary Man," *Ensign* 4 (March 1974): 2-13; and Spencer W. Kimball, *One Silent Sleepless Night* (Salt Lake City: Bookcraft, 1975).

On the Washington Temple and its dedication see the special issue of the *Ensign* 4 (August 1974), and J. M. Heslop, "Majestic Temple Dedicated," *Church News,* November 23, 1974.

Commentaries on historic preservation are Edward Geary, "The Last Days of the Coalville Tabernacle," *Dialogue: A Journal of Mormon Thought* 5 (Winter 1970): 42-49, and Mark Leone, "Why the Coalville Tabernacle Had to be Razed: Principles Governing Mormon Architecture," ibid., 3 (Summer 1973): 30-39.

Comments on the equal rights ammendment include those of Relief Society President Barbara B. Smith, reported in *Deseret News,* December 13, 1974, and *Church News,* December 21, 1974; and editorials in the *Church News,* January 11, 1975, and *Deseret News,* January 22, 1975. Copies of these and other discussions on the issue can be found in "Journal History of the Church," for the months and dates specified.

For reports on Brigham Young University's opposition to federal anti-discrimination regulations, see "Journal History" entries for October 16 and 27, 1975.

INDEX